NORTH CAROLINA HANDBOOK

NORTH CAROLINA HANDBOOK

FROM THE GREAT SMOKY MOUNTAINS
TO THE OUTER BANKS

FIRST EDITION

**ROB HIRTZ AND
JENNY DAUGHTRY HIRTZ**

**MOON
TRAVEL
HANDBOOKS**

NORTH CAROLINA HANDBOOK
FIRST EDITION

Published by
Moon Publications, Inc.
P.O. Box 3040
Chico, California 95927-3040, USA

Printed by
Colorcraft Ltd.

ISBN: 1-56691-130-3
ISSN: 1099-8861

Editor: Gregor Krause
Map Editor: Gina Wilson Birtcil
Copy Editor: Valerie Sellers Blanton
Production & Design: Carey Wilson
Illustration: Bob Race
Cartography: Chris Folks and Mike Morgenfeld
Index: Jeannie Trizzino

Front cover photo: North Carolina, Outer Banks, Courtesy UniPhoto

All photos by Rob Hirtz and Jenny Daughtry Hirtz unless otherwise noted.

Distributed in the United States and Canada by Publishers Group West

Printed in China

Please send all comments,
corrections, additions,
amendments, and critiques to:

NORTH CAROLINA HANDBOOK
MOON TRAVEL HANDBOOKS
P.O. BOX 3040
CHICO, CA 95927-3040, USA
e-mail: travel@moon.com
www.moon.com

Printing History
1st edition—February 1999

*To the memory of
Charles Kuralt (1934-1997),
Tarheel traveler without peer.*

North Carolina is my home,
Home far beyond all praise,
Goodliest home under heaven's dome,
Here I shall spend my days.

—from the song
"North Carolina Is My Home,"
Lyrics by Charles Kuralt

CONTENTS

MAPS

MAP SYMBOLS

═══ Superhighway	★ Point of Interest	·········· Ferry
═══ Primary Road	• Accommodation	✗ Airport
─── Secondary Road	▾ Restaurant/Bar	⅃ Golf Course
------- Trail	▪ Other Location	♠ State Park
⬯ U.S. Interstate	⊛ State Capital	⋏ Campground
⬯ U.S. Highway	○ City	⇞ Waterfall
◯ State Highway	○ Town	▲ Mountain

HANDBOOK DIVISIONS

© MOON PUBLICATIONS, INC.

Great Smoky Mtns. National Park

8 Blowing Rock

Winston-Salem **6**

Durham

5

Corolla

Kitty Hawk

Nags Head

9 Asheville

GREENSBORO

Chapel Hill

RALEIGH

10

7

1

CHARLOTTE

Pinehurst

4

2

Ocracoke Island

Cape Lookout

3

Wilmington

1. **THE OUTER BANKS**

2. **THE MAINLAND CENTRAL COAST**

3. **WILMINGTON AND THE SOUTH COAST**

4. **PINEHURST AND VICINITY**

5. **THE RALEIGH/DURHAM/ CHAPEL HILL TRIANGLE**

6. **THE TRIAD**

7. **CHARLOTTE**

8. **THE NORTHERN MOUNTAINS**

9. **ASHEVILLE AND VICINITY**

10. **GREAT SMOKY MOUNTAINS NATIONAL PARK AND VICINITY**

WE WELCOME YOUR COMMENTS

To compile a complete and current travel guide is impossible. Restaurants and lodgings are perpetually closing or changing owners, new attractions are always opening, and the price of everything continues to rise. Between the time this book went to press and the time you bought it, the precise price listings are virtually guaranteed to have become slightly outdated. We apologize for any such unavoidable discrepancies.

North Carolina is home to countless jewels—accommodations, restaurants, sights, and attractions—worthy of mention. We can't possibly know about all of them. Have we missed any of your favorites? We would deeply appreciate hearing from you about special places and events you've encountered in your travels in this beautiful state. Address your correspondence to:

North Carolina Handbook
c/o Moon Publications
P.O. Box 3040
Chico, CA 95927
email: travel@moon.com

ACKNOWLEDGMENTS

Most important, we thank *you*—for buying this book. Researching and writing the first edition of a travel guide to a state as rich with wonders and attractions as North Carolina—a daunting task requiring a relentless sense of exploratory enthusiasm—took more than two years. While it's demanding, travel writing ranks among the most rewarding of all writing jobs. Often, travel writers have to forego the leisurely fun of exploring without purpose, because they have to spend so much time plotting routes and timelines and recording loads of information that most visitors never have to bother with. But the job also delivers an extraordinarily heightened sense of joy when the writers find a particularly wonderful place and know that their personal discoveries will be multiplied thousands of times—thanks entirely to their readers. Over the past two-plus years, you have always provided our prime inspiration and given us the energy to press on whenever our enthusiasm temporarily flagged.

Thank you, Thomas B. Daughtry, Chair of the Art Department at Clayton College & State University (and Jenny's Uncle Tommy), for your exquisite illustrations of North Carolinian flora and fauna in this book, and for your constant good humor and encouragement.

Countless folks in the North Carolina hospitality and tourism industry deserve our thanks here. Staffpeople at chambers of commerce and convention and visitors bureaus; public-relations professionals at dozens of museums, historic sites, and amusement parks; owners of B&Bs and front-desk clerks at lodgings who always let us inspect their rooms; the waitstaffs, chefs, and restaurant managers who consistently gave us not only great recommendations not only about the fare served at their own establishments but also generous leads to their culinary competitors—we thank you all, and apologize that we don't name every one of you.

Again, with apologies to the hundreds of helpful professionals of the North Carolina hospitality and tourist industry who aided us, we have to single out for special thanks Bridget Maupin, of the North Carolina Travel and Tourism Division, for her repeated, immediate help when we ran into a variety of emergencies in the writing and production of this book.

We are deeply indebted to the great team at Moon Travel Handbooks, who patiently guided us through this first edition of the *North Carolina Handbook*. We extend our grateful thanks: to Becky Brasington Clark, Jenny's perfect friend, who, as a former Marketing Director for Moon, first suggested we submit a proposal to our lunar beacon of publishing; to Bill Newlin, our esteemed, adventurous publisher, who had confidence that our writing voices, heretofore devoted mostly to other areas, would enrich the complex fabric woven by dozens of Moon Handbook authors; to senior editor Pauli Galin, who ceaselessly provided compassionate guidance through our two-plus years of research and writing; and to Gina Birtcil, Bob Race, and Karen Bleske, the wizards who put all of the pieces of this complicated puzzle together into this book.

Our personal thanks to our family and friends for always politely and warmly asking about the progress of this book, and for pretending not to be bored stiff while we regaled them with North Carolina trivia and tales of our travels. A special remembrance goes to Robin Clark (1955-1995), a wandering searcher, writer and friend whose Tarheel soul never truly left home.

Last, we thank the unsung member of our family writing team, our fellow, canine traveler, Sparky, who has shared and energized so many of the outdoor experiences we have related in this book, expertly guided our coverage of pet-friendly lodgings, and provided a perpetual enthusiasm for exploring all of the smells, sounds, sights, tastes, and textures of North Carolina.

INTRODUCTION

North Carolina stretches from the Appalachian Mountains to the Atlantic Ocean, from Great Smoky Mountains National Park to 70-mile-long Cape Hatteras National Seashore. As millions of visitors discover each year, the state boasts alluring weather, spectacular scenery, a rich history, terrain ideal for virtually any recreational pursuit, and a pervasive spirit of friendliness and tolerance.

Covering 52,669 square miles, North Carolina takes in three distinct geographic regions: the coastal plain (which takes in almost half of the state, accounting for the extraordinary fertility of much of the state's soil and abundance of productive farmland), the central Piedmont plateau, and the mountains in the west.

The Outer Banks and the Coastal Plain

North Carolina's coast comprises three major areas: the Outer Banks; the "inland" coast, including the area around the Neuse River and Albemarle and Pamlico Sounds and the towns of "The Crystal Coast"; and the Wilmington, Cape Fear River, and South Brunswick area.

The Outer Banks are a chain of narrow, sandy barrier islands (the largest such chain on the east coast) stretching some 200 miles along more than half of the state coastline. Today, as they have been for generations, the islands are home to dozens of small towns and fishing villages interspersed with secluded stretches of beach—whose shell-rich sands and pristine surf, beneath bright blue skies by day and heavens brimming with stars by night, dazzle with a natural beauty that defies description.

At Kill Devil Hills, hang gliders atop Jockey's Ridge—the tallest sand dune in the eastern United States—catch the same wind currents that send the Wright brothers soaring into history almost 100 years ago. In the ocean just offshore, surfers test themselves aboard different craft in different currents (forming some of the Atlantic ocean's most prodigious waves) while, to the west of the islands, toddlers bob in dinosaur floats in the harbor safety of gently lapping Pamlico Sound.

Ashore from the Outer Banks, the coastal plain extends about 100 miles inland. It is marked by an intricate intracoastal waterway system, forest, swampland, and the state's premier agricultural region. The huge coastal peninsulas that protrude into Pamlico and Albemarle Sounds include vast expanses of isolated, pristine wetlands and nature preserves, laced with dirt roads leading through dense brambles, tangles, streams, and swamps that are home to turtles, alligators, exotic birds, and other shy creatures as well as rare flora such as the Venus flytrap and four other insectivorous genera.

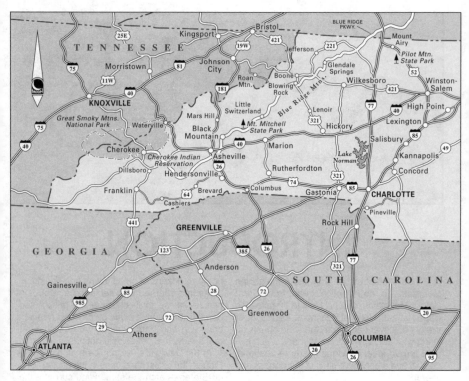

This northern section of the mainland coast is also home to a visitor's paradise of historic attractions, inviting lodgings, superb restaurants, and an assortment of quaint old small towns and villages. Exemplary are the "Crystal Coast" cities of New Bern, Morehead City (home of the annual Strange Seafood Festival), Beaufort, and Atlantic Beach, all boasting an abundance of history and unassuming "local color" accrued and preserved over the course of more than 200 years of sea-oriented commerce.

The southern coast is lined with residential and vacation beach communities, from Wrightsville and Carolina Beach south to Calabash (the self-proclaimed "Seafood Capital of the World"), near the South Carolina border. The principal city in this region is "Hollywood East"—Wilmington, North Carolina's 200-year-old chief seaport, a city not only rich in history, culture, and culinary offerings, but also the third-largest movie-production city in the nation, behind only Los Angeles and New York.

Between the Ocean and the Mountains—the Piedmont

Farther inland from the coastal plain lies the 200-mile-wide heartland of North Carolina, the diverse Piedmont. The Piedmont (Latin for "foot of the mountain"), sprawling from the shadow of the state's mountainous western region, is a land of dense clay soil and powerful rivers, of gently rolling hills, forests, farms, lakes, and quiet small towns as well as North Carolina's most populous and bustling cities. Among the benefits it receives from the mountains are moderating breezes in summer and an abundance of granite—not only a superb building material but also a spiritual symbol of North Carolinians' steadfastness. Here is where most of the state's inhabitants live, from country folks who make

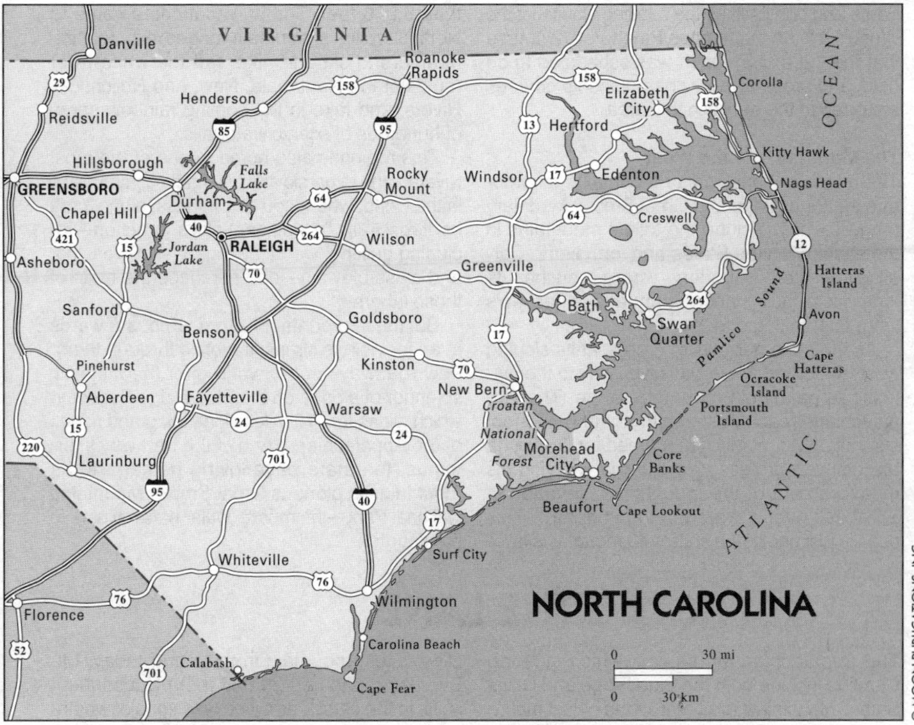

NORTH CAROLINA

0   30 mi

0   30 km

© MOON PUBLICATIONS, INC.

ends meet with tiny tobacco gardens in their back yards to the three-piece suiters of Charlotte (the nation's second-largest banking hub) and the urban scholars who earn the Raleigh-Durham-Chapel Hill "Triangle" its distinctive claim to the highest per-capita concentration of Ph.D. holders of any metropolitan area in the nation. The region is also home to the world's largest natural-habitat zoo—the magnificent 1,400-acre North Carolina Zoological Park, in Asheboro.

The region's inherent diversity is typified by the fact that the living history village of Old Salem, a memorial to the early Moravian settlement of the region, full of old spinning wheels and butter churns, is only minutes from the highly automated R.J. Reynolds cigarette factory, which is capable of producing 275 million cigarettes a *day,* making it responsible for a sizable portion of the 475 *billion* cigarettes manufactured in 1997 in North Carolina. The arts and crafts of the early settlers

aren't lost (even though the methods may have changed considerably)—High Point is known as the "Furniture Capital of the World," and Seagrove is one of the nation's renowned pottery enclaves.

The Piedmont is also an enclave of practitioners of three almost religious pursuits: college basketball, stock-car racing, and golf. Home to four members of college basketball's Atlantic Coast Conference, the Piedmont often sends two or more teams—usually the University of North Carolina Tar Heels from Chapel Hill, the Blue Devils of Duke University in Durham, or Raleigh's North Carolina State University Wolfpack—into competition for the national title. Given that North Carolina is the birthplace of stock-car racing, it is only fitting that NASCAR's biggest annual race, the Coca-Cola 600, is still held here, in Charlotte. And when it comes to golf, it would be hard to beat the Piedmont's Pinehurst area, which is home to the Golf Hall of

Fame and bills itself as the "Golfing Capital of the World." It is on the famous Pinehurst #2 course that the 1999 U.S. Open was scheduled to be held, and more than 40 championship courses are open to the public in this area.

The Mountains of the West

The majestic Appalachian Mountains incorporate the Blue Ridge and Great Smoky Mountain ranges, which include the tallest mountains in the eastern United States and form North Carolina's western boundary, where it pushes its long, west-facing nose in under Tennessee's long, east-facing one.

As the state narrows to a point at its sloping western border, the terrain gives way to the majestic Appalachian mountain range. The Appalachians reach their zenith at the 6,684-foot summit of Mount Mitchell (named for Dr. Elisha Mitchell, the professor who, while verifying his measurement of the mountain's elevation in 1857, fell over a waterfall to his death). This peak is just one of the state's 43 mountains taller

than 6,000 feet. Today, vacationers come to North Carolina's mountain ranges in increasing numbers to ski and hike; raft the whitewater rapids of the Nantahala, New, and Nolichucky Rivers; and take in the cooling rainbow spray of hundreds of scenic waterfalls.

This region is also home to one of the most revered and dynamic arts and crafts communities in the world, where you can witness, along "craft heritage trails," traditional skills in action—including quilting, woodcarving, basket-weaving, and glass-blowing—and purchase the fruits of those labors.

But these mountains afford famous rewards even for visitors simply traveling through them. Few roadways in the world offer the majestic splendor of a drive on the Blue Ridge Parkway, which glides for 470 miles along the grand ridges of the Appalachians. And at the Parkway's terminus, the state pays loving homage to its mountains in glorious Great Smoky Mountains National Park—the most popular national park in the country.

THE LAND

The Appalachian Mountains, which in North Carolina include both the Blue Ridge and Great Smoky Mountains, are some of the oldest mountains on Earth. Geologists date rock from these mountains back to the Archeozoic era—basically, when geologic time began, some 4.6 billion years ago. From pre-Cambrian times, billions of years ago, these mountains slowly eroded into a great, shallow inland sea, which covered all of central North America to Cascadia—an ancient continent that at one time lay east of the Rockies. For about 500 million years, the seas receded and returned as tectonic plates shifted, causing layers of limestone and sediment to be pressed into metamorphic and crystalline rock through a prolonged period of uplift and erosion, intermittent volcanic activity, and continents crashing into one another, then drifting apart.

About 500 million years ago, during the Paleozoic era, Earth's crust underwent a readjustment, called the "Appalachian Revolution." Geologists estimate that the Appalachian mountains were at least 40,000 feet tall at that time.

(The tallest mountain in the world today, Mt. Everest, measures 29,028 feet.) Subsequent shifts in the crust, combined with eons of weather erosion, shaped the Appalachians into their present form. While quite a bit shorter now than in ancient times, they remain the tallest in the eastern United States. North Carolina's portion of the Appalachian range includes the tallest mountain east of the Rockies, Mount Mitchell.

The state's mountains are abundant with rivers, streams, mountain lakes, and more than 300 waterfalls, from Whitewater Falls, near South Carolina (the highest waterfall in the eastern U.S.—a spectacular, two-tiered, 411-foot cascade) to Sliding Rock, near the Blue Ridge Parkway (a more humble example of the species, known as "Bust-Yer-Butt Falls" for its popularity as a natural waterslide). Slowly meandering through the northern mountain region, the New River is actually the *oldest* river in the United States—and the second oldest in the entire world (only the Nile predates it).

Compared to the mountains, the Piedmont Plateau is a geologic toddler, formed only about

THE "TARHEEL" NICKNAME

Thanks to its abundance of pine forests, North Carolina was for centuries America's chief producer of tar, pitch, and turpentine, essential for painting, caulking, and preserving the wood and ropes of naval and merchant vessels. By 1768, North Carolina was producing 60% of the colonies' supply of all three. But the process of heating pine lumber in charcoal beds to catch the oozing extracts was rather messy and resulted in the soles of workers' shoes routinely getting coated with tar.

According to popular legend, following a Civil War battle in Virginia, in which the Virginia troops fled while the North Carolina troops stuck to their positions—as if held fast by tar—Confederate General Robert E. Lee said, "God bless the Tarheel boys." Confederate President Jefferson Davis is reported to have asked jokingly whether there was any surplus tar available from North Carolina, so other commanders could smear it on *their* troops' heels to help them, too, stand fast against Union assaults.

Regardless of whether Lee actually coined the phrase, he certainly popularized it and gave it a positive meaning. And North Carolinians have proudly called themselves Tarheels ever since.

250 million years ago during the Triassic period. Characterized today by rolling hills, lakes, rivers, and forests, this was once an area of highlands and deep troughs. Geologists believe that the red clay soil prevalent in the Piedmont today resulted from erosion from the sides of these deep troughs, compounded by an arid climate that caused the sediment to turn reddish in color. The great pressure of folding and buckling that created the Appalachians reverberated in this region, causing large deposits of granite, which is still quarried throughout the Piedmont today.

The region's numerous lakes and rivers serve as sources of power as well as outlets for recreation and commercial fishing. The scenic Yadkin, Catawba, and French Broad Rivers flow east from the Blue Ridge Mountains to form lakes including Lake Norman, High Rock Lake, Badin Lake, Lake Tillery, Jordan Lake, Falls Lake, Lake Gaston, and Kerr Lake; the last four are man-made dammed lakes that produce electricity. In the Raleigh/Durham/Chapel Hill area, volunteer conservationists work hard to keep the Eno, Haw, and Pee Dee Rivers clean and beautiful for future generations.

During the Jurassic period, about 150 million years ago, the North Carolina shoreline extended many miles farther east into the Atlantic Ocean, and volcanic activity was common. At the end of the Jurassic and the beginning of the Cretaceous (66-144 million years ago) periods, the seas rose and the coastline sank, causing the ocean to come as far inland as Raleigh and Pinehurst. The sandy soil of the Pinehurst area is a consequence of its having been beachfront property at one time. Today, the coastal plain, extending more than 100 miles inland from the Atlantic Ocean, is a region of rich, loamy soil—perfect for farming.

The complex northern North Carolina coast consists of the huge Albemarle and Pamlico Sounds, flanked to the east by the Outer Banks, the longest system of barrier islands on the east coast. The Outer Banks were formed some time after the last Ice Age—about 17,000 years ago. Originally, they were located about 25 miles east of their current location, and they continue to move towards the mainland. There's no need to hurry, however, to enjoy the islands' pristine, sandy beaches or to take advantage of their status as the closest land approach in the U.S. to the fish-filled Gulf Stream: Geologists estimate that it will take about another 17,000 years before the Outer Banks roll into the mainland.

CLIMATE

North Carolinians enjoy four distinct seasons, marked by warm summers and mild winters, with some variation depending on the region. Throughout all seasons, visitors are often struck by the intense "Carolina Blue" skies and the abundance of sunshine (Durham, in the Piedmont, receives an average of more than 300 days a year). Temperatures normally range from 22° to 92° F, and annual precipitation averages 44 inches per year. In general, North Carolina averages five to six inches of snow per year, but that figure can be much larger in the mountains, while snow is rarely witnessed on the coastal plain.

Spring and fall are both long and beautiful in North Carolina. The first crocuses push their heads up in late February. March and April are generally cool but characterized by pleasant, sunny days with highs in the high 60s and low 70s (although chilly temperatures and treacherous ice storms are not unknown in March). Fall imparts a gentle crispness to the air in late September and generally lasts until mid-November or, often, after Thanksgiving. Nights slowly begin to get cooler, and temperatures drop down to the 40s and 50s at night, and a little cooler in the mountains. Millions of visitors make pilgrimages to the North Carolina mountains during the fall "leaf-changing" season when the mountain forests explode in dazzling hues of red and yellow. Peak leaf season in the mountains comes generally during the second through the fourth week in October.

Summer can be rather hot in North Carolina, particularly in the Piedmont and on the Coastal Plain. Temperatures regularly hit the 80s from mid-May to late June and often ascend into the low 90s from late June through August. Fortunately, summer is often marked by violent, cooling thunderstorms, so heat waves lasting more than three or four days are not particularly common.

Winters can vary here. Some years, below-freezing temperatures are frequent and the state may experience a half-dozen snowstorms. Other years little or no snow or ice may occur, with the mercury remaining in the high 30s to low 40s (except in the usually cooler higher elevations in the mountains). While the skies customarily retain their intense blue during winter, rain is common.

FLORA

North Carolina covers 33 million acres of highly varied terrain over elevations ranging from almost 7,000 feet to sea level. Because of its widely diverse natural settings, the state is home to almost every type of vegetation represented on the East Coast. This includes some types unique to North Carolina, such as the Venus flytrap, which continues to thrive in wetlands on the state's coast—the only spot in the world where this plant grows in the wild.

Mountain Flora

The state's mountains are blessed with vegetation diverse enough to please the senses any time of year. In winter, the abundance of blue-green, sharp-scented Fraser firs remind visitors that North Carolina is one of the leading Christmas-tree producing states in the nation. Great balls of mistletoe, with their fat clusters of white, waxy berries, stand out in sharp contrast to the leafless, hibernating skeletons of the hardwood trees in which they nestle. Holly trees and nandina also stand out in the woods, particularly when they're dusted lightly with snow, when their broad green leaves, red berries, and snowy highlights combine to form a series of picture-perfect Christmas postcards.

In spring, the mountains take on the colors of Easter dresses. Rhododendrons unleash their white, rose, and deep lavender blooms against their broad, flat leaves. The mountain laurels explode into clusters of pinkish-white, bell-shaped cups of brilliant blossoms. Flame azalea and trillium dot the forests with lipstick reds, pinks and whites, highlighted against the gentle greens of the ferns and mosses covering the forest floor. Dogwood trees, with their copious white blossoms, donate a dappled appearance to the forest, against the predominant background of deep, dark greens of hardwood, pine, fir and cedar trees.

Summer in the mountains unleashes meadows filled with pink oxalis, white Queen Anne's

---

WHAT PRETTY SHOULDERS THE HIGHWAYS HAVE!

Among the most engaging examples of cultivated plant life in North Carolina are the dazzling roadside gardens you'll see periodically as you travel the state's busiest highways. Funded by state tax dollars, the North Carolina Wildflower Program is a decades-old project whose goal is to beautify North Carolina highways with swaths of wildflowers. Currently, most of these brilliant highwayside gardens feature flowers not native to North Carolina (a bone of contention among floral purists). Nevertheless, you can thank state taxpayers for brightening up your highway horizons and helping to make your trip feel shorter.

lace, and a painter's palette of daisies, asters, berry bushes, and other wildflowers, against a backdrop of green grasses, and brightly green, newly leafed trees.

Fall explodes into a blaze of colors, with beech, oak, maple, poplar, apple, buckeye, and other deciduous trees displaying flaming reds, yellow-golds, and oranges against the evergreen backgrounds of spruce, fir, and pine.

Although most of the North Carolina Appalachians can boast about their remarkable variety of flora, Great Smoky Mountains National Park, shared by North Carolina and Tennessee, and Grandfather Mountain, next to Linville, North Carolina, bear the imprimatur of being designated among 300 or so "international biospheres," protected by the United Nations and international treaties to preserve their place among the most botanically diverse environments in the world. For example, in just Great Smoky Mountains National Park, you'll find more than 120 species of trees—more than exist in all of Europe, from the Mediterranean Sea to Scandinavia.

Piedmont Flora

Between the mountains and the coastal plain, the North Carolina Piedmont is characterized by broad-leaf hardwood trees, pines, and grassy meadows covering rolling hills. Broom sedge, aster, daisy, Queen Anne's lace, wild carrot, evening primrose, daylilies, clover, buttercups, and bluets bloom over the Piedmont's meadows in spring and summer. As the Piedmont is North Carolina's most populous, urban region, it's difficult to definitively describe the native plants of this area, insofar as botanical "imports" like the infamous kudzu vine have, in many spots, taken firm hold of the land. But residents favor many native plants that you'll frequently see in their carefully tended yards.

American chestnut trees once provided colonnades along the broad avenues of the Piedmont, until the "great chestnut blight" obliterated them all soon after the turn of the century. Willow and water oaks have now taken their place. In addition, pines (the state tree) and dogwoods (the state flower, even though it's

a tree) flourish, augmented by healthy hordes of maple, pecan, poplar, sweet-gum, and Bartlett pear trees, whose myriad colors grace many urban and suburban Piedmont streets. The symbol of the South, *Magnolia grandiflora* explodes with cabbage-size, waxy white blooms in early summer, their citrusy perfume scenting the air of yards, campuses, and parks throughout the Piedmont.

The Mimosa, a favorite import from the East, is another common Southern tree pervading the Piedmont. Their touch-sensitive fronds close at night, and they produce a powerfully scented, spiky, sea-urchin-shaped pink blossom in midsummer that the legendary Harper Lee, author of *To Kill a Mockingbird,* described as smelling like "angels' breath." Their heavenly sweet smell will convince you of Lee's descriptive powers.

Coastal Plain Flora

Stretching about 100 miles inland from the Atlantic Ocean, North Carolina's coastal plain features, on its eastern edges, vast stands of towering long-leaf pines, augmented by more diminutive flora like wild iris, pixie moss, and spiderwort. As you travel closer to the coast, maritime forest takes root in the sandy soil, and the botanical scene grows into a veritable riot of exotic diversity, from the ghostly and craggy bonsai-like yaupon, myrtle, bay, saw-palmetto, wild olive, and live oaks, draped with Spanish moss, to the area's tall, thick carpets of grasses, cattails, marsh morning glories, sea lavenders, and sea ox-eye. As pervasive, lush, and attractive as these predominant wetland plants may be, however, they'll always play second-fiddle to their comparatively rare botanical aristocracy: the carnivorous plants.

In the Great Dismal Swamp, crossing North Carolina's northeast border into Virginia, and slightly further south, in the vast Croatan National Forest, America's greatest collection of insect-eating plants make their home. Thriving in the black, mucky soil of these wetlands' "pocosins" (bogs peculiar to the coastal plain), the pitcher plant,

developing seeds of the Magnolia grandiflora

TOMMY DAUGHTRY

sundew, and trumpet plants emit a sweet fragrance that seduces various insects to land on these plants' "throats," where, through a combination of oozing, digestive "glue," and spiky obstacles, flying insects are eventually delivered into a bowl of digestive stew. Even more celebrated, the Venus flytrap (so named because long-ago locals suspected it was delivered to Earth from Venus) makes its only natural, Earthly home in the wetlands near the Cape Fear Coast. This most famous of insectivorous plants, like its close, Croatan, carnivorous relatives, attracts insects with a sweet scent onto a sticky pad that looks a little like a human palm, augmented by sharp, toothy fingers reminiscent of Freddy Kruger. Adjoining this sharp-fingered, sticky palm is another razor-fingered palm. Together these two imposing palms are joined at their base, imitating a supplicant in prayer. As soon as the unsuspecting insect lights upon one of the flytraps' sticky palms, this extraordinary plant snaps shut within a few seconds, imprisoning its insect behind the closely-knit fingers of its palms. Over hours, and sometimes days, the flytrap slowly digests its prey. Athough this description may conjure memories of those malicious, human-eating plants in old Tarzan movies, rest easy: Venus flytraps are, at their tallest, only about six inches high with fronds barely big enough to catch a fly. Nonetheless, from an evolutionary perspective, it's almost impossible to behold these celebrated plants, many of which you'll observe with an imprisoned meal, without wondering where the plant leaves off and the animal begins.

As you travel farther east, to the sands of the Outer Banks and Cape Fear beaches, you can thank the beach grasses and shrubs for their millennia-long struggle to prevent your beach from blowing away. Sea oats, beach grass, salt grass, evening primrose, and a host of other sturdy shrubs and trees are largely responsible (with a little human help) for resisting the erosion of the state's hundreds of miles of beachfront.

cardinal

FAUNA

As diverse as the flora is in North Carolina, the state also enjoys an almost equally diverse population of wildlife. While the prevalent bison and elk described by early colonial settlers are long gone, other endangered species have made dramatic comebacks in recent years, from eagles in the mountains to red wolves on the coastal plain. But most of the state's most unique flora and fauna have survived the modern age. North Carolina even boasts more varieties of salamanders than anywhere else in North America—and, according to many respected experts, more than anyplace else on the Earth.

The red wolf ranks among the North Carolina's more successful rescues of endangered species. In the 1970s, the red wolf was just about extinct. But, thanks to a concerted effort by local conservationists, today you can hear red wolves howling at the Carolina moon in the Great Smoky Mountains and on the coastal plain near Pamlico Sound. While you may hear them, your chance of catching even a fleeting glimpse of these elusive, human-shy wolves is extremely remote.

The populous Piedmont region is home to more common critters, like gray squirrels and cardinals (both state emblems), deer, sparrows, raccoons, opossums, woodpeckers, chipmunks, and chickadees. The common sight of hummingbird feeders (bright red plastic tubes, about four inches in diameter and one or two feet long, filled with rich nectar, hanging from tree limbs or just outside kitchen windows) attest to the presence of one of our favorite Piedmont residents: the ruby-throated hummingbird. These tiny, hypnotically engaging birds beat their wings about 55 times per second and eat more than the equivalent of half their total body weight each day. Keep an eye out for these finger-size, iridescent green and gray-brown bodies with the scarlet throats. You'll be mesmerized by their combination of grace and industry.

The North Carolina coast offers a wealth of sighting opportunities for the orinthologically inclined. At Pea Island National Wildlife Refuge,

TOMMY DAUGHTRY

just south of Nags Head on the Outer Banks, it's possible to spot more than 260 bird species, from great blue herons to snowy egrets and hundreds of winged creatures in between. Farther north, near the Virginia border, Currituck National Wildlife Refuge is home to a number of rare animals, from hundreds of bird species to loggerhead turtles to legendary wild horses (descendants of generations of feral equines who have roamed the coast for centuries).

Although North Carolina's coastal plain offers an almost inexhaustibly varied cornucopia of nature studies, certainly the most popular place to view wildlife in this region is the beach—whether you're spending a late summer or early fall morning casting a line out in the surf for bluefish, seeing a bottlenose dolphin trace an arc in the air to dive over a wave, or watching a flock of pelicans diving for their evening meals like kamikaze pilots on a mission.

HISTORY

EARLY INHABITANTS

North Carolina's Natives
The earliest evidence of human habitation of North Carolina goes back about 10,000 years. These Paleo-Indian inhabitants probably gathered wild foods and hunted small animals, but evidence like stone-cut spear points indicates that they also hunted big game. And the fact that they left no evidence of permanent dwellings, villages, pottery, or agriculture implies that they probably pursued big game—mammoths and bison—in herds through what is now the Piedmont. By about 1000 B.C., the area's inhabitants had come a long way, combining new hunting technology of bows and arrows with new agricultural strategies, building farms and permanent villages, and creating the first examples of pottery (a talent for which present-day North Carolina artisans continue to be renowned).

Little is known about the people who made North Carolina their home before the Europeans landed. The broadest dependable information is that by the time the Spanish arrived, in the early 16th century, about 24 tribes, generally separated into three major groups, resided in North Carolina. Algonquin tribes lived mainly in the eastern section, on the coastal plain. Sioux tribes occupied the present-day Piedmont area, in the central part of the state. Iroquois tribes, including the Cherokee, inhabited the western mountain region. Many of these tribes waged frequent and ferocious war, but the Hatteras and Croatans seem to have lived peacefully—and virtually undisturbed—for about 5,000 years. Until the Europeans arrived.

The Europeans Appear (and Disappear)
In July 1524, Giovanni da Verrazano, a Florentine who was exploring for Francis I of France, became the first European explorer to land in North Carolina. From his ship, hovering off the coast between the Cape Fear River and Bogue Banks, Verrazano noticed people on shore. Verrazano ordered a single sailor to swim ashore to make first contact. He was treated very well and exchanged gifts with the natives. When he attempted to swim back, the waves battered him unconscious. The Indians patched him up, dried his clothes by a fire they built on the shore, and helped him back into the water a few hours later, when the sea had calmed.

Luckily for the native inhabitants, Verazzano, who was obsessed with the idea of discovering gold in the New World, found neither the Outer Banks nor the Cape Fear coast inviting or promising—thanks in part to the ferocious currents of the coastal waters. For the next 60 years, successive European explorers confirmed Verrazano's unflattering evaluation of the region.

In the 1580s, that view began to change. England's Sir Walter Raleigh became interested in staking a claim in North Carolina for Queen Elizabeth. The queen provided Raleigh a ship, and the secretary of state provided another. In 1585, a party of 108 men sailed from Plymouth headed for Roanoke Island (home today of Manteo, a charming town on one of the Outer Banks' most protected barrier islands).

In a letter written on September 3, 1585, less than a month after the expedition's arrival, the colony's leader, Lieutenant Ralph Lane, proclaimed his land "the Goodliest Soile Under the Cope of Heaven." He would not retain that opinion very long. The farming methods that worked so well in cool, moist England—consisting mostly of spreading seeds on top of tilled farmland—didn't enjoy the same success on Roanoke Island. The few seeds that didn't roast to death in the summer sun were overcome by tenacious weeds. Despite the fact that Lane had murdered a few of the natives before he'd gotten to know them, the local Indians for a time came to the colony's assistance. Even so, the following June, when Sir Francis Drake stopped by with a few ships, Lane and most of his men immediately hitched a ride back to England, leaving 15 men on the island to keep the colony going until more supplies arrived from England.

The Lost Colony
Raleigh was embroiled in personal financial difficulties that prohibited him for some time from financing another trip to the goodlie soile. On July 22, 1587 (20 years, incidentally, before Captain John Smith first laid eyes on Pocahontas at Jamestown), another 91 men, 17 women, and nine boys—constituting the first "permanent" English colony in the New World—arrived on Roanoke Island. The only evidence they found of the unlucky 15 men Lane had left behind two years earlier were a few skeletons.

The new colony was headed by John White, whom Raleigh appointed governor of the tiny colony. On August 18, less than a month after landing, White's granddaughter, Virginia Dare, became the first English child born in the New World. Somewhat spoiling that good news, White realized that his colony was in big trouble. They had arrived too late to successfully plant crops to help them through the winter, and they were already running low on food and on hunting and other supplies (apparently, this group was not terribly keen on fishing).

A week after his granddaughter's birth, White and a handful of men set sail back to England, promising to return promptly with supplies to get the colony through the winter. Due to some unfortunate circumstances, White ran a little late—about three years late—getting back to the colony. Thanks to England's engaging in a war with Spain when White returned, Queen Elizabeth wouldn't allow any ships to sail to the New World that could be more productively used to fight naval battles with Spain.

By the time White returned to Roanoke Island, in 1591, all that remained of his colony was an empty fort. Inside the fort, the word "CROATOAN" was carved on a tree. Three years earlier, when White left for England, he had told the colonists that if they left, they should carve their destination on a tree. If they were leaving in distress (including attacks from Indians), the colonists were also to carve a cross

the cryptic last sign of the Lost Colony

on the tree. But upon his return White found no cross. So he and his expedition set sail for Croatan, a friendly Indian village about 50 miles south of Roanoke Island, and home of two Indians, named Manteo and Wanchese, who had befriended earlier expeditions of Raleigh's and had even visited England.

But White's string of bad luck wasn't over. As he sailed towards Croatan, the ship got caught in a mighty storm, was swept severely off course, and developed some pretty bad leaks. Obviously a little lacking as a family man, White decided to abort the mission and sailed back to England, never to return. More than 20 years later, Captain John Smith sent out a ship from the Jamestown settlement to look for signs of the Lost Colony. According to most accounts, however, this effort was halfhearted at best, consisting mostly of sailing once down the coastline and back and then reporting to Smith, basically, "Nope, didn't see any Lost Colony, Captain."

To this day, historians debate the fate of the Lost Colony, with conflicting evidence supporting various conclusions. Some maintain that they were probably slaughtered by unfriendly Indians. We prefer the interpretation of other historians who contend that the colonists moved in with the friendly Croatan Indians, intermarried, and lived happily ever after.

The British Return

In 1663 and 1665, King Charles II conferred a vast tract of land—spreading from the current North Carolina/Virginia border south to Cape Canaveral in Florida—to be controlled by eight aristocratic "proprietors" in England. (In contrast, Virginia was a royal colony, owned and controlled by the Crown of England.) However, although these proprietors were the ultimate heads of state for this vast area, several local governments sprang up. In what is today North Carolina, the first local government was established as the county of Albemarle, which extended from the North Carolina/Virginia border down to Cape Hatteras and Bogue Banks. The proprietors named a governor for the Albemarle area, and the freeholders/citizens of Albemarle elected a legislature.

In what would become a North Carolina tradition, that legislature specialized in rebelling against a succession of governors (who were charged with collecting tariffs and taxes). Of the five men who served as governor of Albemarle between 1672 and 1689, only one served without incident. Of the remaining four men, three were toppled by the citizen legislature and thrown in jail, and one—threatened with the same fate—was intimidated into never entering the colony to assume his office.

Eventually, in 1729, after numerous rebellions and a generally unprofitable tenure, seven of the territory's eight proprietors sold off their land for £7,500 each, and North Carolina became a simple royal colony. (The one holdout, Earl Granville, held onto one-eighth of the land, located mostly in northwestern North Carolina, until the American Revolution, when it was confiscated by the new, independent government.)

In general, the transfer of authority to the Crown resulted in a much more streamlined operation of government. For a while. But as the population increased along the coast, political infighting emerged between the northern counties and the southern and central counties. Since the beginning of the colony, the northern (Albemarle) counties had always controlled the legislature, sending five representatives per county, as opposed to the *two* representatives allotted each of the southern counties. This caused the southern counties and the royal governor considerable consternation.

In 1747, the governor and the southern and central county legislators decided to hold a legislative session in Wilmington, in the south. The northern legislators, who constituted a majority of the legislature, refused to attend. At this "Wilmington Assembly," the governor and southern and central representatives voted to cut the number of northern representatives down from five to two representatives per district.

The result was that the northern counties refused to participate in any legislative sessions for the next eight years—until King George II restored their number of representatives to five per county. In those eight years, the Albemarle counties refused to recognize any laws passed by the Assembly, refused to use the currency issued by the colony, and, most important, refused to pay any taxes and fees owed the colony.

The southern and central counties decided that it wouldn't be fair to pay taxes and fees to the

BLACKBEARD

Into the early 1700s, North Carolina's coastal towns served as haunts for the most treacherous and feared sailors of the day—pirates—including the most infamous of them all, Blackbeard. At one point, Blackbeard, who hid out regularly on the Outer Banks, married and settled down briefly in the town of Bath, about three miles up an inlet off the Pamlico River.

Blackbeard was a master of psychological warfare and placed great importance on a fierce appearance as a crucial strategy in intimidating his enemies and cowing his victims. Blackbeard's notoriety was probably worse than his actual misdeeds (he was more mercenary than murderous). But he went to considerable trouble to at least *look* as if he fully deserved his nefarious reputation. Although he had been born with the unimposing name of Edward Teach (or perhaps Edward Drummond), he earned his nickname for his great, thick, ebony beard. The beard started nearly at his eyes and flowed to below his waist, covering most of his upper body. He frequently braided it and tied the braids with brightly colored ribbons. Particularly when negotiating the surrender of a ship, he augmented the beard by hanging slow-burning cannon fuses from the brim of his hat and then lighting them, thereby shrouding his head in smoke.

In an age of clean-shaven men who wore generally understated clothing and stood about five feet tall, Blackbeard not only cultivated his flamboyant facial hair but was also over six feet tall, broad, and muscular. He accentuated his size by wearing a long cape of brightly colored silk and velvet, gaudy knee breeches and shirtwaists, and high-heeled knee boots. At the mere sight of this bizarre monster of a man, most captains surrendered immediately, gave up their cargo, and considered themselves lucky to have survived the encounter.

In fact, Blackbeard was considered "fair," at least by pirate standards. Any sea captain who surrendered quickly and turned over his cargo was left unharmed with his crew intact (except for any crew members who volunteered to join Blackbeard's band), and the romantic legend is well known to have never harmed any women or children.

Despite their relative civility, Blackbeard and his men weren't exactly the kind of neighbors coastal North Carolinians wanted. However, North Carolina's governor, Charles Eden, had performed Blackbeard's wedding and reputedly received a share of any booty taken at sea. The one time the governor had Blackbeard and his mates arrested for piracy and put on trial, they were all acquitted. So, in the autumn of 1718, North Carolina's colonists called on the royal governor of Virginia, Edwin Spotswood, to dispatch a fleet to capture Blackbeard. Unfortunately, the pirate hadn't bothered to purchase Spotswood's friendship, loyalty, or protection, so the governor dispatched two ships, led by English Navy Lieutenant Robert Maynard.

Under cover of darkness on the evening of November 21, 1718, the two ships sailed into Ocracoke Inlet and waited silently for dawn the next morning. At daybreak, they attacked Blackbeard's sloop, *Adventure,* which was anchored just off Ocracoke Village. In the ensuing battle, 18 men—including Blackbeard, who continued to fight after being shot five times—died. Maynard, who obviously had a flair for the theatrical, cut off Blackbeard's head, stuck it on a spit on the bow of his ship, and sailed back to Virginia like that.

Legend has it that Blackbeard's body continues to swim around the waters of Ocracoke Village in search of its head—good to keep in mind if you're swimming off Ocracoke these days and see something you can't readily identify drifting in the waves.

colonial government if the Albemarle counties weren't. As a result, from 1747 until 1754, none of the counties and towns in North Carolina paid taxes or fees to the royal government.

But since the colony was providing plenty of important materials to the Crown—including corn, wheat, and the wood, tar, pitch and turpentine needed to expand the British navy—the rebellious behavior of the unruly North Carolinians went largely ignored.

In fact, the relatively poor colony of North Carolina often wasn't as big a headache as the more prosperous New England colonies anyway. For example, in 1764, when the British Parliament enacted the Sugar Act, placing duties on products like sugar, coffee, wine, and cloth imported to the colonies, the New England colonies had a fit. But North Carolina's poor colonists weren't importing these kinds of fancy European goods in the first place and so raised virtually no protest.

THE REVOLUTIONARY WAR

The Roots of Rebellion

A year later, however, the Parliament enacted a tax which did grab some North Carolinians' attention: the Stamp Act of 1765. Having been administered successfully for almost a century in England, the Stamp Act required that various paper products, from contracts and licenses to newspapers and playing cards, be made *only* from official paper, which had been made in England and stamped by the British government. The official stamped paper was much more expensive than unstamped paper and was sold only by agents of the Crown.

That same year, North Carolina had been appointed with a new royal governor, William Tryon. Tryon had served as lieutenant governor the previous year and realized that his unruly constituents had a genuine talent for avoiding taxes.

When the Stamp Act was announced, public demonstrations erupted all along the coast. The most colorful protest occurred in Wilmington, where an ad hoc group calling themselves the Sons of Liberty gathered at the harbor and imbibed untold gallons of spirits, repeatedly toasting to "Liberty, Property, and No Stamp Duty!" Then, as the Crown's stamp agent, Dr. William Houston, watched, they hanged in effigy former British Prime Minister and Stamp Act proponent Lord Bute. No dummy himself, Dr. Houston promptly resigned his office.

Governor Tryon realized that the Stamp Act was going to be extremely difficult to enforce in his colony. He tried to negotiate with various business and political leaders to get them to obey the law, but they had enjoyed such success at flouting the Crown's taxation policies in the past that they ignored Tryon's entreaties. A wealthy man, Tryon apparently even offered to pay the stamp act duties himself, but he was rebuffed and told not to bother.

On November 28, 1765, the British ship *Diligence,* delivering stamped paper to the colonies, arrived in Brunswick, just south of Wilmington. A distinguished party—including the speaker of the legislative assembly, the mayor, several assembly members, local officials, wealthy land owners, and several hundred citizens—met the captain of the *Diligence* and courteously informed him that the Crown's stamp agent (the official responsible for receiving and disbursing the stamped paper) had resigned, and that there was nobody in the colony to properly receive the shipment of stamped paper. So the *Diligence* sailed on.

Four months later, the British Parliament repealed the Stamp Act. Tryon, who never condoned the actions of his rebellious constituents, nonetheless had done nothing that might antagonize them. In fact, he may have learned a little something from their clever style. A few months earlier, nine colonies had organized a "Stamp Act Congress" in New York, which heaped abuse on the Crown for its taxation policies. North Carolina, Georgia, Virginia, and New Hampshire declined to send any delegates to this congress. Tryon was following the tried-and-true North Carolina tradition of averting conflict whenever feasible—not through active negotiation, but rather through passive avoidance.

The War of the Regulation

During this time, settlement of the inland "backcountry" was proceeding apace. Governing these areas was increasingly troublesome and wasn't helped by the fact that North Carolina still had no official capital. The seat of government was considered to be any place that the governor lived, or any place he decided the Assembly should meet. Under this system, the capital during the 18th century included Edenton, New Bern, Wilmington, and Bath.

In 1766, the Assembly finally decided to choose New Bern as the permanent capital and passed "An Act for erecting a Convenient Building Within the Town of New Bern, for the Residence of the Governor." The Assembly allocated £15,000—a vast sum at the time—to start construction. The project soon came to be known derogatorily as "Tryon's Palace."

To pay for the construction, the Assembly enacted a poll tax, under which each citizen paid the same amount. This was wildly unpopular in the backcountry. Noting that "a man that is worth 10,000 pounds pays no more than a poor back settler that has nothing but the labour of his hands to depend upon for his daily support," the citizens of Orange County declared on August 2, 1768, that they were "determined not to pay the Tax for the next three years, for the Edifice or

Governor's House. We want no such House, nor will we pay for it."

By this time, the political divisions which had previously pitted the northern against the southern counties had largely evaporated. But it had been replaced by divisions between the established east coast and the frontier west. By 1770, the western counties accounted for more than a third of the free white population. But these counties accounted for only 15 representatives in the 81-member North Carolina Assembly.

In addition, most of the officeholders were strangers appointed by the Crown. Sheriffs, who collected taxes, were the most hated government officials. In the frontier territories, where currency was scarce, sheriffs often confiscated settlers' property to settle tax debts. Many sheriffs also had a proclivity for making up their own tax rates. In addition, they often kept confiscated goods for themselves, failing to pass on their plunder to the colonial government.

The tax to build Tryon Palace resulted in the formation of a backcountry organization whose members called themselves the Regulators. The Regulators' main goal was to cease paying taxes to corrupt sheriffs until assured by the colonial government that the taxes were legal and that the goods collected were actually being passed on to the proper treasuries. Before they would pay any more taxes, they insisted on a strict accounting of how their taxes had been collected and spent and insisted on receiving such accounts in the future. Most county officials immediately arranged to meet with the Regulators in their counties and arrange a mutually acceptable agreement.

One particularly corrupt and haughty sheriff, Edmund Fanning (a graduate of both Yale and Harvard), decided on a different course of action. He deputized some friends and arrested Herman Husband and William Butler—two leaders of the Regulator movement—and threw them in jail in Hillsborough, charging them with incitement to riot.

Simultaneously, Governor Tryon issued an official proclamation that the Regulators disband. In the proclamation, he warned that while the poll taxes were due, any official who collected the tax illegally would be charged with extortion. The Regulators immediately drew up a list of Fanning's transgressions, and Fanning was in-

dicted for extortion by the colonial government.

During the September court term, the trials of Husband, Butler, and Fanning were all to take place. The Regulators wanted to see justice at work, and 3,700 of them gathered in Hillsborough for the trials. Alarmed by the potential for a violent incident, Governor Tryon himself led 1,500 North Carolina militiamen to Hillsborough.

At the trials, Husband was acquitted, but Butler and two other Regulators were found guilty of inciting to riot. Tryon adeptly arranged for the guilty Regulators to be pardoned almost immediately by King George, averting a potential violent clash. Sheriff Fanning was found guilty of extortion. However, the court inexplicably decided that his illegal acts had been accidental, and so he was let go without any punishment.

The Regulators grew increasingly tired of having their grievances dealt with unsatisfactorily. Two years after Fanning's trial, when the court was again meeting in Hillsborough, 150 Regulators decided to take matters into their own hands. Armed with sticks, they stormed the court, forced the judge from the bench, and held a mock court at which they read many spirited, sometimes profanity-riddled statements. They also dragged attorneys through the streets for public ridicule. But they saved their worst for Fanning. It was reported that they dragged Fanning out of the courthouse by his heels—hitting his head on every step—and then on to his house. There, they burned his library, broke up his furniture, and beat him up. Then they left town.

Governor Tryon and a nervous Assembly swiftly enacted a law called "The Bloody Riot Act" of 1770. It allowed the attorney general to move cases involving riot charges to counties other than where the riotous acts were committed. In addition, anyone charged with rioting who failed to show up for a court summons within 60 days could be immediately executed, no questions asked.

The Regulators responded by asserting that they would pay no more taxes and would shoot Fanning on sight, refusing to recognize all courts, and threatening to kill any lawyers or judges sent to the frontier by the Governor or Assembly.

In response, Governor Tryon ordered a special term of the Superior Court to be held in Hillsborough in May 1771. He raised a militia of 1,450 men—mostly from the east—and on May 15, this force camped on Great Alamance Creek, near Hillsborough.

On the afternoon of May 16, about 2,000 Regulators gathered next to the militia, and the Regulators peacefully sought a meeting with Tryon to iron out their differences. Tryon said he would agree to such a meeting only if the Regulators disarmed. Tryon said that if they didn't disarm, his troops would fire on the Regulators. He gave them an hour to decide. An hour later, the Regulators replied, "Fire and be damned!"

Within two hours, the militia had routed the Regulators. Nine militiamen were killed and 61 wounded. The Regulators, who fought Indian-style, took their dead and wounded with them, so their casualties were unknown. Fourteen Regulators were captured and tried in court. Six were hanged and, at Tryon's request, eight were pardoned by the King.

The day after the battle, Tryon issued a blanket pardon for any Regulators who would swear an oath of allegiance to the colonial government. Most Regulators took advantage of the offer—or fled the region. The movement was finished and, within weeks, Tryon moved north to become the governor of New York.

The battle of May 16, 1771, which came to be called The War of the Regulation, was the first (and only) armed battle in the pre-Revolutionary colonies that focused on the individual rights of settlers to protest the rule of colonial and local governments. The battle also spawned the creation of several organized militias, in North Carolina and elsewhere. Within five years, these became the invaluable seeds of an American army, which rose up against and vanquished British rule.

The Edenton Tea Party

When, in 1771, Governor Tryon became Governor of New York, he was succeeded in North Carolina by Josiah Martin. A "Crown Royalist," Martin quickly questioned the powers—and, consequently, earned the antipathy—of the colony's elected Assembly. That Assembly soon helped to organize the Committee of Correspondence, whose members (representatives from the colonies) were assigned to "obtain the most early and authentic intelligence of all . . . Acts and Resolutions of the British Parliament . . . [that] affect the British Colonies and to keep up and maintain a correspondence and communication with our Sister Colonies respecting these important considerations." This secretive, conspiratorial organization served as something of a foundation for the Continental Congress, which would declare the colonies' independence from Britain in 1776.

In December 1773, as every U.S. elementary school student knows, colonists costumed as Indians tossed hundreds of pounds of tea into Boston Harbor to protest the tea import tax. The "Boston Tea Party" was one of the most dramatic and widely publicized protests in colonial history, and it marked the advent of a season of protest throughout the colonies. The following October, a group of 51 women in Edenton, North Carolina, held another sort of anti-tea party. This one was at least more recognizable as a tea party, if no more welcome to the British. Presided over by Mrs. Penelope Barker—wife of North Carolina's official agent to London, Thomas Barker—these relatively aristocratic women staged a meeting in which they aired, in front of the press, objections to various taxations imposed by King George III and his Parliament. One of their resolutions was to thenceforth refrain from buying any tea imported from England.

Although this event has today been omitted from most history books, the media in England at the time leapt upon it as a big story that helped demonstrate to Englishmen that in the brutish Colonies the fairer sex not only failed to restrain their mates but, in fact, perhaps even *fomented* rebellion. The Edenton Tea Party became a cause célèbre for anti-colonist Englishmen. More or less typical of the response is the following excerpt of a letter which was sent from Londoner Arthur Iredell to his brother James—then the Crown's customs officer in Edenton:

I see by the newspapers the Edenton ladies have signalized themselves by their protest against tea-drinking. . . . Is there a female Congress at Edenton too? I hope not, for we Englishmen are afraid of the male Congress, but if the ladies, who have ever since the Amazonian Era, been esteemed the most formidable enemies, if they, I say, should attack us, the most fatal consequence is to be dreaded. So dexterous in the handling of a dart, each wound they give is mortal; whilst we, so unhappily formed by nature, the more we strive to conquer them, the more are conquered! The Edenton ladies, conscious, I suppose, of this superiority on their side, by former experience, are willing, I imagine, to crush us into atoms, by their omnipotency; the only security on our side, to prevent the impending ruin, that I can perceive, is the probability that there are but few places in America which possess so much female artillery as Edenton.

The nickname "Edenton's female artillery" was immediately popularized by the press—which, although the protest may sound a bit tame, widely covered the event. The term, of course, had been intended as a disparaging term. But the ladies of Edenton—rebellious in this, too—wore the title with pride. (Today, an unusual memorial commemorates this group of women: a big bronze teapot mounted on a Revolutionary War cannon on the village green in downtown Edenton.)

A Provincial Congress

As King George III and his Parliament concentrated on punishing Massachusetts for its rebellious actions, the 13 colonies began to call and organize for a Continental Congress, which would meet without the Crown's authority. In North Carolina, Governor Martin prohibited the Assembly from convening to appoint delegates to such a Continental Congress. So North Carolina's various counties decided to assemble independent of the Governor—the first such colony-wide assemblage in the American colonies. The members of the body called it the "North Carolina Provincial Congress" and elected John Harvey to the post of speaker. They pledged their allegiance to the rebellious Massachusetts colony, appointed three delegates to the Continental Congress, and passed several laws, including one stating, "We will not import any slave or slaves, nor purchase any slave or slaves imported or brought into this province by others from any part of the world after the first day of November next" (three months away).

The next month, the first Continental Congress, with representatives from all 13 colonies, met in Philadelphia. Governor Martin, being pressured by King George III to suppress any North Carolina involvement in this seditious Continental Congress, was furious. In March, he called for the Assembly to hold a legislative session in New Bern on April 4, 1775. John Harvey, speaker of the Provincial Congress and a delegate to the Continental Congress, led the effort to co-opt Governor Martin's Assembly. Harvey sent out his own call to the North Carolina Assembly members, calling for a meeting of the Provincial Congress on April 3, one day earlier.

Martin demanded that no member of the North Carolina Assembly attend Harvey's Provincial Congress. The Assembly members ignored him and attended the Second Provincial Congress on April 3. The following day, despite the outraged protestations of Governor Martin, the North Carolina Assembly overwhelmingly elected John Harvey as its speaker.

Four days later, on April 8, 1775, Governor Martin officially dissolved the North Carolina Assembly. He quickly realized, though, that this was bound to be an extremely unpopular move, and on May 31 (after sending his wife and children to New York), he left Tryon's Palace and sought refuge at Fort Johnston. Six weeks later, he fled the fort on a British war ship. His escape was timely—three days later, on July 18, some 500 North Carolinians stormed the fort and burned the buildings inside it, constituting the first act of war against England in the colony of North Carolina.

The Battle of King's Mountain

For most of the Revolutionary War, the colony of North Carolina saw very few major military conflicts. But there were two significant exceptions. By January 1780, the British, under the leadership of Lord Charles Cornwallis, had seized virtually complete control of Georgia and South Carolina. In Camden, South Carolina, Cornwallis assembled an invasion force to take North Carolina in September.

While most of his army marched toward Charlotte, Cornwallis sent a separate force to conquer the sparsely inhabited western region, where "mountain men" had been assembling a Continental force. This separate army of about 1,000 British and Loyalist troops was put under the command of Colonel Patrick Ferguson. Ferguson, whose force was operating along the border of North and South Carolina, sent a message to the North Carolina "Over-Mountain Men," who numbered a few hundred. Referring to them as "a set of mongrels," Ferguson demanded that they disband immediately, or he and his army would come after them, execute their leaders, and burn their mountain settlements.

The Over-Mountain Men of North Carolina did not respond politely to Ferguson's offer, and, after gathering hundreds of extra recruits (amassing a force of close to 1,000), they began advancing on the British army. Thus was the stage set for the Battle of King's Mountain, which took place along the North and South Carolina border on October 7, 1780.

Ferguson, a veteran of many battles and regarded as one of the most competent British military strategists, took the high ground along the ridge of King's Mountain and its surrounding peaks. Considering the equal number of troops on both sides, the superior training of the British army, and the Brits' strategically superior positioning, the Battle of King's Mountain should have proven a convincingly easy victory for the English.

And indeed, when the Over-Mountain Men first charged up one side of the mountain, Ferguson's forces repelled them. About 15 minutes after that first charge began, a separate band of mountain men went charging up the opposite side of the mountain and took Ferguson's troops by surprise. The troops, however, were able to regroup sufficiently to repel this second attack, too. But at that point, a *third* corps of mountain men attacked from another direction. The British army, which for centuries had been trained to fight in one direction, was suddenly having to cope with almost simultaneous attacks from three directions by an army whose members moved across the mountainous terrain with a swiftness more befitting deer than soldiers.

Within an hour, the battle was over. Of Ferguson's army, 119 (including Ferguson) had been killed, 123 wounded, and 664 captured. Only 28 Over-Mountain Men had been killed, and 62 wounded. This was the first major victory for the Americans in the South, and it proved a turning point in Cornwallis' plan to quickly conquer North Carolina and then take Virginia.

Cornwallis Occupies the Hornets' Nest

Cornwallis' army, although constantly harassed by guerilla attacks, had meanwhile struggled over the North Carolina border and, on September 25, occupied Charlotte. Cornwallis' men didn't find Charlotte the inviting city they had been promised by North Carolina Loyalists (including banished royal governor Josiah Martin). Cornwallis' troops were treated not only to open disrespect by the citizenry but also to "terrorist" acts including sniper fire and arson. Cornwallis wrote that North Carolina was "a damned rebellious country" and christened Charlotte "the Hornets' Nest of the Revolution" (two centuries later, this would inspire the moniker of today's professional basketball team, the Charlotte Hornets).

Just 17 days after his army first occupied Charlotte, and after hearing about the Over-Mountain Men's rout of Ferguson's troops, Cornwallis decided that it was time to rethink his plan for the conquest of North Carolina, and he led his army back to central South Carolina.

The Battle of Guilford Courthouse

Two months later, in January 1781, Cornwallis mounted a second invasion of North Carolina. In skirmishes at the border area, the Americans inflicted hundreds of casualties on the British forces but always retreated back into the woods. This tactic had become practiced and proven under the leadership of General Nathanael Greene, whom George Washington had sent to Charlotte to command the North Carolina military. As Cornwallis' army crossed the border into North Carolina, Greene kept his perpetually retreating army always just a step ahead of the British. Greene had meticulously planned his routes of retreat beforehand. His goal was to get Cornwallis' army as far away as possible from the British bastion (and military supplies) of South Carolina.

The strategy worked. With Greene's army serving as a carrot, Cornwallis hungrily pursued. To gain speed along the way in his effort to overtake Greene's forces, Cornwallis abandoned many of his heavier, more cumbersome supplies.

When Greene reached Guilford Courthouse (what is today Greensboro—named for Greene), 230 miles from Cornwallis' main store of supplies in South Carolina and only 40 miles south of the Virginia border, he decided it was time to make a stand. On March 15, 1781, the two

cavalry officers at the Battle of Guilford Courthouse

armies finally met in battle, in the traditional "head-on" style of European war. Several dramatic clashes occurred that day, at the end of which the casualties included 78 Americans dead and 183 wounded, 93 British dead and 439 (almost a quarter of Cornwallis' invading force) wounded.

Even so, at the end of the battle, it was Greene and his American troops who retreated, preferring to save their strength to fight another day. Officially, Cornwallis had won the battle, though many historians suggest that he had just lost the war.

Upon announcing that the colony of North Carolina had officially been brought back under British control, Cornwallis immediately led his men south to Wilmington. After months of regrouping and reinforcing there, Cornwallis' still-weakened army mounted its attack on Virginia by advancing up North Carolina's east coast. It was there, on October 18, 1781, after the battle at Yorktown, that Cornwallis surrendered to George Washington.

DEVELOPING IN THE AFTERMATH

North Carolina: Constitutionally Rebellious?
In 1787, when the Constitution came up for ratification of the colonies, the North Carolina legislature soundly (184 to 84) voted *not* to join the federal Union. (Rhode Island was the only other colony to decline to join.) But North Carolina also resolved to reconsider the vote if an amending Bill of Rights was added to the Constitution, and it submitted to Congress a bill proposing just such an addition. In April 1790, George Washington became President. By November 1789, the first 10 articles of the Bill of Rights had been added and North Carolina finally ratified the Constitution and joined the Union. By 1790, the state had grown to become the third most populous of the 13 colonies, behind Virginia and Pennsylvania.

The State Begins to Prioritize
The 1776 state constitution had called for the establishment and support of public education. In 1789, the state established the nation's first state-funded university, the University of North Carolina, which started taking students in 1795. By 1800, more than 40 tax-exempt academies had been chartered and funded by state government.

In the meantime, the legislature finally decided to build a proper state capitol. Thanks to state senator Joel Lane's persuasive talents (and the bottomless barrels of wine he supplied to the commission making the decision), in 1792 Raleigh was chosen to be the new (and permanent) capital, and the state purchased 1,000 acres of Lane's land for $1,378.

Gold!
In 1799, on a farm outside Charlotte, young Conrad Reed brought home a yellowish rock he'd found while playing in the woods. His father, John, let the boy keep it, and Conrad used it as a doorstop for almost three years, until a jeweler spotted what was, in fact, a 17-pound boulder of gold ore. Word soon spread of the find, and the nation's first gold rush was on. Up until 1828, all of the native gold coined by the U.S. mint came from North Carolina. Almost all of that ore came from the Charlotte area, which led the na-

tion in gold production until 1848, when gold was discovered in California.

The Trail of Tears

In 1835, President Andrew Jackson presided over a heartless federal decision to relocate the Cherokee to a reservation west of the Mississippi. The Cherokee steadfastly refused, and in 1838, General Winfield Scott brutally rounded up the Carolina Cherokee and marched them to Oklahoma. On this death march, known as the Trail of Tears, as many as one in four Cherokee died. Hundreds of Cherokee managed to escape Scott's roundup, led by a warrior named Tsali. Unable to capture Tsali's band, Scott made a bargain that those who escaped with Tsali would be allowed to remain on their North Carolina lands, if Tsali and his family turned themselves in. They did, and Scott had Tsali and all of his sons shot. For once, however, the federal government was good to its word, and the Cherokee were allowed to keep the lands in western North Carolina that prosper today (albeit thanks in great measure to legalized gambling on the reservation).

THE CIVIL WAR

As the Southern states drew closer and closer to brink of secession, North Carolinians continued their long tradition of being reluctant joiners. While other Southern states' economies relied almost completely on agriculture and vast plantations, North Carolina's economy was more diverse and included nascent textile, ship-building, and lumber industries. It had also long been the South's primary seaport state and boasted the region's most complete railroad infrastructure.

Although North Carolina, too, depended primarily on agriculture, the farms of the Tarheel State were generally family affairs. In 1860, of the more than 300 plantations in the South owning 300 or more slaves, only four were located in North Carolina. By that same year, the state was home to 30,463 "free Negroes." Both of these factors mitigated the state's desire to hold on to the institution of slavery (there are no recorded incidents of any slave rebellions in North Carolina). North Carolina's tradition of relative tolerance towards blacks, compared to

---

WHAT DO YOU CALL THE GREAT CONFLAGRATION?

Though everyone knows what is meant by "the Civil War," most Southerners—including native North Carolinians—were not raised to use that term (after all, America's bloodiest war was hardly "civil"). As you travel the state, you may read or hear references to alternative monikers for the war. These may include:

The War Between the States
The War for Southern Independence
The War of Northern Aggression
The Great Unpleasantness

---

other Southern states, would, a century later, give it a pivotal role in the Civil Rights movement of the 1960s.

In November 1860, although Abraham Lincoln failed to receive a majority of the American popular vote (he was not even on the North Carolina ballot), he won a clear plurality in the electoral college. South Carolina seceded on December 20. Mississippi followed on January 9, 1861, Alabama on January 11, Georgia on the 19th, and Texas and Louisiana before the month was out. In February, North Carolina held an election to determine delegates for a constitutional convention to determine whether North Carolina should secede from the Union. The result: 74 against secession, 46 for. Lincoln was sworn in on March 4, 1861. On April 12, forces from the South Carolina Provisional Government fired on Fort Sumpter. Lincoln called on Union states to provide 75,000 troops. Perhaps predictably, North Carolina—though still a Union state—refused to provide any. On April 17, Virginia seceded. On May 6, Arkansas seceded. On May 7, the Tennessee legislature passed an ordinance of secession which was ratified by popular vote on June 8.

On May 13, North Carolinians held another election, and a week later their newly elected delegates held a convention and decided to officially declare North Carolina a separate, sovereign state. This withdrawal from the Union, although it did not formally ally the state with the Confederacy, did in fact put North Carolina in the same category, since the primary goal of the secessionist Confederacy was to establish the supremacy of states' rights over the power of the federal government.

Early in the war—by February 1862—Union forces had taken control of the Outer Banks and a few inland ports, including New Bern. But the Cape Fear coast, surrounding Wilmington, remained in North Carolina's hands. The port, and the railroad extending from Wilmington to Weldon, was christened by Robert E. Lee the "lifeline of the Confederacy." Though the Union tried to enforce a shipping blockade for years, it didn't work. Savvy Confederate captains—like Blackbeard before them—knew the treacherous waters too well and easily outmaneuvered the Union's blockade.

For most of the Civil War, North Carolina was spared serving as a major battleground. In March 1865, however, William Tecumseh Sherman's infamous march to the sea entered North Carolina (Sherman had given orders to cease the plundering and wanton destruction that had characterized his march in Georgia and South Carolina). On March 19, Sherman's troops encountered their only major resistance, at the battle of Bentonville, in which more than 4,000 soldiers were killed or wounded in the bloodiest battle of the war fought on North Carolina soil.

Less than a month later—a week after Robert E. Lee surrendered to Ulysses S. Grant at Appomattox—Sherman accepted the surrender of the Confederacy's largest army, under the command of General Johnston, at the farmhouse of James Bennitt, halfway between the towns of Durham and Hillsborough.

Though the last to join the Confederacy, North Carolinians had served with energy and bravery. In all, more than 40,000 North Carolinian soldiers were killed during the war—more than in any other of the 11 Confederate states—accounting for one of every six Confederate army deaths.

THE POST-BELLUM ECONOMY

The Boom Continues
In contrast to most Southern states, whose economies languished for decades after the Civil War, North Carolina's economy boomed from 1865 through the turn of the century. Many of the names of North Carolina's leading industrialists of the time are still around today. The Duke family made Durham an international tobacco center, and R.J. Reynolds did much the same for Winston-Salem when he established his first tobacco factory there in 1875. Taking advantage of the cotton grown in neighboring South Carolina and Georgia, the Hanes and Cannon families made North Carolina the national leader in the production of textiles. In High Point, several entrepreneurs created a furniture manufacturing center that still ranks today as a world leader.

While North Carolina's traditional industries have continued to prosper, the state has continued to sharpen its commercial and industrial cutting edge. In 1960, in cooperation with the state's three premier universities (Duke University in Durham, the University of North Carolina in Chapel Hill, and North Carolina State University in Raleigh), the state legislature established the nation's first planned research park. Today, Research Triangle Park hosts research and development facilities for more than 100 of the world's foremost research companies, in fields ranging from computing to pharmaceuticals.

Since the banking industry was deregulated in the 1980s, North Carolina banks have grown to

OZELL CALLAHAN

CHARCOAL CURING FOR BRIGHT LEAF TOBACCO

One day in the summer of 1839 on Abisha Slade's plantation, north of Greensboro, a young slave named Stephen was put in charge of keeping the curing fire burning in the tobacco barn. Stephen fell asleep for awhile and, as he slept, pieces of the wood fuel for the fire ignited but didn't burn up—they had become charcoal. Stephen picked up the charcoal and fed it into the smoldering fire. The result was a burst of tremendous heat, which filled the barn and blanched the hanging harvested tobacco leaves a bright yellow color.

Stephen was at first terrified by his mishap, but he and the plantation owner were astonished when they smoked this charcoal-cured tobacco. Stephen had discovered the magical process that would soon make "Brightleaf" the most coveted tobacco in the world. As a free man, Stephen Slade would eventually buy some of his former master's land, become a successful tobacco farmer himself, and live to the ripe old age of 93.

make Charlotte the second-largest financial center in the U.S., behind only New York City—and home to NationsBank/BankAmerica, the largest banking corporation and the second-largest financial institution in the nation, behind only Citi-Corp/Travelers (if and when that proposed merger is approved).

That's not to say that North Carolina has abandoned its early roots in agriculture. Thousands of small tobacco farms still dot the North Carolina landscape, which produces the nation's second-largest tobacco crop (Kentucky produces the largest crop). The state also leads the nation in the production of one of the most beloved commercial crops—the Fraser firs that are the East Coast's most popular Christmas trees. The livestock industry has also exploded in North Carolina, which now leads the nation in turkey production and has risen to number two (behind Iowa) in hog production.

Manufacturing constitutes the largest segment of North Carolina's economy today, and the state leads the nation in its number of manufacturing jobs (although, true to its non-joining tradition, the state ranks 47th out of 50 in percentage of employees who belong to unions).

Tourism is the state's second-largest industry, and the travel and tourism industry continues to grow steadily. More than 40 million people visit North Carolina each year—about two-thirds of them for pleasure—and spend over $10 billion on tourism-related activities.

Visitors and newcomers quickly become accustomed to easy smiles and nods of hello, to chatting with checkout clerks at convenience stores, and to answering small inquiries about your family from your waiter or waitress—in North Carolina, people are genuinely interested in your answer, having internalized the state's Latin motto, *Essi Quam Dittum,* "to be rather than to seem."

While some visitors may initially feel impatient at the slower pace of life in North Carolina, the relentlessly friendly and unpretentious natives, and the refreshing absence of honking horns and tailgating drivers will quickly grow on you.

POLITICS

Among the contributions made by North Carolina statesmen in formulating the structure of American government, perhaps the most significant are the state's efforts to establish and enforce the ultimate control over the abuse of executive power—through the process of impeachment. During the Constitutional Convention of 1787, it was a delegate from North Carolina, Hugh Williamson, who first introduced the notion that impeachment be included in the Constitution. His motion was seconded by another North Carolinian delegate, William Davie.

The issue of impeachment would lead to another distinction for North Carolina almost a century later when, in early 1870, in response to the murders of two prominent Republicans in Alamance and Caswell counties, Republican Governor William Holden declared martial law in those counties and had several powerful citizens arrested and held without being charged with anything. Although these notables were soon released by a federal judge, members of the Conservative party saw their chance and acted swiftly to impeach the governor. Holden was convicted and removed from office—making

STATE SYMBOLS

Beverage	Milk
Bird	Cardinal
Fish	Channel Bass
Flower	Dogwood
Insect	Honey Bee
Mammal	Gray Squirrel
Reptile	Eastern Box Turtle
Rock	Granite
Seashell	Scotch Bonnet
Gem	Emerald
Tree	Pine

him the first governor to be impeached and convicted in the United States.

A century later, in 1973, the senior U.S. senator from North Carolina, former judge Sam Ervin, Jr., chairman of the Senate Judiciary Committee, chaired the Watergate Committee hearings. Ervin's captivating combination of folksy humor, Constitutional expertise, and gentlemanly demeanor—in particular his respectful but firm handling of committee members and the witnesses called to testify—made Ervin the powerfully engaging, entertaining, and informative master of ceremonies for the most-watched government hearings in history. The hearings, of course, led to President Richard M. Nixon's resigning to avoid an impending impeachment trial before the Senate.

Somewhat ironically, 1973 was also the year that North Carolinians elected their first Republican U.S. senator in generations. The candidate was a journalist who had gained notoriety during the late 1960s and early 1970s for irascible, humorous commentaries aired daily on statewide radio and on Raleigh's most popular TV station. He railed on about the demise of American morals during the height of the countercultural movement of those years, attacking everything from rock and roll music and free love to bra burning and Vietnam War protests.

The name of this media personality, Jesse Helms, still ignites controversies at dinner tables throughout the country when he utters one of his inflammatory sound bites designed to get ratings. Curiously, within North Carolina, Helms does not inspire the same intense level of sheer hatred among the solidly liberal half of the state's voters that he draws from liberals *outside* the state. Over the quarter-century that Helms has represented North Carolina, even the most liberal residents and pundits grudgingly admit, his constituent service operation has usually helped at least a few friends and neighbors in need, and his record of "putting North Carolina first" in his legislative agenda has resulted in considerable federal benefits for the state. And everybody has witnessed the media wizardry of Helms' expert campaigns, which have provided prototypes of many of the media and message strategies used so successfully in conservative Republican electoral successes of the 1980s and 1990s throughout the nation.

The high profile of Helms' colorful continued career tends to obscure the generally progressive, Democrat-dominated trends of 20th-century North Carolina politics. (In Helms' last two elections, in 1990 and 1996, his Democratic—and almost victorious—opposition has been Harvey Gantt, the liberal African-American former mayor of Charlotte.)

Along with Helms, North Carolina's most popular living politician is liberal Democrat Governor James B. Hunt, who was elected to his fourth term in 1995. Nationally known for innovative programs like Smart Start, a massive, state-funded program for North Carolina preschools, Hunt is only the most recent in a long line of progressive Democrats elected by North Carolina voters. In 1998, former governor, U.S. senator, and president of Duke University Terry Sanford passed away, leaving an extraordinary legacy—not the least of which was his courageous leadership not only among Southern governors but in the nation as a whole during the early 1960s, when he persuasively argued and acted to advance the cause of civil rights for all Americans.

ON THE ROAD
SIGHTSEEING HIGHLIGHTS

The great charm of the villages and towns is only one reason to visit North Carolina's **Outer Banks.** The islands are perhaps most famous for their hundreds of miles of spectacular beaches, whose waters, warmed by the Gulf Stream, remain comfortably swimmable for almost half the year.

At Kill Devil Hills, you can climb Jockey's Ridge—the tallest sand dune in the eastern United States. This is where the Wright brothers tested their pioneering aircraft, and the Wright Brothers Memorial here is one of the most engaging, informative, and moving sites in the state.

South of Kill Devil Hills, pristine Cape Hatteras National Seashore stretches for 75 miles, to the south end of the cozy island of Ocracoke, and then gives way to the virtually uninhabited 55 miles of Cape Lookout National Seashore.

One of the great attractions of virtually the entire North Carolina coast is the omnipresence of fresh, relatively inexpensive seafood, from tender bluefish fillets and thick Mako-shark steaks to all the cheap clams and oysters you can slurp, to soft and hard shell crabs and lobsters you can munch. But for cuisine you'd be

hard pressed to find anywhere else, you won't want to miss the Strange Seafood Festival, held annually (usually the first weekend in October) in the **Mainland Central Coast** community of Morehead City. The festival gives you the opportunity to sample captivating dishes like a stingray casserole, with a left-handed whelk chowder and a seaweed salad on the side.

An attraction nearby but of an entirely different sort, Croatan National Forest provides an engaging glimpse into the wilds of this region.

The vital port of **Wilmington,** just 20 minutes inland from Atlantic Ocean beaches, has been one of North Carolina's most dynamic cities for two centuries. Today it augments its rich historic heritage, architecture, and culture with abundant opportunities for shopping, entertainment, and nightlife. The city is also home to the battleship *North Carolina,* one of the most popular attractions in the state. Allow two hours for the self-guided tour.

The **South Coast** towns of Wrightsville Beach and Carolina Beach offer a full array of diversions, from neon-bedecked amusement parks and miniature golf courses abristle with dinosaurs to live theater, movie megaplexes, and night clubs showcasing disco, karaoke, and everything in between.

For a sampling of more sedate enjoyments, head to **Pinehurst,** the "Golfing Capital of the World." It is here, site of the Golf Hall of Fame and more than 40 championship courses open to the public, that the 1999 U.S. Open will be held.

All three of the cities that make up the **Triangle** are fanatical about basketball. Each city is home to a member of the nine-team Atlantic Coast Conference: the University of North Carolina at Chapel Hill, Duke University in Durham, and North Carolina State University in Raleigh (a fourth, Wake Forest University, is in Winston-Salem). Tickets for most ACC games are difficult to come by, but the enthusiastic atmosphere is easy to soak up and hard to resist.

In the **Triad** city of Winston-Salem, tour the living-history Moravian settlement of Old Salem. The Triad is a superb showcase for an exceptional array of artisanship, offering a glimpse of how some traditional crafts have evolved over the centuries—from the showrooms of High Point, the "Furniture Capital of the World," to the more than 80 intimate potteries in Seagrove, one of the nation's most renowned pottery enclaves.

Another fascinating stop is the R.J. Reynolds factory museum, in Winston-Salem. The factory, which discontinued floor tours in 1998, is capable of producing 275 million cigarettes *a day,* making it responsible for a sizable portion of the 475 billion cigarettes manufactured in 1997 in North Carolina.

ATTITUDES ABOUT TOBACCO

Beginning soon after the Civil War, North Carolina led the world in cigarette manufacturing for almost a century. But the glory days of tobacco have been gone from the state for decades. Today, the R.J. Reynolds Tobacco Company, now headquartered in Virginia but still operating two plants in Winston-Salem, is the last vestige of "Big Tobacco" in North Carolina. Durham, the city that produced more cigarettes than any other place on earth during the first half of the 20th century, is home now only to a small plant operated by Liggett and Myers Tobacco Company, whose mostly generic brands of cigarettes account for less than two percent of the cigarette industry.

However, while the manufacturing end of the tobacco industry has largely moved elsewhere, thousands of tobacco farmers remain in the state. Tobacco farming here is almost always a family affair. As you drive along the back roads of the coastal plain and eastern Piedmont, you won't see vast fields of tobacco stretching to the horizon. In the coastal plain ("down East" or "East Carolina," as it's called by natives), the typical tobacco field averages 25 to 30 acres. In the eastern Piedmont, you'll see small fields—usually just a few acres or, even more common, little tobacco "gardens," often the size of a tennis court or two, located in side or back yards.

The reason these tobacco fields are so small goes back to the 1930s, when the federal government, in an effort to control tobacco prices, doled out "allotments" to American tobacco farmers. These allotments specified how many pounds of tobacco each grower could sell based on a specific percentage of cleared land that the farmer owned. Still in force, these allotments have been passed down from generation to generation. The smaller allotments, which account for the little tobacco gardens, may sometimes yield less than $1,000 worth of tobacco. But it's more than just the extra income that keeps North Carolinians growing tobacco on their land. People take real pride in tobacco growing as a family tradition. As a consequence, if you've been driving along back roads and you decide to stop at a roadside diner or watering hole, we recommend that you temporarily steer clear of discussions about certain types of class-action suits and the latest government efforts to regulate cigarette smoking.

That said, in all North Carolina cities—and in most small towns, too—restaurants almost always have non-smoking sections, and an ever-growing number of restaurants and coffeehouses are completely smoke-free. Hotels and motels usually have non-smoking rooms, and indoor public places like museums and theaters are virtually always smoke-free (as are bed-and-breakfast inns).

Although North Carolina has been following the national trend toward efforts to reduce smoking, the legislature is unlikely to raise state taxes on cigarettes. Smokers will find cigarettes much less expensive in North Carolina than in the vast majority of other states.

In Asheboro, south of the Triad city of Greensboro, the beautiful 1,400-acre North Carolina Zoological Park (the world's largest natural habitat zoo) is a must-visit.

For fans of stock car racing, the **Charlotte** Motor Speedway is NASCAR Nirvana, regularly drawing more than 160,000 spectators for the Coca Cola 600 on Memorial Day. And the chances are decent that you'll even be able to get a ticket.

In the state's **Northern Mountains,** amidst the cooling, rainbow spray of hundreds of scenic waterfalls, the Blue Ridge Parkway provides what is indisputably (particularly in the fall) one of the world's most spectacular drives, an excursion through the brilliant splendor of the Appalachian Mountains. The 470-mile roadway extends from Shenandoah National Park in Virginia to Great Smoky Mountains National Park.

These mountains are also home to one of the most dynamic arts and crafts communities in the world. The "craft heritage trails" publicized by the revered arts organization Handmade In America clearly map out convenient routes to hundreds of artisans' shops throughout the region. At the various sites, you can observe artisans working at arts including quilting, woodcarving, basket weaving, and glassblowing.

No visitor to **Asheville** should pass up the opportunity to tour the grand halls and gardens of railroad robber baron George Vanderbilt's incomparably magnificent 250-room estate, Biltmore House.

At the terminus of the celebrated Blue Ridge Parkway, on the western edge of the state, lies glorious **Great Smoky Mountains National Park,** the most popular national park in America, attracting over nine million visitors a year.

And adjacent to the park, the Cherokee tribe's Qualla Boundary, including the town of Cherokee, provides the most comprehensive, informative, and entertaining of any Native American site on the east coast of the United States.

OUTDOOR RECREATION

Whether you want to hike the tallest peak east of the Rockies, conquer a really tricky windmill obstacle on a miniature golf course, or pursue almost any outdoor activity in between, you'll probably find some outlet in North Carolina.

Swimming
The warm waters of the Gulf Stream make their closest approach to the United States shoreline in North Carolina. One of the happy consequences of this is that the waters of the Atlantic and the state's several sounds are invitingly warm from mid-May through September and, depending upon weather patterns, remain comfortable (if cool) for swimming even through early October.

Many North Carolina beaches are staffed with lifeguards only part of each day, and some have no lifeguards at all. For safety's sake, you should never swim alone. Also, never leave small children unattended while they're playing in the surf.

Be sure to heed "Danger: No Swimming" signs and watch for posted red flags. These indicate particularly strong and unpredictable currents or the presence of underwater construction materials from structures the sea has reclaimed.

North Carolina's more than 1,500 lakes also provide refreshing swimming opportunities. Most lakes designate specific swimming areas, and you're advised to stay within such boundaries. Boating and water-skiing are popular lake sports, and swimmers and boats don't mix well. Most

NORTH CAROLINA DIVISION OF TOURISM, FILM & SPORTS DEVELOPMENT

COPING WITH A RIPTIDE

You'll almost always find swimming in the Atlantic to be a safe, enjoyable experience. But remember that ocean swimming does have its perils. You don't have to worry about human-eating sharks—they don't frequent North Carolina beaches. But you should be wary of the power of the ocean currents, particularly the phenomenon of the riptide.

Often, riptides are caused by the currents around submerged sandbars, which often lie a few dozen yards from beach. Sometimes, a sandbar develops a narrow valley. As the incoming tide pours over the sandbar on its way into the beach, the *out* rushing tide simultaneously recedes in a rush through "valleys" in the sandbar forming strong opposing currents—essentially a swiftly flowing river in the ocean. (Sometimes, riptides are also caused by changing tides located near a river flowing into the sea or by changes in weather patterns caused by tropical storms or hurricanes.)

Swimmers experience these riptides as a strong undertow, pulling them out to sea. You may not realize you're caught in one until you find yourself trying to swim back to shore and find that you can't make any headway—or, in fact, are going in reverse. If you find yourself in such a situation, don't panic and don't struggle. You're not in any deadly danger, and, although it may feel like it, you're not being swept irreversibly out to sea. Just relax, stay afloat, and calmly swim with the current, parallel to the beach.

Within a few minutes, the riptide will play out, and you'll be able to gradually swim the few dozen yards back to the beach, following a different current. Remember that although you will come out of the surf rather far from where your entered, you *will* get back to the beach. The most important thing to remember is to not tire yourself out by trying to fight the riptide. Just give it a few minutes, and the riptide will tell you when it's time to start swimming back to shore.

---

lakes also have public restrooms and changing areas. The 37,000 miles of North Carolina's rivers and streams can be irresistible temptations to swimmers, especially on hot summer days. Be aware that submerged or partially submerged rocks can be slippery—and, naturally, be extremely careful if you're taking a dip near any rapids or waterfalls.

Other Water Sports

For anyone interested in **scuba diving,** the waters off the Outer Banks, particularly around Cape Hatteras, constitute a veritable museum of dozens of sunken vessels, from pirate ships to German U-boats (these waters, full of treacherous currents and shoals, are deservedly known as "the Graveyard of the Atlantic"). Diving outfits provide guided dives and lessons for folks who want to learn how to scuba dive.

Although **windsurfing** is very popular on Roanoke Sound, off the eastern shore of Nags Head, the East Coast's mecca for windsurfers is Canadian Hole, on Pamlico Sound off the Outer Banks between Avon and Buxton. Windsurfers from around the world flock here all year long, lending these little towns—particularly Avon—the perpetual air of a windsurfers' convention.

The waters off this coast also draw board surfers. Most of the time, the Atlantic waves here are comparatively gentle for **surfing,** posing little threat even to beginners. At times, however, offshore storms and hurricanes can generate fierce wave action.

On the opposite side of the state, in the western mountains, dozens of outfitters offer the thrill of **whitewater rafting.** Trips are usually offered early spring through late fall. The rapids run swiftest during the spring, when rains and melting snow raise the rivers' water levels. During the summer months, water levels usually drop considerably, transforming whitewater adventures into tranquil drifts along mirror-like waters.

Hang Gliding

If you've ever had the slightest desire to try a hang glider, you should visit Jockey's Ridge State Park in Nags Head on the Outer Banks. There, veteran outfitter Kitty Hawk Kites will help you sail aloft on the very same wind currents that sent the Wright Brothers soaring into the history books. It can be enjoyable even if you're afraid of heights—your first few flights probably won't take you above an altitude of about six feet, and even the advanced lessons will rarely put you higher than 10 or 20 feet above soft sand dunes.

Fishing

The Gulf Stream's warming presence makes the sea off North Carolina a site for some of the best fishing in the nation. Up and down the state's coast, you're never far from a marina where dozens of charter boats run half-day, whole-day, and sometimes even overnight fishing expeditions that give you the chance to pursue the largest game fish in the ocean. Fishing licenses are not required for saltwater fishing.

If you are not experienced at ocean fishing but would like to try your hand, visit the closest fishing pier (expect to pay a small fee for the privilege, but you're almost guaranteed to catch something). The proprietor will rent you equipment and set you up with the right kind of bait. Most pier proprietors will help you (if you need it) by identifying any fish you reel in, many will even take a Polaroid of you holding up your catch, and many will also clean and gut your fish for a small fee.

Surf fishing is unrestricted (to the consternation of some swimmers) but requires more skill and strength than you might suspect. Overfishing has greatly reduced the numbers of Gulf Stream schooling fish, like black sea bass and red drum; and others, like grouper and blue fish—which used to swarm all along the coast—are less prevalent today. However, recently instituted commercial fishing restrictions are bringing back many species. Although it is not required by law, you can do your part to ensure more fish for the future by keeping only what you can eat and following catch and release guidelines with undersize fish and any fish that appears ready to spawn.

Inland from the coast, the state boasts more than 1,500 lakes and 37,000 miles of rivers, relatively evenly distributed. Fishing licenses are required for inland fishing and are available at sporting goods stores, bait shops, and some general stores. For more information about fishing licenses, call the North Carolina Wildlife Resources Commission at (919) 662-4370 or (800) 628-3773.

Crabbing is a delightful alternative to fishing, especially if you have small children who aren't

---

BEACH ACCESS

Unlike in some Atlantic coast states, North Carolina's beaches are all public property. While private beachfront homes, condominiums, inns, hotels, and motels may restrict access to their property, private property rights only extend to edge of sand dunes and, by law, do not include the beach. Swimming, beachcombing, surf-fishing, surfing, windsurfing, jet-skiing, kayaking, sailing, and just soaking up the sun are all permitted on any beach in the state.

Parking

Finding a place to park your car can occasionally be tricky. Free Beach Access parking lots are fairly plentiful and relatively evenly spaced all along the more popular beaches. (Note, however, that along some stretches, to provide as much room as possible for beachfront real estate development, these lots are sometimes small and crowded.)

It is also usually possible to park on the streets in most beach communities, but keep in mind that most roads right next to beaches do *not* allow street parking, so you'll usually have to venture inland a block or two.

There are also many beach roads—particularly on the Outer Banks—that tempt you to pull off onto sandy patches, where you may see some 4WD vehicles parked. Resist this temptation and do *not* pull over onto these patches. Many a pleasant afternoon drive along the Outer Banks has been marred by having to wait for a tow truck to pull the car out of these sandy turnoffs.

Boat Ramps

It's permissible to unload most water-bound equipment, including small jetskis, sail and surf boards, kayaks, and small Sunfish-type sailboats at public beach access parking lots, if you want to carry it to the water yourself. However, boats, larger sailboats, catamarans, and larger jetskis should be unloaded at designated boat ramps on beaches or in town harbors. Use of beach boat ramps is usually free, but most harbors charge a small unloading fee. Boat ramps and harbors are plentiful and usually clearly marked, but if you don't encounter any, ask for directions at the local visitors center, gas station, or convenience store, or simply roll down your window and ask a local.

ready to handle fishing poles. Blue crabs are plentiful in North Carolina's sounds and salt marshes. You can either rent a small boat from one of the many little shops that advertise boat or skiff rentals or simply crab from a salt marsh pier. Crabs love mud flats and areas with shallow water. To catch one, all you have to do is tie a little weight—like a fishing weight—to the end of a long string, then tie a piece of chicken (the smellier the better) toward the end of the string. Drop the weight in the water, and wait (usually not very long) until you feel a persistent tug. Draw the crab slowly toward the surface, scoop it up in a net, and toss it in your cooler. Make sure to keep your crabs cool, and don't cook any crab that has died before you get it in the pot. Children, being curious, often want to touch the crabs. But crabs are surprisingly agile, and those claws can snap shut and hold fast. If a crab does grab a finger or toe with its claw, and insists on holding on, tear the claw from the crab's body, then gently pry it loose with your hands, a knife, or a pair of pliers.

Hunting

More than two million acres, spread out over 90 parcels in North Carolina, are designated game lands. Generally, there are three types of game lands: those on which only dove hunting is allowed, only on Monday, Wednesday, and Saturday; those open for hunting all but a few game species, again only on Monday, Wednesday, and Saturday; and those open for hunting of all but a few game species six days a week.

With very few exceptions, anyone entering any game land for the purpose of hunting or trapping must have in his or her possession a game lands license in addition to the appropriate hunting or trapping licenses. For more information about hunting licenses and a free 80-page booklet mapping out all game lands in the state, call the North Carolina Wildlife Resources Commission at (919) 662-4370 or (800) 628-3773.

Hiking

An engaging hike is rarely more than a few minutes' drive away in North Carolina, from the soaring mountains in the west to the isolated beaches and nature preserves of the coast and dozens of parks and preserves in between. The Appalachian Trail winds along the North Carolina/Tennessee border for more than 200 breathtaking miles, including a glorious stretch through Great Smoky Mountains National Park, often at an elevation of more than 6,000 feet.

The northernmost 12 miles of Hatteras Island constitutes Pea Island National Wildlife Refuge, where sea-level trails through lush salt marshes have made this a favorite haunt of birdwatchers (more than 260 feathered species have been identified here).

North Carolina's more than 60 state parks and four national forests are also great sites for hiking. In the east, stretching from the Atlantic Ocean to Pamlico Sound, Croatan National Forest features miles of dark, deep trails through 157,000 acres of woods, maritime forest, marshes, and bogs. The trails lacing Uwharrie National Forest, in the center of the state, take you over 47,000 acres of gentle mountains and along lovely lake shores. In the western mountains, adjacent to Great Smoky Mountains National Park, the vast Pisgah and Nantahala National Forests together form more than a million acres of mountainous terrain, woven with hundreds of hiking trails on which you'll rarely encounter other humans.

Remember, when you're hiking anywhere, *always make sure you take along plenty of water.* Don't plan on finding potable water on any North Carolina hiking trail.

Although we've made a concerted effort to describe a few good hikes in virtually every chapter of this book, if you're a real hiking buff, you'll want to purchase the "bible" of hiking in this state, *North Carolina Hiking Trails,* by Allen De Hart, published by the Appalachian Mountain Club.

Golf

The Pinehurst area is home to more than 40 magnificent championship golf courses, including some of the world's most celebrated. Although slightly less well known, the South Brunswick coast, between the South Carolina border and Cape Fear, also boasts dozens of top-flight championship courses. But the state provides more than 500 18-hole golf courses, so wherever you visit, you're never far from golf. Even in the more rugged sections of the Appalachians, you'll be able to enjoy some of the most revered mountain courses in the nation.

Although renowned for its full-size golf courses, North Carolina is also home to some of the most elaborate *miniature* golf courses in the nation, particularly along the coast, where life-size dinosaurs loom over miniature volcanoes and 10-foot-tall pirates brandish sabers. A new and growing trend in miniature golf in the state is the emergence of courses carpeted in natural grass. While these don't include the kitschy obstacles and themed sculptures for which miniature golf is famous, they do offer a small-scale taste of what it feels like to putt on a "real" golf course.

Skiing and Snowboarding

Over the past 30 years, since artificial snowmaking equipment has become more prevalent and sophisticated, skiing has continued to grow as one of North Carolina's most popular sports. From as early as November through as late as March, hundreds of thousands of skiers and snowboarders flock to the slopes in the state's mountains. (Note, however, that early and late in the season, the "powder" usually consists solely of snow generated by snowmaking machines.)

The premier snow sport destination is the Banner Elk area. The Ski Beech resort, on Beech Mountain, features the highest ski slopes east of the Rockies, topping out at 5,505 feet. Sugar Ski resort, on Sugar Mountain, features the state's deepest vertical drop—1,200 feet over a 1.5-mile run. The resorts of Hawksnest and Appalachian Mountain provide tamer, family-friendly slopes. In all, these four Banner Elk-vicinity resorts offer more than 50 trails, as well as a handful of snowboarding half-pipes.

One of the state's newest and most popular ski resorts, located within a 45-minute drive of Asheville, Wolf Laurel Ski Area includes 14 trails, with a maximum vertical drop of 650 feet. All of North Carolina's ski resorts offer night skiing and a full array of lessons.

Spectator Sports

From November through March, North Carolinians follow the ups and downs of the state's **col-lege basketball** teams with a passion. The Piedmont is home to four members of the nine-team Atlantic Coast Athletic Conference (ACC)—the University of North Carolina at Chapel Hill, Duke University in Durham, North Carolina State University in Raleigh, and Wake Forest University in Winston-Salem. Almost every year, two or more of these teams are ranked in the top 10 in the nation and are in the thick of the chase for the national championship. Tickets for ACC games can be very scarce.

Stock car racing is another major draw in North Carolina. Though the Charlotte Motor Speedway is the premier venue in the state, hosting the Coca Cola 600 NASCAR race in May, you'll find smaller tracks scattered throughout.

Charlotte is also home to three major-league professional sports teams, the **National Football League** Carolina Panthers, the **National Basketball Association** Charlotte Hornets, and the **Women's National Basketball Association** Charlotte Sting. All three teams are enormously popular in town, but the Panthers have been adopted by the entire state—it's not uncommon for North Carolinians from all parts of the state to make the pilgrimage to the city to attend a Panthers game. As a result, tickets can be difficult to obtain.

North Carolina is also home to the **National Hockey League** Carolina Hurricanes. The Hurricanes are playing out of Greensboro through the 1999 season, until construction of their permanent arena, in Raleigh, is complete, in 2000.

Minor-league baseball flourishes in North Carolina, with teams in larger cities including Wilmington, Charlotte, Raleigh, Durham, Winston-Salem, and Asheville, as well as numerous smaller towns like Edenton, Rocky Mount, and Wilson. Watching these low-paid boys of summer play with passionate abandon fills fans with a joy that some find hard to muster watching the millionaires in the majors. Fans particularly flock to watch the Durham Bulls, the most famous minor-league baseball club in America, thanks to the film *Bull Durham*.

ARTS AND ENTERTAINMENT

MUSEUMS

Museum locations are indicated by brown signs alongside major thoroughfares, including interstate highways, throughout North Carolina.

Science Museums
The North Carolina Piedmont boasts three of the nation's most celebrated and emulated science museums, designed to educate children about the natural world: Discovery Place in Charlotte, the Museum of Life and Science in Durham, and SciWorks in Winston-Salem. Hands-on exhibits at all three delight and educate hundreds of thousands of kids and adults every year on the subjects of physics, biology, and chemistry.

In Raleigh, the North Carolina Museum of Natural History has been actively expanding its collection since 1879, making it one of the nation's premier natural history museums.

The Morehead Planetarium in Chapel Hill was the nation's first observatory built by a university, in 1832, and it has been at the forefront of astronomy research ever since. The observatory has served as a NASA celestial navigation training center for Mercury, Gemini, Apollo, Skylab, Apollo-Soyuz, and early space shuttle astronauts. Today, the Morehead complex contains a number of astronomical exhibits and features planetarium shows about the heavens and earth.

Art Museums
Fine arts and arts-and-crafts museums big and small abound in North Carolina. Four fine arts museums stand out particularly: the Mint Museum in Charlotte, the North Carolina Museum of Art in Raleigh, the Ackland Art Museum in Chapel Hill, and Reynolda House in Winston-Salem.

Although dozens of museums showcase the state's renowned tradition of arts and crafts, two are especially mesmerizing: the Museum of Early Decorative Arts in Winston-Salem and the Folk Art Center, located just outside of Asheville on the Blue Ridge Parkway. The contemporary state of arts and crafts, however, is probably best enjoyed in the products of living artisans, whose work is sold in hundreds of stores and galleries statewide.

Historic and Cultural Museums
Hundreds of idiosyncratic little museums, cared for with great love by their curators, line the roads of North Carolina, like the Museum of the Alphabet in Waxhaw, the Angela Peterson Doll Museum in High Point, the Museum of North Carolina Minerals on the Blue Ridge Parkway, and innumerable one-room preserved pharmacies, doctors' offices, and collections of Civil War artifacts. To mention just three favorites that offer insights into the state, the North Carolina Maritime Museum, in Beaufort, brings to life the state's seafaring history; the Duke Homestead, in Durham, discusses the humble origins of the state's tobacco industry, which became the world's most lucrative monopoly at the beginning of the 20th century; and the Museum of the Cherokee Indian, in Cherokee, chronicles the noble and tragic history of the state's best-known Native Americans.

Aquariums
In 1976, the state government created three aquariums on the North Carolina coast—on Roanoke Island near Manteo, at Pine Knoll Shores near Morehead City, and at Fort Fisher near Wilmington. At the time, only a handful of major marine attractions existed in the country. Since then, a host of "mega-aquariums" have gone up across the country—the spectacular aquariums in Baltimore and New Orleans are but two. In comparison, North Carolina's three state aquariums now seem rather humble affairs. (All three are due for significant expansions over the next few years that will nearly double the size of each facility.) But even as they are, these make captivating stops guaranteed to deliver an entertaining and educational couple of hours.

HISTORIC SITES

Historic Homes

During the last year of the Civil War, Union General William T. Sherman obliterated untold thousands of homes and public buildings in the South during his infamous march to the sea. He halted his march in Durham, but he had lifted his slash-and-burn policy of "total war" as soon as his forces crossed the North Carolina border—a gesture of respect for the fact that North Carolina had been the southern state most vociferously opposed to secession and the last to join the Confederacy. As a result, hundreds of still-standing North Carolina homes and buildings date back to the 1700s and early 1800s. Dozens of these have been restored to period splendor (or humility) and are open to the public.

Two historic homes are well worth going out of your way to visit. Tryon Palace, in New Bern, consists of a series of structures, including the Governor's mansion, that made up the state capitol in 1770. Although most of the complex was burned to the ground in 1798, it was meticulously restored in the 20th century. The other, in Asheville, is the spectacular Biltmore Estate, which includes the largest privately owned home in America—250-room Biltmore House, conceived by railroad magnate George Vanderbilt and completed in 1895. In addition to the magnificent house, you'll find restaurants, shops, a winery, and 75 acres of landscaped gardens and grounds. Plan to spend at least one full day here, taking in the splendors of this glorious monument to the grandeur of the Gilded Age.

William Tecumseh Sherman looms large in the military history of North Carolina.

Military History Sites

When it comes to battlefield memorial sites in North Carolina, the calendar begins in the 1770s. In Alamance County, between Durham and Greensboro, little Alamance Battleground commemorates the brief battle in 1771 between the colony's Royalist militia and the rural settlers known as the Regulators, who mounted an armed rebellion against unfair taxation. Five years later, within the space of two weeks, two crucial battles were fought on North Carolina ground that would help decide the outcome of the Revolutionary War. On February 27, 1776, at Moore's Creek Battlefield, about 20 miles northwest of Wilmington, North Carolina patriots routed British forces who were attempting to initiate a major campaign to conquer the southern colonies. Then, on March 15, 1776, at the battle of Guilford Courthouse, in what is now Greensboro, colonial General Nathanael Greene's forces battled the British army's premier force, under the leadership of General Cornwallis. Greene's army inflicted devastating harm, then retreated—staying just close enough to continue harassing Cornwallis' troops. Cornwallis directed his army to Yorktown, where, within a few months, his depleted force surrendered to General George Washington, ending the Revolutionary War. Today, Moore's Creek and Guilford Courthouse Battlefields together offer informative visitors centers and more than 300 acres of preserved, marked battlefield.

Despite its proximity to capital of the Confederacy, in Virginia, very few Civil War battles were fought on North Carolina soil. Nevertheless, Civil War buffs won't want to miss visiting a few celebrated sites. Fort Fisher State Historic Site, at Kure Beach near Wilmington, commemorates the heaviest land-sea battle of the Civil War, when Union ships lobbed more than two million pounds of bombs and other projectiles at this fort, which had protected Wilmington's port as "the lifeline of the Confederacy."

From Fort Fisher, a 90-minute drive northwest along I-40 will take you to the town of Newton Grove, and Bentonville Battleground, site of North Carolina's bloodiest Civil War battle, waged March 19-21, 1865, between the armies commanded by Union General William T. Sherman and Con-

DOVER PUBLICATIONS, INC.

federate General Joseph E. Johnston. These two men met on neutral ground, Bennett Place in Durham, a month later and negotiated the largest surrender of the Civil War. The Civil War did not end when Robert E. Lee surrendered to Ulysses S. Grant at Appomattox Courthouse. After Lee's surrender, Jefferson Davis, president of the Confederacy, urged Johnston—who commanded a far larger force than Lee surrendered at Appomattox—to continue to fight. The outcome of the Civil War ultimately was sealed after several days of negotiations at the little farmhouse in Durham, on April 26, 1865. The drama of these last days of the Civil War is presented in moving detail at Bennett Place State Historic Site.

The World War II battleship *North Carolina* today rests directly across the Cape Fear River from downtown Wilmington. You can take a two-hour self-guided tour—one of the most popular and fascinating offered in the state—of this extraordinary dreadnought, which, when it first rolled into saltwater in 1941, was proclaimed the most unassailably destructive war vessel sailing the open seas.

PERFORMING ARTS

Theater

During the summer months, 11 outdoor dramas are performed nightly in various venues in North Carolina. Three of these productions (all performed nightly except Sunday, mid-June through late August) stand out particularly. In Manteo, *The Lost Colony,* written by Pulitzer Prize-winner Paul Green, is the nation's first and longest-running outdoor symphonic drama, having debuted in 1937. Performed under the stars on the spacious stage of the Waterside Theatre—on the very sands the settlers first colonized—*The Lost Colony* tells the story of the 117 English settlers who came to Roanoke Island more than four centuries ago. It's a great show, complete with colorful costumes, energetic dancing, and a score that ranges from courtly Elizabethan tunes to Native American dances. With a cast and crew of 125, the performance is big and gripping and offers viewers of all ages a more intimate understanding of the courage of these first settlers.

The other two standout outdoor musical dramas, both written by Kermit Hunter, have been performed every summer since the early 1950s. In Boone, *Horn In The West,* complete with Native Americans and redcoats, takes you back to the 1770s and recounts how Daniel Boone and his fellow settlers battled the elements and the British in these rugged hills. Younger kids in particular will find this theater under the stars a wonderfully memorable evening.

In Cherokee, you'll find the state's best attended outdoor drama. *Unto These Hills,* elaborately staged and performed by more than 100 actors, relates the history of the Cherokees from Hernando De Soto's arrival in 1540 through the tragic Trail of Tears. The production includes blazing torch dances and a lively musical score. *Unto These Hills* provides kids and adults alike with an unforgettable, personal understanding of the noble history of the Cherokee.

Indoor theaters host plays throughout the state all year long. Venues in Wilmington, Raleigh, and Charlotte not only present plays but also regularly host touring companies of Broadway shows. In addition, dozens of semi-professional community theater groups have emerged in North Carolina, spawned by the dramatic arts professors and graduates of the dozens of colleges and universities in the state.

Music and Dance

From early June through late July, Durham is the home of the American Dance Festival, hailed as the nation's premier festival of modern dance. During these two months, the neighborhoods surrounding the campus of Duke University, where the festival is held, are populated by hundreds of svelte young people, gliding along the sidewalks and lending the town an exceptionally graceful ambience.

North Carolina is blessed with a fine, state-supported orchestra. The North Carolina Symphony Orchestra is based in Raleigh but frequently travels to give performances throughout the state. All of North Carolina's major cities host national musical acts year-round, sometimes at outdoor theaters and stadiums, and sometimes at indoor venues of varying sizes. Music festivals and special musical performances take place throughout the year all over the state, such as Greensboro's **Eastern Music Festival,** featuring nightly classical music concerts from late June through early August.

Nightlife

Just about anyplace in North Carolina, you'll usually be able to find at least a few places to listen to a variety of live music, trip the light fantastic, and enjoy a drink. The music varies widely, from modern jazz to country to rock. Particularly in the larger cities and towns, you should have little trouble finding a musical atmosphere to suit your taste. Dance clubs are also very popular.

All along the coast and throughout the mountains, establishments cater to vacationers looking for a good time. Wilmington is the nightlife center of the coast, while Asheville earns that title in the mountains. In the central Piedmont, the major cities of Charlotte, Raleigh, Durham, Chapel Hill, Greensboro, and Winston-Salem all offer dozens of hot night spots, from elegant jazz clubs frequented by businesspeople to discos packed with students attending the area's major universities.

FESTIVALS AND CULTURAL EVENTS

Somewhere in North Carolina, something special is happening every day. The North Carolina Division of Travel and Tourism produces a free publication every year listing more than 1,300 festivals, musical performances, and cultural events, including thumbnail sketches and contact phone numbers for each one. For a copy of the comprehensive *North Carolina Calendar of Events*—along with other handy materials, including a detailed map of the state—call the Division of Travel and Tourism at (800) VISIT-NC (847-4862).

Here's a quick list of the state's 10 most-attended annual festivals.

North Carolina Azalea Festival, tel. (910) 754-7177. First or second weekend in April, in Wilmington. Entertainment, home and garden tours, and a parade.

Spring Historic Homes and Gardens Tour, tel. (252) 638-8558, (252) 633-6448, or (800) 767-1560. Last weekend in March or first weekend in April, in New Bern. Tours of Tryon Palace historic sites, gardens, and buildings, along with area homes, gardens, and historic sites.

Festival of Flowers, tel. (828) 274-6333 or (800) 543-2961. Early April through early May, at Biltmore Estate in Asheville. A profusion of flowers inside Biltmore House and in the extensive gardens, along with special activities and performances to celebrate spring.

National Hollerin' Contest. Usually the third Saturday in June, at Midway High School, in Spivey's Corner. Contest focuses on hog-calling as a traditional form of communication. Crafts, food, entertainment, and a chance to witness live performances that appear on virtually all news programs across the nation later that day.

American Dance Festival, tel. (919) 684-6402. Early June through late July, at Duke University. Arguably the nation's premier modern dance festival, featuring almost daily performances.

Eastern Music Festival, tel. (336) 333-7450. Late June through early August, at Guilford College in Greensboro. Professional concert series, including orchestras, chamber ensembles, recitals, and other special events.

Grandfather Mountain Highland Games and Gathering of the Scottish Clans, tel. (828) 733-1333. Usually the second weekend in July, at MacRae Meadows, at the base of Grandfather Mountain, in Linville.

Folkmoot, USA, tel. (828) 452-2997. Last two weeks in July, at Waynesville and Maggie Valley locations. International folk music festival.

Candlelight Christmas at Biltmore, tel. (828) 274-6333 or (800) 543-2961. Mid-November through the end of December. Elaborate Victorian Christmas experience, complete with live musical performances.

Tryon Palace Christmas Celebration, tel. (252) 514-4900 or (800) 767-1560. Third week in December. Tours (some by candlelight) of elaborately decorated historic sites and other special events.

ARTS AND CRAFTS

Artists and artisans are drawn to North Carolina in serious numbers, attracted by the natural beauty and the longstanding craft traditions. Throughout the state, but particularly along the coast and in the mountains, gift stores and galleries feature works by local artists. Sometimes many galleries are clustered together—as in Raleigh's downtown City Market, where, in a visual arts center called ArtsSpace, you can watch artists work in one of the 25 studios open to public view, browse three exhibition galleries, and purchase pieces by the resident artists in the sales gallery. You'll also find a high density of artists in the tiny town of Seagrove, near Asheboro, in the center of the state. World famous for its pottery, Seagrove boasts a population of just 200, but that number includes more than 40 potters whose artistry has been passed on through generations. In all, the Seagrove area is home to more than 80 potteries.

The mountains are the true paradise for lovers of North Carolina arts and crafts. Pick up a copy of *The Craft Heritage Trails of Western North Carolina,* published by the arts organization HandMade In America, Inc., tel. (828) 252-0121, and available at most stores and visitors centers in the western part of the state. This invaluable book describes hundreds of craft stores and galleries and not only maps out how to get to each one but also organizes routes for you to make your arts and crafts hunting more efficient.

But you don't need the Craft Heritage Trails guide to find craft stores and galleries. One of the easier alternatives is to simply stop in towns on or near the Blue Ridge Parkway. Blowing Rock and Boone, in particular, feature some of the finest sales galleries in the state for traditional local arts and crafts, as well as newer styles. Seven miles north of the Parkway in the little town of Penland, next to Spruce Pine, half a dozen marvelous galleries are located near the Penland School, one of the finest craft schools in the nation, preserving old and creating new craft traditions since 1929.

Another particularly worthwhile stop on your crafts tour is the Folk Art Center on the Blue Ridge Parkway, just outside Asheville. This museum and sales gallery represents a guild of more than 700 artists expert at a variety of craft traditions, from quilting and glass-blowing to woodworking and jewelry-making. The Folk Art Center is the descendant of Allanstand Cottage Industries, started in the late 1800s by Frances Goodrich. Goodrich founded Allanstand to preserve traditional mountain crafts, expose the rest of the world to the exquisite beauty of the then-dying mountain craft traditions, and develop sources of income for the artisans. Goodrich would be thrilled to know that the artistic heritage of these mountains has not only thrived but today fuels a thriving tourist economy.

SHOPPING

As a very general rule, most places to shop in North Carolina are open Monday through Saturday, usually from 10 a.m. to 6 or 7 p.m. In areas frequented by tourists, such as the beach during the summer months, you're likely to find places open on Sunday and for longer hours. Covered malls are usually open 10 a.m.-9 p.m.

For the most sophisticated shopping in North Carolina, head to the historic district of Wilmington. Front Street, which runs the length of the historic district near the Cape Fear River, is full of unique gift boutiques, designer shops, antique stores, and plenty of places to stop for a drink and a bite to eat when your strength starts to flag. The side streets in between Front and Third Streets are also packed with unusual stores. Chandler's Wharf and the Cotton Exchange offer not only interesting shopping but also a look at two beautifully restored buildings—one an old warehouse, the other the former home of the largest cotton exporting company in the world. Wilmington's shops are generally upscale, so bring your credit cards.

In Charlotte, the South End area of town showcases unusual home furnishings, antiques, and decorative accessories. Cannon Village, in Kannapolis, 26 miles northeast of downtown Charlotte via I-85, is the ideal place to go if you need to restock your linen closet. The "village" includes about 40 stores including Cannon Bed & Bath Outlet, where you can buy towels by the pound and search among hundreds of styles of linens and blankets.

In Raleigh, don't miss the quaint shops of downtown's City Market. On Saturday, local farmers sell flowers and fresh produce here—fun to browse, even if you don't buy anything. City Market also features some hip shops and great restaurants, so you can spend most of a day here.

If you need a new sofa, rug, or dining room table, head to High Point. While many of the city's showrooms are open only to the trade (furniture store owners, interior decorators, and the like), many are open to the general public. Only some of the furniture is discounted, but the selection is peerless, and you *can* find some real bargains. Virtually any showroom in High Point can ship merchandise anywhere.

If you're heading to the northern mountains, be sure to stop by the Mast General Store in Valle Crucis. Established in 1883, this is a true "general store." In his *On the Road* television series, Charles Kuralt claimed that you could find the "soul of the South" at the Mast General Store. Although today it overflows with visitors, this place has not lost its authentic feel, and locals still come by all the time, simply to pass the time with their neighbors.

The town of Blowing Rock is well known for antiques, terrific gift and craft shops, and summer art shows and fairs, as well as simply for being a great place to sit on a downtown park bench and watch other shoppers go by. Blowing Rock is an extremely inviting little mountain town, and one of the best ways to experience its charms is on an afternoon's shopping expedition.

Asheville is fast becoming one of the hippest towns in North Carolina. The city's exceptionally walkable downtown is filling up with all kind of trendy little shops. Outside of downtown, next to the Grove Park Inn, the Biltmore Homespun Shops sell lovely quilts, handwoven woolen items, and more.

Just off I-40 and NC 191, the Western North Carolina Farmers Market features a cornucopia of produce, flowers, homemade jellies, honeys, and pies, as well as lots of local color.

In Cherokee, you'll find beautiful beadwork, baskets, pottery, dolls, paintings, and carvings at the Qualla Arts and Crafts Mutual, Inc., a craft cooperative owned and operated by the Cherokee tribe. These are all authentic Native crafts. While they emphasize items tourists enjoy, the goods for sale here are not in any way kitschy or unrepresentative of Cherokee life (something you can't say about many other gift shops in Cherokee).

ACCOMMODATIONS AND FOOD

ACCOMMODATIONS

Bed and Breakfasts

Sherman's infamous march through the south, from Atlanta to the area near Raleigh, largely spared North Carolina. As a result, the state offers one of the richest collections of historic homes in the region. Many of these now serve as bed-and-breakfast inns. Of course, not all B&Bs here are historic inns. Services vary widely—some cater to business travelers, offering everything from jacuzzis to data ports in the rooms; others, more getaway-oriented inns where the owners purposely don't offer distracting modern conveniences like private phones and cable TV. If you have any questions, be sure to call ahead for details. Unless otherwise specified, all inns recommended in this book provide private bathrooms.

Hotels, Motels, Inns and Resorts

The most comprehensive descriptions of hotels, motels, inns, and resorts in this book are of establishments operated by independent owners. Because chain and franchise establishments can generally be counted on to fulfill dependable, pre-

dictable standards of cleanliness and comfort, such accommodations are detailed only when specific individual accommodations offer an unusual number or quality of amenities.

Pet-Friendly Accommodations

An extra effort has been made to identify pet-friendly accommodations in the vast majority of locales covered in this book. No matter where you travel, you can usually count on Motel 6 and Red Roof Inn to welcome pets.

OZELL CALLAHAN

ACCOMMODATIONS RATINGS
Based on high-season, double-occupancy rates

Budget	under $35
Inexpensive	$35-60
Moderate	$60-85
Expensive	$85-110
Deluxe	$110-150
Luxury	$150+

Camping
Camping opportunities abound in North Carolina—particularly in the mountain region. While most campgrounds are privately owned and operated, the state park campgrounds have much to recommend them: relative ubiquity, dependable cleanliness, attractiveness, scenic surroundings, and low prices. Reservation policies vary from campground to campground, and many don't have RV hookups, so be sure to call ahead to confirm details.

If you'll be camping in summer, *make sure to bring bug repellent.*

A Note About Pricing
The vast majority of North Carolina lodgings listed in this handbook, including most of the franchise lodgings, charge significantly varying rates, depending on seasons and events. For example, an oceanfront suite on the Atlantic that runs $150 a night with a three-night minimum stay in July may cost $50 for a single night November through February.

Although prices listed in this book are as accurate as possible at press time, prices can always change. Don't use the prices quoted in this book as the basis for arguing with desk clerks or hoteliers. For the most up-to-date prices, *always call ahead.*

HOME RENTAL SEASONS

This is an *approximate* breakdown of the seasons for home rentals.

IN-SEASON	June 20-August 20
PRE-SEASON	June 5-20
POST-SEASON	August 20-31
OFFSEASON	September 1-June 5

FOOD AND DRINK

A few things to keep in mind about North Carolina cuisine:

- "Barbecue" usually describes slow-cooked pork, preferably shredded but possibly sliced, seasoned with a variety of spices and served with vinegar- and/or tomato-based sauces. If you crave a ketchup-based red sauce, order barbecued ribs—in restaurants and barbecue joints throughout the state, these come with a succulently spiced, thick red sauce.

- In North Carolina, the second-biggest pork producer in the nation, pork is almost considered a health food.

- For breakfast, grits are eaten with salt, pepper, and lots of butter, or with red-eye gravy (a clear, reddish gravy made from country ham) and maybe a dash of Tabasco, but *never* with sugar, honey, or syrup. Grits, a close relative of polenta, can also be served at any other time of day—with shrimp, mixed with cheese, reheated as a casserole, or just devoured any way you like them any time you need a little comfort.

- Few things brighten a North Carolina day like seeing the neon Hot Doughnuts Now sign at a Krispy Kreme Doughnuts shop. This ubiquitous North Carolina institution makes a perfect glazed doughnut. The recent opening of a Manhattan shop has brought about a frenzied craving for these confections in other cities, and once you taste a fresh one, you'll see why.

- Remember that fish always really *does* taste better fried—if it's done right. In these health-conscious times, most of us try to steer clear of fried foods, but Calabash-style fried fish and seafood is a treat you don't want to miss. The batter is crispy and lighter than air and will usually only leave a drop or two of grease on your plate. Inside this protective shell of fried batter, fish and shrimp retain a moistness that simply can't be achieved by grilling, broiling, or sautéing.

There is a trend toward reducing the fat content of some of the delicious traditional foods of North Carolina and incorporating them into nouvelle American and gourmet European cuisine. The various combinations make for heady eating in the state's best restaurants. Be advised that great restaurants are located virtually everywhere in the state, so come with an empty stomach and an adventurous palate. You won't be disappointed.

Finally, though, a note of caution: descriptions in this book cover many mouth-watering dishes tasted and enjoyed by the authors. However, due to the fact that many of North Carolina's best restaurants are constantly refining, reshaping, adding to, and removing items from their menus, some of the dishes described may not be available when you sit down to a meal at a particular restaurant. The hope is that the descriptions will serve not as a precise guide to the menu but rather as a general indication of the kinds and quality of cuisine you're likely to encounter.

A NOTE ON ALCOHOLIC BEVERAGES

As everywhere in the U.S., you have to be 21 years old to consume alcoholic beverages in North Carolina. Wine and beer are sold in grocery stores, general stores, gas stations, and wine and gourmet shops. Hard liquor is sold only at state-owned and -operated stores, which are called ABC (Alcoholic Beverage Control) stores. ABC stores are individually managed, so their hours vary, but all are closed on Sunday. You can, however, buy beer and wine on Sunday after noon. Alcoholic beverages cannot be sold or served 2-7 a.m. in North Carolina.

State law mandates that public establishments serving alcoholic beverages must generate at least 51% of gross sales by serving food. Consequently, you won't find many little bars serving only alcohol. Exempt from the 51% rule, though, are "private clubs."

In most instances, such "private clubs" in North Carolina are indistinguishable from regular neighborhood bars found elsewhere in the United States. Most clubs will simply require you to pay a membership fee at the door to allow you entrance—sometimes just a few dollars, sometimes more. Usually, only one person has to pay the membership fee and can then bring along as many guests as are in his or her party. If you're only planning to visit one of these private clubs once and don't want to pay the membership fee, your best bet is to hang around outside until you find a member willing to take you in as guests. (It won't hurt to include an offer to buy the accommodating member or members a round.)

As has been stated elsewhere, don't drink and drive in North Carolina or anywhere else. It's a serious offense, and checkpoints make it easy to get caught.

TRANSPORTATION

GETTING THERE

Airports

North Carolina is home to three major airports. The largest is **Douglas International Airport,** tel. (704) 359-4027, in Charlotte. A major hub for USAirways, Douglas offers nonstop flights to more than 150 domestic and international cities. The second-largest is the Raleigh/Durham airport, known as **RDU,** tel. (919) 840-2123, providing more than 200 flights a day to more than 40 destinations, including nonstop flights to Toronto, London, and the Caribbean. The third major airport is **Piedmont Triad International,**

tel. (336) 665-5666, adjacent to the city limits of Greensboro, off I-40 about 22 miles from Winston-Salem, and about 12 miles from High Point. Piedmont Triad International is served by 13 airlines—including American, Delta, United, US-Airways, Continental, and Northwest—and offers more than 80 flights a day, including international connections.

Two regional airports might make your trip a little easier. **New Hanover International Airport,** tel. (910) 341-4333, is located about three miles from downtown Wilmington. Four carriers—US-Airways, Midway, United Express, and Delta Express—offer about 25 flights a day. On the western side of the state, **Asheville Regional**

Airport, tel. (828) 684-2226, is located about 20 minutes from downtown Asheville. Five airlines, including USAirways and Delta, offer about 25 flights a day.

Rail and Bus Service

Amtrak, tel. (800) 872-7245, does not offer service to either the coast or the western mountains, but it does reach a dozen cities and towns in the Piedmont—from south to north, Gastonia, Charlotte, Southern Pines, Salisbury, High Point, Winston-Salem, Greensboro, Burlington, Durham, Raleigh, Wilson, and Rocky Mount. Most of these destinations are served only once or twice a day.

Greyhound Bus Lines, tel. (800) 231-2222, serves all of the major cities in North Carolina as well as many smaller towns popular with tourists.

By Car

Auto travelers enter North Carolina primarily along five major roads.

Interstate 95, which runs almost the entire length of the eastern United States, cuts vertically through North Carolina about 100 miles inland from the coast. The interstate roughly divides the state's coastal plain from the Piedmont and offers the closest interstate access to the Outer Banks (lack of direct interstate access accounts for part of the Outer Banks' off-the-beaten-path charm). Be warned, however, that *getting* to the barrier islands from I-95 can be slow going, along two-lane roads and through many small towns.

On its run from Virginia to Alabama, Interstate 85 drops down into North Carolina, cuts west, then descends again. In the process, it serves the Triangle (Durham), Burlington, the Triad (Greensboro and High Point), and Charlotte. Stretching from Cleveland, Ohio, to Charleston, South Carolina, I-77 runs directly north-south through North Carolina, providing convenient access to the state's northern mountains, as well as a swift route directly through Charlotte.

Another favorite north-south route into the state is, of course, 470-mile-long Blue Ridge Parkway, which extends from Virginia's Shenandoah National Park to Great Smoky Mountains National Park, roughly paralleling North Carolina's western state line as it passes through Pisgah National Forest and the northeastern corner

of Nantahala National Forest. This engineering marvel took almost 50 years to complete, but it merits its reputation as "the nation's most scenic highway."

East-west Interstate 40, which stretches from Barstow, California, enters North Carolina about one-third of the way up the sloping western boundary, just north of Great Smoky Mountains National Park. It drops into Asheville and then runs east, arching up to pass through Winston-Salem, Greensboro, and Burlington, and then down again as it descends through Durham and Raleigh to end at the coast, in Wilmington.

GETTING AROUND

Automobiles are virtually a necessity when visiting almost any part of North Carolina. Airplanes, buses, and trains may be able to get you *to* the destination of your choice in the state, but once you arrive, you'll have a tough time finding a taxi—and an even tougher time trying to negotiate the lackluster public transportation systems that do exist. The attractions of North Carolina's biggest cities—Charlotte, Raleigh, Greensboro, and Winston-Salem—are generally spread out and not conveniently accessible by public transit. You'll find car-rental counters at all of North Carolina's airports (in many cases, even in larger cities, the closest airport is usually the best place to go if you need to rent a car). Call the airport phone numbers listed above or the car rental company of your choice to find out which companies are located at which airports. All of the major car rental companies serve North Carolina, including (but not limited to) Alamo, tel. (800) 327-9633; Avis, tel. (800) 331-1212; Budget, tel. (800) 527-0700; Dollar, tel. (800) 800-4000; Hertz, tel. (800) 654-3131; National, tel. (800) 328-4567; and Thrifty, tel. (800) 367-2277.

Driving Tips and Laws

Take special precautions when driving after or during an ice or snow storm. Many North Carolina towns do not have snow plows or salt trucks, and conditions can be treacherous. Be particularly wary of "black ice"—thin patches of ice virtually invisible on black asphalt until you find yourself skidding on them. The best course of action is usually to do as the natives do—stay off the roads during icy conditions. If you do venture out onto the roads when it's icy, allow lots of extra space between you and the vehicle in front of you.

In general, North Carolinians are too polite to tailgate and don't like it when visitors follow too closely (this is true even on beautiful sunny days, let alone when road conditions make it potentially lethal).

Always wear your seat belt when driving in North Carolina. Every year, thousands of visitors are ticketed for not obeying this strictly enforced state law. All front-seat passengers must wear them, children ages four or younger must be secured in child safety seats, and children ages 4-12 must ride in a safety seat or wear a seat belt.

Do not drink and drive in North Carolina. It's also against the law to have an open container of alcohol in a car, even if the passengers are the only ones partaking. The police set up checkpoints to catch violators of either of these offenses.

INFORMATION AND SERVICES

SPECIAL INTERESTS

Traveling with Children
North Carolina offers a wealth of entertaining diversions suitable for children. Miniature golf courses, waterparks, and tiny amusement parks dot the coast, and you'll find several larger-scale amusement parks elsewhere in the state, like Paramount Carowinds, just south of Charlotte, and the comparatively tame amusements offered by the Tweetsie Railroad near Blowing Rock and the Ghost Town in the Sky in Maggie Valley.

The state also boasts some of the nation's most noted children's museums, including Discovery Place, in Charlotte; the Museum of Life and Science, in Durham; and SciWorks, in Winston-Salem.

And of course, the abundance of outdoor recreation should appeal to virtually all kids.

If you're traveling with young children, you can expect something less than an open-arms welcome at bed-and-breakfast inns, but you'll find other family-friendly accommodations and places to eat everywhere in North Carolina.

Travelers with Disabilities
Detailed information for travelers with disabilities is available in *Access North Carolina: A Vacation and Travel Guide for Disabled Persons,* compiled by the North Carolina Department of Human Resources. The guide is available free of charge by contacting the North Carolina Division of Travel and Tourism, tel. (800) VISIT-NC.

As in all American states, North Carolina is working toward complete compliance with the federal Americans With Disabilities Act. While the state is making significant progress, it still has a long way to go.

Gay and Lesbian Travelers
North Carolina's deserved reputation for hospitality and tolerance extends across the board. However, particularly in smaller towns not fre-

Touch tanks make the North Carolina Aquariums favorite stops for young visitors.

NORTH CAROLINA AQUARIUM

TOURIST INFORMATION SOURCES

The following is not a comprehensive list, but rather a guide to some of the most useful and popular sources of information for travelers to North Carolina.

STATE AGENCIES

Department of Transportation: (919) 733-2520, www.state.nc.us

Department of Transportation/Ferry Division: (800) BY-FERRY or (919) 726-6446, www.state.nc.us/transit/ferry

Division of Parks and Recreation: (919) 715-3085

Division of Travel and Tourism: (800) VISIT-NC or (919) 733-8582

Historic Sites: (919) 733-7862

Office of Bicycle & Pedestrian Transportation: (919) 715-4422

GENERAL INFORMATION

Appalachian Trail Conference: (828) 254-3708

Blue Ridge Mountain Host: (800) 807-3391

Blue Ridge Parkway: (828) 298-0398

Cape Hatteras National Seashore: (252) 473-2111

Cape Lookout National Seashore: (252) 728-2250

Great Smoky Mountains National Park: (423) 436-1200

North Carolina Association of Bed and Breakfasts & Inns: (800) 849-5392

North Carolina Campground Owners Association: (919) 779-5642

North Carolina Coast Host: (800) 948-1099

North Carolina High Country Host (for the Northern Mountains): (800) 438-7500

North Carolina Ski Areas Association: (828) 295-7828

Smoky Mountain Host of NC: (800) 432-HOST

CONVENTION AND/ OR VISITORS BUREAUS

Ashe County Visitors Bureau: (336) 626-2626

Asheville Convention and Visitors Bureau: (800) 257-1300

Banner Elk Chamber of Commerce: (800) 972-2183

Beech Mountain Chamber of Commerce: (800) 468-5506

Blowing Rock Chamber of Commerce: (800) 295-7851

Boone Convention and Visitors Bureau: (800) 852-9506

Brunswick Islands: (800) 795-7263

Cape Fear Coast Convention and Visitors Bureau: (800) 222-4757

Cashiers Travel and Tourism Authority: (828) 743-9446

Chapel Hill/Hillsborough Visitors Bureau: (888) 968-2060

Charlotte Convention and Visitors Bureau: (800) 231-4636

Cherokee Visitors Center: (800) 438-1601

Dare County Tourist Bureau: (800)446-6262

Durham Convention and Visitors Bureau: (800) 446-8604

Greensboro Covention and Visitors Bureau: (800) 344-2282

High Point Convention and Visitors Bureau: (336) 884-5255

Highlands Chamber of Commerce: (828) 526-2112

Maggie Valley Convention and Visitors Bureau: (828) 926-1686

Northeastern North Carolina Tourism: (888) 872-8562

Outer Banks/Dare County Tourist Bureau: (800)446-6262

Pinehurst Area Convention and Visitors Bureau: (800) 346-5362

Raleigh Convention and Visitors Bureau: (800) 849-8499

Topsail Area Chamber of Commerce and Tourism: (800) 626-2780

Wilmington/Cape Fear Coast Convention and Visitors Bureau: (800) 222-4757

Winston-Salem Convention and Visitors Bureau: (800) 331-7018

quented by tourists, gay and lesbian couples are well advised to avoid public displays of affection (a caution, incidentally, that applies to straight couples as well), which are considered rude by some. In general, gay and lesbian travelers will find the state's major cities and tourist towns friendly and welcoming. Wilmington and Charlotte feature the largest network of gay- and lesbian-oriented entertainment establishments—including dance clubs and bars—but Asheville and the Triangle and Triad cities are also home to sizeable openly gay and lesbian communities.

HEALTH AND SAFETY

Heat and Sun Exposure

North Carolina's summer weather is usually fairly comfortable, albeit warm and humid. However, if you're not careful, the combination of heat and outdoor activity can increase your chances of suffering heat exhaustion or heat stroke, which can be serious. Early warning signs of heat illness are heavy sweating, clamminess, nausea, cramping in the stomach and/or legs, dizziness or lightheadedness, and sudden weariness. If you or a fellow traveler experiences any of these signs, immediately get to a cool place and drink plenty of nonalcoholic fluids—preferably an electrolyte-rich sports drink such Gatorade or Powerade, although water will usually suffice. In the event that a heat illness victim passes out, immediately immerse him or her in cold water or place ice packs on the person's neck, armpits, and groin area—and immediately call 911.

If you're hiking in the mountains, *always make sure to take plenty of water along.*

If you're headed to the beach, be sure to exercise a little "sun sense." The North Carolina sun can get intense on the coast and in the mountains. Remember that white sand and snow reflect the sun and considerably multiply its burning rays. If you're accustomed to sunning yourself in more northerly climes, keep in mind that you won't be able to withstand the North Carolina sun as long as you can your "home" sun, without significant sun protection. Invest in a good sunblock with an SPF of at least 15, as well as a pair of sunglasses or ski goggles with UVA and UVB protection. When visiting the beach, you also won't regret taking a hat. If you love to sit for

hours at the water's edge, purchase or rent a beach umbrella. Also, consider bringing some lightweight opaque cover-up clothing.

If you do end up with a painful sunburn, you can get some relief. First, drink plenty of nonalcoholic fluids—over several hours. Apply cool, moist compresses (but not ice) to the affected skin. Take aspirin or ibuprofen, and apply a topical sunburn cream or lotion (the most effective balms usually include aloe vera extract). If you or someone in your traveling party tries these remedies but remains in agonizing pain—particularly if the symptoms include nausea—seek medical help.

Encountering Wildlife

Hiking through the wilds of North Carolina offers magnificent rewards. But it's important to exercise common sense—not all the wild creatures are friendly. The wetlands of the coastal plain are home to a few alligators and water moccasins, so it's wise to have an experienced guide along, or at least pick up a copy of safety guidelines from a park ranger's office, before you go traipsing through a swamp. Although if you venture deep into some wetland marshes, you may see some locals fishing within just a few yards of alligators, you're not advised to follow their lead. These folks have been sharing turf with gators for generations and have a keen sense of when the animals' internal "snack time" bell goes off.

Similarly, the forests of the central Piedmont and western mountain region are home to a few (rarely encountered) creatures you should shy away from. Poisonous snakes are not unknown in North Carolina's woods. You probably won't ever see one—they're extremely shy and will do all they can to stay out of your way. If you're tramping through some dense underbrush, you can avoid a surprise encounter with a snake by simply whistling while you walk. Any snakes close by will get out of your way. However, if by some happenstance, someone in your party is bitten by any kind of snake, do *not* follow the ill-advised example you may have seen in movies—slicing the skin over the bite and sucking out the poison. Rather, just proceed directly to the closest point of civilization and get some medical help.

In the western mountains—particularly around Great Smoky Mountains National Park, you might, if you're lucky, get a fleeting glimpse of a black bear. Don't try for more than a glimpse. Never pursue a bear or try to attract one. If you leave them alone, they'll leave you alone. Of course, many other mammals make their homes in North Carolina, and like the bears, they'll generally stay out your way. However, if anyone you're traveling with is bitten by any species of mammal, again, head back to civilization and get medical help. While rare, rabies has not been eradicated from North Carolina.

You have little grounds for worry about being harmed by anything in the Atlantic Ocean off the North Carolina coast, except for the very occasional pinch from a crab you've kicked or stepped on or the sting of a small jellyfish.

Mosquitoes and Ticks

Mosquitoes love North Carolina natives and visitors alike—they're out from late spring through early fall. The best mosquito repellent is a spray or lotion containing the pesticide DEET. Remedies such as Avon's Skin-So-Soft (and its imitators) and newer soybean-based concoctions are also effective, without containing chemicals that may irritate some users.

Of the 16,000 new cases of Lyme disease reported in the U.S. every year, over 80% of them are located in the northeast U.S. corridor, from Maryland north to Massachusetts. Nonetheless, Lyme disease does make a very occasional appearance in North Carolina. This tick-borne disease, if left untreated, results in arthritis-like symptoms that can sometimes take years to get rid of. The vast majority of ticks *don't* carry *Borrelia burgdorferi,* the bacteria that causes Lyme disease, but you want to avoid ticks just the same. You can take several precautions. Wear light-colored clothing so you can spot ticks more easily. When you're hiking through underbrush, wear long-sleeved shirts and long pants tucked into your shoes or boots. Apply an insect repellent containing DEET. And, most important, be sure to look for ticks *everywhere* on your skin—especially in patches of body hair—after venturing into the woods. If you happen to find a tick on you, pull gently and steadily on its body until the tick disengages. Do *not* crush the tick, burn it with a match, douse it in alcohol, or any other "home remedy," as these actions can cause the tick to regurgitate bacteria into its bite, increasing your chance of infection. Again, al-

though Lyme disease is very rare in North Carolina, just for your peace of mind, here are the symptoms: a red "bulls-eye" shaped rash (a ring of small red bumps) around the bite, which will appear about two days after the bite, followed by flu-like symptoms, including muscle aches, appearing about two to four weeks later.

Crime

As a rule, North Carolina cities do not have high crime rates (one reason the cities appear so often near the top of Best Places to Live in America lists). Still, don't be lulled into assuming that *no* crime occurs in the state. Just take the usual common-sense precautions: lock your doors, don't walk alone late at night, keep your purse close to your body and your wallet deep in a secure pocket, and don't leave luggage and valuables exposed in your car.

MONEY

You will have no trouble finding North Carolina bank branches, or automated teller machines, anywhere in the state. Travelers checks and credit cards are accepted by the vast majority of accommodations, restaurants, and stores (though it's always sound policy to check first, particularly before making a lodging reservation or sitting down to eat).

If you're looking to exchange foreign currency, your best bet is to convert your currency into U.S. dollars before you arrive. Even the currency exchange operations in some of North Carolina's international airports don't keep dependable hours. If you find yourself in a situation in which you *must* convert some foreign currency, stop in at the nearest bank branch—customer service staff will probably be able to help you out.

COMMUNICATIONS AND MEDIA

North Carolina is blessed with dozens of wonderful local newspapers. The Raleigh *News and Observer* and the Charlotte *Observer* are nationally known, award-winning publications. In most major cities, many street corners invite you to select from several newspaper boxes offering lots of different options—from local daily and weekly newspapers to national papers like *USA TODAY* and the *New York Times.*

Wherever you drive in North Carolina, you'll always be able to receive clear signals from dozens of radio stations all along the AM and FM bands. Fans of National Public Radio and television's Public Broadcasting Service will find North Carolina a paradise—a cooperative venture among all the NPR and PBS affiliates has made both services available, free, to virtually every radio and TV in the state. To get one or more NPR stations on your radio, check the stations located between 89 and 92 on the FM band.

FILM AND PHOTOGRAPHY

Film is readily available in shops throughout the state. If you're headed to the Outer Banks or some of the more remote areas of the mountains, stock up on film ahead of time at a camera shop, chain drugstore, grocery store, or Kmart-type store. Not only will you get better prices this way, but the higher turnover in big stores ensures that the film is fresher. We have heard of independently owned stores in isolated areas being victimized by "black market film" sellers, who pawn off old film they've bought from an offshore distributor on unsuspecting store owners. While this is rare, remember that a dash to a roadside Mom-and-Pop store for film before you catch a ferry may result in ruined pictures. Always check film expiration dates before you buy, in any type of store.

As far as photo etiquette goes, you'll find that most North Carolinians will generally be flattered if you want to take their picture. The one place to practice extra politeness is within the Qualla Boundary reservation in Cherokee. Here, several Cherokee make their living by dressing up in full tribal regalia and charging a small fee for posing with tourists. If you're taking pictures of Cherokee who are not in this business, exercise common courtesy and ask your subject if you can take a picture before snapping away.

TIME ZONE

North Carolina is situated in the Eastern time zone, five hours ahead of Greenwich mean time. The state shifts to daylight saving time, "springing" one hour ahead, on the first Sunday in April, and "falls" back an hour on the last Sunday in October.

WEIGHTS, MEASURES, AND ELECTRICAL APPLIANCES

The United States has steadfastly refused to adopt the metric system. If you're unfamiliar with the way the U.S. measures weights, lengths, and temperature, see the conversion chart at the back of this book.

Electric current in the U.S. is 110-120 volts, 60-cycle; appliances manufactured for use in most Asian and European countries will need an adapter to operate safely outside their typical system of 220-240 volt, 50-cycle current—as well as a plug adapter, for the flat two-pin style of the U.S. plug.

THE OUTER BANKS

For generations, this chain of barrier islands has beckoned to beach lovers in search of a remote getaway. More than 150 miles long and often less than a mile wide, this thin thread of sand between the Atlantic Ocean and the U.S. mainland retains much of its natural splendor—thanks in great measure to the fact that so much of this shoreline has been designated as protected national seashore and wildlife refuge. In fact, it was here that, in 1953, the federal government created the country's *first* "national seashore"—the 70-mile stretch of Cape Hatteras National Seashore, stretching south from Nags Head to Ocracoke Island. Less than 10 years later, the National Park Service added the adjacent 55-mile long Cape Lookout National Seashore, extending south from Portsmouth Island to Cape Lookout.

The maritime forests that lie behind the beaches of these protected seashores take you back in time, making it easy to visualize what a brambly tangle used to lie inland from these inviting, sandy beaches. Even during the peak summer season, you can find long stretches of beach and woods on these protected seashores where, over several hours, you may encounter no more than a handful of other visitors.

Even today, visitors to the Outer Banks can enjoy the rare experience of sunbathing or

strolling along a public beach without forsaking a sense of remoteness or having got away from it all. The mystique of the Outer Banks derives in part from its relative inaccessibility. Only two bridges—at Nags Head and Kitty Hawk, both in the northern section—connect the Outer Banks with the mainland. The only other way to reach these barrier islands is by ferry or private boat.

Not all of the Outer Banks exude an aura of splendid isolation, however. The 20-mile stretch along Route 12, parallel to the ocean, north from Duck to the end of the paved road at Corolla, opened to public traffic only in 1984. Before that, the road was privately maintained—by the few hundred folks who owned land on this isolated strip of sand. But after some landowners won a lawsuit demanding that the North Carolina Department of Transportation assume control of the road, developers arrived and apparently made offers that landowners couldn't refuse. The result is a 20-mile stretch of luxury oceanfront and oceanview homes offering spacious quarters that can easily accommodate a large family or two, maybe even a small scout troop.

The area beginning at Duck and extending south—through Kitty Hawk, Kill Devil Hills, Nags Head, and Manteo—has developed a burgeoning tourist industry that supports hundreds of commercial enterprises, from miniature golf courses to outlet malls, with loads of restaurants, shops, and motels in between.

South of Nags Head, on Hatteras Island, you'll find mostly protected National Seashore areas. Dotting this area, though, are seven formerly sleepy villages now slowly awakening to ways they can beguile visitors to stay and sample their slow-paced charms. Visitors to Hatteras Island are treated to unsullied beaches, dense forests, and lush salt marshes—protected havens for hundreds of species of birds and other wildlife (including the once-threatened red wolf). The northernmost 12 miles of Hatteras Island constitute Pea Island National Wildlife Refuge, a favorite haunt of birdwatchers, who have identified more than 260 species here.

A two-hour drive (including the 40-minute ferry crossing from Hatteras) south from Nags Head takes you to Ocracoke Island. Ocracoke boasts a centuries-long history as a fishing village and pirate haunt as well as a newer reputation as a low-key vacation destination with an unpretentious charm.

Swimming in the Atlantic Ocean off the Outer Banks becomes popular around mid- to late May and remains comfortable through the end of September, thanks to the moderating influence of the nearby Gulf Stream, which keeps the water warm and the air temperature moderate.

The Outer Banks offer a wide variety of other recreational diversions as well, from fishing, surfing, and hiking through brambly maritime forests and salt marshes to windsurfing the ocean and the sounds, scuba-diving into shipwrecks, and hang-gliding on the same winds the Wright Brothers first flew. But the "Banks" won't disappoint if you're interested in more commercial attractions—miniature golf courses, amusement and water parks, and diverse shopping are all present here in great abundance.

Virtually anywhere you go along the length of the Outer Banks, you're never far from a restaurant serving savory, fresh-from-the-boat fish and other seafood—served fried, broiled, or on the half-shell. And you'll never have to dress for dinner. Unless you want to make a spectacle of yourself, feel free to leave the ties and high heels at home.

Having served as a popular vacation destination for more than a century, the Outer Banks provides a substantial and varied range of accommodations, particularly with respect to rental properties. You're assured of finding a beach getaway to suit your tastes whether you choose to stay in a high-rise hotel in Nags Head, a luxury beach house in Corolla, a cottage in Kitty Hawk, a secluded motel in Buxton, a B&B in Ocracoke, or a tent on Portsmouth Island.

To obtain a wealth of free information about the Outer Banks, contact the **Dare County Tourist Bureau,** 704 S. Hwy. 64, P.O. Box 399, Manteo, NC 27954, tel. (252) 473-2138 or (800) 446-6262.

The Sands and Time

Scientists are uncertain about when the Outer Banks were formed, but most agree that it was sometime after the last Ice Age, which ended about 17,000 years ago. Geologists think that all or part of the barrier islands were originally formed about 25 miles east of their current location. If you could view a time-lapse film of these islands over the past five millennia, you'd see a strip of sand constantly migrating westward, toward the mainland, with hundreds of inlets being constantly narrowed and widened, filled in and created. However, the movement of the Outer Banks averages only a few feet per year, and it's something of a mystery as to why these islands are so stable, since they're without any underlying rocky ridges or coral reefs to keep them in place. In fact, the Outer Banks are really just big sandbars.

The remarkable resilience of these islands, constantly battered by the ocean, owes much to their tenacious flora—sea oats, beach grass, bayberry bushes, wax myrtle, hearty oaks, pines, and red cedars. As hurricanes blast the islands' ocean shores, much of the blown beach sand that washes over the islands in great waves ends up collecting in the maritime forests, compensating for the erosion of the oceanside beaches by building up the beaches on the mainland-facing sides of the islands. Essentially, the islands have survived by slowly rolling over themselves, towards the mainland.

Impediments to Settlement

After the unexplained disappearance of Sir Walter Raleigh's colony on Roanoke Island in the late 1500s, further European settlement of the region was forestalled for more than a century by the unpredictable ocean currents and occasional hurricane-strength winds that have always buffeted these islands. Indeed, the shores here have genuinely earned their reputation as "the Graveyard of the Atlantic"—more than 700 ships have sunk in these waters.

And the winds and waves weren't the only dangers to sailors—the Outer Banks were also home to many pirates, including Blackbeard. The Atlantic Coast's most notorious pirate in the early 1700s, Blackbeard is said to have commanded in his heyday four ships and a crew numbering more than 100.

With the increasing colonization of the mainland of the eastern seaboard during the 1700s, a few fishing villages sprouted up on the Outer Banks. This drove most of the islands' Native Americans, including the Hatteras Indians and most of the Croatan tribe, to move to the mainland and to other islands south of the Outer Banks to escape the encroaching colonists. (Some of the Croatans stayed, and hundreds of their descendants still live on North Carolina's coastal plain.)

The Outer Banks remained sparsely populated long into the 20th century. The population of the most populous town, Kill Devil Hills, provides a good example. When Orville and Wilbur Wright came here at the turn of the century, the town was little more than a life-saving station, a few modest homes, and some fishing shacks. With the construction of the first two bridges between the Outer Banks and the mainland in the 1930s, the population around Kill Devil Hills began to swell—but only slightly. When residents became the first folks on the Outer Banks to incorporate their town, in 1953, the voting rolls had swelled to a whopping 93 citizens.

But the beaches around Kill Devil Hills and neighboring Nags Head had been discovered, and between 1980 and 1990 the population more than doubled—from 1,796 to 4,238. Today, more than 2.2 million people visit the Outer Banks every year, and the percussive sounds of new construction often augment the laughter of the gulls and the pounding of the surf.

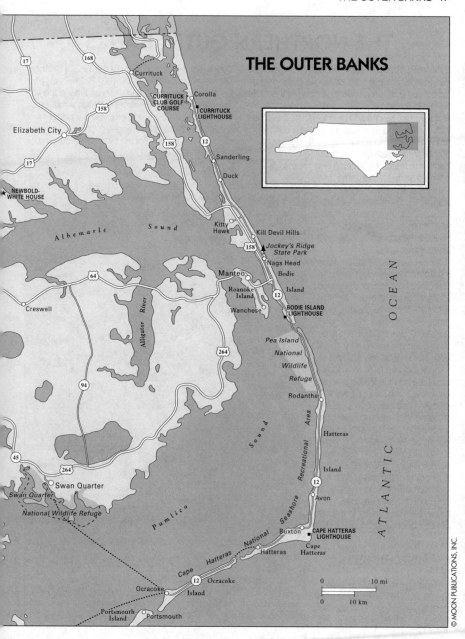

THE OUTER BANKS

17

168

Currituck

CURRITUCK
CLUB GOLF
COURSE

Corolla

CURRITUCK
LIGHTHOUSE

158

158

12

Elizabeth City

17

NEWBOLD-
WHITE HOUSE

Sanderling

Duck

Albemarle   Sound

Kitty
Hawk

Kill Devil Hills

158

*Jockey's Ridge
State Park*

Nags Head

64

Manteo

Bodie

Roanoke
Island

Island

Creswell

Wanchese

12

BODIE ISLAND
LIGHTHOUSE

94

Alligator River

264

Pea Island

National

Wildlife

Refuge

Rodanthe

45

264

Swan Quarter

Swan Quarter

National Wildlife Refuge

Pamlico

Sound

Recreational   Area

Hatteras

Island

12

Avon

National   Seashore

Buxton

Cape   Hatteras

12

Ocracoke

Hatteras

Hatteras

CAPE HATTERAS
LIGHTHOUSE

Cape
Hatteras

OCEAN

ATLANTIC

ATLANTIC

OCEAN

Ocracoke

Island

Portsmouth
Island

Portsmouth

0   10 mi

0   10 km

© MOON PUBLICATIONS, INC.

THE NORTHERN OUTER BANKS

Extending about 50 miles, from the Virginia border to the southern tip of Bodie (pronounced "body") Island, the northern section of the Outer Banks is the most popular with visitors. The resort towns of Manteo, Nags Head, Kill Devil Hills, Kitty Hawk, and Duck are all within a half hour's drive of each other, united by the only stretch of four-lane roadway on these barrier islands, US 158. This 25-mile stretch contains the Outer Banks' densest concentration of commercial enterprises, including plenty of hotels, motels, restaurants, strip malls, fishing piers, aquariums, and historic sites.

Local residents have long lamented the commercial buildup of these areas. But compared to its nearest brother beach-mecca—Virginia Beach, Virginia—these few developed acres of the northern Outer Banks are almost rural. Beachfront hotels and motels are interspersed with generous tracts of private homes. With a few exceptions, you won't see two high-rise hotels side-by-side. As a result, the beaches don't get as densely packed with beachgoers as do those in Virginia Beach, Virginia, or, to the south, Myrtle Beach, South Carolina. Even during the peak July-August summer season, you usually won't have to tote your beach blanket very far to get out of earshot of other boom-boxes.

HISTORIC SITES

Wright Brothers Memorial
In Kill Devil Hills, at milepost 8 on US 158, you can see in the distance the striking sight of the soaring granite monument of the Wright Brothers Memorial, tel. (252) 441-7430. Before you hike up to the monument, spend some time at the visitors center. Inside, a self-guided tour, which takes less than half an hour, leads you past dozens of exhibits explaining the intriguing origins of human flight, detailing many of the pitfalls and successes

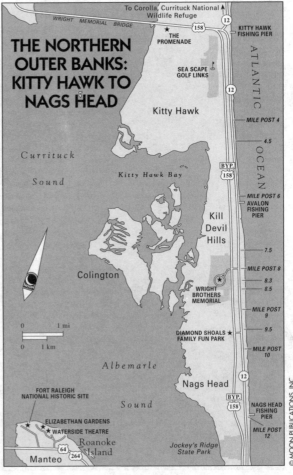

THE NORTHERN OUTER BANKS: KITTY HAWK TO NAGS HEAD

of the first aeronautical engineers. Working by trial and error, 18th-century scientists discovered that strapping on sets of large, bird-like wings and flapping like mad didn't work out so well—especially if you were jumping off a steep cliff.

As it chronicles the development of the brothers' historic manned glider, the tour extensively documents their experimental tenacity. In addition to scientific exhibits such as the ingenious tabletop wind tunnel created by the brothers, you'll find endearing "human-interest" tidbits including letters and cables describing the intense family pressure the brothers were under to finish their experiments so they could get home in time for Christmas.

Interpretive material at the exhibits are a bit text-heavy for kids. But visitors of all ages will understand the entertaining 30-minute presentations delivered by park guides every hour on the hour (except in winter, when some hours may be skipped). These mini-lectures are presented in the auditorium, which houses a meticulous, full-size replica of the Wrights' first successful airplane (the original is in the Smithsonian). In addition to manipulating various levers to show how the pilot controlled the plane, the guide will give you a brief, enlightening overview of the history and science behind the brothers' efforts.

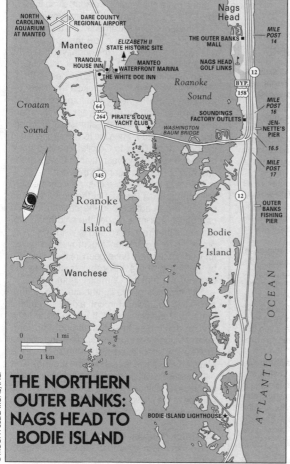

THE NORTHERN OUTER BANKS: NAGS HEAD TO BODIE ISLAND

© MOON PUBLICATIONS, INC.

Take a few minutes to peek into the huts on display next to the visitors center. These replicas of the humble quarters the Wright brothers stayed in help further set the historical scene. A few yards from the huts, concrete blocks mark off the distances of the Wright brothers' first four flights on that brisk day in 1903. The markers show the swift progress of those first baby steps in aviation: 100 feet, then 175, 200, and, finally, 852 feet (the final flight damaged the plane, prompting the brothers to pack up quickly and go home—for Christmas).

From the huts and markers, take the 10-minute hike up to the monument. Perched atop 90-foot Kill Devil Hill, the monument, shaped a bit like a bird's wing, reaches another 60 feet toward the clouds. As you ascend the gentle slope, you'll feel the wind gradually strengthen. Even when you don't feel a breeze at the visitors center, by the time you reach the base of the monument, you'll feel the gusting winds that sent the Wright brothers soaring into history.

Visit the memorial early in your trip, to give you an appreciation of the omnipresent winds that buffet these barrier islands. Admission to the memorial costs $2 per person, $4 per vehicle.

If you want to use more than your imagination to get a feel for the Wright brothers' feats, **Kitty Hawk Aero Tours,** tel. (252) 473-2227, take off from the airstrip behind the memorial. Rates range $19-24 per person for 30-minute flights in a modern Cessna to $48/person for a couple willing to take a thrilling 15-minute flight back in time on an antique Waco biplane.

THE WRIGHT BROTHERS

At the turn of the century, a pair of Ohio bicycle mechanics, Orville and Wilbur Wright, sent letters to the postmasters in various parts of America that had two highly desirable features: they were windy and they were sandy. The Wright brothers had an insatiable curiosity about the possibility of human flight. Although they had no formal scientific training, they had used the equipment in their bicycle shop to construct a sophisticated glider that they wanted to test someplace that had more wind (for longer, better rides) and more sand (softer landings) than Dayton. They explained in their letters that they wanted to perform some flying experiments and requested information about topography and wind conditions.

The brothers received only one response, from a Captain William Tate, husband of the postmistress at Kitty Hawk, North Carolina. Despite his apparent suspicion that the Wrights were a couple of kooks, Tate nonetheless felt unencumbered by the prevailing religious philosophy of the time—namely, that if man were meant to fly, the Lord would have given him wings. Tate's reply to the Wrights was an invitation to the Outer Banks.

As a result of their periodic excursions to Kitty Hawk between 1900 and 1903, Orville and Wilbur Wright became the state's most famous tourists ever. Almost a century later, hang gliders still pick up the winds at Kill Devil Hills, and the memory of those pioneering bikers of the air is commemorated on North Carolina's license plate, which bears the slogan "First in Flight."

Lighthouses

Two lighthouses stand on the sands of the Northern Outer Banks. Eight miles south of the intersection of highways US 64 and 158, the **Bodie Island Lighthouse** rises 150 feet. Visitors can't climb this tower, but the old lighthouse keeper's quarters have been restored and are now used as a visitors center where you can learn about the structure, workings, and history of this 1872 facility, whose beacon reaches 19 miles out to sea. Brief walkways and trails guide you through the lush marshlands near the tower.

For a more challenging workout, climb the 212 steps to the top of **Currituck Lighthouse** in Corolla. At the top, you're rewarded with a breathtaking series of views as you circle the catwalk surrounding the beacon. To the north, you'll see the subdivisions along the oceanfront give way to dense maritime forest, which stretches as far as binoculars can see. As you circle the tower toward the southern views, you can see an endless progression of oceanfront development stretching to the horizon—almost all of it constructed since 1984, when the road was opened to the public from Duck to Corolla. You also get a bird's-eye view of the vast Atlantic Ocean to the east and of Pamlico Sound to the west.

Climbing to the views costs $4 per person, but you can visit the rest of the grounds at no cost. In a pen adjacent to the parking lot, you can get a look at a few of the wild horses of Corolla (if they're in the mood to visit). This pen, protected by electric fencing, provides a haven for wild horses who have been injured—usually by getting hit by 4WD vehicles cruising the beaches north of the Currituck lighthouse.

The grounds of the lighthouse also feature an inviting boardwalk through a dense maritime forest to Roanoke Sound. If you visit the lighthouse, don't miss this stroll through the foreboding foliage, replete with spiders and snakes (don't worry about the snakes—the boardwalk is elevated about five feet above the ground). This half-hour walk will give you a memorable insight into how tenaciously plants used to cling to the surface of the shifting sands of the Outer Banks, before the bulldozers arrived.

Currituck National Wildlife Refuge

A five-minute drive north of the Currituck Lighthouse brings you to the northern terminus of

Currituck Lighthouse

NC 12. The pavement ends rather abruptly at this point, at the beach on the southern edge of the refuge. Currituck is a fabulous place to explore a maritime forest, but you need a 4WD vehicle to gain access to the refuge. The only public parking available within miles is on the sand along the beach—something you definitely do *not* want to attempt with a two-wheel-drive vehicle (unless you want to contribute to the thriving tow-truck industry of the Outer Banks).

If you *are* driving a 4WD, you won't want to miss a drive along this pavement-free stretch of beach for another 20 miles, pulling off occasionally to explore this home of wild horses, feral boars, exotic birds, and a dense network of sand-clinging shrubs, grasses, and evergreen trees. (By the way, don't get too cocky about your 4WD—it, too, can get stuck in soft dunes. Stay on the moist, harder-packed sand near the water.)

This is definitely not the stretch to choose for solitary sunbathing, however—the beach constitutes the only route from Corolla to the Vir-

ginia border, and truck-tire tracks can really make a mess of a tan.

Amusements
Driving along the US 158 Bypass, you'll be hard pressed to forget that you're in a tourist mecca. Roadside amusements abound, beckoning to your inner child—and any real children in the car. The vast majority of these parks are small operations, usually including a couple of steep water slides, a handful of rides that spin you around in various ways, and a miniature golf course or two. None of the parks charge a general admission fee, instead charging per ride.

The biggest entertainment park in the area is the **Promenade,** on US 158 in Kitty Hawk, at the Wright Memorial Bridge, tel. (252) 261-4900. Although it doesn't, as it happens, have water slides or spinning rides, it does offer lots of other diversions. Miniature golf is the major one: a 19-hole course features lots of waterfalls and rapids ($4), and another course features 27 holes on natural-grass greens ($3-5). There's also a driving range ($5 for a bucket of 52). The Family Arcade includes pool tables, pinball machines, video games, and favorites like skee ball and the aggression-releasing Wac-a-Mole, in which plastic moles pop up through an array of holes, and you try to whack them on their heads before they disappear again. Located directly on Albemarle Sound, the Promenade also rents a variety of watercraft, including inner tubes, canoes, kayaks, windsails, catamarans, and jet skis. Little tykes will have a ball at the huge Smilin' Island soft-play park ($5 ages three and up, $2 for two-year-olds, $1 for one-year-olds). The park has a snack bar (good for a hot dog or an ice cream sundae) and a coffee and draft house (where you can load up on cappuccino or beer), but you can also bring your own fixings and enjoy a homemade picnic meal on Roanoke Sound. Parking is free. The Promenade is open March-November, 8:30 a.m.-midnight in summer.

The hottest new water park on the Northern Outer Banks is **Diamond Shoals Family Fun Park,** at milepost 9.75 on the 158 Bypass in Kill Devil Hills, tel. (252) 480-3553. The park includes paddle boats, a video arcade, batting cage, and 36 holes of natural-grass miniature golf. But the big attractions here are the three "state-of-the-art" water slides—full of twists, turns, and tunnels. Passes to the water slides are $10 if you want to slide, $4 if you just want to watch the stunned, wide-eyed kids as they skid off the ends of the slides into the shallow pool, regain their footing, and invariably ask, "Can I do it again?"

ROANOKE ISLAND ATTRACTIONS

Just east of Bodie Island, where US 64 and 158 meet, lies historic Roanoke Island, site of the first English settlement in America. Four attractions offer glimpses into the history of the English explorations of the Outer Banks in the 1580s, including the 117 members of the "lost colony."

Elizabeth II State Historic Site

At the waterfront in downtown Manteo, you can look across a narrow inlet of Shallowbag Bay to see the Elizabeth II, a faithful replica of the vessel that transported 54 sailors and soldiers to explore the region in 1585. This is a wonderfully fun and informative place to learn about the rich history of this island.

The visitors center, tel. (252) 473-1144, offers a vast amount of information about the British voyages to this island in the 1580s. In addition to artifacts, dioramas, and interactive and print displays, the center shows two films. The 20-minute Roanoke Voyage details the hardships of the 1585 voyage of the Elizabeth II. The terrific 40-minute film The Legend of Two-Path, by Academy Award-winner Sam Grogg, director of Kiss of the Spider Woman and The Trip to Bountiful, presents the story of the 16th-century explorations of Roanoke Island from the point of view of the inhabitants at the time, the Algonquin Indians. Make sure to view this film before you leave the park—it gives you an intimate, historical frame of reference when you explore other unspoiled, protected parts of the Outer Banks, which tend to look more like the landscape of the late 1500s.

From the visitors center, take the short path to the meticulous replica of the Elizabeth II, docked in Shallowbag Bay. At first glance, this lovely vessel inspires romantic visions about how glorious it must have been to sail across the Atlantic Ocean four centuries ago. But then, as you tour the decks of the 69-foot-long craft, the gritty details of the ship's 1585 voyage surface.

This was a densely cramped ship, manned by 24 sailors and 30 soldiers. For the soldiers in particular, the 12-13 week voyage across the Atlantic was extraordinarily grueling—they spent the entire trip below the top deck, except when they briefly stopped at the Canary Islands and Puerto Rico. The food—consisting mostly of soured beer, moldy and buggy hard tack (a rock-like mixture of flour and water); salted fish, pork, and beef; and dried beans, peas, and lentils—encouraged flatulence, diarrhea, and vomiting. For these excretions, the soldiers were provided with buckets, but much of this waste found its way into the bilge of the ship. (The bilge is the bottommost level of a ship; in the days before watertight hulls arrived in the 20th century, the bilge frequently filled with seawater from inevitable leaks in the old wooden hulls. Pumps were then employed to remove water from the bilge. On the 1585 crossing, Elizabeth II's chief mariner, Thomas Cavendish, made several frustrated references to the fact that the bilge pumps were constantly getting stopped up with human waste.) Luckily, the living history presented here doesn't include an olfactory component. Living history guides include some in period dress who remain in 16th-century character; some (arguably the most entertaining) "ghost guides," who pretend to have sailed on the 1585 voyage and have no knowledge of all the intervening time between then and now; and contemporary guides who give you history from a familiar perspective.

To reach the site, follow the signs on US 64, then drive over the Cora Mae Basnight Bridge on Ananias Dare St., next to the Tranquil House Inn. Open daily 10 a.m.-6 p.m. April 1-Oct. 31, closed Monday Nov. 1-March 31. Several new additions, including many more interactive exhibits and an outdoor stage, were in the works as this book went to press. The admission price is expected to be in the $5-10 range.

More Manteo Historic Sites

At the northern end of Roanoke Island, on US 64/264, about three-quarters of a mile west of the bridge crossing Croatan Sound, you'll see signs for The Lost Colony, Fort Raleigh National Historic Site, and the Elizabethan Gardens.

Roanoke Island is not only the site of America's first English settlement, but also the home of the nation's first (and longest-running) outdoor symphonic drama. For a dramatic and entertaining night of theater, don't miss the celebrated musical drama *The Lost Colony.* Performed under the stars on the spacious sound stage of the Waterside Theatre (on the very sands the settlers first colonized), the play tells the story of the 117 English settlers who came to Roanoke Island more than four centuries ago and vanished without explanation. It's a great show, complete with colorful costumes, energetic dancing, and a score that ranges from courtly Elizabethan tunes to Native American dances. Written by Pulitzer Prize-winner Paul Green, *The Lost Colony* has captivated audiences here every summer since 1937. With a cast and crew of 125, the performance is big and gripping and makes a great vehicle for visitors of all ages to gain a greater sense of the courage of these first settlers. The play starts at 8:30 p.m. every night except Saturday from early June through the end of August. Tickets cost $14 for ages over 11, $7 for ages 11 and under. The production is popular, so reserve ahead. Call the box office at (252) 473-3414 to book your seats in advance or to locate the most convenient of the play's 65 ticket outlets on the Outer Banks.

Adjacent to the Waterside Theatre off US 64/264 lie the lush **Elizabethan Gardens,** tel. (252) 473-3234. More than a thousand varieties of flora are meticulously maintained in these dazzling gardens. Something here is blooming on any given day of the year—rhododendrons, azaleas, dogwoods, hydrangeas, bulb flowers, and spring annuals peak in mid-April; roses, gardenias, magnolias, crape myrtle, lilies, and other annuals in midsummer; chrysanthemums and impatiens in early autumn; and camellias and pansies in winter. Various walking trails lead through structured parterre gardens and wooded paths, along the beach of Roanoke Sound, and past sculptures and fountains. It's easy to spend at least an hour touring the 10.5 acres of this botanical paradise. Admission is $3 for adults, $1 for ages 12-17, free for ages under 12.

Adjacent to the Elizabethan Gardens and the Waterside Theatre, **Fort Raleigh National Historic Site,** tel. (252) 473-5772, features a reconstruction of the "fort"—consisting of sandy mounds surrounding a space about 50 yards

square—built by the Lost Colony. You won't see any buildings—or even any fences—so you have to use a considerable degree of imagination to give much meaning to this site. Stopping first at the visitors center can help you along. There you can watch a 17-minute video chronicling the early history of these sands. The center also includes a 400-year old room brought over from Kent, England, furnished in authentic Elizabethan fashion, complete with lots of 16th- and 17th-century furnishings.

A self-guided interpretive trail leads about a quarter of a mile from the visitors center to the fort. A new path was added in 1998—the three-mile (roundtrip) **Freedom Trail**—through a maritime forest and out to the site of the **Roanoke Island Freedmen's Colony.** Consisting mostly of escaped slaves, this colony was a temporary home for 3,000-6,000 people during and for a few years after the Civil War. As with Fort Raleigh, the trail, consisting only of interpretive panels and displays, will take some imagination to appreciate. Park admission is free; open 9 a.m.-8 p.m. June-Aug., 9 a.m. to 5 p.m. the rest of the year.

North Carolina Aquarium at Manteo

About three-quarters of a mile southwest of Fort Raleigh (between the fort and downtown Manteo), take Airport Road off US 64/264, to get to the North Carolina Aquarium at Manteo, tel. (252) 473-3494. Like the two other state aquariums, the one in Manteo is on a smaller scale than many large, new aquariums across the nation. But the few dozen exhibits here are guaranteed to fascinate and educate all ages.

Kids love the touch-tank, where you can handle lots of sea critters, including starfish, whelks, and horseshoe and hermit crabs. The Shark Gallery features an 8,400-gallon shark tank, along with continuous videos about sharks. In addition to other favorites, including exhibits of live turtles and young alligators, the aquarium recently installed a popular exhibit about fishing. Called *It's the Big One!,* this exhibit highlights the rich variety of game and food fish that have drawn anglers to the Outer Banks for hundreds of years. An informative computer program delivers lots of information about 34 species pursued in deep sea, surf, sound, and freshwater fishing. In addition, the exhibit includes a replica of an old fishing shack, complete with antique fishing equipment and memorabilia. Another fun new feature is the *Big Backyard,* which describes the ecology of a typical backyard, from birds to in-sects to underground animals. The aquarium is open daily 9 a.m.-7 p.m. Memorial Day through Labor Day, 9 a.m.-5 p.m. the rest of the year. Admission is $3 for adults, $1 for ages 6-17.

RECREATION

Jockey's Ridge State Park

Don't miss exploring Jockey's Ridge State Park, at milepost 12 on Route 158, tel. (252) 441-7132. The tallest natural sand dune system in the eastern United States, this area gives you an unspoiled glimpse into the sandy, hilly, and windy conditions that attracted the Wright brothers at the turn of the century. Jockey's Ridge provides an exotic environment, particularly attractive to hikers, hang-gliders, and kite-flyers.

The park, which you shouldn't miss, features several examples of medanos—sprawling hills of shifting sand, barren of vegetation. Although some of the valleys between these towering dunes support small pockets of beachgrass and an occasional thicket of wax myrtle and bayberry bushes, hiking through the park will give you more of a feeling that you're trudging across the Sahara rather than strolling along some sand dunes at the beach. If you head out into the dunes, keep the desert metaphor in mind. Particularly in the summer, the heat on the sand can be blistering—literally. Wear shoes (not sandals), a hat, sunglasses, and high SPF sunscreen, and tote *plenty of water.* Although pets are permitted in the park, don't bring them in the summer. Even a brief hike on the scorching sands of the dunes can give a dog heat stroke.

Although the sparseness of the vegetation gives you free reign to ramble almost anywhere in the park, the vast majority of hikers follow the trail beginning at the visitors center parking lot, just off the milepost 12 marker on Route 158. The **Tracks in the Sand Trail** is a self-guided 1.5-mile nature trail from the parking lot to the shrub forests and the beach at Roanoke Sound. Pick up the pamphlet at the visitors center to read about the 14 stations marked on this intriguing trail. For a more solitary trek to Jockey's Ridge, start out at the parking lot on the sound side of the park, located at the end of Soundside Road on the southern border of the park.

DIVING IN THE GRAVEYARD

For such a popular and inviting beach destination, the ocean waters of the Outer Banks have a rather off-putting moniker—"the Graveyard of the Atlantic." But this treacherous stretch of ocean fully earned its nefarious nickname over the past four centuries, thanks to its wicked storms and currents, unpredictable creation of sandbars, and the generally narrow, shallow inlets between the barrier islands through which ships have to pass on their way to ports on the North Carolina mainland.

More than 600 shipwrecks lie beneath the waves off the shores of the Outer Banks. About 200 have been identified, ranging from ships lost in the 1700s (archaeologists think they may have recently discovered the remains of Blackbeard's flagship, *Queen Anne's Revenge*) to dozens of wrecks from the 20th century, including some German U-boats and some big ships torpedoed during World War II.

These hundreds of wrecks draw thousands of scuba divers to the Outer Banks every year, and divers describe the diving sites here as breathtaking beautiful and solemn.

This is not an activity you can simply "jump into," however. In order to dive these wrecks, you must be scuba-certified. Four dive shops service the Outer Banks. In the Northern Outer Banks, **Sea Scan Dive Centre**, milepost 10 on Virginia Dare Trail (the beach road), tel. (252) 480-3467, and **Nags Head Pro Dive Center,** milepost 13 on U.S. 158, tel. (252) 441-7594, both rent and service scuba equipment and offer scuba instruction and diving charters. **Hatteras Divers** on Route 12 in Hatteras, tel. (252) 986-2557, and **Ocracoke Divers, Inc.** on Oyster Creek Rd. in Ocracoke Village, tel. (252) 928-1471, rent and service scuba equipment and provide diving charters.

Beginning hang gliders can receive instruction at Jockey's Ridge.

Again, bring plenty of water if you take either of these routes, since you'll be out in the desert sands for at least an hour and a half roundtrip.

Although the Jockey's Ridge dune is less than 100 feet tall, it takes 10 or 15 minutes to ascend to its summit from its base. All along the way, you get ever grander views of the ocean, the sound, and the undulating mounds of migrating sand all around you. From the top, you'll find an airy, 360-degree, panoramic view of the Atlantic Ocean, Outer Banks, and Roanoke Sound. You'll also find the stiff breezes that buffeted the Wright brothers' first flights. Chances are that you won't be alone atop Jockey's Ridge. In addition to fellow hikers, there's a good chance that you'll share the summit with hanggliders. It can be intoxicating to watch these folks run off the top of the ridge and soar out into the air. But you don't have to remain just an onlooker if you're so inclined; **Kitty Hawk Kites,** on Route 158, tel. (252) 441-4124 or (800) 334-4777, just across the street from the dune, has swept more than 200,000 people off their feet over the past 25 years. As you'll see from observing the hang gliders in action, gliding at Jockey's Ridge is not a death-defying, daredevil sport. The highest altitude achieved by beginning gliders is about 15 feet. Nonetheless, gliding here is likely to give you a thrill you won't soon forget. A wide range of lessons are available for all levels of expertise. If you've never tried it, the "hang gliding demo" sampler for beginners includes a training film, ground school,

and three flights on the park's sand dunes, all for $49 (two extra flights cost $20 more). Call Kitty Hawk Kites for more information.

Incidentally, the high elevation of the ridge makes it extremely susceptible to lightning strikes, so don't make a pilgrimage to Jockey's Ridge if you see any hint of storms on the horizon. If you look closely at the sands, you'll probably see a few examples of what look like little glass tubes. Those are fulgurites, formed when lightning has fused the sand. *Don't remove them from the park*—it's against park regulations, the staff is very protective of these crystalline reminders of lightning strikes, and you risk being asked to leave (without your souvenirs).

The park has recently made efforts to improve access. Park staff will arrange to take visitors with physical disabilities on a tour on an all-terrain vehicle. If possible, call at least 24 hours ahead so the staff can make the proper arrangements. The park also includes a wheelchair-accessible, 360-foot boardwalk that leads through a shrub forest to an overlook of Jockey's Ridge. Admission is free, and the park is open from dawn to sunset.

Miniature Golf
More than a dozen miniature golf courses flank the US 158 Bypass on Bodie Island. Miniature golf is a competitive business on this island; as a result, all of the courses are top notch, complete with special effects including waterfalls, 10-foot-tall dinosaurs, and the ever-popular windmills.

A popular new trend in miniature golf on Bodie Island is "natural grass" courses. Instead of the thin green carpet laid over concrete that characterizes the traditional "goofy golf" course, these new facilities consist completely of natural bent grass putting greens. These courses don't have artificial obstacles—no windmills, pirate statues, or T-Rexes—but they do present challenges including sharp corners, bumps, mounds, and water hazards.

Full-Size Golf

Bodie Island also boasts a few championship golf courses, open to the public. The three courses described here are extremely popular, so you won't regret reserving a tee time weeks—even months—in advance. The most recent, finished in the summer of 1996, is the **Currituck Club,** located on NC 12 at Corolla, tel. (252) 453-9400 or (888) 453-9400. This magnificent course, designed by the brilliant Rees Jones, earned a spot in *Golf Magazine's* 1997 "Top Ten New Courses You Can Play." Winding through woods, wetlands, and dunes, the course provides stunning views of Currituck Sound. Greens fees in the summer of 1998 were $95 from 7 a.m. to 11:30 a.m., $75 11:30 a.m.-4 p.m. The rest of year, fees range $45-75, depending on season and time of day. Fees include carts (walking is not permitted).

In Kitty Hawk, a combination of sand and subdivisions provide for an unusually challenging round of golf at the **Sea Scape Golf Links,** 300 Eckner St., off US 158. at milepost 2.5, tel. (252) 261-2158. This is a rather tight course—if you have a pronounced hook or slice, you might want to keep your woods in the bag on a few holes, just to keep from driving a shot through a window of a neighboring home. Most of the holes have gorgeous views of Roanoke Sound. Trickier than the water and house hazards, however, are the devious network of sand traps (recently redesigned by none other than Jack Nicklaus). Summer greens fees are $65 until 11:30 a.m., $55 11:30 a.m.-4 p.m., and $40 after 4 p.m. (fees drop by about $15 during non-summer months). Open year-round. Carts are mandatory, included in listed prices.

As with the other breezy courses on the Outer Banks, you can always blame the wind for a bad shot at the **Nags Head Golf Links,** 5615 S. Seachase Dr., off US 158 at milepost 15, tel. (252) 441-8073 or (800) 851-9404. Most holes offer views of Roanoke Sound and pretty water hazards, which can make for a frustrating but guaranteed breathtaking round. Dense maritime woods also gobble up more than their share of errant shots. During the summer, greens fees are $80 until 11:30 a.m., $65 11:30 a.m.-4 p.m., and $50 after 4 p.m. (fees go as low as $40 in winter). Open year-round. Rates include mandatory carts.

FISHING (AND OTHER BOATING ACTIVITIES)

Whether you just want to toss in a line from the beach, stroll out onto a pier, or take a boat out onto the waters, the Northern Outer Banks offers a variety of fishing options. The Gulf Stream, about 15-20 miles offshore, offers the chance to land big-game fish like marlin and tuna. Closer by, the inland backwaters of Dare County offer the sumptuous beauty of the Alligator River and lots of superb coves, where you can reel in largemouth and striped bass, flounder, drum, perch, catfish, and trout. If you want to stay on the beach, you might hook spots, bluefish, flounder, red drum, and others.

Pier Fishing

For the highest ratio of fish to time, effort, and budget, you might want to try one of the several fishing piers along Bodie Island. A day's fishing pass usually costs $5 and includes the popular option of night fishing. If you've never fished off a pier before, you can walk out on the pier (it might cost you a dollar or two) and watch the practiced pier anglers reel them in by the bucketful. All of the piers are popular and can get a bit crowded, but the communal atmosphere can be fun. The piers will rent you equipment and supply you with bait for $5-10. You're almost guaranteed to reel in enough spot, bluefish, croaker, or other fish for a few meals, and you might even catch something exotic like amberjack or tarpon. Piers along Beach Road (Route 12), from north to south, include **Kitty Hawk Fishing Pier,** milepost 1, tel. (252) 261-2772; **Avalon Fishing Pier,** milepost 6, tel. (252) 441-7494; **Nags Head Fishing Pier,** milepost 12, tel. (252) 441-5141: **Jennette's Pier,** milepost 16.5, tel. (252) 441-6116; and the **Outer Banks Fishing Pier and Fishing Center,** milepost 18.5, tel. (252) 441-5740.

Charters, Headboats, and Sightseeing Cruises

In case you're unfamiliar with the phrase "head-boat fishing," headboats (named for the "per head" charge, usually $20-30) are the least expensive option for fishing off a boat. As many as 50 anglers board a single boat for excursions lasting around four hours or more. Charters offer a lot more privacy and typically run $600-900 for six or so fishermen for a full day, $350-500 for a half-day. If you want to charter a boat for the Gulf Stream, you'll have to go for a whole day. The following four marinas provide a full assortment of options: the **Oregon Inlet Fishing Center,** on NC 12, just north of the Herbert C. Bonner Bridge, tel. (252) 441-6301; the **Pirate's Cove Yacht Club,** on the Manteo-Nags Head Causeway, tel. (252) 473-3906 or (800) 367-4728; the **Salty Dawg Marina,** US 64 in Manteo, tel. (252) 473-3405; and the **Manteo Waterfront Marina,** in downtown Manteo, tel. (252) 473-3320.

Several boats offer various **sightseeing cruises,** from tours of the backwaters, to twilight cruises on the high seas. For more information, call or stop by the marinas listed above.

Kayaking

If you'd like to power your own vessel, then contact **Kitty Hawk Kites and Outer Banks Outdoors,** tel. (800) 334-4777, about their menu of guided kayaking excursions. Most of the tours explore calm waters—marshes, creeks running through maritime forests—and therefore don't require any prior experience. These "eco-tours," led by experienced, knowledgeable, and entertaining guides, last two to three hours and are available at several spots along the entire length of the Outer Banks. Kitty Hawk Kites' main store is located on US 158 in Nags Head, at milepost 13 opposite Jockey's Ridge State Park, but this veteran outfitter also has branches in Corolla, Duck, Manteo, Avon, Hatteras Village, and Ocracoke Island. From these branches, you can arrange to go on one or more of these fascinating tours through the various complex ecosystems of the Outer Banks; cost ranges $20-40.

Surfing and Windsurfing

Although the best surfing and windsurfing is to be found on Hatteras Island, both sports are nonetheless also popular on Bodie Island, with more than a dozen equipment outfitters to choose among. If you've never tried either sport, a few places offer lessons. For surfing (lessons run $25 an hour), try the **Cavalier Surf Shop,** on US 158, milepost 13.5, tel. (252) 441-7349. For windsurfing instruction, go to **Kitty Hawk Watersports,** on US 158, milepost 16, tel. (252) 441-2756 (three-hour beginner class costs $44).

SHOPPING

The Outer Banks have better, more varied, and more interesting shopping than you might expect at "the beach." While you'll find plenty of traditional beach stores specializing in T-shirts, flip-flops, sand pails, and $1.99 souvenirs made from seashells, you'll also find stores to satisfy more discriminating tastes.

Timbuck II is an upscale shopping center on the southern edge of Corolla, along route 12. More than 60 shops are located here, including two wonderful art galleries, clothing stores with up-to-the-minute fashion (including swimsuits, of course), an extensive book shop. In addition, you'll also find one of the Outer Banks' most popular stores here, **Kitty Hawk Kites,** (which also has stores in Corolla, Nags Head, and Avon), where you'll find the biggest selection of kites you're ever likely to see.

If you're tired of the beach and you need a potent shopping fix, go to Duck, where you'll find the biggest variety of interesting shops within the smallest area on the Outer Banks. All of the shops are along Route 12. Visit the wonderful **Greenleaf Gallery,** where you'll find traditional works, upscale handmade crafts, pottery and sculpture, as well as sophisticated, cutting-edge work from respected artists. (Greenleaf has another location in Nags Head at milepost 16 on US 158.) Across the street, the five stores of the **Duck Soundside Shops**—offering gifts, Christmas decorations, mens' and womens' fashions, and exotic seashells—feel more seasoned and relaxed than many other shopping centers on the Outer Banks. Adjoining **Scarborough Faire** and **Scarborough Lane,** in downtown Duck, provide an inviting, shady atmosphere, rising two stories and winding around like a little village. Exploring the 30 shops housed here can feel a little like searching for buried treasures as you peruse the selections of antiques, art galleries, clothing boutiques and gourmet shops.

In Kitty Hawk, at milepost 4.5 on US 158, **The Crafter's Gallery** is a great stop if you're in search of local crafts and other unique handmade items, from jewelry to furniture. In Kill Devil Hills, at milepost 10 on US 158 the **Beach Barn Shops** feature several interesting shops and two good bookstores. Make a point to stop in at the **Carolina Moon**, which offers a wide selection of unusual gifts, jewelry and Christmas ornaments in a calming atmosphere with soothing music (also for sale).

Nags Head offers dozens of interesting shops, particularly along US 158. **The Outer Banks Mall,** at milepost 14 on US 158, offers your typical mall chain stores and a cineplex. Bargain hunters like the **Soundings Factory Outlets** mall at milepost 16 on the US 158 Bypass in Nags Head, featuring 26 shops selling gifts, clothing, shoes, fragrances, jewelry, cookware, books, and a great deal more. In addition, you'll see dozens of spots to pick up beach equipment like lounge chairs, beach balls, T-shirts, sun hats, sandcastle molds, and the ever-popular kites.

Despite the considerable variety of shopping available in this region, there is one shop that truly stands out in the Northern Outer Banks, the **Christmas Shop and Island Gallery,** on Highway 64 near downtown Manteo, tel. (252) 473-2838 or (800) 470-2838. Located next to the Weeping Radish Brewery and Bavarian Restaurant, this store is the Christmas shop to beat all Christmas shops, a 33-room maze where you can wander through over 20,000 square feet of retail space, the entire complex crammed with every type of Christmas paraphernalia imaginable, including thousands of ornaments, dolls, and an exhaustive collection of miniature Christmas villages. Even if it's 95 degrees outside, you'll find yourself expecting to see snow falling when you leave this Christmas wonderland. Watch the delighted faces of the young kids as they first enter the big Christmas room. Even though the Christmas shop doesn't have many toys, the kids look as pleased as if they'd landed in Santa's village at the north pole. In addition to the massive Christmas collection, there's a fully stocked Halloween Room, and the Island Gallery portion of the store features artworks, mainly paintings, from local artists. A Manteo institution since 1966, the Christmas Shop and Island Gallery is a shopping stop you won't soon forget.

ACCOMMODATIONS

Hotels and Motels

In addition to an assortment of chain hotels and motels, dozens of family-run motels adorn the shores and roadways of Kitty Hawk, Kill Devil Hills, and Nags Head. These family-run operations vary widely in quality, not so widely in price. Everyplace fills up during the summer season—and even the not-so-nice places can charge fairly high rates. From Memorial Day to Labor Day, expect to pay at least $75 per night, even for a motel with sagging mattresses and mildew-tinged bathrooms, located next to an RV park. That said, there are plenty of clean and comfortable independent hotels and motels in the Kill Devil Hills/Kitty Hawk/Nags Head area. It's well worth your while to reserve ahead—particularly during the summer season. All of the places listed here are located directly on the beach and, un-

less specified otherwise, are open year-round.

Families are fond of the **Sea Foam Motel,** 7111 Virginia Dare Trail, tel. (252) 441-7320, which features a swimming pool, wading pool, and playground (not just for kids—it includes two shuffleboard courts and a hammock-for-two). Open March 1-Dec. 15, rooms start at $75 in summer and drop to $42 off-season. Most rooms have balconies and ocean views; all have refrigerators, microwaves, and phones. If you're staying for at least a week, opt for one of the 18 efficiencies (which rent only by the week during the summer season but daily in the off-season). Efficiencies range $510-610 for a weeklong stay in the summer, as low as $330 a week in the off-season. Moderate.

You can find another family-run bargain at the 14-room **Vivianna Motel,** 6905 Virginia Dare

Trail, tel. (252) 441-7409. Run for almost 40 years by the Midgett-Senf family, all of the rooms in this kitschy 1950s-style, one-story motel provide ocean views and include refrigerators and cable TV. Nine rooms also include coffeemakers, microwaves, and kitchenettes. None of the rooms have phones. Open March 1-Nov. 30; rates begin at $70 during peak summer season, range $36-52 during the other seasons they're open. The Vivianna also has one one-bedroom suite, which rents by the week. Moderate.

Among the plethora of smaller, family-run motels on the beach, the **Blue Heron Motel,** 6811 Virginia Dare Trail, at milepost 16 on NC 12, tel. (252) 441-7447, rises a cut above the rest. Comfortably furnished rooms all include refrigerators, microwaves, coffeepots, cable TV, and phones. The Blue Heron has *two* outdoor pools, as well as an indoor pool and a whirlpool. Run by the friendly Gladden family, the motel has 19 guest rooms and 11 efficiencies, all with ocean views. Rooms on the second and third floors have private balconies. The rates begin at $95 during the summer and dip as low as $45 during the winter. The efficiencies are a great deal, costing only about $5 more than the rooms without kitchenettes. Weekly rates are also available. Expensive.

The **Surf Side Motel,** 6701 Virginia Dare Trail, at milepost 16 on NC 12, tel. (252) 441-2105 or (800) 552-SURF, provides 76 clean and comfortably furnished guest rooms, 11 suites, and six efficiencies on the oceanfront. All of the rooms offer ocean views, private balconies, and little refrigerators—but some ocean views are better than others. The main, rectangular structure rises five stories, from which a third of the rooms face the ocean directly while the other rooms offer "side" views of the ocean from their balconies. Be aware, too, that while the rooms on the upper floors may give you a better view, you have to work a bit for it: the Surf Side doesn't have any elevators. But it does have a spacious outdoor oceanfront pool and an indoor pool with an adjacent whirlpool. Weekdays during peak summer season, rooms with side views begin at $99, rooms directly facing the ocean run $134 (add $15 on weekends). Luxury suites with jacuzzis cost $170 during the summer. Room rates drop considerably the rest of the year, to as low as $39 in the winter. If you're traveling with kids, you might consider trying one of seven "loft suites," which include a small, separate room just underneath the motel's roof, with double beds and a skylight. Kids in particular seem to enjoy these neat little "attic-style" cubbyholes. Expensive/Premium.

Of the 100 rooms at the five-story **Nags Head Inn,** 4701 S. Virginia Dare Trail, at milepost 14 on NC 12, tel. (252) 441-0454 or (800) 327-8881, 50 face the ocean and come with private balconies (the other 50 lack balconies and face the town of Nags Head—but do provide expansive views across the island to Roanoke Sound). All rooms are well maintained and include small refrigerators, cable TV, and free HBO. Other amenities include a sun deck with a hot tub (which easily accommodates a dozen people) and a heated indoor/outdoor oceanfront pool. Oceanfront rooms run $150, street-facing rooms $100, from the third week in June through the third week in August. Rates dip to $105 and $70 during the weeks surrounding the peak season, in May, June, August, and September, and drop much lower the rest of the year—to as low as $60 and $40 during the winter. Premium.

National Chains

If you prefer the dependability of chain motels, the Northern Outer Banks has plenty of choices. Almost all are located in the towns of Kill Devil Hills and Nags Head. Unless specified otherwise, rates quoted below are for single rooms during peak summer season. Many of these places increase their rates on weekends, and/or charge more for a room with a direct ocean view, which accounts for more than one rate range being quoted. During the rest of the year, rates drop by as much as half to two-thirds, with most of the motels listed below dipping to the moderate and inexpensive range.

Days Inn Oceanfront-Nags Head Beach, 101 Virginia Dare Trail, milepost 8.3 on NC 12 in Kill Devil Hills, tel. (252) 441-7211 or (800) DAYS-INN. Oceanfront. Pool. Some efficiencies available. Moderate/Expensive.

Holiday Inn Express, 3919 N. Croatan Highway, milepost 4 on US 158 Bypass in Kitty Hawk, tel. (252) 261-4888 or (800) 836-2753. Short walk to ocean. Pool, refrigerators in all rooms. Moderate/Expensive.

Comfort Inn, 401 Virginia Dare Trail, milepost 8.2 on NC 12 in Kill Devil Hills, tel. (252)480-

2600 or (800) 854-5286. Oceanfront. Small pool, game room. Expensive/Premium.

Comfort Inn Oceanfront South, 8031 Old Oregon Rd., milepost 17 on beach road in South Nags Head, tel. (252) 441-6315 or (800) 334-3302. Oceanfront. Pool. Expensive/Premium.

Quality Inn-John Yancey, 2009 Virginia Dare Trail, milepost 10.3 on NC 12 in Kill Devil Hills, tel. (252) 441-7141 or (800) 367-5941. Oceanfront. Pool, playground, some efficiencies. Expensive/Premium.

Quality Inn Sea Oatel, 7123 Virginia Dare Trail, milepost 16.5 on NC 12 in Nags Head, tel. (252) 441-7191 or (800) 440-4FUN. Oceanfront. Pool. Expensive/Premium.

Ramada Inn at Nags Head Beach, 1701 Virginia Dare Trail, milepost 9.5 on NC 12 in Kill Devil Hills, tel. (252) 441-2151 or (800) 635-1824. Oceanfront. Heated indoor pool, whirlpool, pets allowed for extra $10. Expensive/Premium.

Holiday Inn, 1601 Virginia Dare Trail, milepost 9.5 on NC 12 in Kill Devil Hills, tel. (252) 441-6333 or (800) 843-1249. Oceanfront. Pool, whirlpool. Premium/Luxury.

Best Western Ocean Reef Suites, 107 Virginia Dare Trail, milepost 8.5 on NC 12 in Kill Devil Hills, tel. (252) 441-1611 or (800) 528-1234. Oceanfront. All rooms are suites and include kitchens. Heated pool, sauna, whirlpool, exercise room. Premium/Luxury.

Inns

Three inns provide the most luxurious accommodations on the Northern Outer Banks. About 10 miles north of Kitty Hawk, along NC 12, lies the posh **Sanderling Inn Resort and Conference Center,** 1461 Duck Rd., tel. (252) 261-4111 or (800) 701-4111. Housed in cedar-shingled, three-story buildings are 88 rooms, most with private porches or balconies and expansive views overlooking the ocean or Currituck Sound (views from first-floor rooms are obscured by dunes). The lobby is embellished with marvelous pine woodwork, artworks including intricate, carved duck decoys, porcelain birds, and wildflower sculptures. The rooms are spacious and airy and come with little extras like bathrobes, and a gift basket of bath gels and lotions. The furnishings in the rooms emphasize comfort—such as cushioned wicker chairs that invite you to curl up with a book and listen to the surf in the background. In addition to the private beaches, other amenities include an indoor pool, a health club, tennis courts, nature and walking trails, and a marvelous restaurant. Many of the rooms include kitchens, and some come with hot tubs. Rates, which include a buffet breakfast and afternoon tea, begin at $190 from mid-May through the end of September, and $125 the rest of the year. Luxury.

In Nags Head, at milepost 12 on SR 12, you'll find the zenith of luxury in the entire Outer Banks at the extraordinary **First Colony Inn,** 6720 South Virginia Dare Trail, tel. (252) 441-2343 or (800) 368-9390. Each of the 26 guest rooms is immaculately furnished with gorgeous antiques and includes TV, telephone, and refrigerator. The three-story shingle-style structure has two wraparound porches replete with inviting rocking chairs. The beach is just across Virginia Dare Trail, a minute's walk from your door. For freshwater fans, an outdoor pool is also available. What makes the First Colony extraordinary is its history. The last surviving "beach-style hotel" from the early days of Nags Head's advent as a vacation destination, the inn first opened in 1932. By 1988, the "Grand Old Lady" had fallen into grave disrepair and was slated for destruction—to make way for six beach cottages. That's when the Lawrence family, from Lexington, North Carolina, stepped forward with a bold proposal. After surmounting a myriad of obstacles, the Lawrences sliced the First Colony into three huge sections, packed them onto tractor-trailer rigs, and reassembled the inn on land they owned three miles south of its original site; this is the present location of the inn. After three years of painstaking restoration—and the addition of modern touches like central heat and air conditioning, sparkling bathrooms, and truckloads of fine antiques—the inn reopened to rave reviews, deservedly earning awards for historical preservation and restoration as well for its luxurious lodgings. Rates start at $130 in the summer, $70 November-March, and $105 the rest of the year for first-floor rooms (rooms on the upper two floors run $20-60 more, and weekend and holiday nights often cost $10-20 more), including a continental breakfast in the sunny breakfast room. Thursday nights are free for stays running Sun.-Thurs. night. Premium/Luxury.

In Manteo, the **Tranquil House Inn,** 405 Elizabeth St., tel. (252) 473-1404 or (800) 458-7069, provides 23 guest rooms and two one-bedroom suites. Situated on the Manteo waterfront overlooking the *Elizabeth II,* this inn was built just over 10 years ago (though its turn-of-the-century feel pays homage to its predecessor, the old Tranquil House, which stood at this site from the Civil War until the 1950s). All the rooms are individually and tastefully decorated, with touches like canopied beds and Oriental rugs. Rates begin at $159 in the summer, and dip as low as $79 in the off-season. Luxury.

Bed and Breakfasts

Traditional bed-and-breakfast inns are extremely scarce in the Northern Outer Banks. If you're looking for an elegant, antique-filled atmosphere, you should plan on staying at the **The White Doe Inn,** 301 Sir Walter Raleigh St., tel. (252) 473-9851 or (800) 473-6091. Located in downtown Manteo, this gorgeous Queen Anne-style home provides six guest rooms and one suite, all with private baths and antique or reproduction Victorian furnishings. Owners Bebe and Bob Woody serve a full breakfast and an afternoon tea. The White Doe provides a peaceful atmosphere in which you can lounge on the wraparound porches or in the library or parlor, or stretch your legs by strolling around the downtown Manteo waterfront. Rates during the peak summer season begin at $135 and drop $10-20 the rest of the year. Premium.

For something a bit more modern, the **Advice 5 Cents,** 111 Scarborough Lane, tel. (252) 255-1050 or (800) ADVICE-5, provides a casual atmosphere in a newly constructed beach house. You can still smell the freshness of the juniper wainscoting. A short walk from downtown Duck, and a couple hundred yards from the beach, this friendly B&B includes four guest rooms and one suite, all of them bright, airy, and comfortable—as are the common rooms. The innkeepers, Donna Black and Nancy Caviness, provide a buffet-style continental breakfast featuring homemade muffins, fresh fruit, juices, and cereals. Rates begin at $125 May through September and drop to $80 the rest of the year. Premium.

House Rentals

The Northern Outer Banks are a favorite spot for extended summer vacations. If you plan on spending a week or more, we recommend that you rent a house from one of the many realty companies who serve this area. All will provide detailed brochures, including photos and brief written descriptions of each of the houses they rent. Rates vary widely depending on season, proximity to the water, and size of the home. The rates are determined, ultimately, by the respective homeowners, so it's impossible to give a precise range of price variance between the seasons. As a rule of thumb, pre- and post-season rates drop about 30-50% from peak rates, and off-season rates drop 40-60% from peak.

The homes themselves vary widely, but here's an extremely general idea of the prices charged for various types. North of Kitty Hawk, in towns like Duck, Sanderling, and Corolla, the homes are almost all of recent construction, clumped together subdivision-style. They tend to look very much alike and are generally quite large (particularly in Sanderling and Corolla), with four or more bedrooms—capable of accommodating 10 or more people. Oceanfront homes range $2,200-3,500 per week. Non-oceanfront homes run about $1,200-2,000 a week.

In the towns of Kill Devil Hills, Kitty Hawk, and Nags Head, the homes are generally smaller, older, have more individual character *and* are considerably less expensive. Small oceanfront homes (two to three bedrooms) can cost $500-1,000 a week; large oceanfront homes (four to six bedrooms) usually top out near $2,000. Non-oceanfront homes in these towns, depending on the size and location, generally cost $350-1,000 per week.

Get detailed brochures from any of the realty companies below. To get a feel for the wide variety of rental homes available, request brochures from at least two realtors. There are several small realty companies in the area that specialize in limited neighborhoods. The following are larger companies, extremely reputable, and pride themselves on matching your desires with available options. The companies below manage at least 200 properties, all along Bodie Island.

Atlantic Realty, tel. (800) 334-8401

Joe Lamb Jr. & Associates, tel. (800) 552-6257

Kitty Dunes Realty, tel. (800) 334-DUNE

Kitty Hawk Rentals, tel. (800) 635-1559

Resort Realty, tel. (800) 458-3830

Southern Shores Realty, tel. (800) 334-1000

Stan White Realty, tel. (800) 338-3233

Camping

You don't have much choice if you're looking to camp near Nags Head. Operated by the National Park Service, the campground at Oregon Inlet, just north of the Herbert C. Bonner Bridge on N.C. 12, tel. (252) 473-2111, amidst the dunes is the best choice. It's capable of serving trailers and motor homes, but there are no utility connections available. With 120 sites, most of them for tents, the campground has modern restrooms (with unheated showers) and potable water. The fee is $12 per site. All campsites are assigned on a first-come, first-served basis, with no reservations possible. If the National Park Service campground is full or if you prefer the reliability of a reservation (and the luxury of a hot shower), try the **Colington Park Campground** on Roanoke Sound (on Little Colington Island, near Kitty Hawk), tel. (252) 441-6128. All sites have water, power, and picnic tables, and the bathrooms include hot showers. Bring plenty of bug repellent to either site.

FOOD AND DRINK

The Northern Outer Banks—particularly the Nags Head/Kill Devil Hills/Kitty Hawk area—are crammed with eateries. Except for a smattering of breakfast places and barbecue joints, the specialties of the house consist almost always of critters freshly hauled from the local waters—usually fish, shrimp, scallops, and crabs (lobsters, when you see them on a menu, are probably shipped in from out of town). Although plenty of restaurants give you the option of draping your seafood with exotic-sounding sauces, the traditional haute cuisine of the region comes in basically three varieties: fried, broiled, or sautéed in a butter and lemon sauce. The freshness of the seafood served at Outer Banks restaurants makes for superb dining with minimal embellishment.

The restaurant industry is a big business on the Northern Outer Banks, with dozens of good restaurants to choose from, serving a variety of fare. We have listed a few of our favorites to help get you started on exploring the culinary scene of the area, but we have left out many deserving dining spots. The free *Restaurant Guide to the Outer Banks*, available at the Kitty Hawk and Manteo visitors centers and elsewhere, is a good, informative guide, about 100 pages long, listing dozens of detailed menus (including prices), and will help you navigate the wide array of eateries.

Incidentally, casual attire is almost mandatory at Outer Banks restaurants. Although men won't be turned away if they show up in suit and tie, they might be seated near the kitchen door, so as not to discombobulate the sandal-clad majority of the clientele.

North of Kitty Hawk

About ten miles north of Kitty Hawk, the **Sanderling Inn Restaurant,** 1461 Duck Rd, tel. (252) 261-3021, serves outstanding fare for breakfast, lunch, and dinner in a casually elegant atmosphere. Made up of more than a half dozen separate dining rooms, the structure was built in 1899 and served as the Caffey's Inlet U.S. Life Saving Station. After a massive restoration/makeover in 1982, the Sanderling Inn Restaurant was born. All of the dining rooms feature superbly restored woodwork, lending them a warm ambience. Starters include specialties like tomato and herb focaccia, packed with local crabmeat and artichokes, topped with a summer tomato relish (serves two for $10), or the Sanderling Classic shrimp, corn and crab chowder, blended with cream and garnished with bacon, scallions, and red peppers ($5). Dinner entrees include seafaring options such as Carolina fish Creole, with fresh local seafood and smoked sausage, sautéed with peppers, onions, and yams in a rich Caribbean-style fish broth ($17). If you're all fished out, the Sanderling also offers steaks, veal chops, chicken, vegetarian dishes, and the popular tamarind honey barbecued baby back ribs, slow roasted and served over Wonder Bread with rice, beans, and marinated vegetables ($16). Full breakfasts cost about $6. Lunch options feature an array of sandwiches, salads, and appetizers, with sandwiches running from $6 for a tuna melt to $10 for a luscious crab cake on a Kaiser roll. Sunday brunch—including specialties like crab crêpes and smoked salmon eggs Benedict—is served 11:45 a.m.-1:30 p.m. and costs about $15. Partly because it's one of the few restaurants between Corolla and Duck, the Sanderling is extremely popular. In the summer, be sure to make reservations for dinner or brunch.

If you decide to have one blowout of a gourmet meal on the Outer Banks, we recommend without hesitation **Elizabeth's Cafe & Winery,** at the Scarborough Faire shops on Route 12 in downtown Duck, tel. (252) 261-6145. Reservations are an absolute must at this French bistro-style restaurant. The menu changes daily, but you're guaranteed glorious options of seafood, poultry, steaks, and vegetarian fare. Dinner entrees usually run $20-30, but if you're in a mood to splurge, go for the prix fixe wine dinner, which usually costs about $80 per person. A perennial winner of the *Wine Spectator* Best Award of Excellence, Elizabeth's offers one of the most outstanding wine lists in the nation. Included with the wine dinner are no fewer than five magnificent vintages. One unforgettable wine dinner began with a Deutz Classic Brut champagne and an appetizer of jumbo shrimp brushed with barbecue sauce, flame grilled and served with a mango chutney, accompanied by a glass of Josmeyer Pinot Blanc 1991 mise du printemps; a salad of selected Napa greens and fruit with French bourgogne Chardonnay white wine walnut dressing was accompanied by a glass of Preston Vineyards Viognier 1992 Dry Creek Valley Sonoma; fresh Norwegian salmon, shrimp, and lobster poached in French white burgundy wine, ginger, pepper, and fresh herbs topped with a lobster and shrimp cream sauce, served with peasant country rice and wine-poached vegetables complemented the glass of Carpe Diem Chardonnay 1994 with which it was paired; the entree of flame-grilled lamb chops with a shiitake French burgundy reduction sauce, served with flame-grilled yams and wine-poached vegetables came with a glass of Joseph Douhin Cambolle-Musigny Les Amoureuses Premier Cru 1990; and dessert was coffee and crème brûlée. In summer only, Elizabeth's also serves lunch—a much less expensive proposition ($7-15).

A couple hundred yards north of Elizabeth's, in the village of Duck, you'll find the delightful **Barrier Island Inn and Duckside Tavern,** tel. (252) 261-3901, whose menu includes mottos like "All the right stuff, never stuffy," and "More fun than you can shake a shark at." With both indoor and outdoor seating, the Barrier Island Inn sits directly on Currituck Sound, offering expansive waterside views, making it a premier choice to enjoy a sunset as you sip a Blue Duck, made with light rum, blue curaçao, pineapple juice and a splash of sour ("It'll quack you up," the menu promises, and you get to keep the plastic hurricane glass and the little parasol). Open year round for lunch and dinner, the restaurant offers appetizers like "super nachos" or oysters Rockefeller (both $7), big sandwiches like the grilled marinated tuna ($8) or steak and cheese sub ($7), or even heftier entrees like a broiled or fried seafood combination ($19), or a wide variety of surf and turf options for $22-25. The Barrier Island Inn is also the "Home of the Pizza Dude," with 12-inch pies starting at $14. Live music, mostly contemporary rock or rhythm and blues, is featured nightly at the friendly Duckside Tavern, which also boasts a pool table and tabletop shuffleboard game.

Restaurants from Kitty Hawk to Nags Head
For breakfast, go with the specialists at **Stack 'em High,** who have been serving breakfasts only for over 20 years at two locations on US 158, in Kitty Hawk at milepost 4.5, tel. (252) 261-8221, and in Kill Devil Hills at milepost 9.5, tel. (252) 441-7064. You'll be hard-pressed to spend more than $5 at this cafeteria-style spot, where your pancakes, waffles and/or eggs are cooked to order and brought to your table. If you're famished, you can order pancakes, two eggs and bacon or sausage for just $4.25. Open from early spring until Thanksgiving, Stack 'em High closes at noon.

Awful Arthur's, at milepost 6 on Virginia Dare Trail (the beach road) in Kill Devil Hills, tel. (252) 441-5955, is one of the most popular hangouts in the area. Serving lunch and dinner year round, Arthur's, "Home of the Happy Oyster," exudes a casual, festive atmosphere fostered by aging wooden booths, large lobster tank, and a bar running the entire length of the dining room. For a snack or meal with a view, visit the second floor Ocean View Lounge. Featuring a full raw bar, Arthur's is a great place to fill up on a variety of seafood for a moderate price. Sandwich offerings cost $4-6 and range from shrimp, softshell crab, oyster, fresh fish, or scallop sandwiches to hot dogs and hearty burgers, including the Backfin Burger topped with cheese and backfin crabmeat, and "the burger that Arthur eats," the 10-ounce "Awesome Burger." Dinner options feature a host of seafood (no fancy sauces here), as well as chicken, steak and barbecue. A crowded nightspot for the youthful beer-drinking crowd, Arthur's features live music in the upstairs lounge during the summer, and downstairs on Monday nights during the off-season.

Restaurateur John Kirchmier runs two fun spots close to each other on the beach road in Kill Devil Hills. Decorated with a West Indian, tropical fish motif, you can slurp an oyster, sip a blue cocktail, or munch on alligator ("He's harmless, he's fried, he's $5.95") at **Goombays Grille and Raw Bar,** milepost 7.5 on Virginia Dare Trail in Kill Devil Hills, tel. (252) 441-6001. Open year round for lunch and dinner, the fare features seafood with a Southwestern and Caribbean flare, like the Goombay Sampler, which includes coconut shrimp, parmesan scallops, jalapeño crab balls and chicken wings ($7), or the blackened shrimp burger ("favorite of the Jamaican bobsled team"). Dinner entrees, which range $10-14, include fresh catches of the day, crab cakes, West Indian curried chicken, and various mixed grills, as well as the ever-popular rasta pasta.

Kirchmier's other festive spot, less than a half mile down the beach road in Kill Devil Hills, is the oceanfront **Quagmire's on the Beach,** at milepost 8 on Virginia Dare Trail, tel. (252) 441-9188. Dedicated "to the kids who never grew up . . . or rarely color between the lines," Quagmire's features a great ocean view, colorful big and little kids' drinks, a children's menu, and a variety of games for both kids and adults, including volleyball, horseshoes, ring toss, boccie ball and paper football. With both indoor and outdoor seating, you can eat barefoot on one of the oceanview outdoor decks, or in sandals in the dining room overlooking the ocean. Seafood and Southwestern fare predominate here, or sometimes both, like the shrimp quesadilla ($6) or shrimp enchilada ($12). A popular night spot, Quagmire's features live acoustic music nightly in the summer.

For waterfront dining on the sound side of the island, try the spacious, comfortable dining room of the **Penguin Isle Soundside Grill and Bar,** in Nags Head at milepost 16 on US 158, tel. (252)

441-2637. Overlooking Roanoke Sound, the Penguin Isle makes a great, romantic choice to linger over a sumptuous dinner while watching the sun set over the sound. In addition to straightforward broiled seafood, beef and poultry, specials change every evening, taking advantage of the freshest ingredients. One example of the Penguin Isle's regal specials, often offered in the summer, is the cream sautéed lobster, shrimp, and sea scallops with shiitake mushrooms, tomatoes, sweet bell peppers, Cajun crawfish ravioli, parmesan cheese and cream (yes, that's one entree), all for just $19. Entrees generally cost $14-24. A perennial winner of the *Wine Spectator's* coveted award of excellence, the Penguin Isle has a world-class wine list to complement your meal. Closed January and February, the Penguin Isle is open for dinner only. Reservations are strongly encouraged.

If the Penguin Isle is booked, and you want a soundside view, try the **Windmill Point Restaurant** down the street in Nags Head, at milepost 16.5 on US 158, tel. (252) 441-1535. Located near the causeway to Roanoke Island, Windmill Point's dining room looks out over Roanoke Sound. Although the specialties of the house are (surprise!) seafood, you can also dine on beef, duck, poultry and pasta dishes ($16-24). Open only in the evening, you can choose to have a full course meal, or enjoy a cocktail and an appetizer or two in the S.S. *United States* Lounge upstairs, which, like the dining room, is decorated with memorabilia from the luxury ocean liner S.S. *United States.* The upstairs lounge, with its expansive view of the sound, makes it an ideal spot to catch a sunset.

For a tradition of dining excellence on the Outer Banks, you can't beat **Owens' Restaurant,** in Nags Head at milepost 16.5 on Virginia Dare Trail (the beach road), tel. (252) 441-7309. Since 1946, this casual yet elegant restaurant has been owned and operated by the Owens family, whose extensive collection of memorabilia from early seafaring days lends a special warmth to this charming dining spot, modeled after a life-saving station and replete with wonderful woodwork. Serving classic coastal cuisine, the menu highlights are the fresh-off-the-boat seafood and shellfish, as well as whole Maine lobster, pasta, beef and poultry. Although the restaurant can seat 200 in its dining rooms, reservations are suggested. If you have to wait or just want to enjoy a cocktail in a friendly atmosphere, visit the Station Keeper's Lounge upstairs. Open from mid-March through New Year's Eve, Owens' serves dinner only. Entrees run $14-25.

Sam & Omie's, milepost 16.5 on Virginia Dare Trail, tel. (252) 441-7366, has been a favorite with locals for decades. Serving three meals a day year-round, Sam & Omie's exudes the casual atmosphere of a beach pub, complete with a pool table and pinball machine. A breakfast of eggs, bacon or sausage, grits or hash browns, and toast or biscuits costs $4.50. For lunch or dinner, you can choose from a wide variety of sandwiches, from burgers ($3), to fresh fried fish sandwiches ($6), to the Garbonzo Treat, with garbonzo spread, melted cheddar cheese, cucumber, mushrooms, lettuce, tomato and mayo ($4.50), as well as several salads. For dinner, in addition to nightly seafood specials, you can select a variety of fish and seafood, or go for both with the Whale of a Seafood Platter—fried or broiled shrimp, scallops, oysters, fish, clams and soft shell crab ($19). Don't bother trying to make a reservation at Sam & Omie's—they don't accept them. If there's a wait for a table, most folks just hang out at the bar.

Manteo Food and Drink
For a bit of Bavaria at the beach, try **Weeping Radish Brewery and Bavarian Restaurant,** on Highway 64 near downtown Manteo, tel. (252) 473-1157. An authentic German atmosphere prevails at the Weeping Radish (even their beer glasses are made in Germany), decorated with woodwork and artifacts reminiscent of a Bavarian country inn. Although you can choose from a several "American" dishes, like sandwiches, prime rib or stuffed chicken breast, the highlights of the menu are, not surprisingly, the German specialties, with schnitzels, sauerbraten, variously seasoned pork loins, and an array of sausages to choose from. Entrees range $10-16. The beers, brewed on the premises, are fabulous, adhering to the *Reinheitsgebot,* the German Purity Law of 1516 dictating that only hops, malt, yeast and water may be used in brewing beer. In addition to the inside seating, where you can choose between the warm dining rooms or the

friendly bar, you can also sit outside in the Beer Garden. The Weeping Radish is open for lunch and dinner year-round.

NIGHTLIFE

Many of the most popular nightspots in the Northern Outer Banks—Barrier Island Inn, Awful Arthur's, Goombays Grille and Raw Bar, Quagmire's, Sam & Omie's, and the Weeping Radish—are listed above). Another restaurant whose bar is immensely popular is **Kelly's Restaurant and Tavern,** milepost 10 in Nags Head, tel. (252) 441-4116. During the summer, live bands perform Tues.-Sun., packing patrons in on the big dance floor; on Monday, you can try your luck in a karaoke contest.

If you're looking to two-step or line-dance to country tunes, try **George's Junction,** at milepost 11 on Virginia Dare Trail (the beach road), tel. (252) 441-0606. George's provides a full bar, and a separate lounge area. For something a little different, you can yuk it up at the **Comedy Club at the Carolinian,** at the Carolinian Hotel, "smilepost" 10.5 on Virginia Dare Trail, tel. (252) 441-7171. Shows go on Mon.-Sat. at 10 p.m. (veterans of the Carolinian include Sinbad, Drew Carey, and Brett Butler).

INFORMATION

The Aycock Brown Welcome Center is the main visitors center for the entire Outer Banks, and well worth the stop to collect helpful information like the invaluable *Restaurant Guide to the Outer Banks.* The center is staffed with several well-informed and friendly townsfolk. Located at milepost 1.5 on US 158 in Kitty Hawk, just east of the Wright Memorial Bridge, the center is open 8:30 a.m.-5 p.m., sometimes later in the summer. If you're coming to the Outer Banks through Manteo, stop by the information kiosk at the Roanoke Island Visitors Center, which, while not as comprehensive as the Aycock Brown Center, still provides a healthy collection of brochures, including the *Restaurant Guide* and the *Outer Banks Visitors Guide.* For more information, call or write to the Dare County Tourist Bureau, tel. (252) 473-2138 or (800) 446-6262, P.O. Box 399, US 64 and Budleigh St., Manteo, NC 27954.

SOUTHERN OUTER BANKS

HATTERAS ISLAND

Driving south along NC 12 from Nags Head, you'll cross Oregon Inlet via the grand spans of the three-mile long Herbert C. Bonner Bridge. You'll immediately notice the difference between Bodie Island and the island you're about enter. Most of Hatteras Island's shoreline is undeveloped, protected by the National Park Service as part of the Cape Hatteras National Seashore. When you cross the bridge, you're in the **Pea Island National Wildlife Refuge,** a tranquil wildlife preserve managed by the U.S. Fish and Wildlife Service. About four miles south of the southern terminus of the Bonner bridge, you'll come to the **Pea Island Refuge Headquarters and Visitors Center,** tel. (252) 987-2394, where you can pick up free information about birdwatching as well as some nature trail maps. While you're there, take a stroll along the **North Pond Interpretive Trail,** beginning at the visitors center parking lot. This trail offers a magically peaceful introduction to the unspoiled beaches of Hatteras Island. The beginning of this trail—a favorite among birders—leads along a dike built between two ponds and includes observation decks with viewing binoculars. Although most visitors hike in only about one-half mile for birdwatching, you can continue along a service road that winds 2.5 miles around the pond and lets you out on NC 12 about two miles from the visitors center.

Rodanthe

Exiting the Pea Island Refuge, about 15 miles south of the Bonner Bridge, you'll pass three villages—Rodanthe, Waves, and Salvo—all within a four-mile stretch. These three little towns are among the seven villages allowed to remain on Hatteras Island when the national seashore was formed in 1953. In Rodanthe (pronounced "ro-DAN-thee"), you can visit the restored **Chicamacomico Lifesaving Station,** on Route 12, tel. (252) 987-2394. Inside the station, you can peruse

exhibits recounting the heroic efforts of the lifesavers who toiled here from 1876 to 1954, working under the harshest weather conditions to rescue crewmembers from sinking ships. Usually, this involved shooting a lifeline from a powerful Lyle gun to the foundering ship, and then trying to reel it in. When that didn't work, lifesaving crews had to swim and/or row out into the savage waves to rescue the sailors. On Thursday afternoons during the summer, usually around 2 p.m., the National Park Service puts on demonstrations of lifesaving drills. Admission is free. When this edition went to press, the station's hours of operation were Tuesday, Thursday, and Saturday10 a.m.-4 p.m.

Also located in Rodanthe, along Route 12, you can experience the thrills and chills provided by **Waterfall Action Park,** tel. (252) 987-2213. By far the biggest amusement park on Hatteras Island, this park offers 18 different amusements, most of which cost $6 a pop (less if you purchase a combination ticket). In addition to 36 holes of miniature golf, waterslides, bumper boats, and speed boats, Waterfall Action Park features several go-cart racetracks and about a dozen different kinds of miniature race cars,

great blue heron

TOMMY DAUGHTRY

BEWARE ROADSIDE SANDTRAPS!

All along Hatteras Island's main drag, NC 12, you'll see isolated, inviting spots to pull off the paved road onto sandy semicircles. Often, you'll even see four-wheel-drive pickup trucks parked here, the owners having gone off to fish on the beach. Less often, you'll see two-wheel-drive cars parked in these pulloffs; and you'll notice that these vehicles are usually accompanied by one or more people not fishing but waving energetically at you, sometimes with both hands. These are not, generally speaking, tourism representatives enthusiastically greeting passersby. Rather, the chances are excellent that their car has become hopelessly mired in one of these deep-sand pulloffs, and they're desperately seeking transportation to the nearest gas station so they can get their car towed out of the sandtrap.

These sandy pulloffs are *not* marked with signs warning you that if you're driving a 2WD vehicle you're pretty sure to get stranded. So be forewarned: DON'T PULL OFF UNLESS THE PULLOFF IS PAVED!

(Even 4WD vehicles aren't immune, and you should really avoid the pulloffs in any event unless you're experienced at driving in deep sand.)

from Barbie Jeeps for kids age three and up and Kiddie-Indy Racers for kids age four and up to mini-Grand Prix race cars and Winston NASKARTS for kids over age 11. The park is open from May through the end of September.

Rodanthe also boasts the only oceanview restaurant on Hatteras Island, the festive **Down Under Restaurant and Lounge,** tel. (252) 987-2277, at the Hatteras Island Fishing Pier. Open for lunch and dinner, you might want to time your visit here for 3-6 p.m., for the popular Happy Hours, when steamed or spiced shrimp go for a mere 10 cents apiece. In addition to a full selection of burgers, crab cakes and fish sandwiches for $5-6, you might want to try a Great White Shark for $2.50, a taco with freshly grilled tuna and black beans wrapped with a blend of jalapeños and cream cheese, garnished with homemade Down Under seafood salsa. Dinner entrees feature various seafood selections and pastas, ranging in price from $11-13. While the food is good, it's the view and friendly Australian atmosphere that make the Down Under a local favorite. If you prefer to catch your own meal from the sea, chances are you'll get lucky at the adjacent **Hatteras Island Fishing Pier,** tel. (252) 987-2323. It's open round the clock during the summer; a 24-hour pass costs $5. The pier is closed Thanksgiving through Easter.

Most folks visiting the Rodanthe area rent houses by the week or month. Some cottages also offer three-day weekend stays. For the best selection, call **Outer Beaches Realty,** tel. (252) 995-4477 or (800) 627-3150. Located in Avon, Outer Beaches manages more than 400 properties on Hatteras Island and will send you a free brochure to help you make a selection to fit your taste and budget.

Motels are scarce in the Rodanthe/Waves/ Salvo area. The best bet in these towns is the **Hatteras Island Resort,** tel. (252) 987-2345 or (800) 331-6541, next to the Hatteras Island Fishing Pier in Rodanthe. Open April through November, the 25-acre complex includes 18 motel rooms, 14 efficiencies, and 35 cottages. During the peak summer season, motel rooms run $80 a night or about $500 for a week; efficiencies cost about the same; the cottages, which include two, three or four bedrooms, cost $650-880 per week. During the off-season, rates are lower by at least a third, and the efficiencies and cottages can be rented on a nightly basis. The resort has a swimming pool and a wading pool for the tykes. Rooms don't have phones but do have cable TV.

The biggest campground on Hatteras Island can be found at Rodanthe's **Cape Hatteras KOA** campground, with more than 300 camping sites (including 33 tent sites with water only for $28 a night). Full hookups with water, power and sewer, cost $32 a night. Sparsely furnished cabins are also available from $40. The KOA includes extras like two pools, a hot tub, game room, playground, and a 200-foot pier on the sound.

At the **Pamlico Station** shopping center on Route 12 in Rodanthe, **Lee's Collectibles** provides a fascinating collection of gifts, books, and toys, in addition to one of Hatteras Island's best collections of arts and crafts by local folks, including paintings, jewelry, furniture and other works.

Avon

About 13 miles south of the town of Salvo, you'll enter the little village of Avon, a mecca for windsurfers who flock to **Canadian Hole,** generally acknowledged as providing the most exciting windsurfing on the East Coast of the United States. Located about 1.5 miles south of town, Canadian Hole is marked by a spacious, paved parking lot along the sound side of Route 12. Even if you're not planning to ride the waves yourself, you should stop here just to watch the windsurfers in action, their colorful sails soaring through and over the waves. If you do want to try your hand at windsurfing, you'll find at least a half dozen shops that provide equipment, including the veteran outfitter **Kitty Hawk Water Sports,** in Avon along Route 12, tel. (252) 995-5000.

For food, drink and nightlife, look no further than the **Froggy Dog Restaurant,** on Route 12, tel. (252) 995-4106, serving breakfast, lunch and dinner year-round. The Froggy Dog, offering seafood, beef, poultry and pasta dishes, has different dining rooms to choose from, from wood-paneled rooms catering to families to the similarly warm, woody lounge that fills up nightly with locals and visiting windsurfers. Breakfast and lunch cost around $5, with dinner ranging $10-15.

For house rentals, we again recommend **Outer Beaches Realty** for this area. Call (800) 627-3150 for a free brochure. Avon is also home to one of the best motel/resort buys on Hatteras Island. Spacious rooms at the **Castaways Oceanfront Resort,** on Route 12, tel. (252) 995-4444 or (800) 845-6070, begin at $99 during the summer season, and drop to as low as $49 during the off-season. Featuring an Olympic-size heated indoor pool, tennis courts, and a sauna and hot tub, the five-story Castaways resort offers great ocean views (above the first floor), and a fun restaurant/lounge on the premises, where you can sip on the tropical cocktail of your choice. For $20 you can also try your hand at the 9-hole golf course. The Castaways is closed in December. Expensive.

Buxton

About seven miles south of Avon, the town of Buxton boasts the most visited attraction on Hatteras Island, the towering **Cape Hatteras Lighthouse**—at 208 feet, the tallest lighthouse in the United States. Distinctive black and white "bar-

ber-pole" striped Hatteras Light is probably the most frequently reproduced image of the North Carolina coast. You see it not only replicated in miniature and portrayed in paintings but also depicted on postcards, Christmas ornaments, ashtrays, and any number of other varied items for sale. You may feel that the real thing would be anticlimactic, but a visit to this premier symbol of the Graveyard of the Atlantic is unlikely to leave you unmoved.

There's no admission fee to climb to the top of the lighthouse, though the 268 steps up the spiral staircase to the top can exact a toll on your knees. But the view from the observation deck is well worth the climb, providing an unparalleled, panoramic view of Hatteras Island. When it was built in 1870, the lighthouse was a safe 1,500 feet from the ocean. Constructed on a "floating foundation," the structure is now threatening to float out to sea, with the waves pounding away just a few dozen yards from its base. The Army Corps of Engineers has constructed three jetties and fortified the beach with thousands of huge sandbags to halt the erosion in front of the lighthouse, but virtually all the experts agree that this is a losing proposition and that within the next decade or so the lighthouse will fall into the ocean unless it's moved inland. After the appropriation of several million tax dollars to study the feasibility of moving the lighthouse (another $2.2 million in federal funds was appropriated for further studies in 1997), most experts now agree that moving the structure is theoretically feasible, though practical estimates of how much the move would cost tend to vary a bit, usually falling somewhere between $10 and $20 million. While it's still standing, the lighthouse is open Easter through Columbus Day.

Just off the "bent elbow" of Hatteras Island, in front of Hatteras Light(house), lies one of the **surfing** meccas of the East Coast. This is not a spot for beginners. The dangers posed by wicked currents and unpredictable waves are compounded by the iron-reinforced rock jetties built to preserve the lighthouse.

The second-largest town on Hatteras Island, next to Hatteras, Buxton offers arguably the widest array of restaurants on the island. The favorite of the locals is **Billy's Fish House,** on Route 12, tel. (252) 995-5151, a homey little seafood eatery, with blue-and-white-checkered tablecloths and blue cafe chairs. You might notice that the floors are slightly slanted—that's intentional. Originally a fish market, Billy's has slanted floors to make for easier cleaning. Though it's located on the waters of Pamlico Sound, you actually don't get much of a view of the water due to some taller structures on the docks. Billy's serves lunch and dinner; sandwiches run $3-6. Although you can get steak, chicken or pasta ($7-13) for dinner, the seafood entrees are what draws the locals. No fancy sauces here, your choices are basically broiled or fried. Prices range from the fried bay scallops for $9 to the popular fried seafood platter, a hefty combination including fish, clams, scallops, shrimp, a crab cake, hushpuppies, and two vegetables, for $16. Billy's is also a popular choice for take out.

For a dazzling view of Pamlico Sound, you can't beat the **Soundside Restaurant,** about 100 yards south of Billy's Fish House in Buxton on Route 12, tel. (252) 995-6778. Situated on the second floor of a building directly on the sound, the Soundside is an ideal spot to enjoy a cocktail and a snack or a meal as the sun sinks into the Pamlico Sound, often lighting up the sky with heavenly hues. Open for breakfast, lunch and dinner, Soundside offers a cheeseburger for $3 or a fresh fish sandwich for $4. In addition to steaks, chicken, and ham entrees for dinner ($10-13), you can choose fried or broiled seafood combinations for $9-14.

Another favorite soundside spot in Buxton is the **Pilot House** on Route 12, tel. (252) 995-5664. Set right on the water and serving dinner only, the Pilot House is slightly more pricey ($15-20 for entrees) but well worth the extra few bucks if you're looking for a top-notch meal and slightly more gourmet fare, such as the oysters Rockefeller appetizer. The lounge on the second floor provides a fabulous view of the sound and a friendly, laid-back atmosphere.

Buxton provides the largest number of motel rooms of any town on Hatteras Island, though most of these lodgings are a good 10-minute hike away from the ocean. One of the exceptions is the oceanfront complex of the **Lighthouse View Motel and Cottages** on Route 12 at the northern edge of Buxton, tel. (252) 995-5680 or (800) 225-7651. The Lighthouse View offers a wide variety of well-maintained accom-

modations, including motel rooms, efficiencies, cottages, two-bedroom apartments, and one- and two-bedroom villas. Amenities include an outdoor pool and hot tub, and all rooms have refrigerators and cable TV. If you're going to stay at least a week, you can reserve an efficiency for just $400 during the summer, one of the better deals on the Outer Banks. Nightly stays range $80-100 (with a three-night minimum for apartments and cottages), and the two-bedroom villas run $850 a week in summer. Rates drop by half or more during the off-season.

Another good buy in Buxton is the **Falcon Motel,** in town on Route 12, tel. (252) 995-5968 or (800) 635-6911. Located on the sound side of the island, the Falcon offers 30 clean and comfortable motel rooms and five apartments. Extras include a swimming pool, boat ramp, and soundside nature area. Its convenient location is within easy walking distance of restaurants and shops. Rooms don't have phones, and the motel's location right on busy Route 12 is not the most serene locale, but with a peak season price of $75, the Falcon still offers one of the better buys on Hatteras Island.

Buxton is also home to one of the two chain motels on Hatteras Island (the other is a Holiday Inn in Hatteras). Located in the heart of town, at Route 12 and Lighthouse Road, the **Comfort Inn,** tel. (252) 995-6100 or (800) 432-1441, has 60 rooms costing $99 during the summer; prices gradually drop to as low as $49 in the off-season. In addition to an outdoor swimming pool, the Comfort Inn provides refrigerators and phones in all rooms.

If you're looking to rent a house in the southern portion of Hatteras Island (Buxton, Frisco, or Hatteras) we recommend **Midgett Realty** on Route 12 in the town of Hatteras, tel. (252) 986-2841 or (800) 527-2903.

The National Park Service operates two large campgrounds in the Buxton area. About a mile and a half south of the Cape Hatteras Lighthouse, on Park Road, the **Cape Point Campground** provides 202 sites, most of them out in the open in dunes, a three- or four-minute walk from the ocean. About 3.5 miles south of Buxton, another Park Road leads toward the beach, the Billy Mitchell Airport, and the **Frisco Campground.** The superior of the two, the Frisco campground's 127 sites provide a lot more privacy, nestled among dunes and scrub pines. Although RV's are welcome, neither campground has utility hookups. Unless you count the picnic table and charcoal grill provided at every site, the most luxurious amenities are flush toilets and cold showers at the rest stations. Open from Memorial Day to Labor Day; reservations are not accepted. For more information on either National Park Service campground, call (252) 473-2111. If you prefer camping luxuries like hot showers, a swimming pool, playground, laundry, and utility hookups, try the nearby **Frisco Woods Campground** on Pamlico Bay, tel. (252) 995-5208 or (800) 948-3942. Tent sites cost $18, and full hookups for RV's run $23. Reservations are accepted.

As you pass through the town of **Frisco,** just south of Buxton, you'll pass a popular attraction, the **Frisco Native American Museum,** tel. (252) 995-4440. Don't get your hopes up too high. Although it's billed as a museum, and suggests a $2 donation to tour the place, we suggest you hold off on the donation until you leave. At least half of the square footage of the building is a gift shop, selling Native American jewelry and other artifacts from around the country. The quality of the exhibits—well, you won't think you're in the Smithsonian. Nonetheless, it doesn't take long to visit, it's fun for adults and kids alike, and if one of the adults wants to spend some quality shopping time alone, the rest of the family can wander around the short nature trails out back. The Frisco Native American Museum is closed on Monday.

Hatteras

With a year-round population of 2,600, the town of Hatteras is by far the most populous on Hatteras Island. But, as that rather humble population figure suggests, Hatteras is hardly a numbing metropolis. Exuding the casual, no-frills atmosphere of a working fishing village, the town of Hatteras is remarkably free of the new construction which has come to characterize so much of the Outer Banks. Decades before Route 12 connected Hatteras Island to the mainland in the 1960s, the town of Hatteras was an active fishing center. Not surprisingly, fishing is still the main game in town. In restaurants and in several display cases on storefronts in town, you'll see mounted game fish that would have had

Ernest Hemingway screaming for his mommy.

The town includes four marinas, the biggest being **Hatteras Harbor Marina,** in the heart of downtown, on Route 12. Call the Marina at (252) 986-2166 or (800) 676-4939 for information on charter fishing excursions and sightseeing (including sunset) cruises in Hatteras Village.

When you eat out here, you can expect to see both the weather-beaten faces of the local professional fishermen and plenty of flushed cheeks on enthusiastic amateur anglers in from drink-fueled fishing charter to the Gulf Stream. The village of Hatteras has two restaurants of particular note, both serving dinner only. The best choice for both ambience and food quality is the **Breakwater,** at Ogden's Dock in the heart of town, tel. (252) 986-2733. The bar, dining room, and screened-in deck, all on the second floor, overlook Pamlico Sound, making this a great spot to catch a sunset. In addition to landlubber options like prime rib and chicken gorgonzola, the Breakwater whips up tantalizing seafood specials nightly in addition to the mandatory fried and broiled fare, all of it fresh from the boat. Indeed, the seafood served here usually comes directly from the boats delivering their hauls to the dock of the fish market on the first floor below the restaurant. Entrees cost $14-23. The Breakwater is open nightly during the summer, and most of the time during the off-season. However, the owners recommend that you call for their hours of operation in the off-season.

The other noteworthy restaurant in Hatteras is the **Channel Bass,** directly on Route 12 in the northern section of town, tel. (252) 986-2250. A Hatteras institution for more than 30 years, the Channel Bass is located beside a peaceful canal, which adds to the warm atmosphere of this friendly eatery. The broad menu will have something to appeal to every taste, including, of course, a full selection of fried or broiled seafood. If you're sick of surf, you might want to consider the popular turf option of charbroiled steaks, cut on the premises. Entrees range $9-20. Open mid-March through the end of November, the Channel Bass serves beer and wine, and like most Hatteras eateries, allows brown-bagging.

For breakfast or lunch, try **Gary's Restaurant** on Route 12 in town, tel. (252) 986-2349. If you're feeling adventurous, try the crabmeat omelette for breakfast. An extremely friendly, casual place, Gary's doesn't discriminate against folks who like to eat in their bare feet, which you'll deduce from a quick survey of the clientele. Surprisingly, the carpeting seems to remain remarkably clean, and you won't have any sanitary complaints about this family-friendly eatery. Expect breakfast or lunch to cost $4-6.

Lodging in Hatteras is also, typically, a few-frills affair. The biggest exception to this generalization is the bright and lovely **Seaside Inn,** on Route 12 in town, tel. (252) 986-2700. Built in 1928, this venerable, shingled inn served as Hatteras Island's first hotel, built to provide accommodations for the wealthy businessmen and industrialists who traveled to the island to make like Hemingway and land a huge game fish to stuff and hang over their mantel at home. Thoroughly and lovingly renovated in the 1990s by the friendly innkeepers, Sharon and Jeff Kennedy, the hotel has 10 guest rooms eclectically decorated with local antiques and artwork. Five of the rooms have separate sitting areas, and all have modern bathrooms, some with jacuzzis. Sharon serves a full breakfast, usually including the option of a succulent slice of ham. The beach is a five-minute walk along a path winding through densely shrubbed dunes. Summer rates range $85-150, with rooms dropping to $75-95 in the off-season. Pets are allowed in one of the inn's rooms.

The four-legged members of the family can stay in one of several (though not all) of the rooms at the friendly U-shaped **Hatteras Harbor Motel,** on Route 12 in town next to Oden's Dock, tel. (252) 986-2565. Popular with fishermen and families, this motel has an outdoor pool and clean, comfortable rooms, all of which come with phones, cable TV, and refrigerators. The rates begin at $61 for motel rooms, $70 for small efficiencies, and $75 for large efficiencies. During the off-season, rates drop by $10. The Oden family runs the place, as well as their namesake dock, various charter boats, and the Breakwater Restaurant, next to the motel. Moderate.

The **Sea Gull Motel** in the northern section of town, along on Route 12, tel. (252) 986-2550, also offers well-maintained rooms. Although the Sea Gull doesn't have a pool, it is the closest motel to the ocean in Hatteras. A short walkway leads to the beach. The prices begin at $55 during the summer and drop to $40 in the off-season. Inexpensive. For the reliability of chain motel

lodgings, you can stay at the **Holiday Inn Express & Suites,** next to the ferry docks on Route 12 at the southern end of town, tel. (252) 986-1110 or (800) 361-1590. There's a pool, and amenities in all rooms include phones, microwaves, and refrigerators. Rooms start at $109 during the summer and drop to as low as $59 in the off-season. Expensive.

If you're looking to rent a house in Hatteras, try **Midgett Realty** on Route 12 in town, tel. (252) 986-2841 or (800) 527-2903.

OCRACOKE

Maybe it's because you have to take a ferry to get here that makes you feel privy to some special secret when you make the journey to Ocracoke. Or maybe it's because there's only one small town, at the southernmost tip of the 16-mile-long barrier island.

The sole town, Ocracoke Village, is only about three miles long and less than two miles wide, a sleepy little world you might find difficult to leave—indeed, a significant portion of the village's population of about 700 are descendants of the 30 families who established the first permanent settlement on the island in the 1700s. The heart of Ocracoke Village hugs Silver Lake, a picturesque harbor where old and new buildings blend harmoniously and where you can lazily pass several pleasant hours just watching the marine traffic come and go.

If you like to ride bicycles, Ocracoke Village is an ideal place to pedal around—most points of interest are a few minutes' ride from any given point in the town. This small town also invites walks along its friendly streets—although, if you prefer a sedate (15-20 mph) Sunday drive, no one will ever honk at you to speed up.

History

During the 16th and 17th centuries, pirates discovered that they could elude colonial navy captains out to arrest them and recover stolen goods by sailing from the Atlantic Ocean through Ocracoke Inlet and hide out in one of the many hidden coves and creeks on Pamlico Sound. The most famous of these pirates was the notorious Blackbeard—actually Edward Teach (namesake of Teach's Hole Channel, a renowned fishing spot just west of Silver Lake Harbor). Although Blackbeard never lived on Ocracoke, the island was a favorite hideout—and the site of his grisly death at the hands of the colonial navy of Virginia. In fact, local legend claims that Blackbeard gave the island its name, when, in pitch darkness, unable to distinguish the land from the sea so he could steal into a hiding place on Ocracoke to escape his pursuers and unload his booty, he shook his fist at the night sky and impatiently beckoned the sunrise by yelling "O crow, cock!" (It *is* a bit of a stretch, and there's pretty clear evidence that the name actually derives from the Wokokon Indian tribe, but the legend does give a sense of the romantic atmosphere surrounding the island.)

Ocracoke was not actually settled until the 1700s. Until then, it had been known primarily as a pirate hideout and not considered safe for law-

abiding settlers. In 1715, North Carolina's colonial assembly passed an act calling for "settling and maintaining Pilots at Roanoke and Ocacock Inletts." The purpose of this act was to improve navigation and trade along the North Carolina coast by providing experienced pilots and two assistants to safely guide all vessels entering Ocracoke and Roanoke Inlets into the deeper waters of the offshore sounds. It wasn't until the 1730s that pilots actually started working at Ocracoke. By that time, after Blackbeard's death in 1718, the heyday of pirating had waned, giving way to more genteel corruptions. The early Ocracoke pilots spent most of their time guiding trading vessels through Ocracoke Inlet and leading them to smaller ships hiding in the same coves used by pirates a few years earlier, whereupon these "law-abiding" (tax-avoiding) captains would unload much of their cargo onto the smaller

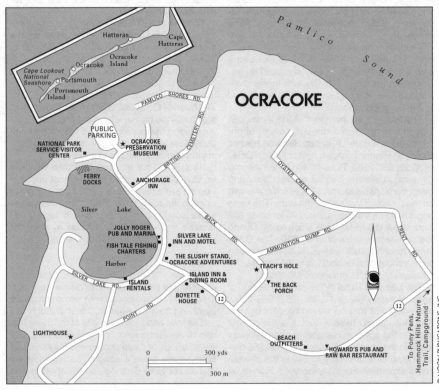

ships, then proceed to Bath, 30 miles across Pamlico Sound, where they would pay duty on the reduced cargo. The smaller cargo ships sold their duty-free merchandise directly to ports along Pamlico Sound and its many tributaries, enriching the wily captains and pilots and depriving England—and the colony of North Carolina—of untold revenues.

During the Revolutionary War, Ocracoke's veteran pilots used their knowledge and skill to smuggle goods to the American rebels (and sometimes to George Washington himself). The population of Ocracoke after the Revolutionary War amounted to about 30 families, all of whose men made their livings as pilots and many of whose descendants own commercial enterprises in Ocracoke today.

By 1850, there were 536 folks living on Ocracoke, not many fewer than today's 700 residents. Most of these antebellum families made their living piloting; fishing; raising cattle, sheep, and chickens; and sailing aboard the great schooners that sailed the world. Ocracoke pilots played a crucial role in the Civil War, smuggling supplies to the Confederacy. After the Civil War, Ocracoke's status as a major port began to wane, with the gradual displacement of the grand masted schooners by bigger steam- and coal-powered ships that required bigger ports and deeper waters.

By the early 1900s, fishing became the major livelihood on the island. Today, Ocracoke retains the aura of a quaint fishing village whose rhythms are driven by the sound and sea. Although the economy now is supported mostly by tourism, commercial fishing is still a viable industry here. Many seasoned fishermen have begun to combine the two and found that taking visitors on sport fishing charters can be quite lucrative. Modern Ocracoke balances its rich seafaring past and its tourist-friendly present with a breezy ease, the new charms of fine restaurants and lodgings mixing with the unaffected social atmosphere engendered by the pirates and pilots who forged the community.

Sights

If, like most visitors, you arrive on the northern shores of Ocracoke via the Hatteras ferry, you still have a 12-mile ride ahead of you along Route 12 to get to Ocracoke Village. These 12 miles, protected by the National Park Service, are completely undeveloped and invite you to pull over to the side of the road and take a solitary wander along the beach or sound. (Remember, though, that you should only pull off the road onto a *paved* surface, unless you're commanding a 4WD vehicle.)

Stop at the **Ocracoke pony pens** on your way to town. Located on the sound side of the island about five miles south of the Hatteras-Ocracoke ferry docks, the pens won't take you long to visit. Get out of the car when you reach the parking lot on Route 12. At the parking lot you'll see the fenced-in pen, but there's a good chance you won't see any wild ponies in this section (leading many visitors to quickly pull back on to the road). To get a view of the ponies, take the 600-foot boardwalk leading north from the parking lot through a shady bower and stopping at an elevated observation platform at the edge of the woods. You'll be able to see at least a few ponies in the pasture spreading out before you to the sound.

Legend has it that the "Banker horses of Ocracoke" arrived when Sir Richard Grenville's ship, *Tiger*, ran aground just off the coast of Ocracoke in 1565. The horses were thrown overboard to lighten the load so the ship could be refloated, and the mustangs eluded recapture. At one time, as many as 300 wild horses freely roamed the island. But by 1959, due in great measure to the numerous accidents that happened after the northern 12-mile-long stretch of Route 12 was completed two years earlier, the herd was rounded up and restricted to their current, fenced-in, 180-acre home of pasture and maritime woods. Today the herd numbers between 25 and 30 and is assiduously cared for by National Park Service personnel. Although these wild ponies create a portrait of perfect serenity, grazing in their pasture, don't even think about hopping the fence to go pat one on the nose. For one, the National Park Service personnel will fine you for trespassing; for two, these are wild horses—quite likely to bite or kick you if you approach them.

The sightseeing attractions in Ocracoke Village, the most popular being the 75-foot-tall lighthouse (which you can't climb), are not why most folks come here. The chief attraction of Ocracoke is the seductive atmosphere engendered by the picture-postcard beauty and casual bustling of Silver Lake Harbor in the heart of town, the tranquility of the village's side streets, and the seclusion of the island's beaches.

Your feet provide the best locomotion for exploring Ocracoke Village. Next to the National Park Service docks in Ocracoke Village, at the entrance to Silver Lake Harbor, stop by **National Park Service Visitors Center,** and/or the **Ocracoke Preservation Museum,** across the parking lot from the visitors center, to pick up a free map of Ocracoke Village to guide you on a walking tour of the village. While you're at the Preservation Museum, in a charming little white frame house, take a few minutes to peruse the modest collection of artifacts and brief printed exhibits about Ocracoke's history.

Ocracoke's other "museum" makes no such claims of modesty. **Teach's Hole,** on Back Road, tel. (252) 928-1718, "Home of the Outer Banks Original Blackbeard Exhibit," is actually a gift shop, specializing in anything and everything relating to pirates, from treasure maps, skull-and-crossbones flags, pirate hats, and sabers, to books, jewelry, costumes, T-shirts, and toys. Despite the rather commercial atmosphere, this is an enjoyable place to learn about Blackbeard and practice your delivery of phrases like "Arrrgh, Matey" and "Shiver Me Timbers!"

Recreation

To explore both the village and the more secluded, northern beaches, you should consider **renting a bicycle,** a mode of transportation possessing the advantage of not requiring a tow-truck when foundered in sand. Several shops rent bikes, the most popular being **The Slushy Stand,** on Route 12 at Silver Lake Harbor, tel. (252) 928-1878. Rentals are $4 an hour or $12 a day. You can rent bikes, as well as other vacation supplies, from Nintendo games to linens, from **Beach Outfitters** on Route 12 at the northern edge of town, tel. (252) 928-6261, or **Island Rentals** on Silver Lake Rd., tel. (252) 928-5480. (Incidentally, both shops mentioned above are associated with the island's two realty companies, so if you call them and get a real estate agent, you haven't dialed the wrong number.)

A dozen or so charter boats provide half- or full-day **fishing.** All are located on small marinas on Silver Lake. Stroll along the docks for de-

NORTH CAROLINA AQUARIUM

tails, or if you'd like to reserve a trip in advance call one or more of the following: Capt. David Nagel's *Drum Stick,* tel. (800) 825-5351, Capt. O'Neal's *Miss Kathleen,* tel. (252) 928-4841, Capt. Outlaw's *Outlaw,* tel. (252) 928-4851, or Capt. Miller's *Rascal,* tel. (252) 928-6111. Capt. John Ferrara offers a wide selection through his **Fish Tale Fishing Charters** on the marina, tel. (252) 928-3403, including four-, six- and eight-hour trips ($50-100/person); a two-hour, "catch your dinner special" for $25; and a special educational four-hour trip for families with kids 5-12 on calm, safe, inland waters, where kids can have fun catching flounder, trout, croaker, bluefish, and more, while Capt. Ferrara teaches you about each species caught, all for $40/person (including bait, tackle and fish filleting).

If you want to explore the local waters under your own power, stop by **Ocracoke Adventures,** at Route 12 and Silver Lake Rd., tel. (252) 928-7873. You can **rent kayaks** or sign up for **guided eco-tours** from these friendly and knowledgeable outfitters.

If you're staying on Ocracoke, you should strongly consider taking a few hours to explore

Portsmouth Island, accessible only by private boat. About 23 miles long by often less than a mile wide, this fascinating island is today uninhabited—except for a handful of National Park Service personnel who maintain the island, including the "ghost town" of Portsmouth Village. When we say "ghost town," we're not referring to a wild west theme park, like Maggie Valley's "Ghost Town In the Sky." This is the real thing, reputedly the only true "ghost town" east of the Mississippi.

In the early 1800s, Portsmouth Village, at the northern tip of the island, bustled with shipping activity. Oceangoing ships and fleets of fishermen passed daily through Ocracoke Inlet, between Ocracoke and Portsmouth Islands, often stopping to unload cargo (and load up at the taverns) at the ports on either side of the inlet, Ocracoke Village to the north, and Portsmouth Village to the south. By the mid-19th century, Portsmouth Village was actually the bigger of the two towns, with about 700 residents. Then, in 1846 a massive hurricane filled in the inlet, and opened up the Hatteras Inlet to the north. Most of Portsmouth Village's seafaring population eventually moved north. By the time another storm reopened the inlet years later, the more developed harbor at Ocracoke Village attracted most of the new residents. By 1950, Portsmouth Village was home to just 14 residents. Ten years later, Portsmouth Island was designated as part of the Cape Lookout National Seashore, and 11 years after that, in 1971, the last three residents moved on (one to that great ghost town in the sky).

Today, you can wander through the remarkably well-preserved, abandoned village, and stop by the National Park Service Visitors Center in the Dixon/Salter House (the only house open to visitors) to learn more about the history of this intriguing ghost town. After exploring the village, take your time to wander along the deserted beaches and dunes, and bask in the island's aura of splendid isolation. Incidentally, the proliferation of waterfowl won't be the only winged wildlife to grab your attention. The mosquitoes on Portsmouth Island have ravenous appetites, so make sure to bring bug repellent with you. For $20, Rudy Austin or his brother, Donald, will ferry you to the island (a 20-minute trip), and pick you up, usually allowing visitors about four hours to visit this magical barrier island. Call Rudy at (252) 928-4361 or Donald at (252) 928-5431 for details and reservations.

For a captivating stroll on Ocracoke Island, take half an hour to amble along the **Hammock Hills Nature Trail,** opposite the Ocracoke Campground, about .75 miles north of the town limits on Route 12. This lush trail begins near sand dunes, plunges through dense maritime forest, and then curls through a salt marsh, giving you an insightful view of the ecosystems characterizing these hardy barrier islands. Again, bring bug repellent with you on this nature hike.

Accommodations

Although many folks make their visit to Ocracoke a one-day affair, not staying overnight, the island does offer lots of superb lodging choices at surprisingly modest prices. Most of the hotels, motels, and inns are relatively new, having arrived within the past 15 years. One big exception is the historic **Island Inn** bed and breakfast on Route 12 and Lighthouse Road, tel. (252) 928-4351. Built in 1901 as part Oddfellows Lodge and part school, the inn features Ocracoke's only heated swimming pool, but that's one of the few modern touches (along with air conditioning and cable TV in every room). The 35 rooms are spacious and exceedingly comfortable, evoking the languorous, casual atmosphere that pervades Ocracoke. Though the structure shows some of the wrinkles of its age, you'll quickly feel at ease and at home. Open year round, the moderate rates begin at $75 during the summer, and drop to as low as $48 during the off-season. Cottages are also available for $500/week during the summer (less during the off-season).

Although the **Silver Lake Inn and Motel,** Silver Lake Rd., tel. (252) 928-5721, was just built in 1983, this lodging exudes an older feel, from the handsplit cedar shakes covering the exterior to the warm wood floors and paneling of the rooms. During the summer, motel rooms run $75, dropping to as low as $45 during weekdays in the off-season. The Silver Lake Inn recently added another building housing 12 luxurious suites with private balconies overlooking Silver Lake harbor. Some of the suites include pine-paneled hot tub rooms overlooking the harbor, offering the ultimate in romance. Suites run $135-180 during the summer and $95-170 in the off-season.

THE OCRACOKE FERRY

Most visitors traveling to Ocracoke take the free ferry from Hatteras. The 40-minute crossing breezes by quickly, taking you and your car past the undeveloped beaches of southern Hatteras Island and a few tiny islands, usually chock full of birds. May 1-Oct. 31, the ferries depart every half hour, and often more frequently, beginning at 7 a.m. from Hatteras and 8 a.m. from Ocracoke, until 7 p.m. at both ferry docks. Both docks also have ferries departing at 5, 6, and 7 a.m., and 8, 9, 10, 11 p.m., and midnight. Nov. 1-April 30, ferries depart from both locations every hour 5 a.m.-midnight, with additional departures scheduled as needed.

Particularly during the summer, don't be surprised if you have to wait in line—occasionally up to an hour or more, after you arrive at the ferry dock. The Hatteras-Ocracoke ferries have a maximum capacity of just 30 cars. But you'll find that the lines move faster than those at most amusement parks—and, anyway, the high density of humans and vehicles only makes your release onto the pristine shores of Ocracoke Island all the more appealing.

If you're coming to Ocracoke from the south, you should consider taking the ferry leaving from Cedar Island on the mainland. If you decide to ride this ferry, which accommodates up to 50 cars, costs $10 per vehicle under 20 feet in length, and lasts a bit over two hours. Be sure to make a reservation first by calling (800) 856-0343 (if you're east of the Mississippi) or (252) 225-3551, between 6 a.m.-6 p.m. Reservations can be made up to 30 days in advance and have to be confirmed in person 30 minutes before boarding. This ferry runs at odd increments of time, 10 or more times a day from Cedar Island and Ocracoke during the summer, and four to six times a day during the off-season. If you're just curious about the scheduled times, call the toll-free, recorded schedule line for all North Carolina ferries at (800) 293-3779 (BY-FERRY).

If you're coming from directly west of the Outer Banks, you may want to consider riding the 28-car, 2.5-hour ferry from Swan Quarter to Ocracoke. This ferry, which costs $10 for vehicles under 20 feet long, usually runs only three times a day from each location, from Swan Quarter at 6:30 a.m., 12:30 p.m., and 4 p.m., and from Ocracoke at 7 a.m., 9:30 a.m., and 4 p.m. If you're planning to take this ferry, definitely make a reservation by calling the Swan Quarter ferry docks up to 30 days in advance, tel. (800) 773-1094 (east of the Mississippi) or (252) 926-1111.

For a dynamic view of the Silver Lake harbor, and the sound beyond, you can't beat the five-story **Anchorage Inn,** Silver Lake and British Cemetery Roads, tel. (252) 928-1101. The rooms are comfortable and meticulously maintained, though you'll probably spend a good bit of your time out on the private balcony overlooking Silver Lake. The inn, which includes an outdoor swimming pool, is open year-round, with rates ranging $89-109 in the summer and dropping to $49-89 in the off-season. **Boyette House** on Route 12, tel. (252) 928-4261, provides similarly clean and pleasant rooms, without the harbor view (and without air conditioning). It's located a block and a half from Silver Lake harbor. Rooms begin at $65 for smaller motel rooms, $85 for larger rooms with microwaves, refrigerators and coffeemakers, and $145-160 for the grand, 700-square-foot luxury suites complete with jacuzzis. Prices drop by $10-20 in the off-season.

Two realty companies manage about 100 rental properties apiece on Ocracoke, a few allowing pets. For free brochures, call **Sharon Miller Realty,** tel. (252) 928-5711 or **Ocracoke Island Realty, Inc.,** tel. (252) 928-6261.

Camping

About three miles north of Ocracoke Village, the National Park Service manages a popular campground with 136 tent and RV sites nestled among the oceanfront dunes. The campground is open only during the summer and, as with the other NPS campgrounds on the Outer Banks, amenities are minimal: cold-water showers, restrooms, and charcoal grills. Unlike the other NPS campgrounds, however, the Ocracoke campground not only accepts reservations but very strongly encourages them. In fact, your chances of getting a site here without a reservation are pretty slim. Call (800) 365-2267 to reserve.

Food, Drink, and Nightlife

The premier dining spot on Ocracoke, **The Back Porch** on Back Road, tel. (252) 928-6401, combines a casually elegant atmosphere with the most creative cuisine on the island, like the luscious crab beignets appetizer. This is one of the few spots on the Outer Banks where you can trust the chefs to drape your seafood, beef, or poultry selections with savory, exotic sauces. In addition to the great food, The Back Porch provides cozy surroundings, either on the screened-in back porch or inside the warm, wood-paneled dining rooms. Open for dinner only from mid-April to mid-October, The Back Porch charges $11-18 for entrees. This is a very popular restaurant, drawing folks from the length of the Outer Banks, so call for a reservation during the peak summer season.

The Island Inn Dining Room at Route 12 and Lighthouse Road, tel. (252) 928-7821, provides three meals a day at modest prices in a casual, inviting atmosphere, either inside or on the airy porch. The cuisine isn't as exotic as the Back Porch, but there are a few surprises, like the delightful oyster omelette for breakfast. Expect to pay $4-6 for breakfast or lunch and $12-16 for dinner.

For terrific, straightforward fish and seafood and hearty homemade soups and sandwiches, all at modest prices, you can't beat the ultra-casual ambience of the **Jolly Roger Pub and Marina** on Silver Lake Harbor, tel. (252) 928-3703. Order your food from the bar, and it will be brought out to your table on the covered, open-air deck on the marina. Open for lunch and dinner, the big burgers start at $4, and fish sandwiches cost $6. You can also choose heftier entrees, like the huge seafood combo of shrimp, scallops, oysters, and fish (broiled or fried) for just $11. This is a great spot to kick back and enjoy a snack and a beer while you watch the water traffic in the harbor. The raw bar serves oysters and clams for $5 a half dozen, $9 for a dozen. The smoked fish is particularly splendid, available as a large appetizer with wasabi, soy and crackers for $7, or with baked brie, fresh fruit and a baguette for $11. The Jolly Roger is one of the few places on Ocracoke featuring live music during summer evenings.

Open 365 days a year 11 a.m.-2 p.m., **Howard's Pub and Raw Bar Restaurant,** Route 12 on the north edge of town, tel. (252) 928-4441, reliably provides friendly company. The menu features fresh local shrimp, clams, oysters, and fish, as well as burgers, subs, salads, and pizza. The ambience is casual and lively, with live bands on most weekends and sometimes during the week. This is the only restaurant we know of where you can relax in a rocking chair on a screened-in porch and drink in an ocean view and a beer. While you're at Howard's, don't miss sampling the renowned oyster shooters—a healthy shot of good draft beer with a freshly shucked raw oyster and a dash of Tabasco sauce, for only $1.50. Chances are you won't be able to shoot just one.

Information

If you call for information, Ocracoke's visitors centers won't fill your mailbox with fat brochures. However, if you call the Ocracoke Civic and Business Association, at (252) 928-6711, you will get a complete listing of all the businesses and attractions in town, along with a marvelously precise map of Ocracoke Village, plotting the exact location of virtually every commercial enterprise in town. If you make your pilgrimage to Ocracoke in person and want to peruse a collection of books and brochures, stop by the **Ocracoke Preservation Museum** or the **National Park Service Visitor Center.** Take a right at the terminus of Route 12 onto Silver Lake Road and follow it to the end, next to the village ferry docks.

GETTING THERE AND AWAY

Driving to the Northern Outer Banks from the south or the west, you have three main routes to choose from—US 17, 64, or 264. For helpful information about attractions along these routes, contact **Historic Albemarle Tour, Inc.,** P.O. Box 1604, Washington, NC 27889, tel. (252) 974-2950 or (800) 734-1117. If you're not in a hurry, you'll find some interesting stops along the way.

US 17

The most interesting (though also the slowest) route runs west along US 17, from its junction with US 64. Four miles northeast of Windsor, you can take a four-mile detour on NC 308 east to the **Hope Plantation,** 132 Hope House Rd., tel. (252) 794-3140. Built in 1803, this estate features the elegant mansion built by David Stone, one of North Carolina's most popular public servants—he served seven terms in the state House of Representatives, one term each in the state Senate and the U.S. House of Representatives, and two terms each as Superior Court Judge, North Carolina Governor, and U.S. Senator. Admission is $6.50 for adults, $2 for students.

Continuing north along US 17, you'll come to historic **Edenton,** a charming town with colonial roots. Dozens of beautifully preserved and restored 18th- and 19th-century homes flank the picturesque waterfront parks and tree-lined streets in the downtown historic district, home to delightful shops, restaurants and bed-and-breakfast inns. Though several downtown B&Bs offer elegant lodgings, for something a bit different you might want to try the fascinating **Granville Queen Themed Inn,** 108 South Granville St., tel. (252) 482-5296. Furnishings throughout the house include fine pieces from Italy, China, Holland, Thailand, and England. Each of the nine guest rooms, most of which have fireplaces and private balconies, feature a different theme, from the Queen's cottage, which resembles a French country cottage, to the slightly outlandish but very memorable Egyptian Queen bedroom, complete with two large bronze sphinxes and a sumptuous bath with cobra-handled faucets.

Rates are $95-105. For more information about Edenton, call the **Tourism Development Authority** at (252) 482-3400 or (800) 775-0111, or stop by the **Historic Edenton Visitors Center,** 108 North Broad St., tel. (252) 482-2637.

Proceeding northeast about 12 miles, just before Hertford, take a 1.5-mile detour south on SR 1336 to visit the **Newbold-White House,** the oldest house in North Carolina. Built in 1730 by a Quaker named Abraham Sanders, this sturdy brick two-story home features large fireplaces with great wooden lintels, pine woodwork, and a winding corner staircase—surprisingly stylish for a farmhouse. Period furnishings and household goods help capture the rugged charm of the Sanders' domestic life. Admission is $2 for adults, 50 cents for kids. This detour will take about half an hour.

About 17 miles northeast of Hertford, you'll come to **Elizabeth City.** Although this town has a long history, stretching back to the early 1700s, it lacks the colonial charm of Edenton. With a population of more than 15,000, Elizabeth City offers plenty of restaurants if you need to take a meal break before driving the last leg to the Outer Banks. If you're up for a brief history lesson on the region, stop by the **Museum of the Albemarle,** 1116 US 17 South, tel. (252) 335-1453. Admission is free. If you're headed for the Outer Banks, don't forget to get off US 17, just past the museum, and on to US 158 East.

US 64

If you coming directly from the west, off I-40 or I-95, the most direct route to the Outer Banks is US 64. Along this route you'll pass through numerous small towns, mostly farming communities with few restaurants, but interesting snapshots of local color, including numerous roadside yard sales, where you can occasionally pick up nifty trinkets like carved duck decoys, or, more frequently, outdated clothing or rusty farm implements. The one big attraction along this route, however, is truly memorable and well worth taking this route. That's **Somerset Place,** 2572 Lake Shore Rd., tel. (252) 797-4560. Located seven miles south, off US 64 just west of Creswell (follow the Somerset Place signs from US 64), this preserved and restored antebellum plantation offers insightful views of what life was like on this 100,000-acre estate, which was an active plantation 1785-1865. The lavishly furnished, 14-room main house, built in the 1830s, stands in poignant contrast to the restored and re-created buildings where the plantation's more than 300 slaves toiled and lived. Since the early 1950s, archeological excavations have been ongoing at this site to elaborate on the African-American aspect of the plantation's history. Reconstruction of several more buildings in the slave community are planned for the future, which will make this an even more outstanding historical site. Somerset Place is operated by the state; admission is free. From April through October, hours are Mon.-Sat. 9 a.m.-5 p.m., Sunday 1-5 p.m. From November through March, hours are Tues.-Sat., 10 a.m.-4 p.m., Sun 1-4 p.m. Plan to spend at least an hour here. From Creswell west to the Outer Banks, you'll encounter few towns, as you pass through lush wetlands including the foreboding-looking, aptly named Alligator River National Wildlife Refuge.

US 264

Beginning at US 17 and proceeding east, this route takes you through charming, historic little towns, beginning with Washington at the US 17/264 junction. But if you're going to stop in just one town, make it **Bath,** North Carolina's oldest official town, incorporated in 1705. You should stop by the **Historic Bath Visitors Center,** in town, on NC 92, tel. (252) 923-3971, where you can start your visit by taking in the 20-minute orientation film, which will fill you in on the long and colorful history of this town, including its being the occasional home and haven for the notorious pirate, Blackbeard, and his crew. A walking tour includes several historic

homes, as well as St. Thomas Episcopal Church, the state's oldest existing church, built in 1734. The Bath Visitors Center is well worth the detour along NC 92 (and then NC 99 to return to US 264). If you want to enjoy a meal here, stop by the **Tide and Thyme** just east of the bridge leading into town on NC 92, tel. (252) 923-1300. You can't sit down here, but you can get terrific take-out meals for lunch or dinner, including sandwiches, desserts, and full seafood platters, which can enjoy at picnic tables at nearby Bonner Point on the Pamlico River (ask for directions at the restaurant). Proceeding east along NC 92, and then north along NC 99, you'll join back up with US 264 at Belhaven, another scenic historic town on the Pamlico river. From Belhaven east to the Outer Banks, you'll pass few towns, but you will see magnificently pristine wetlands, including the Swan Quarter and Alligator River Wildlife Refuges, which include several "wildlife viewing areas" that beckon for you to take little side trips.

Ferries

One of the most pleasurable ways to reach various points on the Outer Banks from the mainland coast is aboard one of 13 state-operated ferries. When you call the North Carolina Division of Travel and Tourism, tel. (800) VISIT-NC, and ask for a travel packet, the state map they send includes precise details about the routes and departure and arrival times of these state ferries. Pamphlets offering the same details are available at visitors centers, most accommodations, and many stores all along the North Carolina coast. If you don't mind listening to a recorded phone message with many options, you can also get the information by calling (800) BY-FERRY. You can also find much relevant information online at www.dot.state.nc.us/transit/ferry or www.nccoast.com.

THE MAINLAND CENTRAL COAST

Although North Carolina's mainland central coast is not as well known a travelers' destination as the Outer Banks region, the charms of this area include an array of historic attractions, inviting lodgings, and superb restaurants—particularly in the bigger towns of New Bern, Morehead City, Beaufort and Atlantic Beach. With few exceptions, the rest of the vast central coastal area of North Carolina is composed of small towns and villages.

NEW BERN

Incorporated in 1710, the historic city of New Bern is the second-oldest town in North Carolina (Bath is the oldest). Founded by German and Swiss settlers, the town was named after Bern, Switzerland, although the North Carolina port city had virtually nothing topographically in common with its mountainous namesake. One thing the two towns *do* have in common is a love of bears ("Bern" is German for "bear"). You see representations of the creatures all over town— from the signs and floral displays of the city's coat of arms to life-size stuffed versions for the kids to take home.

Situated at the confluence of the Neuse and Trent Rivers, which flow into Pamlico Sound, New Bern has been a bustling center of seafaring commerce since the earliest days of the 18th century. This prosperity led to its selection as the seat of North Carolina's colonial government and the state's first capital. The city continues to bustle with commerce today. Still an active port, New Bern has diligently retained a sense of its architectural past, with lovely old churches and hundreds of grand historic homes, some now converted into bed and breakfasts, restaurants, and shops.

TRYON PALACE

The jewel of historic New Bern is **Tryon Palace,** 610 Pollock St., tel. (252) 514-4900 or (800) 767-1560, an extraordinarily meticulous reproduction of the home of British Royal Governor

William Tryon. On October 10, 1764, Lt. Colonel William and Margaret Tryon and their four-year-old daughter, "little Margaret," arrived at Cape Fear, near Wilmington, after a long, rough voyage from England. They were accompanied by a spirited young British architect, John Hawks. Tryon had persuaded Hawks to sail across the ocean to build a structure that would house his family and provide a meeting place for the North Carolina colony's Governor's Council. This new building, Tryon hoped, would provide a sense of permanence and stability to the young colony and establish New Bern as North Carolina's permanent seat of colonial government.

Completed in 1770, Hawks' building fulfilled its purpose, providing a comfortable, graceful home for Governor Tryon and his family, a meeting place for the Colonial Assembly, and plenty of room for entertaining statesmen of the day, (though he didn't sleep here, George Washington dined and danced at the Palace). From the gala ball celebrating its official opening on December 5, 1770, word spread about this "biggest and most beautiful home in North Carolina."

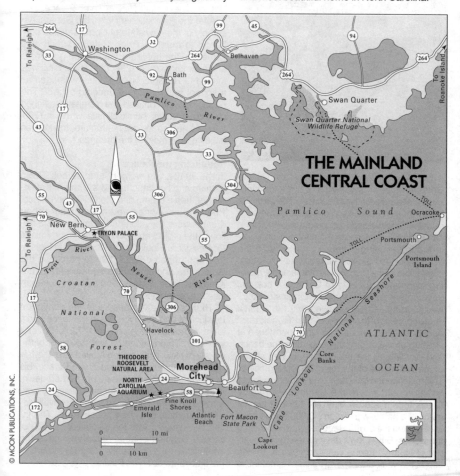

THE MAINLAND CENTRAL COAST

TRYON PALACE HISTORIC SITES AND GARDENS

Not all North Carolinians were pleased by the Governor's new digs, which is not surprising, since a separate tax had been levied on colonists to pay for the construction of the Georgian-style mansion. Disaffected taxpayers, referring pejoratively to the excesses of the construction, christened the building "Tryon's Palace," and the name stuck. In the western regions of the state, completion of the "Palace" further fueled a growing resentment that North Carolina's colonial government, ruled by the "eastern aristocracy," was abusing settlers elsewhere in the colony. A group calling themselves the "Regulators" openly rebelled, bursting into the courthouse at Hillsborough, dragging the judge from the bench and vandalizing the courthouse as well as the property of some of the town's colonial officials. Tryon responded by leading the eastern militia to Hillsborough, where the Battle of Alamance Creek took place on May 16, 1771. It wasn't much of a battle, with Tryon's 6,000 troops easily defeating the 2,000 Regulators, who fled into the woods. But Tryon's days as the royal governor of North Carolina were numbered. By the end of the year, after spending just 13 months in

his "palace," Tryon was transferred to be the governor of the colony of New York.

Tryon's successor, Josiah Martin, didn't fare any better. After three and a half years of growing anti-British fervor, Governor Martin eventually couldn't even exert any control over the colonial assembly. In April 1775, Martin, in a pique of frustration, dissolved the entire assembly. Soon after, Martin realized that he would be lucky to survive long in New Bern, so he immediately hopped on a ship to England, leaving all of his belongings behind at the palace. He was the last royal governor to live at Tryon Palace.

After the Revolutionary War, the General Assembly of the new state of North Carolina continued to meet at Tryon Palace, which also served as the home for the elected governors and their families. In 1794, the state capital was moved to Raleigh. Tryon Palace was used as a school and then as a dancing school. The palace had fallen into severe disrepair, hastened by neglect and the humid climate, when, in 1795, a fire destroyed the main structure, the kitchen building, and most of the grounds.

Rebuilding the Palace

In the 1940s, two women, Mrs. James Edwin Latham and her daughter, Mrs. John A. Kellenberger, had a dream of restoring Tryon Palace. Putting their money and efforts where their dreams were, they donated more than $1.3 million to the project and founded the Tryon Palace Commission. Finally, in 1953, the state legislature appropriated $227, 000 to purchase the land in the original palace square and authorized the Tryon Palace Commission to supervise the restoration.

Thanks in great measure to the continued bad luck of William Tryon, the commission had a lot of information to go on. In 1773, just over a year after Tryon became royal Governor of the colony of New York, having moved all of the furnishings with which he filled Tryon Palace, his governor's mansion in New York burned down. In seeking compensation for his losses, the governor and his wife compiled an exhaustively detailed inventory of all their possessions. This inventory, coupled with the discovery in 1939 of Hawks' detailed original blueprints, gave the commission a remarkably accurate picture of the first years of Tryon Palace.

Completed in 1959, Tryon Palace today is a painstakingly faithful reproduction of the original main building, the adjoining kitchen/office building, and the stables and gardens (the stables in the West Wing are the lone remnants of the actual 18th-century Palace).

Touring the Tryon Palace Complex

Begin your visit by watching the 15-minute audio-visual presentation at the Reception Center. From there, well-informed and engaging guides will lead you through the main residence, adding plenty of historical tidbits like "here in the parlor, George Washington led the minuet at a ball in 1791." Despite is regal title, the complex isn't palatial in size. Even the chamber where the colonial council met is only slightly larger than your average suburban living room. But there's nothing suburban about the furnishings of the Palace. The furniture, chandeliers, and fabrics are all faithful to the Tryons' sophisticated tastes, consisting mostly of antiques from the period, along with a few reproductions to reflect what the house looked like when the Tryons lived there. From the dazzling marble and woodwork to the canopied beds, silk draperies, delicate china, and silver, the residence oozes a rare colonial elegance. Among the artworks, you'll find an early portrait by Thomas Gainsborough, and a study for a painting that hangs in Buckingham Palace of Queen Charlotte and her children.

After the 40-minute guided tour of the main residence, take the self-guided tours of the adjacent kitchen building, where costumed re-enactors frequently demonstrate the cooking, laundering, candle-making, and fabric spinning that kept this place hopping during Tryon's time. Then take your time to wander the resplendent gardens, a mix of formal English and French styles replete with topiary and classical statuary, giving the gardens a haunted, old-world feel.

Exiting the Palace gates, proceed to two other restored homes; admission is included with your ticket to the Palace. Just outside the gates, at 609 Pollock St., stands the **Dixon-Stevenson House,** an elegant Federal-style home built between 1826 and 1833 on a lot that was originally a part of Tryon Palace's gardens. Furnished today with lovely antiques, this home served as a hospital for Union troops during the Civil War, lending its pristine rooms an intriguingly ghostly ambience.

Also included with your Tryon Palace admission is free access to the **John Wright Stanley House,** at 307 George Street, next to the Palace Reception Center. Authentically furnished with late 18th-century pieces, this stately Georgian home, built in 1779, can boast that George Washington really did sleep here, for a couple of nights in 1791. Touring this grand home of Washington's friend, the wealthy shipping magnate John Wright Stanley, you'll see why Washington described his pal's home as "exceeding good lodgings."

Open 9 a.m.-4 p.m. Mon.-Sat., and 1-4 p.m. Sunday, admission to the Tryon Palace historical complex costs $12. Plan to spend at least two to three hours.

If you didn't get your fill of history at the Tryon Palace complex, visit the **Civil War Museum,** a block away from the palace at 301 Metcalf St., tel. (252) 633-2818. Featuring an extensive private collection of Civil War memorabilia (including lots of muskets, knives and swords), this little museum pales in comparison to the grandiose operation at Tryon Palace, but if you're a Civil War buff, you'll want to stop by. Open Tues.-Sat. year round, admission is $2.50 for adults, $1.50 for students.

ACCOMMODATIONS

Bed and Breakfasts

You can choose among half a dozen lovely bed-and-breakfast inns in downtown New Bern. We recommend selecting one of the following three, all located on the same block of Pollock Street, between Craven and East Front Streets (US 70 Bus.), a tranquil, tree-lined block, within a couple of blocks of several restaurants and shops. **Howard House,** 207 Pollock St., tel. (252) 514-6709 or (800) 705-5261 is one of New Bern's few surviving examples of Queen Anne-influenced architecture. This gracious and comfortable Victorian-style bed and breakfast, with its corner tower, stained glass windows and oriental rugs, has three elegant guest rooms adorned with fine period antiques and family heirlooms. Each room includes phone, cable TV, and private bath with hair dryers, robes and other bath amenities. Innkeepers Steven and Kimberly Wynn serve a full breakfast as well as evening desserts and refreshments, included in the $85-95 rates. Expensive.

The Greek Revival style **Harmony House Inn,** 215 Pollock St., tel. (252) 636-3810 or (800) 636-3113, provides eight spacious guest rooms and two suites, tastefully appointed with antiques, reproductions and historic memorabilia. All rooms include private telephones and cable TV. The $85-95 rates ($130 for the suites), include a full gourmet breakfast, wine and soft drinks in the evening, as well as port and sherry at bedtime. Expensive. Across the street, the **King's Arms Colonial Inn,** 212 Pollock St., tel. (252) 638-4409 or (800) 872-9306 provides seven clean, comfortable guest rooms and one suite, decorated in a colonial style with a mix of antiques and reproductions. Innkeepers Richard and Patricia Gulley give you the option of sharing breakfast on the porch, or having it served by candlelight to your room. Rates are $90 ($60 for one person), and $130 for the suite. Expensive.

Chain Lodgings

A number of chain hotels serve New Bern, including several riverfront locations. Located one block west of US 70 Business and Tryon Palace Drive, on the waterfront at the confluence of the Neuse and Trent Rivers, the **Sheraton Grand New Bern** at One Bicentennial Park, tel. (252) 638-3585 or (800) 326-3745, offers tranquil river views along with the most convenient downtown location of any of the chains. The Sheraton actually consists of two separate structures. The older five-story "hotel" provides 100 rooms, all with a river view, beginning at $120. The newer three-story "inn, " whose 72 rooms have either river or city views, provides slightly more luxuriously appointed rooms beginning at $140. You'll find three restaurants on the premises, including the **Cityside Cafe,** which often features live bands in the evening, making it New Bern's most popular dancing spot. Premium.

On the other side of the Trent River, directly across from the Sheraton just off US 70 Business, the **Ramada Inn Waterfront Marina,** 101 Howell Rd., tel. (252) 636-3627 or (800) 228-2828, provides 112 rooms, all with a splendid river view of the Trent and Neuse Rivers. Including a swimming pool, coffee makers in every room, and a spacious covered, riverfront deck, where you can enjoy a meal or a snack, this hotel is the best buy of the chains in New Bern, with the rates beginning at $65 (more for suites with jacuzzis). Moderate.

If the Ramada is booked, the Moderate-Expensive **Comfort Suites Riverfront,** tel. (252) 636-0022 or (800) 228-5150, includes 100 suites, consisting of a bedroom with a sitting area. Suites with a city view start at $60, and riverfront suites with a balcony run $99. The more luxurious Jacuzzi suites cost $129.

FOOD AND DRINK

Chances are, you've come to New Bern to visit Tryon Palace. To continue your history-packed visit, try the **Harvey Mansion,** 221 Tryon Palace Drive, tel. (252) 638-3205, for dinner. This three-story brick home, built 1797-1804, includes a half-dozen high-ceilinged dining rooms exuding colonial charm and allowing plenty of space between the tables, which are draped with white tablecloths. If you arrive between 5 and 6 p.m., you can take advantage of the best meal deal in town, which includes soup, salad and an entree for just $10. The entrees for this special vary nightly and are usually confined to your choice of just two entrees, but those choices are usually delicious. On our latest visit, the soup was fish chowder, and the entree choices were Hungarian veal served with spinach linguine in cream sauce, or blackened trigger fish with a jambalaya sauce. In addition to this "early-bird special," the Harvey House offers gourmet entrees of surf or turf, costing $17-24, like the Assiette Neptune, grilled crab cake, shrimp and scallops baked with bell peppers, onion, and olives served with a Kansas rice medley (wild rice, white long-grain and wheat berries). To get a feel for the age of this home, consider enjoying a cocktail and/or appetizer in the popular bar in the cellar. This evocative, underground rathskeller, whose low ceilings are less than half the height of the upstairs dining rooms, used to be where Mr. Harvey's slaves cooked for the family, but today, these brick walls rock to jukeboxes and DJs, making it one of New Bern's more popular night spots.

For similar gourmet fare, you won't be disappointed by the classy dining rooms in **Hender-**

son House, 216 Pollock St., tel. (252) 637-4784. Located between US 70 Business and Craven St., on the same block as the bed and break-fast inns listed above, this smoke-free restaurant has several dining rooms with walls adorned with noble portraits and majestic landscapes in gilt frames. Although gents don't have to wear a jacket and tie, you won't feel out of place if you dress a bit more formally at this pinnacle of fine dining in New Bern, where the entrees begin in the $25 range.

For a more casual, lively atmosphere, including a bit of history, you should try the **The Chelsea,** 335 Middle St., tel. (252) 637-5469, open for lunch and dinner. Built in 1912, this building initially served as Caleb Bradham's drug store (Caleb's most celebrated concoction being "Brad's Drink," which evolved into a libation known as "Pepsi-Cola"). The first floor of this local favorite, which includes the popular bar, retains the original pressed-tin ceiling, along with the restored tile mosaic of Caleb's original drug store. Renovated in 1996, the upstairs dining rooms evoke a more romantic feel, with high ceilings and warm woodwork. Regardless of where you sit, you'll be treated to a sumptuous selection of enticing gastronomic pleasures, from appetizers like the Arroyo rolls, a western blend of roasted chicken, herbs, spices and cheese, in crispy egg roll wrappers, served with black bean salsa and pico relish, ($6), to entrees like the black strap pork tenderloin, marinated in dijon and molasses, grilled and served with butter-milk "smashed" potatoes, and peach chutney ($15). Lunch selections, like the Maryland crab cake or pecan-crusted catfish run $5-6.

If you're just looking for a quick snack before or after visiting Tryon Palace, your best bets are the **Pollock Street Deli,** 208 Pollock St., tel. (252) 637-2480 or the groovy, late '50s-early '60s-style **Kress Cafe,** 309 Middle St., tel. (252) 633-9300, which remains open until about 1 a.m., serving sandwiches and snacks to the beat of Buddy Holly, Elvis, the Beach Boys, the Bea-tles and other hot bands of the era.

Information

For information about New Bern, contact the **Craven County Convention and Tourist Bu-reau,** 314 Tryon Palace Drive, New Bern, NC 28463, tel. (252) 637-9400 or (800) 437-5767. You might want to stop by their office when you first arrive in town to pick up one of the wealth of free brochures and helpful maps.

CROATAN NATIONAL FOREST

From New Bern, stretching south about 20 miles almost to the coast, the sprawling Croatan Na-tional Forest consists of 157,000 acres of woods and pocosins (vast bogs peculiar to the North Carolina coastal plain) that are inviting, dark and deep. Hiking trails and unpaved roads lead to several lakes, taking you past exotic flora like five species of insect-eating plants, including the famed Venus flytrap. A rich variety of wildlife make the Croatan their home, from the endan-gered red-cockaded woodpecker to the rare southern bald eagle, to more common critters like white-tailed deer, black bears, and wild turkeys. It's best to keep to the trails here, since some of the residents of the forest can be un-friendly if disturbed, including rattlesnakes, cop-perheads, and cottonmouths, not to mention al-ligators. This forest being so diverse, you should stop by the park headquarters, next to US 70 about 9 miles southeast of New Bern, to pick up maps and brochures before embarking into the woods. For more information about this na-ture preserve, including its selection of primitive camping sites, call or write to: District Ranger, Croatan National Forest, 141 E. Fisher Ave., New Bern, NC 28560, tel. (252) 638-5628.

THE INSECTIVOROUS PLANTS OF CROATAN

The Croatan National Forest is home to five genera of insect-eating plants, a concentration rarely seen in the U.S. These unusual plants supplement their diets (particularly with nitrogen) by attracting, trapping, and eating insects. Although they can survive without their buggy meals, they do much better with them—particularly since the plants often live in typically poor growing sites—in soils that are sandy, very wet, or highly acidic, and inhospitable to many other types of plants.

Each of the five types of insectivorous plants in Croatan National Forest uses a different technique to capture its prey. The most infamous is the **Venus flytrap** (Dionaea muscipula), whose leaves resemble and function as traps. When an insect touches sensitive hairs on the inner surface of the lobes, the hinged leaves close swiftly, and interlocking teeth on the edges of the leaves form a cage that captures the intruder. Glands in the leaves then secrete juices that digest the unfortunate captive. The Venus flytrap's traps lie close to the ground, at the base of fairly long stalks whose ends bloom with white flowers in May and June.

Two species of "pitcher plants" also grow here, the **parrot pitcher plant** (Sarracenia purpurea) and the **trumpet pitcher-plant** (Sarracenia flava). They're distinguished by erect, vase-shaped, tubular leaves and showy flowers that hang face-downward from tall stems. The flowers attract insects, luring them onto the hollow tubes at their bases. The inside of the tube is lined with hairs that point downward. Once an insect creeps onto the hairs, it finds that it can't reverse direction. Fluid in the tubes eventually drowns and slowly digests the hapless flower-hopper. The parrot pitcher-plant has red leaves; the trumpet pitcher-plant has yellow-green leaves and bright yellow flowers. Both species grow in bogs of pine forests in the coastal plain.

The **round-leaved sundew** (Drosera rotundifolia) is named for the "dewdrops" that cover its leaves. The numerous hairs on the leaves are tipped with glands that secrete tiny droplets of a glistening, sticky substance. This dewy glue also contains an anesthetic that helps subdue the victim. When a small bug touches the hairs it is held fast by the sticky fluid. Surrounding hairs bend toward the struggling insect, further enmeshing it. The bug is then slowly digested by juices that ooze from glands in the leaf, allowing the plant to absorb the nourishment directly into its leaves. The round-leaved sundew is easily identified by its leaves—each has a pinkish circular lobe at the end of a long thin stalk, giving it something of a look of a land-based sea anemone.

Butterworts have broader leaves, forming rosettes at the bases of the flower stems. The leaves are covered with a sticky glue that, like those of the sundew, contains an anesthetic. When an insect gets stuck, the leaf curls up and entombs it. Substances then secreted from the leaves do the digestive work. Butterworts grow in moist sites in bogs and pinelands on the coastal plain. Their flowers, blooming in the early spring, can be blue, yellow, white, violet, or pink.

Bladderworts are mostly aquatic, floating on the surfaces of ponds, lakes, and roadside ditches. They are named for the inflated leaves (bladders) that not only buoy up the plants but also serve as traps to catch small forms of aquatic fauna, including the larvae of such insects as mosquitoes (you may find yourself wishing the forest grew a lot more of these bladderworts as you hike through the mosquito-heavy woods). The air-filled bladders have unique valves that allow prey to enter but keep out the water that would destroy the plant's buoyancy. Trapped insects or small marine animals are digested by secretions and bacterial action. Of the four bladderworts found in Croatan National Forest, the **floating bladderwort** (Utricularia inflata) is perhaps the most picturesque. Its inflated leaves arranged like spokes on a wheel, it sails across water with the breeze, trailing its bladder-laden stolons behind it.

For more information about these intriguing insectivorous plants, including which trails you'll find them on, stop by the Croatan National Forest visitors center, on U.S. 70 about nine miles southeast of New Bern, before heading out into the woods.

pitcher plants

TOMMY DAUGHTRY

THE CRYSTAL COAST

Relatively little-known as vacation destinations, the towns of "The Crystal Coast"—particularly **Morehead City, Beaufort, Atlantic Beach** and **Pine Knoll Shores**—offer visitors an enticing combination of pristine beaches, attractive lodgings, terrific restaurants, and interesting shops in a tranquil atmosphere relatively free of crowds.

Morehead City, a bustling port and the largest town in the area, boasts about 6,000 residents and a thriving waterfront district, complete with lots of shops and eateries. The historic village of Beaufort has a warm, colonial charm, preserving its centuries-old traditions as a port and fishing village. Atlantic Beach and Pine Knoll Shores, on the eastern side of the barrier island of Bogue Banks, provide miles of inviting, uncrowded, sandy beaches. All these towns are within a 10- to 15-minute drive of each other.

Historic Sites and Museums

At the corner of Turner and Ann Streets, half a block from the waterfront in downtown Beaufort, you can roam the two acres of the **Beaufort Historic Site,** tel. (252) 728-5225 or (800) 575-7483. Consisting of 13 historic structures, you can take guided tours with costumed docents through seven restored homes and public buildings built in the 1700s and 1800s. The site is open year-round, seven days a week; admission is $5. The guided tours are conducted Monday through Sunday. The tour of the restored homes leaves at 11 a.m. and 1 p.m. and takes about an hour. The tour of the public buildings, including the courthouse, county jail, apothecary shop and doctor's office, also takes about an hour and departs at 11:30 a.m. and 3 p.m. In the summer, you should also take advantage of the guided tours on a British-style double-decker bus, which leave periodically from the historic site and cruise around Beaufort's historic district, which includes more than 100 historic homes, many dating back to the 1700s.

While you're in Beaufort, stop by the **North Carolina Maritime Museum,** 315 Front St., tel. (252) 728-7317. Despite its cavernous, 18,000 square feet of exhibit space, it won't take long to explore the exhibits of full-sized watercrafts,

models of various boats and ships, collections of decoys and seashells, small aquariums, and historical dioramas. In the affiliated **Harvey W. Smith Watercraft Center,** across the street from the museum, you can watch the construction and restoration of wooden boats. Open seven days a week year-round; hours are Mon.-Fri. 9 a.m.-5 p.m., Saturday 10 a.m.-5 p.m., and Sunday 1-5 p.m. Admission is free to both the museum and the watercraft center.

About three miles east of Atlantic Beach, at the eastern terminus of Route 58, lies **Fort Macon State Park,** tel. (252) 726-3775, the most visited state park in North Carolina. The attraction that draws more than 1.4 million visitors to the park is the captivating Fort Macon, built 1826-1834, the scene of a fierce attack during the Civil War. On April 25, 1862, Union troops surrounded Fort Macon by land and sea and bombarded the fort with cannon fire. After being hit by 560 cannon balls over a period of 11 hours, the Confederate forces surrendered the next morning.

Begin your exploration of the fort by visiting the handful of rooms, re-created in authentic 19th-century detail, augmented by informative audio presentations, narrated by the ghosts of the commandants and soldiers stationed here a century ago. You'll quickly learn that being stationed at this seaside fort was no picnic. The soldiers had to endure dark, dank, cramped quarters infested with bedbugs, fleas, and relentless swarms of mosquitoes. Indeed, thanks to the sunken design of the fort, which tends to gather moisture, you won't have to use your imagination when it comes to the historical descriptions of the mosquitoes—bring bug repellent when you visit.

Visiting the re-created rooms will help your imagination populate the dozens of other eerie, empty rooms of the fort with the ghosts of the fort's former tenants. Watch your step when exploring these rooms. As a sign at the entrance of fort states, "Fort Macon was made for war, not safety. Please be careful." This warning mainly refers to the uneven brick floors, so watch your step, particularly in the darker rooms. You won't have to worry about your footing if you take the quarter-mile **Ailed Coues Nature Trail,** next to the fort. This inviting, shady trail (also popular with mosquitoes), leads through wax myrtle, Virginia creeper vines, live oaks, crape myrtle, and poison ivy before emerging onto Bogue Sound.

Swimming is not allowed near the fort, these waters being particularly populated by motor boats and commercial watercraft, but you can take a dip at the popular beach near the entrance to the park, which includes a seaside bath house, with rest rooms, and a refreshment stand. Admission to the park, including the fort, is free.

North Carolina Aquarium at Pine Knoll Shores

Traditional sightseeing attractions are few and far between on the Crystal Coast. One significant exception, however, is the fun and popular North Carolina Aquarium at Pine Knoll Shores, five miles west of Atlantic Beach on Route 58, tel. (252) 247-4003. Like the other two state-run aquariums on the North Carolina coast, the aquarium at Pine Knoll Shores is a rather modest affair, featuring 24 display tanks with an overall capacity of about 26,000 gallons. But it's a very fun and informative place to spend an hour or more, well worth the admission price of $3 for adults and $1 for kids 6-17. Animals on display include a wide variety of North Carolina species, including gar, bass, catfish, grouper, snapper, triggerfish, octopus, eels, alligators, and tropical reef fish. In addition, the aquarium serves as a nursery for sea turtles, and several are always on display. The touch tank is always a big winner with kids, and aquarium staff also periodically bring around exotic species like snakes and turtles on carts for the kids to interact with, up close and personal. A number of interactive and video exhibits make the learning here easy and entertaining. Call ahead to see if the aquarium is offering any special programs when you're in the area, or request one of their detailed calendars of special events by calling (252) 247-4003, or writing to the North Carolina Aquarium at Pine Knoll Shores, Atlantic Beach, NC 28512-0580.

Be sure to take half an hour to hike the half-mile **Alice G. Hoffman Nature Trail,** which leads from the back of the aquarium through lush salt marsh and maritime forest in the **Theodore Roosevelt Natural Area.** Don't forget to bring along the handy 11-by-17-inch laminated trail guide,

NORTH CAROLINA AQUARIUM

keyed to 19 numbered markers along the trail, telling the story of this unique maritime forest. And don't forget bug repellent, either.

Recreation

Swimming in the ocean is the predominant recreation on the Crystal Coast, most folks choosing the sandy, uncrowded beaches of Atlantic Beach. For even more isolated swimming and hiking, you should consider visiting one or more of the uninhabited islands in the region, especially **Shackleford Banks,** home to dozens of wild ponies. **Beaufort Belle Tours,** 300 Front St. at the downtown Beaufort waterfront, tel. (252) 728-6888, provides ferry service and/or guided tours of three islands in the area. Ferries to Shackleford Banks cost $14, while a three-hour guided tour of the island runs $22.

Next to swimming, **fishing** is easily the second most popular recreational diversion on the Crystal Coast. No fewer than 35 marinas dot the waterfronts of this small area, providing a vast variety of fishing charters to suit any angler's desires. If you want to take a short cruise without casting a rod and reel, the 82-foot paddlewheeler

Crystal Queen 600 Front St. in Beaufort, tel. (252) 728-2527, offers 1.5-and two-hour cruises through the region's waters, departing Mon.-Sat. at 2 p.m., 4:30 p.m. and 7 p.m. The 1.5-hour cruise costs $8 ($4 for kids 6-12), and the two-hour cruise costs $10 ($6 for kids).

Beaufort and Morehead City are also among the most popular **scuba-diving** destinations on the East Coast, thanks in great measure to the hundreds of shipwrecks off the coast (see "Diving Into the Graveyard" in the Outer Banks section). Two first-class operations in the area offer charter dives and scuba instruction, including the **Olympus Dive Center,** 713 Shepard St. in Morehead City, tel. (252) 726-9432 or (800) 992-1258, and **Discovery Diving Company,** 414 Orange St. in Beaufort, tel. (252) 728-2265. Discovery also offers snorkeling instruction.

ACCOMMODATIONS

Lodgings in the three towns of Morehead City, Beaufort, and Atlantic Beach are quite distinct, with Morehead City offering inexpensive chain motels, Beaufort featuring elegant bed and breakfasts, and Atlantic Beach providing attractive oceanfront digs. Just a few miles east of Atlantic Beach, rental homes abound along the unspoiled beaches of Emerald Isle.

Morehead City

Staying overnight in Morehead City pretty much means choosing between chain motels. The superior choice, and the only one on the water, is the **Hampton Inn,** 4035 Arendell St., (US 70), tel. (252) 240-2300 or 800-HAMPTON. It's located on Bogue Sound about three miles west of downtown. Most of the Hampton's rooms offer tranquil views of the water. You won't find a spacious, sandy beach for sunbathing here, and swimming in the sound is a bit hazardous because of boating traffic, but the swimming pool next to the sound helps make up for those deficiencies. Moderate summer rates begin around $75 on weekdays and $85 on weekends. Off-season rates, Oct.-March, dip to around $50.

Three other chain motels provide clean, comfortable rooms and swimming pools. None are located in particularly scenic spots within easy walking distance of downtown, but they all offer Inexpensive to Moderate rates. About 2.5 miles west of downtown, a block north of US 70 at 35th St., you'll find the **EconoLodge,** 3410 Bridges St., tel. (252) 247-2940 or (800) 424-4777, whose rooms begin at around $70 during the summer, and drop to as low as $35 in the winter. The **Comfort Inn,** 3100 Arendell St. (US 70), tel. (252) 247-3434 or (800) 422-5404, provides rooms in the summer beginning around $60 during the week, rising to about $80 on weekends. In the off-season, rates dip as low as $40. Also on US 70, the **Best Western Buccaneer Inn,** tel. (252) 726-3115 or (800) 682-4982, offers the convenience of an on-site restaurant and lounge, the **Anchor Inn.** Rates begin at $85 during the summer, dropping as low as $45 during the winter, and include a free full breakfast.

Beaufort

You won't find any chains in this historic port town, which provides a bounty of inns and historic bed and breakfasts. For a combination of history and comfortable elegance, you won't beat **The Cedars by the Sea,** 305 Front St., across the street from the waterfront in the heart of the historic district, tel. (252) 728-7036. Sitting proudly behind a stand of old cedars, the original portion of the inn has been watching over the Beaufort harbor for more than two centuries. Consisting of two stately homes, built circa 1768 and 1851, the Cedars has 12 rooms and suites with comforting touches like fireplaces and antique bathtubs. Rates, which include a full breakfast, range $85-115 for rooms, and $140-165 for suites. Lower winter rates are available. Expensive.

Half a block from the waterfront, in the historic district, stands the grand, Victorian **Pecan Tree Inn,** 116 Queen St., tel. (252) 728-6733. Built in 1866, the inn features characteristic Victorian porches, turrets and gingerbread trim, enhanced by antiques collected by the innkeepers, Susan and Joe Johnson. In addition to five lovely guest rooms, the inn offers two deluxe rooms, complete with Jacuzzis and king size canopy beds. Rates, which include a full breakfast, range $85-125 April 1-Oct.1, and drop to $65-110 the rest of the year. Expensive-Premium.

Two larger, modern inns in the Expensive-Premium rate category provide comfortable rooms and private porches with romantic water views. The three-story **Inlet Inn,** 601 Front St., tel. (252) 728-3600, offers 37 rooms, most with great views of the harbor across the street. The harbor-front rooms include seating area, ceiling fans, cable TV and a bar with a refrigerator and ice-maker. In many rooms, French doors open onto private porches with rocking chairs, where you can relax and drink in the views of the harbor, and in the distance, the wild ponies on Carrot Island. Rates, including a free continental breakfast brought to your room, range $100-120 in the summer and gradually drop to $50-70 during the winter. The 44 rooms of the **Beaufort Inn,** 101 Ann St., tel. (252) 728-2600 or (800) 726-0321, all provide private porches with rocking chairs, overlooking Beaufort Channel at the eastern edge of downtown Beaufort. Rates, including an expanded continental breakfast, range $100-120 during the summer and gradually dip to $50-70 during the winter.

Atlantic Beach and Pine Knoll Shores
With inviting, uncrowded, sandy beaches, the areas of Atlantic Beach and Pine Knoll Shores provide the Crystal Coast's most plentiful oceanfront lodgings, from reputable chains to marvelous independent lodgings.

You, along with any four-legged members of the family, will enjoy your stay at **The Atlantis,** milepost 5 on Salter Path Rd., tel. (252) 726-5168 or (800) 682-7057. Most of the 42 units at this three-story oceanfront motel are spacious efficiencies with kitchens and small living and dining areas. Amenities include the peaceful swimming pool set amidst maritime woods and a third floor library and adjoining lounge, including a game table, video games, and pool table. The Atlantis is one of the best buys at the beach, with summer rates beginning at $86 for regular rooms, and $105 for efficiencies, gradually falling to $51 and $57 during the winter. Expensive.

Next to the Atlantis, to the west on Route 58, the **Royal Pavilion Resort,** milepost 5.2 on Salter Path Rd., tel. (252) 726-5188 or (800) 533-3700, provides 115 rooms, many of them efficiencies, looking out on the 1,500 feet of the Royal Pavilion beachfront and inviting oceanfront swimming pool. Summer rates begin at $85 for poolside rooms, $100 for oceanfront ($10 more for Friday and Saturday), and gradually reduce to as low as $60 and $45 during the winter. Expensive.

On the other side of the Atlantis, to the east on Route 58, the five-story **Windjammer Inn,** milepost 4.8 on Salter Path Rd., tel. (252) 247-7123 or (800) 233-6466, offers a swimming pool, and 45 spacious rooms, all with an ocean view and private balconies. Even if you're not staying on one of the upper floors, take a ride in the glass-enclosed elevator and watch the ocean dramatically spread out before your eyes. Summer rates begin at $85-110 and gradually drop to as low as $45 during the winter. Expensive.

If you prefer the dependability of chain lodgings, you have several options in this area. The following chain operations all feature oceanfront rooms with private balconies, swimming pools, and restaurants on the premises. The nine-story **Sheraton Atlantic Beach,** milepost 4.5 on Salter Path Rd. (US 58), tel. (252) 240-1155 or (800) 624-8875, features its own 600-foot fishing pier, game room, both indoor and outdoor pools, spa, and fitness room. In addition to the on-site restaurant, the Sheraton features lounges that are popular night spots. Summer rates begin at $155 for oceanview rooms, $180 for oceanfront rooms, and $235 for oceanfront suites, gradually dropping to as low as $50-95 in the winter. Luxury. Just down the road, to the west on US 58, you'll find the **Holiday Inn on the Ocean,** milepost 4.75 on Salter Path Rd., tel. (252) 726-2544 or (800) 733-7888. Summer rates begin at $100 and gradually decline to as low as $50 in the winter. Expensive. At milepost 8.5 on Salter Path Rd., (in Pine Knoll Shores, despite its name), the seven-story **Ramada Inn Atlantic Beach,** tel. (252) 247-4155 or (800) 338-1533, offers rooms beginning at $85 during the summer ($99 on Friday and Saturday), and gradually drop to $33-44 during the winter. Expensive.

Rental Homes
Hundreds of homes and condominiums are available for weekly, monthly, and in non-summer months, weekend rentals. Most of these properties are located in the residential communities just west of Atlantic Beach and Pine Knoll shores, in **Salter Path, Indian Beach** and **Emerald Isle.** More than a dozen real estate companies handle rentals in this area. For a selection of more than 1,000 properties, call for the free, detailed brochures (including color photos of each property) supplied by the following

three realtors, the biggest operations in the area: **Emerald Isle Realty,** tel. (800) 849-3315, **Bluewater Associates,** tel. (252) 354-2323 or (888) 258-9287, and **Sun-Surf Realty,** tel. (252) 354-2658 or (800) 553-SURF.

FOOD AND DRINK

Morehead City and Beaufort offer superb dining, often with romantic water views. If you're staying in Atlantic Beach or Pine Knoll Shores, it's worth the short drive to Morehead City and Beaufort to eat. Not surprisingly, the specialties featured at the best restaurants in the area usually involve fish and shellfish, fresh off the boat.

Morehead City Restaurants

For a great selection of waterfront restaurants offering fresh seafood, proceed to the Morehead City waterfront, between 5th and 7th Streets. At 501 Evans Street, the **Sanitary Fish Market,** tel. (252) 247-3111, has been serving fish and seafood since 1938. Open for lunch and dinner, the Sanitary's long wooden dining rooms look out onto Bogue Sound and have the casual, no-frills atmosphere of an old-style fish house. Although you can get steaks, ham and chicken here, folks come here for the straightforward fried or broiled, wonderfully fresh fish and other treats from the sea, like the fried east coast oysters and crab cakes. The menu includes a wide choice of hefty seafood combination platters, ranging $13-23 depending on your appetite. Smaller entrees, like broiled bluefish, jumping mullet or spots in-the-round, begin at $9. Alcoholic beverages are limited to wine and beer. In slight contrast to the Sanitary's traditional style, the menu includes the unusual option of microwave-broiled sea scallops, shrimp, oysters and fish, which doesn't brown the food, but helps it retain a surprisingly natural, juicy flavor. Incidentally, the unusual name derives from the folks who first ran the Sanitary, whose lease demanded that they keep the place neat and clean—a tradition that continues today. If you want to cook your own, stop by the adjoining fish market.

Next door, **Blue Peter's Cafe,** 509 Evans St., tel. (252) 808-2904, is a bit more upscale. Owned by the same folks as the Sanitary, this romantic spot offers more elegant waterfront surroundings, with white tablecloths and fresh flowers on the tables. Seating is also available on an outdoor deck over the water. This cafe, which offers a full bar, is a great spot to enjoy a cocktail and a tasty appetizer like the Blue Peter's sautéed crab cakes, served with a low country remoulade ($7). The lunch menu includes a wide selection of sandwiches from burgers ($6) to salads and pasta specials ($3-8). The dinner entrees include creative options like Thai-Creole Sauté, shrimp, sea scallops, and black mussels sautéed in a Thai-Creole sauce.

Even the most ravenous appetites will be sated by the "Fabulous Seafood Buffet," laid out 5-11 p.m. at **Ottis' Restaurant,** overlooking Bogue Sound a couple blocks away on the waterfront at 711 Shepard St., tel. (252) 247-3474. Utilizing fresh fish and seafood from the adjoining fish market, this renowned buffet offers more than 50 items, including fried and steamed shrimp, fried scallops, crab cakes, seafood Alfredo, blackened tuna, and oysters, both fried and on the half shell, along with landlubber fare like hand carved roast beef. This all-you-can-eat buffet costs $17 ($20 if you want to add snow crab legs); kids under 10 pay half-price. Ottis' has a full bar and offers a la carte menu selections beginning at half the price of the buffet. For a scaled-down version of the buffet, stop by for lunch between 11:30 a.m.-2:30 p.m.

Beaufort Restaurants

For waterfront dining with an intimate, friendly atmosphere, try the **Spouter Inn,** 218 Front St., tel. (252) 728-5190. Tables in the warm, wood-paneled interior provide lovely views of Taylor's Creek, and the tables on the small outdoor deck offer the enchanting serenity of dining directly over the water, where you can watch the harbor traffic cruising by and schools of hungry fish compete for morsels of bread tossed over the railing. Open for lunch and dinner, the Spouter Inn offers delightful options either time of day. For lunch, you can choose among a variety of salads and sandwiches ($5-8), including the marvelous Out Island sandwich, a shrimp melt with whole boiled shrimp, portabella mushrooms, covered with melted provolone cheese, with sweet onions, lettuce and tomato on toasted wheat bread ($6.50). If you're up for a gourmet lunch, consider the delectable Admiral's pasta, a combination of sautéed shrimp and scallops simmered in lobster bisque served over linguine. In addition to different nightly specials, dinner entrees change seasonally, including steaks, poultry, and, of course, fresh seafood, like the tantalizing crab cakes, fresh blue crab with a touch of Reggiano, lightly sautéed and served with roasted garlic aioli and your choice of potatoes or basmati rice. Entrees range $14-18.

For a more casual, waterfront dining atmosphere, the bright, spacious dining rooms and outdoor deck of **Loughry's Landing,** 502 Front St., tel. (252) 728-7541, provide grand views of Taylor Creek, the Beaufort harbor, and Carrot Island, across the creek, where you can often see wild horses grazing. In addition to a few land-lubber choices, Loughry's offers Beaufort's widest selection of fresh fish and seafood, fried, broiled, or covered in savory sauces. The prices are among Beaufort's most moderate, with lunch fare running $5-7 and dinner entrees mostly ranging $11-16.

Although it's not on the water, you'll be charmed by the airy ambience of the **Beaufort Grocery Co.,** 115-117 Queen St., tel. (252) 728-3899. Located just off the Beaufort waterfront, behind the Inlet Inn, this humbly named restaurant displays the subtle grace of a French country bistro. Open for lunch, dinner and Sunday brunch, this extremely popular restaurant offers terrific sandwiches for lunch, like the Joshua tree, with tomato, alfalfa spouts, cucumber, mushrooms, onions, cashew butter, smoked gouda cheese and vinaigrette on rye bread ($6), and Mrs. Abby's crabby sandwich, two sautéed crab cakes wedged into a croissant with lettuce, tomato, provolone and spicy remoulade sauce ($8). Dinner entrees, ranging from $16-25, include tempting nightly specials, along with dependable options like the charbroiled veal chop, half standing rack of lamb, and the marvelous

Mediterranean seafood and pasta—sautéed shrimp, scallops, clams and mussels tossed with linguine, roasted garlic, white wine, kale and sun-dried tomatoes ($17).

Beaufort is blessed with several other wonderful restaurants, enough for you to enjoy a different one every night for more than a week. Across the street from the waterfront, the **Front St. Grill,** 419 Front St., tel. (252) 728-3118 serves creative fare, like goat cheese quesadillas, in an American bistro atmosphere. Though it doesn't have a view of the harbor, the friendly yet chic atmosphere provides for pleasurable dining, and the varied menu appeals to a wide variety of tastes. The bar in the front of the bistro is also a popular night spot for locals. Prices range around $6 for lunch, and $11-16 for dinner. Another popular waterfront restaurant lies several blocks north of the historic district, at Town Creek Marina, overlooking Gallant's Channel. As you cross the bridge from Morehead City, **The Veranda** at 232 W. Beaufort Rd., tel. (919) 728-5352, is visible to your left (make a left on Turner Street after the bridge). Closed on Wednesday, the Veranda serves "seasonal American fare with a Southern accent," like the pecan-crusted triggerfish with a lemon cream sauce. The good food and great views of the water make this an extremely popular restaurant, well worth the five-minute drive from the downtown historic district. Lunch ranges $4-7, dinner $15-20. The covered, second-floor deck overlooking the marina is a great spot to enjoy a meal, or a cocktail and a snack, any time of the day or night.

Information

For a bounty of brochures, maps and friendly guidance, stop by the **Crystal Coast Welcome Center** 3409 Arendell St. (US 70), in Morehead City, or call (800) 786-6962 for helpful advice and/or a free, informative travel packet.

WILMINGTON AND THE SOUTH COAST

North Carolina's chief seaport for over two centuries, Wilmington boasts a sizable downtown historic district, comprising more than 200 square blocks. The majestic oak- and sycamore-lined streets invite you to stroll past hundreds of beautifully preserved and restored mansions from the 18th and 19th centuries. Although Wilmington embraces its historic Southern traditions with a languid ease, there's a lot more to do in downtown Wilmington than just sip mint juleps on the veranda. The Wilmington waterfront buzzes with the activity of dozens of interesting shops, delightful restaurants, and energetic live-music venues.

Longtime residents of Wilmington have witnessed a startling transformation of their city during the 1980s and '90s. It all started with the arrival in 1984 of "the movie people," as they're always referred to by the locals. That year, movie mogul Dino DeLaurentiis came to Wilmington to shoot the movie *Firestarter,* starring Drew Barrymore, at nearby Orton Plantation. He became enamored of the area, with its beautiful and diverse locations and ample supply of artists and craftspeople, and immediately built himself a movie studio on the outskirts of downtown, in hopes of making Wilmington a kind of Hollywood East. DeLaurentiis' dream is coming true, and Wilmington is now the third-largest film city in the country, behind Hollywood and New York. With the arrival of the movie people and their cosmopolitan tastes, Wilmingtonians have made a few adjustments to help the visitors feel at home. Local clothiers beefed up their selections of all-black ensembles. Restaurateurs added a continental flair to their Southern fare.

In 1990, the $23 million expansion of New Hanover International Airport encouraged US-Airways (still the only major carrier servicing Wilmington) to expand its service. In 1991, the last links of I-40 were completed, leading into Wilmington. These access-enhancing steps helped engender a vast increase in the number of visitors to the area. These visitors frequently return, drawn by the city's harmonious blend of old Southern manners and civility with cutting-edge Hollywood savoir-faire.

For free information about the Cape Fear area—particularly the Wilmington vicinity—contact the **Cape Fear Coast Convention and Visitors Bureau,** 24 N. Third St., Wilmington, NC 28401, tel. (910) 341-4030 or (800) 222-4757, in Canada (800) 457-8912, or stop in at the office to collect an armful of brochures.

WILMINGTON AND THE SOUTH COAST

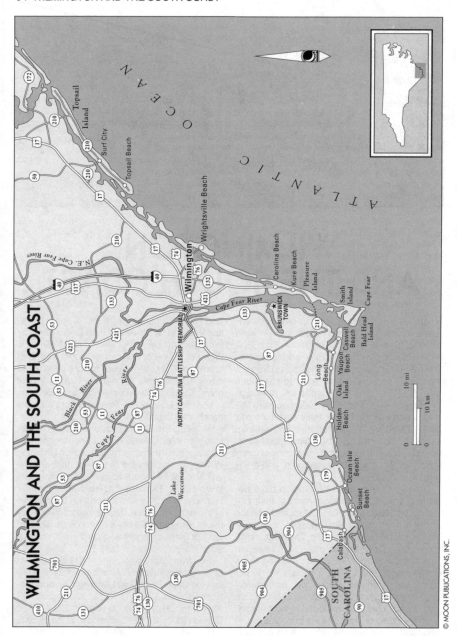

© MOON PUBLICATIONS, INC.

SIGHTS

USS *North Carolina*

Despite its subtle "Measure 32" camouflage paint scheme, you won't have any trouble spotting the massive USS *North Carolina,* docked across the Cape Fear River from the downtown Wilmington waterfront. Commissioned in 1941, this fearsome 728-foot-long floating arsenal took part in every major U.S. naval offensive in the Pacific during World War II, becoming the most decorated U.S. ship of the war. When the *North Carolina* was decommissioned in 1960, then-Governor Terry Sanford called upon the school children of North Carolina to save up their pennies, dimes and nickels to save her from the scrap heap. Their efforts raised $330,000, enough to buy her and bring her to Wilmington. But this terror of the Pacific did not yield to riverside retirement with humble resignation. As a flotilla of tugboats guided her along the Cape Fear River to within sight of her retirement home, she managed one final, defiant stroke of destruction, bursting free of the tugs and ramming straight into the floating restaurant called Fergus' Ark (although the Ark sank to a watery grave, the battleship kindly claimed no human casualties in her last attack).

On self-guided tours, you can enter gun turrets, inspect the bridge, view the crew's quarters, sick bay, engine room, and a host of other interesting spots throughout the dizzying nine decks of this dreadnought, whose crew numbered more than 2,300 during her fighting prime. You have your choice of two self-guided tours, one abbreviated tour that takes about an hour, and the more interesting, in-depth tour that involves more climbing and takes about two hours. Along the tour, there's plenty to read, lots of audio program buttons to push, and authentic shipboard announcements that add further to the sense of realism. Kids really get a bang out of touring this ship, whose main batteries could fire shells weighing as much as a midsize car for a distance of 20 miles. As you leave the ship, don't forget to look for Charley the alligator: Almost as friendly as his tuna namesake, this wild reptile often suns himself on the riverbank just below the exit gangplank, awaiting bits of hot dogs and potato chips from tourists who ignore the clearly posted "Please don't feed the alligators" sign.

Located at the junction of US Routes 17/74/76/421, the battleship is open for tours every day, 8 a.m.-8 p.m. May 16-Sept. 15, and 8 a.m.-5 p.m. the rest of the year, tel. (910) 350-1817 for taped information, tel. (910) 251-5797 for live information.The last tickets are sold an hour before closing time. Admission is $8 for adults, $4 for kids 6-11, and free for children 5 and under. Instead of driving, you can also take a "River Taxi" from the downtown waterfront across the river to the ship, a five-minute ride well worth the couple of bucks it'll cost you.

USS North Carolina

DOWNTOWN WILMINGTON

To Poplar Grove Historic Plantation and Chain Lodging

COAST LINE INN

WILMINGTON RAILROAD MUSEUM

THE COTTON EXCHANGE

WILMINGTON HILTON

BESSIE'S

BATTLESHIP NORTH CAROLINA

PORT CITY JAVA

BELLAMY MANSION MUSEUM OF HISTORY AND DESIGN ARTS

CAPE FEAR MUSEUM

ROY'S RIVERBOAT LANDING

DELUXE

JAMES PLACE/ CAFFE PHOENIX

BURGWIN-WRIGHT HOUSE

THE INN AT ST. THOMAS COURT

GRAYSTONE INN

ROSEHILL INN

CAPONE'S

MICKEY RATZ'

BARBARY COAST

ZEBULON LATIMER HOUSE

THE ICE HOUSE

CROOK'S BY THE RIVER

ST. JOHNS MUSEUM

TASTE OF COUNTRY

CHANDLER'S

CURRAN HOUSE

ELIJAH'S

WHARF

THE PILOT HOUSE

THE VERANDAS

THE WORTH HOUSE

CATHERINE'S INN

SCALE NOT AVAILABLE

To NC Aquarium, Zoo, Fort Fisher, Carolina Beach State Park

To Airlie Gardens

© MOON PUBLICATIONS, INC.

Fort Fisher

During the Civil War, Wilmington remained the last major port open to the Confederacy, thanks almost completely to its protection by Fort Fisher. At the dawn of the war, the Confederacy took control of a spit of land near the mouth of the Cape Fear River, just south of what today is Kure Beach, and constructed the largest earthwork fortifications in the South. Unlike older fortifications built of brick and mortar, Fort Fisher was made mostly of earth and sand, consisting of a series of 25 12-foot-high gun batteries distributed between 15 huge earthen mounds, each rising 32 feet, with interior rooms used as bomb

shelters ("bombproofs") or powder magazines connected by underground passageways.

Though the Union planned several attacks on Fort Fisher, none were deemed feasible until the Union Army and Navy staged a massive, surprise assault on Christmas Eve 1864. After two days of fierce fighting, making little headway, Union commanders withdrew their forces. Realizing this wasn't going to be easy, the Union geared up for another assault. Beginning on January 12, 1865, the Union unleashed the heaviest naval bombardment ever seen up to that time, using 50 ships as well as a land attack of artillery batteries and more than 8,000 Union infantry. On January 15, after six hours of bloody combat, the Union captured Fort Fisher. Within weeks, Union forces overran Wilmington, severing a major supply line of the Confederacy, further guaranteeing its imminent surrender.

Though the fort's construction materials of earth and sand were ideal for absorbing the shock of heavy explosives during the war, it was not exactly ideal with respect to preserving the fort's architectural integrity. Most of the fort has slipped under the ocean, and it takes a bit of imagination to re-create it in your mind's eye. Only one gun emplacement remains at the fort, and visitors can't walk inside any of the remaining bombproofs. Nonetheless, the slide presentation at the visitors center and the half-hour guided tours of the earthworks help this site come alive. Admission is free to the fort, located on US 421 just south of Kure Beach, about two miles from the North Carolina Aquarium at Fort Fisher, tel. (910) 458-5538. Open Mon.-Sat. 9 a.m.-5 p.m. and Sunday 1-5 p.m. April 1-Oct. 31, the fort is closed on Monday Nov. 1-March 31, when its hours are Tues.-Sat. 10 a.m.-4 p.m. and Sunday 1-4 p.m.

Moore's Creek National Battlefield

Administered by the National Park Service, this site comprises a museum, an audio-visual program, and self-guiding history and nature trails through a picturesque battlefield—the scene of the South's first major clash of the Revolutionary War. The decisive outcome of the battle of Moore's Creek ended royal authority in North Carolina and emboldened the legislative assembly to become the first American colony to vote for independence from England. Considering the details of this engagement, it's easy to see why the North Carolina patriots felt so confident. On the morning of February 27, 1776, British General Donald MacDonald was leading his army of Tory Scottish Highlanders from Fayetteville south to join Cornwallis and his army in Wilmington. On the way, at Moore's Creek, they were intercepted by Col. Richard Caswell's patriot

HOORAY FOR WILMYWOOD

In addition to dozens of made-for-TV movies (from the *Mayberry Reunion* to Hallmark Hall of Fame productions including *What the Deaf Man Heard* and *Ellen Foster*) and episodes of TV series including *Matlock* and *The Twilight Zone,* the Wilmington studios have hosted a growing number of feature films. Here's a chronological list—beginning in 1984 and running through 1998—of features filmed in "Wilmywood":

Firestarter	Collision Course	The Crow
Cat's Eye	Track 29	Chasers
Marie: A True Story	Cyborg	My Summer Story
Silver Bullet	Loose Cannons	The Horror Story
Maximum Overdrive	Little Monsters	Radioland Murders
Blue Velvet	Weekend at Bernie's	The Road To Wellville
Manhunter	Everybody Wins	When We Were Colored
Raw Deal	The Exorcist III	Empire Records
No Mercy	Teenage Mutant Ninja Turtles	The Grave
King Kong Lives	Tune In Tomorrow	Lolita
The Bedroom Window	Betsy's Wedding	To Gillian on Her 37th Birthday
Trick or Treat	Sleeping With The Enemy	Traveler
Crimes of the Heart	Alan and Naomi	Bloodmoon
From the Hip	Rambling Rose	Jackal
The Squeeze	Teenage Mutant Ninja Turtles II	Virus
Weeds	29th Street	I Know What You Did
Traxx	Billy Bathgate	Last Summer
Date With An Angel	Amos and Andrew	Shadrach
Hiding Out	Household Saints	
Dracula's Window	The Hudsucker Proxy	

troops, far fewer in number, but armed with the advantage of surprise. And what a surprise it turned out to be. Caswell's minutemen fully earned their nickname, vanquishing the Scots within a few minutes. Only one of Caswell's men was killed and one wounded, while General Macdonald's forces suffered 50 casualties, along with 850 prisoners taken (including the general). Located five miles west of the junction of US 421 and US 210, on US 210, the admission-free park is open daily 9 a.m.-5 p.m.

Historic Home Museums

Strolling along the grand, tree-lined residential streets in Wilmington's downtown historic district, you'll see that most of the homes bear a plaque mounted next to the front door. These plaques tell about the early lives of these houses, most of which have been standing for at least a century and sometimes two. Three of these homes are open to the public, offering guided tours. If you're planning to visit all three, you can purchase a combination ticket for $13 at any of these homes (it costs $16 if you pay separate admissions). The oldest of the house museums, the **Burgwin-Wright House,** 224 Market St., tel. (910) 762-0570, was built in 1770 by John Burgwin, planter, merchant, treasurer of the Colony of North Carolina, and loyal British subject. In 1799, Joshua Grainger Wright (whose family Wrightsville Beach is named after) bought the house, continuing its tradition of opulent elegance. Today, the rooms are meticulously restored to their 18th-century splendor, and the guided tour provides an interesting mix of architectural, interior design, and historical detail, including nifty facts like how British General Cornwallis made this home his headquarters shortly before taking off for his defeat and surrender at Yorktown. Open Tues.-Sat. 10 a.m.-4 p.m.; admission is $5.

The **Zebulon Latimer House,** 126 S. 3rd St., tel. (910) 762-0492, is a gorgeously preserved, Italianate-style mansion. It was home to the Latimer family from 1852, when Zebulon, one of Wilmington's wealthiest merchants, built it, until 1963, when the Lower Cape Fear Historical Society took over and fully restored the home to its 19th-century grandeur. Open Mon.-Fri. 10 a.m.-4 p.m., year-round, and Sat.-Sun. noon-5 p.m. March-Dec. (it's closed weekends in January and February); admission is $5.

Built on the eve of the Civil War, the stately **Bellamy Mansion Museum of History and Design Arts,** 503 Market St., tel. (910) 251-3700, stands as a majestic monument to Wilmington's antebellum opulence. From the grand wraparound porch adorned by 14 two-story Corinthian columns, to the cozy belvedere atop the four-story mansion, this home shines with an unabashed splendor. The guided tours emphasize the architecture, construction, and restoration of the house, as well as the history of its occupants. Two gallery spaces also feature changing exhibits on historic preservations, architectural history, and the design arts. As this edition went to press, extensive archeological research was underway in preparation for the reconstruction of the original slave quarters in the back yard, an addition that should make a tour of the Bellamy Mansion all the more fascinating. Open Wed.-Sat. 10 a.m.-5 p.m., and Sunday 1-5 p.m.; admission is $6.

Among Wilmingtonians who care about history, a heated debate rages concerning the presentation of the region's involvement with slavery. Some feel it's critically important to present a full portrait of antebellum life as it was, while others would prefer to present it as they wish it had been. At **Poplar Grove Historic Plantation,** 10200 US Route 17, nine miles north of Wilmington, tel. (910) 686-4868, tours of the manor house and outbuildings led by costumed guides focus on the history and daily life of the Foy family, who owned this grand estate 1795-1971. Today, the 16-acre site re-creates the life and look of the plantation during the 1800s, when Poplar Grove was a self-sufficient 628-acre estate. In the antebellum years, the plantation's workforce included 64 slaves, but you won't find any slave quarters here today, and the tours tend to shy away from that embarrassing ugliness, concentrating instead on the wealthy owners. Otherwise, the tours, which include craft demonstrations, are exceedingly informative about the workings of the plantation. Open Mon.-Sat. 9 a.m.-5 p.m. and Sunday noon-5 p.m., (closed in January); tours cost $6.

Other Museums

Informative and fun for both adults and kids, the **Cape Fear Museum,** 814 Market St., tel. (910) 341-4350, presents a wealth of information about the history and ecology of the Cape Fear region. From the life-sized diorama of Native Americans catching fish in a salt marsh, to the 16- by 21-foot scale model of the Wilmington waterfront in 1863, the historical exhibits at this museum are first-rate (many of them designed by the same fellow who designed the Holocaust Museum in Washington D.C.). Audio presentations augment many of the exhibits, like the seven-minute, sound-effects-filled tape that augments the 31-foot diorama of the battle of Fort Fisher. Kids will particularly get a kick out of the interactive exhibits in the Michael Jordan Discovery Center, which focuses on the ecosystems of the Cape Fear region and how humans affect the environment. And, speaking of the Wilmington-born-and-raised basketball superstar, who has given very generously to this museum, you'll also get a chance to look at a fun little display case of Michael Jordan memorabilia, which includes some quaint and unusual items like Michael's certificate of perfect attendance from middle school, a modest hinged box he made in wood shop, and a well-worn copy of an elementary sports primer titled *Basketball for Young Champions*. Open Tues.-Sat. 9 a.m.-5 p.m. and Sunday 2-5 p.m.; admission to the museum is $2 for adults, and $1 for kids ages 5-17.

For a more specialized insight into Wilmington's history, stop by the **Wilmington Railroad Museum,** at Red Cross and Water Streets, at the northwest terminus of the river walk, tel. (910) 763-2634. Wilmington, in addition to its early roots as one of America's premier shipping ports, also constituted one of the young nation's pioneering railroad hubs, transferring cargo from ships directly onto trains. In fact, when the Wilmington and Weldon railroad was completed in 1840, its 161 miles of track, stretching from Wilmington north to Weldon, NC (today located along I-95, just south of the Virginia/North Carolina border), comprised the longest continuous railroad line in the world. The museum is a labor of love of the Wilmington Railroad Museum Foundation, a group founded in 1979 by retired railroad employees, their families, businessmen and historians. Although you won't confuse it with the Smithsonian, you'll feel the sincere love of trains that permeates the exhibit spaces, filled with hundreds of bits of railroad memorabilia, from old train schedules, conductors' uniforms, and communications equipment, to the replica of

a 1940s waiting room, complete with the Unfinished Portrait of FDR on the wall.

The entire second floor houses the Cape Fear Model Railroad Club's elaborate model railroad exhibit, featuring three or four simultaneously running model trains chugging through villages and valleys, to the delight of every railroad-magnate wannabe who ever assembled a Lionel train set in the basement. In addition to enjoying the inside exhibits, you can climb onto the 1910 Old Copperhead Engine #250 and stroll through a box car and the furnished Seaboard red caboose, a favorite with kids (and incidentally, available for rental for birthday parties). Open Mon.-Sat. 10 a.m.-5 p.m. and Sunday 1-5 p.m. (closed on Monday Nov.-March); admission to the museum is $3, or $1.50 for kids 6-11.

Housed in three restored, architecturally distinctive buildings dating to 1804, including St. John's church, the **St. John's Museum,** 114 Orange St., tel. (910) 763-0281, highlights the works of two centuries of North Carolina and American masters, including one of the world's major collections of color prints by 19th-century American artist Mary Cassatt, as well as an extensive collection of Jugtown pottery, one of North Carolina's most time-honored crafts. In addition to the permanent and traveling collections, the museum also features the dynamic Art Sales Gallery, representing more than 80 contemporary North Carolina artists and craftsmen. Open Tues.-Sat. 10 am.-5 p.m. and Sunday noon-4 p.m.; admission is $2 for adults and $1 for ages 6-17 (admission is free the first Sunday of each month).

An Aquarium and a Zoo

At the **North Carolina Aquarium at Fort Fisher,** located a couple of miles south of Fort Fisher, near Kure Beach, on US 421, tel. (910) 458-7468, you'll get to view, and, in some cases interact with, critters living in the waters of the Cape Fear region. The state-run Fort Fisher aquarium packs a lot of information and fun into its dozen-tank display, including several hands-on exhibits. From the 20,000-gallon Shark Tank and the ever-popular touch tank, where kids thrill to handle crabs and various mollusks and bivalves, to the outdoor nature trails where you might spot a few alligators, the aquarium is a great spot to entertain yourself and any kids for a hour or so. Open daily 9 a.m.-7 p.m. June-Aug., and 9 a.m.-5 p.m. the rest of the year; admission is $3 for adults, $1 for kids. You might want to call ahead to time your visit so that you can take advantage of the numerous special programs and events offered by the aquarium, from canoe trips to shark-feeding times.

If you have kids in the backseat, and you're driving along US 421 between Wilmington and Carolina Beach, you might as well just give in, and stop at the **Tote-Em-In Zoo,** 5811 Carolina Beach Rd., tel. (910) 791-0472. Located about 10 miles southeast of Wilmington, this kitschy tourist attraction first opened in 1953. Entrance doors lay inside the jaws of a 15-foot-high concrete model of a lion's face. After you enter the lion's mouth, you can stroll along outside walkways that lead through the five-acre zoo, past exotic animals like zebras, camels, tigers, leopards, jaguars, bear-cats, and lots of monkeys and exotic birds, to name just a few of the zoo's more than 130 species. In addition to the menagerie-style zoo, the Tote-Em-In includes a gift shop and two indoor museums, one of exotic mounted specimens, and the other an eclectic collection of artifacts from around the world. Open daily from early March through mid-November; admission is $5 for adults, $3 for kids 2-11.

canna (Cannaceae)

Gardens and Parks

Two lush gardens lie within half an hour's drive of Wilmington. The **Airlie Gardens,** on Airlie Road off US 76, two miles west of Wrightsville Beach, tel. (910) 763-9991, are open March 23-Oct. 31. Dazzling year-round, with native and exotic plants, and many rare species, the gardens are most celebrated from the end of March to the beginning of May, when the blooming azaleas create explosions of color. During this azalea extravaganza, admission is $6, with children under 10 admitted free. After the first week of May, admission is $5. Although strolling through the 20 acres is the preferred way of experiencing the gardens,

you can also drive through a good bit of them. The other grand gardens in the area lie about 20 miles southeast of Wilmington, off NC 133, at the **Orton Plantation Gardens,** tel. (910) 371-6851, open daily March through November. Something's always blooming amidst these formal and natural gardens, which feature spectacular displays of native plants like azaleas, camellias, magnolia, crape myrtle, oleander and hydrangea. Admission is $8 for adults, $3 for kids 6-12.

At the rugged **Carolina Beach State Park,** just off US 421, on Dow Road a mile north of the town of Carolina Beach, tel. (910) 458-8206, you can explore five miles of hiking trails leading through a remarkable diversity of maritime forest, swamps, tidal marshes, and sand dunes. A mecca for birdwatchers, the park is also home to rare flora, including the celebrated Venus flytrap and other carnivorous plants. Admission to the park is free.

TOMMY DAUGHTRY

Tours

Wilmington abounds with touring opportunities, by land, sea and air. For an intimate, entertaining and informative introduction to the historic streets of downtown Wilmington, join guide Bob Jenkins for one of his **Wilmington Adventure Walking Tours,** tel. (910) 763-1785, embarking from the riverfront at Market and Water Streets Mon.-Sat. at 10 a.m. and 2 p.m. April-October. Jenkins, a tall, slim fellow with a straw hat and cane, who has personally witnessed more than 70 years of Wilmington history, leads you at a brisk pace through the streets of the downtown historic district, filling you in on centuries of history. The tour takes about an hour and costs $10.

If you'd prefer to rest your legs and let a horse do the work, hop on a **horse-drawn carriage or trolley** for a narrated tour from the folks at Springbrook Farms, tel. (910) 251-8889. Originating at the same spot as Jenkins' tour, at Market and Water Streets on the riverfront, the half-hour rides cost $8 for adults, $4 for kids under 12. Hours April-Oct. are Tues.-Sun. 10 a.m.-10 p.m. In March, November, and December, hours are Friday 7-10 p.m., Saturday 11 a.m.-10 p.m. and Sunday 11 a.m.-4 p.m. Call ahead for rides in January and February.

Several outfits conduct a variety of **sightseeing, dinner, and entertainment cruises** along the waters of the Wilmington area. Docked by the Hilton on the downtown Wilmington riverwalk, the *Henrietta II,* tel. (910) 343-1611 or (800) 676-0162, North Carolina's only true sternwheeler riverboat, offers a full range of cruises, including 90-minute, narrated sightseeing cruises, two-hour sunset dinner cruises, two-and-a-half-hour dinner and dancing cruises, and 90-minute moonlight cruises. Costs range $9-35. At the marina in Carolina Beach, **Winner Cruise Boats,** tel. (910) 458-5356, provides a similar selection, including very popular dancing cruises in the evenings. At Wrightsville Beach, **Blockade Runner Scenic Cruises,** at the Blockade Runner Resort Dock, tel. (910) 350-2628, provides harbor cruises and sunset cruises on its 40-foot pontoon boat ($10 and $18), and terrific **nature excursions to uninhabited Masonboro Island** guided by a marine biologist from the NC Aquarium ($25). Call ahead for reservations for these popular nature excursions.

For a bird's eye view of Wilmington's coastal region, the seaplanes of **Kitty Hawk Air** at the Wilmington International Airport, tel. (910) 791-3034, will deliver unforgettable coastal views, as well as a thrilling water landing. The low-altitude flights cost $25 per person for a half-hour flight, and $50 for a one-hour tour. **Air Wilmington,** tel. (910) 763-0146, provides similar sightseeing flights, without the water landings, at slightly lower rates.

For something a bit different, focusing on Wilmington's recent emergence as one of the nation's biggest movie meccas, **Silver Screen Tours,** 1223 N. 23rd St., tel. (910) 675-8479, will take you on a behind-the-scenes tour of **Screen Gems Studios.** The walking tours, which last 90 minutes to two hours, take you through portions of the eight sound stages and the three-block-long, four-story backlot, a marvelous structure with tall, thin facades capable of standing in convincingly for just about any big-city downtown. Enthusiastic and knowledgeable tour-leader James Crews will fill you in on Wilmington's meteoric rise into prominence in the film industry, as well as lots of details about current productions. Tours don't include any glitzy special effects, like King Kong or Jaws lunging out at you, but you're sure to emerge from the studio with a liberal sprinkling of movie magic. The tours, which began running in late 1997, are conducted on Saturday and Sunday at 10 a.m., noon and 2 p.m. This schedule is subject to change, so you should call ahead. The cost is $10.

RECREATION

The most popular recreational activities in the Wilmington area are swimming and sunbathing on the inviting, uncrowded sandy beaches, particularly Wrightsville, Carolina and Kure beaches. But if you need a break from the languorous demands of sun-worshipping, you'll find some recreational variety, particularly if you like to fish or golf.

Fishing

In addition to surf fishing, which is popular all along the Cape Fear coast, the almost two dozen piers along the coast are favorite hangouts of anglers in search of filling up a cooler with bluefish, flounder, spot, king mackerel and other kinds of fish. We won't bother listing them all here, but suffice it to say that from Topsail Beach in the north to Sunset Beach in the south, you're never far away from a fishing pier. The cost to fish at the piers ranges $3-5, and most are open for night fishing. If you seek the adventure of reeling in big game, like blue marlin, tuna, or shark, you'll want to take a day to fish in the Gulf Stream. The hubs for fishing charters in the Cape Fear region are the marinas in Wrightsville and Carolina Beach, where you can take your pick among dozens of boats owned and operated by experienced captains. Though there are many great charters available, we'll list just a few here who provide toll-free numbers. In Wrightsville Beach, **Sea Lady Charters,** tel. (800) 242-2493, books several boats. In Carolina Beach, try **Flapjack & Gung Ho,** tel. (800) 288-FISH, **Large Time Charters,** tel. (800) 582-5524, **Musicman, tel. (800) 294-5482, or** Sea Filly, tel. (800) 732-3455.

Golf

If you wanted to play a different course every day, you'd have to stay more than three weeks to exhaust the supply within an hour's drive of downtown Wilmington. Listed here are some of the more celebrated courses in the area, but it's hardly an exhaustive list of the marvelous courses permeating the Cape Fear coast. All greens fees below include cart rental. About six miles north of Wilmington, **Porter's Neck Plantation and Country Club,** 8403 Vintage Club Circle, tel. (910) 686-1177 or (800) 423-5695, has earned the distinction of being named North Carolina's #1 coastal golf course by *Golf Digest*. Winding through woods and a private residential area alongside the Intracoastal Waterway, this beauty, designed by Tom Fazio, challenges you with sand and water hazards galore. Greens fees March-Nov. range $55-75, and $10-20 less the rest of the year.

For a feeling of extraordinary exclusivity, it's hard to beat the renowned course at the **Bald Head Island Club,** tel. (910) 457-7310 or (800) 234-1666. Designed by George Cobb, this breathtaking course curls through marshes and maritime forest and features several stunning oceanside fairways and greens. One of the things that makes playing Bald Head Island's isolated course so unique is how you get there. Accessible only by ferry, the entire island is devoid of cars; residents and visitors travel the few streets on bicycles and in golf carts, which lends an unusually golf-friendly atmosphere to the whole island. One round of golf, including the roundtrip ferry ride, costs around $95 during the peak summer season and drops as low as $55 in the winter. Call the 800 number above to schedule tee times, make ferry reservations, and inquire about golf-getaways, including rental properties, on Bald Head Island.

The southern beaches between Bald Head Island and the South Carolina border boast a host of terrific coastal courses, among which two stand out particularly. Both are near the little island of Sunset Beach, next to the South Carolina border, about 45 miles southwest of Wilmington. The **Oyster Bay Golf Links,** tel. (910) 579-3528 or (800) 552-2660, selected as Best New Resort Course of 1983 and currently ranked in the Second 25 of America's 75 Best Public Courses by *Golf Digest,* provides glorious vistas along the Intracoastal Waterway, plenty of sand, and some unusual oyster shell hazards. Greens fees begin at $55 during the summer, dipping to $45 during the winter. The other standout is the **Sea Trail Plantation,** tel. (910) 579-4350 or (800) 624-6601, which includes three superb courses. Of the three, the most renowned is the Rees Jones Course, one of 100 American courses meriting *Golf Digest's* coveted "Great Value" designation. Although it is not oceanside, being about a mile from the beach, you'll be around plenty of water on the Jones course, with its 11 water holes. Greens fees are $50 in the summer, $40 in the winter.

SHOPPING

By far, the best shopping in the area lies near the waterfront in downtown Wilmington. From the river north to Third Street, between Ann and Walnut Streets, you'll find a diverse range of stores, from antique shops that look like vast, cluttered attics transported directly from the 1800s, to cutting-edge, New York City-style boutiques, where the rule seems to be "the less merchandise, the better." In the latter, you may be able to spot two or three outfits inconspicuously displayed in a 500-square-foot space, perhaps augmented by a little area for cosmetics and perfume.

At the northern end of the downtown Riverwalk, **The Cotton Exchange,** 321 N. Front St., tel. (910) 343-9896, occupies eight buildings that mostly served as warehouses and factories for over a century, before being converted in 1976 to a shopping complex housing 33 specialty shops and restaurants connected by brick walkways and open-air courtyards. The shops run the gamut from toy stores to bookstores, bead shops to jewelers, fine art galleries to gift shops featuring sculptures made from seashells. At the southern end of the downtown waterfront, **Chandler's Wharf,** at the corner of Ann and Water Streets, includes about a dozen specialty shops, located conveniently next to the premier riverfront restaurants in town, Elijah's and The Pilot House.

Antique hounds should start their exploration of Wilmington's bountiful antique scene by strolling along the five square blocks bounded by

Front, Water, Walnut and Dock Streets, where, at last count, ten marvelous antique dealers sell their eclectic wares. Another, smaller, hub for antiquers is located on Market Street between 16th and 17th Streets, home to the **Cape Fear Antiques Center,** 1606 Market St., tel. (910) 763-1837, the largest multi-dealer antique store in Wilmington.

ACCOMMODATIONS

Downtown Bed and Breakfasts

The intimate lodgings provided by more than two dozen downtown bed-and-breakfast inns are an ideal way to experience the gracious style of this historic and elegant port city.

For sheer grandeur, the **Graystone Inn,** 100 S. Third St., tel. (910) 763-2000, tops the list. Completed in 1906 as a private residence for one of Wilmington's wealthiest industrial magnates, this neoclassical revival stone mansion with soaring Ionic columns could easily be mistaken for an embassy. Located within easy walking distance of all of Wilmington's waterfront attractions, the Graystone has served as a popular film set, as well as a favored lodging for movie stars filming at nearby Screen Gems Studios. You'll get your first taste of the stately sumptuousness of this magnificent mansion as you enter the front door and stand in the marble-floored foyer, gazing up at the hand-carved oak staircase rising three stories high. The "common rooms" exude an equally uncommon grandeur, including the spacious, mahogany-paneled library. The large guest rooms, and even more spacious suites, are all elegantly appointed and equipped with phones, full baths and televisions. Innkeepers Paul and Yolanda Bolda provide delicious full breakfasts and beverage service throughout the day, including wine and sherry at night. The rates range $165-200 during the summer, gradually declining to $145-165 in the winter.

Just a few doors down, the **Rosehill Inn,** 114 S. Third St., tel. (910) 815-0250 or (800) 815-0250, once was the home of Henry Bacon, Jr., architect of the Lincoln Memorial in Washington, D.C. Built in 1848 and redone in 1909, Rosehill has an interior architecture that combines the styles of both periods, with a mix of Queen

Anne and Victorian antiques and furnishings from the 1920s and 1930s. Gracious innkeepers Laurel Jones and Dennis Fitsch have decorated each of the six guest rooms in an individual style, though all are elegant, with king- or queen-size beds, comforters, and plush robes to use while staying at Rosehill. Though all rooms have private bathrooms, not all have bathtubs, so if you plan on a luxurious hot bath, be sure to specify your preference. A full breakfast is included in the rates, which range $90-165.

From the Victorian turrets and lace curtains to the spacious outdoor porches and gardens, the **Worth House,** 412 S. Third St., tel. (910) 762-8562 or (800) 340-8559, offers the ultimate in Victorian B&Bs in Wilmington. Period antiques and paintings pervade the parlor, library, formal dining room, and seven guest rooms. Each room includes a sitting area, and some feature a fireplace and/or an enclosed porch. Innkeepers Francie and John Miller provide a full breakfast, and coffee, tea and soft drinks are available throughout the day. Rates range $80-120.

The graceful, Italianate **Catherine's Inn,** 410 S. Front St., tel. (910) 251-0863 or (800) 476-0723, built in 1884, is furnished like a grand, old-fashioned Southern home, with a comfortable mix of Queen Anne and Victorian antiques in the common rooms and three guest rooms. The gracious hosts, Catherine and Walter Ackiss, provide a full breakfast in the morning, along with liquors and turn-down service at night. In addition to the open-air, wraparound front porch and two-story, screened back porch, Catherine's features perhaps the most scenic backyard of any Wilmington B&B, a sloping back lawn with gardens and a gazebo, complete with views of the Cape Fear River. Rates range $85-99.

If you like staying in B&Bs, but don't particularly desire an ambiance characterized by antique furnishings, try the **Front Street Inn,** 215 S. Front St., tel. (910) 762-6442. Proprietors Stefany and Jay Rhodes have created a peaceful haven in the heart of the historic district that strikes a harmonious balance of providing friendly service without being intrusive, making this inn a favorite of business travelers, vacationers, and movie people alike. Each room and suite is decorated in a theme—Nutcracker, Monet, Pearl Buck, Kipling, Segovia, O'Keeffe, Molly Brown, and Cousteau. Though the names of these

rooms and suites might imply an excess of kitschiness, the furnishings and decor are tastefully understated. Some rooms include balconies overlooking the courtyard garden and the Cape Fear River. The Front Street Inn was the 1996 winner of Wilmington's Historic Preservation Award. Some suites include fireplaces, jacuzzis, full kitchens, and wet bars. All rooms include a healthy continental breakfast in the morning and soothing libations in the evening at the inn's Sol y Sombra bar and breakfast room. Rates range $95-165. Expensive to Luxury.

Three blocks down the street, toward downtown, three inviting guest rooms star at the 1909 **James Place,** 9 S. Front St., tel. (910) 251-0999 or (800) 303 9444, where you can relax in the private hot tubs or in a rocker on the front porch. Rates are $55-95. The **Curran House,** 312 S. Third St., tel. (910) 763-6603 or (800) 763-6603, a Queen Anne beauty from the late 1800s, provides three immaculate guest rooms decorated with English and American antiques. Rates range $70-85.

The Verandas, 202 Nun St., tel. (910) 251-2212, is a gorgeously restored 1853 Victorian Italianate mansion that deservedly won 1997 Interior Restoration Award from the Historic Wilmington Foundation. All eight corner rooms feature state-of-the-art amenities, including private climate control and modem jacks, in addition to an on-site fax machine and copier. Rates range $110-165.

If the listings above don't suit your fancy, or if they're all booked, and you still would like to experience the gracious grandeur of Wilmington through the lodgings of a first-rate B&B, call the Cape Fear Coast Convention and Visitors bureau at (800) 222-4757 for further guidance. The folks there will steer you towards more than a dozen other historic Wilmington B&Bs in homes dating from the mid-1800s to early 1900s, whose elegant ambience and professional, courteous innkeepers won't disappoint discerning B&B aficionados.

Other Downtown Lodgings

Surprisingly, only two lodgings sit directly on the Cape Fear riverfront in downtown Wilmington. The **Coast Line Inn,** 503 Nutt St., tel. (910) 763-2800, a few dozen yards from the northern terminus of the downtown Riverwalk, boasts a river view from each of its 50 clean and comfortable rooms, some with sitting rooms. Decorated with historic photographs of the Wilmington riverfront from the early 1900s, the rooms aren't especially spacious, but they do provide a relatively good deal for downtown accommodations—particularly considering the river views—with rates ranging from $85-100 during the summer to $75-90 in the off-season. Expensive.

At the northern terminus of the Riverwalk, downtown Wilmington's other riverfront hotel looms over the Cape Fear River like the concrete convention center that it is. With 178 rooms, half overlooking the river, the **Wilmington Hilton,** 301 N. Water St., tel. (910) 763-5900 or (800) 445-8667, provides peerless riverfront amenities in downtown Wilmington, including a swimming pool, poolside jacuzzi, on-site restaurant and lively hotel lounge, and an exercise room. Rates range $145-170 during the summer, gradually declining to $120-155 during the winter. Premium-Luxury.

The **Inn at St. Thomas Court,** 101 S. Second St., tel. (910) 343-1800 or (800) 525-0909, is a small luxury inn that caters to guests staying for an extended period, whether for business or vacation. Located in the heart of the historic district within easy walking distance of all downtown attractions, this tasteful professional inn features one- and two-bedroom suites, most with balconies overlooking a small but well-designed garden and courtyard area. Many of the spacious, two-room suites are bi-level. The Inn often provides a short-term home for guests involved with Wilmington's burgeoning film industry, so don't be surprised if you see a familiar face from television or the big screen. The suites are individually decorated in styles from "Country French" to nautical themes; several have classic movie themes like *Gone With the Wind* and *Casablanca*. Some suites are equipped with kitchenettes, washer/dryers, wet bars, jacuzzi tubs, VCRs, fireplaces, and data ports. Amenities include a daily breakfast basket, delivered to your door with the morning newspaper, an exercise room, a book and video library, and business services including faxing, copying, and shipping. From March to November, rates begin at $135 for a one-bedroom and $210 for a two-bedroom suite. Rates decline a bit during the winter. Premium-Luxury.

Wilmington Motels

The Wilmington area teems with motels, most of them chain operations. One of the exceptions—and one of the only accommodations in the area that accepts pets—is the **Waterway Lodge,** close to Wrightsville Beach (though still technically in Wilmington) at 7246 Wrightsville Ave., tel. (910) 256-3771. The three-story motel offers a swimming pool and 42 clean and comfortable units, 15 of them efficiencies. Rates range $80-100 during the summer, and dip as low as $45 during the winter.

You'll find motel chains galore along Market Street (U.S. 17/74), a five- to 10-minute drive from either downtown Wilmington or Wrightsville Beach. All of the following corporate motels lie along this busy stretch of roadway and provide the typical chain amenities, including, unless specified otherwise, a swimming pool. The rate descriptions, as throughout this guide, are: Inexpensive=$35-60, Moderate=$60-85, Expensive=$85-110, Premium=$110-150, Luxury=$150+. Where more than one rate description is listed, the more expensive rates apply to the summer season.

Best Western Carolinian, 2916 Market St., tel. (910) 763-4653 or (800) 528-1234. Moderate.

Days Inn, 5040 Market St., tel. (910) 799-6300 or (800) 325-2525. Inexpensive-Moderate.

Fairfield Inn By Marriott, 4926 Market St., tel. (910) 791-8850 or (800) 348-6000. Inexpensive-Moderate.

Hampton Inn, 5107 Market St., tel. (910) 395-5045 or (800) 426-7866. Moderate-Expensive.

Holiday Inn of Wilmington, 4903 Market St., tel. (910) 799-1440 or (800) 465-4329. Inexpensive-Expensive.

Howard Johnson Plaza Hotel, 5032 Market St., tel. (910) 392-1101 or (800) 654-4656. Moderate.

Rodeway Inn, 2929 Market St., tel. (910) 763-3318 or (800) 228-2000. No pool. Inexpensive.

FOOD AND DRINK

Wilmington is loaded with terrific restaurants of all types, hip or traditional, sophisticated or "downhome." You'll find most of the establishments described below within the concentrated culinary wealth of the convenient downtown historic district.

If you're looking for some great seafood with peerless views of the Cape Fear River, you should proceed directly to Water and Ann Streets, on the riverfront. There, you'll find two Wilmington culinary institutions, managed by the same folks, both open for lunch, dinner and Sunday brunch. The slightly more formal of the two restaurants, the **Pilot House,** tel. (910) 343-0200, occupies the gorgeously restored interiors of the Craig House (circa 1870), decorated with antiques and reproduction furniture, and a covered outdoor deck over the flowing waters of the Cape Fear River. The front of the menu includes a quote from Jonathan Swift, "They say a fish should swim thrice . . . first it should swim in the sea, then it should swim in butter, and last, sirrah, it should swim in good claret." That aptly describes the attitude of the Pilot House, which provides polished service and superbly prepared cuisine in an air of luxury and leisure. For starters, try the famed Carolina bisque, a sumptuous soup with shrimp, scallops, fish and clams in cream, fresh herbs, butter, sherry and clam stock ($3 a cup, $4 a bowl). Lunch selections run $6-9 and range from seafood delights like shrimp Newburg to a variety of sandwiches, like the grilled salmon BLT or grilled portabella mushroom sandwich with fresh mozzarella cheese, tomato, red onion, sprouts, and avocado mayonnaise. Dinner entrees ($16-23) include a wide variety of fish and seafood prepared with a southern twist, like the sweet potato-crusted grouper or the crunchy catfish with grits. Landlubber entrees include more conventional options like rack of lamb, filet mignon, and pan-seared duck breast, along with some continental fare with a southern flair, like the delightful veal scallopine with fried green tomatoes.

Next door at **Elijah's,** tel. (910) 343-1448, you have your choice of two restaurants-in-one, both overlooking the river. The "Elijah's Restaurant" side has the feel of an old ship's dining room and lounge, with nautical prints and appointments, white tablecloths, wood paneling and dark green carpet. Serving lunch and dinner, the restaurant side offers a lunch menu of salads and sandwiches ranging $4-7. Dinner entrees ($12-19) include pastas like shrimp Alfredo, steak and chicken dishes, and a full range of relatively straightforward fish and seafood, like shrimp panned in butter, crab cakes, catfish, and soft shell crabs. The other side of Elijah's, called "The Oyster Bar," is open 11:30 a.m.-midnight. This festive, informal eatery includes indoor seating at a spacious bar, indoor tables, and an airy outdoor deck built over the waters of the Cape Fear River. Except for salads, burgers, and a chicken sandwich, everything on the Oyster Bar menu features fish or seafood, from the fried oyster sandwiches ($7) to the renowned Carolina Bucket, a sumptuous seafood feast including steamed clams, snow crab legs, oysters, mussels, shrimp and sausage with new potatoes and corn ($18 for one, $32 for two). This is also the place to gorge yourself at a raw bar. Oysters and clams, steamed or on the half shell, run $5 for a half dozen, $8 for a dozen. If you've got a powerful hankering for steamed oysters, or want to share with a few other folks, go for the bucket of steamed oysters for $22.

Another North Carolina institution, imported from the Triangle, is **Crook's by the River,** 138 S. Front St., tel. (910) 762-8898, affiliated with Crook's Corner in Chapel Hill, where, in the 1970s, legendary restaurateur and chef Bill Neal began his influential experiments in making traditional Southern fare more sophisticated and appealing to cosmopolitan palates. This hip and truly Southern restaurant features intimate dining rooms and a spacious deck with views of the Cape Fear River. On the cover of Crook's menu, you'll see the quote "simplicity to extravagance, but always the best!" We agree that this aptly describes the gastronomic pleasures you're sure to enjoy here. Although their signature dish, shrimp and grits, may sound humble, it's absolutely sensational, with fresh shrimp saut_ed with bacon, mushrooms, and scallions, served over a bed of creamy cheese grits ($17). The menu changes seasonally (though the shrimp-and-grits dish is always available), but there are always plenty of savory choices for folks looking for splendid, creative dishes, like the Explorer Plate, with braised venison tenderloin and Carolina quail with port wine sauce, accompanied by potato pancakes, tomato relish, alligator and Andouille sausage, and collard greens ($18). Open daily for dinner 5-10:30 p.m., and for Sunday brunch 11 am.-2 p.m., Crook's also serves a late night menu with lighter fare 10:30 p.m.-2 a.m.

Roy's Riverboat Landing, at Market and Water Streets, tel. (910) 763-7227, occupies the Eiler's Building, a former dry goods warehouse built in 1857. Today, Roy's is decorated in traditional Queen Anne style, with white tablecloths and blue and white china. The two downstairs rooms are a little less formal, with bare wood floors and casual seating areas with views of Market Street. One of these rooms features an understatedly elegant bar. For a romantic treat, reserve one of the private balcony tables for two, providing an expansive view of the Cape Fear River. Although fish and seafood are the specialties here, like lobster Imperiale and grouper Royale, Roy's also provides plenty of other options, including steaks, quail, lamb, veal, and vegetarian dishes, ranging $14-24. Open daily for dinner, Roy's is also open for lunch on weekends ($6-12).

If you've always thought of German cuisine as consisting of heavy sausages and mounds of sauerkraut, the **Nuss Strasse Cafe,** in the Cotton Exchange at Grace and Front Streets, tel. (910) 763-5523, will disabuse you of that notion. While your meal may not be classified as "lite" fare, it will be fresh, authentically prepared, and delicious. The Nuss Strasse's atmosphere is pure German, complete with cuckoo clocks, paintings of alpine scenes, exposed wood beams, red carpeting, quaint little tables, and waitstaff dressed in alpine garb, right out of a St. Pauli Girl ad. All of the schnitzel dishes are sensational, prepared with veal or pork loin. If you are in the mood for a sausage-fest, you won't leave feeling hungry after consuming the wurst platter, which includes Oktoberfest bratwurst, knockwurst, and kielbasa for $12. Needless to say, there's a full selection of German beers, on tap and in bottles. If possible, save room for the luscious desserts, which you can view in the pastry case at the entrance. Open for lunch and dinner, the prices range from $6-9 for lunch, and $11-17 for dinner.

Caffé Phoenix, 9 S. Front St., tel. (910) 343-1395, has a soothing, sophisticated appeal, with wood floors, high ceilings, and black-and-white color scheme, embellished by lots of plants, paintings by up-and-coming artists, and tables with candles and fresh flowers. The menu leans towards Italian, with appetizers like the tempting Torta Rustica, an Italian egg and cheese pie with four cheeses, egg, vegetables, and Italian meats or seafood. In addition to nightly specials, entrees include fish selections like the delicious horseradish-encrusted salmon with dill-butter sauce; a New York strip steak with wild mushroom risotto cakes; and Italian delights from individual-sized pizzas to a broad selection of pastas. Appetizers range $6-8, entrees $12-18 for dinner. Serving dinner seven nights a week, and lunch ($5-10) Mon.-Sat., the Caff_ Phoenix is also one of Wilmington's more popular late-night spots for folks seeking a calm, soft-jazz atmosphere.

Another Italian-leaning restaurant, the **Deluxe,** 114 Market St., tel. (910) 251-0333, exudes a warm feel, with its wood floors, modern stained glass, exposed brick wall, iron light fixtures, and surprisingly comfortable wooden chairs. Fresh flowers and candles on each table complement the warm ambience. Open Mon.-Sat. for lunch and dinner, the Deluxe offers lunch selections featuring a variety of sandwiches, salads, and pastas for $4-8. The dinner menu changes seasonally, but you can depend on a tempting selection of appetizers ($5-8), like the tequila-lime gravlax, roasted garlic prawns, and the spicy, crackling calamari. Entrees ($10-17) include a variety of seafood, chicken, beef, pork and lamb dishes, like the pan-roasted loin of lamb, stuffed with gorgonzola cheese and roasted garlic, with a demiglace of rosemary and port wine. The Deluxe also serves a wide selection of pasta dishes, like the Tuscan seafood pasta, with shrimp and fish sautéed with garlic, basil and roma tomatoes. Save room for the delicious desserts, like the chocolate créme brûlée, or praline mocha Napoleon (both $5). On Sunday, the Deluxe serves a popular brunch, featuring standards like eggs Benedict and eggs Florentine, and more unusual choices like smoked salmon in brioche, and the sophisticated-yet-homestyle crab and country ham *vol au vent,* with sautéed backfin crabmeat, ham, and fresh asparagus in a light cream sauce served on a buttermilk biscuit (all of the above cost $8).

Bocci, 811 Mercer Ave., tel. (910) 763-0067, is such a popular favorite and such a splendid restaurant that it's worth the trip a bit farther afield. Specializing in Mediterranean, wood-fired cuisine, Bocci has a fitting Mediterranean atmosphere, with tile floors and an extended mural running along the walls, along with a little reminder that you're still in the South—reproduction Chippendale chairs. Wood-fired specialties, ranging $12-20, feature meaty entrees like steaks and the brochette of lamb, chicken and sausage, or the fresh fish catch of the day, dressed with marinades of your choice, including virgin olive oil, garlic, lemon, oregano, tropical fruit chutney, soy, ginger, lime, serrano chilis or Cajun spices. Bocci also provides a full medley of pastas ($9-14), from traditional dishes like linguine pomodoro, to novel Bocci creations like cannelloni—fresh pasta stuffed with sirloin, spinach, herbs, and three cheeses, topped with a béchamel and basil tomato sauce. If your appetite isn't quite so ravenous, you can choose among a variety of appetizers, salads, or "small plates" ranging $5-7, including such savory options as blackened Carolina oysters with pancetta and spinach, finished with light pesto and hollandaise, or the wood-grilled portabella mushroom with warm, toasted goat cheese and eggplant and olive relish. Open Mon.-Sat. for dinner only; reservations are recommended. To get there from the downtown historic district, take Market Street toward I-40 and Wrightsville Beach, to just past 30th Street and the Best Western Carolinian motel on your right.

Take a right at the light, onto Mercer Street. Bocci is located at the second traffic light, on your left, at the corner of Mercer Street and Wrightsville Avenue.

For true, down home Southern country cooking, you'll never leave hungry at the all-you-can-eat buffet at **Taste of Country**, 226 S. Front St., tel. (910) 343-9888. This friendly and casual restaurant, with the feel and aromas of grandma's house, offers a huge buffet with beef, fish, seafood, and poultry, in addition to sides like potatoes, butter beans, collards and turnip greens, as well as several desserts. At $6 for lunch and $8 for dinner, your wallet won't feel much lighter than your stomach when you leave.

For a jolt of good, strong coffee, and a place to relax, you'll feel welcome at **Port City Java**, 7 N. Front St., tel. (910) 762-5282. Its quirky decor of mismatched tables and chairs and comfortable couches provide a soothing place to rest your feet, read the paper, or just watch the pedestrians strolling along Front Street. In addition to the extensive selection of coffees and teas, served hot or iced, Port City Java also offers frappes and freezes, fresh juice and smoothies, and an assortment of cookies, biscotti, scones, muffins, bagels, cake, and pie, all under $5. The coffeehouse opens daily at 6:30 a.m., and closes Sun.-Thurs at 10 p.m. and Fri.-Sat. at midnight.

NIGHTLIFE

If you're looking for a popular bar to enhance some evening imbibing, Wilmington offers you dozens of choices. The Caff_ Phoenix and Crook's By the River, described above, both provide a stylish atmosphere for enjoying a late night cocktail. On the other side of the style spectrum, the **Barbary Coast**, 116 S. Front St., tel. (910) 762-8996, serving beer and wine only, draws a hefty college crowd and others who don't choose a bar based on the pristine cleanliness of its bathrooms. **Bessie's**, 133 N. Front St., tel. (910) 762-0003, offers the widest variety of entertainment we've encountered. It's actually two bars; one is pub style, and the other includes a half dozen pool tables. Live performances occur in one or the other on most nights of the week. The usual schedule features a mix of dancing to live bands and DJs on Tuesday and Thurs.-Sat., a live comedy troupe on Wednesday, live theater on Sunday, and, on Monday nights, the continuing saga of the live, satiric soap opera *Shelf Life*, based on local Wilmington happenings. Cover charges usually run $3-4.

You'll never pay a cover at **The Ice House**, 115 S. Water St., tel. (910) 763-2084. A thriving Wilmington institution, located just across Water Street from the Cape Fear River, the Ice House features live bands every night and most afternoons during the summer, when the spacious outdoor patio throbs to the beat of blues, rock, jazz, and even some folk tunes. Often packed with music lovers of all ages, the Ice House is a great place to listen to music under the sun or stars and enjoy beer, wine, and a snack like steamed shrimp, raw oysters, or a hefty bratwurst. The Ice House is open daily year-round, beginning at lunch; the patio closes during cold weather, but the inside still hops to energetic tunes, with live bands usually appearing Thursday, Friday, and Saturday.

If you're looking for a more disco-oriented dance floor, complete with high-tech lights and sound systems that will make your body quake to the bass beat, **Capone's**, 107 S. Front St., tel. (910) 251-1623, won't let you down. Neither will **Mickey Ratz'**, a few doors down at 115 S. Front St., tel. (910) 251-1289, which attracts a largely, but not exclusively, gay crowd. DJs provide most of the music at both clubs, though live bands appear occasionally.

Last, and largest, the cavernous **Palomino Club**, 2649 Carolina Beach Rd., tel. (910) 452-0102, encompasses more than 25,000 square feet and frequently hosts big-name country acts. On Tuesday, Thursday, and Sunday, line-dancing rules. Friday and Saturday are devoted to live bands, sometimes country, sometimes rock (call ahead to see who's playing). Although it's a private club, don't worry about having to take out a loan to join—it's only $3 for a year's membership.

SOUTH COAST BEACHES

In a region with more than 100 miles of coastline, stretching south from the quiet sands of Topsail Island past the hopping beaches near Wilmington, and then east, from Cape Fear past the quiet, residential beach communities of the South Brunswick islands to the South Carolina border, you'll find a beach getaway to suit your tastes on North Carolina's southern coast.

Visitors have lots of choices for a beach getaway in the Wilmington vicinity. Wrightsville, Carolina, and Kure Beaches—the easiest to reach from Wilmington and I-40—attract the most visitors and provide the broadest choices of accommodations, restaurants, and nearby attractions. The other beaches are more residential in character, featuring long rows of private homes along the oceanfront. Most of these homes are available for vacation rentals—ideal for anyone in search of a laid-back stay on pristine, uncrowded beaches.

AVERAGE SOUTHERN COAST TEMPERATURES

With the Gulf Stream only about 45 miles offshore, the ocean moderates temperatures in the winter and provides soothing breezes during the hot summer months, making the Southern Coast a favorite destination year-round for millions of visitors.

MONTH	HIGH	LOW
Jan.	56° F	35° F
Feb.	58° F	37° F
March	65° F	43° F
April	74° F	52° F
May	81° F	60° F
June	86° F	67° F
July	89° F	71° F
Aug.	89° F	71° F
Sept.	84° F	66° F
Oct.	75° F	54° F
Nov.	67° F	44° F
Dec.	59° F	37° F

TOPSAIL ISLAND

Accessible about 25 miles north of Wilmington, Topsail Island stretches for 24 miles along the Atlantic Ocean. Most of the island is quiet and residential, the biggest exceptions being **Surf City,** located at the junction of NC 210 and 50, and **Topsail Beach,** about seven miles south of Surf City along NC 50. Topsail Island is a favorite choice for North Carolinians who want to rent a house on the beach and spend some quiet time with the ocean, relatively free from the out-of-state visitors who flock to many other North Carolina beaches.

Beach Properties, 320 New River Drive in Surf City, tel. (800) 753-2975, handles about 60 rental properties including oceanfront homes, townhouses, and condos, ranging $400-2,500 per week during the summer, and less in the off-season. Call for a free color brochure. **Ward Realty,** 116 S. Topsail Drive in Surf City, tel. (800) 782-6216, also will send you a free color brochure showing their more than 120 various properties, which rent during the summer for $600-3,000 per week, less during the off-season.

If you want to visit for a night, or stay a week, the oceanfront **Jolly Roger Inn by the Sea,** 803 Ocean Blvd. in Topsail Beach, tel. (910) 328-4616 or (800) 633-3196, provides a wide variety of 65 roomy, clean and comfortable choices, including efficiencies, one- and two-bedroom suites, and apartments at extremely modest prices—$60-165 per night and $300-900/week during the peak summer season, plummeting to as low as $39-90 during the winter. In addition to the on-site restaurant, serving three meals a day, the Jolly Roger features an 854-foot long pier, ideal for catching your dinner or taking a romantic stroll over the water.

Figure Eight Island

While President Clinton and his family have often chosen Martha's Vineyard for island vacations, Al and Tipper Gore and their portrait gallery of good-looking kids and pets chose Figure Eight Island for theirs. In addition to the commercial-free, secluded atmosphere, the Gores can also take advantage of swimming in waters significantly warmer than those off the Vineyard. The only commercial company on the island, **Figure Eight Realty,** tel. (910) 686-4400 or (800) 279-6085, handles about 75 luxury properties, ideal for anyone with a fat bank account and a hankering for privacy.

WRIGHTSVILLE BEACH

The most popular beach on the Cape Fear coast—and the closest to Wilmington—this barrier island, barely three miles long, bustles with beach lovers all summer long and hums with the activity of both visitors and residents year-round. Despite their popularity, Wrightsville's sandy beaches remain relatively uncrowded, because of the predominance of homes rather than hotels along the oceanfront. An ideal destination for folks who want a beachy base from which to explore the diverse attractions of Wilmington, just six miles inland, Wrightsville Beach also fulfills the desires of vacationers who just want to lay back and enjoy the sunny and sandy pleasures of a residential beach community where you won't have to hop in the car to dine, shop, swim and sunbathe. For a recreational break from the demands of swimming and sunbathing, the several marinas at Wrightsville Beach offer a grand selection of charters for nature excursions on uninhabited nearby islands or fishing for big game in the Gulf Stream.

Accommodations

Although Wrightsville has a few hotels and motels to choose from, you should seriously consider renting a home if you're staying for a week or more (as you'll see, it's not cheap to stay in a hotel or motel in Wrightsville Beach—all but one of the accommodations below are in the Luxury price category at $150+ per night). To receive colorful brochures detailing hundreds of rental properties, renting from $600 to more than $3,000/week, call **Bryant Real Estate** at (800) 322-3764, **Intracoastal Realty** at (800) 346-2463, or **Fran Brittain Realty** at (800) 362-9031. All three of these veteran companies are located in Wrightsville Beach and will serve you well.

On a narrow stretch of the island, you'll get expansive views of the ocean or the intracoastal waterway at the oceanfront **Blockade Runner Resort Hotel,** 275 Waynick Blvd., tel. (910) 256-2251 or (800) 541-1161. The Blockade Runner's amenities include a health and fitness center, a good restaurant on the premises (the Ocean Terrace Restaurant), and a heated indoor/outdoor pool. All 150 units, distributed between a four-story and a seven-story structure, consist of single rooms. The units in the four-story building feature private, oceanfront balconies. Rates in the summer range from $210 for a harbor room, $245 for an oceanfront view, and $295 for an oceanfront room with a private balcony. These rates are for just one night. The hotel also offers three-, five- and seven-night packages at reduced but still Luxury rates ($150+). Rates gradually reduce to $90-110 during the winter.

The only chain operation on Wrightsville Beach is the oceanfront **Holiday Inn SunSpree Resort Wrightsville Beach,** 1706 N. Lumina Ave., tel. (910) 256-2231 or (800) 532-5362. All 144 rooms have at least a partial view of the ocean and include a refrigerator, microwave, coffeemaker, hair dryer and data port. In addition to the Shades Bar and Grill, adjoining the oceanfront swimming pool, you can dine at the hotel's Beach Club and Cafe or grab a sandwich at the on-site market/delicatessen. A fun place for kids, the resort has a playground, kid's room, and, during

TOMMY DAUGHTRY

brown pelican

SHELL ISLAND RESORT vs. ATLANTIC OCEAN

After Hurricane Fran in 1996 ravaged much of North Carolina's southern coast—particularly devastating Topsail Island's oceanfront dwellings—a number of policy issues arose with respect to the state's regulation of oceanfront development. The governor and state legislature couldn't decide whether homeowners should be allowed to rebuild their storm-smashed houses on beaches so susceptible to future hurricanes. After months of withholding permission, the state relented—and homeowners immediately set about rebuilding and repairing their homes.

Fran's destruction also gave rise to a reappraisal of North Carolina's policy of prohibiting construction of "hardened structures" (including cement jetties and barrier walls) on any North Carolina beach. The folks who made the loudest cry for repealing this policy were the owners of the Shell Island resort. When developers first proposed the construction of the $23 million resort condominium complex, in the early 1980s, state officials warned them that the ocean inlet—which at the time lay more than 200 yards away from the proposed structure's founda-

tion—could, over time, move south or widen to the point that the sea might wash the development away. The officials specifically warned the Shell Island developers that the state would not allow the construction of a seawall to prevent that eventuality.

Ignoring these cautions, the developers built the complex in 1985, and managed to sell more than 400 condominium units. Unfortunately, the owners of those units are now in the unhappy position of seeing the ocean lapping virtually at the edge of the resort's foundation. It will take more than crossed fingers and wishful thinking to forestall the further approach of those waters. Specifically, it would require redredging of the inlet (a move that's been nixed by the owners of Figure Eight Island, across the inlet) or construction of a big, protective seawall. As this book went to press, the state was standing firm in upholding the state's prohibition against hardened beach structures—even facing the prospect of $23 million worth of condo units washing out to sea.

If your plans include a stay at the Shell Island resort, we highly recommend calling ahead, tel. (910) 256-8696 or (800) 689-6765.

---

the summer, a supervised children's activity program. Rates begin at $150-180 during the peak summer season, when there's a two-night minimum on weekends, and drop to as low as $75-125 during the winter.

The most talked-about accommodations on Wrightsville Beach lie at the **Shell Island Oceanfront Suites,** 2700 N. Lumina Ave., tel. (910) 256-8696 or (800) 689-6765. All 165 one-bedroom suites in the nine-story condominium/hotel are oceanfront, sleep up to six people, and include 1.5 baths, a kitchen and private balcony. In addition, the resort features indoor and outdoor pools, a fitness room and sauna, two on-site restaurants, and a convenience store. But it's not the rooms and amenities that have everyone talking about Shell Island. Located at the northern edge of the island, at the inlet between Wrightsville Beach and Figure Eight Island, this beach resort has gained statewide notoriety for giving new meaning to the term "oceanfront." As this book went to press, the waters of the inlet were less than 20 yards from the northern face of the high-rise and closing fast. Rates are

$250 in the summer but gradually decline to $90 during the winter.

In addition to the outdoor swimming pool, the four-story **Surf Motel Suites,** 711 S. Lumina Ave., tel. (910) 256-2275, provides 46 one-bedroom suites, all of them oceanfront, with kitchens and private patios or balconies. Rates begin at $175 for weekends during the summer, gradually declining to as low as $60 in the winter. The **Summer Sands Motel,** 104 S. Lumina Ave., tel. (910) 256-4175 or (800) 336-4849, on the harbor side of the island, in downtown Wrightsville Beach, is yet another "motelminimum" with a swimming pool and 32 efficiencies, many with a view of the harbor. During the summer, rates range $120-160, gradually dipping as low as $60 in the winter.

Food and Drink

Befitting its beach-mecca character, the culinary specialties at Wrightsville Beach are relatively straightforward, featuring broiled or fried fish and seafood, along with landlubber options like steak and poultry. If you want to dine by the water, Wrightsville Beach won't let you down, with lots of oceanfront and marineside restaurants offering romantic views of the Atlantic and the Intracoastal Waterway. As at virtually every restaurant on the North Carolina coast, you'll never have to wear a suit or high heels to any Wrightsville Beach restaurant—casual beach attire is welcome at any venue.

Every table provides views of the Atlantic at the oceanfront **Oceanic Restaurant,** 703 Lumina Ave., tel. (910) 256-5551. With three floors available for indoor dining and about 20 tables on an outside pier, this popular place buys its seafood twice a day for maximum freshness. If you can't quite make up your mind about which kind of seafood you prefer, you might consider the seafood lasagna, with pasta noodles, shrimp, scallops, fresh fish, and three cheeses, in a tomato basil cream sauce ($15). Dinner entrees range $12-19, and lunch, including salads, sandwiches, and slightly more elaborate fare like pastas, run $6-11. Noted for its rich she-crab soup and seafood gumbo ($3.25 for a cup, $4.25 for a bowl), the Oceanic also offers a full raw bar. Open daily.

An oceanfront view, combined with a background of soft, live jazz, provides a romantic setting for dinner at the **Ocean Terrace,** at the Blockade Runner Resort, 275 Waynick Ave., tel. (910) 256-2251. Typical dinner entrees, ranging $17-24, include the pan-seared, herb-encrusted tuna—a fresh cut tuna loin seared with fresh herbs, served on a bed of fresh green lentils with grilled portabella mushrooms and herb jus-lie ($18). Also open for lunch ($6-9), the Terrace features a popular New Orleans-style jazz brunch on Sundays.

Two popular restaurants on Airlie Road, just off the east side of the drawbridge to downtown Wrightsville Beach, both provide tranquil views of the marinas and water traffic along the Intracoastal Waterway. Open for lunch and dinner, both restaurants provide indoor seating as well as outdoor decks over the water. Both restaurants feature fresh fish and seafood, broiled or fried, along with a smattering of landlubber options. Dinner entrees at the **Bridge Tender,** 1414 Airlie Rd., tel. (910) 256-4519 range $17-23, and lunch is $6-10. At the **Dockside,** 1308 Airlie Rd., tel. (910) 256-2752 dinner entrees range $8-17, and lunch costs around $5. The Dockside, slightly less formal than the Bridge

Tender, is a great place to sit at a dockside table at a marina in a T-shirt and flip-flops and enjoy a cocktail and appetizer.

On the other side of the Intracoastal Waterway, at the west end of the drawbridge, **Pusser's Landing** 4 Marina Ave., tel. (910) 256-2002, offers casual dining on the first floor, called Pusser's Pub, particularly on the popular outdoor deck overlooking the marina. Or patrons can choose the slightly more formal second floor, complete with white tablecloths and a wait staff wearing black-and-whites (though patrons certainly don't need to dress up—no ties needed). The second floor also includes a spacious outdoor deck. The specialties of the house are Caribbean-style fish and seafood, like the blackened stuffed flounder, stuffed with shrimp, scallops, and blue crab ($16). Open seven days a week for lunch and dinner, dinner entrees on the second floor range $12-21, and lunch $5-16. The Pub also serves sandwiches and appetizers during dinner hours and hops with a lively bar crowd in the later evening.

In addition to popular bars at the above-mentioned restaurants, as well as at the Holiday Inn SunSpree Resort, Wrightsville Beach also boasts of two venues for **stand-up comedy.** On Thursday evenings, the Ocean Terrace restaurant transforms into **The Comedy Zone,** tel. (910) 256-2251, and on Saturday night, the lounge at the Holiday Inn becomes **Laff Trax,** tel. (910) 256-2231. Tickets are usually about $7 and are discounted slightly if you have dinner at the respective restaurants beforehand.

CAROLINA AND KURE BEACHES

Located about 15 miles south of Wilmington, on the barrier island dubbed Pleasure Island, the neighboring communities of Carolina Beach and Kure Beach may lack some of the sophistication of Wrightsville Beach, but that only adds to their unassuming charm. Carolina Beach retains the flavor of a beach town from earlier decades: its beachside arcade with old bumper cars and skee ball games; the tiny **Jubilee Amusement Park's** acrophobic-friendly Ferris wheel; and the handful of slightly dusty, but nonetheless hopping dance halls. Just south of Carolina Beach, Kure Beach is a more family-oriented little town, where a big night out features buying an ice cream cone and strolling along the downtown fishing pier and the moonlit beach. If you need a break from the beach, nearby attractions include **Fort Fisher** and the **North Carolina Aquarium at Fort Fisher,** just south of Kure Beach; the diverse ecosystems of **Carolina Beach State Park,** just north of the town of Carolina Beach; and the cruise boats and fishing charters offered at Carolina Beach Marina. Peppered with dozens of small, family-owned and -operated motels, Pleasure Island has no chain accommodations. You won't find any glitzy gourmet restaurants either, but, particularly in Carolina Beach, you can enjoy some savory fare at modest prices in a friendly, casual atmosphere.

Accommodations

Rising 11 stories, the oceanfront **Atlantic Towers,** 1615 S. Lake Park Blvd., tel. (910) 458-8313 or (800) 232-2440, includes 137 one- and two-bedroom suites, all oceanfront, with private balconies and full kitchens. By far the biggest lodging operation in Carolina Beach, the Towers is actually a condominium, though it has daily housekeeping service. Except for walk-ins, there's a two-night minimum stay. During the summer, one-bedroom suites begin at $130 ($700 for a week), and two-bedroom suites at $170 ($900/week). Rates gradually drop to as low as $60 and $100 during the winter. Premium.

The four-story, oceanfront **Cabana de Mar,** 31 Carolina Beach Ave. N., tel. (910) 458-4456 or (800) 333-8499, located in the heart of downtown Carolina Beach, offers 71 one- and two-bedroom suites, all with kitchenettes, some with private balconies looking out on the ocean. Although technically a condominium, the Cabana is run more like a motel, with rooms available for one night, daily housekeeping service, and an oceanfront swimming pool. During the peak summer season, street-facing one-bedroom suites start at $110, oceanfront one-bedrooms $130, and oceanfront two-bedrooms $145. Rates gradually decline the rest of the year to as low as $60. Premium.

From the Cabana De Mar north along the Carolina Beach oceanfront, a half dozen smaller, family-owned and -operated motels provide lodgings slightly frayed around the edges—not particularly luxurious, but friendly places to stay. The moderately priced **Surfside Motor Lodge,**

THE FORT FISHER FERRY

To explore the various sightseeing, culinary, and entertainment attractions on Pleasure Island (Carolina and Kure Beaches), you can save yourself an hour's worth of driving on the South Brunswick Islands—and get out on the water—by riding the ferry across from Southport, just inland from Oak Island at the southwestern terminus of NC 21, to Fort Fisher. The trip takes 30 minutes. Fare is 50 cents for pedestrians, $3 for vehicles under 20 feet long. The ferry has a capacity of 38 cars and doesn't accept reservations, so get there early to wait in line.

The following schedules have rarely changed over the years, but if you want to be sure, call the Southport ferry office at (910) 457-6942 or (800) 368-8969, or the state's automated ferry information line at (800) BY-FERRY (293-3779).

April to mid-November, ferries depart Southport at 5:30, 7, 8:30, 9:15, 10, 10:45, and 11:30 a.m., and 12:15, 1, 1:45, 2:30, 3:15, 4, 4:45, 6:15 and 7:45 p.m. They return from Fort Fisher at identical times 9:15 a.m.-4:45 p.m., and also at 6:15 a.m., 7:45 a.m., 5:30 p.m., 7 p.m., and 8:30 p.m.

Mid-November through March, ferries depart Southport every 90 minutes 5:30 a.m.-4 p.m. and return every 90 minutes 6:15 a.m.-4:45 p.m.

---

234 Carolina Beach Ave. N., tel. (910) 458-8338, offers a wide range of lodgings, from small motel rooms to three-bedroom cottages, ranging $70-140 during the summer, and dipping to as low as $25-70 during the winter. If you're bringing a pet along, Fido won't be alone at the pet-friendly **Sandstep Motel,** 618 Carolina Beach Ave., N., tel. (910) 458-8788. Most of the 20 units, including 10 single rooms, four efficiencies, and four two-bedroom apartments, have diagonal views of the ocean. The four two-bedroom apartments share two oceanfront porches. The Sandstep just changed ownership, and new rates were not available as this edition went to press, though rates are expected to remain in the Moderate-Expensive range. At any rate(s), the new owners have pledged to retain the Sandstep's long, canine-accepting tradition.

In the heart of Kure Beach, the oceanfront **Docksider Inn,** 202 N. Fort Fisher Blvd., tel. (910) 458-4200, provides 34 units, half of them efficiencies, along with an inviting oceanfront swimming pool and sun deck. Depending on whether you want an oceanfront efficiency with a private balcony, or an oceanside, single room without a balcony, rates range $95-125 in the summer (plus another $25 for weekends), to as low as $50-90 during the winter. Premium. For something a little more secluded and romantic, the **Ocean Princess Inn,** 824 Fort Fisher Blvd., tel. (910) 458-6712 or (800) 762-4863, is a contemporary bed and breakfast with eight comfortable rooms, three of them with jacuzzis. The rooms contain only one queen-size bed, and children are not really welcome. A full breakfast is served in the main dining room, and there's a full bar on the premises (guests get a voucher for a free cocktail during the evening social hour). Rates are $90-140 during the summer, and decline to $70-90 during the off-season. Expensive-Premium.

Food and Drink

If you're staying on Pleasure Island and in search of a good meal, Carolina Beach offers several marvelous choices. For a casual, romantic setting on the water, your best bet is the **Sweetwater Cafe,** 106 Carl Winner Ave., tel. (910) 458-0500, open for lunch and dinner seven days a week. Overlooking the picturesque Carolina Beach marina, the Sweetwater provides three dining areas. The enclosed room behind big glass windows provides a slightly more formal setting with white tablecloths. The covered first-floor deck puts you right on the water—you can even look down between the floors' wood slats to the water beneath. This deck, curtained with plastic during cooler weather, and the open-air, rooftop dining area, both exude a festive, waterfront ambience enjoyed by folks who want to sample Sweetwater's wide selection of Caribbean-style cocktails, full raw bar, and varied selection of sandwiches and entrees. The waitstaff at Sweetwater perpetually achieve the golden mean between friendliness and professionalism, the mark of a first-class beach restaurant. Oyster fans can get a dozen raw for $8, or a steamed peck (about 25) for $9. In addition to tantalizing nightly fish and seafood specials, you

can opt for dependable choices like the Rasta grouper with fettucine Alfredo for $12; the mixed-grill with grouper, fresh catch-of-the-day, and jumbo shrimp for $17; or surf-and-turf prime rib and lobster tail for $20. Or you can choose from a variety of sandwiches in the $5-7 range for either lunch or dinner.

The Cottage, at 1 N. Lake Park Blvd., tel. (910) 458-4383, housed in a cozy bungalow built in 1916, has a casual, elegant atmosphere with white tablecloths and candlelight on the intimate tables inside the cottage and umbrella-covered tables on the more festive outdoor dining deck. The stars of the menu are the sensational pasta dishes, including several mouth-watering cream sauces, like gorgonzola cream, pesto cream, roasted garlic cream, and sun-dried tomato cream, as well as tomato-based sauces and Fred's Fabulous Feta, a spicy, chunky sauce of feta, roasted red peppers, red onions, olives, fresh thyme, lemon juice and extra virgin olive oil. All of the pastas cost a mere $7 for dinner (a dollar or two less for lunch), and you have the option of adding various toppings, like bay scallops, shrimp, prosciutto, chicken breast, and andouille sausage for $2-4 per topping. In addition to tantalizing nightly specials, the dinner menu includes fresh fish and seafood, filet mignon, chicken, and a zesty jambalaya made with chicken, andouille sausage, and Cajun-spiced shrimp. Most entrees fall in the $10-15 range. Lunch sandwiches average $5. Open Mon.-Sat., the Cottage also provides one of the best wine lists on Pleasure Island, along with a full bar.

If Sweetwater's and the Cottage have too long a wait, try the **Marina's Edge,** 300 North Lake Park Blvd., tel. (910) 458-6001, which, despite its accurate name, doesn't offer views of the Carolina Beach marina. Located next door to Sweetwater Cafe, the Marina's Edge offers a full menu of seafood and landlubber choices—live Maine lobster, a full raw bar, fish and seafood, steaks, and chicken. In addition to the rather sedate indoor dining rooms, the more festive outdoor veranda and bar areas give you a variety of atmospheres to choose from.

The most popular dining institution on Pleasure Island is located in Kure Beach, in the form of the highly publicized **Big Daddy's Seafood Restaurant,** 206 K Ave., in downtown Kure

Beach at the town's only stoplight, tel. (910) 458-8622. Since the 1960s, folks have been flocking to this dependable, family-friendly establishment. It can seat more than 500 people in several dining rooms, all decorated with a morass of maritime memorabilia. The menu features fried or broiled fish and seafood, in addition to steaks, prime rib, and poultry. You can augment your entree with heaping helpings from the salad bar. A full bar is also available. Dinner entrees fall in the $10-15 range.

Nightlife

Particularly on Friday and Saturday nights, downtown Carolina Beach rumbles with the thundering beats of live bands. The center of the action revolves around the intersection of Harper and Carolina Avenues, a block from the small beach boardwalk. The rocking **Club Astor,** 110 Harper Ave., tel. (910) 458-7883, attracts a younger crowd, while across the street, at the **Ocean Plaza Ballroom,** tel. (910) 458-8898, folks over 30 won't be alone, Shagging to Beach Music (the Ballroom maintains that its hardwood floors witnessed the birth of the Shag, but the same claim is also made by places in Myrtle Beach, South Carolina, and the dispute is heated). Don't be intimated by all the Shaggers, though—Beach Music resembles Motown and is adaptable to many dance styles. Cover charges vary but usually don't exceed $5.

SOUTH BRUNSWICK ISLANDS

From Cape Fear southwest to the South Carolina border, four barrier islands offer some of the most uncrowded beaches in the state. That's not to say that these islands would be confused with nature preserves. On the contrary, most of the oceanfront land on these islands is developed, but with a relatively low density of private residences; there are very few hotels and motels. The vast majority of visitors to these islands rent private homes and stay for a week or more. Besides swimming in the clear ocean waters and sunbathing on the sandy beaches, the major recreation for visitors is the plethora of golfing opportunities, located a few miles away on the mainland. For free information, including a complete list of golf courses in the area, call the South Brunswick Islands Chamber of Commerce, at (910) 794-6644 or (800) 426-6644.

Oak Island includes **Caswell Beach, Yaupon Beach,** and **Long Beach.** At the eastern end of the island, the ruins of **Fort Caswell,** on Caswell Beach Rd., tel. (910) 278-9501, provide one of the only "sights" on the southern islands. Built in 1838 of earthen ramparts enclosing a pentagonal brick fort and citadel, the facility was abandoned in January 1865, soon after the fall of Fort Fisher. The Confederate troops exploded the powder magazine on their way out, destroying much of the fort and citadel. Admission to the grounds costs $2, but it's *not* open to the public from early June through Labor Day, when the Baptist Assembly of North Carolina, which owns the property, hosts a summer camp on the site for about 1,200 kids.

Just west of Oak Island, across the Lockwood Folly Inlet, lies the almost commercial-free community of **Holden Beach,** a barrier island 11 miles long that appeals to folks seeking a serene, neon-free stay at the beach. The next island to the west, **Ocean Isle Beach,** provides eight miles of sandy oceanfront, along with the biggest selection (though only a handful) of motels and restaurants of any of the four southern islands. Last, and smallest at only three miles long, the island of **Sunset Beach** next to the South Carolina border provides another, almost commercial-free atmosphere, ideally suited for people looking for a secluded beach getaway. Accessible by car only by driving over a one-lane, pontoon bridge, laid-back Sunset Beach does offer one bit of daily excitement—during low tide, you can walk across a shallow inlet to tiny, unspoiled **Bird Island,** a nature treat for both adults and kids.

As we mentioned, the preferred way to vacation on the South Brunswick Islands is to rent a home for a week or more. The experienced rental agencies listed below provide detailed brochures on each of their rental properties. The wide price ranges quoted do refer to the peak summer season, but, with a few exceptions, you should be prepared to spend at least $1,000/week for oceanfront properties. **Margaret Rudd Realty,** 210 Country Club Dr. in Yaupon Beach, tel. (910) 278-6523 or (800) 733-5213, manages 250 rental properties on Oak Island, ranging $450-2,500/week. On Holden Beach, **Alan Holden Realty,** 128 Ocean Blvd., tel. (910) 842-

6061 or (800) 720-2200, manages more than 400 homes and a few condos on its namesake island, $500-2,500. **Sloan Realty,** 16 Causeway Dr. in Ocean Isle Beach, tel. (910) 579-6216 or (800) 843-6044, handles about 400 properties on Ocean Isle Beach, $600-3,000. **Sunset Properties,** 419 Sunset Blvd. in Sunset Beach, tel. (910) 579-9900 or (800) 446-0218, manages 225 homes on Sunset Beach, ranging $600-2,500/week.

Dining on the South Brunswick Islands is always a casual, family-friendly affair. With no special spots worth going out of your way for, the best choices among the few restaurants on these islands are the ones closest to your lodgings. Virtually all of the islands' eateries carry a full menu including fresh fish and seafood. On the opposite side of the restaurant-density spectrum, the little seaport town of **Calabash** (which bills itself "The Seafood Capital of The World") boasts perhaps the highest number of restaurants per capita in North Carolina. The city is lo-

cated next to the South Carolina border on NC 179, within a 10- to 15-minute drive from Sunset Beach and Ocean Isle Beach.

All along the North and South Carolina coasts, you'll see restaurants advertising that they serve "Calabash-style seafood," which basically consists of fish and seafood fried in a light batter, usually accompanied by hush puppies and coleslaw. For a taste of "the real thing," you can choose among this little town's more than 30 seafood restaurants, most of them located on River Road between NC 179 and the waterfront. Considering the fierce competition, all of Calabash's restaurants serve first-rate fresh fish and seafood. All of the restaurants are casual and family-friendly. To add a little scenic ambience, we recommend trying one of the several waterfront restaurants at the end of River Road, like **The Original Calabash Restaurant,** tel. (910) 579-6875, where, depending on how high you want to pile your plate with seafood, entrees range $6-15 for lunch and dinner.

white ibis

TOMMY DAUGHTRY

PINEHURST AND VICINITY

Visitors flock to the Pinehurst area for three major reasons: golf, golf, and golf. Home to more than 40 magnificent championship courses, including some of the world's most celebrated, this area isn't over-hyping itself when it boasts of being "the Golf Capital of the World." The Pinehurst area is known locally as the "Sandhills region," which is also its geographic designation, aptly describing this undulating terrain of sandy soil. Millions of years ago, these hills formed the coast of the Atlantic Ocean—which now lies 100 miles to the east. Today, the gentle hills reach as high as 600 feet above sea level, providing a topography perfect for golf—not too flat, not too steep, and with plenty of variety to give each hole an individual character. The soil is also perfectly suited to the game, since it allows fairways and greens to drain quickly and evenly after a rain, and since, unlike so much of North Carolina's clay-rich soil, it resists hardening during droughts.

Most of the area's lodging, dining, and legendary golf courses lie in or between the villages of Pinehurst, Southern Pines, and Aberdeen, three small towns located within five miles of each other. The combined population of these three little burgs totals about 17,000, most of whom are connected somehow with the golf and hospitality industries. These small towns radiate a contagiously languid, Southern ease combined with a cosmopolitan expertise at making all varieties of visitors feel immediately comfortable and welcome.

As you make your plans to visit the area, contact the **Pinehurst, Southern Pines and Aberdeen Convention and Visitors Bureau,** 1480 Highway 15-501, Southern Pines, NC 28387, tel. (910) 692-3330 or (800) 346-5362. As you would expect of any visitors bureau, this one provides several helpful brochures listing a variety of lodgings and restaurants, as well as sightseeing, shopping, and other diversions. But this bureau goes a classy step beyond most in providing travel information to prospective visitors who want to play golf. Request your free copy of the bureau's annually updated *Play & Stay Golf Vacation Guide,* a glossy, 70-page magazine detailing hundreds of golf packages provided by the area's lodgings, most of which have relationships with a dozen or more championship courses in the neighborhood.

History

Thick forests of Carolina longleaf pines once dominated this thin slice of sandy hills that separate the clay-based North Carolina Piedmont from the coastal plain. But by the early 1890s, loggers had sheared the land so completely that the area was referred to as "the Sahara of North Carolina." The stand of pines at the Weymouth Woods Sandhills Nature Preserve in Southern Pines is supposedly the only original stand remaining in the area.

Then, in 1895, Boston philanthropist James Walker Tufts, who had amassed a fortune selling soda fountains, visited this land of sand and somehow envisioned it as an inviting setting for a resort. Purchasing 5,000 acres a few miles from the main Boston-to-Miami rail line for about $1 an acre, Tufts assembled a small army of ar-

chitects, engineers, planners, and workers to build his resort and create a New England village on the sandy North Carolina property. First, he hired legendary landscape architect Frederick Law Olmstead, designer of New York City's Central Park and Asheville's Biltmore Estate gardens and grounds, to shape the village of Pinehurst. Olmstead designed the town around an oval village green, from which radiates a series of intricately winding roads and paths with no right angles. Then Olmstead set about reforesting the area by planting more than 220,000 tree

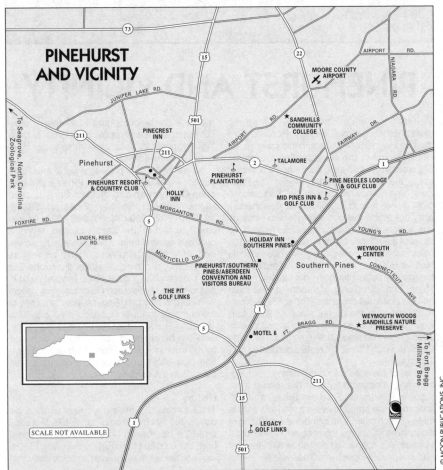

PINEHURST AND VICINITY

To Seagrove, North Carolina Zoological Park

73

15

22

AIRPORT RD.

NIAGARA RD.

MOORE COUNTY AIRPORT

JUNIPER LAKE RD.

501

211

AIRPORT RD.

SANDHILLS COMMUNITY COLLEGE

FAIRWAY DR.

PINECREST INN

Pinehurst

211

2

TALAMORE

1

PINEHURST RESORT & COUNTRY CLUB

PINEHURST PLANTATION

PINE NEEDLES LODGE & GOLF CLUB

HOLLY INN

MORGANTON RD.

MID PINES INN & GOLF CLUB

FOXFIRE RD.

5

LINDEN, REED RD.

YOUNG'S RD.

MONTICELLO DR.

HOLIDAY INN SOUTHERN PINES

WEYMOUTH CENTER

CONNECTICUT AVE.

PINEHURST/SOUTHERN PINES/ABERDEEN CONVENTION AND VISITORS BUREAU

Southern Pines

THE PIT GOLF LINKS

1

WEYMOUTH WOODS SANDHILLS NATURE PRESERVE

5

MOTEL 6

FT. BRAGG RD.

To Fort Bragg Military Base

211

SCALE NOT AVAILABLE

1

15

LEGACY GOLF LINKS

501

© MOON PUBLICATIONS, INC.

seedlings, shrubs, and flowers, beginning the reclamation of the area's lush greenery.

When it opened, the complex consisted of a modest hotel, a general store, some boarding houses, and 16 cottages. Tufts knew that supplying recreational opportunities would help draw visitors, and he provided an abundance, including horseback riding, hunting, polo, tennis, trapshooting, croquet, bicycling, and archery—but no golf. Not a golfer himself, Tufts didn't initially believe that building a golf course would attract visitors. It was his guests—and an annoyed neighbor—who sold him on the idea. According to Pinehurst lore, in 1898 a neighboring dairy farmer complained that some of Tuft's guests were traipsing into his dairy pastures, chasing little white balls that they were whacking around with thin little clubs. Tufts hired Dr. D. Leroy Culver of New York City to lay out a nine-hole golf course. It was such an immediate and thorough hit with guests that it was expanded to 18 holes within the year.

Tufts realized that this golf thing had real potential, and he decided he needed someone to pilot his fledgling operation. In 1900, during a trip to Massachusetts, he ran into a young Scottish immigrant named Donald Ross, who had been tutored in golf by one of the original masters—Old Tom Morris—at St. Andrews, Scotland, the legendary cradle of the game. On a whim and a handshake, Tufts hired the 27-year-old Ross, launching the career of America's most revered golf course architect. That year, Ross completely redesigned the resort's course. By 1919, Ross had completed three more courses at Tuft's resort, transforming it into one of the premier golfing destinations in the nation.

The popularity of Pinehurst golfing soon grew beyond Tufts' resort. Developers realized that if they built a course in the area, the golfers would come. But with so many splendid courses to choose from, any new additions had to be first-rate in order to compete, so the developers hired the best course designers they could find. As Pinehurst enters its second century as a golfing mecca, the list of architects who have built golf courses in the Pinehurst area reads like a "who's who" of America's greatest course designers, including, among other notables, Donald Ross (7), Ellis Maples (6), Dan Maples (3), Gene Hamm (3), Robert Trent Jones (2),

Rees Jones (2), Tom Jackson (2), Tom Fazio (2), Arnold Palmer (2), Peter Tufts (1), Gary Player (1), and Jack Nicklaus (1).

Today, Moore County—with a population of about 65,000 people—offers 648 holes of golf, covering the equivalent of more than 2,600 football fields with fairways. And new courses continue to be added at a brisk pace. As this edition went to press, 72 more holes were being built. The neighboring towns of Pinehurst, Southern Pines, and Aberdeen have preserved their welcoming, small-town charm while growing gracefully to accommodate the ever-increasing number of golfers making pilgrimages to Pinehurst.

GOLF

Playing golf in these sandhills is like taking part in a living-history experience. Over the past decade or two, for instance, most of America's most beautiful (and expensive) courses decided to make cart rentals mandatory. But that trend hasn't infected most courses in the Pinehurst area. True to tradition, when you play this area's great courses, you can follow, step-by-step, in the footprints of the greats of the game, from Bobby Jones, Byron Nelson, and Babe Zaharias to Arnold Palmer, Jack Nicklaus, and Tiger Woods. (You aren't *required* to walk these courses—carts are universally available—but so many golfers walk that if you do rent a cart, you may spend a fair amount of time waiting for the foursome ahead to get out of range.)

Greens fees and area accommodations rates fluctuate considerably during the year. Most golfing visitors to the Pinehurst area take advantage of one of the golf packages offered by virtually every lodging. Greens fees at various courses and preferred tee times are included in the packages. However, you certainly can play almost any of the area's courses on your own, not tied to any accommodations package.

Greens Fees

There are four seasons for greens fees. Peaks are spring (March through mid-June) and autumn (early September through mid-November), during which a premier course might charge $75 or more for a round. In summer (mid-June through early September), the fees drop—to about $55. Winter (mid-November through February) boasts the lowest rate—about $40 a round.

Within the seasons, there are other variables—day of the month, day of the week, and time of day.

Pinehurst Resort & Country Club

If you've never golfed in this area, then you shouldn't start anywhere but at the **Pinehurst Resort & Country Club,** One Carolina Vista, tel. (910) 295-6811 or (800) ITS-GOLF. Since the turn of the century, the legends of golf have honed their skills on these fairways, particularly on course No. 2. Take your pick from any of the resort's eight fabulous courses, each of which will give you a spectacular round. But for a guaranteed memory of a lifetime, go for the legendary Pinehurst No. 2, built in 1907 by Donald Ross and widely considered by folks as knowledgeable as *Golf Magazine* and *Golf Digest* to rank among the top ten golf courses in the *world.* Site of the 1999 U.S. Open, this course truly looks and feels like living history. If you want to play No. 2, your travel planning will be a little simpler, because you only have one choice about where to stay: with very few exceptions, only guests of the resort (and members of the country club) get to play No. 2. The same goes for the celebrated No. 7 course, designed by Rees Jones, which opened in 1986. If you manage to become one the few who don't stay at the resort but get a shot at No. 2 or 7, expect to pay between $85-150 for the privilege. Greens fees for the other six classic courses, designed by Ross, Robert Trent Jones, Ellis Maples, or George and Tom Fazio, generally range $40-80 for nonguests of the resort.

After the venerable Pinehurst Resort's courses, the next-highest-rated course in the town of Pinehurst (according at least to *Golf Digest* readers) is a relative upstart opened in 1993, the **Pinehurst Plantation,** Midland Rd., tel. (910) 695-3193. Designed by Arnold Palmer, one of the all-time great putters, this challenging course features, not surprisingly, a series of great greens, as well as superb use of the naturally undulating topography of the region. Fees range $55-110, including carts (some walking is allowed, with restrictions). Another young course, opened in 1991, that has received heaps of praise is the **Legacy Golf Links,** located two miles south of Pinehurst on US 15-501, tel. (910) 944-8825 or (800) 344-8825. The first American design by Jack Nicklaus, Jr., this course features lots of variety, utilizing water, sand, and hills to give each hole an individual character. The site of the 2000 U.S. Women's Public Links Amateur Championship, Legacy's greens fees (including mandatory carts) run $35-75.

Reverting back to classic courses of past *and* present, you can experience two Donald Ross, full-service beauties in Southern Pines, at the **Mid Pines Inn & Golf Club,** 1010 Midland Rd., tel. (910) 692-2114 or (800) 323-2114, and its sister property across the street, **Pine Needles Lodge & Golf Club,** 1005 Midland Rd., tel. (910) 692-7111 or (800) 747-7272. The Mid Pines Inn

*the Pinehurst Resort
and Country Club*

NORTH CAROLINA DIVISION OF TOURISM, FILM & SPORTS DEVELOPMENT

and course was built in 1921, and the Pine Needles Lodge and course soon followed in 1927, both featuring courses by Ross. Although the Mid Pines course is world-class, the favorite daughter among the two remains the Pine Needles course, site of the 1996 and 2001 U.S. Women's Open Championship. Your most economical way to play these courses is to stay at the Mid Pines Inn or Pine Needles Lodge; if you don't stay on-site, expect to pay $30-65/round (carts cost about $20 extra).

Although at least another dozen fabulous courses in this area merit special attention, we're going to hold ourselves back and mention only two more (for more comprehensive coverage, start by calling the Pinehurst/Southern Pines/Aberdeen Convention & Visitors Bureau at (800) 346-5362). **The Pit Golf Links,** on NC 5 about three miles south of Pinehurst, tel. (910) 944-1600 or (800) 574-4653, was designed by Dan Maples and opened in 1985 to absolutely rave reviews. By 1994, The Pit was still ranked by Golf Digest's readers as one of the top 50 public courses in America. It feels a little like a 6,500-yard miniature-golf course, so you'd be well advised to leave your bag when descending into The Pit. It's one of the tightest great courses you'll ever play, complete with lots of water, sand, wicked doglegs, and other hazards you'll love or hate. Fees range $25-65.

The last course we recommend here isn't included just because they provide llamas as caddies. Yes, we said llamas. At **Talamore ,** 1595 Midland Rd., tel. (910) 692-5884 or (800) 552-6292, you can splurge (for an extra C-note) to have your golf bag strapped onto a llama, who, under the guidance of an experienced llama-handler, will serve as your caddie (for advice about how the green breaks, we recommend consulting the llama-handler more than his or her four-legged charge). Sound like a gimmick? Well, it is, but it's a gimmick that delivers a golfing experience that you can discuss at length at cocktail parties. And, with or without llamas (most folks go for the otherwise mandatory carts instead), this Rees Jones masterpiece, which opened in 1991, combines sand, water, and doglegs with dramatic elevation changes, guaranteed to deliver a terrific, memorable round of golf, even if you don't encounter any llamas along the way. Greens fees range $40-90, not including llama caddies.

OTHER PINEHURST VICINITY DIVERSIONS

The main recreation in Pinehurst, aside from golf, is **shopping.** The village defines the adjective "quaint." You can easily spend a leisurely day exploring the couple dozen antique shops, gift stores, clothing boutiques, and specialty shops in the heart of the village, as well as the hotel shops at the Pinehurst Resort and Country Club. If you exhaust the opportunities at Pinehurst Village and still want more, the even tinier downtown in the village of Southern Pines, five miles from Pinehurst, offers more of the same. A couple minutes' drive from downtown Southern Pines, the **Weymouth Center,** 555 E. Connecticut Ave., tel. (910) 692-6261, located on 24 scenic acres, is the area's major center for the arts and humanities. The former home of author and publisher James Boyd (1888-1944), the center sponsors numerous concerts and lectures and provides the setting for the **North Carolina Literary Hall of Fame,** a shrine to many of North Carolina's great writers, including Thomas Wolfe, William Sydney Porter (O. Henry), Paul Green, and dozens of others, complete with displays and photographs.

If you have the slightest inkling to shop for some pottery, the dozens of truly ethereal potteries in the little town of **Seagrove** (see section on Triad Side Trips) lie about an hour's drive northwest from Pinehurst, along US Route 220A. Another 10 miles north of Seagrove, you'll find the deservedly famed **North Carolina Zoological Park,** one of the finest zoos in the world.

About an hour's drive west of Pinehurst and Southern Pines will take you to the visitors entrance of sprawling **Fort Bragg Military Base,** located on NC Route 87 between Spring Lake and Fayetteville. Many parts of the base are open to the public, including two military museums. The **John F. Kennedy Special Warfare Museum,** at Ardennes Street and Reilly Road, tel. (910) 432-1533, features military art, cultural items, and weaponry from around the world, used by special forces like the Green Berets. The **82nd Airborne Division War Memorial Museum,** tel. (910) 432-3443, contains more than 3,000 artifacts used by this famed division from World War I to Desert Storm. Both museums are closed on Monday. Call (910) 396-5401 to inquire about extensive guided or self-guided tours of the base. Tours are available 9 a.m.-4 p.m. weekdays.

Nature lovers don't have to travel far to escape the seeming omnipresence of fairways and greens. The **Sandhills Horticultural Gardens,** 2200 Airport Rd. in Pinehurst, tel. (910) 695-3882, located on the Sandhills Community College campus behind Heutte Hall, includes nine resplendent gardens covering 25 acres. The wonderful walking trails are free to the public and open every day of the year from dawn to sunset. The **Weymouth Woods Sandhills Nature Preserve,** 1024 Fort Bragg Rd. in Southern Pines, tel. (910) 692-2167, is a splendid, 571-acre nature preserve of longleaf pine forest. In addition to more than 4.5 miles of year-round hiking trails, the preserve includes a visitors center and small museum. Open Mon.-Sat. 9 a.m.-6 p.m. (9 a.m.-7 p.m. during daylight savings time), and Sunday noon-5 p.m.; admission to this lush preserve is free.

ACCOMMODATIONS

If you're planning to stay overnight in the Pinehurst area, you're probably spending the night here so that you can play some world-class golf during the day. As we mentioned earlier, virtually every lodging in the area, from luxury resorts to intimate bed-and-breakfast inns to every franchise in between, offers golf packages, including reduced fees to play at a variety of the area's 40-plus championship courses. For a comprehensive guide, call the **Pinehurst/Southern Pines/Aberdeen Convention and Visitors Bureau** at (800) 346-5362 to get a free copy of the *Play & Stay Golf Vacation Guide,* detailing several dozen of the available golf packages offered by local lodgings.

Pinehurst Resorts

Although visitors can choose from among more than 35 superb accommodations in the Pinehurst/Southern Pines/Aberdeen area, three resorts combine gracious service and elegant lodgings with a historical ambience that sets them apart from the attractive competition. Another facet that puts these three resorts above the

rest is their Luxury rates. If you're looking to "go all the way" for a Pinehurst area resort experience and get a package including meals and golf privileges, expect to pay at least $200 per person per night, and more during the peak spring and fall seasons.

Everything is world-class at the legendary **Pinehurst Resort & Country Club,** Carolina Vista Dr., tel. (910) 295-8553 or (800) 487-4653. Long known as "the Queen of the South," this resort employs more than 1,000 folks dedicated to ensuring your comfort. In all, the resort offers more than 500 rooms through five different venues. Though golf certainly reigns, you'll find plenty of other recreational diversions provided here. The 24 clay and Har-Tru tennis courts have hosted the USTA Men's Clay Court Championships and earned the distinction of being ranked among the top 50 tennis resorts in the world by *Tennis Magazine.* For something a little less strenuous, but nonetheless world-class, try a round or two on the meticulously groomed lawns of the croquet courts. And if your preferred exercise involves water and sun-worshipping, choose between five of the resort's swimming pools. To help you assuage the aches of your Pinehurst Resort exertions, call the concierge to arrange a therapeutic massage.

The centerpiece of the resort is the **Pinehurst Hotel,** located a five-minute walk along a sandy path from the couple dozen shops and restaurants of picture-postcard-perfect Pinehurst Village. Opened on New Year's Day 1901, this grand Victorian structure, originally christened the Carolina Hotel, remains the oldest wooden hotel in North Carolina. From the wide verandas with their inviting rocking chairs to the airy lobby with its understated hotel shops to the utterly immaculate grounds, this place exemplifies class. The recently renovated and refurbished 222 guest rooms and 12 suites are all likewise immaculate and graciously furnished. The numerous amenities feature the hotel pools, fitness center, tennis courts, and concierge service. The elegant Carolina Dining Room, complete with dozens of crystal chandeliers, serves breakfast, lunch and dinner, and the Ryder Cup Lounge provides lighter fare and cocktails. For the ultimate Pinehurst experience, stay at the hotel. Luxury rates, including meals and golf privileges, range $450-700.

If the hotel's booked, you still have the opportunity to stay in historic lodgings at the resort. Two blocks from the Pinehurst Hotel, in the heart of quaint Pinehurst Village, you can enjoy the slightly more intimate comforts of the 45-room **Manor Inn,** 5 Community Rd., tel. (910) 295-8472 or (800) 487-4653, or the 70-room **Holly Inn,** 2300 Cherokee Rd., tel. (910) 295-2300 or (800) 487-4653. Both offer full access to all of the Pinehurst resort's many amenities. The Manor Inn is a small, four-story hotel built in 1923 and recently fully refurbished. The inn also features Mulligan's, a casual sports bar and restaurant. Rates for the Manor Inn, including meals at the Pinehurst Hotel's Carolina Dining Room and golf privileges at the resort, range $350-600. The Holly Inn, a rambling, 70-room hotel, was actually the first structure built for the resort, in 1895. Sold by the resort's owners in the mid-1970s, the inn was bought back by the resort in late 1997 and has been closed since then, undergoing an extensive renovation and refurbishing. We expect that the Holly Inn will reclaim its rightful place as one of Pinehurst's premier lodgings, but we won't be sure until it opens in mid-1999. Rates for the Holly Inn were unavailable as this edition went to press.

The Pinehurst Resort & Country Club also offers a number of modern villas and "condotels." The villas consist of four guest rooms that each connect to a central parlor, which provides a spacious and comfortable hospitality area. The condos, located on courses No. 3 and No. 5 and the 200-acre Lake Pinehurst, offer a choice of one, two, or three bedrooms. They feature completely furnished kitchens and living rooms. On-call shuttle service is provided for condo guests to all of the resort's amenities. As throughout the resort, Luxury rates apply for these alternative lodging options.

Pine Needles Lodge & Mid Pines Inn

These sister properties, located across Midland Road from each other in Southern Pines, both feature classic golf courses built by the legendary Donald Ross. Staying at one of these inns gives you golf privileges at both. The stately Mid Pines Inn, 1010 Midland Rd., tel. (910) 692-2114 or (800) 323-2114, an elegant, three-story, 66-room Georgian-style hotel, has been providing gracious comfort and hospitality to guests since 1921. In addition, this resort offers 66 villas containing three to 10 bedrooms each. Amenities at Mid Pines include a restaurant, cocktail lounge, pool and tennis courts, and the fabulous golf course. Luxury rates, including meals and golf privileges, range $400-600. Pine Needles Lodge, 1005 Midland Rd., tel. (910) 692-7111 or (800) 747-7272, began as a resort in 1927, featuring a Donald Ross golf course and its main, two-story brick lodge. In 1953, the resort was transformed by adding 10 more lodges; each includes between five and 12 hotel-style bedrooms. In all, the resort offers 72 rooms, most of which exude an elegantly rustic decor, many with exposed beam ceilings. In addition to the great golf course, Pine Needles provides a restaurant, lounge, pool, hot tub, and sauna. Luxury rates, including meals and golf privileges, range $270-600, depending on the time of year.

Other Pinehurst Area Accommodations

The **Pine Crest Inn** on Dogwood Road, tel. (910) 295-6121 or (800) 371-2545, was built in 1913 and owned by Donald Ross from 1921 until his death in 1948. Located in the heart of Pinehurst Village, tucked away in a shady stand of pine trees, this informal, homey inn consists of 40 rooms, a restaurant, and a popular lounge. Expensive-to-Luxury rates, including breakfast and dinner, range $100-150. Golf privileges are available at all local courses but cost extra.

Along US Route 1, in Southern Pines and Aberdeen, more than half a dozen franchise lodgings provide dependably comfortable rooms at less expensive rates. All the local chain operations offer a variety of golf privileges at various local courses for an extra fee. At the top of the franchise line, the **Holiday Inn Southern Pines,** US Route 1 and Morgantown Road, tel. (910) 692-8585 or (800) 262-5737 provides 160 rooms at moderate rates, around $75. At the least expensive end of the franchise spectrum, the **Motel 6,** 1408 Sandy Hills Dr., tel. (910) 944-5633 or (800) 466-8356, is located a third of a mile off US 1 in Aberdeen and offers 81 inexpensive (including some pet-friendly) rooms, around $45.

FOOD AND DRINK

All of the lodgings listed above except the Motel 6 have at least one restaurant, plus a lounge.

In addition, if you stay at any of these spots, meals are usually included with the cost of your stay. Nonetheless, we will point out a few inviting culinary choices in Pinehurst Village. For the ultimate in fine dining, make a reservation at the **Carolina Dining Room,** at the Pinehurst Resort and Country Club, tel. (910) 295-8434. Jackets are required for dinner at this luxurious restaurant, where you'll be treated to a prix-fixe, five-course, gourmet meal for about $40/person. If you just want to sample the ambience, the Carolina Dining Room also serves breakfast and lunch buffets for $10-12.

For delicious, down-home country cooking in a more casual, yet historic atmosphere, try the restaurant at the **Pinecrest Inn,** Dogwood Road in Pinehurst, tel. (910) 295-6121. The house specialty is stuffed pork chops, but you can also choose from a variety of other delightful dishes, including beef, seafood, and poultry. Dinner entrees range $12-22. The inn also serves breakfast for $3-6. Reservations are requested for dinner. The place is also home to one of the liveliest nightspots in Pinehurst Village, **Mr. B's Bar,** a welcoming spot to share the highlights and lowlights of your day's golf round over cocktails.

The **Pinehurst Playhouse Restaurant,** in the Theater Building, West Village Green, tel. (910) 295-8873, is a popular spot for the soup-and-sandwich crowd. Lunches run about $4-8; it's not open for dinner. The **Pinehurst Sundry & Soda Fountain,** 40 Chinquapin St., in the heart of the village, tel. (910) 295-3193, doesn't have much in the way of ambience, with its Formica tables and sandwiches served in plastic baskets. But the burgers are splendid and the milk shakes memorable. Open Mon.-Sat. 8:30 a.m.-5:30 p.m. and Sunday 10 a.m.-5 p.m., a sandwich and shake will run $5-6. A few doors down the street, tucked away behind some Pinehurst Village shops, you can find one of the very few ethnic restaurants in this area at **Theo's Taverna,** 140 Chinquapin St., tel. (910) 295-0780. Open Mon.-Sat. for lunch ($4-9) and dinner ($8-25), Theo's serves authentic Greek fare in an intimate, elegant setting.

GETTING THERE

If you're staying at one of the premier resorts, particularly the Pinehurst Resort & Country Club, you can leave your car at home and fly into Moore County Airport, tel. (910) 692-3212. Shuttles from the resorts will pick you up at the airport and drive you from place to place once you arrive. The airport is mainly served by USAirways Express, tel. (800) 428-4322. Otherwise, your best bet is to drive to the Pinehurst area, located about 70 miles from the Raleigh/Durham Airport, about 90 miles from the Piedmont Triad International Airport (between Greensboro and Winston-Salem), and about 105 miles from Charlotte's Douglas International Airport. One note about driving to Pinehurst: there are no interstates that lead directly to this area, so be prepared for some slow going. For example, though the Raleigh/Durham airport is only about 70 miles away, you'll drive at least two hours before arriving at Pinehurst.

THE RALEIGH/DURHAM/ CHAPEL HILL TRIANGLE

For most of the 19th and 20th centuries, the "Triangle" cities of Raleigh, Durham, and Chapel Hill retained separate and distinct personalities. Raleigh, located 23 miles from Durham and 28 miles from Chapel Hill, had the somewhat antiseptic ambience of a small city whose main purpose was to serve as the state capital. Durham and Chapel Hill were closer to each other geographically—about 12 miles apart—but had little in common. In Durham—long a North Carolina manufacturing hub—the air held the sweet scent of curing tobacco mixed with the smell of smoke from textile mills. In Chapel Hill, students and faculty breathed the rarefied air of higher learning at the oldest state university in the nation.

Research Triangle Park

Today, the cities of Raleigh, Durham, and Chapel Hill are much more closely intermingled, and one of the unifying elements is sprawling Research Triangle Park (known locally as "RTP"), an internationally recognized center for cutting-edge research and development. Spanning 6,900 acres just off I-40, near Raleigh/Durham International Airport, RTP lies just 20 minutes from each of the Triangle cities. The research park

was created in the late 1950s, when leaders from state and local government, private businesses, and universities developed the idea of a campus that would combine research and development with a diversified tax base. They also sought to reverse the trend of young scientists and engineers graduating from the three major universities in the area—Duke University in Durham, the University of North Carolina in Chapel Hill, and North Carolina State University in Raleigh—only to leave the state for more lucrative employment opportunities elsewhere. In 1958, $1.5 million in private funding was used to purchase land for RTP, and the nonprofit Research Triangle Foundation was established. The purpose of RTP was to provide an ideal setting for research that would attract companies at the forefront of technological research and development in the burgeoning scientific and technological fields.

In 1965, IBM and the National Institute of Environmental Health Sciences both established facilities in RTP, and the park began to grow in earnest. By 1989, 66 companies had established research and development facilities in RTP. The next decade brought even faster growth. Home, at last count, to about 140 private, government, and nonprofit companies and organizations, the park provides a major economic hub for the area, employing more than 37,000 scientists, technicians, support personnel, and other professionals, whose combined salaries total more than $1.2 billion a year. Including the scientists working at RTP and the faculties of the area universities, the Triangle boasts the highest per capita concentration of Ph.D.s in the nation.

The Rest of the Triangle
When they discuss their home turf with "outsiders," the folks who live in these three cities proudly consider themselves residents of "The Triangle," a metropolitan area of about a million people. The residents of the area beamed with pride when, in 1994, *Money Magazine* proclaimed the Triangle the best place to live in the United States. But when you probe the residents, deeper loyalties to the individual cities emerge. As much as the Triangle presents itself to the world as a unified, metropolitan area on the move, the citizens in the Triangle area are passionately protective of their respective cities. The rivalry among the Triangle cities is based on a laundry list of quality-of-life issues. Raleigh residents are proud of their ever-more-

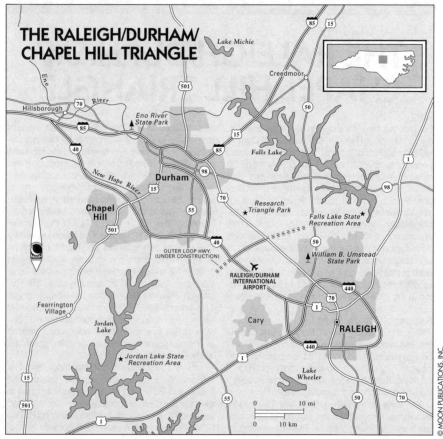

THE RALEIGH/DURHAM/ CHAPEL HILL TRIANGLE

© MOON PUBLICATIONS, INC.

cosmopolitan capital city—complete with traffic jams. Durham devotees are proud of the blue-collar heritage of their tobacco and textile industry roots and their nationally known minor league baseball team, the Durham Bulls. Chapel Hill's citizens are proud of the intellectual heritage of their college town, home to the first state university in the nation, founded in 1795.

But the most heated rivalry among the Triangle cities revolves around their respective college basketball teams—the University of North Carolina (known locally as simply "Carolina") Tar Heels in Chapel Hill, the Duke Blue Devils in Durham, and the North Carolina State Wolfpack in Raleigh. College basketball is close to being a universal religion in the Triangle. Particularly when Duke and Carolina play each other, the game assumes the feverish character of a Super Bowl: every local bar is jammed with vociferous

fans, parties are pervasive, and the streets are almost barren of traffic except for pizza delivery trucks and folks making frantic runs during half-time for more chips and brew. When visiting the Triangle, particularly during college basketball season (November through March), be aware that there are only three opinions that can get you into trouble: 1) that North Carolina native and former Carolina star Michael Jordan (known locally simply as "Michael") isn't the best basketball player of all time; 2) that former Carolina coach Dean Smith isn't the greatest coach of all time; and 3) that college basketball isn't the most exciting sport in the world. Say whatever you want about Jesse Helms, North Carolina's senior U.S. Senator (everyone else does), but be very careful what you say about Michael, Coach Smith, or anything else having to do with college basketball. Consider yourself warned.

RALEIGH

In 1792, the members of North Carolina's state government confronted a problem that had plagued the colonies and, later, the state's legislators—namely, that the seat of state government could change from year to year, depending on which bloc of lawmakers controlled the most votes. Over the previous century, more than a half dozen towns had alternately served as the state capital. The issue was finally settled, thanks primarily to the persuasive powers of state senator Joel Lane, a tavern owner in the tiny village of Raleigh who convinced a plurality of his legislative peers that his little tract of land would be a perfect compromise for a state capital. Nobody in the legislature was envious of Raleigh, because, basically, there was nothing there. And so the legislature bought 1,000 acres of Senator Lane's land and made plans for designing a capital city. Two years later, the brick statehouse was completed, and Raleigh was immediately dubbed a "city of streets without houses." Indeed, state government was slow to build its big bureaucracy. By 1800, the entire permanent population of Raleigh numbered just 699 folks.

The 1800s witnessed the creation of a half dozen colleges in Raleigh (all of them still going strong today). In 1842, one of the nation's first colleges for women was founded here; St. Mary's

college remains the only Episcopal women's college in the United States. In 1857, the Presbyterians, not to be outdone, founded their own women's campus, Peace College, which still occupies a lush section of downtown Raleigh, near St. Mary's. A bike ride away, Meredith College for women was formed in 1891 and has grown into today's largest four-year women's college in the Southeast, with more than 2,500 students. Women weren't the only nontraditional students getting college educations in Raleigh in the 1800s. Within the first couple of years after the Civil War, two of the nation's oldest four-year institutions for freed slaves and other African-Americans were established downtown; St. Augustine's College and Shaw University both still thrive today.

Then in 1889, a few blocks away from the Capitol, the state legislature established the North Carolina College of Agriculture and Mechanical Arts; this eventually evolved into today's massive North Carolina State University (known locally as "State"), which enrolls more than 27,000 students each year.

Raleigh continued its tradition of economic diversification through the 1900s, balancing government business with manufacturing and education and continually seducing more and more folks to make Raleigh their home. Within the past 25 years, Raleigh has doubled in population—to its current 240,000 residents—and the ubiquity of construction equipment around the city today attests to the fact that the boom shows no sign of slowing.

But true to Raleigh's advent as an unassuming compromise as a state capital, the phrase "downtown Raleigh" could be considered slightly misleading, despite the city's noticeable skyline of skyscrapers. That's not to say that downtown Raleigh is a ghost town. The downtown City Market area, the Hillsborough Street area of the North Carolina State campus, and the historic neighborhoods of Hayes Barton and Oakwood buzz with activity both day and night. But most of the activity in this capital city is quite diffuse, taking place in hundreds of strip malls and office parks spread rather evenly throughout the city limits. If you venture outside of downtown, you're well advised to first pick up some detailed maps at the downtown **Capital Area Visitors Center,** 301 N. Blount St., at the corner of Blount and Lane Streets, tel. (919) 733-3456. Or, better

yet, before you visit, get an information packet by contacting the **Greater Raleigh Convention and Visitors Bureau,** 225 Hillsborough St., Suite 400, P.O. Box 1879, Raleigh, NC 27602, tel. (919) 834-5900 or (800) 849-8499.

SIGHTS

One of the great perks about visiting North Carolina's capital city is that, thanks to state taxpayers, you can visit a lot of spots, from fascinating museums to lush state parks, without having to pay an admission fee. With a few notable exceptions—especially the Museum of Art and some parks—most of Raleigh's major attractions are located in the downtown area, within walking distance or a short drive of each other. Negotiating the streets of downtown Raleigh is pretty easy. The streets are laid out on a square, grid system, there's plentiful parking, and traffic is generally light, except during rush hours when thousands of bureaucrats fill and empty downtown's state government buildings.

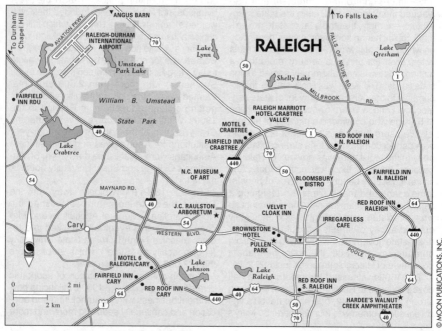

© MOON PUBLICATIONS, INC.

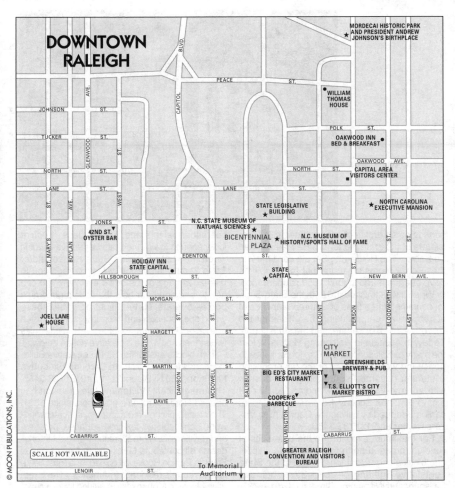

DOWNTOWN RALEIGH

MORDECAI HISTORIC PARK AND PRESIDENT ANDREW JOHNSON'S BIRTHPLACE

WILLIAM THOMAS HOUSE

OAKWOOD INN BED & BREAKFAST

CAPITAL AREA VISITORS CENTER

NORTH CAROLINA EXECUTIVE MANSION

STATE LEGISLATIVE BUILDING

N.C. STATE MUSEUM OF NATURAL SCIENCES

BICENTENNIAL PLAZA

N.C. MUSEUM OF HISTORY/SPORTS HALL OF FAME

42ND ST. OYSTER BAR

HOLIDAY INN STATE CAPITAL

STATE CAPITAL

JOEL LANE HOUSE

CITY MARKET

GREENSHIELDS BREWERY & PUB

BIG ED'S CITY MARKET RESTAURANT

T.S. ELLIOTT'S CITY MARKET BISTRO

COOPER'S BARBECUE

SCALE NOT AVAILABLE

GREATER RALEIGH CONVENTION AND VISITORS BUREAU

To Memorial Auditorium

© MOON PUBLICATIONS, INC.

Government Buildings

To get the flavor of this capital city, start your visit by exploring a couple visitor-friendly government buildings. The **North Carolina State Capitol,** 1 Edenton St., tel. (919) 733-4994, is located in the center of downtown Raleigh. Taking up two city blocks, the Capitol Square is bordered by seven streets, including the main drags of Hillsborough and Salisbury Streets. Built 1833-40, this masterpiece of Greek Revival-style government building architecture exudes the grace-

ful, marbled majesty you might expect of an early 19th-century American state capitol. But unlike many of its contemporary counterparts in other states, where the state capitol buildings seek to emulate the vast indoor spaces of the grand U.S. Capitol in Washington, D.C., the North Carolina State Capitol gives a much more intimate feel. Every room is only as large as it needed to be at the time. The legislative chambers for the state Senate and House of Representatives are particularly humble for the time,

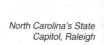

North Carolina's State Capitol, Raleigh

serving as an architectural reminder to the legislators of the state motto, "To Be Rather Than To Seem." The House and Senate don't meet in these cozy rooms anymore, but these spaces have been restored to their 1850s appearance.

When it was finished in 1840, the State Capitol contained the offices of all three branches of state government, including the offices for the Governor, House, Senate, and the state courts. Today, in addition to welcoming visitors to tour the many exhibit spaces, the Capitol continues to house the working offices of the governor and lieutenant governor, so the place still bustles with energy. Visitors are welcome Mon.-Fri. 9 a.m.-5 p.m. and Sunday 1-5 p.m. Guided tours can be arranged by calling the Capital Area Visitors Center at (919) 733-3456.

For maximum exposure to the blue suits of Raleigh, proceed north from the State Capitol one block along Bicentennial Plaza to the **State Legislative Building,** on Jones Street, between Salisbury and Wilmington Streets, tel. (919) 733-7928. Completed in 1961, this home of the North Carolina Senate and House of Representatives is relatively unique because it is solely devoted to the legislative branch of state government (almost all other states combine the executive and legislative branches in the same building). Throughout the State Legislative Building, provisions are made for easy public access and observation of the legislative process. However, you may want to heed Otto Von Bismarck's sage advice, that law is like sausage—you don't want to see either being made. Nonetheless, if you're lucky enough to visit the State Legislative Building when the North Carolina State House and/or State Senate in session, we encourage you to take advantage of the bird's eye view you can get, to see and hear how the state's governing bodies operate. Natural light pervades these grand open spaces, and the public is free to listen and observe from comfortable seats in balconies two stories above the legislative action below.

Two blocks east of the State Legislative Building stands the stately **North Carolina Executive Mansion,** 200 N. Blount St., tel. (919) 733-3456. This magnificent, Victorian-style mansion has housed North Carolina's governors since 1891. The steeply pitched roofs, cupola, intricate woodwork, richly colored textured surfaces, porches, and pavilions, and breathtakingly elegant interior design all contribute to making this mansion, as Franklin Delano Roosevelt opined, "the most beautiful governor's residence in America." The Executive Mansion is open only to guided tours, scheduled by the Capital Area Visitors Center, tel. (919) 733-3456. Tours are frequent but not on a set schedule, as they are led by dozens of devoted volunteers whose schedules vary, so be sure to call ahead before you visit. You can usually count on tours being offered on Tuesday and Friday.

Museums

After your introduction to the living governmental history of Raleigh, you can gradually work your way back in time hundreds, and then thousands, of years by just walking across Jones Street, from the State Legislative Building to Bicentennial Plaza. On either side of the plaza you'll find two engaging, free-admission state museums. The **North Carolina Museum of History,** 5 E. Edenton St., tel. (919) 715-0200, opened in 1994. This modern museum succeeds in its attempt to make learning about the state's history a relatively entertaining enterprise. Videos, hands-on exhibits, and more than 300,000 artifacts and photographs fill the four galleries, each with a different focus. Collections feature North Carolina women, folk life, a chronological history of the state, and the **North Carolina Sports Hall of Fame.**

Stroll across the Bicentennial Plaza promenade to widen your history focus from centuries to millennia at the marvelous **North Carolina State Museum of Natural Sciences,** 102 N. Salisbury St., tel. (919) 733-7450. The museum's zoological collections were started in 1879, and this place has been providing delightful and informative romps for kids and adults alike ever since. The museum currently includes seven major natural history exhibits, including Freshwater Wetlands, Fossil Hall, Bird Hall, and Gems and Minerals. The exhibits are detailed, finely crafted, and absorbing, reflecting the work of its full time research staff. As this edition went to press, this popular, well-funded museum was in the process of completing a major expansion, scheduled to open in spring 1999. The new building, at 11 W. Jones St., will be four times larger than the current museum, adding 200,000 new feet of exhibit space. The new exhibits sound spectacular, like the "Mountains to the Sea" exhibit, a walk through an immersion diorama with both live and mounted animals in six native North Carolina habitats ranging from mountain spruce forest to the Atlantic Ocean, including interactive learning stations and a two-story waterfall. Another big attraction will be the new "Prehistoric North Carolina" exhibit, displaying replicas of the state's ancient habitats, with their curious plants and animals, including the new crown jewel of the museum, the 40-foot-long fossilized skeleton of *Acrocanthosaurus atokensis,* acquired in 1997. This astoundingly rare skeleton, nicknamed "The Terror of the South," is the only one exhibited in the world and, fittingly enough, once roamed the state's turf.

The museum is not closed for this expansion project, so you can still visit while the new halls are being completed. When the new 200,000-square-foot space is finished, you'll be able to browse among 600,000 specimens of animals, vegetables, and minerals running the gamut from ancient fossils to live critters, in addition to lots of interactive exhibits including a hands-on science experiment center. The free-admission museum is open Mon.-Sat. 9 a.m.-5 p.m. and Sunday 1-5 p.m.

It's too far to walk, but it's worth a short drive to visit the **North Carolina Museum of Art,** 2110 Blue Ridge Rd., tel. (919) 839-6262. In 1956, North Carolina became the first state in the nation to use public funds to purchase an art collection and appropriated $1 million, most of which was used to purchase artworks from the private collection of millionaire merchant Samuel Kress. Originally housed in a renovated office building downtown, the museum moved in 1983 into its grand, present structure, a $15 million, 180,000-square-foot masterpiece designed by Edward Durrel Stone, architect of the original Museum of Modern Art in Manhattan.

In addition to frequently changing, traveling exhibits of the highest caliber, the museum today provides a wealth of works, presented in historical sequence through eight major collections: Ancient, European, American, 20th Century, Jewish ceremonial art, African, Oceanic, and New World. The museum's collections of paintings are particularly dazzling, ranging from old European masters like Sandro Botticelli and Peter Paul Rubens to more modern Europeans like Claude Monet and John Singleton Copley, as well as an extensive American collection includingWinslow Homer and Georgia O'Keefe. Guided tours are offered daily at 1:30 p.m., an ideal way to get to know the collection. The museum also presents films in an outdoor sculpture garden/amphitheater, as well as concerts and lectures.

The museum is about a 10-minute drive west from downtown, and only five minutes from either I-40 or I-440. From downtown Raleigh, take Downtown Blvd. northwest (which will become Wade Ave.), turning right (north) on Blue Ridge Rd. after you pass the I-440 Interchange. From either I-40 or I-440, take the Wade Avenue exit (exit 289 on I-40 or exit 4B from I-440). Proceed on Wade Avenue to Blue Ridge Road. Turn north on Blue Ridge, following the signs to the museum. Admission is free. Hours are Tues.-Thurs. and Saturday 9 a.m.-5 p.m., Friday 9 a.m.-9 p.m., and Sunday 11 a.m.-6 p.m. The museum is closed on Monday.

Historic Homes

In addition to the magnificently elegant Executive Mansion, two other homes in the downtown Raleigh area combine beautiful architecture and gardens along with interesting historical insights. Eight blocks west of the State Capitol, the **Joel Lane House,** at the corner of St. Mary's and W. Hargett Streets, tel. (919) 833-3431, stands as Raleigh's oldest dwelling, constructed in the 1760s. The one-and-a-half-story, wood-frame home was built by the "Father of Raleigh," Colonel Joel Lane, a colorful character and savvy negotiator who combined his talents as a tavern owner and state senator to pull off quite a legislative coup in 1788.

Prior to that year, the state capital was moved between half a dozen cities, depending on the fluctuating influence of various legislators and governors. In 1788, the state legislature appointed a commission of senators and representatives to approve "an unalterable seat of state government," and state Senator Joel Lane saw an opening. Since choosing a capital city was such a big decision, with so many competing interests, Lane suggested to the commission members that they should contemplate this decision at some neutral site, like his home, with its adjacent tavern. The commission members agreed and stayed at Lane's house for two weeks, during which Lane's tavern continually supplied libations to the commission members. The negotiations were often heated, as every commission member wanted to locate the state capital in his district. After two weeks of unsuccessful wrangling, the commissioners realized they had to choose a neutral site that would displease them all equally. Inspired no doubt by their host's hospitality (including several barrels of ale), the commission concluded its business by choosing to buy 1,000 acres of Joel Lane's land for $1,378 and making Raleigh the permanent capital city of North Carolina. The Joel Lane House and its formal city garden and herb garden are open to the public Tues.-Fri. 10 a.m.-2 p.m. and the first and third Saturdays of each month, 1-4 p.m. Tours begin on the half hour, with an admission charge of $4.

Eight blocks northeast of the State Capitol, at the intersection of Wake Forest Road, Mimosa Street, and Person Street, lies the **Mordecai Historic Park and President Andrew Johnson's Birthplace,** tel. (919) 834-4844. The 1785 plantation house with original furnishings, in addition to the Ellen Mordecai Garden, a kitchen outbuilding, and other historic structures grouped together along a restored 18th century village street, provide an evocative glimpse into 18th-century Raleigh life.

Included among the historic structures is the tiny 1795 house in which President Andrew Johnson was born. Just 12 by 18 feet, this humble cabin provides a moving introduction to the life of one of our nation's most fascinating, underappreciated presidents. Born in 1908, Johnson spent his first 16 poverty-stricken years in Raleigh, never spending a day in school and being apprenticed to a tailor when he was 10 years old. At age 16, he rebelled against his tailor master and fled to Greeneville, Tennessee, where he plied his tailor trade, continued his self-education, and made friends with customers and neighbors.

At the age of 21, Johnson ran for the post of alderman, representing his working-class peers against a slate of Greeneville's aristocracy. He won, the first of a string of successful elections in which he became mayor, state representative, state senator, U.S. congressman, U.S. senator, and U.S. Vice President. Honest Abe Lincoln, a Yankee Republican, had chosen Johnson, a Southern Democrat, as his running mate in 1864, to signal his goal to reunite the United States. The Lincoln/Johnson administration was just 42 days old when John Wilkes Booth assassinated Lincoln, propelling Andrew Johnson into the Presidency. Shortly thereafter, the Republicans in Congress voted to impeach Johnson because he had illegally fired Lincoln's Secretary of War, the infamous Edwin Stanton. This is especially ironic because several historians later suspected that Stanton had some degree of complicity in Lincoln's assassination. The U.S. Senate put Johnson on trial. He was found not guilty by a margin of just one vote. He finished out his term, supervising the peaceful reunification of the United States, from 1865 until 1869, when he was succeeded by Ulysses S. Grant, whose Reconstruction policies imposed much harsher punishments upon the Confederate states. Six years after voluntarily leaving the Presidency, Johnson was elected again to the U.S. Senate, the only ex-President who ever served in that body. After visiting his birthplace, you'll never think of Andrew Johnson again as just "the only impeached President," which is how he's dismissed by most history textbooks. Closed on Tuesday, the park is open Monday and Wed.-Sat. 10 a.m.-3 p.m. and Sunday 1-3 p.m. Tours cost $4 and begin every half hour.

Gardens, Parks, and Lakes

Greenery abounds throughout Raleigh. Inviting, 65-acre **Pullen Park**, 408 Ashe Ave., tel. (919) 831-6468, located on the outskirts of downtown, adjacent to the North Carolina State University campus, offers lots of diversions. You can rent a paddle-boat to navigate the small lake, swim in one of the pools of the grand new aquatic center, or ride on one of the horses of the Denzel Carousel, restored in the mid-1990s at a cost of

the Executive Mansion

more than $200,000. The **J.C. Raulston Arboretum**, 4301 Beryl Rd., tel. (919) 515-3132 provides a more natural getaway. Featuring more than 8,000 varieties of native trees, shrubs and perennials, these elegantly landscaped gardens encompass eight acres and are interlaced with wide walking paths ideal for those seeking a peaceful hour's stroll.

For a more dramatic escape to nature, **William B. Umstead State Park**, tel. (919) 677-0062, stretches for 5,300 lovely, dark and deep acres of forest between I-40 and US Route 70. Dozens of miles of hiking trails and 11 miles of bicycling and horseback riding trails make Umstead State Park Raleigh's premier nature oasis. With 28 campsites, the park also provides the best of the few camping opportunities in the Raleigh area.

If you're looking to spend a few hours on a lake beach, **Falls Lake** 13304 Creedmoor Rd., less than half an hour's drive from downtown Raleigh, tel. (919) 676-1027, will fill the bill. This manmade reservoir, created in 1983, stretches for 22 miles from the north of Raleigh to the north of Durham. To get to the lake's recreational areas and closest beaches, proceed north from downtown Raleigh on NC Route 50 (Creedmoor Road), and then take NC Route 98 East to Falls Lake Recreation Area or Blue Jay Point County Park.

SPECTATOR SPORTS

As this book went to press, Raleigh was preparing for its first major league sports franchise, the National Hockey League's **Carolina Hurricanes**, tel. (919) 467-PUCK or (888) NHL-TIX-1. They are scheduled to make their hometown debut sometime in 1999, when the new sports arena will be completed. In the meantime, the Hurricanes will continue to play their home games in Greensboro, their temporary North Carolina home. The Hurricanes, however, cannot hope to supplant Raleigh's favorite team, the North Carolina State Wolfpack, tel. (919) 515-2106. As we mentioned earlier, college basketball is a religion in the Triangle, so be prepared for a passionate sporting experience if you can wrangle a seat at a Wolfpack game at the 20,000-plus-seat Reynolds Coliseum.

PERFORMING ARTS

Founded in 1932, the taxpayer-subsidized **North Carolina Symphony** 2 E. South St., tel. (919) 733-2750, travels throughout the state, delivering about 200 delightful performances every year. Based in Raleigh, the symphony performs most frequently at Memorial Auditorium, box office tel. (919) 733-2750, ext. 260, and often features internationally renowned soloists. Touring Broadway shows, ballets, and operas also make their way to Memorial Auditorium periodically during the year. At **Hardee's Walnut Creek Amphitheater,** 3801 Rock Quarry Rd., tel. (919) 831-6400 or (800) 48-CREEK, the biggest acts in music strut their stuff before folks sitting in the 7,000 seats in the open-air pavilion, and up to 13,000 more lounging on the surrounding, sloping lawn. Call the automated Concert Line at (919) 831-6666 for upcoming events and/or directions to the amphitheater.

ACCOMMODATIONS

Bed and Breakfasts

The **William Thomas House,** 530 N. Blount St., tel. (919) 755-9400 or (800) 653-3466, is located along one of Raleigh's ritziest residential rows, within walking distance of downtown's attractions. Built circa 1881, this majestic Victorian home offers four spacious guest rooms, all with private telephones, baths, and cable TV. If you're in Raleigh to lobby state government on a difficult issue, this is the perfect spot to stay, not only for the comfortable quarters and business amenities including fax and copying services, but also because you'll get some expert advice from owners Sarah and Jim Lofton, veteran insiders of the Raleigh and North Carolina political scenes (Jim is a former state secretary of administration). Rates range $100-135 and include a full Southern breakfast, snacks, soft drinks, late afternoon wine and cheese, and evening turndown service. Expensive-Premium.

Nestled in the historic Oakwood neighborhood, which is known for its quiet, tree-lined streets and restored homes, the **Oakwood Inn Bed & Breakfast,** 411 N. Bloodworth St., tel. (919) 836-9712 or (800) 267-9712, offers six rooms, each furnished with Victorian antiques and equipped with private baths and phone lines. Fax and copier services are also available. Rates run $75-130 and include a full breakfast and afternoon tea. Moderate-Premium.

Hotels and Motels—Downtown Vicinity

The vast majority of hotel/motel lodgings in the Raleigh area are of the franchise variety. A notable exception lies about two blocks from the NC State campus, at the unassumingly tasteful 170-room **Velvet Cloak Inn,** 1505 Hillsborough St., tel. (919) 828-0333, (800) 334-4772 outside NC, or (800) 662-8829 inside NC. Though the exterior suffers from the boxlike configurations popular during the early 1960s when the hotel was built, the inside reveals marbled lobbies, sunlit atriums, and arguably the most personalized and polished service available at any Raleigh hotel, including the city's best hotel restaurant, the **Charter Room,** and one of the best hotel bars, the **Baron's Lounge,** a favorite haunt of the capital city's politicos. Amenities include the enclosed swimming pool, surrounded by a tropical garden. Premium rates start at $120. Two blocks down the street, next to the NC State campus, the **Brownstone Hotel,** 1707 Hillsborough St., tel. (919) 828-0811 or (800) 237-0772, is a former Hilton that was purchased by private owners in 1985. In addition to amenities like the swimming pool, restaurant, and lounge, the Brownstone offers free HBO in every one of its 210 rooms. Next door, the YMCA provides full fitness facilities for guests. Rates start at $100. Expensive.

If you're visiting Raleigh on government business, the most convenient choice is the downtown **Holiday Inn State Capital,** 320 Hillsborough St., tel. (919) 832-0501 or (800) HOLIDAY, within walking distance of most state government buildings. The cylindrical tower reaches 20 stories into the downtown Raleigh skyline, just two blocks from the State Capitol Building at the center of town. In addition to the indoor pool on the second floor, the 200-room hotel features the **Top of the Tower** restaurant, providing the most elevated restaurant view in Raleigh. Rates range $85-105. Expensive.

Chain Lodgings along I-440 and I-40

More than 50 franchise motels surround Raleigh, all providing clean, decent rooms. In general, the motels in north and east Raleigh, along the I-440 Beltline, are a bit less expensive than the more traveled I-40 stretch, which shares the southern section of the I-440 Beltline.

For inexpensive lodgings, try the pet-friendly rooms at one of four **Red Roof Inns** in Raleigh, including one on I-40/440 at I-40 exit 293 (exit 1 on I-440), 1800 Walnut St. in Cary, tel. (919) 469-3400 or (800) 843-7663, and one in northeast Raleigh at exit 13 of I-440, at 3520 Maitland Dr., tel. (919) 231-0200 or (800) 843-7663. **Motel 6** also provides two inexpensive, Rover- and Garfield-friendly locations on the Beltline, including one at exit 293 on I-40 (exit 1 on I-440), 1401 Buck Jones Rd., tel. (919) 467-6171 or (800) 4MOTEL6, and one at exit 7 on I-440 in north Raleigh, 3921 Arrow Dr., tel. (919) 782-7071 or (800) 4MOTEL6. For I-40 lodgings in the moderate range, around $60, try the **Fairfield Inn,** 2641 Appliance Court, just off I-40 exit 11B, tel. (919) 856-9800 or (800) 348-6000.

The biggest hotel in Raleigh is the 375-room, six-story **Raleigh Marriott Hotel-Crabtree Valley,** 4500 Marriott Dr., tel. (919) 781-7000 or (800) 228-9290. Half a mile off Exit 7 on I-440, located directly across the street from Raleigh's premier shopping mall, Crabtree Valley Mall, the Marriott offers both indoor and outdoor pools, an exercise room with whirlpools, restaurants, and lounges on-site. Rates begin around $75 on Friday and Saturday to around $120 the rest of week. Moderate-Premium.

For accommodations at Research Triangle Park, see the Durham accommodations section.

FOOD AND DRINK

Downtown Restaurants
For breakfast, lunch, dinner, and drinks in the downtown area, make your way to the cobblestone streets of **City Market,** located three blocks southeast of the State Capitol at Martin and Blount Streets. The Spanish Mission-style marketplace served as the city's farmers market from 1914 to 1957. In the mid-1980s, in an effort to revitalize the downtown area, the market house and surrounding buildings were renovated to provide an inviting atmosphere for eating, shopping and entertainment. Intermingled amongst art galleries and specialty shops, you'll find a variety of restaurants.

Y'all will know you're in the South when you bite into a biscuit or take a gulp of the sweet tea at **Big Ed's City Market Restaurant,** 220 Wolfe St., tel. (919) 836-9909. This is the place to find down-home Carolina cooking, including country ham with red-eye gravy, grits, fried chicken, and lots of succulent, slow-cooked vegetables. The homey atmosphere, accented with an eclectic array of farm implements, makes you feel like you're sitting down to mama's kitchen table. Almost everything on the menu is $5 or less. Open Mon.-Sat. for breakfast and Mon.-Fri. for lunch.

Day or night, beer aficionados will feel at home at either of City Market's popular pubs. **Greenshields Brewery & Pub,** 214 E. Martin St., tel. (919) 829-0214, brews a wide variety of delightful beers, all brewed on the premises, and serves standard American pub fare, along with British staples like fish and chips and shepherd's pie ($5-10). When the weather cooperates, Greenshields' patio area is a relaxing spot to kick back and people-watch. **T.S. Elliott's City Market Bistro,** 205 Wolfe St., tel. (919) 839-0405, offers 25 microbrews and imported beers on tap, and an eclectic selection of bistro cuisine in an English-tavern atmosphere ($5-10).

If your historical wanderings through downtown Raleigh work up an appetite for some traditional eastern Carolina barbecue (vinegar, not tomato-based), make your way to one of the dozens of humble booths in **Cooper's Barbecue,** a couple blocks west of City Market and three blocks south of the State Capitol, at 109 East Davie Street, tel. (919) 832-7614. Dusty paintings of swine engaging in various pursuits adorn the walls around this down-home barbecue-mecca, a Raleigh landmark since the 1920s. At every booth, you'll have a chance to sample a full panoply of the many, sometimes mysterious, "barbecue" sauces you'll find on tabletops throughout the South, including "pepper sauce," a delectable jalapeño-vinaigrette-in-a-bottle.

Five blocks northeast of the State Capitol, you'll find the best seafood in town at the **42nd Street Oyster Bar,** 508 W. Jones St., tel. (919) 831-2811. Located *not* on 42nd Street but at the corner of Jones and West Streets, the Oyster Bar has reigned as the capital city's premier gathering place for politicians since it opened up its tin-trimmed doors for business in 1931.

Open and airy inside, exuding a bustling bistro-like atmosphere, the Oyster Bar provides a veritable extravaganza of fresh fish and seafood, most of which is caught by its own boats, immediately processed by its Southport Fish Market on the Outer Banks, and whisked straight to the Oyster Bar. From traditional fish and seafood saut°s using white wine, lemon and butter, to spicy Cajun-style preparations—and a full raw bar—the Oyster Bar will satisfy your every craving for a culinary trip to the beach. Dinner entrees range $11-25 and also include a variety of landlubber delights like beef and poultry dishes. Open daily for dinner, the Oyster Bar also serves lunch ($5-10) on weekdays. The spacious bar section of the bistro draws comfortable crowds every night of the week, particularly from Thursday through Saturday nights, when live R&B bands perform.

Decidedly *not* a favorite haunt for North Carolina's tobacco- and pork-friendly politicos, the **Irregardless Cafe,** 901 W. Morgan St., tel. (919) 833-9920, located nine blocks west of the State Capitol, nonetheless represents a proud Raleigh tradition of its own, having burst onto the Raleigh restaurant scene in the 1970s with an unprecedented, vegetarian-only menu. The fare has since expanded to include seafood and poultry dishes, and the cafe was forced to completely renovate its comfy environs after a fire in 1994, but the Irregardless retains its unpretentious, Bohemian (though totally smoke-free) atmosphere. And it still serves the juiciest bean burger in town. Lunch runs $4-6, dinner $10-15. Open Mon.-Sat. 11:30 a.m.-2:30 p.m. and 5:30-10 p.m., and Sunday 10 a.m.-2 p.m. Live, digestion-friendly jazz is performed nightly.

Other Raleigh Restaurants
As the city's population has almost doubled since the 1970s, Raleigh's restaurant scene has similarly exploded, today offering a vast variety of international options (albeit many of them located in Raleigh's perpetually expanding number of neighborhood strip malls). If you get a craving for a particular style of food not mentioned in these pages, ask your accommodations' hosts for some suggestions, and, chances are, you'll find gastronomic fulfillment nearby. If, however, you're seeking a memorable meal in Raleigh, we heartily recommend the following two restaurants, well worth any extra driving time it may take you to reach them.

Since its opening in 1962, the **Angus Barn,** 9401 Glenwood Ave., tel. (919) 781-2444, has served as Raleigh's traditional favorite restaurant to celebrate life's rites of passage, be it earning a diploma, landing a new job or promotion, going to the prom, or observing a 50th anniversary. This venerable steak house features a rustic, barn-like atmosphere, filled to the rafters with the echoes of patrons' past (and current) triumphs. The specialty of the house is cuts of prime Angus beef, though the menu also offers an extensive selection of other choices, including rack of lamb, pork baby back ribs, and fresh fish and seafood (including, of course, lobster tails to go with your filet mignon). Most of the entrees (except the surf-and-turf) cost about $20. Don't forget to check out the luscious desserts or the wine and beer list, which alone covers some 30 pages of the menu. Located on US 70 (Glenwood Ave.) near Aviation Parkway, the Barn is open nightly for dinner.

The **Bloomsbury Bistro,** 509 W. Whitaker Mill Rd., in the Eckerd Shopping Center at Five Points, tel. (919) 834-9011, is a relative newcomer to the Raleigh restaurant scene. This charmingly informal bistro, through the talents of chef John Toler, has set a new standard of creative culinary excellence for the capital city. From the sprigs of fresh herbs on the tables and the perfectly professional wait staff to the dazzling food, the Bloomsbury Bistro arguably serves the finest innovative cuisine in Raleigh. The menu changes seasonally, and chef Toler concocts dazzling daily specials to take advantage of the freshest available ingredients, like grilled leg of wild boar with parsnip puree, fresh sage and dried fruit bordelaise, or, for the slightly less adventurous, pan-seared tuna with pickled ginger and basmati rice salad; entrees range $20-30. Open Tues.-Sat. for dinner 5:30-10 p.m., and Sunday 5:30-9 p.m.

Raleigh Nightlife
With a half dozen colleges in the city limits, there's no shortage of nightlife in Raleigh. In addition, Raleigh's pervasive strip malls almost invariably offer at least one neighborhood hangout within walking distance of wherever you may be staying. Raleigh's undisputed hub of supercharged evening and late-night activity is Hillsborough

Street, on the NC State campus. Between Gorman Street and Oberlin Road, about four dozen hot spots radiate with the intermingled throbbings of pounding bass beats and youthful libidos, accompanied by the percussive clunks of empty beer mugs returning to bars and tables. Rather than singling out a few of the interchangeable many, we recommend strolling along this strip to select the sizzling ambience of your choice.

GETTING AROUND

One particularly confusing roadway is the I-440 "Beltline," a circular interstate whose southern portion shares the road with the coast-to-coast I-40. Inspired no doubt by the deservedly maligned North Carolina Department of Transportation employees who design the often-unhelpful directional signs on state roadways, signs direct you to the "Inner Beltway" and the "Outer Beltway" when you take an exit or entrance on I-440. The Inner and Outer Beltlines are the same road, (not to be confused with Raleigh's Outer Loop highway, currently under construction). At any rate, when faced with an immediate decision of whether to take the Inner or Outer Beltline on I-440, remember that the Inner Beltline runs clockwise, and the Outer Beltline runs counterclockwise.

DURHAM

The city of Durham gets its name from Dr. Bartlett Durham, honored not for his medical wizardry but rather for providing a small portion of his land to build the Durham railroad station in 1823. The seeds of the town weren't planted until April 1865, when Union General William T. Sherman and Confederate General Joseph E. Johnston negotiated the largest surrender of the Civil War, a few miles from Durham Station. During the two weeks that negotiations proceeded, the combined armies' 80,000 troops occupying the area had little to do but sit around, smoking and chewing the Brightleaf tobacco that many local farmers grew. After these 80,000 soldiers returned to their homes all across the country, they retained a longing for the bright leaves grown around Durham Station, and inquiries began pouring in, asking how they could get their hands on more of the weed.

A dirt-poor tobacco farmer named Washington Duke, himself just returned to his farm near Durham Station, took advantage of this new demand. By the turn of the century, he had amassed the wealthiest monopoly in the world, in the form of his Durham-based American Tobacco Company. The Duke family and Durham became synonymous with tobacco. The infrastructure built by the Dukes' tobacco empire soon spawned other industries in Durham, including the first mill to produce denim and the world's largest hosiery maker.

The city's newfound wealth at the turn of the century was shared by seven enterprising African-Americans, who, in 1898, established the North Carolina Mutual Life Insurance Company, which soon became the largest African-American-owned and -managed financial institution in the world; today the Durham-based company remains the largest African-American-owned and -managed insurance company in America. Through the early 1900s, downtown Durham's Parrish Street was referred to as "Black Wall Street," a moniker popularized by figures like Booker T. Washington and W.E.B. Dubois, who held up Durham as a model for African-Americans in other cities to emulate. The Durham Committee On the Affairs of Black People, first organized in 1935—and, later, a major force behind the sit-in movement of the 1960s—remains a vital and influential political organization in Durham.

As Durham approaches the 21st century, the textile mills are long gone, and the tobacco industry has, with one small exception, moved to other locales. The huge, abandoned American Tobacco Company factory, with its looming Lucky Strike Water Tower, now keeps watch over the sparkling new Durham Bulls Athletic Park, serving as a ghostly backdrop for fly balls on warm summer nights. Durham's lone remaining tobacco plant, headquarters of Liggett & Myers Tobacco Co.—formerly a major player in the tobacco industry with nationally best-selling brands including L&M, Chesterfields, and Larks—today controls less than five percent of

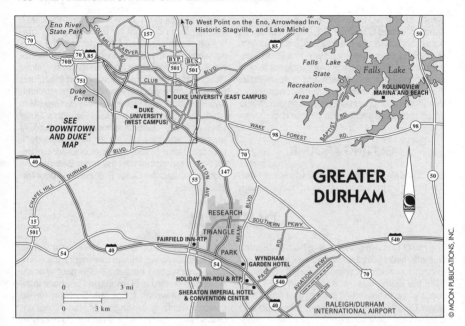

the cigarette market. To the consternation of its peers in the tobacco industry, Liggett & Myers has cooperated with the U.S. Justice Department, settling numerous class action suits filed by dozens of state Attorney-Generals and voluntarily releasing historic, damaging reports about how American tobacco companies for decades targeted much of their marketing at youngsters while engaging in various research and development projects to manipulate the level of nicotine in cigarettes to maximize their addictive power. Despite the fact that its operation continues shrinking, the Liggett & Myers plant periodically contributes a nostalgic olfactory reminder of Durham's history, as the sweet smell of curing tobacco curls out of the flues and wafts through the air for miles.

Nicknamed "The Bull City" at the turn of the century—after Bull Durham, the world's most popular chewing tobacco during most of the 1900s—Durham today has a new, official moniker: "The City of Medicine, USA," befitting a city named for a country doctor. With a population of slightly over 200,000 and a workforce of

about 110,000, nearly one in three Durham residents work in a health-related field. The City of Medicine, home of the world-renowned Duke University Medical Center, also boasts more than 300 other medical and health-related companies and medical practices, with a combined payroll exceeding $1 billion annually.

Further bleaching the collars of Durham's workforce from blue to white is the thriving Research Triangle Park. The park continues to attract America's, and indeed, the globe's, sharpest cutting-edge research and development companies while retaining decades-old R&D tenants including IBM, the Environmental Protection Agency, and Glaxo-Wellcome, Inc. (the largest pharmaceutical company in the world), whose U.S. headquarters are one of the more than 100 companies in RTP.

The neighborhoods surrounding downtown Durham—home to generations of prosperous executives, supervisors, and laborers for Durham's once-thriving manufacturing industries—exude a time-honored grace. The streets are lined with colonnades of century-old willow oaks, crape myrtles, and grand old turn-of-the-century houses, interspersed with the slightly more modest homes of neighboring foremen and senior workers. Today, as you drive through the streets of the neighborhoods between downtown Durham and the Duke University campuses, you'll notice most blocks show the steady influx of white collars to this famed blue-collar city, arguably the state's most dynamically diverse.

For a helpful packet of information on the Bull City, contact the **Durham Convention and Visitors Bureau,** 101 E. Morgan St., Durham, NC 27701, tel. (919) 687-0288 or (800) 755-1755.

SIGHTS

Bennett Place

On April 17, 1865, two battle-weary adversaries, Confederate General Joseph E. Johnston and Union General William T. Sherman, met under a flag of truce to discuss a peaceful surrender of Johnston's Confederate forces, the largest army of the Confederacy (larger even than that of Robert E. Lee, who had surrendered at Appomattox two weeks earlier). Johnston's and Sherman's armies had clashed 70 miles away at the battle of Bentonville less than a month earlier,

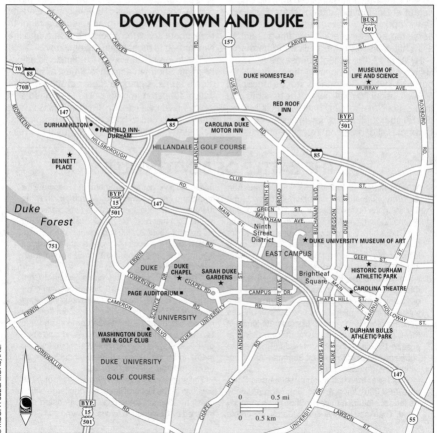

March 19-21, in North Carolina's bloodiest battle. Johnston's army had been forced to retreat, and the Confederate general knew that if he led his troops against Sherman's again, the result would be the same, or worse.

After the Battle of Bentonville, Johnston felt strongly that he had little choice but to surrender to Sherman. On April 11, Johnston met with Jefferson Davis, the President of the Confederacy, who had fled Richmond, Virginia, before Lee's surrender and was currently staying in Greensboro, North Carolina, about 50 miles away. Davis told Johnston that the Confederacy, despite Lee's surrender at Appomattox, could continue the war. Johnston, fresh from his bloody defeat at Bentonville, did not share President Davis' optimism. A savvy negotiator, Johnston persisted and succeeded in getting Davis to allow him to simply have a talk with Sherman.

By April 17, the bulk of Johnston's army occupied the area surrounding the town of Hillsborough, while Sherman's troops occupied Raleigh, about 30 miles away. The generals and their escorts met midway between their lines on the Hillsborough Road, seven miles from the Durham Railroad Station. Needing a place for a conference, Johnston suggested a simple farmhouse nearby, the home of James and Nancy Bennitt. Before officially beginning negotiations, Sherman shared a telegram he'd just received, informing him of President Abraham Lincoln's assassination three nights before.

General Johnston, realizing that the Union's chain of command had been suddenly, and perhaps disastrously, disrupted, took a hard line in the bargaining, encouraged by his earlier conversation with Jefferson Davis, who was still opposed to surrender. Johnston sought not only the military terms of surrender that Lee and Grant had agreed to, but also a range of political guarantees that would preserve and protect many of the Confederate states' sovereignties. General Sherman told Johnston he needed a night to think about Johnston's bold proposals, and the two agreed to meet again the next day.

The following afternoon, to Johnston's astonishment, Sherman agreed to almost all of Johnston's terms, signing a "basis of agreement," which Johnston immediately also signed and which would take effect in 48 hours, unless either party was forced to back out by their superiors. Johnston quickly gained the approval of Presi-

THE BATTLE OF BENTONVILLE

From March 19 to 21, 1865, the Confederate army mounted its last major offensive of the Civil War, the Battle of Bentonville. This major battle, the largest ever fought in North Carolina, was the Confederacy's most significant attempt to defeat General William T. Sherman's army after he left Georgia. Departing from Savannah in January 1865, Sherman had met little resistance on his march northward. Union forces advanced through South Carolina, capturing Columbia and devastating the countryside. Only North Carolina lay between Sherman's army and General Ulysses S. Grant's forces in Virginia. Confederate forces in the Carolinas were widely scattered. General Joseph E. Johnston was ordered to unite these troops and attempt to prevent Sherman from combining his army with Grant's.

With fewer than half as many soldiers as Sherman's 60,000 Union troops, Johnston patiently waited for a chance to catch Sherman's army divided. Thanks to heavy rains in March, miserable road conditions compelled Sherman to separate his command into two wings. By March 18, knowing that Sherman's two sections were temporarily separated by a half-day's march, Johnston organized his army of about 20,000 into a sickle-shaped line, hidden along the Goldsboro road near the village of Bentonville, and lay in wait for Sherman's advancing Federals.

"Nearer and nearer they came," wrote a Confederate soldier on March 19. "When not over 40 or 50 paces from us, the order so anxiously awaited was given, and a sheet of fire blazed out from the hidden battle line . . . that was demoralizing and fatal to the enemy. They battled, reeled, and staggered, while we poured volley after volley into them, and great gaps were made in their line, as brave Federals fell everywhere."

The surprise Confederate ambush overran large sections of the Federal lines, but one large Union division managed to hold on, despite being surrounded by Confederate forces. Knowing that Sher-

dent Davis, but Sherman had no such luck with his superiors in Washington, who were still reeling from the Lincoln assassination. General Ulysses S. Grant commanded Sherman to settle for no less—and no more—than the complete military surrender that Grant had obtained from Robert E. Lee. When Jefferson Davis heard of this Union turnabout, he commanded Johnston to not accept the terms, instructing the general to disband his army's infantry and make an escape with his mounted troops.

Johnston, realizing that prolonging the war would achieve nothing but needless suffering, disobeyed his President's orders, and, on April 26, met again with Sherman at the Bennitt farm, negotiating the largest troop surrender of the Civil War. The final agreement was simply a military surrender, along the Appomattox lines, and ended the war in the Carolinas, Georgia, and Florida, affecting 90,000 Confederate soldiers. Two more surrenders followed Johnston's: General Richard Taylor in Alabama on May 4 and General E. Kirby Smith at New Orleans on May 26, the final Confederate surrender of the Civil War.

The site of Johnston's and Sherman's momentous negotiations today is the **Bennett Place State Historic Site,** 4409 Bennett Memorial Rd., tel. (919) 383-4345 (for some inexplicable reason, the Bennitts' last name has been misspelled for over a century). The visitors center offers an audiovisual presentation and includes a modest collection of Civil War artifacts. Guided tours take you through the immaculately reconstructed, humble, and ghost-filled structures of the Bennitts' place (the original buildings burned down in 1921). Admission is free. Hours April 1-Oct. 31 are Mon.-Sat. 9 a.m.-5 p.m. and Sunday 1-5 p.m. Hours Nov. 1-March 31 are Tues.-Sat., 10 a.m.-4 p.m. and Sunday 1-4 p.m., closed Monday. From I-85/US 70, follow signs from exit 172 southbound or exit 170 northbound.

Duke Homestead

The events that transpired at Bennett Place would soon transform the rural area surrounding the Durham train station. During the weeks that Sherman's army, infamous for a "total war" policy that included burning everything in their path, occupied the Raleigh/Durham area, neighbors supplied Sherman's troops with tons of material to burn—in the form of locally grown Brightleaf tobacco. The locals also supplied Johnston's

---

man's other, stronger wing would soon arrive, Johnston pulled his troops back into more defensible positions. Sherman arrived early the next morning, March 20. For two more days, the opposing armies repeatedly battled each other over an area covering more than 6,000 acres. Johnston, realizing he was now hopelessly outnumbered and outgunned, retreated towards Hillsborough, from where he would negotiate a surrender of his forces to Sherman on April 26.

More than 4,000 soldiers were reported killed, wounded, or missing over the three-day battle. During the confrontation, wounded Union soldiers—and some Confederate soldiers as well—were taken to the farm home of John and Amy Harper, where a Federal field hospital was established. Lieutenant Colonel William of the Ninth Ohio Cavalry wrote, "A dozen surgeons and attendants in their shirtsleeves stood at rude benches cutting off arms and legs and throwing them out of the windows, where they lay scattered on the grass. The legs of infantrymen could be distinguished from those of the cavalry by the size of their calves, as the march of 1,000 miles had increased the size of one and diminished the size of the other."

The Harper House still stands, furnished as a field hospital. A Confederate cemetery and a section of Union trenches are also located on the grounds, part of the **Bentonville Battleground State Historic Site,** 5456 Harper House Rd., in Four Oaks, North Carolina, tel. (910) 594-0789. Located about 35 miles southeast of Raleigh, the battleground is located on NC 1008, just off US 701, about eight miles south of I-95 exit 90, and eight miles north of I-40 exit 343. Admission is free, and a visitors center presents exhibits, including an audiovisual program about the battle and Civil War artifacts. Roads in the area are marked with plaques highlighting the events of the Battle of Bentonville. The hours of the historic site are Mon.-Sat. 9 a.m.-5 p.m., Sunday 1-5 p.m., April-October. The site is open Tues.-Sat. 10 a.m.-4 p.m. and Sunday 1-4 p.m. Nov.-March.

THE DUKES OF DURHAM

At the end of the Civil War, Washington Duke trudged home to his wife and three sons and found that his home and farm had been pilfered of almost all the Dukes' worldly goods. One exception was a carefully hidden 25-pound sack of raw tobacco leaves. The Duke men roasted the leaves, shredded them by beating them with sticks, and sold the tobacco for a surprisingly high price. During the war, thousands of soldiers from the North and South alike had discovered the rich Brightleaf tobacco that grew abundantly in the area. These former soldiers were willing to pay extra for the "Bright Leaves."

So Washington Duke became a full-time tobacco farmer. He was soon able to expand his enterprise by building a tiny "factory" (smaller than most of the one-room schoolhouses in the region) where the tobacco was roasted, shredded, and packaged in pouches. The W. Duke & Sons Tobacco Company was born.

The company remained profitable but small until 1884. That year, an inventive young mechanic in Lynchburg named James Bonsack created what many dismissed as a silly machine—a mechanized cigarette roller. Washington Duke didn't think the machine was silly and bought the patent rights as soon as he heard about the contraption.

Thanks to the cigarette machine and a clever—some would say cutthroat—talent for business, Washington Duke (and then his son, Buck) soon owned a virtual worldwide monopoly on cigarette production. Durham was the tobacco hub of the world, with thousands of workers toiling in the city's massive tobacco warehouses and factories.

The success of the tobacco industry led directly to further prosperity for the area—the commercial and industrial infrastructure built by tobacco money soon attracted the textile industry. Among several mills established in the region was the first American mill to manufacture denim. By the turn of the century, Durham was one of the South's major manufacturing cities.

In 1907, the U.S. Department of Justice filed petitions to break up the Dukes' American Tobacco Company, but by that time the family's assets were estimated to be a cool—or perhaps a *smoking*—three hundred million dollars, a sum that, converted into today's dollars, would give Bill Gates a run for his money.

In 1924, inspired by some of the philanthropic educational investments of some of his fellow robber barons, Buck Duke decided to create a world-class university. He chose Trinity College, which had an enrollment of 200 students. Washington Duke had already established a tradition of rather lavish funding for the little school, including an $85,000 grant in 1892 to move Trinity from rural Randolph County (about 40 miles east) to Durham. Buck established a combination endowment/construction fund allocating about $19 million to the university, and construction began on dozens of buildings, including the libraries, classroom and laboratory halls, and thousands of dormitory rooms (still used by Duke University students today). To make sure his ivory tower wouldn't easily tarnish, Buck also bought the lush, green, 20,000-acre woods that still surround the campus. As a final stroke, he funded construction of a Canterbury Cathedral knockoff—magnificent Duke Chapel, which towers over the campus.

After visiting the majestic Chapel and lush Sarah Duke Gardens, a couple hundred yards away, it's well worth the 10-minute drive to visit the Duke Homestead, to see the humble (restored) shacks where the Dukes began their rise to billionairedom.

NORTH CAROLINA DIVISION OF TOURISM, FILM & SPORTS DEVELOPMENT

Duke Chapel

troops with plenty of the same. After the surrender at Bennett Place, the Union and Confederate soldiers eventually went home, but they carried with them the memory of the tastiest tobacco they'd ever smoked.

By the time a poor Durham farmer, Washington Duke, trudged home from his Confederate army service on the North Carolina coast, his tobacco-growing neighbors were already getting requests for the area's golden leaves. Over the next 40 years, Washington Duke and his sons would construct one of the world's most successful monopolies, the American Tobacco Company. The humble roots of the Dukes' vast tobacco empire can be visited today at the **Duke Homestead State Historic Site and Tobacco Museum,** 2828 Duke Homestead Rd., tel. (919) 477-5498. The visitors center offers a fun and informative movie about the history of tobacco and includes a number of museum exhibits displaying a variety of early equipment used to make cigarettes. The museum gives an entertaining history of tobacco and cigarette marketing, including the first print and radio ads, as well as the TV ads so familiar to baby-boomers and their predecessors. If you grew up viewing these ads, you'll be nostalgically struck by their totally unimpressive production values and find yourself laughing out loud at the unabashedly dubious "health benefits" touted by various brands.

After touring the museum, take the guided tour of the restored and preserved humble structures of Washington Duke's farm, including his family's home and the "tobacco factory" outbuildings, which by today's standards are more like big sheds than small factories. Admission is free. Hours April-Oct. are Mon.-Sat. 9 a.m.-5 p.m. and Sunday 1-5 p.m. The rest of the year, hours are Tues.-Sat. 10 a.m.-4 p.m. and Sunday 1-4 p.m., closed Monday.

Historic Stagville

About 10 miles northeast of downtown Durham on Old Oxford Highway, Historic Stagville is the nation's first state-owned research center for the archaeological study and historic preservation of wooden buildings. Headquartered in a 1787 plantation manor house, this research center is in the midst of a long process aimed at eventually making this a premier, visitor-friendly state historic site with potentially intriguing restorations of the plantation's slave quarters and other buildings. The historic site is open to the public Mon.-Fri. 9 a.m.-4 p.m., and no admission is charged.

Duke University

Duke University—consistently rated the best university in the southern U.S. and among the top half-dozen universities in the nation—traces its origins to 1838, when Methodist and Quaker families in rural Randolph County united to educate their children by founding Union Institute. Renamed Trinity College in 1859, the campus was moved to Durham in 1892, thanks to a donation of $85,000 from tobacco magnate Washington Duke (and a Duke-encouraged gift of land from Durham tobacco dealer Julian Carr). Over the next several years, Washington Duke donated another $300,000 to Trinity College's endowment—an enormous sum at the time—enabling the college to hire able, ambitious faculty trained at the new graduate schools of Johns Hopkins, Columbia, and other northern universities, making the 200-student college one of the leading liberal arts colleges in the South.

In 1924, Washington Duke's son, James Buchanan "Buck" Duke established a vast, $40-million philanthropic foundation known as The Duke Endowment, the annual income of which was to be distributed in North and South Carolina among hospitals, orphanages, the Methodist church, and a few colleges, including Trinity. As part of this massive endowment, Buck Duke allocated $19 million to renovate and rebuild the Trinity College campus, and to create a new campus nearby, surrounded by a vast forest. When the wise president of Trinity College immediately told Buck Duke that he wanted to rename Trinity College "Duke University," Buck humbly consented on the condition that the university's name be a memorial not to him, but to his father and family.

Today, Duke University's undergraduate student body of about 5,700 and graduate/professional school enrollment of about 3,800 consistently draws top students from all 50 U.S. states and approximately 70 foreign countries, contributing acosmopolitan and sophisticated flavor to Durham's blue-collar roots.

The university actually comprises two separate campuses, about a mile apart but united by buses constantly shuttling between the two campuses. The **East Campus,** originally the site of Trinity College, is today where all Duke freshman reside. The invitingly walkable campus is constructed in Georgian architectural style, complete with lots of Ionic columns and spacious greens. On the East Main Street side of the campus, the **Duke University Museum of Art,** tel. (919) 684-5135, features changing exhibits and an impressive permanent collection of ancient Greek and Roman pieces, European and American paintings, and a variety of other sculptures and drawings. The free-admission museum is open Tues.-Fri. 9 a.m.-5 p.m., Saturday 11 a.m.-2 p.m., and Sunday 2-5 p.m.

The **West Campus,** about a mile away, constitutes the main campus of Duke University. With an English Gothic atmosphere you'd associate with the centuries-old structures of Oxford and Cambridge, the original buildings of the campus were actually built between 1930 and 1932. The centerpiece of West Campus is the magnificent **Duke Chapel,** at the terminus of Chapel Drive, tel. (919) 684-2572. Modeled after the Canterbury Cathedral, albeit on a slightly smaller scale, the chapel seats 1,800 and soars 210 feet toward the sky, remaining visible from most parts of the campus. The chapel is also within hearing distance of most of the campus, thanks to the 50-bell carillon, with bells weighing from 10 pounds to more than 5.5 tons. Music students are periodically allowed time to practice on the carillon, contributing an angelic timbre to the campus atmosphere.

A couple hundred yards from Duke Chapel, the 55-acre **Sarah Duke Gardens,** tel. (919) 684-3698, provide spacious greens for Duke students to simultaneously study and suntan. Miles of walking trails wind through a wide variety of gardens, from blossoms-blazing terraced gardens to lakeside Japanese-style gardens, to woodsy walks along subtly designed paths leading through thousands of species of native North Carolina flora. The gardens have no admission fee and are open from sunrise to dusk. The gardens are an ideal way to explore Duke's West Campus, not only because of their beauty, but also because they provide the most convenient place for visitors to park (West Campus is generally a maze of permit-only parking). The free parking lot for Sarah Duke Gardens is located along Anderson Road, between Erwin Road and Campus Drive.

Surrounding West Campus and stretching almost to Chapel Hill, the 8,300-acre **Duke Forest** contributes a bucolic air to the university's environs. Managed by Duke's School of Forestry and Environmental Studies, the forest is laced with dirt roads and intimate trails, offering Duke students and the public secluded outlets for hiking, running, bicycling, and horseback riding. For more information about Duke Forest, call (919) 613-8013.

Museum of Life and Science

Founded in 1946 as a tiny trailside nature center with a few dozen specimens, the **North Carolina Museum of Life and Science,** 433 Murray Ave., tel. (919) 220-5429, was one of the nation's first science museums. Today, with 55,000 square feet of interior exhibit space and a few outdoor acres that house a collection of barnyard critters, this trail-blazing museum shows its age to best advantage. Most modern science museums are jam-packed with primary-colored plastic gizmos that pop, buzz, and generally try to imitate the energy of the latest video games. In contrast, the Museum of Life and Science features absorbing and thoughtful interactive exhibits made of solid, familiar materials (like well-worn wood and metal), reminiscent of timeless toys like Lincoln Logs and Erector Sets.

Kids will be enthralled by dozens of engaging exhibits, such as the interactive virtual-reality room and the weather exhibits, where you can touch a cloud and a tornado. Adults will be utterly captivated by the extensive aerospace exhibits donated to the museum by NASA, including the tiny Mercury Atlas 5 capsule, which was the first American spacecraft to orbit the Earth with a passenger, on November 29, 1961. The two-orbit flight lasted three hours and 21 minutes, and the passenger was Enos, a chimpanzee. As you can see from other NASA-donated exhibits, Enos' incredibly cramped capsule was barely bigger than the capsules in which the early Mercury and Apollo astronauts circled the Earth. The highlight of the museum's terrific aerospace collection is a two-story exhibit featuring the final prototype of the Lunar Landing Module that first landed on the moon, in 1969. When you actually see this magnificent contraption right before your eyes, in this humble Durham museum, you can't help but drop your jaw, and whisper, "Wow!"

The museum has been rapidly expanding its exhibits of live animals, almost all of which were injured critters rescued from the wild. Inside, the Carolina wildlife area features owls, alligators, opossums, raccoons, skunks, snakes, and lots of other Carolina natives. Outside exhibits feature domestic critters like sheep, goats, cows, turkeys, and chickens—and, most poignantly, a pen shared by a goose and a pot-belly pig, an inseparable duo whose obviously close, emotional attachment compels a re-evaluation of the supposedly fictional components of favorite barnyard movies and stories, like *Babe* and the everlasting *Charlotte's Web*.

Last but hardly least, the museum's most recently heralded exhibit features a total-immersion Butterfly House, open only in summer. Beginning in spring 1999, the museum will open the **Magic Wings Butterfly House,** one of only ten permanent, total-immersion butterfly houses in the United States. The largest butterfly house east of the Mississippi, this magical exhibit, open year-round, will be a three-story glass structure with luxuriant flowering plants and more than 1,000 exotic butterflies in flight. In addition, the Butterfly House will include the state-of-the-art, interactive **Rhone-Poulenc Insectarium,** presenting a vast assortment of exotic bugs from around the globe.

The museum is open Mon.-Sat. 10 a.m.-5 p.m. and Sunday noon-5 p.m. (open daily until 6 p.m. Memorial Day-Labor Day). Admission is $5.50 for adults, $3.50 for kids ages 3-12 and seniors over 65 (kids under 3 admitted free).

RECREATION

Water Recreation
About eight miles northwest of downtown Durham, the meandering 2,600 acres of **Eno River State Park,** tel. (919) 383-1686, provide some of loveliest hiking in the North Carolina Piedmont, with ten trails winding about 18 miles along the narrow, steep-walled Eno river and through dense woods and flowering meadows. The Eno River is the focus of activity at this state park. Upstream, rapids smash against rocks daring to stand in the river's path, forming Class III rapids, while further downstream the river surface barely shimmers, like a slow-moving plate of

glass. While some canoe and rafting enthusiasts paddle the Eno, it's generally not especially conducive to these pursuits, requiring a significant amount of portage, unless you catch the river after some hefty rainstorms. (The park doesn't rent canoes or rafts, by the way.) The draw of the river centers around the terrific hiking trails that follow the currents. Because the park is so narrow, it's hard to get lost; but you probably won't regret picking up a trail map when you enter the park at one of five access points, most of which can be reached by taking the Cole Mill Road exit off I-85 from the north, and exit 170 from the south. The most visited access point is called **West Point On the Eno,** 5105 N. Roxboro St., across from the Riverview Shopping Center, tel. (919) 471-1623, where you can visit a couple historic mill buildings and the **Howe-Mangum Museum of Photography** on Saturday and Sunday 1-5 p.m.

For further aquatic fun and frolic, **Falls Lake State Recreation Area,** tel. (919) 846-9332, provides pleasant swimming beaches and very tame hiking. You can't rent boats on Falls Lake, but you can launch your own from several sites. To get to the recreation area from Durham, take I-85 N to US 70 Bypass, exit at NC 98 and follow signs for Rollingview Marina and Beach. Open 8 a.m.-8 p.m. daily; access to Rollingview costs $3 per car.

You'll find boat rentals, a tiny swimming beach, and some of the area's best hiking (easy to moderate) at **Lake Michie,** tel. (919) 477-3906. To reach this park from Durham and I-85, take US 15/501/Roxborough Rd. north 10 miles. Turn right on Bahama Road, at the traffic light just past the sign for the Treyburn development, and proceed on Bahama Road for 3.5 miles. Park access is free, and the park is open sunrise-sunset.

Golf
Among the dozen or so golf courses in the Durham area, two particularly stand out. The **Duke University Golf Course,** at the Washington Duke Inn & Golf Club on Cameron Boulevard and Science Drive, tel. (919) 681-2288, is the premier course in the region, ranked the 11th best course in North Carolina by *Golf Digest.* Originally designed by Robert Trent Jones, then brilliantly redesigned in 1994 by his son, Rees, the challenging, tree-festooned course features few level areas. Greens fees range

$38-53, and carts cost $17 extra. The **Hillandale Golf Course,** at Hillandale and Sprunt Streets, tel. (919) 286-4211, designed by George Cobb, provides an invitingly walkable, very gently sloping design. The greens fees are also particularly inviting, at $15-20.

PERFORMING ARTS AND SPECTATOR SPORTS

The hub of Durham's thriving arts scene is the **Carolina Theatre,** 309 W. Morgan St., in downtown Durham, tel. (919) 560-3040 or box office tel. (919) 560-3030, a restored and renovated, three-theater complex combining the grandeur of yesteryear with state-of-the-art cinematic and theatrical mechanics. The largest theater, a holdover from Hollywood's Golden Age, features stage plays and musicals, operas, and concerts by top-of-the-line national acts. Whether your tastes lean towards Rigoletto or Rocky Horror, the Carolina Theatre probably offers something to fill the bill. Duke University also hosts several world-class acts throughout the year— such as the **American Dance Festival,** one of the most respected dance festivals in the world, in June and July. For information about who's coming to town when you're there, call **Page Auditorium,** on Duke's West Campus, next to Duke Chapel, at tel. (919) 684-4444.

Baseball and Softball

Thanks to the movie *Bull Durham,* made in 1987, the **Durham Bulls** are America's most famous minor league baseball team. In 1996, the Bulls moved into a glorious new stadium built by the same folks who designed the Baltimore Orioles' elegant new home, Camden Yards. The **Durham Bulls Athletic Park,** 409 Blackwell St., tel. (919) 687-6500, provides intimate, comfortable environs, ideal for discovering the unique camaraderie and fun provided by minor league ball, complete with lots of audience-participation contests between innings. As at virtually all sports venues, food and drink can be a little pricey, but this ballpark's food is both various and of surprisingly high quality. The Bulls, a AAA-affiliate of the Tampa Bay Devil Rays, play April-September. For tickets, call the Bulls box office at (919) 956-2855. Most tickets run $3-7.

DURHAM'S CONTRIBUTIONS TO THE ENGLISH LANGUAGE

By incorporating the city's name into the name of its principal product, one of Durham's earliest major companies hit upon a combination so catchy that it has worked its way into the language in a variety of ways. At the turn of the century, Bull Durham was the most popular chewing tobacco in the world.

The brand's popularity gave rise, for a start, to the phrase "shooting the bull." The phrase springs from the then-common spectacle of chewers of Bull Durham punctuating idle conversation by spitting tobacco juice.

In 1939, the town got its own minor-league baseball team, the Durham Bulls. (The latter-day version of the team was immortalized in the 1987 baseball film *Bull Durham,* starring Susan Sarandon, Kevin Costner, and Tim Robbins.) Realizing that young boys idolized baseball players, most of whom played with significant chaws in their mouths, the company supported the team with big advertising billboards along the foul lines in the home park. Liking the way this looked (and worked), the company soon did the same thing in as many other ballparks as it could manage, establishing a presence just above the spot where the relief pitchers traditionally warm up during a game. Voila— the "bullpen" was born.

The process that began with the company's borrowing the name of the city has come full circle, and Durham now returns the honor—its nickname is "the Bull City."

In July and August, you can watch women's fast-pitch softball in the nostalgic *former* home of the Durham Bulls, where the movie *Bull Durham* was filmed. Beginning in the summer of 1997, the **Durham Dragons** became one of just six professional women's fast-pitch softball teams in the nation. They play in the historic **Durham Athletic Park,** bounded by Corporation, Foster, Morris, and Geer Streets. Call (919) 680-3278 for schedule and ticket information about this exciting new addition to the Triangle's sports scene.

Blue Devil Basketball

Last, yet foremost, is college basketball. We can't leave out what many national sports commentators call the single most exciting sports venue in the nation: attending a Duke Blue Devil basketball game in the intimate-but-deafeningly-loud Cameron Indoor Stadium. We mention the Blue Devils last in this section on spectator sports, because your chances of actually getting a seat in the stadium to see a Blue Devil basketball game are extremely remote, unless you're intimate friends with a season-ticketholder or involved in a marriage-track relationship with a Duke student. Even Duke students are regularly forced to camp out for several nights, sometimes weeks, in front of the Cameron ticket office, to get a ticket for a Blue Devil game. Nonetheless, if obtaining a Blue Devil ticket is your goal, start by calling the Duke University Athletics ticket center at (919) 681-2583 or (800) 672-BLUE.

ACCOMMODATIONS

With more than 60 lodgings providing over 7,000 guest rooms, Durham offers the largest variety of accommodations in the Triangle. Bed and breakfast fans have a half dozen options, the best of which is the **Arrowhead Inn,** 106 Mason Rd., tel. (919) 477-8430 or (800) 528-2207. This 1775 inn is situated on four woodsy acres located about six miles north of downtown Durham, just off Roxborough Road (US 501 Bypass). The eight elegant guest rooms and two suites, including the two-room carriage house, are all tastefully decorated with colonial and Victorian furnishings. Expensive-Premium rates begin at $95 for individual rooms, $145 for the suites.

If you're visiting Duke University—and seeking the most luxurious quarters in Durham—choose the **Washington Duke Inn & Golf Club,** 3001 Cameron Blvd., at the junction of Cameron Boulevard and Science Drive on the perimeter of Duke University's West Campus, tel. (919) 490-0999 or (800) 443-3853. Many of the handsomely appointed 171 guest rooms overlook the perfectly maintained golf course on the edge of Duke Forest. Amenities at this five-story, full-service hotel include the great golf course, six lighted tennis courts, heated outdoor pool, first-rate restaurant, and upscale cocktail lounge. The immaculate public areas feature lots of homey memorabilia about the Duke family (see "The Dukes of Durham").

If the Washington Duke Inn is booked, you won't be forced to slum it in Durham. The six-story **Durham Hilton,** 3800 Hillsborough Rd., tel. (919) 383-8033 or (800) 445-8667, provides a restaurant, cocktail lounge, swimming pool, and health club, along with typically high-class Hilton service and spacious, attractive rooms. Set off a bit from the dense commercial strip of Hillsborough Road, in a wooded copse, the Hilton is easily accessible to I-85 (exit 173) and Duke University. Premium rates begin around $110. Next door, the **Fairfield Inn-Durham,** 3710 Hillsborough Rd., tel. (919) 382-3388 or (800) 228-2800, provides hospitable lodgings and a swimming pool. Moderate prices begin at $60.

For inexpensive Durham accommodations, you'll find clean and comfortable rooms and an outdoor pool at the **Carolina Duke Motor Inn,** just off I-85 exit 175, at 2517 Guess Rd., tel. (919) 286-0771 or (800) 438-1158. Off the same exit, you'll find the equally inexpensive **Red Roof Inn,** 1915 North Point Dr., tel. (919) 471-9882 or (800) 843-7663. You can't swim under the red roof, but you can cuddle with your pet for no extra charge.

Research Triangle Park/Airport Area

A number of franchise lodgings hug I-40 along a four-mile stretch from Raleigh/Durham International Airport (RDU) and Research Triangle Park (RTP). Several full-service hotels cater to researchers and other professionals making an expense-account-subsidized trip to RTP. Consequently, these full-service hotels, complete with restaurants, lounges, and swimming pools, generally charge Premium rates Sunday through Thursday, and drop down to Moderate on Friday and Saturday nights. Among the glitzier full-service RTP hotels is the **Wyndham Garden Hotel,** 4620 S. Miami Blvd., at exit 281 of I-40, tel. (919) 941-6066 or (800) 972-0264. At exit 282, take your pick from the interchangeably large and hospitable **Sheraton Imperial Hotel & Convention Center,** 4700 Emperor Blvd., tel. (919) 941-5050 or (800) 325-3535, or the **Holiday Inn-RDU & RTP,** 4810 Page Rd., tel. (919) 941-6000 or (800) 465-4329.

Though it doesn't have a swimming pool or restaurant on-site, the **Fairfield Inn-RTP,** off exit 278 of I-40, on NC 55, at 4507 SR 55, does include a free continental breakfast, along with an exercise room and whirlpool, at some of the best rates in the RTP area, $55-75. Inexpensive-Moderate.

FOOD AND DRINK

Durham has long been on the cutting edge of "nouveau" regional fare, infusing traditional Southern foods like pork with innovative continental twists since the 1970s. Today, several Durham restaurants are consistently rated among the best in the South by sources like *The New York Times* and *Southern Living* magazine. In addition to Durham's more inventive restaurants, several "old reliable" eateries, featuring down-home barbecue and Carolina seafood dishes, round out Durham's restaurant scene. Durham can brag about dozens of terrific dining spots; here are a few standouts.

Ninth Street Vicinity
The Ninth Street neighborhood offers a bohemian selection of cuisines, from burgers and bagels to burritos and babaganoush. Along the two-block-long main commercial corridor of Ninth Street, extending from Main Street to Hillsborough Road (where Hillsborough turns into Markham Street), an eclectic collection of small restaurants included, at last count, three pizza and sub places, an old-fashioned diner, a bar featuring live music, a bagelry, two Mexican restaurants, an Irish pub, and a Middle Eastern restaurant. And topping off this list, there's the cavernous **George's Gourmet Garage,** 737 Ninth St., tel. (919) 286-4131. Housed appropriately enough in a former supermarket converted to an "industrial chic" decor, the Garage is a full-service restaurant specializing in (but not limited to) seafood—in addition to a bakery, plus a market featuring dozens of hot, prepared dishes, everything from lasagna to soups, salads to flank steak. And then, of course, there's the full sushi bar. As if that weren't enough, the Garage also includes a bar that, since the Garage's opening in 1997, has grown into one of Durham's hottest night spots, with jazz on Tuesday, guitar on Friday, and dancing on Saturday. Not your typical beer-guzzling, college crowd, the clientele at George's is a youthful, fashionable, martini-and-cigar crowd.

You'll find neither martinis nor cigars at the family-friendly **Pizza Palace,** 2002 Hillsborough Rd., tel. (919) 286-0281. Located across Hillsborough Road from the Garage, the Pizza Palace provides a warm, friendly place to sample some of the best pizzas, calzones, and strombolis in the Triangle. The menu also includes a number of sandwiches and other Italian dishes. Though the food is delicious, it's the welcoming atmosphere that has made the Pizza Palace a Durham institution for decades. If you come during early evening hours, you'll probably be welcomed by owner and former Durham mayor Harry Rodenhizer, a delightful raconteur, as well as able restaurateur (and politician par excellence).

From George's Garage and the Pizza Palace, a two-block stroll north along Ninth Street, to the corner of Knox and Ninth, will land you at one of the most celebrated restaurants in the South, the **Magnolia Grill,** 1002 Ninth St., tel. (919) 286-3609. Unassuming from the outside—a boxy, one-story structure with gray-painted stone—the restaurant's inside exudes an invitingly intimate bistro-like atmosphere, drawing a diversely dressed clientele, some in suits, some in just shirts and slacks. But it's not the atmosphere that's the main attraction here—it's the utterly fabulous, creative food. The menu is constantly changing, utilizing the freshest ingredients, but for appetizers you'll be tempted by such cosmic creations as grilled quail in pomegranate molasses jus with wild sour cherries, Moroccan-spiced walnuts, and sun-dried cherry tabbouleh ($8). You'll have an equally difficult time choosing among the tantalizing entrees ($18-25), which might include grilled hickory-smoked pork tenderloin in zinfandel-port jus with wild mulberries, cane spaetzle with broccoli rabe, pancetta haricot verts, and baby carrots ($18). The Magnolia Grill serves dinner only, Monday through Saturday. Reservations are strongly advised.

A long city block northeast of Ninth Street, in the towering First Union Plaza, between W. Main and Hillsborough Road, you can explore many creative, Mediterranean-inspired delights for lunch or dinner at **Cafe Parizade,** 2200 W. Main St., tel. (919) 286-9712. Founded by Giorgious Bakastias, the same bold restaurateur who created George's Gourmet Garage, the spacious dining area at Cafe Parizade has an airy atmosphere, with high ceilings, an open kitchen, and loads of decorative pressed copper. Lunch selections include a variety of salads ($4-9) and several pastas, including the mildly adventurous angel hair with calamari, garlic, crushed red pepper, lemon and butter ($8) and the divine risotto with shrimp and artichokes in a caramelized citrus broth ($8.50). Pizzas, calzones and sandwiches fill out the lunch menu. The dinner menu offers a much wider selection, including about 20 appetizers and salads, leaning towards Greek fare, like the Mezze platter, with dolmas, Greek olives, feta cheese, roasted red peppers, roasted artichokes, and grilled eggplant ($8.50). Entrees include about a dozen pastas, and another dozen specialties of the house, including rack of lamb, filet mignon, roast duck, and the superb paella with clams, mussels, shrimp, sausage, chicken, and vegetables seasoned with saffron and wine. Entrees range $10-23. (Incidentally, the paella is $16.50 per person, for a minimum of two people.) Parizade is open Mon.-Fri. for lunch and dinner, and dinner only on Saturday. Dress is dress-casual to jackets.

Brightleaf Square Vicinity

From the intersection of Ninth and Main streets, about half a mile southwest along Main Street toward downtown Durham is the Brightleaf Square complex, consisting of dozens of specialty shops and restaurants housed in converted tobacco warehouses. On the back side of Brightleaf Square, on W. Peabody Street between Duke and Gregson Streets, **Pop's Trattoria,** 810 W. Peabody St., tel. (919) 956-7677, emanates an informal, city-chic atmosphere, complete with an open kitchen with wood-fired ovens and hulking sculptures of recycled, rusted metal. The menu features Italian dishes with creative Southern twists, like the tagliatelle pasta with pan-seared scallops, smoked bacon, and melted leeks ($14), or the linguini with rock shrimp, clams, grilled corn, and sweet pickled jalapeños ($14). Wood oven-fired pizzas are also a favorite, including novel combinations like the pizza with barbecued duck, smoked mozzarella and fresh cilantro ($9). Open for dinner 5:30-10 p.m. Tues.-Sunday.

Half a block from intersection of Main and Gregson Streets, **Anotherthyme,** 109 N. Gregson St., tel. (919) 682-5225, is a local favorite with a friendly atmosphere enhanced by brick walls, strings of miniature lights, and lots of plants. Always featuring fresh, innovative fare with a leaning toward seafood, poultry, and vegetarian offerings, the menu changes frequently to take advantage of the freshest ingredients, like the favorite *salade niçoise* with fresh, grilled tuna. The fried chicken and mashed potatoes are a reliable and delectable staple. Entrees generally range $9-15 for dinner, served Mon.-Sat., and $5-10 for lunch on weekdays only. The Sunday brunch at Anotherthyme is among the most popular in Durham. In addition, the long, curving mahogany bar is a favorite hangout at night for non-student locals.

Fishmonger's Seafood Market, Crab & Oyster House, 806 W. Main Street, between Gregson and Duke Streets, tel. (919) 682-0128, is another venerable, Durham institution. Its huge storefront-type windows, high ceilings with fans and exposed pipes, and wooden picnic tables with butcher paper for placemats will remind you of New Orleans, but the fare is straight from North Carolina waters. Specials change daily, but sure bets are fresh, pick-your-own lobsters, the grilled shrimp, and whatever the fish special is that day. Fishmonger's often smokes its own fish—if you don't see it on the daily menu, be sure to ask—it's out of this world as an appetizer. There is an upstairs room that opens on busy nights, with bar seating and a few tables decked out in sort of an old beach bar, nautical theme. Fishmonger's upstairs is the place to be Friday 3-6 p.m., when oysters on the half shell are just a quarter apiece. Fishmonger's has an extensive beer list and unsophisticated but drinkable wine selections. There is nothing fancy about this place, but you won't find fresher, better prepared fish or colder beer to wash it down with anywhere in North Carolina—even on the coast. Fishmonger's is open seven days a week for dinner, and every day except Monday for lunch. Entrees range $5-10 for lunch, $8-20 for dinner.

Other Famed Durham Restaurants

Since its opening in 1993, when *Esquire Magazine* selected it as one of the best new restaurants in the nation, **Nana's Restaurant,** 2514 University Dr., tel. (919) 493-8545, has enjoyed a deluge of glowing reviews from such auspicious sources as the *New York Times* and *Food and Wine Magazine* about the work of chef and owner Scott Howell. The dining room is classy yet inviting, with white tablecloths, fresh flowers, lots of displayed wine bottles, and artwork from local artists. The menu changes frequently but shows Howell's dedication to Southern regional cuisine, with strong Italian and French influences evident in dishes like his famed risotto with smoked bacon, silver queen corn, and caramelized vidalia onions. Other entrees might include hickory-smoked venison loin with a sweet potato gratin, or the ethereal pan-seared halibut over sugar snap peas and fennel in an ocean broth with littleneck clams. Entrees range $15-25, and reservations are strongly encouraged. Open Mon.-Sat.for dinner.

For fine dining, the **Fairview** at the Washington Duke Inn & Golf Club, 3001 Cameron Blvd., tel. (919) 493-6699, provides the most formal dining experience in Durham (gentlemen, wear a tie with your jacket for dinner). Overlooking the postcard-perfect golf course, the restaurant's inside decor is luxurious, with Oriental rugs covering the hardwood floors. As the main restaurant for the first-class Washington Duke Inn, the Fairview serves dinner nightly, breakfast and lunch Mon.-Sat., and brunch on Sunday. Breakfast options range from cereal and fresh fruit, eggs and omelets ($4-7), to eggs Benedict, Nova Scotia salmon, and the hearty Angus ribeye steak and eggs ($9-14). The lunch menu changes seasonally but can be counted on to include a variety of salads ($5-11), along with more complete meals, like the outstanding pan-seared backfin crab cakes with sweet red pepper and cucumber salsa, yellow pepper coulis, and grilled bruschetta ($14). The dinner menu also changes seasonally but dependably includes brilliant New American renditions of seafood, poultry, beef, and lamb, in addition to more adventurous fare like the seared antelope with cremini mushroom and leek rye bread pudding; carrot, apple, and celery ragout; and wild blueberry sauce ($29). Dinner appetizers run $6-13 and entrees $20-36, topping out with the pan-seared veal chop with roasted potatoes, porcinis, and artichokes, with foie gras garlic sauce. Reservations are strongly advised for dinner.

In addition to its national reputation for innovative, epicurean creations, Durham is also home to one of the nation's most celebrated "pig palaces." **Bullock's Barbecue,** 3330 Quebec Drive, tel. (919) 383-3211, has the look of an unassuming family restaurant, with wall-to-wall carpet, hotel room art, and comfortable booths. The food and the down-home service, not the ambience, are the main attractions here. Bullock's represents Eastern North Carolina country cooking at its very best. By all means, try the barbecue—for the uninitiated, this means, chopped pork with a side of slaw—and be sure to have some fresh vegetables, which change daily. You aren't served dinner rolls here, but your waitress will bring you the most heavenly hush puppies you've ever tasted. Don't know what hush puppies are? They are delightful, deep-fried confections of corn meal, onion, spices, and some secret ingredient that we have never been able to duplicate at home. If barbecue isn't your thing, try the fried oysters, fried chicken, or pork chops. Bullock's won't be good for your waistline, but nothing is better for your soul. Quebec Drive is almost impossible to find on a map, but Bullock's isn't. It's located just a block north of Hillsborough Road a couple of blocks east of exit 174 of I-85, at its junction with US 15/501, next to the parking lot of the Coca-Cola plant on Hillsborough Road. Bullock's doesn't accept reservations, but the line moves fast, and as you get closer to the hostess station, you'll pass the "Wall of Fame," packed with dozens of the autographed photos, testimonials, and thanks of celebrities ranging from Lucille Ball and Robert Duvall to Reba McIntire and Berra. Bullock's serves lunch and dinner, Tues.-Sat., and accepts cash only. Most entrees run $5-10.

Nightlife

Durham residents and students combine to lend Durham a lively nightlife. In addition to popular hangouts like **George's Gourmet Garage,** described above, and the several hotel cocktail lounges in the area, the Brightleaf Square area is a favorite focus for the college crowd. Beer-guzzling university students reign at night at **Satisfaction Restaurant & Bar,** 905 W. Main St. in Brightleaf Square, tel. (919) 682-7397, and across the street at **Devine's Restaurant & Sports Bar,** 904 W. Main St., tel. (919) 682-0228.

CHAPEL HILL

In 1789, North Carolina state government chartered the first taxpayer-funded state university in the nation, the University of North Carolina. It took the legislature a few years of wrangling before a site for the university was chosen—at a prominent road crossing on a hill, near New Hope Chapel. Work began on the university's first building in 1793, and town lots were auctioned off (although it would be another two years before the first Chapel Hill residents occupied permanent homes). By January 1795, the university's Old East building was completed and the faculty hired—a total of two professors.

On January 15, the faculty accepted their first student, Hinton James, a resident of Wilmington. As soon as James got the news, he and his fam-

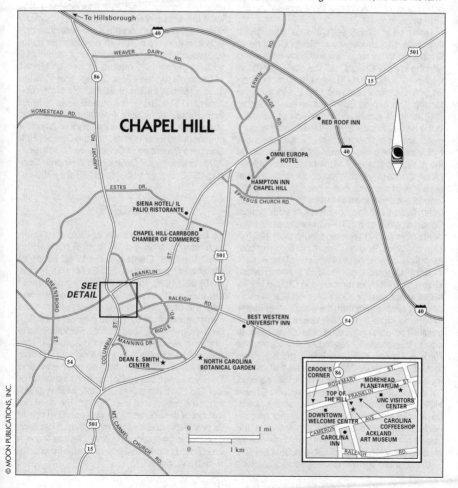

ily became the first of millions of UNC freshmen and their families to get ready to go off to college. After packing him up, his mother waved goodbye to her son, no doubt with tears welling up, just like mothers today—but with one slight difference. To get to college, young Hinton had to walk the 150 miles to Chapel Hill, bearing all his belongings (lucky they didn't have stereos in those days). He arrived in Chapel Hill on February 12, after a journey of more than two weeks. Over the next two weeks, 40 more students arrived, forming the class of 1798—the only graduating class of an American state university in the 18th century.

Referred to simply as "Carolina" throughout the state, the University of North Carolina at Chapel Hill today remains inextricably interwoven with the town of Chapel Hill. The city's population numbers about 45,000, including more than 24,000 Carolina students and 2,400 full-time faculty. The central Carolina campus, covering 729 acres, is easily among the most beautiful in the nation. Brick walkways lead under ancient trees and past flowering shrubs and meander by the campus's 190 permanent buildings. Unlike the main campuses of many huge state universities, Carolina—thanks no doubt to its gradual growth over two centuries—has the feel of a college located in a town with its own historic character (albeit not the character of your typical Southern small town). The university admits students from all 50 states and more than 100 foreign countries, lending Chapel Hill the most cosmopolitan atmosphere of any city in the state.

North Carolina's senior U.S. senator, Jesse Helms, is widely remembered in Chapel Hill for his infamous remark about Chapel Hill's distinctly different atmosphere from the state's other towns. When the state legislature was considering a multimillion-dollar allocation of taxpayer funds to create the wonderful North Carolina Zoological Park in Asheboro, Helms had a more cost-effective suggestion. "Why waste all that money for a new zoo," Helms is reported to have asked, "when we could just put a fence around Chapel Hill?" (This comment by North Carolina's notoriously conservative Republican senator also reflects Chapel Hill's deserved reputation as the state's premier bastion of liberal politics—Helms receives only a handful of votes in Chapel Hill.)

Unlike most sprawling state university towns with their pre-fab strip malls, Chapel Hill has a real downtown with long-established shops and restaurants. At the edge of the central campus downtown, Franklin Street bustles day and night with folks from all over the Triangle enjoying a multitude of shopping, dining, and entertainment opportunities. Another perk of visiting this state university town is that most of the attractions are taxpayer-supported, and consequently, free to the public.

A note of caution to parents of teenagers: if you have your heart set on sending your children to a college *other* than Carolina, you may want to pass up a visit to Chapel Hill—its many charms make it among the most seductive college towns in the nation. If, on the other hand, you wouldn't mind being parents of alumni of a college perennially ranked as one of *Money Magazine's* top ten "Best College Buys" in the nation (with a tuition of $2,183 for state residents and $10,716 for out-of-staters, as of 1998) then, by all means, visit. For helpful information about the town, including a jam-packed calendar of scheduled local events, call the **Chapel Hill-Carrboro Chamber of Commerce** at (919) 967-7075, or stop by the **Downtown Welcome Center,** 137 E. Franklin St., tel. (919) 929-9700.

SIGHTS

To begin your exploration of Carolina's campus, stop in Mon.-Fri. 10 a.m.-5 p.m. at the **UNC Visitors' Center,** in the West Lobby of Morehead Planetarium, 250 E. Franklin St., tel. (919) 962-1630. Watch the short video about the college, then strap on your Walkman and take the recorded, historic walking tour of the campus, narrated by Wallace Kuralt (Charles' brother, owner of The Intimate Bookshop, one of many revered Chapel Hill bookstores). This delightful and informative walking tour will take about an hour, depending on your gait, and lead you past dozens of campus landmarks like Old East, the oldest public university building in the nation, and the Old Well, the unofficial symbol of the university, having provided one of its few water sources for more than a century. The tour is free, requiring only that you leave a credit card or driver's license to ensure you return the Walkman.

While at the visitors center, take some time to explore its immediate environs, in **Morehead Planetarium,** 250 E. Franklin St., tel. (919) 962-1236. The nation's first observatory built by a university, in 1832, Morehead has been at the forefront of astronomy research ever since. Beginning in the 1960s, it served as a NASA celestial navigation training center for Mercury, Gemini, Apollo, Skylab, Apollo-Soyoux, and early Space Shuttle astronauts. The Morehead complex contains a number of engaging astronomical exhibits—including a walk-in model of the solar system—as well as a small art gallery and lush garden, complete with a giant sundial. Open daily; admission is free. Nightly planetarium shows are complemented by matinees on weekends. Special programs at the planetarium's observatory are also held periodically. Movie and special program admissions are usually $3.50 for adults, $2.50 for students. Call (919) 549-6863 for a recording of events information. Open Tues.-Fri. noon-5 p.m. and 7-9:30 p.m., weekends 10 a.m.-5 p.m. and 7-9:30 p.m., and Monday noon-5 p.m.

To explore further heavenly beauties, along more human-made lines, take a five-minute walk west along Franklin Street, and turn left onto Columbia Street, where, 50 yards away, you'll find the **Ackland Art Museum,** tel. (919) 966-5736, containing an astonishingly diverse collection of centuries of paintings, sculpture, photography, furniture, and every other conceivable art and craft from around the globe, including North Carolina. To give you an idea, just the painting collection includes works by Peter Paul Rubens, Edgar Degas, and Eugene Delacroix. Open Wed.-Sat. 10 a.m.-5 p.m. and Sunday 1-5 p.m.; admission is free.

Two more of the University's top attractions lie a short drive away. When you get back to the intersection of Franklin and Columbia Streets, turn left as if you're going to the Ackland Art Museum and keep going along S. Columbia half a mile. Turn left onto Manning Drive, continuing to follow the signs for the **Dean E. Smith Center** on Skipper Bowles Drive, tel. (919) 962-7777. Though the University of North Carolina at Chapel Hill can brag about more than two centuries worth of monumental intellectual achievements, the Smith Center houses the heart and soul of this great university. This is where the Carolina Tar Heels basketball team plays, a cavernous indoor stadium seating over 21,000 passionate Carolina fans. The Center is dedicated to the living legend, former coach Dean Smith, who retired in 1997 after 36 years of coaching the Tar Heels, having won 879 basketball games, more than any other coach in NCAA history. Although "Coach Smith," as he is reverently referred to by Carolina fans, had some help along the way from players like Michael, Smith earned a legendary reputation as a relentlessly innovative genius of the game, perhaps best known for his insistence on his players always operating as a fluid, five-man team on the floor, never relying too much on any single player's talents. Among the endless praises sung to Coach Smith by Tar Heel fans, one of the most resonant is that "Coach Smith was the only living being who could hold Michael to under 20 points a game." The Smith Center includes the 3,000-square-foot **Carolina Athletic Memorabilia Room,** displaying artifacts, highlight tapes, and other memorabilia from the university's rich athletic history. Open Mon.-Fri. 8 a.m.-5 p.m.; admission is free. For tickets to all Carolina Tar Heel sports events, call the **Sports Ticket Office** at (919) 962-2296.

From the Smith Center's parking lot, follow the signs for the three-minute drive to the **North Carolina Botanical Garden** on Old Mason Farm Road, just off the US 15/501 Bypass, tel. (919) 962-0522. The largest natural botanical garden in the Southeastern U.S., the garden covers 600 acres and offers miles of inviting nature trails that pass carnivorous plant collections, herb gardens, and extensive collections of North Carolina and Southeastern plants arranged by various habitats. From mid-March through mid-November, the grounds are open every day 8 a.m.-5 p.m., the rest of the year, Mon.-Fri. 8 a.m.-5 p.m. Admission is free.

ACCOMMODATIONS

The worst aspect of a visit to Chapel Hill is usually trying to find a convenient place to stay that doesn't require driving to and from the campus. A number of terrific lodgings, including some nationally renowned inns, are located within a half-hour's drive of downtown Chapel Hill. Although I-40 passes along the edge of the official city limits, even this coast-to-coast interstate offers only three franchise motels, all located at least a 10-minute drive from downtown Chapel Hill. If you're visiting during a busy weekend, like graduation or Homecoming, you're well advised to consult the earlier listings for Durham and Raleigh accommodations.

The one exception to this rule of lodging inconvenience is the venerable **Carolina Inn,** 211 Pittsboro St., tel. (919) 933-2001 or (800) 962-8519. Located in the heart of the Carolina campus, bounded by S. Columbia and Pittsboro Streets and Cameron Boulevard, this graceful, 185-room, Colonial-style hotel was built in 1924, and in 1995 received a tasteful, $13.5 million facelift, restoring the inn to its early status as one of the finer hotels in North Carolina. With spacious, elegant public areas and handsomely appointed (though not terribly large) guest rooms, this is your only choice for lodgings on the UNC campus. There's no swimming pool, but there is a fine on-site restaurant, the **Carolina Cross-roads,** tel. (919) 933-2001, that serves three luxurious meals every day, in addition to providing room service—just one facet of the comprehensively first-class service provided by this historic hotel. Rates generally range $130-145. Premium.

If you don't mind walking about a mile to the downtown campus, the next-closest hotel is the equally renowned and first-rate **Siena Hotel,** 1505 E. Franklin St., tel. (919) 929-4000 or (800) 223-7379. This classic, three-story, 80-room hotel provides personalized, professional service and elegantly appointed, spacious rooms with a warm Italian decor. Combining European styling with North Carolina hospitality, the Siena constitutes a seductive microcosm of Chapel Hill's cosmopolitan charms, including fabulous food. The Siena's on-site restaurant, Il Palio, arguably tops the list of North Carolina's Italian restaurants.The Siena's Premium rates begin at $135. This top-flight hotel will accept small pets, for a $50 surcharge.

Also about a mile from campus, on NC 54, the **Best Western University Inn,** 1310 Raleigh Rd., tel. (919) 932-3000 or (800) 528-1234, provides comfortable quarters and a swimming pool at Moderate-Expensive rates, ranging $70-105. Other franchise lodgings are located off exit 270 of I-40, about three or more miles from the campus. The relatively classy **Omni Europa Hotel,**

1 Europa Drive, tel. (919) 968-4900 or (800) 843-6664, located on six wooded acres, features original artwork by regional artists in each of the 168 guest rooms. The Europa's amenities also include a swimming pool, on-site restaurant, and cocktail lounge. Expensive-Premium rates range $90-140. The **Hampton Inn-Chapel Hill** 1740 US 15/501, just off I-40 exit 270, tel. (919) 968-3000 or (800) 426-7866, provides a pool and predictably clean and comfy rooms in the $75 Moderate range. For inexpensive, pet-friendly accommodations, hit the **Red Roof Inn-Chapel Hill,** also off exit 270 of I-40, at 5623 Chapel Hill Blvd., tel. (919) 489-9421 or (800) 843-7663.

FOOD AND DRINK

Chapel Hill and its Triangle neighbor, Durham, together provide the state's most exciting and innovative epicurean delights. As with our coverage of Durham restaurants, we regret the omission of several terrific Chapel Hill restaurants, whose ambience and cuisine merit mention. But, to avoid turning this book into the *Chapel Hill Restaurant Handbook,* we'll limit ourselves to our very favorites.

Downtown Restaurants

Chapel Hill provided the shining light for developing and popularizing "nouveau" Southern gourmet cuisine decades ago, in the person of a legendary chef, the late Bill Neal. Often compared to Alice Waters' famed "California cuisine" creations at Berkeley's Chez Panisse, Neal's groundbreaking creations utilized the basics of the beloved dishes of his Carolina childhood and incorporated the freshest available ingredients to lend these dishes a European flair, with unusual twists geared toward exciting the modern palate. At **Crook's Corner,** 610 W. Franklin St., tel. (919) 929-7643, Neal's first and most beloved restaurant, you can still experience the marvel of his signature dish, shrimp and grits, a heavenly yet simple combination of fresh shrimp saut°ed with bacon, mushrooms and scallions served over cheese grits ($16.50). The menu at Crook's changes daily in order to take advantage of the freshest ingredients, but the wonderful shrimp and grits is a dependable staple.

Chapel Hill's
Franklin Street

Or, you might choose something like the equally ethereal catfish amandine with brown butter and almonds, served with collards and cheese grits ($15). No matter what you choose, you won't be disappointed. The atmosphere of Crook's Corner comes in two varieties. Weather permitting, we highly recommend making a reservation to dine on the delightfully intimate outside patio, enclosed by bamboo fencing. Complete with subtle lighting and a cascading waterfall sculpture, the patio creates the illusion of a cozy ocean paradise, totally obscuring the fact that you sit just a few yards away from a busy street. Inside Crook's, a funky bistro atmosphere reigns, with a black-and-white tile floor and bright, eye-popping paintings by local artists. The inside also includes a small bar. Open Mon.-Sat. for dinner and on Sunday for brunch (enjoying a Bloody Mary and Crook's Eggs Benedict on the patio on a sunny Sunday is one of life's purest pleasures). Be sure to call ahead and specify that you want a table on the patio. Dress is generally dress-casual.

For purely stupendous Southern country cooking (sans European twists), make your way to **Dip's Country Kitchen,** 405 W. Rosemary St, tel. (919) 942-5837. Owner and former Chapel Hill elected official Mildred Council Dip, or "Mama," as she's known to locals, started her restaurant in the early 1980s with the catchy slogan "Put a little South in your mouth." At Dip's, you'll find true Southern cookin', the kind your grandma probably made after church on Sun-

day if you grew up in the rural South. Dip's is a family affair, with some of Mama's children and grandchildren helping to run the place—but her progeny are always toiling under the firm supervision of Mama Dip, who insists that everything be done exactly (and deliciously) right. Dip's serves breakfast, lunch and dinner seven days a week and offers beer and wine. The menu changes daily, but you can usually get fried chicken, pork chops and gravy, greens and black-eyed peas—and even real chit'lins (although if you weren't raised on them, beware; keep in mind that chitterlings are rather pungent pig intestines boiled for hours). If you're not a Southerner and are seeking to taste authentic Southern cooking at its best, come to Dip's—Mama Dip herself may come to your table and ask you how you're enjoying your food: be sure to mind your manners and tell her it's the best you've ever had, ma'am, (trust us, you'll probably be telling the truth). Lunch and dinner entrees run $7-11, and breakfast is less expensive.

To experience the same ambience enjoyed by Carolina students and faculty for generations, visit the **Carolina Coffee Shop,** 138 East Franklin St., tel. (919) 942-6875. It's the oldest original restaurant in the Triangle, opened in 1922, and the building actually has older roots, first serving as the Carolina student post office. The wainscoting, counter, and back bar are remnants of its early days as a soda shop. Today, its soft lighting, brick walls and wood booths befit its graceful old age, complemented by the Mozart,

Beethoven, and other classical music composers whose works gently fill the place. This is no traditional college hang-out joint, but rather, a tasteful, warm place to savor any one meal or all three of them. Breakfast runs $2-7, including eggs, omelets, eggs Benedict, and the Coffee House's fabulous signature breakfast dish, eggs Neptune—poached eggs with blue crab meat and Hollandaise sauce on an English muffin. Lunch options range $5-8 and include a wide variety of sandwiches, soups, salads, or slightly heartier fare like crab cakes or salmon. Dinner ($8-17) features the widest variety at the Coffee House, with beef, poultry, vegetarian, and seafood choices, but, staying with this restaurant's brilliant use of crabs, we heartily recommend the homemade crepes with crabmeat stuffing, artichoke hearts, Swiss cheese, and Hollandaise sauce. Closed on Monday, the Coffee Shop is open Tues.-Thurs. 8 a.m.-11 p.m., Fri.-Sat. 8 a.m.-midnight, and Sunday 8 a.m.-10 p.m.

The food is fine at **Top of the Hill,** at the southeast corner of Franklin and Columbia Streets, tel. (919) 929-8676, but the view is sensational. Located three stories above Chapel Hill's busiest intersection, this relative newcomer to the established Chapel Hill restaurant scene has been drawing consistent crowds since its opening in 1994. Open 11 a.m.-2 a.m., Top of the Hill has lunch and dinner menus ranging from salads and sandwiches to pastas, poultry, and steaks (lunch $4-8, dinner $8-20), along with an eclectic collection of marvelous beers and a full bar.

Il Palio Ristorante, 1505 E. Franklin St., tel. (919) 918-2545, arguably the finest (and certainly the most lauded) Northern Italian restaurant in the state, is located in the classy Siena Hotel, less than a five-minute drive from downtown Chapel Hill. Serving lunch daily 11:30 a.m.-2:30 p.m. and dinner 6-10:30 p.m., the Siena's intimate dining rooms include sculptures, French doors, and fresh flowers. Both lunch and dinner offer a tantalizing selection of soups, appetizers, pastas, and entrees. The menu changes seasonally and features fabulous daily specials, made from that morning's shopping. For lunch ($7-10), try one of the pastas, like the *Linguine Ai Gamberi,* pan-seared shrimp and prosciutto with Swiss chard and ricotta ($9.50), and/or one of the *secondi piatti,* like *capesante con semolina,* semolina-crusted scallops, seasoned lentil and mesclun salad with a saffron chive broth ($9). For dinner, if you're willing break the $100 barrier (for two), you can luxuriate in an hours-long Italian blowout, with soup, salad, antipasti, pasta, fish, meat, and dessert. With about a half dozen seductive choices for each category, you won't be disappointed by any choice you make, like the *risotto d'Anatra,* smoked muscovy duck breast, butternut squash and morel mushroom risotto ($8 as a "pasta course" or $16 as an entree), or the *pesce al Monaco,* pan-seared monkfish, pancetta, sage, sweet garlic, roasted tomato, calamata olives, and braised Swiss chard with seasoned risotto. Just one appetizer plus one entree will cost about $25. Dress is dress-casual, though you won't feel out of place in semi-formal attire at dinner, when reservations are advised.

NIGHTLIFE

As you might expect from a university campus with 24,000 students, Chapel Hill comes alive at night. Stroll the several blocks along Franklin Street, on the edge of the central campus, and take your pick. Of the city's many lively nightspots, two truly stand out.

Since its opening in 1970, **Cat's Cradle,** 300 E. Main St. (just continue west along Franklin Street, and it turns into Main), tel. (919) 967-9053, has earned its reputation as one of the most cutting-edge live-music clubs in the Southeast. The tradition continues today, as the club books such diverse acts as reggae band Burning Spear, folk musician Gillian Welch, and punkers Offspring. Cat's Cradle serves soft drinks, beer, and wine, which you can imbibe sitting on the benches, in the booths surrounding the stage, or while standing, for more popular bands. Cover charges range $3-13 depending on the acts.

Hell, at the corner of Henderson and Rosemary Streets, tel. (919) 929-7799, started luring souls into its dank, red and black basement environs in 1997. Run by first-time club owners Mark Dorosin and Bronwyn Merritt, respectively a lawyer and an artist, Hell supplies a "comprehensive selection of the finest Frito Lay products" to accompany a wide variety of beers, and a dazzling wine list, complete with suggestions of complementary foods: a sample from Hell's wine list reads, "Bridgeview Pinot Noir. From the grape that put the upstart Pacific Northwest on the vinifying map, Bridgeview combines a Kafka-esque, neurotic humility with all the cloying, devil-may-care exuberance you might expect from such a fine breakfast wine. The perfect Cartesian foil for salt-and-vinegar-laced potato chips." You won't find any live music in Hell, but you will find one of the most diverse and entertaining jukeboxes in America, including, among many other timeless stylists, James Brown, the Jam, Frank Sinatra, Motor Head, Louis Prima, AC/DC, and Sammy Davis, Jr. Open Mon.-Sat. 4 p.m.-2 a.m. and Sunday 7:30 p.m.-2 a.m., Hell is a private club, for members only. But don't let that scare you off—membership costs $5 a year.

CHAPEL HILL VICINITY

Hillsborough

Sometimes referred to as "a museum without walls," historic Hillsborough, an inviting small town of 5,000, boasts more than 100 homes and other buildings built in the late 1700s and early 1800s. During that period, Hillsborough was known as "the capitol of the back country," because its courthouse was North Carolina's western-most government building for most of the 18th century. The scene of many protests against British rule prior to the Revolutionary War, Hillsborough provides a pleasant afternoon's stroll. Stop in at the **Orange County Visitors Center,** 150 East King St., tel. (919) 732-7741, to view an informative 15-minute video about the town and pick up a pamphlet about the self-guided "Historic Hillsborough Walking Tour."

Established in 1754 where the Great Indian Trading Path crossed the Eno River, Hillsborough retains its roots as the site of a major transportation intersection, today located next to the junction of Interstates I-40 and I-85, about a 15-minute drive from both Chapel Hill and Durham.

If you're looking to stay in a historic bed-and-breakfast inn in the Triangle area, you won't find any more historic than Hillsborough's trio of terrific, centuries-old inns. The **Colonial Inn,** 153 W. King St., tel. (919) 732-2461, dates back to 1759, and some of the furnishings are original to the inn. The eight guest rooms with private baths are cozy—not terribly spacious, but at least you'll

know that you're sleeping in the same rooms once occupied by Aaron Burr, Lord Cornwallis, and a slew of other colonial bigwigs. The Colonial Inn also houses a nice restaurant, open to the public for lunch and dinner. A good buy for all that history and convenient good food, the Colonial Inn's rates range $55-65. Inexpensive-Moderate.

The neighboring **Inn at Teardrop,** 175 W. King St., tel. (919) 732-1120, exemplifies elegance. Built in 1768, this museum-quality inn provides six guest rooms, all with private baths. Moderate-Expensive. The youngster among Hillsborough's historic inns, built circa 1790, the **Hillsborough House Inn,** 209 E. Tryon St., tel. (919) 644-1600, is an Italianate mansion located on seven acres, convenient to Hillsborough's historic district and furnished with antiques, original art, and an extensive library. The Moderate-Expensive rates include a full breakfast.

Fearrington Village

In 1974, R.B. and Jenny Fitch purchased the old 640-acre Fearrington Dairy Farm. Located about eight miles south of Chapel Hill along US 15/501, the farm had passed for two centuries through generations of the Fearrington family. Since 1974, the Fitch family has been developing the farm into a charming residential community, with more than 800 families nestled in homes in the woodlands surrounding the Village Center, a quaint collection of shops, along with a nationally-renowned inn and restaurant. To keep the feel of the old dairy farm, the Fitches continue to breed the Fearringtons' Belted Galloway cows (or "Belties," as they're known for their unusual marking of a wide, white swath running like a belt around their midsections). The Belties are the first Fearrington villagers you'll see, in pastures along US 15/501.

The **Fearrington House Country Inn** and the **Fearrington House Restaurant,** the centerpieces of this planned community, have amassed awards from virtually every gourmet and travel magazine in the nation. Although through the course of writing this book we have often been mystified by the checklists used by various "rating guides," like the AAA guide, to determine how many stars or diamonds a place deserves, we have no quarrel with other guides when it comes to the inn and restaurant at Fearrington Village (recipient, for example, of AAA's rare and coveted "Five Diamond" rating for both lodging and dining).

The Fearrington House Country Inn, 2000 Fearrington Village Center, tel. (919) 542-2121, opened in 1986. Each of the 31 rooms is individually decorated with English country antiques, the finest fabrics, and original artwork. All rooms incluéde private baths, phones, and cable TV. Four types of rooms are available, from the spacious, airy "standard" rooms, beginning at $165, to the grand suites, beginning at $325. The personalized service at the inn is already legendary. Luxury.

The Fearrington House Restaurant, 2000 Fearrington Village Center, tel. (919) 542-2121, opened in 1980 and has been receiving rave reviews ever since, from sources including *Gourmet, Food and Wine* and *Bon Appétit,* to name a few. Housed in the renovated 1927 family homeplace of the Fearringtons, the dining rooms look out onto lovely gardens and arbors. The prix-fixe menu ($60/person) changes monthly. Meals begin with a taste-bud-teasing hors d'oeuvre and soup, followed by your choice of one of the eight to 10 first course items, like crispy sweetbreads with red wine truffle vinaigrette and warm potato salad, or air-cured antelope carpaccio with fresh basil and tomato concassé, sprinkled with Balsamic vinegar and extra virgin olive oil. Next, take a quick, palate-cleansing break with some sorbet or a small

salad before moving on to your choice of eight to 10 magnificently prepared main courses, like roast veal medallions with green apple chutney and baby turnips, or seared snapper filet with lobster fennel fricassee and lobster sauce. Then finish with one of the heavenly desserts, like the hot chocolate soufflé with whipped cream and chocolate sauce, or the coffee crème brûlée, served with currant doughnuts and banana-chocolate chip crullers. The fabulous wines and full selection of other drinks, including brandies, are not included in the fixed price (the fine wines begin at $5.50/glass, ranging up to $300 or more for a half bottle). Dress is semi-formal, and reservations are a must. Dinner is served Tues.-Sat. 6-9 p.m. and Sunday 6-8 p.m.

For a taste of the famed Fearrington cuisine without having to hit three figures for your bill, the **Fearrington Market & Cafe,** 2000 Fearrington Village Center, tel. (919) 542-5505, provides lunch and dinner during the week, and brunch on weekends. Housed in the converted old granary of the Fearrington farm, the market is a great place to enjoy a light meal, pick up some take-out food and a nice bottle of wine for a picnic, or just snatch a copy of the *New York Times* and enjoy a cup of cappuccino at the bar. Meals are served Mon.-Fri. 11:30 a.m.-2:30 p.m. and 6-8:30 p.m. Brunch is served Sat.-Sun. 9:30 a.m.-3 p.m. It's considerably less expensive than Fearrington House; most meals cost under $10.

TOMMY DAUGHTRY

iris

THE TRIAD

Nestled in the gently sloping, fertile northern Piedmont, where they are caressed by cool mountain breezes out of the Blue Ridge and Sauratown Mountain ranges, the thriving cities of Greensboro, Winston-Salem, and High Point make up what is known as "The Triad."

For the visitor, the Triad cities offer a wealth of historic attractions, from the living history of the centuries-old town of Old Salem to the restored lunch counter at Greensboro's downtown Woolworth's, site of the famed 1960 civil-rights sit-in. Thanks in part to its situation on two major interstate freeways—I-40 and I-85—the Triad is also a bustling hub of business and arts. More than 125 furniture manufacturing plants make their homes in and around High Point. And Winston-Salem, birthplace of the R.J. Reynolds tobacco empire, is also home to one of the nation's largest banks, Wachovia. Substantial corporate contributions by the many businesses headquartered in the Triad have spawned, among other enhancements, dozens of interesting museums and a number of performing arts groups. The area is also blessed with a profusion of city parks and several captivating state parks spread out in the nearby mountain ranges.

GREENSBORO

With a population of about 200,000, Greensboro is North Carolina's third-largest city (behind Charlotte and Raleigh). Although the town was named after Revolutionary War general Nathanael Greene, the name is also appropriate for the overall look of this city, which is home to more than 100 municipal parks. Five colleges and universities—the University of North Carolina at Greensboro, NC A&T State University, Guilford College, Greensboro College, and Bennett College—give the city a youthful flavor and also provide a variety of cultural and sporting events for the community. Greensboro provides a convenient geographical base for exploring not only the city's own attractions but also those lying nearby, such as the fabulous North Carolina Zoo, 25 miles south in Asheboro.

The folks who planned the streets of Greensboro shunned the grid system, favoring a laissez-faire design that yields an area map resembling a tangle of spaghetti noodles. You won't regret stopping when you arrive and picking up a map from the **Greensboro Convention and Visitors Bureau,** 317 S. Greene St., tel. (336) 274-

THE TRIAD

Hanging Rock State Park

Pilot Mountain State Park

Reidsville

Winston-Salem

Browns Summit

GUILFORD COURTHOUSE NATIONAL MILITARY PARK

PIEDMONT INTERNATIONAL AIRPORT

GREENSBORO

Clemmons

High Point

Thomasville

Lexington

High Rock Lake

Asheboro

NORTH CAROLINA ZOOLOGICAL PARK

0   10 mi

0   10 km

Uwharrie National Forest

Seagrove

© MOON PUBLICATIONS, INC.

2282 or (800) 344-2282, open Mon.-Fri. 8:30 a.m.-5:30 p.m., Saturday 10 a.m.-4 p.m., and Sunday 1-4 p.m. Better yet, call ahead to receive several helpful brochures to supplement the map provided here.

History

The first colonial settlers in the Greensboro area were mostly Quakers of Welsh and English descent, along with some Germans and Scotch-Irish. Throughout the 1700s, the area was sparsely populated, almost exclusively by farmers. In 1807, these farmers voted to create a more centrally located seat of government, and the following year, elected officials mapped out a 42-acre tract of land and ponied up a whopping $98 to purchase it. They named it for patriot General Nathanael Greene, who led his troops in the 1781 Battle of Guilford Courthouse.

The town remained a relatively quiet place through the early 1800s. But the strong influence of the area's Quaker population led to some

IF YOU'RE PLANNING TO VISIT THE TRIAD IN APRIL OR NOVEMBER . . .

. . . be forewarned that for a couple of weeks in April and October-November (the dates vary from year to year), the International Home Furnishings Market is held in High Point. During these two-week events, more than 70,000 furniture buyers and exhibitors from around the globe descend on the Triad, take up most of the available lodging space, and usually drive up the prices of most of the things visitors need or want. For exact dates, call the International Home Furnishings Market Association, tel. (336) 889-0203.

quiet but significant "rebellious" activities that would put Greensboro in the forefront of the fight for human rights. From 1830 until the end of the Civil War, Vestal Coffin, an abolitionist Quaker, and his cousin Levi helped to operate the "Greensboro station" on the famed Underground Railroad, providing shelter and assistance to hundreds of escaped slaves fleeing to the North. In 1837, area Quakers established Guilford College, the first coeducational institution in the South. Indeed, Greensboro was a pioneer in placing an emphasis on higher education for women and African-Americans. In addition to Guilford College, the town established the Normal and Industrial School for White Girls (now the University of North Carolina-Greensboro); Greensboro Female College (now coeducational Greensboro College); the Bennett Seminary (originally for African-American students, now Bennett College); and the Agricultural and Mechanical College for the Colored Race (now North Carolina Agricultural and Technical State University). In 1960, four black students from NC A&T sent shock waves through the nation and inspired countless other activists (including Martin Luther King, Jr.) when they sat down at the segregated lunch counter at Greensboro's downtown Woolworth's and asked for service—the first civil rights "sit-in" in the nation.

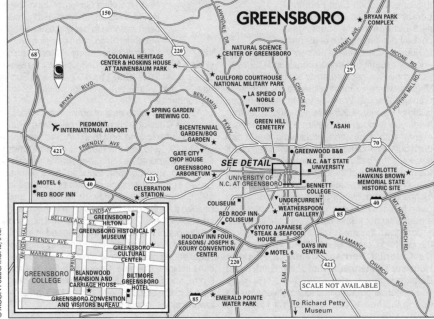

SIGHTS

Historic Sites

One of most pivotal and bloody battles of the Revolutionary War was fought on the 220 acres that now make up **Guilford Courthouse National Military Park,** 2332 New Garden Rd., tel. (336) 288-1776. Make sure to stop by the visitors center to view the 20-minute video that summarizes the events of March 15, 1781. On that fateful day, Continental Army General Nathanael Greene (after whom Greensboro is named) led his army of 1,400 veterans, augmented by 3,000 raw-recruit militiamen into battle against the 2,000 seasoned soldiers led by British general Lord Cornwallis. The Brits had recently suffered some embarrassing defeats, and Cornwallis was determined to win this one. Despite being outnumbered, Cornwallis' army held the field and won the day, but at great cost. About one quarter of his army fell during this battle. The continued threat of another assault by Greene convinced Cornwallis to move his crippled army east to Yorktown, Virginia, where six months later he'd surrender to General George Washington in the climactic battle of the war. A 2.5-mile self-guided car tour leads you through the battleground and monuments, with occasional stops where you can push buttons and hear audio presentations about details of the battle and its participants. One of the more colorful of these, Peter Francisco, "the Goliath of the Revolution," stood six-feet, six-inches tall and swung a lethal five-foot sword given to him by George Washington. Open 8:30 a.m.-5:30 p.m.; admission to the park is free.

General Nathanael Greene

Just down the street from the visitors center at the Guilford Courthouse National Military Park, the **Colonial Heritage Center & Hoskins House at Tannenbaum Park,** New Garden and Battleground Ave., tel. (336) 545-5315, gives you a more intimate glimpse into everyday life during the late 1700s, including a variety of hands-on exhibits. The site includes the preserved 1778 Hoskins House, along with a kitchen, blacksmith shed, and barn. Living history weekends, complete with costumed docents and demonstrations of weaving, blacksmithing and other activities, are usually held about once a month. The Hoskins House is only open on weekends, Saturday 10 a.m.-5 p.m. and Sunday1-5 p.m. The Colonial Heritage Center, with a gift shop and gallery of exhibits, is closed on Monday, and open Tues.-Fri. 9 a.m.-5 p.m., Saturday 10 a.m.-5 p.m., and Sunday1-5 p.m. The park is open Mon.-Sat. 8 a.m.-5 p.m. and Sunday 1-5 p.m. Admission is free.

Blandwood Mansion and Carriage House, 447 W. Washington St., tel. (336) 272-5003, was built as a farmhouse in the late 1700s and then completely renovated and redesigned into an elegant Italian villa in 1844. The former home of North Carolina Governor John Motley Morehead, the mansion has been restored to depict the era when Morehead lived in the mansion, from 1827 to 1866, and includes many of Morehead's original furnishings. Closed on Monday, the mansion is open Tues.-Sat. 11 a.m.-2 p.m. and Sunday 2-5 p.m. Admission is $5 for adults, $2 for kids under 12.

About eight miles east of downtown Greensboro, the **Charlotte Hawkins Brown Memorial State Historic Site** on US 70 in Sedalia, tel. (336) 449-4846, on the campus of the former Palmer Memorial Institute, honors the African-American educator who founded the Institute. Brown started the black preparatory school in 1902, when she was only 19 years old, and headed it for the next 50 years. The visitors center shows a brief video on Dr. Brown's life and the history of her school, which closed in 1971. Other exhibits chronicle the pioneering educational efforts of Brown and other African-Americans in North Carolina. Open Mon.-Sat. 9 a.m.-5 p.m. and Sunday 1-5 p.m.; admission is free. To get to the site, take exit 135 on I-85, and follow the signs for about a mile.

Museums

The **Greensboro Historical Museum,** 130 Summit Ave., tel. (336) 373-2043, housed in a Romanesque church built in 1892, traces the history of Greensboro through a variety of well-designed exhibits. The informative museum details the area's early settlement, military, and transportation history, as well as more modern events, like the 1960 Woolworth lunch counter sit-in. You'll also learn about the lives of several Greensboro natives, including First Lady Dolley Madison, journalist Edward R. Murrow, and author William Sydney Porter, alias O. Henry. Closed on Monday, the museum is open Tues.-Sat. 10 a.m.-5 p.m. and Sunday 1-5 p.m. Admission is free.

A combination science museum, zoo, and planetarium, the **Natural Science Center of Greensboro,** 4301 Lawndale Dr., tel. (336) 288-3769, is a big hit with kids. Emphasizing an interactive approach, the museum gives kids an opportunity to have fun with many hands-on science and technology exhibits, like the rocket room, where kids can assemble toy rockets. In the Marine Gallery, a bioscanner, aquarium, and touch tank reveal secrets of the sea. A dinosaur gallery features includes several impressive species—no bones here—the T-Rex and his dino friends come complete with skin and penetrating eyes. Slithery snakes and other reptiles and amphibians populate the herpetarium. Perhaps the most popular spot at the center is the petting zoo, where kids can stroke a donkey or deer, hold a rabbit, and meet other friendly, furry critters. Visitors can also get close (but not too close) to jaguars, black bears, and other imposing animals. The planetarium shows multi-media productions about the heavens, with showtimes weekdays at 2 and 3 p.m. and Sat.-Sun. at 2, 3, and 4 p.m. The science center is open Mon.-Sat. 9 a.m.-5 p.m. and Sunday 12:30-5 p.m. The zoo is open Mon.-Sat. 10 a.m.-4:30 p.m. and Sunday 12:30-4:30 p.m. Admission is $4.50 for adults, $3.50 for kids 4-13. Kids 3 and under are admitted free. Planetarium shows cost $1 extra.

On the campus of the University of North Carolina at Greensboro, the **Weatherspoon Art Gallery,** at the corner of Tate and Spring Garden Streets, tel. (336) 334-5770, features an impressive collection focussing on 20th century American art, with works by Robert Rauschenberg, Willem de Kooning, among many other noted American artists. The museum's biggest draw is the collection of lithographs and bronzes by Henri Matisse. Admission is free. Hours are Tuesday, Thursday, and Friday 10 a.m.-5 p.m., Wednesday 10 a.m.-8 p.m., and Sat.-Sun. 1-5 p.m.

The **Greensboro Cultural Center,** 200 N. Davie St., includes five small, individual art galleries, all with free admission. **African American Atelier, Inc.,** tel. (336) 333-6885 exhibits artwork by local African-American artists and has a gift shop. Hours are Tues.-Sat. 10 a.m.-5 p.m. and Sunday 3-5 p.m. The **Green Hill Center for North Carolina Art,** tel. (336) 333-7460, promotes the visual arts of North Carolina through a variety of changing exhibits. The sales gallery features a range of works by North Carolina artists, including glass, ceramics, jewelry, wood, fiber, and paintings. Hours are Tues.-Sat. 10 a.m.-5 p.m. and Sunday 2-5 p.m. The **Greensboro Artists' League Gallery and Gift Shop,** tel. (336) 333-7485, has changing exhibits of work by local artists. Hours are Tuesday, Thursday, and Friday 10 a.m.-5 p.m., Wednesday noon-7 p.m., Saturday noon-5 p.m., and Sunday 2-5 p.m. The **Guilford Native American Art Gallery and Gift Shop,** tel. (336) 273-6605, exhibits and sells traditional and contemporary Native American arts and crafts. Hours are Tues.-Sat. 10 a.m.-5 p.m. The **Mattye Reed African American Heritage Center Satellite Gallery,** tel. (336) 334-7108, features traveling exhibits of a wide range of African works. Hours are Tues.-Fri. 10 a.m.-5 p.m. and Sat.-Sun. 1-5 p.m. A couple blocks away from the Cultural Center, you can take in one of the nation's best collections of African art at the **Mattye Reed African American Heritage Center,** 1601 E. Market St., tel. (336) 334-7874. Located on the NC A&T State University campus, the museum houses more than 3,500 art and craft works from over 30 African nations.

If you're a NASCAR (stock car racing) fan, you won't to pass up a visit to the **Richard Petty Museum,** 311 Branson Mill Rd., tel. (336) 495-1143. Race cars, awards, and photos honor the seven-time Winston Cup Series champion, known simply as "the King" in NASCAR circles. A minitheater shows highlights of Petty's career, with interviews and racing footage including some dramatic crashes. A gift shop provides a

GREENSBORO: CIVIL RIGHTS FLASHPOINT

In the fall of 1959, four young African-Americans began taking classes at Greensboro's North Carolina Agricultural and Technical College (one of the city's two African-American colleges). Ezell Blair, Jr., Franklin McCain, Joseph McNeil, and David Richmond were born and bred North Carolinians. McNeil had been raised in Wilmington, but the other three were lifelong Greensboro residents. Over more than a century, Greensboro had earned a reputation as being generally supportive of civil rights. This is not to say that Greensboro's color lines weren't always clearly drawn. "Separate but equal" was a goal Greensboro had come as close to achieving as had any other city in the South, but the four freshmen knew firsthand the inherent inequality of the prevailing "separate but equal" policy.

That December, for instance, following his first semester at NC A&T, Joseph McNeil took a trip to New York and upon his return was refused food service at the Greensboro Trailways Bus Terminal. Such discrimination wasn't unusual in Greensboro at the time.

On February 1, 1960, the four young men went into the Woolworth's general store and bought school supplies (making sure to keep their receipts).

Then they sat down at the store's lunch counter and politely requested coffee. The counter was reserved only for whites, and the freshmen were refused service. In silence, they remained seated at the counter. The manager of the store came up and tried to persuade them to leave. He failed. Blair, McCain, McNeil, and Richmond all remained seated—and informed the manager of their intention to come back the next day, and the next, and the next after that, and to keep coming back until they were served at the lunch counter like any other Woolworth's customer. The store steadfastly refused them service but took no other action. None of the young men could later recall any single, crystallizing event that inspired their action. "The thing that precipitated the sit-ins," explained McCain later, "was that little bit of incentive and that little bit of courage that each of us instilled within each other."

Overnight, word spread of their courageous and dignified act, and the freshmen gained an enthusiastic ally, the talented, charismatic student-body president of NC A&T. This man was Jesse Jackson, and, quickly demonstrating the strategic, political, and organizational brilliance that have characterized his career ever since, he helped turn the initial

---

variety of gifts and souvenirs ideal to bring back home for a favorite car racing fan. Open Mon.-Sat. 9 a.m.-5 p.m., the museum is located about 10 miles south of downtown Greensboro, in the little town of Level Cross. From the junction of I-40 and I-85, take US 220 south to the Level Cross exit and follow the signs. Admission is $3 for adults, $1.50 for students.

Gardens
Three marvelous gardens located within a few minutes of each other provide lovely walking paths. The **Greensboro Arboretum,** on West Market Street between Wendover Avenue and Ashland Drive, features nine permanent plant collections consisting of species native to North Carolina. From autumn's flaming

*arrow
arum*

leaves to winter's red berries, to spring and summer's explosive blooming flowers and shrubs, the arboretum's 17 acres provide colorful strolls year-round, through a varying topography that ranges from steep slopes to flat, meadow-like plains. On Hobbs Road, just north of Friendly Avenue and Holden Road, two smaller gardens located next to each other provide startling contrasts. At the 7.5-acre **Bicentennial Garden,** the bright colors of blossoming flowers in formal gardens, like the spectacular rose garden, are particularly splendid during the spring and summer. At the adjacent **Bog Garden,** a half-mile-long elevated wooden walkway leads you through a lush, swampy area replete with more than 8,000 individually labeled trees, shrubs, ferns, bamboo, and wildflowers. Open from sunrise to sunset, all

humble act of protest into a flashpoint for the national civil rights movement.

By the next day, Tuesday, the four freshmen were joined by 29 fellow African-American NC A&T students—including several ROTC cadets in full dress and four immaculately dressed women. Again, the protest remained peaceful, but Woolworth's still refused to serve the African-Americans at the lunch counter.

On Wednesday, students from surrounding African-American colleges joined the sit-in, taking up 63 of the 65 seats available at the counter.

On Thursday, the protesters included three white women.

By Friday, more than 300 students took turns at the Woolworth lunch counter. That day, police made the only arrests of the entire demonstration: two white men were arrested for disturbing the peace with their hate-mongering heckling of the demonstrators, and another white man was arrested for using his cigarette lighter to try to set fire to the coat of a student sitting at the lunch counter.

By Saturday, hundreds of students, both black and white, had rallied to the four freshmen's cause. (Hundreds of white "counter-protesters" also crowded Woolworth's, to jeer the "sit-inners.") That day, the NC A&T football team joined the fray, forming peaceful but effective "flying wedges" that allowed fresh demonstrators to relieve those who had been sitting at the counter for hours. Again, the day was ruled by nonviolence, and no arrests were made. That evening, 1,600 mostly African-American students gathered in a meeting and decided that they had made their point. They called a halt to the sit-in and embarked on an ultimately successful strategy to "negotiate and study" a repeal of Greensboro's separatist practices.

But the four freshmen had ignited a fire, and it spread quickly. The following Monday, African-American students in Durham and Winston-Salem held sit-ins at lunch counters; on Tuesday, students did the same in Charlotte; Wednesday, students sat-in in Raleigh. Before long, such protests were occurring throughout the nation. The civil rights struggles of the 1960s and early 1970s included thousands of sit-ins, attended by millions of civil rights advocates.

That old Woolworth's, which closed in 1993, is now in the process of being restored and converted into the **International Civil Rights Center and Museum,** 134 S. Elm St., tel. (336) 274-9199. Near the turn of the new millennium, you should be able to obtain an intimate perspective on that catalytic event by visiting (and being served at) the historic lunch counter itself.

three gardens offer free admission. For information about any of these gardens, call Greensboro Beautiful at (336) 373-2558.

RECREATION

Water and Amusement Parks

You can splash and slide your way through more than three million gallons of water at **Emerald Pointe Water Park,** 3910 South Holden Road, tel. (336) 852-9721 or, in NC or VA, tel. (800) 555-5900. The largest water park in the Carolinas, Emerald Pointe includes 22 water rides, from sloshing wave pools to towering slides. Admission is $20 for folks over 45 inches tall, and $14 for folks under that height (some rides have a 45-inch height requirement). Located off I-85 exit 121 on Holden Road, the park is open Mon.-Thurs. 10 a.m.-7 p.m. and Fri.-Sun. 10 a.m.-8 p.m., from mid-May through early September.

There's more than just water at **Celebration Station,** 4315 Big Tree Way, just off I-40 at the Wendover Avenue exit, tel. (336) 316-0606. In addition to the water bumper boats, you can try your hand at miniature golf, go-carts, batting cages, and more than 80 arcade and video games. You can also grab a meal or snack at two restaurants, the 1950s-style Dixie Diner and a pizza place for young kids that features an animated band of bears and dogs that sing songs and tell jokes. Open Sun.-Thurs. 10 a.m.-10 p.m. and Fri.-Sat. 10 a.m.-11 p.m. year-round. There's no admission fee to the park. Prices for individual activities vary, with combination tickets available for $10-16.

Golf

The cream of a pretty good crop of area golf courses can be found at the **Bryan Park Complex,** off US 29 North on Bryan Park Avenue in Browns Summit, about 10 miles from downtown Greensboro. At the complex, you can choose between two superb public courses. The **Champions Course,** designed by Rees Jones and completed in 1990, was named that year's runner-up as the nation's best new public course by *Golf Digest.* It features 100 sand and grass bunkers and six holes bordering scenic Lake Townsend. Greens fees, including a mandatory cart, are $34 on weekdays, and $38 on Saturday and Sunday, which has earned this gorgeous course a place among *Golf Digest's* 100 U.S. courses rated a "Great Value." Also on the premises, the **Player's Course,** designed by George Cobb, features 84 bunkers and 8 ponds. You can play this beauty for $32 weekdays, and $34 weekends including a cart, or you can walk the course for $20-22. Both courses offer twilight rates ($11-19) beginning at 2 p.m. in the winter, 4 p.m. in the summer. Metal spikes are not allowed. To reserve a tee time, call (336) 375-2200.

If you're planning an extended stay, you also won't want to miss a shot at two other magnificent public courses in the Triad area. The **Tanglewood Park Golf Club** in Winston-Salem is also one of *Golf Digest's* 100 "Great Values," as well as one of the top 25 public courses in the nation, and **Oak Hollow Golf Course** in High Point, just eight miles from Greensboro, has earned *Golf Digest's* designation as one of the 75 best public courses in the nation.

ACCOMMODATIONS

Greensboro's location along I-40 and I-85 and proximity to Piedmont International Airport has spawned a large number of lodgings. In fact, you can choose among more than 60 hotels and motels, the vast majority of them of the franchise variety. At last count, Greensboro was home to three Days Inns, three Holiday Inns, four Howard Johnsons—you get the idea. For a complete list, including a precise locator map, contact the Greensboro Convention and Visitors Bureau, tel. (800) 344-2282.

Despite its rich history, the city has few small bed-and-breakfast inns. The superior **Greenwood Bed & Breakfast,** 205 North Park Drive, tel. (336) 274-6350 or (800) 535-9363. Known as the "Chalet in the Park," this inviting 1905 home, located on North Park in the central historic district, is eclectically decorated with antiques and contemporary furnishings. Hosts Dolly and Bob Guertin describe their inn as a "culinary escape where great conversation is standard fare." Indeed, you'll be hard pressed to find a better B&B cook than Bob, a former New Orleans chef who'll create a full breakfast for you and serve it to order at the time of your choosing (5-10 a.m.). On Sunday, Bob serves up a three-course New Orleans-style brunch, complete with crΩpes Suzette. Rates range $95-105 for each of the five charming rooms. Expensive.

Also in the central historic district, the 100-year-old **Biltmore Greensboro Hotel,** 11 W. Washington St., tel. (336) 272-3474 or (800) 332-0303, provides 25 graceful rooms, including a few suites, decorated with antiques, early American reproductions, and some with splendid, canopied king-size beds. The hardwood floors and high ceilings give this renovated hotel an airy, historic feel you won't find at the franchise lodgings. Rates range from $75 for a single room to $110 for a two-room suite. Moderate-Expensive. Nearby, the 281-room **Greensboro Hilton,** 304 N. Greene St., tel. (336) 379-8000, or (800) 533-3944, provides all the typical Hilton amenities, including an indoor pool and a health club with Nautilus equipment, free weights, sauna and whirlpool. Rates range $99-129. Expensive-Premium.

If bigger is better, you can't beat the massive 17-story **Holiday Inn Four Seasons/Joseph S. Koury Convention Center,** 3121 High Point Road, tel. (336) 292-9161 or (800) 242-6556. North Carolina's biggest hotel, with 1014 rooms, this place offers a vast number of amenities, including babysitting services, an indoor/outdoor pool, health club, racquetball courts, four on-site restaurants, three bars, a dance club with live bands Mon.-Sat., and an adjacent shopping mall with more than 200 retail stores. In addition, golf privileges are provided for two courses at the Grandover Resort a five-minute drive away. Noncorporate rates start at $135.

Dozens of franchise motels dot I-40 and I-85 in the Greensboro area, providing interstate travelers with a bounty of clean and comfortable overnight lodgings. The following is just a sampling of the many motels offering rooms in the $40-60 range. Two Red Roof Inns on I-40 provide not only some the least expensive rates in the area, but also allow small pets. At exit 217B, the

Red Roof Inn-Coliseum, 2101 W. Meadowview Rd., tel. (336) 852-6560, offers 108 rooms, and at exit 210, the Red Roof Inn-Greensboro/High Point, tel. (336) 271-2636, has 112 rooms. To make toll-free reservations at either Red Roof Inn, call (800) THE-ROOF. At the junction of I-40 and I-85, Motel 6, 831 Greenhaven Dr., tel. (336) 854-0993 or (800) 4-MOTEL-6, houses 150 standard rooms at Inexpensive rates. Along I-40/I-85 at exit 125, relatively close to downtown Greensboro, the Day's Inn Central, 120 Seneca Rd., tel. (336) 275-9571 or (800) DAYS-INN, offers 122 rooms and a swimming pool.

FOOD AND DRINK

With more than 500 eateries to choose from, you're never far from a restaurant in Greensboro. The Convention and Visitors Bureau, tel. (800) 344-2282, provides a fairly comprehensive dining brochure, listing more than 400 places. Here are a few standouts.

Located in the city's historic district, **Undercurrent**, 600 Elm St., tel. (336) 370-1266, is an inviting bistro with a metropolitan atmosphere, housed in a comfortable space with high ceilings, ceiling fans, white tablecloths, and comfortable, cushioned blue chairs. The menu, which changes frequently, displays a Mediterranean influence, mostly Greek, Italian and French, but always features delectable seafood and meat dishes in the $17-22 range. Two terrific examples of the creative fare are the grilled Chilean sea bass and fresh mussels with saffron-Chardonnay broth over cracked black pepper fettuccine, finished with Spanish-style Romesco ($19), and the herb-crusted grilled leg of lamb over trecce del orto pasta, basil-cured tomatoes, and kalamata olives, finished with lamb broth ($18). A perennial winner of the coveted *Wine Spectator* award of excellence, Undercurrent is open Tues.-Sat. for dinner only.

On Battleground Avenue, between Wendover and Cornwallis Road, you can choose between two popular Italian restaurants. **La Spiedo Di Noble**, 1720 Battleground Ave., in the Irving Park Plaza, tel. (336) 333-9833, is a Tuscan-inspired restaurant, complete with wood grill oven, grill and rotisserie, murals of Italian landscapes on the walls, ivy-covered trellises, and, on the second floor, an impressive marble sculpture of a rooster. The fare and service here are first-rate, and entrees range $12-25. The atmosphere is "faux-formal," with paper over the white tablecloths. For appetizers, try one of the several delectable options, like the fried oyster and baby spinach salad with roasted red peppers, applewood-smoked bacon, and creamy balsamic vinaigrette. Among the many tantalizing entrees, you can choose the spit-roasted chicken; the yellowfin tuna grilled rare over sesame quinoa, with a wasabi ginger and mint crème fraiche; or the cassoulet of duck comfit, with Italian sausage, smoked duck, and Tuscan white beans, a bargain at $15. To complement your meal, a jazz trio performs Wednesday through Saturday. La Spiedo Di Noble is open for dinner every day but Sunday; as this edition went to press, the owners were planning to open for lunch as well.

Just down the street, **Anton's**, 1628 Battleground Ave., tel. (336) 273-1386, is a Greensboro institution, run by third-generation Italian restaurateurs in the Triad area. The owners, Chris and Stephen Anton, hold true to their grandfather's motto, "Always offer friendly service and great food at a good value." The atmosphere is casual and homey, with wood beam ceilings, cozy booths, and spacious tables. There's nothing pretentious about Anton's, from the tumblers that serve as both wine and water glasses to the straightforward menu of Italian favorites like lasagna and manicotti (under $9), veal dishes and steaks for under $12, and the Shrimp Anton's—shrimp saut°ed in scampi butter, with fresh garlic, parsley, white wine and light cream, served over angel hair pasta, for $12. Anton's is open Mon.-Sat. for lunch and dinner, with prices ranging $6-13.

Steak houses are very popular in Greensboro, and none is more popular than the **Gate City Chop House**, 106 S. Holden Rd., at the corner of Holden and W. Market Street, tel. (336) 294-9977. With its wood-paneled interiors and patio areas with fireplaces (yes, outdoor fireplaces), the Chop House is the kind of place that students from the local colleges book when the folks ask them to make a dinner reservation. Despite the elegant surroundings and entrees ranging $16-34, you won't feel out of place if you don't wear a tie or high heels here, and you won't feel out of place if you do. The emphasis is on certified Angus beef, along with fresh fish, veal, pork, and lamb. The Chop House is also open for lunch, for about $8-11.

If you're just looking for a spot to enjoy a good beer and sandwich, or a good beer and steak, rotisserie ribs, duck, or chicken, try the **Spring Garden Brewing Co.**, at the corner of Friendly Avenue and Guilford College Road, just two miles from exit 314 on I-40, tel. (336) 299-3649. The beers are brewed on the premises according to the Bavarian Purity Law of 1516, and they're sure to please. Meal prices range $5-16. Open daily for lunch and dinner.

Greensboro is home to several excellent Japanese steak houses and sushi bars. Two of the best for succulent raw fish, or a flashy tableside performance by a master itamaesan, try **Asahi,** 4520-B W. Market St., tel. (336) 855-8883, or **Kyoto Japanese Steak & Seafood House,** 1200 S. Holden Rd., at the junction of Holden and Peterson Street. Entrees range $12-20.

Entertainment

For a meal and show that transcends even the pyrotechnics of a Japanese steak house, the **Barn Dinner Theater,** 120 Stage Coach Trail, tel. (336) 292-2211, is one of the nation's oldest dinner theaters. Since its opening in 1963, this dinner theater has been bringing old Broadway shows to enthusiastic Greensboro audiences. A buffet dinner featuring baked halibut and carved roast beef, ham, and turkey, as well as a salad and dessert bar, precedes the show. The buffet is actually set up in the middle of the room, 6:30-7:45 p.m. At 8 p.m., after the buffet has been cleared away, the "magic stage" descends from the ceiling, forming a theater-in-the-round. Open year-round, with performances Wed.-Sun. (seven nights a week in December); the cost for dinner and the show usually ranges $28-35 per person. Call first for reservations.

From late June through early August, Greensboro hosts the **Eastern Music Festival.** Nightly concerts often feature internationally renowned soloists accompanied by the Eastern Philharmonic Orchestra, composed of about 80 professional musicians from around the country. The more than 40 performances feature diverse musical fare. For more information, call (336) 333-7450.

WINSTON~SALEM

In the early 18th century, the Moravians—a band of German-speaking religious dissidents from Bohemia and Moravia (later Czechoslovakia)—settled in Bethlehem, Pennsylvania. In 1753, a party of these Moravians set out in search of inexpensive, fertile land in a warmer climate. They found what they were looking for in what is today Winston-Salem, bought about 100,000 acres, and dubbed it "Der Wachau," after the ancestral home of their sect's leader. Der Wachau soon was Americanized into "Wachovia." (Somewhat ironically, the name given to the community by its hard-working, simple-living founders is today carried on principally by the 17th-largest bank in the nation.)

The original Moravian settlement was located at Bethabara. They were soon joined by dozens of their fellow Moravians from Bethlehem, among whose agricultural pursuits included the raising of herds of sheep and fields of cotton. Although some Moravians stayed on at Bethabara, most moved in 1772 to newly acquired land in the town of Salem. During the first half of the 19th century, the Salem area was home to a wool and cotton mill that would later help establish the area as a leading textile hub of the South.

After the Civil War, a fellow named R.J. Reynolds started selling tobacco and built his first factory in the town of Winston in 1875 (the same year the Western North Carolina railroad came to town). With Reynolds' tobacco empire leading the way, the adjoining towns of Salem and Winston sprouted dozens of textile and tobacco factories, which soon gave birth to several banks eager to lend money to the agricultural and industrial interests in the area. By 1913, the towns of Winston and Salem had expanded to the point where they joined together to form a single municipality.

The diverse influences that established this town in the foothills of the Blue Ridge and Sauratown Mountains yielded a graceful city of many faces—from modest, 200-year-old structures along the narrow streets of Old Salem to high-rise office buildings towering over the bustling one-way streets of downtown, to attractive homes situated on the rolling green hills outside town. Having sprung from roots as a religious settlement to emerge as a manufacturing and financial center, Winston-Salem has a home-grown yet cosmopolitan atmosphere, inviting to travelers of all stripes.

SIGHTS

You'll be transported back to life in this Moravian church town in the late 18th and early 19th centuries when you visit **Old Salem,** a living history village on Old Salem Road and East Academy Street, just south of downtown, tel. (336) 721-7300 or toll-free (888) OLD-SALEM. More than 90 structures have been preserved and restored, dating back to as early as 1766. As you explore the homes, outbuildings, trades shops, swept yards, kitchen gardens, and orchards, you'll meet costumed interpreters who still do things the old fashioned way, from chopping wood to cooking over wood fires. Though it has a few similarities to the massive reconstructed town of Williamsburg, Virginia, the village of Old Salem is far more understated. You get the feel

Old Salem, in Winston-Salem, preserves and demonstrates traditional ways of life in living-history displays.

NORTH CAROLINA DIVISION OF TOURISM, FILM & SPORTS DEVELOPMENT

that this is still a working village, and that real people, not just costumed actors, actually live here—and in fact, they still do. Many of the homes in the village are privately owned, and in addition, the campus of Salem College (for women) is interwoven with the village, lending the historic village a surprisingly complementary, youthful, and contemporary tone. Of the more than 90 restored structures in the village, only about 15 can be visited by the public.

Although there's no admission fee to enter the streets of Old Salem, you do have to pay $14 for adults, $8 for kids 6-16, to take advantage of the in-depth tours of the historic sights and buildings in the village ($18 and $10 if you include the Museum of Early Southern Decorative Arts-see below for description). To purchase your ticket, stop first at the visitors center at Old Salem Road and East Academy Street, where you should also take in the 14-minute slide presentation, showing every half hour. Your admission ticket, good for two days, gives you entrance to eight "museum/houses" like the fascinating **Single Brothers House.** This big building, built in 1769 and expanded in 1786, was aptly named, since this was where all of the young, unmarried Moravian men of the village lived, beginning at the age of 14 (the unmarried women lived communally across the square). In addition to the meeting hall, dining room, kitchen, and living quarters, the building includes a number of trade shops, where today you can observe and interact with costumed artisans casting pewter, blacksmithing, tailoring, and making furniture, among other demonstrations. Other historic tour stops include a doctor's home and apothecary, a silversmith's home and shop, a boys' school, a tobacconist's home and shop, a fire house, a restored tavern, and an art gallery.

At the edge of Old Salem on Main Street, three blocks south of Salem Square, the comprehensive **Museum of Early Decorative Southern Arts,** tel. (336) 721-7360, is dedicated to exhibiting and researching the regional decorative arts of the early South. Through more than 20 period rooms and six galleries, this museum showcases the furniture, paintings, textiles, ceramics, silver and other metalwares made and used in the Carolinas, Maryland, Virginia, Georgia, Kentucky, and Tennessee through 1820. In the impressive period rooms, you'll experience a wide range of atmospheres, from a 17th-century Virginia great hall and an elegant Charleston parlor, to a log house from North Carolina's backcountry and a Maryland plantation shack. Tours, which last about an hour, begin every 30 minutes Mon.-Sat. 9:30 a.m.-3:30 p.m. and Sunday 1:30-3:30 p.m. Separate admission to this museum is $9 for adults, $5 for kids 6-16, but the vast majority of visitors purchase a "combination ticket" for $18 ($10 for kids 6-16), which includes this museum, as well as all the other tours in Old Salem.

Even if you don't want purchase any tour tickets in Old Salem, you'll still enjoy spending an hour or two just strolling along the streets, watching the docents do their Moravian things, and looking into the various shops. Don't miss stopping at the **Winkler Bakery,** on Main Street, just north of Salem Square, to sample, among the other wood-fired wares, the astonishingly thin and tasty Moravian cookies; the most popular are the spice cookies, similar to ginger snaps, about the diameter of an Oreo cookie, but about one-tenth the thickness. Once you try them, you'll be sure to buy a tin for yourself, as well as for the folks back home. Speaking of eating, as you tour Old Salem, you should seriously consider having lunch or dinner at the historic Old Salem Tavern (see Food and Drink).

About a 15-minute drive north from Old Salem will take you to the first Moravian settlement in the area, at **Bethabara Park,** 2147 Bethabara Rd., tel. (336) 924-8191. First, stop by the visitors center to get some background, including a slide presentation about this 1753 settlement. From there, you can explore this lush yet ghostly 110-acre park, which includes more than 40 archaeological ruins, along with a few restored structures, including a 1788 church and a reconstructed palisade fort. Admission is free, and costumed docents add historical color and information to this interesting site, open Mon.-Fri. 9:30 a.m.-4:30 p.m. and Sat.-Sun. 1:30-4:30 p.m. The grounds are open all day year-round, but some exhibit buildings are only open April 1-Nov. 30.

Modern Moravians still populate Winston-Salem, though most have moved to the suburbs. However, the Moravians still lend a unique flavor to Winston-Salem, especially at Easter and Christmas. In the pre-dawn hours on Easter Sunday, brass bands parade through Winston-Salem, calling residents to a sunrise service on Salem Square, followed by a walk to God's Acre, the original Moravian cemetery. At Christmastime, candlelight "love feasts" with coffee, music, and delicious and fragrant spice buns, are held throughout Winston-Salem. The most popular love feast is the **Candle Christmas Tea** in Old Salem, sponsored by the Home Moravian Church. During the Christmas season, softly illuminated, many-pointed, three-dimensional Moravian stars adorn many Winston-Salem porches, and the air is pervasively perfumed with the tantalizing scent of Moravian spice cookies.

Museums

Kids will have a blast at **SciWorks,** 400 Hanes Mill Rd., tel. (336) 767-6730. Interactive science exhibits in the 45,000-square-foot Science Center include a parabolic dish that you can whisper into and be clearly heard 40 feet away. Kids can also mix chemicals to create reactions, including the dramatic old standby of vinegar and baking soda; flashier demonstrations are performed by museum staff. At the 120-seat planetarium, the heavens will unfold, while at the small aquariums and touch tank, you can get up close and personal with a number of marine critters. Outside, in the 15-acre environmental park, you can stroll along nature trails and meet with deer and farmyard animals. Open Mon.-Sat. 10 a.m.-5 p.m. and Sunday 1-5 p.m. Admission is $4 for adults, $3 for kids 6-19, and $1 for 3- to 5-year-olds. To get to SciWorks, take US 52 north from downtown and get off at the Mill Road exit. Brown signs for SciWorks on US 52 will announce that the exit is coming up.

One of the nation's most superb collections of American art lives at **Reynolda House** on Reynolda Road between Coliseum Drive and Silas Creek Parkway, tel. (336) 725-5325. This gracious country home, built by tobacco magnate R. J. Reynolds and his wife Katharine, opened as a museum in 1965, but the place still retains the flavor of a warm inviting home. The collection spans the course of American art from 1755 to the present, including colonial portraits by Jeremiah Theus and John Singleton Copley; dramatic landscapes by Frederic Church and Thomas Coles; stunning works by late 18th-century masters Mary Cassatt and Thomas Eakins; more modern works by Georgia O'Keeffe, Jasper Johns, and Frank Stella; and contemporary pieces by Alexander Calder and David Smith. The house preserves personal touches of the family, from the clothes and toys of the Reynolds children to Katharine Reynolds' elegant wardrobe, dating back to 1905, including her handsewn wedding dress and exquisite gowns from the 1920s. Other parts of Reynolda House that set it apart from more sterile art museums include the recreational facilities, like the indoor swimming pool, squash courts, bowling alley, and shooting gallery. Open Tues.-Sat. 9:30 a.m.-4:30 p.m. and Sunday 1:30-4:30 p.m.; admission is $6 for adults, $3 for students, and free for college students.

THE CIGARETTE MUSEUM

In 1998, one of Winston-Salem's most enduring tourist attractions bit the dust. After 80 years of leading people behind the scenes at its cigarette manufacturing facilities in town, the R.J. Reynolds Tobacco Co. put an end to its guided tours. In the 1970s, more than 60,000 people were led onto the manufacturing floor of the Whitaker Park plant. By 1997, that number had dipped to 20,000, and the company decided to dump the tours. However, if you're interested in exploring Winston-Salem's tobacco roots, you can still visit R. J. Reynolds' informative and entertaining museum at the Whitaker Park Manufacturing Center on Reynolds Boulevard between Cherry Street and Indiana Avenue, tel. (336) 741-5718.

Richard Joshua Reynolds' company has come a long way from the days in 1875 when he was hand-packing and bagging his first chewing tobacco. Museum exhibits describe the history of the business from its humble origins to the astonishingly efficient automated facility that today produces up to 275 million cigarettes a day (and that's just at the Whitaker Park plant).

The museum's collection of tobacco memorabilia will take you back in time to the days when TV commercials blitzed the airwaves with catchy slogans such as "You can take Salem out of the country, but you can't take the country out of Salem" and "Winston tastes good, like a cigarette should." Other displays in the exhibition hall outline current tobacco industry issues in a manner that tends to shy away from some pesky health issues in favor of issues such as individual liberties and tobacco incomes for family farmers and factory workers.

You can also check out the souvenir shop, offering some kitschy gifts to take back to any puffers back home. A quick way to get to the Whitaker Park factory from I-40 or Business I-40 is to take US 52 north from downtown, get off at the Akron Drive exit, and follow the signs. Admission is free.

Across Reynolda Road from Reynolda House is another lavish home, built in 1929 by textile giant James G. Hanes and now converted into the **Southeastern Center for Contemporary Art,** 750 Marguerite Dr., tel. (336) 725-1904. This museum doesn't have the warmth of Reynolda House, and much of the artwork is housed in a modern addition to Hanes' home. Nonetheless, the constantly changing exhibits presented here represent some of the finest contemporary art being produced in the southeastern U.S., in a variety of media. SECCA is also a thriving education center, offering a variety of art and art appreciation courses. The galleries are open Tues.-Sat. 10 a.m.-5 p.m. and Sunday 2-5 p.m. Admission is $3 for adults, $2 for students and seniors, with children under 12 admitted free.

Winston Salem's two universities offer some diverse collections. On the campus of Wake Forest University, a five-minute drive from Reynolda House, you'll find the intriguing **Museum of Anthropology** just off University Parkway on Wingate Road, tel. (336) 759-5282. Founded in 1963, this museum features a permanent collection with objects from the Americas, Africa, Asia, and Oceania. Household and ceremonial items, textiles, hunting and fishing gear, and objects of personal adornment are presented thematically and clearly. During the summer a family Discovery Room offers hands-on exhibits and activities. Open Tues.-Sat. 10 a.m.-4:30 p.m.; admission is free, though donations are accepted and appreciated. **Diggs Gallery,** 601 Martin Luther King Jr. Drive, tel. (336) 750-2458, located in the lower level of the O'Kelly Library on the campus of Winston-Salem State University, opened in 1990. Its 6,500-square-foot exhibition space hosts 10-15 visual art exhibitions a year, in addition to a growing permanent collection of works that focus on African, African-American and regional art. Open Tues.-Sat. 11 a.m.-5 p.m.; admission is free.

RECREATION

Two state parks about 25 miles from Winston-Salem, Pilot Mountain and Hanging Rock State Parks, provide stunning views and exciting hiking opportunities. Closer to town, about eight miles west of Winston-Salem on US 158, off I-40 in Clemmons, NC, you'll find a dizzying array of recreational opportunities at **Tanglewood Park,** off exit 182 on I-40, tel. (336) 778-6300. Some of the activities you can engage in at this 1,200-acre park include boating in paddleboats and canoes, tennis, horseback riding, fishing, bicycling, hiking a number of nature trails, and splashing around in the Olympic-size swimming pool.

But the biggest attraction of these rolling green hills are the **Tanglewood Park golf courses,** tel. (336) 778-6320, two of the nation's premier public courses, both designed by Robert Trent Jones. Both courses offer terrific golf, especially the Championship Course, site of the 1974 PGA Championship and now the proud home of the annual Vantage Championship, the second richest tournament on the Senior PGA Tour. A tight course, demanding accuracy, finesse, and a steady stroke with a putter (and sand wedge), the beautiful and challenging Championship Course has earned its *Golf Digest* ranking as one of the top 25 public courses in the nation. The other course, the Reynolds Course, is also a beauty and plays a little fairer. Greens fees including carts are $55 for the Championship Course ($40 for North Carolina residents), and $40 for the Reynolds Course ($32 for locals). In addition to the two championship-level courses, Tanglewood Park offers an 18-hole par-three course. The park also offers a number of lodgings for visitors (see below). Admission to the park is $2 per car.

ACCOMMODATIONS

Inns

If you're looking to stay within the town limits of Old Salem, you have one choice, the **Augustus T. Zevely Inn,** 803 S. Main St., tel. (336) 748-9299 or (800) 928-9299. Built circa 1844, this 7,000-square-foot, brick home offers 12 elegant guest rooms, individually furnished in authentic Moravian style with lovely antiques and reproductions. All rooms have private baths, TVs, phones, and queen- or king-size beds; some also include whirlpool/steam baths and working fireplaces. A spacious covered porch, shaded by a spreading magnolia tree, offers a serene outdoor space to enjoy your breakfast or relax after a day of exploring the historic neighborhood. The Moderate-Luxury rates range $80-185.

You can experience the turn-of-the-century opulence enjoyed by one of Winston-Salem's wealthiest citizens, who co-founded the Wachovia Loan and Trust Co. in 1893, at the **Henry F. Shaffner House,** 150 S. Marshall St., tel. (336) 777-0052 or (800) 952-2256. Built in 1907, this Victorian-style mansion provides six guest rooms and two suites, decorated with antiques and reproductions. In addition to the continental breakfast, guests can enjoy afternoon tea with savory snacks in the tea room, as well as complimentary wine and cheese in the sun room. Expensive-Luxury rates range $90-190.

In the historic West End, replete with beautifully restored, turn-of-the-century homes, you can stay at one of two adjacent historic homes comprising the **Colonel Ludlow Inn,** 434 Summit St. (at W. 5th St.), tel. (336) 777-1887 or (800) 301-1887. Although the 10 rooms in these two homes, built in 1887 and 1895, exude a stately Victorian elegance, the inn features a host of modern amenities, including stereo systems, TV/VCRs, hair dryers, microwaves, mini-refrigerators, and in most rooms, a two-person jacuzzi, complete with bubble bath and candles. Moderate-Luxury rates range from $75 ($85 on Friday and Saturday) to $160, with higher rates during special-event periods.

Also in the West End neighborhood, the Georgian Revival-style **Thomas Welch House,** 618 Summit St., tel. (336) 723-3586, provides four meticulously decorated rooms, with private baths, phones, and TVs, as well as a full exercise room and a kitchenette for guests, for $70-120, including a continental breakfast weekdays, and full breakfast on weekends. Moderate-Premium. **Mickle House,** 927 West 5th St., tel. (336) 722-9045, is a beautiful, immaculate 1892 Victorian cottage offering two rooms with private baths. Your gracious host, Barbara Garrison, serves a full breakfast, included in the $80-90 rates. Moderate-Expensive.

Hotels

With 71 rooms and suites spread over four stories, the **Brookstown Inn,** 200 Brookstown Ave., tel. (336) 725-1120 or (800) 845-4262, is housed in a converted 1837 cotton mill, just a few blocks from Old Salem. The rooms are warmly furnished with antiques and handmade quilts, and some include jacuzzis. In addition to a complimentary breakfast in the morning, you can also enjoy complimentary wine and cheese in the afternoon. Popular with visiting business executives, rates range $125-130 Mon.-Thurs., falling to $90-120 Friday to Sunday. Expensive-Premium.

Also popular with the traveling business set, the towering, downtown **Adam's Mark Winston Plaza,** 425 and 460 N. Cherry St., tel. (336) 725-3500 or (800) 444-2326, provides more than 600 rooms in its twin towers, one 17 stories and the other, nine stories high. Amenities include indoor pools, exercise rooms with sauna, restaurants, and lounges providing nightly entertainment. The Moderate-Premium rates vary considerably from season to season, and weekday versus weekend, from as low as $80 during a weekend to as high as $145 during a special-event weekday (like during the International Home Furnishings Market in April and October). The six-story **Holiday Inn Select,** 5790 University Parkway, tel. (336) 767-9595 or (800) 553-9595, provides a pool, data ports, restaurant, and on-site bar with entertainment. Expensive rates begin at $90.

Whether or not you're traveling with a pet, you'll be welcome and find comfortable lodgings at the seven-story **Hawthorne Inn & Conference Center,** 420 High St., just off Bus. I-40 near downtown, tel. (336) 777-3000 or (800) 972-3774. With 159 rooms, an outdoor swimming pool, exercise room, and an on-site restaurant, the Hawthorne's year-round rate is $79, with no extra fee for pets, unlike some other pet-friendly chains in Winston-Salem, who charge a sometimes exorbitant (up to $150!), non-refundable fee to accept pets. Moderate.

Motels

Three blocks from Old Salem, the **Salem Inn,** 127 S. Cherry St., tel. (336) 752-8561 or (800) 533-8760, offers clean rooms, including some rooms ideal for folks traveling on business, with spacious desks, data ports, and a recliner, as well as rooms with two queen-size beds. In addition to the outdoor swimming pool, the Salem Inn also provides an exercise room. Moderate rates begin at $60 (if you bring a pet, there's a one-time, $25 non-refundable fee). The Inexpensive **Motel 6,** located at the Patterson Avenue exit on US 52, six miles north of I-40, at 3810 Patterson Ave., tel. (336) 661-1588 or (800) 466-8356, allows pets with no extra fee.

With more than two dozen franchise motels to choose from, it's easy to find a room at Moderate ($60-85) or Inexpensive ($35-60) rates. The **Comfort Inn Cloverdale Place,** 110 Miller St., tel. (336) 721-0220, off the Cloverdale exit on Bus. I-40, provides a pool and exercise room with sauna and whirlpool. Moderate. **Days Inn/Hanes Mall,** 3330 Silas Creek Parkway, off exit 189 on I-40, tel. (336) 760-4770 or (800) DAYS-INN, offers a swimming pool, and some rooms with jacuzzi. Inexpensive. **Hampton Inn,** 1990 Hampton Inn Ct., off exit 189 on I-40, tel. (336) 760-1660 or (800) HAMPTON, has a swimming pool and exercise room. Moderate.

Tanglewood Park Lodgings and Camping

In Tanglewood Park, about eight miles southwest of downtown Winston-Salem, in Clemmons, NC, you can take advantage of a number of Inexpensive-Moderate accommodations located on the plush 1,200 acres of this recreation-filled park (see Recreation above). The **Manor House Bed & Breakfast** is housed in the restored 1859 home of William Neal Reynolds, R.J.'s brother. The ten lovely rooms of varying sizes are all tastefully decorated with antiques and reproductions. Rates, including the complimentary breakfast, range $80-110. Moderate-Expensive. Next to the Manor House you'll find 18 basic, motel-style rooms, each with two double beds, at the Inexpensive **Tanglewood Lodge,** where prices start at just $45. In addition, you can rent a three-bedroom lodge apartment, or one of four, two- and three-bedroom rustic cottages for about $425 a week, or a four-bedroom guest house for $575/week. **Camping** options include more than 100 tent and full-hookup RV sites, which cost $10 and $17 per night. To get to the park, take exit 182 on I-40, and follow the signs.

FOOD AND DRINK

Winston-Salem is blessed with a bounty of terrific restaurants. Wherever you stay in this urbane town, you'll usually be able to find a neighborhood haunt that provides good food and professional service.

Located in the heart of Old Salem, the 1816 **Old Salem Tavern,** 736 S. Main St. tel. (336) 748-8585, with its costumed servers and six atmospheric dining rooms, provides a memorable lunch or dinner for Old Salem visitors. For lunch, try the oyster Po Boy, fried oysters on a hoagie roll with lettuce and tomato served with Cajun mayonnaise and steak fries ($7). For lunch or dinner, if you want to continue your historical research, you'll want to sample the authentic Moravian double-crusted chicken pie, served with fresh vegetables. Dinner entrees generally range $14-20 and include some tantalizing choices like the roasted vegetable Napoleon—layers of roasted vegetables with mozzarella and ricotta cheese, served with a spicy tomato sauce, ($14)—and the succulent roast duck, half a duck, slow roasted, breast-boned, and served with dried cherries and wine sauce. The rack of lamb and seafood options are also delightful. Save room for a dessert, like the Moravian gingerbread, made with fresh ginger root and grated orange peel, topped with Tavern-made lemon ice cream.

Another marvelous choice for those seeking historic surroundings for dinner is the upscale **Zevely House,** 901 W. 4th St., tel. (336) 725-6666. The brick home, built in 1815, features working fireplaces in the intimate dining rooms, as well as an outside garden patio. The menu abounds with rich, tempting choices, like the potato cake appetizer with caviar, sour cream and scallions ($9). Entrees range $18-25 and include choices of fish and seafood, roast pork, grilled duck, and steaks. A representative and delightful example of Zevely House entrees is the famed scallops with apricot and Jarlsberg gratinee ($19). Open for dinner Mon.-Sat. and Sunday for brunch 11 a.m.-2 p.m.; reservations are recommended. The patio provides a wonderful space for Sunday brunch, when you can enjoy eggs Benedict, Moravian chicken pie and other brunchy fare for $8-10.

For an atmosphere evoking a more recent era of history, you can rediscover what "fine dining" was like in the 1950s and '60s by visiting **Staley's Charcoal Steak House,** 2000 Reynolda Rd., tel. (336) 723-8631. With its painted white brick exterior (looking a little like an old funeral home, except for the fountain in front of the entrance) interior softly lit with oil lamps on the white tablecloths, and cushioned, red vinyl chairs, Staley's is the kind of place that for over 40 years has been where people go to celebrate winning the big game, getting accepted to college, and other milestones. Located across the street from the entrance to Reynolda House, Staley's specialty is (surprise!) char-broiled steaks, with a dozen superb beef entrees to choose from, generally ranging $20-25, from prime rib, filet mignon, T-bone and porterhouse steaks to the ethereal Chateaubriand for two and the sensational char-broiled shish kabobs, doused with 151-proof Ron Rico rum and served on a flaming sword. A variety of hearty seafood, pasta, and fowl dishes are also available if you've been dragged against your will to Staley's by a steak-lover—even vegans can choose the flaming veggie shish kabob. Open for dinner only, Staley's is closed on Sunday.

If you're looking for slightly more innovative cuisine with a cosmopolitan, bistro atmosphere, try the intimate **Leon's Cafe,** 924 S. Marshall St., tel. (336) 725-9593. The menu changes daily to take advantage of the freshest ingredients, but you're sure to be offered luscious fare. On a recent visit, the menu included dazzling choices like an appetizer of lamb loin brochette on a painted plate of raspberry and citrus beurre blanc ($9), and entrees like a mixed grille of boneless duck breast, pork tenderloin, and shrimp, with fire-roasted pepper prosciutto sauce ($19), or fresh scallop saut° with sun-dried tomatoes, shallots, and a compound butter over linguine ($16). The menu also offers dishes with chicken, fish, pork, and lamb chops for $16-22. Outdoor seating is also available, weather permitting.

In the NationsBank Building, **Noble's Grille,** 380 Knollwood St., tel. (336) 777-8477, is a favorite haunt of visiting business folk on an expense account who want to walk from a meeting to a snazzy restaurant, complete with high ceilings and black-and-white dressed wait staff. The fare leans towards nouveau Mediterranean, with most menu selections grilled in the open oak- and hickory-fired ovens. In addition to the variety of grilled items available, which change daily, you can also choose some unusual, tasty pizzas, like the grilled duck, chèvre, and shiitake mushroom pizza ($10). Open daily for lunch and dinner; prices range $8-12 for lunch, $20-30 for dinner.

One of Winston-Salem's hot spots, for both popularity and spice level, can be found at **South by Southwest,** close to Old Salem, at 241 S. Marshall St., tel. (336) 727-0800. Open for dinner Tues.-Sat., this lively restaurant, complete with pink adobe walls adorned with hanging bunches of chili peppers, offers an upscale selection of Mexican dishes you'd be more likely to find in San Diego than Mexico City, like the Zarzuela, fresh shrimp, scallops, mussels, crab, and fish in a roasted red pepper-saffron sauce on a grilled tortilla ($16). Regardless of its roots, the food is superbly prepared, and the margaritas are guaranteed to warm your spirit. Entrees range $11-17.

For inexpensive eats in highbrow Reynolda Village, stop in at the **Village Tavern,** 221 Reynolda Rd., tel. (336) 748-0221. Open Mon.-Thurs. 11 a.m.-midnight Fri.-Sat. 11 a.m.-1 a.m., and Sunday 9 a.m.-10 p.m., this popular, relaxing hangout features a bevy of tasty sandwiches in the $5-8 range, including beef and veggie burgers, club sandwiches, grilled tuna, and Maryland-style crab cake sandwiches, in addition to a variety of salads and a full bar. Outdoor seating is available on a patio, a relaxing spot to linger over the tavern's superb Sunday brunch. The same menu is available at its newer branch location at 2000 Griffith Rd., at the corner of Hanes Mall Boulevard and Stratford Road, tel. (336) 760-8686, just off the Stratford Rd. exit on I-40.

If your spiritual roots lie in Bohemia, you'll feel right at home at the **Rainbow News & Cafe,** just off the Broad Street exit on Bus. I-40, at 712 Brookstown Ave., tel. (336) 723-5010. Housed within two turn-of-the-century homes (1895 and 1905) that are seamlessly tied together, these invitingly warm rooms draw university students, professors, and visitors in equal numbers. Parts of the place include a wonderfully eclectic bookstore, a smoker-friendly coffee bar, and several intimate dining rooms. Vegetarians and carnivores alike will find solace in the Rainbow's menu, which offers appetizers like the Rainbow Combo, hummus and spinach dip with fresh vegetables, tortilla chips, and pita triangles. A wide variety of salads are available, featuring portabella mushrooms, fried oysters, chicken, tuna, and—yes, lettuce, too. Entrees, $7-15, run an even larger gamut, from a dozen sandwiches with oysters, mushrooms, tofu, beef, tuna, or turkey to heartier fare like spinach lasagna and grilled pork tenderloin. Outdoor seating is also available most of the year.

Finally, no description of Winston-Salem's culinary scene would be complete without mentioning **Krispy Kreme Doughnuts,** founded and headquartered in Winston-Salem. With dozens of locations sprinkled throughout the Triad, and hundreds more elsewhere in the Southeast, Krispy Kreme creates arguably the best doughnuts in the world. In 1997, Krispy Kreme gained national prominence with an opening of a Manhattan franchise, which, as this edition went to press, continued to take the Big Apple by storm with long lines stretching around the block at all hours of the day and night. Also in 1997, Krispy Kreme was invited to place one of its doughnut-manufacturing machines in a permanent exhibit in the Smithsonian Institution in Washington, D.C., the only doughnut in the world so honored. You don't have to make a special trip to the Smithsonian to watch the Krispy Kreme machines in action. At virtually all franchises, when the neon "Hot Donuts" sign is illuminated in the window, you can view the assembly line and follow the doughnuts through the entire, magical process, culminating in the ethereal moment when you take that first bite of one of North Carolina's most majestic creations: the original plain glazed Krispy Kreme doughnut.

HIGH POINT

About 10 miles southeast of Greensboro, along business route I-85, lies High Point. If you're not looking closely, a drive through this town presents a mysterious paradox. Although you'll see few cars and even fewer pedestrians, High Point's downtown—which extends about seven blocks in each direction—appears to be thriving, filling a dozen towering buildings and boasting virtually no empty storefronts. Closer examination of the storefronts reveals High Point's obsession: furniture. Nine out of ten stores carry furniture, and the big buildings have names like the International Home Furnishings Center and the Furniture Plaza Building. Welcome to the "Furniture Capital of the World."

History

In the early 1850s, two transportation routes crisscrossed this region of the state: the North Carolina and Midland Railroad and the 130-mile-long, Salem-to-Fayetteville plank road. These two routes intersected at the highest point in the North Carolina Midland Railroad route. This "high point" became a minor transportation hub. Thanks to the ready availability of this affordable transit for goods, the area swiftly became a major manufacturing center.

For most of the 20th century, High Point was the world's leader in hosiery production, but most of the stocking and sock mills have moved elsewhere in the past few decades. High Point has also long been—and remains today—the nation's leader in the manufacture of school buses.

But stockings and school buses aside, High Point's high points have always revolved around furniture. After the plank road and the railroad converged here in the 1850s, the area around High Point immediately became a much sought-after source of hardwood, which was boundlessly plentiful in the area. Trees were harvested, cut to various specifications in local lumber mills, and shipped to furniture makers throughout the nation.

One of the most successful entrepreneurs in the area was William Henry "Captain" Snow, a Vermont Quaker who relocated to High Point after marching through the area as an officer in the Union army during the Civil War. Here he started Snow Lumber, which cut and dressed lumber to send to furniture makers from Michigan to Massachusetts. The Captain's son, Ernest Angel Snow, was working for the lumber company after the war when, in the mid-1880s, had an inspiration. They were chopping down the trees, cutting them up, and dressing the pieces according to what they were told by Northern furniture manufacturers. They were making a good living—but the manufacturers were making a *fortune*. Ernest suggested that they control the whole process and reap all the profits.

The Captain admitted that it was a good idea but declined to invest in the venture himself. So the enterprising Ernest went off to seek investors elsewhere. He found two local lumber barons who *were* willing to invest in his idea. In 1888, the High Point Furniture Company was born—the first furniture manufacturing company in America in which felled trees entered at one end and finished furniture emerged at the other. By the turn of the century, High Point was home to 25 major furniture companies who had copied Ernest Snow's vision.

In 1909, High Point's furniture moguls embarked on a bold experiment. They decided to display all of their wares in a few buildings and invite furniture buyers to come and see their splendid furnishings. In 1913, the Southern Furniture Market became a semiannual affair, occupying 30,000 square feet of space in eight buildings to showcase the work of more than 100 furniture manufacturers. That first year, more than 400 buyers came to view the merchandise.

Today, the event—now called the International Home Furnishings Market—is still held twice a year in High Point, but the demographics have changed a bit. The biggest furniture market in the world, it's now held for two weeks every April and October, attracts more than 70,000 furniture buyers and makers from over 85 countries, and occupies more than seven *million* square feet of showroom space.

These four weeks are the peak times you do *not* want to visit High Point. Hotels and motels are booked solid (at increased rates), parking is extremely hard to find (local businesses with lots charge $10 per space), and the streets, stores, and restaurants are crammed with frazzled furniture buyers wearing the special registration badges required for admission to most showrooms during the Market.

SIGHTS

The **High Point Historic Park and Museum,** 1805 East Lexington Ave., tel. (336) 885-6859, provides a delightful, informative, and free-admission introduction to the economic and social history of the area. Here you'll see pictures of the town at the turn of the century and its subsequent transformation and exhibits on furniture making, including examples of the earliest furniture made here. You'll learn some intriguing tidbits, like how a High Point fellow named James Gibson, during the Depression, invented what he called the "Gibson Fli-Back," a silly contraption consisting of a handheld wooden paddle, rubber band, and rubber ball, and how he marketed it to make it one of the most successful toys in history. In addition, the museum frequently features dazzling traveling exhibits.

But for the full effect of the High Point Historical Park and Museum, come on a weekend. That's when costumed guides will take you through the original small house and reconstructed (operational) blacksmith barn, built in 1786 by the notable High Point civic leader, John Haley, Quaker sheriff and blacksmith. Call ahead to make sure the blacksmith will be there, because watching the blacksmith work is a real treat.

When we read the brochure describing the **Furniture Discovery Center,** 101 W. Green Dr., tel. (336) 887-3876, we anxiously awaited our visit. "You will experience the furniture manufacturing process in a way that becomes not only an informative event that will expand your horizons, but also an adventure," the brochure proclaims. "The mysteries of upholstery are unveiled at the production area . . . grab an air powered nail gun and experience the 'hands-on' sensation of assembling a frame for an upholstered love seat." In fact, the museum consists mostly of static exhibits, many featuring several large, immobile machines that require a considerable amount of imagination to figure out how they might work, if they were plugged in.

Kids may be bored by this museum, although adults will learn some fun facts. We learned that, on average, every American uses the equivalent of a 100-foot-tall tree every year, largely in the form of paper products, and that lumber mills utilize 98% of a harvested tree. Did you know that today, there are 269 million acres of hardwood forests in the U.S., and that thanks to nature and the lumber industry, there are lots more hardwood trees now than there were 40 years ago?

If you're really curious about how furniture is made, then you'll be glad you visited the Furniture Discovery Center—and you'll know when you leave that you have visited the only museum in the world dedicated solely to unveiling the mysteries of upholstery and furniture manufacturing. Open Mon.-Sat. 10 a.m.-5 p.m. and Sunday 1-5 p.m. (closed on Monday Nov.-March); admission is $5 for adults and $2 for kids 6-15.

The adjacent **Angela Peterson Doll Museum,** 101 W. Green Dr., tel. (336) 885-3655, features more than 1,600 dolls, all collected by the museum's namesake. This international collection, from 53 countries across five centuries, is truly a treasure trove for doll lovers. Exhibits include dressed "flea dolls," which you need to look through a magnifying glass to appreciate, and the huge case of dozens of Shirley Temple dolls, including one of Shirley in a Navy outfit. Open the same hours as the Furniture Discovery Center; admission is $3 for adults, $1.50 for kids 6-15.

Last *and least,* no list of High Point attractions would be complete without a mention of one of the silliest sites you'll find in North Carolina, the semi-legendary **World's Biggest Bureau,** 508 N. Hamilton St., which was built in 1926 and billed as a gigantic, three-story chest of drawers. Today, the Word's Biggest Bureau still stands, a magnificent monument not to furniture nor architecture, but to the PR minds that in the past have given memorable thrills through exhibits like "See the Headless Woman—Still Alive!" The "bureau" is simply an ill-disguised, six-inch facade on the front wall of a three-story brick building. When we last saw it, the building was vacant and the bureau looked like it had been left out in the rain for a few decades—paint peeling, missing a few handles on the three "drawers," and some of the rotting molding had fallen off.

RECREATION

At 1,500-acre **Oak Hollow Lake Park and Marina,** 3431 N. Centennial St., tel. (336) 883-3494, you can enjoy boating, sailing, fishing, and tennis. But what makes this park particularly renowned is the **Oak Hollow Public Golf Course,** 3400 N. Centennial St., tel. (336) 883-3260. Ranked by *Golf Digest* as one of the 75 best public courses in the U.S., this beauty, designed by Pete Dye, harmoniously blends hills and water for a memorable round of golf. The low greens fees make this a particularly great golfing bargain, at $13 on weekdays, with carts optional for $10. On weekends, carts are mandatory, bringing the total fee to $26.

PRACTICALITIES

Accommodations

If you're planning to spend a day or two shopping in the downtown stores, the most convenient lodgings, both equipped with swimming pools, are the **Radisson,** 135 South Main St., tel. (336) 889-8888 or (800) 333-3333, and the **Holiday Inn,** 236 S. Main St., tel. (336) 886-7011. Both are Moderate.

Food and Drink

High Point's culinary scene is characterized mostly by mediocre fast-food and family-style chain restaurants, with one significant exception. **J. Basul Noble's,** 114 S. Main Street, tel. (336) 889-3354, is in the heart of downtown and, although it's a little pricey ($17-22), it offers fine continental cuisine with a Southern flair, from beef, veal, and poultry to seafood and vegetarian delicacies. As befits a restaurant in the "Furniture Capital of the World," Noble's inviting "woody" decor includes a magnificent mahogany bar, and fancy wooden chairs. On most nights, you can enjoy a drink and listen to live jazz upstairs.Noble's serves dinner Mon.-Sat. from 6 p.m.

Shopping

During the 48 weeks of the year when the International Home Furnishings Market is not being held, High Point offers a dizzying selection of home furnishings in dozens of stores and outlets. (During Market weeks, most showrooms are off-limits to the public.) Information about many of them is available at the Convention and Visitors Bureau at 300 South Main Street. If you're looking to be immediately overwhelmed, try **The Atrium,** 430 S. Main St., a block from the Visitors Bureau, where 36 vast showrooms display more than 700 lines of furniture and accessories.

SIDE TRIPS

NORTH CAROLINA ZOOLOGICAL PARK

As devoted animal lovers prone to anthropomorphism (encouraged by our dog, Sparky, who understands everything we say), we are usually a bit wary of zoos, thanks in great measure to sad, youthful memories of visiting zoos that served as animal jails—small cages with iron bars and lots of concrete. We mention our bias only to reassure fellow animal lovers that they'll suffer few "compassion pangs" at the North Carolina Zoological Park, 4401 Zoo Parkway (NC 159), off US 220 and US 64, six miles southeast of Asheboro, tel. (336) 879-7200 or (800) 488-0444. The designers of this 550-acre zoo have created cozy, natural habitats for its 1,100

resident animals—and over 30,000 plants, for you floral-rights advocates—encouraging them to behave as they would in the wild, with the exception that animals in predator-prey relationships are separated so they won't eat each other.

Although the zoo's location in Asheboro is a bit off the beaten path, about a half-hour's drive south of I-40 from Greensboro, this marvelous zoo is well worth the extra effort. It's easy to spend most of a day here, strolling along five miles of paths, past about two dozen major habitat exhibits (spaced a five- to 10-minute walk apart). If your feet get tired, you can always hop on the free trams that roll along every 15 minutes or so. (The zoo also offers wheelchair and stroller rentals.) The park is separated into two sections, the 250-acre North American area and the 300-acre African section. The two areas are con-

PROTECTING THE ZOO'S EXOTICS

In the North Carolina Zoological Park, elephants, giraffes, gorillas, gazelles, lions, zebras, chimpanzees, rhinos, warthogs, antelope, and other favorite *National Geographic* creatures roam the African plains that have been re-created in the foothills of North Carolina's Uwharrie Mountains. But no matter how effectively the zoo simulates equatorial Africa, there's no getting away from the fact that these animals are built to cope with heat, not cold, and would freeze to death during a typical North Carolina winter.

With some exceptions (lions, for instance, can withstand temperatures as low as the 30s F), most of the African species in outdoor habitats retire to heated, off-exhibit shelters when the mercury dips to 45° F or lower. In many cases, the decision to seek heated shelter is left up to the animals. For example, the chimpanzees and antelope can come and go freely between their shelters (outside public view) and their outdoor spaces.

Some of the most temperature-sensitive animals are protected from the elements year-round. Birds, lizards, snakes, fish, primates, and other residents of the R. J. Reynolds Forest Aviary, Sonora Desert, African pavilion and Streamside exhibits live in climate-controlled indoor homes, providing both the animals (and their human visitors) with comfortable temperatures when the weather outside is frightful. Indeed, most of the zoo's animals can be enjoyed even during the depth of winter—which is the favorite time of year for the polar bears, Arctic foxes, harbor seals, and California sea lions.

Arctic fox

JIM PAGE

tiguous, but not intermingled, so you have to decide which continent you'd like to visit first. The African exhibits feature creatures like elephants, rhinos, zebras and giraffes; in general, they're in areas spacious enough that you might want to slip a quarter into the binocular viewers to get a close look. The North American habitats are more intimate, and you can find yourself nose-to-nose (against an intervening glass wall) with a polar bear or sea lion. You can even pet a furry, barnyard mammal at the Hardee's Touch and Learn Center.

In addition to the outside habitats, several indoor exhibits provide climate-controlled atmospheres ranging from the moist, tropical rain forest environs of the R.J. Reynolds Forest Aviary, densely inhabited by more than 75 exotic birds and 1,700 tropical plants, to the bone-dry Sonora Desert exhibit, home to tarantulas, gila monsters, ocelots, road runners, and a host of other desert-dwelling critters.

The zoo is located on Zoo Parkway (NC 159), six miles southeast of Asheboro off US 220 and US 64. Visitor amenities include restaurants, picnic facilities, gift shops, free parking, and al-most-irresistible photo-booths, where you can purchase souvenir polaroids of your mugs surrounded by a variety of the zoo's residents. The zoo is open year-round except Christmas Day; hours are 9 a.m.-5 p.m. April-October and 9 am.-4 p.m. November-March. From March through November, admission is $8 for adults, $5 for children 2-12 and seniors 62 and older. From December through February, admission is half-price (in part because some of zoo's critters may be residing in their heated, private quarters during cold winter days).

SEAGROVE

About 13 miles south of the zoo, at the junction of US 220 and NC 705, you'll find the pottery paradise of Seagrove. Long before you reach the town limits from any direction, you'll know you're getting close by the increasing frequency of the roadside potteries advertising their wares. Whether you're looking to buy or just browse, you'll be welcome in the Seagrove area, home to some of the most exquisite pottery made anywhere in the world. More than 80 potteries are located here, some of them run by eighth-generation potters. With all the competition, you're guaranteed to be wide-eyed by the artistry you see on the shelves of Seagrove's magnificent potteries.

Almost every pottery carries a map brochure pinpointing the 80-plus potteries in the area. If you'd like a map in advance, contact the **Friends of the Pottery Center,** P.O. Box 500, Seagrove, NC 27341, tel. (336) 873-7887.

THOMASVILLE AND LEXINGTON

A five-minute drive south from High Point along Business Interstate 85 will take you to the little town of Thomasville, famed as the home of the once-pervasive Thomasville Chair Company, which is still headquartered here and which affords some terrific outlet shopping at the **Thomasville Furniture Outlet,** 401 E. Main St., tel. (336) 476-2211.

You'll know you're close to the outlet store when you see the **World's Biggest Chair,** perched on a 10-foot-high concrete platform

along Thomasville's downtown Main Street, next to the railroad. Although obviously hokey (like the World's Biggest Bureau), the biggest chair is at least in terrific shape (in part because it's made mostly of well-maintained, painted concrete). Nonetheless, it's a great illusion, and it does have a history—in the 1960 elections, Texas Senator Lyndon B. Johnson jumped off the train during a whistle-stop tour, climbed a ladder to the platform, and delivered a rousing speech from the seat of the massive chair to enthusiastic Thomasvillers.

For a bite to eat in Thomasville, look no further than the **T-ville Diner,** 132 West Main St., tel. (336) 472-3322. When it first opened its doors in 1936, it was completely housed in an old dining car from the Southern Railway. Alas, the passage of time demanded the demolition of the antique railroad car, whose last meals were served on Christmas Eve 1986. A few mementos, like brass shelves, light fixtures and air vent covers have been retained in the plain, current structure. But the traditions of fabulous home-cooking, friendly service, and almost depression-era prices remain. If you're on a tight budget and don't mind a slight diversion from the traffic of main I-85, take Business I-85 to Thomasville and find the T-Ville Diner. The fried chicken can't be beat, but if you're especially starved and have a hankerin' for some meat, try the dinner specials available after 3 p.m., including the center-cut country ham or the pork tenderloin, both of which include your choice of two vegetables and mouth-watering cobblers or puddings for dessert. The entire dinner special is most expensive item on the menu at just four bucks.

At the southern terminus of Business I-85, you'll find another "World Capital." In this case, it's **Lexington,** billed as the "Barbecue Capital of the World." Lexington is a charming little town, and if you want to explore it, you'll find several shops worthy of a short diversion from your interstate driving. In your wanderings you'll no doubt run across some of the 20 or so barbecue restaurants in the tiny "metro area."

If you're just looking for a quick barbecue fix, then **Lexington Barbecue,** 10 Highway 29/70 S., at the junction of Bus. I-85 and US 64, tel. (336) 249-9814, yields as delectable a plate of barbecue and/or ribs as you'll find anywhere. You can either dine inside at the bright green

MOUNT AIRY—A LITTLE BIT OF MAYBERRY

About five miles south of the Virginia border, the little town of Mount Airy is the birthplace of actor Andy Griffith. And even today the place gives the visitor an unmistakable sense that it is the real-life counterpart to the town Griffith made a household name—Mayberry, that timeless haven that was home to Sheriff Andy Taylor and his son, Opie, deputy Barney Fife, mechanics Gomer and Goober, Floyd the barber, and the rest of the characters who live on in reruns of *The Andy Griffith Show*.

Mount Airy's Main Street is dotted with gift shops selling a dizzying array of Mayberry memorabilia and diners offering inexpensive, down-home meals worthy of that culinary legend Aunt Bea. For lunch, you can't beat the eats at **Snappy Lunch,** 125 N. Main St., tel. (336) 786-4931, where nothing on the menu costs more than $2.50, including Snappy's celebrated pork chop sandwich—a boneless chop dipped in a light batter, fried, and served on a steamed bun with tomato, onion, chili, coleslaw, and a light slathering of mustard.

Although the town warmly welcomes visitors year-round, it explodes with Mayberry fervor the last weekend in September, when, from Thursday to Saturday, it hosts the **Mayberry Days** festival. During the festival, Mount Airy seems to absorb a significant amount of the good will and good humor available on the planet. Folks dressed up as Mayberry characters roam the streets, lectures on the subtle nuances of *The Andy Griffith Show* are delivered, and favorite episodes of the series are shown in the downtown movie house. There's also a big pie-eating contest, presided over by David Browning, an uncannily convincing reincarnation of Barney Fife.

For more information about Mount Airy and Mayberry Days, contact the **Mount Airy Chamber of Commerce,** 134 Renfro St., tel. (336) 786-6116.

---

seats and Formica tables, or take advantage of the old-fashioned carport/drive-in service, where you can find a parking spot and someone will come to you to take your order and deliver it to your car.

NORTH FROM THE TRIAD

Chinqua-Penn Plantation

About 25 miles north of Greensboro, just north of the town of Reidsville, lies the stunning Chinqua-Penn Plantation on Wentworth Street, tel. (336) 349-4576, built in 1925 by tobacco and utility magnates Jeff and Betsy Penn. The 22-acre estate includes lodge houses, greenhouses, gardens, orchards, a pagoda, arboretum, and the dazzling 27-room mansion, adorned with an extensive collection of art created between 1100 B.C. and the 1950s. The globetrotting Penns' taste in art was all over the map, and their collection is nothing if not eclectic, with works from Russia, Egypt, Europe, Nepal, China, and just about everywhere else. The plantation is open March 1-December 31, and admission is $13 for adults, $6 for kids 6-18. Hours are Tues.-Sat. 9 a.m.-5 p.m. and Sunday noon-5 p.m. To get to the plantation, take US 29 north from Greensboro, get off at the third Reidsville exit, and follow the plentiful signs. From Winston-Salem, take US 158 east and follow the signs when you get to Reidsville.

State Parks

North and northeast of Winston-Salem, two state parks offer distinctly different, mountainous experiences. **Hanging Rock State Park** on Hanging Rock Road, about a 45 minute drive from Winston-Salem between NC highways 66 and 89, tel. (336) 593-8480, encompasses 6,340 acres in the Sauratown Mountains. The park includes more than 18 miles of splendid hiking trails that take you to soaring overlooks on rocky ridges, and past numerous streams, waterfalls, and caves. Almost all of the trails interconnect, making it easy to lose your way, so make sure to pick up a trail map before you go exploring. Waterfall fans looking for an easy hike will particularly enjoy the 1.6-mile roundtrip route that includes the Hidden Falls, Window Falls and Upper Cascades trails. For a similarly short, but steeper, climb, climaxing with a superb summit view, try the 1.4-mile roundtrip Hanging Rock Trail. For a more challenging day hike, try the 6.8-mile roundtrip network of trails that lead up and down rocky terrain to the breathtaking vistas at

Moores Knob and Devils Chimney. Admission to the park is free. The park also offers about 80 campsites for $12 per night ($8 Dec.-March).

You won't have any problem finding **Pilot Mountain State Park,** about 25 miles northeast of Winston-Salem alongside US 52, tel. (336) 325-2355. The striking knob-shaped peak of the Big Pinnacle surges almost straight up, 1,400 feet above the surrounding valley, becoming easily visible just outside Winston-Salem. The park includes a network of about a dozen inter-connecting hiking trails, but, somewhat curiously, access to most of these trails begins at the summit parking lot of Little Pinnacle Mountain, the highest point accessible to visitors (Big Pinnacle is off-limits to humans). But even though you don't have to work to gain access to the summit of Little Pinnacle, you'll find the view utterly breathtaking, on a clear day encompassing more than 3,000 square miles. Campsites with hot showers and flush toilets are also available at the park for $12.

brown thrasher

TOMMY DAUGHTRY

CHARLOTTE

North Carolina's largest city (pop. 470,000), Charlotte is a gleaming metropolis with a heart of gold. And that's not just a figure of speech. In 1799, a local farm boy named Conrad Reed discovered a 17-pound gold rock in the woods. The boy's family, not realizing what it was, used the nugget as a doorstop for three years, until a Fayetteville jeweler saw it, bought it for $3.50, then sold it for $3,600, igniting the nation's first gold rush. Up until 1828, all of the native gold coined by the U.S. Mint came from North Carolina, and most of that came from the Charlotte area. Charlotte led the nation in gold production until 1848, when gold was discovered in California.

Charlotte continues to earn its reputation as a town with a Midas touch—the city is the second-richest banking center in the U.S. (behind New York City), home to mega-banks Nations-Bank and First Union. The city's banks today control almost a trillion dollars in assets. The affluence of the city is evident as you stroll along the wide, litter-free sidewalks downtown and gaze up at some of the tallest skyscrapers in the southeastern U.S., or peer into their Trump-scale lobbies complete with dazzling public art, or as you drive through the stately, tree-lined, residential streets of Charlotte's tonier neighborhoods, past countless mansions with vast rolling lawns. The wealth of this city stretches far beyond just the banking sector. At last count, nine of the top 10, 44 of the top 50, and 292 of the nation's "Fortune 500" firms are represented here.

Nicknamed "The Queen City" because it was named for King George III's wife in 1762, Charlotte reigns as North Carolina's most glittering symbol of the burgeoning, business-friendly New South, complete with noted museums, a flourishing performing arts scene, professional sports teams, abundant restaurants, a bustling international airport, and rush-hour traffic jams befitting one of the nation's largest cities.

Start your exploration of Charlotte by stopping by the **Info! Charlotte** visitors center, 330 S. Tryon St., tel. (704) 331-2700 or (800) 231-4636. It's packed with information, including the handy 150-page *Charlotte Visitors Guide* and extremely helpful maps. Charlotte's maze of roadways is a brambly tangle of curving streets that can be very confusing to negotiate. The exception is the easily walkable, grid-system streets of "Uptown" Charlotte (actually the "downtown" business district).

CHARLOTTE SIGHTS

Discovery Place
If you're traveling with kids, don't miss visiting one of the nation's premier kid-friendly science mu-

seums, Discovery Place, 301 N. Tryon St., tel. (704) 845-6664 or (800) 935-0553. The 140,000-square-foot space hums with the energy of a massive arcade, complete with flashing lights and a hodgepodge of sound effects, as young folks and their parents manipulate dozens of hands-on science exhibits.

Exhibits appeal to a wide variety of ages. At Kidsplace, a play area designed for ages seven and younger (including an area for infants and toddlers), parents and youngsters are encouraged to interact, learning science through play. The grade-school crowd are particularly attracted to all the popping, buzzing, and flashing exhibits. At the "Sparks Anyone?" exhibit, kids can make their hair stand on end or become mesmerized by the electromagnetic Light Sculpture. The Amateur Radio Education Center shows kids how radio waves work and lets them hear radio programs from around the globe. At the Life Center, kids can see and touch an actual human heart, and see how a baby develops in the womb. Junior high and older students are drawn to the Computer Center, a self-paced pro-

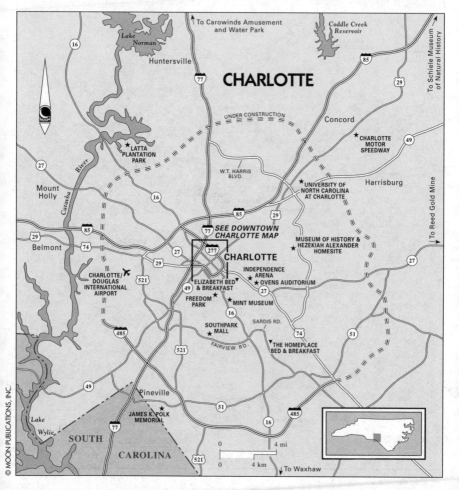

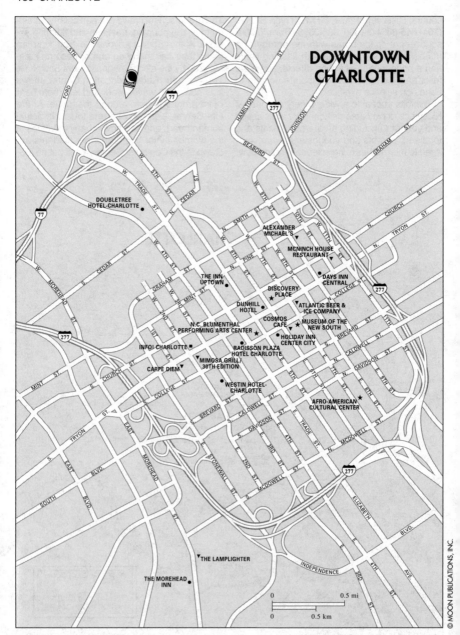

DOWNTOWN CHARLOTTE

DOUBLETREE HOTEL-CHARLOTTE

ALEXANDER MICHAEL'S

MCNINCH HOUSE RESTAURANT

THE INN UPTOWN

DAYS INN CENTRAL

DISCOVERY PLACE

DUNHILL HOTEL

ATLANTIC BEER & ICE COMPANY

COSMOS CAFE

N.C. BLUMENTHAL PERFORMING ARTS CENTER

MUSEUM OF THE NEW SOUTH

HOLIDAY INN CENTER CITY

INFOI CHARLOTTE

RADISSON PLAZA HOTEL CHARLOTTE

MIMOSA GRILL/ 30TH EDITION

CARPE DIEM

WESTIN HOTEL CHARLOTTE

AFRO-AMERICAN CULTURAL CENTER

THE LAMPLIGHTER

THE MOREHEAD INN

INDEPENDENCE

0   0.5 mi

0   0.5 km

© MOON PUBLICATIONS, INC.

DISCOVERY PLACE, INC.

Kids of all ages love the interactive displays and exhibits at Discovery Place.

format, vary considerably in content but usually take you to exotic places like the heights of Mt. Everest or the depths of the oceans (call to see what's playing). The theater also is home to the "Starball" projection system, which transforms the domed screen into the compelling **Kelly Space Voyager Planetarium,** using 200 computer-coordinated special effects projectors to take you on a thrilling ride through space. The third "extra" option is the **Challenger Learning Center,** where kids can experience what it's like to take the controls at the Operations Deck of a space station and at Mission Control.

Museum hours are Mon.-Fri. 9 a.m.-5 p.m. (until 6 p.m. June-Aug.), Saturday 9 a.m.-6 p.m., and Sunday 1-6 p.m. OMNIMAX films and planetarium shows are shown regularly throughout the day during museum hours and also during the evening on Friday and Saturday.

Charlotte Nature Museum

About a five-minute drive from Discovery Place will take you to the Charlotte Nature Museum, 1658 Sterling Rd., tel. (704) 372-6261 or (800) 935-0553, on the edge of Freedom Park. Managed by the same folks as Discovery Place, the Charlotte Nature Museum is a similarly delightful and classy act, though on a much more modest scale. Geared toward grade-school-age children, the museum features a variety of hands-on exhibits about natural history, like some fun "discovery boxes" where you stick your hand in the box and try to figure out what you've got a hold of. The museum also includes some live animal displays, like a butterfly pavilion, and an educational nature trail, complete with talking trees. Museum hours are Mon.-Fri. 9 a.m.-5 p.m., Saturday 10 a.m.-5 p.m., and Sunday 1-5 p.m. Admission is $2, and free to kids under three.

Museum of the New South

Returning to uptown, a block away from Discovery Place, the Museum of the New South, 324 N. College St., tel. (704) 333-1887, focuses on the region's history from the turn of the century to the present. In the first exhibit room of this visitor-friendly museum, kids have been invited to write comments on Post-It notes, and stick them next to exhibits. For example, at an exhibit of a bank's night depository safe, containing shredded old money, one kid noted

gram for beginners to experts, with one-on-one instruction from the Center's helpers.

Folks of all ages will enjoy exploring the tropical rain forest, a three-story habitat complete with exotic plants, colorful birds, small animals, and waterfalls. At the aquarium section, you can observe a variety of animals in fresh and salt water environments, pet the critters in the touch tank, and watch the staff feed the sharks and electric eels. General admission is $6.50 for ages 13-59, $5 for folks 6-12 and 60 or over, and $2.75 for ages 3-5.

In addition to the myriad of general admission exhibits, which include first-class traveling exhibits, Discovery Place offers three other options that cost an additional $2 apiece. The most amazing of these additional options takes you into the cavernous, domed theater. Here, you can recline and be catapulted into the action on the nation's largest domed film screen, stretching five stories above you. Two different shows alternate playing in the theater. The **OMNIMAX** films, in the IMAX

"These people must be on drugs to tear up money!" A note next to an exhibit of a Ku Klux Klan hood read "The KKK is dorkey!" In addition to its permanent displays, the museum creates first-class exhibits that change every six months or so, concentrating on different cultural and historical facets of the New South. Two terrific recent exhibits included the history of radio in North Carolina and the lives of North Carolinians who worked in the cotton industry. Museum hours are Tues.-Sat. 11 a.m.-5 p.m. Admission is $2 for adults, $1 for students.

Afro-American Cultural Center
About five blocks away, the Afro-American Cultural Center, 401 N. Myers St., tel. (704) 374-1565, features changing exhibits on African and African-American art and history. Housed in a majestic Greek Revival building that used to be a church, the center's exhibits are first rate. Programs and performances are held frequently in the center's two theaters (call for details). The art gallery hours are Tues.-Sat. 10 a.m.-6 p.m., Sunday 1-5 p.m., closed Monday. Admission is free.

Wing Haven Gardens and Bird Sanctuary
Tucked away in a posh, residential neighborhood between SouthPark Mall and Freedom Park, the Wing Haven Gardens and Bird Sanctuary, 248 Ridgewood Ave., tel. (704) 331-0664, provide a peaceful escape from the bustling cityscape. Enclosed on all sides by brick walls, the three acres of gardens are a serene delight, with brick paths threading through formal gardens and wooded areas, past several pools, recirculating fountains and dripping bird baths. Throughout the gardens, the emphasis is on plants that attract birds and provide cover, nesting sites, and food. The gardens are a little tricky to find, located on Ridgewood Avenue, just off Selwyn Avenue, between Woodlawn and Queens Roads. The gardens are open year-round, Sunday 2-5 p.m., Tuesday 3-5 p.m., and Wednesday 10 a.m.-noon. Admission is free, although donations are appreciated.

Charlotte Museum of History & Hezekiah Alexander Homesite
About four miles east and 200 years from uptown Charlotte stands the city's oldest surviving structure, at the Charlotte Museum of History & Hezekiah Alexander Homesite, 3500 Shamrock Dr., tel. (704) 568-1774. The two-story "Rock House" (the walls are made of stone) was built in 1774 by Hezekiah Alexander, cofounder and treasurer of Queens College in 1771, coframer of the first North Carolina State Constitution and Bill of Rights, and signer of the 1775 Mecklenburg Declaration of Independence, which renounced British rule a year before Jefferson's Declaration. Furnished with period antiques, the house is open to the public only through guided tours that last about an hour, departing Tues.-Fri. at 1:15 and 3:15 p.m. and Sat.-Sun. at 2:15 and 3:15 p.m. Tour admission is $4 for adults and $2 for kids 6-16. There's no admission, however, to tour the lovely, wooded grounds of the seven-acre site or to explore the history museum, which contains exhibits interpreting the Alexander homesite and a variety of antiques and historic artifacts from pre-colonial times to the 20th century. The museum and grounds are open Tues.-Fri. 10 a.m.-5 p.m. and Sat.-Sun. 2-5 p.m. The homesite, museum, and grounds are closed on Monday.

Mint Museum
For fine art on a grand scale, visit North Carolina's first fine arts museum, the Mint Museum, 2730 Randolph Rd., tel. (704) 337-2000, about five miles southeast of the uptown loop. Originally the first branch of the United States Mint, coining $5 million in gold from 1836 until the outbreak of the Civil War, the Federal-style building was saved from demolition, moved from its previous uptown location to its present site, and opened as a museum in 1936. The first page of the visitor registry is on display, with its first signature— President Franklin D. Roosevelt. The size of the museum has since expanded more than three-fold, but the grandeur of the original structure's architecture has been seamlessly preserved. The museum's impressive permanent collections focus primarily on the art of the Americas, including paintings, furniture, and decorative arts. The collection of American paintings is particularly outstanding, including works by Thomas Eakins, Winslow Homer, James Whistler, William Morris Hunt, and several masters from the Hudson River School. In addition, the museum features works by Italian "Old Masters" including Rosetti and Ghirlandaio; African, Pre-Columbian,

BANKING ON CHARLOTTE

The first images that spring to mind upon mention of North Carolina are probably the sandy, secluded beaches of the Outer Banks, the towering ancient peaks of the Appalachians, or the tobacco fields of the Piedmont. The state certainly deserves this kind of idyllic memorialization, but it's also true that the state has distinguished itself in other realms as well. Perhaps most notably, Charlotte has risen to become the second-richest banking center in the United States (behind only New York City), surpassing such traditional financial centers as Chicago, Boston, San Francisco, and Philadelphia.

Charlotte's rise into the highest spheres of the banking world has been rather meteoric, beginning only in the mid-1980s. In 1985—partly due to local jitters over the prospect of being consumed by giant New York banks, North Carolina and 12 other southeastern states banded together to open up their borders to each others' banks. North Carolina's banks were uniquely poised to dominate the region. Most states in the region (and, indeed, throughout the nation) historically limited the reach of banks, but North Carolina had allowed its banks to establish multiple branches in multiple counties as far back as the early 1900s. By the time the southeastern states banded together, North Carolina's banks had been long familiar with operating networks across various zones. It didn't take long for the branches of Charlotte's banking network to extend throughout the southeastern United States.

The two largest Charlotte banks—which led the way to national prominence—are NationsBank Corp. and First Union Corp., currently ranked third and sixth in the nation with respect to total assets. Fueled by federal and state governments' recent and ongoing fondness for banking deregulation, these two Charlotte institutions have been gobbling up other banks from coast to coast at an astonishing rate. Between 1985 and 1998, these two companies have swallowed up more than 70 banks, and some of these acquisitions have required some mighty big swallows. For example, in the summer of 1997, NationsBank arranged the largest banking acquisition in history when it bought Florida-based Barnett Banks, Inc. for $15.5 billion. Three months later, First Union topped its Charlotte neighbor by acquiring Philadelphia's Corestates Financial Corp. for $16.6 billion, signifying First Union's ability and desire to expand swiftly and aggressively from a strong, North Carolina-oriented bank with $2 billion in assets in 1984 to national prominence and assets totalling more than $150 billion today.

As this book went to press, NationsBank had just announced its absorption of San Francisco's massive BankAmerica. If and when that merger is finalized, sometime in 1999, NationsBank/BankAmerica Corp., which will be headquartered in Charlotte, will have about $575 billion in assets, making it the largest bank in America, and (if and when the merger of CitiCorp and Travelers is approved) the second-largest financial institution in the nation.

---

and Spanish Colonial art; and acclaimed collections of North Carolina works in porcelain, studio glass, and pottery. World-class traveling exhibitions frequently enhance the permanent collections, but whether or not any special show has come to town, you'll find plenty of enriching art to enjoy in this wonderful museum. Hours are Tuesday 10 a.m.-10 p.m., Wed.-Sat. 10 a.m.-5 p.m. and Sunday noon-5 p.m. Admission is $4 for adults, $3 for seniors, $2 for students, and free for kids 12 and under.

The Mint Museum is preparing to open a new museum uptown in early 1999, the **Mint Museum of Craft and Design,** 218-220 N. Tryon St. between 5th and 6th Streets. This new facility will include 16,000 square feet of galleries focusing on studio crafts, with emphasis on building premier collections of ceramics, glass, wood, and fibers. Hours, admission information, and phone numbers were not available at press time, but the Mint Museum on Randolph Road, tel. (704) 337-2000, should be able to provide any information you need.

CHARLOTTE VICINITY SIGHTS

Historic Latta Place
and the Carolina Raptor Center
About 13 miles northwest of uptown Charlotte, located within lush Latta Plantation Park, Historic Latta Place, 5225 Sample Rd., tel. (704) 875-

JOHN REED'S GOLDEN RULE

John Reed (born Johannes Reith) was a Hessian soldier who left the British army near the conclusion of the Revolutionary War and came to settle near fellow Germans living in North Carolina's southern Piedmont. Most of the people in this region, including Reed and his family, dwelt on modest family-run farms in rural areas, where they raised small grain crops such as corn and wheat.

One Sunday in 1799, Reed's son, Conrad, found a 17-pound rock in Little Meadow Creek, on the Reed farm. Recognizing a good-looking rock when he saw one, John let his son keep the rock, using it for a doorstop for three years. Then, in 1802, a jeweler from Fayetteville happened by and recognized the gold ore in the rock. To his credit, the jeweler asked John Reed to "name his price" for the rock. Less to his credit, he nonchalantly accepted Reed's asking price of $3.50, for a profit of about $3,600.

Reed soon realized his folly and began his own mining operation by forming a partnership with three local men—his brother-in-law, Frederick Kizer; Martin Phifer, Jr., a wealthy landowner; and the Reverend James Love, a Baptist minister. The partners supplied equipment and workers, including slaves and hired hands, and Reed supplied the land. Returns were to be divided equally. This was not a sophisticated mining effort. Reed, his partners, the slaves, and the hired hands dug in creek beds and banks, using frying pans to sift for the gold. The primitiveness of the enterprise notwithstanding, at the end of their first year, Peter, a slave owned by Rev. Love, unearthed a 28-pound nugget. Almost immediately, other Piedmont farmers and their families began exploring *their* creeks—and finding gold in them.

For two decades, all of the gold mining in the area used the placer method of sifting surface dirt and gravel. The Reed farm led the pack, recovering about $100,000 worth of gold between 1803 and 1824. Then, in 1825, farmer Matthias Barringer discovered veins of gold running through quartz on his farm in nearby Montgomery County, launching a search for "lode," or vein, gold.

At first, this underground mining was characterized by the frying-pan sophistication of the early placer efforts: farmers simply began randomly digging huge pits in their land. But thanks in great measure to the influx of capital from wealthy "outsiders" and the arrival of skilled Cornish miners from England, European mining techniques soon came into play—digging deep shafts with branched

---

2312, is a meticulously preserved and restored cotton plantation, built circa 1800. The two-story federalist-style mansion is painted in the original colors and furnished with authentic period antiques. The home site is enhanced by an original smokehouse and several faithfully reconstructed outbuildings. Costumed docents take you on informative guided tours of the plantation buildings and fill you in on what life was like for the original residents, including the plantation's 20 slaves. The tours cost $4 for adults, $3 for students and seniors. From March to October., tours depart Tues.-Fri. at 1:30 and 3:30 p.m. and Sat.-Sun. at 2, 3, and 4 p.m. In November and December, tours depart Tues.-Fri. at 1:30 p.m. and Sat.-Sun. at 2 and 3 p.m. In January and February, tours are Sat.-Sun. only, at 2 and 3 p.m. If you're traveling from Charlotte, take I-88 north to exit 16B, and take Sunset Road west to Beatties Ford Road. Turn right and proceed north for 4.8 miles, then turn left on Sample Road.

Also located on Sample Road in Latta Plantation Park, you can get up close and personal with some fierce critters at the **Carolina Raptor Center,** tel. (704) 875-6521. The center is dedicated to caring for injured and abandoned birds of prey, with the goal of returning them to the wild. Some of the raptors you may encounter here include eagles, peregrine falcons, ospreys, owls, harriers, hawks, and vultures. The center's environmental education building is full of informative exhibits about the raptors' importance to the environment. Outdoors, an inviting, rustic nature trail meanders through quiet woods, past constructed aviaries containing 20 different species of live birds of prey. Open Tues.-Sat. 10 a.m.-5 p.m. and Sunday 12-5 p.m.; admission is $4 for adults, $2 for students.

Schiele Museum of Natural History

About 20 miles directly east of Charlotte, along I-85 at the New Hope exit, you'll come to the

networks following underground veins and using sophisticated equipment to extract the gold from the ore. A full-scale gold rush was on, and for several years, gold mining employed more North Carolinians than any other endeavor except farming.

John Reed was skeptical of these expansive new operations, with their fancy and expensive technology. Nearby, mines were investing thousands of dollars hiring professional miners, and the gritty, gurgling whisper of creekside panning was replaced by the rumble and roar of dynamite explosions and the perpetual chugging of steam engines powering stamp mills pounding tons of mined quartz down to gravel and dust (the dust was mixed with water, then intermingled with mercury, which attracts gold. The mercury was then distilled out, leaving a gold mush that could be melted into bars).

The complexity and cost of this kind of operation didn't appeal to Reed, a simple, illiterate farmer. Since the 1803 discovery of the 28-pound nugget, Reed had kept his mining business a small family operation, his workforce composed almost solely of his sons and other relatives, who worked profitably in the creekbeds of the Reed farm using spades and pans. Reed's relatives heard about the success of the nearby lode mining operations, though, and tried to convince the old man to modernize. By 1931, at the age of 75, Reed finally relented and began permitting lode mining at the Reed farm.

Three years later, Reed promoted his sons and a son-in-law to partnership in his mining operation. The deal was that Reed would receive one-third of the mine's income, and the other partners would share the other two-thirds. Within the year, the partnership fractured over ownership of a recovered 13-pound nugget. Everyone went to court, the ensuing litigation stretched on for years, and mining at the Reed Gold Mine ceased for a decade.

The case was finally settled in 1844, after which John Reed, by then 88 years old, promptly died. In accordance with Reed's will, the mine was put up for sale. It was purchased by one of his grandsons and sons-in-law. They failed to turn a profit, and, after eight years, sold the mine in 1852 to "outsiders," ending the Reed family's involvement in the Reed Gold Mine. Although the mine was worked intermittently through the early 20th century and occasionally turned up finds (including a 23-pound placer nugget found three feet beneath the ground in 1896), the "sophisticated" mining operations on the Reed farm would never approach the profits turned by John Reed's simple method of using his extended family to rummage through the soil of his farm's creekbeds.

splendid Schiele Museum of Natural History, 1500 East Garrison Blvd., tel. (704) 866-6900. Exhibition galleries include dioramas of North American habitats and wildlife, archaeological and ethnographic displays, and an extensive collection of fossils and minerals. Outside, a half-mile nature trail winds through 16 acres of forest to an 18th-century backcountry farm and a Native American village. The museum also includes a planetarium, which transports you to the heavens on Saturday at 11 a.m., 2 and 3 p.m. and on Sunday at 2 and 3 p.m. The museum is open Mon.-Sat. 9 a.m.-5 p.m. and Sunday 1-5 p.m. Admission to the museum and grounds are free; planetarium shows cost $2.50.

Reed Gold Mine

On the opposite side of Charlotte, a 20-mile drive east from uptown will take you to the site of the first documented discovery of gold in the United States, at Reed Gold Mine, 9621 Reed Mine Rd., tel. (704) 721-4653. Today, the area resembles a woodsy state park. As you stroll along the trails between mine shafts and along creekbeds, you can't help but wonder if you're treading over a 10- or 20-pound gold nugget like ones that have been unearthed here. The visitors center contains exhibits of gold and historical mining equipment, and an orientation film highlights the first gold discovery on this land. Tours, which last about 30 minutes, take you through portions of the mine shafts and show how the ore was processed into gold. The tours depart every hour on the half-hour during busy season (usually April-Oct.), slightly less frequently during off-times. During the summer, you can pan for gold. A pan of ore costs $2, and, if you let water slowly wash away the soil and gravel the way you're supposed to, it'll take you about half an hour to sift through your pan. Admission and tours of the mine are free. Hours April-Oct. are Mon.-Sat. 9 a.m.-5 p.m. and Sunday 1-5 p.m.; Nov.-

John Reed's gold mine

J. DYSART

March the mine is open Tues.-Sat. 10 a.m.-4 p.m. and Sunday 1-4 p.m.

James K. Polk Memorial
Just outside the southeastern Charlotte city limits, off US Route 521 just south of Pineville, you can learn about one of the nation's most unsung but influential Presidents at the James K. Polk Memorial, tel. (704) 889-7145. The 11th President of the United States, from 1845 to 1849, Polk was elected in part because of his pledge to serve only one four-year term, a promise he kept. Polk's four-year administration would exert an extraordinary impact on American history, from his free-trade-promoting tariff reductions to his savvy negotiation of the Oregon Compromise, to his brilliant and brutal waging of the Mexican War, which resulted in adding California, New Mexico, and Texas to the United States.

Born in 1795, Polk spent his first 11 years in the humble cabin and outbuildings reconstructed on this site. Though his family moved to Tennessee in his 12th year, and Tennessee is the state that elected him to two terms as Governor and several terms in the U.S. Congress, where he served two terms as Speaker of the House, North Carolina claims Polk as a native son. The claim is bolstered by Polk's temporary return to the state when he attended the University of North Carolina at Chapel Hill for both his bachelor's and law degrees. The visitors center features a film on Polk's life, along with exhibits on the Polk Presidency and life in Mecklenburg County during his youth. Admission is free. Hours April-Oct. are Mon.-Sat. 9 a.m.-5 p.m. and Sunday 1-5 p.m.; Nov.-March, hours are Tues.-Sat. 10 a.m.-4 p.m. and Sunday 1-4 p.m.

Museum of the Waxhaws
About 14 miles southeast of Pineville, you can explore the Museum of the Waxhaws on NC Route 75, a half-mile east of downtown Waxhaw, tel. (704) 843-1832. The small museum is devoted in great measure to the very early life and times of our colorful seventh president, Andrew Jackson, who was born nearby at the border of North and South Carolina. Though Jackson always maintained that he was born in South Carolina, he was apparently a few yards off, as geographers have pretty much proven that, in fact, Old Hickory was born a Tarheel. The museum is open Wed.-Sat. 10 a.m.-5 p.m. and Sunday 1-5 p.m. Admission is $2 for adults, and $1 for folks 7-12 and over 65.

Museum of the Alphabet
While you're in the area, you might want to stop by the intimate Museum of the Alphabet on Davis Road, just east of downtown Waxhaw off Route 75, tel. (704) 843-6066. Not for everyone, the print-heavy exhibits trace the developments and varieties of written languages from hieroglyphics to today's alphabets. Located in the headquarters of the JAARS Bible translators, the museum is open Mon.-Sat. 9 a.m.-noon and 1:30-3:30 p.m., and admission is free.

RECREATION

Paramount's Carowinds Amusement and Water Park

A 15-minute drive south from uptown Charlotte to I-77 exit 90 will take you to the premier amusement park in North Carolina. Paramount's Carowinds, Carowinds Boulevard, tel. (704) 588-2600 or (800) 888-4386 covers 100 acres and straddles the North and South Carolina border, features more than 40 action-packed rides, live entertainment, and a 12-acre water park. Although the park has been a popular destination since its opening, in 1973, the place has really taken off since Paramount Communications bought it 1992. In addition to the water park, opened in 1997, Paramount has added a number of state-of-the-art attractions. The latest, added in 1998, is the Paramount Action FX Theater, where guests sit in seats synchronized to move to *James Bond 007: A License To Thrill,* a compilation of film clips of harrowing stunts from the Bond series.

Roller-coaster aficionados will enjoy the Hurler, which achieves speeds up to 50 mph; the Vortex, a stand-up coaster that combines 50-mph speeds with gravity-defying loops and dramatic drops; the Carolina Cyclone, with four consecutive 360-degree loops and a 450-degree helix; and Thunder Road, which may lack twists but more than makes up for that in sheer height. The Scooby-Doo Ghoster Coaster and the Carolina Goldrusher, considered "ideal" for younger riders, are tame by comparison—but only by comparison.

The Drop Zone Stunt Tower sends you plummeting—at 56 mph—through a 100-foot free fall. The Frenzoid is a giant ship that rocks back and forth, eventually completing a series of 360-degree loops, suspending riders upside down 80 feet in the air. For an extra $22, the Xtreme SkyFlyer hoists you 153 feet in the air, at which point you pull a ripcord to free-fall back to earth (definitely not for the faint of heart).

Milder forms of amusement include arcade games, live performances, and rides where your stomach will remain relatively close to your navel. There are plenty of rides and amusements geared for young children. Admission is $30 for adults; $18 for ages 4-6 and 55 and above, and heights under 48 inches; after 5 p.m., admission for all ages is $15. The park is open weekends only beginning in mid-March, daily from the first weekend in June through mid-August, and weekends only mid-August to mid-October (and a couple of Saturdays in late October). In 1998, the park closed for a couple of weekdays during July, for maintenance—so if you're making a special trip, call ahead to make sure it will be open when you're planning to visit.

Parks and Lakes

With half an hour's drive from uptown Charlotte, you can visit a variety of parks providing a wide range of recreational diversions. **Latta Plantation Park,** 5225 Sample Rd., tel. (704) 875-1391, covers 2,247 acres adjoining Mountain Island Lake. Although swimming in the lake is prohibited, you can test the waters by renting canoes, paddleboats and johnboats for about $6/hour. For $1, you can obtain a fishing permit for a day and hook some bass or catfish. An equestrian center rents horses, with whom you can explore about seven miles of bridle trails. The horses cost $15 for a 45-minute ride. To reserve a horse, call the equestrian center at (704) 875-0808. If you prefer using your own feet, the park has 10 miles of tranquil hiking trails. For something a little less physical, visit the Carolina Raptor Center and Latta Place historic plantation (see entries under "Charlotte Vicinity Sights"). From Charlotte, take I-88 north to exit 16B, and take Sunset Road west to Beatties Ford Road. Turn right and proceed north for 4.8 miles, then turn left on Sample Road.

For a lake you can swim in, your best bet lies just north of Mountain Island Lake in the vast waters of **Lake Norman,** North Carolina's largest lake, covering 32, 500 acres. Ten recreation areas are sprinkled about the lake's 520 miles of shoreline. You can swim at most of these areas, including the much-more-bucolic-than-it-sounds **Duke Power State Park,** State Park Road, tel. (704) 528-6350. Named after the company who donated the land, and who flooded the valley to create Lake Norman in 1963, the park covers 1,450 acres, including 13 miles of shoreline. There's no admission to enter the park and explore the hiking trails, but it does cost $2 for adults $1 for kids to swim at the beaches. Campsites are available for $12 per night. **Jetton Park,**

19000 Jetton Rd., just off Route 73, tel. (704) 896-9808, is one of the most popular stretches of Lake Norman shoreline. Set on a peninsula jutting into Lake Norman, this small but scenic 105-acre park provides bike rentals, picnic tables, and concessions, but no swimming. There's a $5 charge per vehicle to enter the park on weekends and holidays.

If you're looking for a leisurely nature stroll, try the 10 miles of hiking trails in 956-acre **McDowell Park and Nature Preserve,** Route 49, tel. (704) 588-5224. Adjoining Lake Wylie on the North and South Carolina border, the park offers canoe and boat rentals. Although the park has an inviting, sandy beach, you can only sunbathe or play beach volleyball on its sands—because, again, this park prohibits swimming. An ideal camping spot for folks who want to spend a full day at nearby Carowinds amusement park, McDowell offers 14 RV sites and 29 tent sites that cost about $20 per night. Or, you can stay at one of the 30 primitive tent sites, accessible only by foot, costing about $10 per night.

For a spectacular, though fairly strenuous, mountain hike in the Charlotte vicinity, proceed directly to **Crowder's Mountain State Park,** Sparrow Springs Road, tel. (704) 867-1181. Located 25 miles west of Charlotte, and six miles southwest of Gastonia, this rustic 2,083-acre park features the striking twin peaks of Crowder's Mountain and King's Pinnacle. Although these twins might sound rather puny by North Carolina mountain standards, at elevations of 1,625 and 1,705 feet respectively, they nonetheless provide breathtakingly dramatic views, surging 800 feet above the surrounding valleys of gently rolling hills. A network of interconnecting trails allows you to explore either or both of the mountaintops with relatively little backtracking. Unless you're a veteran mountain hiker, achieving just one of the summits will give you plenty of exercise for one day. The trails leading to either peak get mighty steep as you reach the summit. Choose either mountain—they're both terrific, though Crowder's Mountain is the favorite, providing dazzling views from atop the summit's sheer 150-foot cliffs, which are often speckled with daredevil cliff-climbers. Make sure to stop by the park headquarters for a trail map, so you can take advantage of the interconnecting trails. The park is easily accessible from I-85 at its junction with US 29/74. From there, follow the signs along Freedom Mill Road to the park entrance. Admission to the park is free. Primitive campsites are also available, starting at $5 per site.

Race Car Driving

At the Charlotte Motor Speedway, you can actually get behind the wheel of a stock car and tear around the track. Before you start conjuring images of spinning out of control, smashing into retaining walls and other cars, and bursting into flames, rest assured that all activity is safely supervised by the professionals of **The Richard Petty Driving Experience,** 6022 Victory Lane, tel. (704) 455-9443 or 800-BE-PETTY. In 1997, more than 100,000 folks took advantage of what Jay Honeycutt, director of NASA, described as "next to the Space Shuttle, the most exciting ride you can experience." You don't need any race car driving experience to partake of the Petty Experience, although if you take the wheel, you do need to know how to operate a standard transmission. The Petty folks offer several levels of NASCAR experiences. In the Ride Along program, a professional driver whips you around the track for three laps, for $89. In the Rookie Experience, which takes three hours, *you* take the wheel—for two eight-lap sessions—at a cost of $329. In addition, you can take more advanced programs ranging $700-2,500.

Golf

Long considered one of North Carolina's poorest golfing destinations, the Charlotte area has witnessed a golf-course building boom in the 1990s. Although these new courses generally pale in comparison to the dozens of world-class courses found in the Pinehurst area 100 miles to the east, Charlotte's golfing scene has improved considerably thanks to these new arrivals. Among the new kids on the block, the **Highland Creek Golf Club,** 7001 Highland Creek Parkway, located 10-15 minutes from uptown Charlotte off exit 46B of I-85, tel. (704) 875-9000, leads the pack. Opened in 1993, this elegantly designed course on lush, rolling terrain is intermingled with a residential development, though most holes are rather secluded. Eleven holes feature water. The course's greens fees, including carts, range $44-54.

Highland Creek's newfound reputation as the top course in the area may soon be eclipsed by the sensational 1997 addition of the **Rocky River Golf Club at Concord,** 6900 Speedway Blvd., located a half mile from I-85 at the Speedway Boulevard exit in Concord, tel. (704) 455-1200. Designed by Dan Maples, the course features several scenic holes with natural wetland settings and striking rock outcroppings. Greens fees, including carts, range $39-49.

SPECTATOR SPORTS

The Big Leagues
In 1988, the **NBA's Charlotte Hornets,** tel. (704) 522-6500 for tickets, played their first game in the 23,000-seat Charlotte Coliseum. That first year, the Hornets drew more home fans than any NBA expansion team in history, and area basketball fans have been raising the rafters ever since, and spawning high hopes for the **WNBA's Charlotte Sting,** a founding franchise in 1997 of the Women's NBA, tel. (704) 424-WNBA.

The success of the NBA's Hornets also paved the way for Charlotte to land a pro football team, and in 1996, the **NFL's Carolina Panthers,** tel. (704) 358-7800, moved into brand-new 72,000-seat Ericsson Stadium. That year, in just their second season, the Panthers came within one game of going to the Super Bowl by defeating the defending Super Bowl-champion Dallas Cowboys in the NFC Western Division Championship game. Although the Panthers lost the next week to the Green Bay Packers (who went on to win the Super Bowl), the Queen City and the Panthers established an immediate, passionate, and continuing love affair.

But as popular as football and b-ball have become in Charlotte, these sports take a backseat when NASCAR roars into town. The **Charlotte Motor Speedway,** tel. (704) 455-3200, hosts races throughout the year. One day a year, usually in late May, about 150,000 stock car racing fans jam the Speedway for the NASCAR Coca Cola 600, the second-most-attended spectator sporting event in the U.S. (behind the Indianapolis 500, usually held the same day).

Performing Arts
The premier venue for symphonic, operatic, choral, dance, and other musical productions lies in the heart of uptown, at the **N.C. Blumen-**thal Performing Arts Center,** tel. (704) 333-4686, ticket office tel. (704) 372-1000, home of the Charlotte Symphony Orchestra and the Opera Carolina company. The **Afro-American Cultural Center,** 401 N. Myers St., tel. (704) 374-4700, on the edge of the uptown business district, stages frequent performances, including dance and theater. A five-minute drive from uptown southwest along Independence Boulevard will take you to **Ovens Auditorium,** 2700 E. Independence Blvd., tel. (704) 372-3600. This performance center, with a capacity of 2,500, hosts a variety of performances from Broadway productions to children's shows. At the same complex, the cavernous, 20,000-plus seat **Independence Arena,** 2700 E. Independence Blvd., tel. (704) 335-3100, hosts concerts and a variety of family shows.

ACCOMMODATIONS

Bed and Breakfasts
For such a large city, containing thousands of lodging rooms, Charlotte has surprisingly few bed-and-breakfast inns, although the short roster is starting to grow. Nonetheless, B&B buffs do have a few outstanding choices. If you'd like to stay within walking distance of uptown's many attractions, **The Inn Uptown,** 129 Poplar St., tel. (704) 342-2800 or (800) 959-1990, puts you in the thick of it all. A three-story, chateau-esque home built in 1890, this bed and breakfast provides seven elegantly decorated rooms, some with whirlpools and/or gas fireplaces. Premium-Luxury rates range $120-170. A couple of blocks from the I-277 uptown loop in the tony Dilworth neighborhood, the stately **Morehead Inn,** 1122 E. Morehead St., tel. (704) 335-1110 or (888) MOREHEAD, built in 1917, provides spacious common areas and 12 luxurious rooms decorated with fine antiques. Premium-Luxury rates range $110-160. The inn also offers a two-bedroom apartment with full kitchen for $225.

About a five-minute drive from uptown will take you to the tree-lined streets of the Elizabeth neighborhood and the hospitality of **The Elizabeth Bed & Breakfast,** tel. (704) 358-1368. Eclectically decorated with antique furnishings, arts and craft works, books, and lots of other interesting artifacts, the Elizabeth offers four comfortable rooms, including one suite. Rates are $75-105. Moderate-Expensive.

If you're looking to get back to nature yet stay within the city limits, try the **The Homeplace,** 5901 Sardis Rd., tel. (704) 365-1936. Built in 1902, this Country Victorian inn, situated on two and a half wooded acres in southeast Charlotte about 15 minutes from uptown, provides a peaceful oasis from the bustle of this rapidly growing city. Ease yourself into a rocking chair on the wraparound porch, stroll the secluded gardens, or rest in spacious bedrooms with 10-foot ceilings, heart-of-pine floors, antiques, quilts, and fine linens. Innkeepers Peggy and Frank Dearien will serve you a full Southern breakfast in the morning. Named one of *Southern Living's* top ten Southern inns in 1994, the Homeplace includes two rooms and one suite, ranging $98-125. Expensive-Premium.

Uptown

Befitting the city with North Carolina's most impressive skyline, uptown Charlotte features a number of high-class, high-rise hotels, almost all of them of relatively recent vintage and operated by major chains. With uptown serving as the city's financial hub, the uptown hotels charge more to stay on weeknights, when business travelers bump up the demand for rooms. Rates for Friday through Sunday nights are generally less expensive.

If you want to stay uptown but don't feel like sleeping at a chain hotel, try the graceful old **Dunhill Hotel,** 237 N. Tryon St., tel. (704) 332-4141 or (800) 354-4141. Located across 6th Street from Discovery Place, this 10-story European-style hotel was built in 1929. Each of the 60 inviting guest rooms is tastefully and comfortably furnished with 18th-century reproductions, along with elegant touches like the handsewn draperies. The service is splendid and the ambience utterly charming, from the pianist in the lobby to the four-poster bed in your room. Rates range Expensive-Luxury, beginning at $99 Fri.-Sun. and climbing to $149 on weekdays. The on-site restaurant, **Morrocrofts,** serves fine continental fare and also offers outdoor dining.

If you're looking for the polish of a modern high-rise hotel that comes with a full package of amenities, you have a few to choose from in the center of uptown, all of them offering on-site restaurants and cocktail lounges, swimming pools and exercise rooms. All of them fall into the Premium category on weeknights and drop to Expensive on weekends, charging $130-140 Mon.-Thurs. and about $100 Fri.-Sunday. The **Westin Hotel-Charlotte,** 222 E. Third St., tel. (704) 377-6664 or (800) 228-3000, towers over the competition, at least in height. Soaring 22 stories, the 407-room hotel also houses the Uptown YMCA, free to guests. The **Radisson Plaza Hotel Charlotte,** One Radisson Plaza (Trade and Tryon Streets), tel. (704) 377-0400, or (800) 333-3333, provides 365 rooms in its 15 stories, the top floor of which features a rooftop pool. The **Holiday Inn Center City,** 230 N. College St. (between 5th and 6th Streets), tel. (704) 355-5400 or (800) 465-4329, spreads 300 rooms through its 14 stories and also features a rooftop pool.

The two-story **Days Inn Central,** 601 N. Tryon St., tel. (704) 333-4733 or (800) 325-2525, doesn't have a pool, exercise room, or cocktail lounge on-site, but it can boast of the least expensive rates in uptown. Within walking distance of all uptown attractions, the Day's Inn's Inexpensive weekend rates begin at $49, rising into the Moderate range, around $70, during the week. The **Doubletree Hotel-Charlotte,** 895 W. Trade St.tel. (704) 347-0070 or (800) 222-8733, lies a 10-15 minute walk from the center of uptown, at the Gateway Center business park. The Doubletree's comfortable 187 guest rooms include amenities like irons and ironing boards, coffeemakers, and data ports. The hotel also offers an on-site restaurant and lounge, as well as a fitness center and a small outdoor pool. Rates on Friday and Saturday nights fall in the Moderate range, around $70, and rise the rest of the week into the Expensive category, around $100.

SouthPark Area

Located about 12 miles south of uptown, the SouthPark neighborhood, anchored by upscale South Park Mall, offers lots of interesting shopping, enticing restaurants, and some desirable lodgings. The **Park Hotel,** 2200 Rexford Rd., tel. (704) 364-8220 or (800) 334-0331, provides some of the poshest accommodations in Charlotte. The public areas sparkle with brass and marble, and the 194 guest rooms are decorated with fine furnishings and original artwork. The Park Hotel offers a heated pool, fitness center, and on-site restaurant and lounge. Luxury rates begin at $150 on Friday and Saturday, rising higher the rest of the week.

If you're looking for the conveniences of a home away from home, try the **SouthPark Suite Hotel,** 6300 Morrison Blvd., tel. (704) 364-2400 or (800) 647-8483. All 208 units are spacious one- and two-bedroom suites, supplying a full kitchen with stove, refrigerator, dishwasher, coffeemaker, toaster, iron, and ironing board. The SouthPark also includes a large outdoor pool, and a full fitness facility, as well as an on-site restaurant and lounge. Luxury rates for one-bedroom suites begin around $190 Sun.-Thurs., dropping to Premium rates, around $110, on Friday and Saturday. For something a little less expensive in the ritzy SouthPark section, your best bet is the **Courtyard By Marriott-SouthPark,** 6023 Park South Dr., tel. (704) 552-7333 or (800) 443-6000. With tastefully decorated, comfortable rooms, a swimming pool and coffee shop, rates at this Courtyard are Premium, around $120, Sun.-Thurs. and decline to the Moderate range, around $75 on Friday and Saturday.

Along I-85

Near the **University of North Carolina at Charlotte,** you'll find a large selection of lodgings just off exit 45A of I-85. The **Charlotte Hilton at University Place,** 8629 J. M. Keynes Dr., tel. (704) 547-7444 or (800) 445-8667 fronts a small lake and fulfills the high Hilton standards of comfort, with a fine restaurant, the **Upper Deck Grill,** and a popular lounge, the **Upper Deck Beach Club,** providing live entertainment, a pool setting, and a beach volleyball court. The Expensive rates begin around $105 Sun.-Thurs., dipping to around $90 on Friday and Saturday. If you're looking for a less expensive place near the university to rest your head, try the **Microtel University Place,** 132 E. McCullough Dr. tel. (704) 549-9900 or (800) 276-0613, also located off I-85 exit 45A. You won't find a swimming pool here, but you will find Inexpensive rates, in the $50-60 range.

Four miles west of the university exit on I-85, you'll find a cluster of comfortable chain lodgings. Take your pick at exit 41 between nine relatively interchangeable competitors. The **Best Western Luxury Inn,** 4904 N. I-85 Service Rd. tel. (704) 596-9229 or (800) 252-7748, and the **Fairfield Inn-Northeast,** 5415 N. I-85 Service Rd., tel. (704) 596-2999 or (800) 348-6000, both have swimming pools and charge Inexpensive rates, $55-60. If you're a light sleeper, ask for a room on the opposite side from I-85.

Another cluster of about a dozen franchise motels lies another 10 miles west, near the airport between I-85 exits 32 and 34. Be forewarned, however, that **Charlotte-Douglas International Airport** is the busiest airport in North Carolina, and despite the most valiant soundproofing efforts, you will be able to hear the rumble, if not the roar, of the jet traffic. The **Microtel Charlotte-Airport,** 3412 S. I-85 Service Rd., tel. (704) 398-9601 or (800) 840-2972, doesn't offer a pool but accepts pets. Inexpensive rates range $50-60. **La Quinta Inn-Airport,** 3100 S. I-85 Service Rd., tel. (704) 393-5306 or (800) 531-5900, provides a pool and accepts pets, at Moderate rates of about $70.

Along I-77

Between uptown Charlotte and the South Carolina border, a distance of about 10 miles, more than a dozen franchise hotels and motels provide predictably comfortable lodgings. Starting at the top of the line, the six-story **Charlotte Hilton Executive Park,** 5624 Westpark Dr., tel. (704) 527-800 or (800) 445-8667, offers the usual, highclass Hilton amenities, including spacious rooms, fitness center, whirlpool, and a large, heated outdoor pool. In addition, you can dine conveniently at the hotel's **Veranda Restaurant** and enjoy cocktails and live entertainment at the hopping **Gershwin's Lounge.** Located just off exit 5 of I-77, the Hilton has Premium rates Mon.-Thurs., beginning around $130, which drop to the Expensive category, around $100, on weekends. For an extra $20, you can bring pets. Also just off exit 5 of I-77, you'll find comfortable rooms and a swimming pool at the **Hampton Inn-Executive Park,** 440 Griffith Rd., tel. (704) 525-0747 or (800) 426-7866, for Moderate rates, around $70.

A mile south, just off exit 4 of I-77, you can take your pick between two franchises in the Moderate rate category. The **Red Roof Inn-Coliseum,** 131 Red Roof Dr., tel. (704) 529-1020, allows pets. Rates begin around $60. For about $10 more, **La Quinta South,** tel. (704) 522-7110 or (800) 531-5900, 7900 Nations Ford Rd., provides a swimming pool. Another mile south along I-77, at exit 3, you can stretch out in the roomy quarters at **AmeriSuites,** 7900 Forest Point Blvd., tel. (704) 522-8400 or (800) 833-1516, located a few hundred yards away from the roaring truck sounds of I-77. Every suite at this all-suite motor hotel includes a refrigerator, microwave, wet bar, and coffeemaker (with coffee). In addition, you can take advantage of a heated outdoor pool and an indoor fitness center. In the morning, help yourself to a free *USA Today* and a free deluxe continental breakfast, including heartier fare like French toast and waffles, as well as pastries and fruit. Popular with corporate visitors, the rates rise during weekdays, ranging $119-139. On weekends, rates dip to $89-119, and often lower during winter weekends. Moderate-Premium.

Spending a full day at Paramount Carowinds amusement park can be utterly exhausting, so you may want to take an afternoon break. The I-77 lodgings mentioned above are all less than 10 miles away from the park. But if you want to stay someplace really close, that you don't even have to drive to, then you can stay right outside the park gates, just across the border in South Carolina at the **Comfort Inn-Carowinds,** 3726 Avenue of the Carolinas, tel. (803) 548-5200 or (800) 228-5150. Equipped with a swimming pool and fitness center, the motel also serves a free breakfast buffet, with fare including eggs, waffles, bacon, sausage, pastries, and fruit. When the amusement park is open, the Moderate rates peak at around $85. The rest of the year, rates run about $65.

FOOD AND DRINK

As you might suspect from its position as North Carolina's biggest and richest city, Charlotte offers a wealth of delightful culinary options. No matter what kind of cuisine and atmosphere you're in the mood for, you'll be able to find it in the Queen City. The official visitors guide from Info! Charlotte lists about 150 restaurants, cate-

gorized by neighborhood and cuisine. You'll quickly see that exploring Charlotte's gastronomic scene presents you with a daunting array of choices. Here are a few suggestions to get you started.

Uptown and Vicinity

Directly across Tryon Street from the Info! Charlotte visitors center, the **Mimosa Grill,** 327 S. Tryon St., tel. (704) 343-0700, exudes an airy atmosphere. With its high ceilings and field stone walls and floors, you'll feel more like you're eating at a mountain lodge than at the base of the Two First Union Center skyscraper. Winner of *Charlotte Magazine's* awards for Best After-Work Watering Hole, Best Sunday Brunch, and Best Chocolate Desserts, the Mimosa Grill specializes in Southern regional fare served with creative flair. Lunch options include local standards like Brunswick stew—pulled barbecue with corn in a tomato base ($4)—and country gumbo with shrimp, oysters, and sausage ($4.50-8), as well as innovative dishes like the spicy Carolina shrimp, sausage, and tasso gravy over creamy cheddar grits ($10). The wood-burning oven churns out delectable pizzas for lunch and dinner, like the Cajun pizza with jumbo shrimp, crawfish, tasso ham, roasted peppers, and hot garlic sauce ($10). Main course salads come in a dozen savory varieties ($7-10), like the warm smoked trout with apple-walnut salad, organic greens, and horseradish aioli; and the pecan beer-battered chicken with organic greens, tomatoes, and basil-buttermilk blue cheese dressing. Although it departs from the regional theme of the Mimosa's menu, another salad deserves special mention, the lunch favorite, grilled tuna loin with soba noodle-cucumber salad, pickled ginger, Asian vegetables, and sweet chili sauce. Burgers and other sandwiches are available at lunch for $8-9. For dinner, try the appetizer of smoked Carolina trout and

azalea

TOMMY DAUGHTRY

crabmeat cake with Charleston asparagus salad and cracked mustard sauce ($8). You won't regret it. In addition to the pizzas and salads available for dinner ($7-10), you can choose from a variety of tempting fish, seafood, beef, pork, and poultry entrees, like the crackling wood-oven half chicken with roasted corn spoonbread, port wine, and cranberries ($16).

The **30th Edition** 301 S. Tryon St., tel. (704) 372-7778, jauntily flaunts its skyscraper location, in the same building as the Mimosa Grill. That's because the 30th Edition is located on the 30th floor of Two First Union Center, with a bird's eye view of the city. Although jackets aren't required, you won't feel out of place here if you do wear one. The interior is softly lit, and the service impeccable. As their motto accurately states, "The only thing we overlook in our service to you is the city below." This is a good choice for dinner if you're on an expense account, seeking to impress your date, or desire a fine dining atmosphere close to the clouds. Entrees range $20-25 for high-end American fare like roast rack of lamb and filet mignon with blackened scallops. An extensive wine list is available.

Just a block down the street, returning to ground level, you'll find more intimate, historic environs at **Carpe diem,** 431 S. Tryon St., tel. (704) 377-7976, open for lunch and dinner. Ingeniously renovated into a restaurant, Carpe diem was the home of Ratcliffe's Flowers from 1929 until 1984. The slate flooring, chestnut woodwork, Tiffany stained glass, columns, and mezzanine are all original. The menu is decidedly eclectic. Lunch choices run $6-9 and include a variety of sandwiches, pastas, and some superb salads, like the Indonesian rice salad with basmati rice, toasted almonds, golden raisins, red peppers, and chives, tossed in a light curry vinaigrette served with grilled shrimp and side of fruit. Dinner entrees range $8-18 and include a variety of pastas and salads, as well as duck, chicken, pork, and shrimp dishes.

The **Atlantic Beer & Ice Company,** 330 N. Tryon St., at the corner of 7th and Tryon, tel. (704) 339-0566, takes its name and congenial spirit from the business that supplied the citizens of Charlotte with the creature comforts of coal, ice, and beer 1936-1956. Located in a structure built in 1918, the dining and tap room areas offer a variety of appealing lunch and dinner choices, including beef, poultry, pasta, pizza, fish, seafood, and salads. You can also count on a variety of marvelous micro-brewed beers. For a terrific lunch sandwich, try the Ybor-style Cuban, with fresh roasted pork, manchego cheese, smoked ham, pickles, mustard, and mayonnaise sauce, pressed on Cuban bread ($6). Dinner entrees ($13-19) include superb choices like the grilled, seared duck breast with lingonberry demi-glace, the honey pistachio-crusted pork loin with a dijon port wine sauce, and the penne pasta with grilled salmon and shiitake mushrooms in a vodka tomato cream sauce. The pub menu at the A.B.I. Cellar downstairs is available for either lunch or dinner. On Wednesday evenings, the dining areas are soothed by live, acoustic jazz. On Friday and Saturday, journey into the Cellar for hotter sounds, from jazz and blues to modern and funk rock.

A couple blocks away, at the corner of 6th and College Streets, **Cosmos Cafe,** tel. (704) 372-3553, caters to a wide range of tastes for lunch and dinner. The cosmopolitan menu leans toward Mediterranean fare, including lots of Greek appetizers and entrees, but also includes pastas, wood-fired pizzas, quesadillas, spring rolls, burgers, salads, and a full sushi bar. Open and airy, with 20-foot ceilings that accommodate an intimate mezzanine level of tables, this converted warehouse space stylishly combines old with new, from the modern fixtures to the frescoes on the walls. This is a perfect place for folks desiring a tapas-style meal, with a couple dozen small-plate choices available for $4.50-7, like the Greek trio, with caviar mousse, grilled eggplant salad, tzatziki, and toasted pita points, or the steamed ginger-lobster dumplings with scallion-soy sauce. If you prefer a hefty entree for dinner, choose among pasta, pizza, pork, beef, lamb, and fish dishes ranging $8-19.

If you feel like escaping from all the skyscrapers, you don't have far to go. The quiet streets of the 4th Ward neighborhood, adjoining the uptown business district, are within easy walking distance, including the intimate hideaway of **Alexander Michael's,** 401 E. 9th St., tel. (704) 332-6789. Tucked away from the uptown traffic, at the corner of 9th and Pine Streets, this friendly spot is not pub-*like,* it's a true neighborhood pub, built in the late 1890s. The decor features soft lighting, dark green walls, a bead-board ceiling (with a pressed tin section), wooden booths, tables with gaslights, a long wooden and brass bar, and a smattering of Tiffany-style lamps. The food is good, but it's the welcoming atmosphere that makes this a special place. The fare ranges from burgers and buffalo wings to blackened catfish and London Broil ($6-11). For something a little different, you may want to venture into some more creative dishes, like the 4th Ward Stroganoff, aged beef with fresh mushrooms in a red wine and sour cream sauce, over rotini ($10). Alexander Michael's is closed on Sunday.

Just a couple of blocks away, even closer to the business district, another century-old structure provides the setting for Charlotte's most memorable fine-dining experience, the extraordinary **McNinch House Restaurant,** 511 N. Church St., tel. (704) 32-6159. Housed in a meticulously decorated 1892 Victorian home, the restaurant has nine tables but generally only seats six of them. That's in part because seatings are always spaced at least 30 minutes apart, so that you can be given a welcoming tour of the house as you sip your introductory glass of champagne, sit for a few minutes in the parlor and indulge in a specially prepared hors-d'oeuvre in front of the crackling wood fireplace (one of 10 working wood fireplaces in the house). Then, you'll be led to your candlelit table, complete with a fresh bouquet of flowers and antique china and crystal. Once seated, you're guaranteed to be treated to a prix-fixe, six-course meal that you'll long remember. The service is peerless, and the food heavenly. The menu changes every day, but one fabled, frequent entree is the rack of lamb with rosemary and mustard crust. During the winter, you also might be offered the succulent rack of venison, marinated in burgundy, cloves, ginger, and nutmeg, with shiitake mushroom and port wine sauce. This is a dining experience not to be undertaken if you're worried about maxing out your credit card; the food costs about $80 per person, but that doesn't count the aperitifs, wine, and after-dinner drinks that you'll want to complete this extraordinary dining experience. The McNinch House requires both jackets and reservations.

If you're seeking a memorable, fine-dining experience in a luxurious, old home, and the McNinch House is booked, then try for a reservation at **The Lamplighter,** 1065 E. Morehead St., tel. (704) 372-5343. Just outside the uptown, I-277 loop, technically in the Dilworth neighborhood, this venerable restaurant, housed in a 1926 Mediterranean-style mansion, exudes romantic intimacy, with candles, gaslights, and first-class service. Begin your meal with one of dozen delectable appetizers ($8-10), like the prawns served cold with a Cajun tartar sauce and sweet potato pommes frites, or the marinated grilled quail with a Chambord and red currant sauce. Then move on to a soup and/or salad, like the wild mushroom and crawfish bisque ($5) or the duck salad with sliced duck breast, hearts of palm, bleu cheese, capers, walnuts, peppers, and onions ($8). The entrees range $18-30 and include a seductive variety of seafood, beef, veal, game, fowl, pasta, and lamb, like the sensational Lamb Rockefeller, stuffed with spinach and oysters, with a roasted fennel and anise star cream sauce.

South End

The South End neighborhood, popular with shoppers for its wealth of antique shops and boutiques, features an eclectic collection of restaurants appealing to a wide variety of tastes. The **Pewter Rose,** 1820 South Blvd., just southeast of its intersection with East Blvd., tel. (704) 332-8149, open for lunch, dinner, and Sunday brunch, radiates a funky, romantic, almost bordello-like atmosphere, with stuffed sofas in the bar, little bee lights all over the place, and table lamps from the 1930s and '40s. Lunch offerings include nine salads ($8), from goat cheese and arugula to spicy Thai chicken and noodles; five soups ($4-8), including pumpkin bisque and Thai shrimp soup; a host of sandwiches and pastas ($6-8), from a portabella hoagie to the smoked salmon baguette; and other wide-ranging options like the hummus ba tahini ($7), or the duck and gnocchi—vanilla-cured duck breast, grilled and served over pumpkin gnocchi with cider cream and a crispy fried mushroom ($9). Dinner choices run a similarly eclectic path. For appetizers ($6-9), you can rely on standards like baked almond brie, or be adventurous with the snail and sausage—a garlicky mix of snails, Italian sausage, and leeks tossed with angel hair pasta. Dinner entrees ($13-18) include pork, beef, and poultry, as well as some delightful fare from the sea, like the lobster pasta, which is spinach tagliatelle pasta tossed with a silky smooth lobster sauce loaded with crunchy shrimp and sweet lobster meat ($16), or the whiskey crawfish gumbo, thick with chicken, crawfish, tasso ham, and chorizo and andouille sausages, slow simmered for hours, with a pepper and whiskey kick, served over white rice ($13).

Just another block down South Boulevard., at the Atherton Mills/Interiors Marketplace shopping complex, **Pastis,** 2000 South Blvd., tel. (704) 333-1928, is a modern French bistro, with modern art on the walls and tiny lamps suspended over the tables. In its opening year, 1997, Pastis was voted Best New Hot Spot by *Charlotte Magazine,* and its reputation continues to build. The menu changes frequently, but for lunch, appetizers ($5-8) will likely include a variety of soups and salads, from the predictable onion soup to the unique skate wing salad with fennel and pastis sauce. Lunch entrees ($9-15) might feature tempting offerings like shrimp crepes with champagne sauce, or peppered beef tenderloin with gratin potatoes in brandy sauce. Dinner includes similarly savory, French-inspired creations, with appetizers running $7-13, and entrees $19-23.

Across the parking lot from Pastis, the specialties of the house are a bit more predictable at the **Southend Brewery & Smokehouse,** 2100 South Blvd., tel. (704) 358-4677. Located in a cavernous warehouse with 30-foot ceilings and huge, gleaming copper and stainless steel brewery tanks behind glass walls, Southend is a favorite yuppie hangout, complete with a spacious bar area where you can sample fancy cigars with your single malt scotch or small batch bourbon. As the name implies, the beer is terrific, especially the ones brewed on the premises. As the name doesn't necessarily hint, the food is surprisingly good and varied. You can get buffalo wings ($6), burgers ($6-8), wood-fired pizzas ($9), and barbecued ribs and chicken ($11), but that's not all. You could also opt for some more unusual fare, like the oak-smoked portabella mushroom with polenta ($6); the blackened salmon on mixed greens with orange-sherry vinaigrette, chèvre, raspberries, and glazed pecans ($11); the garlic fettuccine with shrimp, bay scallops, and roma tomatoes ($11); or the venison fajitas with black beans and saut°ed onions, peppers, and mushrooms ($13).

Just a couple of blocks away, the atmosphere turns family-friendly at **The Spaghetti Warehouse, Italian Grill** 101 W. Worthington, tel. (704) 376-8686. The spaghetti dinners range $4-8, and other pastas, from the hearty 15-layer lasagna to the grilled shrimp Alfredo, run $6-11. Other offerings include pizza ($6-7), veal Marsala ($9), and chicken Cacciatore ($8). Though it might be a little tricky to located the Spaghetti Warehouse on a map, it's easy to find. Just drive along S. Tryon or South Boulevard to their intersections with East Boulevard, and look up. You'll see a water tower on the skyline, with the Spaghetti Warehouse name painted in bold green letters (the sign's lit up at night).

NIGHTLIFE

Far and away, Charlotte boasts the liveliest and most diverse nightlife of any city in North Carolina. We're only going to barely scratch the surface here and assure you that you'll get a few good suggestions for local haunts by talking with the folks who work wherever you're staying. The ever-handy *Charlotte Visitors Guide,* available free from Info! Charlotte, 330 S. Tryon St., tel. (800) 231-4636, also lists a few dozen popular night spots.

To begin with, almost all the big hotels uptown have lounges with live entertainment. And so do many of the restaurants, like the **Atlantic Beer & Ice Co.** The sidewalks of the neighborhood around the University of North Carolina at Charlotte throb with the pounding bass of live bands and state-of-the-art sound systems. But pretty much wherever you find yourself in Charlotte, you won't be far from some bar, lounge, or club open till 2 a.m. or later. Many of Charlotte's hotspots feature live bands and/or DJs presenting various versions of modern rock.

For a quick trip to New Orleans, head on over to the no-cover-charge **Cajun Queen,** 1800 East 7th St., two blocks south of its intersection with Independence Boulevard, tel. (704) 377-9017. Open for dinner, this is *the* ideal spot for folks with a powerful hankering to snap the heads off some crawfish and suck out the juice, as well as to take in live, New Orleans-style jazz. Just a few blocks farther southeast along Independence Boulevard, at its intersection with Albemarle Road, **Jeremiah's Copa Cabana,** open Wed.-Sun. 8 p.m.-3 a.m., sizzles with the beats of salsa, merengue, and cumbia, as well as some retro '70s and '80s. Women are admitted free before 10 p.m. At least as of 1998, Jeremiah's promised in an ad in the *Charlotte Visitors Guide* that if you present a copy of the Guide at the door, you won't be charged a cover.

If you're looking to kick up your heels to some country tunes, check out **Coyote Joe's,** 4621 Wilkinson Blvd., tel. (704) 399-4946. Near the airport, about a half-mile east of the junction of Billy Graham Parkway and Wilkinson Boulevard near I-85, Coyote Joe's features live bands nightly except Monday, when it's closed. The **Palomino Club,** 9607 Albemarle Rd., tel. (704) 568-6104, has two sections: one features national country acts, and the other local rock bands. Call ahead to see who's playing and how much the cover charge is.

For a Terpsichorean trip back in time, boogie over to **Swing 1000,** 1000 Central Ave., just outside the I-277 uptown loop, tel. (704) 334-4443. The Big Band Orchestra consists of just seven players, but they manage to sound like considerably more, as they swing through the works of Benny Goodman, Glenn Miller, Count Basie, and other swing-meisters. Occasionally, the club steps up the tempo a bit with more modern, jazzy swing bands, like the incomparable Big Bad Voodoo Daddy. You can make a whole night of it by dining here (three-, four-, and five-course meals run $45-65), or you can come just for the dancing ($10 cover charge). Open Tuesday through Saturday.

SHOPPING

As uptown Charlotte continues its blossoming into a truly urban city center, its shopping opportunities lag a bit behind the ever-expanding skyline. That's not to say, however, that you won't find sufficient opportunities to cool off any credit cards starting to burn through your wallet. Simply for the architecture, you should start your shopping excursion at Founders Hall, at the corner of Trade and Tryon Streets. The cathedral-scale glass atrium sets the stage for exploring the 20 or so upscale specialty shops. If you want to take a shopping break and enjoy a snack, meal,

or drink, stop in at the elegant **Bistro 100,** tel. (704) 344-1515, on the ground level.

More spread out, but offering the city's most interesting shopping, are the South End and South Park areas. For a dazzling array of antiques and home furnishings, proceed directly to the **Interiors Marketplace,** 2000 South. Blvd., between East Boulevard and Tremont Street, tel. (704) 377-6226. Located in a stylishly converted textile factory built in the late 1800s, Atherton Mills (the name the locals still call this complex) Interiors Marketplace includes 85 shops selling unique collections of antiques, fine art, furnishings, and accessories from around the globe. The South End area near the Interiors Marketplace, particularly on South and East Boulevards, is sprinkled with other interesting and varied shopping, accessible by foot. If the weather or your pleasure attracts you to the "huge mall" experience, then take a five-minute drive from the South End to SouthPark Mall, at the corner of Sharon and Fairview Roads, tel. (704) 364-4411, where you can explore four department stores, and, at last count, 115 specialty shops, like J. Crew, Coach, Pottery Barn, and Tiffany & Co.

If you'd like to spend a day antiquing in a soothing, small town, then head to **Waxhaw,** about 25 miles south of uptown Charlotte on NC Route 16. Along Main Street alone, you'll find more than 20 antique stores, plus a smattering of galleries. Have a down-home, country lunch at the **Bridge and Rail,** 112 Southeast Main St., tel. (704) 843-5005, a Waxhaw institution. For a different kind of shopping break, visit the nearby Museum of the Waxhaws and the Alphabet Museum (see Charlotte Vicinity Sights).

GETTING THERE

By Car
Two major interstates, I-85 and I-77, converge at Charlotte, and the nation-spanning I-40 runs fairly close by. If you're coming from the northeast, take I-40 to Greensboro (from Chapel Hill to Greensboro, I-40 and I-85 occupy the same roadway). Take the I-85 split at Greensboro; Charlotte lies another 90 miles away. If you're coming from the northwest, take I-40 to Statesville, and from there, take I-77 about 40 miles directly into Charlotte.

By Air

Charlotte/Douglas International Airport, 5501 Josh Birmingham Parkway, tel. (704) 359-4027 (welcome center), is a major hub for **USAirways,** tel. (800) 428-4322 (reservations). Several other carriers also fly there, including American, British Airways, Delta, Lufthansa, and TWA, among them offering nonstop service between Charlotte and more than 150 domestic and international cities. The airport has a full complement of car rental agencies. A taxi ride from the airport to uptown Charlotte costs $12; the shuttle bus costs $8.

By Train

Amtrak runs daily trains between New Orleans and the Northeast corridor, stopping at several North Carolina cities. The Charlotte Amtrak station is located at 1914 Tryon St., tel. (704) 376-4416 or (800) 872-7245 (reservations).

By Bus

Greyhound Bus Lines has an uptown station at 601 West Trade St., tel. (704) 375-9536. For toll-free Greyhound information, call 800-231-2222.

TOMMY DAUGHTRY

THE NORTHERN MOUNTAINS

The natural splendors of the Northern Mountains region—also known as "The High Country"—entice visitors year-round. In spring, wildflowers burst with blossoms along the region's majestic slopes and valleys. During summer's dog days, while the "flatlanders" swelter and fight off the mosquitoes, mountain breezes keep the High Country cool. Autumn inaugurates another "colorfest," as the forests flame with brilliance, and winter brings legions of skiers to the area's slopes.

Although the misty majesty of the Blue Ridge Mountains has been drawing throngs of visitors for over a century, the High Country retains a rugged rural character. The biggest city in the region is Boone, with 13,000 permanent residents, while the town that draws the most vacationers—Blowing Rock—is home to only one-tenth that many citizens.

The High Country's vibrant hospitality industry has a long tradition of excellence, dating back to the days when the region's resorts hosted guests including the Roosevelts, the Rockefellers, and their friends, out for a sojourn in the country. The vast majority of lodgings and restaurants are independently owned, staffed by experienced professionals dedicated to enhancing your comfort. If you prefer chain cuisine and motels, you're pretty much out of luck in the High Country (except in the metropolis of Boone).

Visitors will find a bounty of diversions here. Although many, like the Tweetsie Railroad amusement park, are man-made, the spotlight in the High Country falls primarily on sights and activities in the magisterial mountains, which earned this area the turn-of-the-century nickname of "America's Switzerland."

History

Although hospitable to visitors today, these rugged mountains resisted settlement for a long time. Native American remains and tools have been found here dating back to 10,000 B.C., but the people who left these artifacts behind were probably just visitors—there's no further sign of them for thousands of years. Other evidence does indicate that a group briefly tried farming along the Wautaga River in the late 1400s.

Three centuries later—about the time of the Revolutionary War—"over-mountain men," including Daniel Boone, blazed a few trails through this area of the Blue Ridge Mountains. With few exceptions, roads weren't laid for another century, until after the Civil War—and even those roads were extremely rare and crude, used mostly by loggers and the occasional family's carriage winding its way to one of Blowing Rock's resort hotels.

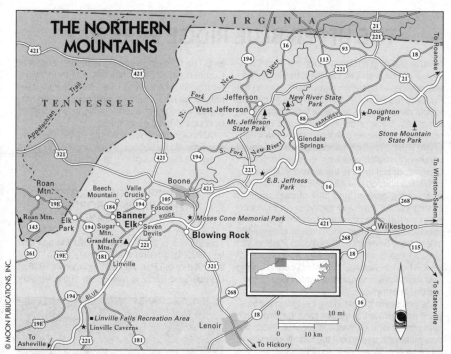

THE NORTHERN MOUNTAINS

© MOON PUBLICATIONS, INC.

The most significant stage in the development of this region came in the 1930s, when construction began on the Blue Ridge Parkway. With the coming of the parkway, tourism soon supplanted logging as the major industry in the High Country. Even today, the vast majority of the High Country's visitor attractions and amenities lie within a ten-minute drive of the Parkway's scenic curves.

Getting There and Getting Around
The closest major airports to the High Country are in Asheville and Winston-Salem, each about a two-hour drive away. Another hour or so farther away, the Charlotte and Raleigh-Durham airports may offer cheaper fares.

Don't even think about relying on mass transit to get around the High Country. A car is a must here (and there are no car rental agencies in the area—virtually everyone drives to get here). The back roads are astonishingly breathtaking—as well as extremely steep, tortuous, and generally slow going. Due to the adventurous contours of the backroads, tailgating is a major hazard here. Don't do it. And if you find some jerk's front bumper threatening to crawl into your backseat, don't keep staring into your rear-view mirror, or you might find your vehicle sliding off one of the multitude of hairpin turns.

If you're at all uneasy about driving mountain roads, stick to the main U.S. highways that traverse this region—namely US 105, 221, 321, and 421, and, in particular, the majestic Blue Ridge Parkway.

THE UPPER BLUE RIDGE PARKWAY

If you're planning a route through the High Country, our advice is simple: use the Blue Ridge Parkway whenever possible. If you're in a hurry, the Parkway (as it's known here) will usually get you to your destination as fast as or faster than the alternatives. If you're not in a hurry, the Parkway also provides scenic overlooks every few miles, where you can pull off the road onto a little paved parking lot, stretch your legs, enjoy an impromptu picnic, or just drink in the mountain vistas.

With its comfortable 45 mph speed limit (slower on some curves) and lack of stop signs or stoplights, the Parkway provides an intoxicating nonstop glide through forests and along spectacular mountain ridgelines stretching 469 miles, from Shenandoah National Park in Virginia to the Great Smoky Mountain National Park. The Parkway has a timeless quality, rolling past log cabins and split-rail fences free of commercial interruptions.

As you seem to float along the mountain tops, you'll appreciate the tender care that went into every facet of this massive project. From the designers who carved out the relentlessly scenic route to the stonemasons who chiseled the scores of little bridges, to the crack maintenance crews who keep the roadway clean and pothole free, this is a first-class act from start to finish.

History
It all started during the first year of Franklin Roosevelt's presidency, when FDR began to consider a public works project promoted enthusiastically by Senator Harry Byrd from Virginia, who kept nudging Roosevelt to get out and take a look at the Blue Ridge Mountains. Byrd's notion was to construct a scenic road stretching from the southern terminus of Skyline Drive in Virginia's Shenandoah National Park to the entrance of Great Smoky Mountain National Park in Cherokee, North Carolina. After sharing a particularly compelling and apparently persuasive journey along Skyline Drive with Byrd, Roosevelt agreed to help find the federal funds for the project.

By 1935, the states of Virginia and North Carolina had bought the necessary land, and Congress gave the budgetary green light to the project. The following year, construction began at Cumberland Knob, a mile south of the Virginia border. Workers were hired from the welfare rolls of the local counties, and construction materials were purchased locally, in an effort to beef up the local economies.

Although the great majority of the Parkway was finished far sooner, it took another 50 years to lay the last links of this grand road.

PARKWAY HIGHLIGHTS: THE VIRGINIA BORDER TO LINVILLE CAVERNS

This section of the Parkway marks the first and last links laid along the 469 mile route. Construction of the Parkway commenced in 1936 at Cumberland Knob, a mile south of the Virginia

the Blue Ridge Parkway

NORTH CAROLINA DIVISION OF TOURISM, FILM & SPORTS DEVELOPMENT

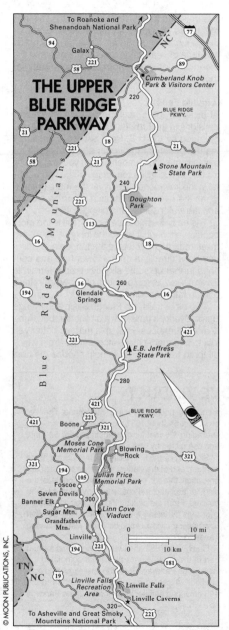

border, and was completed at Linn Cove Viaduct, alongside Grandfather Mountain, in 1983.

In addition to the picnic areas and trails carved by the Civilian Conservation Corps in 1936 and '37, the **Cumberland Knob visitors center** at milepost 217.5 offers a bounty of information about the Parkway, from free copies of "The Parkway Milepost" tabloid and other informative brochures to more encyclopedic volumes about the attractions along the way. You can also buy film here, a commodity that tends to go fast along this spectacular drive.

South of Cumberland Knob, **Stone Mountain Overlook** at milepost 232.5 offers a view of the unusual Stone Mountain. It rises only about 500 feet, but its treeless white granite pate makes for a dramatic sight.

At milepost 235.7, two craggy mountain faces form a dramatic niche, through which you can peer out over the piedmont stretching far below and into the distance. Rattlesnakes and copperheads are said to have a particular proclivity for hiding in the rocks around this spot, aptly named **Devil's Garden.**

Just down the road, **Doughton Park,** between mileposts 238.6 and 244.8, provides miles of hiking trails, as well as a coffee shop, restrooms, a

---

WEATHER ON THE PARKWAY

The elements can provide some non-scenic thrills on the Parkway. No snowplows or salt trucks keep the road open or safe, so **snow and ice** can make parts of the Parkway a little tricky in the winter. (When the road is impassable, the Parkway's entrance gates are closed.) If it's been snowing lately, contact the Parkway's information hotline, tel. (828) 298-0398, for details about winter weather conditions along any stretch of the Parkway you plan to travel.

Fog presents a different kind of thrill. If you find yourself suddenly enshrouded in a dense cloud of fog, slow down, turn on your windshield wipers and headlights (use your *low* beams—high beams only make the fog more opaque), and seriously consider getting off at the next exit.

Thunderstorms are also disconcerting. During the heaviest waves of rain (which often pass within 10 or 15 minutes), you may want to pull off at the next overlook and sit it out.

lodge, and camping and trailer facilities. The park, which was originally named The Bluffs, was renamed in 1951 in honor of Robert Lee "Muley Bob" Doughton, a colorful local congressman who was a staunch advocate for the Parkway.

At milepost 260.3, take the woodsy, one-mile hike to the easily walkable **Jumpin' Off Rocks Trail,** which provides expansive views, all the more dramatic after you emerge from the darkly shaded trail. A similarly easy, shorter trail begins at **E.B. Jeffress State Park** at milepost 271.9. The looping half-mile **Cascades Nature Trail** leads from the parking lot through dense thickets of rhododendron and mountain laurel, and stands of evergreens, Frasier magnolias, hemlocks, and birch trees. The trail follows along Falls Creek, which curls languidly through the foliage, until you get to the cascading waters that give the trail its name.

Moses Cone Memorial Park and the adjacent **Julian Price Memorial Park** stretch from milepost 293 through 300. At Cone, you'll find a visitors center, which will inform you about the bounteous recreational opportunities in these parks, everything from hiking and picnicking to fishing and horseback riding (for more information, see the Blowing Rock section).

For some hearty hiking, you can hook in to the **Tanawha Trail** from several overlook parking lots between mileposts 298 and 305. This trail meanders 13.5 miles around majestic Grandfather Mountain and provides a diverse introduction any time of year to the unique splendors of the mountain (for more information, see Grandfather Mountain).

Linville Falls

At milepost 316.5, exit the parkway and follow the signs to the **Linville Falls Recreation Area,** operated by the U.S. Park Service. Experiencing the beauty of the upper and lower falls requires some effort; depending on your trail choice it's one to two miles roundtrip. Of the two waterfalls, the lower ones are by far the more dramatic, as the river plows through a narrow canyon and the water spirals and plunges 45 feet.

The easy-to-moderate Erwin Trail is the most popular, although it's also the longest, about two miles roundtrip if you take the tangents to Chimney View directly atop the lower falls and continue farther up some slightly steeper terrain to Erwin's View, which provides photo-worthy views of both falls from on high.

Two other trails, the Plunge Basin and Plunge Basin Overlook trails, are a bit shorter, but slightly more strenuous. Pick up a map, or better yet, talk to a ranger at the visitors center (from which all three trails diverge) to help choose the best

THE LINN COVE VIADUCT

Between mileposts 304 and 305, you'll find yourself floating along an unusual bridge, the renowned Linn Cove Viaduct. Truly a marvel of modern engineering, this S-shaped structure appears to curl alongside Grandfather Mountain without touching it. It's a magical sight in the fog, when the road seems to float completely unsupported. In fact, the 1,243-foot-long viaduct touches the mountain in only seven spots—where vertical piers have been sunk into the mountainside.

One of the extraordinary features of the viaduct is that those seven spots constitute the only places touched on the environmentally precious Grandfather Mountain throughout the construction of the viaduct. In contrast to the usual method of blasting and bulldozing roads through mountains, the Linn Cove Viaduct was laid segment by segment—always working from the previously attached segment of the bridge rather than the ground. The final product consists of 153 uniquely curved segments, averaging 8.6 feet long, weighing about 50 tons, and connected by wire cables and epoxy.

Stopping by the Linn Cove Visitors Center at the northern end of the viaduct will give you a fuller appreciation, through photographs and models, of the singular architectural challenges overcome by the builders. From the parking lot here, you can stretch your legs by taking a walk on the hiking trail that runs under the viaduct and connects with the inviting Tanawha Trail.

Finished in 1983, the Linn Cove Viaduct formed part of the final 7.5-mile piece that completed the Blue Ridge Parkway. Given the challenge of its construction, it served as a fitting culmination to the 469-mile-long architectural wonder of the Parkway as a whole.

trail for you. You won't be alone: lots of folks, many with dogs, hike these scenic trails.

Linville Caverns

For an insider's view of the mountains, nearby Linville Caverns offers North Carolina's only commercial cavern tour. Visiting this mystical world of stalagmites and stalactites is a guaranteed eye-popper for young kids, and adults will find their jaws dropping, too. You'll wind your way through eerie, cathedral-like halls, past a creepy underground stream inhabited by blind trout. The temperature is a constant 52 degrees, so dress appropriately. Admission is $4 for adults and $2.50 for children ages 5-12. To get to the caverns, exit the Parkway at the Linville Falls Village marker, and take US 221 South for four miles. The caverns are open daily 9 a.m.-6 p.m. June 1-Labor Day; 9 a.m.-5 p.m. April, May, September, and October, and weekends only Nov.-March. For more information call (800) 419-0540.

ASHE COUNTY

Tucked away into the tri-state corner of North Carolina, Virginia, and Tennessee, Ashe County has managed to maintain its decidedly rural character; most folks must hop in their pickups and take a short drive to get to the nearest neighbor's house.

The little town of West Jefferson is the closest thing to a hub of activity in Ashe County. To get the flavor (literally) of this region, visit the **Ashe County Cheese Company** at Main and Fourth Streets, tel. (336) 246-2501. As the brochure proudly proclaims, "Ashe County, with its fertile soil, lush green pastures and friendly, hardworking people, brings together the ideal ingredients for cheesemaking. In 1930 the Ashe County Cheese Company put these abundant resources to work, and the result was wholesome cheese that captured all the rare qualities of this countryside."

In fact, the cheese is fabulous, and you can even watch it being made. The tour of the factory, from behind a windowed wall, takes 10 minutes and is free—except for the cheese you'll probably end up buying at the store across the street after you taste some of the free samples.

Outdoor Recreation

For some ethereal nature-worship, two state parks are located near Jefferson. **Mount Jefferson State Park,** tel. (336) 246-9653, awaits you, just off US Route 221 between the towns of Jefferson and West Jefferson. A road built by FDR's Works Progress Administration winds up the mountain's gentle slopes to a parking lot near the summit. From there, it's a third of a mile to the top via the Summit Trail, although the mountain's wooded summit doesn't provide much of a view. To get the most out of Mount Jefferson, take the Rhododendron Trail, a moderate 1.1-mile loop that begins a hundred or so yards before the terminus of the Summit Trail. If you're looking to bone up on your botany, grab a copy of the trail guide booklet from the box at the trailhead, and you'll be able to tell your rhododendrons from your dogwoods and flame azaleas. In early June, the Rhododendron Trail's namesakes achieve their most spectacular blooms.

Just a couple of miles away, on Route 88, one mile east of its intersection with Route 16, **New River State Park** follows along the ancient New River. Though the narrow, winding park covers more than 1,000 acres along 26.5 miles of the river, it contains only three access points— two accessible by vehicles, one by canoe only. Calculated to be the second oldest river in the world (the oldest being the Nile), the New River, particularly this protected section, provides a pristine setting for paddlers and anglers.

A half dozen outfitters in the area offer a variety of back-to-nature packages, from one-hour canoe, rafting, or inner tubing trips to two-day camping and canoeing excursions. The veteran **New River Outfitters** in Jefferson, tel. (800) 982-9190, offers the full menu, ranging $5-75 per person. If you're looking for white-water adventure, this section of the New is *not* for you. This part of the river has been trying to level itself out for billions of years, and it's almost got it right. One segment near the Virginia border boasts modest Class II rapids, but for the most part, floating along the New provides a languid glide through unspoiled wilderness.

The river is stocked with smallmouth and redeye bass, which draw their share of rod-and-reelers. However, the New's crystal-clear currents particularly appeal to fly fishermen in pursuit of the populous brown and rainbow trout. If you're looking to sharpen your angling expertise or need help educating a neophyte, you might want to check out **McIntyre's Mountain School of Fishing and Guide Service,** tel. (336) 877-2140. Open mid-April to mid-November, the school offers half-day smallmouth and fly-fishing clinics and guided trips, as well as two-day fly-fishing clinics and two-day camping and fishing trips.

If you feel like tearing up some turf, the **Jefferson Landing** golf course, tel. (336) 246-5555, in Jefferson, lays out the most beautiful links in Ashe County. Greens fees are $35 Mon.-Thurs. and $59 Fri.-Sunday.

Accommodations and Food
You'll find the area's finest lodging and dining under the same roof, at the **Glendale Springs Inn & Restaurant,** on NC Route 16 a third of a mile west of the Blue Ridge Parkway exit at Milepost 259, tel. (336) 982-2103 or (800) 287-1206. The inn dates back to 1892 but was meticulously restored in 1995, true to its late 19th-century character but including some stylish, modern amenities. The nine guest rooms range $95-115, depending upon whether or not you'd like a fireplace and jacuzzi. Expensive. Full breakfast is included. The inn's restaurant, which contains three intimate dining rooms, offers fine dinners like rack of lamb, venison chops, or cinnamon grilled pheasant. Most entrees range $20-30.

For heaping servings of southern fare like country ham and fried chicken, the **Shatley Springs Inn** on Highway 16, five miles north of Jefferson, tel. (336) 982-2236, piles on the food for breakfast ($2-6.50), lunch ($5.50-8) or dinner ($5.50-12).

If you prefer staying at a motel chain, your only option is the **Best Western Eldreth Inn** at Mount Jefferson, at Highways 211 and 88, tel. (336) 246-8845 or (800) 221-8802.

Inexpensive. The Eldreth also offers a convenient home-style restaurant, **Ashley's,** tel. (336) 246-7574.

In nearby Glendale Springs, the **Mountain View Lodge and Cabins,** tel. (336) 982-2233 or (800) 209-8142, PIN # 0595, offers a choice between the inexpensive cabins or the more expensive, comfy suites in the lodge. The cabins are duplexes consisting of two one-bedroom units, each with their own furnished kitchenettes. For $100 a night ($110 for the first night), you can rent both halves of a cabin. Four-footed members of the family are welcome to stay with you in the cabins at this pet-friendly place. The driveway for the Mountain View is directly on the Parkway, at milepost 256. Inexpensive-Expensive.

Just down the road, adjoining the parkway, between mileposts 257 and 258, **Raccoon Holler** camping area, tel. (336) 982-2706, has over 170 camp sites to choose from. Budget. In the shadow of Mountain Jefferson State Park, **Greenfield Resort and Campground,** tel. (336) 246-9106 also offers campsites and cabins at Budget rates.

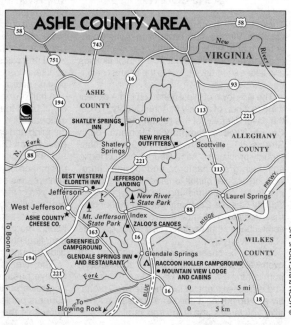

ASHE COUNTY AREA

© MOON PUBLICATIONS, INC.

THE FRESCOES OF ASHE COUNTY

Two turn-of-the-century Episcopal churches in Ashe County draw more than 80,000 visitors a year. Although the plain, wooden structures exude a certain inspiring charm, it's not the architecture that attracts the hordes. (Lack of interest, in fact, led the parish to close Holy Trinity Church from 1946 to 1980.) In 1974, Priest-in-Charge J. Faulton Hodge invited a local boy, from nearby Statesville, to paint a series of frescoes in St. Mary's Church, on Route 194 in West Jefferson.

Having spent years in Italy learning the rare and difficult art of fresco painting in Italy, Ben Long returned home to his native North Carolina in 1974 to begin began work on three frescoes for St. Mary's. Smaller (window-size) portraits, *John the Baptist* and *Mary, Great With Child,* flank the ghostly *Mystery of Faith* crucifixion scene which towers behind the altar. By the time Long finished this trinity of frescoes in 1977, local interest and activity in the parish had increased considerably, and word had spread of the inspiring work, drawing pilgrims and art-lovers alike.

In 1980, a decision was made to resurrect Holy Trinity Church, just off Route 16 in nearby Glendale Springs. Here, Long painted his fresco *The Last Supper,* a grand rendering of the famous scene, using local townsfolk as models for the disciples.

Audio presentations fill you in on the history of Long's creations and deliver comprehensible thumbnail analyses of the works. Anyone seeking an intimate religious service on Sunday morning won't go wrong attending either of these churches. If all you want is a look at the frescoes, however, you don't have to wait for a Sunday—both churches are open 24 hours every day of the year. The parish phone number is (910) 982-3076.

For more information about Ashe County, contact the **Ashe County Chamber of Commerce,** P.O. Box 31, West Jefferson, NC 28694, tel. (336) 246-9550.

Entertainment

If you're around on a Saturday and your feet are itching to move to some energetic bluegrass and old-time mountain music, get over to the **Mountain Music Jamboree,** at the **Burgiss Barn** at Highways 18 and 113 in Laurel Springs. Cover charge is $4 per person. Inside, you can inexpensively grab a sandwich or something a little more substantial, and rehydrate with nonalcoholic libations. For more information, call the New River County Travel Association at (800) 233-1505.

BOONE

With 13,000 permanent residents—augmented during the school year by the 12,000 students attending Appalachian State University (ASU)—Boone is the closest you'll come to a city in the High Country. It's one of the very·few spots in this region where, if you happen to sport a green mohawk haircut and multiple body piercings, you won't feel like an outcast (although most of the students prefer a more blow-dried look).

Most of the diversions in downtown Boone are college-related. There're lots of spots to grab a sandwich and a beer and hear live music. One exception to the beer and band rule is the outdoor drama *Horn In the West,* which runs nightly except Monday late June-late August at the Horn In the West Theatre, a mile east of downtown on Horn In the West Drive, just off US 42, tel. (828) 264-2120. It may not be Shakespeare, but Kermit

The Horn in the West *outdoor drama is a highlight of a visit to Boone.*

Hunter's two-hour historical melodrama has been packing them in every summer since it debuted in 1952. The tale takes you back to the 1770s and recounts how Daniel Boone and his fellow settlers battled the elements and the British in these rugged hills. Complete with Indians, Red Coats, and music, younger kids will find this a wonderfully memorable evening at this theater under the stars. Admission is $12 for adults, $6 for kids under 13.

If you get to the theater early (the shows begin at 8:30 p.m.) you can visit the **Daniel Boone Native Gardens** next door, where you can stroll the winding trails through woods, across rocky terrains and foot bridges, and past a historic cabin and several informal gardens. The gardens are open May-November. Admission is $2.

The **Appalachian Cultural Museum,** tel. (828) 262-3117, provides a superb introduction to the culture and history of the High Country. From Indian artifacts dating back millennia to African American history going back 200 years, to one of NASCAR legend Junior Johnson's stock cars, this museum presents a vast amount of information in a user-friendly manner. A wide selection of arts and crafts are peppered throughout the museum, which also offers slide presentations, videos, and lots of intriguing historical exhibits. Admission is $2.

ACCOMMODATIONS

Boone is not a big bed and breakfast town. The class act of Boone's small B&B scene is the lovely **Lovill House Inn,** half a mile west of downtown, a stone's throw from US 421 at 404 Old Bristol Road, tel. (828) 264-4204 or (800) 849-9466. All five of the nicely appointed rooms in this restored 1875 farmhouse have private baths, telephones, and TVs. Moderate-Expensive.

The **High Country Inn,** tel. (828) 264-1000 or (800) 334-5605, offers comfortable rooms, plus an indoor/outdoor pool, hot tub, and sauna. This big motel also houses the Waterwheel, a fine, friendly German restaurant, and Geno's Sports Lounge (see Food and Drink, below). It's located on NC 105 about a mile south of its junction with US 321. Inexpensive-Moderate.

For folks who prefer the predictability of chain-operated lodgings, Boone offers the region's largest selection, most of them clustered around the junction of US 321 and NC 105. Some of these neighboring motels include the **Hampton Inn** on NC 105, tel. (828) 264-0077, Expensive; the Moderate **Quality Inn Appalachian Conference Center** right at the 321/105 intersection, tel. (828) 262-0020; and the slightly more Moderate **Holiday Inn Express** on US 321 N., a mile south of the NC 105 junction, tel. (828) 264-2451.

Pets are welcome at the **Red Carpet Inn,** tel. (800) 443-7179, and **Greene's Motel,** tel. (828) 264-8845, both on US 321 (Blowing Rock Road) within half a mile of the US 105 junction. Inexpensive-Moderate. (A bit run-down, Greene's merits inclusion chiefly for its pet-friendliness.)

FOOD

As you might expect of a town with a sizable college population, you'll find plenty of places to down a beer and a burger or some buffalo wings. For slightly more creative pub fixings, **Macado's,** 539 West King St., tel. (828) 345-8034, serves chicken sandwiches, salads, and vegetarian pita sandwiches for about $5. Don't confuse Macado's pub with its homonym, **Makato's,** an enjoyable Japanese seafood and steak place on NC 105 South, on the outskirts of Boone, tel. (828) 264-7976, where dinners average $15-20.

The **Dan'l Boone Inn,** tel. (828) 264-8657, is one of the most popular downtown spots. You might have to wait a few minutes in line to get in to this alcohol-free family restaurant, located at the intersection of US 421 and US 321, but once you're seated in the rustic, wood-paneled dining room (upturned buckets serve as light fixtures), you'll soon be rewarded with an impressive parade of bread, ham biscuits, and a variety of beef, pork, and poultry entrees with various vegetable sides, all for about $11. Everybody gets the same meal, but there's enough choice to suit anybody with a hankering for country home cooking. For dessert, choose from a variety of cakes and pies.

On the opposite side of the food spectrum, but only a few feet across the street, the **Mother Ship Restaurant,** tel. (828) 262-1991, specializes in vegan-only fare (meat- and dairy-free). Lunch hovers around the $5 range. Dinner goes for $7-10.

You'll find fewer sets of overalls or tie-dyed T-shirts at the more romantic **Red Onion Cafe,** tel. (828) 264-5470. Located on US 321, half a block south from its junction with US 421, this eatery has a wide selection of wine and beer to go with menu offerings like the grilled yellowfin tuna salad ($8) or the Cajun chicken fettuccini ($12).

For something culinarily unique in the High Country, the **Waterwheel Restaurant,** at the High Country Inn, tel. (828) 264-1000, 1785 US 105 South, on the outskirts of Boone, is the region's only eatery specializing in German cuisine. Although you can choose from a variety of American-style entrees, like steaks and burgers, you'd do well to try the schnitzels, wursts, and other Teutonic options ($8-15). Adjoining the Waterwheel, **Geno's Sports Lounge** is a popular hangout whose energetic decor includes the front end of a Volkswagen beetle (with a rotating cast of characters—JFK and Marilyn Monroe, Popeye and Brutus, and others—in the driver's and passenger's seats) bursting through the wall.

The **Bean Stalk Coffee Shop** on King Street, tel. (828) 262-0999, is popular with the college crowd, not only for the coffee but also for live music.

SHOPPING

In a region with enough antique stores to keep an antique hound nosing around for weeks, the **Boone Antique Mall** at 631 W. King St., tel. (828) 262-0521, is a good place to get started. With 58 dealers covering three spacious floors of the 1930s Belk store, the Boone Antique Mall has everything from buttons to bureaus.

Not to be confused with the celebrated original in Valle Crucis, the **Mast General Store** at 630 W. King St. in Downtown Boone, tel. (828) 262-0000, contains a more spacious, and in some cases, fuller selection than its noble ancestor. In addition to a diversified line of men's, women's, and children's clothing and shoes, you'll find large mercantile and gift departments, including a full line of camping gear. Although a century younger than its Valle Crucis counterpart, the Boone store retains some similar touches of antiquity, from its old-fashioned wood display cases to the creaking wood floors.

Information

The **visitors center** on US 321/221 (Blowing Rock Road) provides a bounty of information on Boone, as well as the whole High Country region. Write to **High Country Host,** 1700 Blowing Rock Road, Boone, NC 28607, or call (828) 264-1299 or (800) 438-7500.

BLOWING ROCK

Nine miles south of Boone, the little town of Blowing Rock has reigned as the premier vacation spot of the High Country for more than a century—and for good reason. The charming downtown village includes dozens of delightful restaurants, shops, and lodging options, as well as attractions like a large village park complete with gardens, carriage rides, and a small lake. Outdoor recreational opportunities abound, from hiking, fishing, and skiing to tennis, golf, and horseback riding. Cultural diversions include the Tweetsie Railroad amusement park (a must for young kids) and a thriving arts scene, including lots of live music and the summer stock of the prestigious Blowing Rock Stage Company.

Despite the wide array of visitor attractions and amenities, Blowing Rock retains its character as a cozy mountain retreat, bereft of strip malls, McDonald's, and traffic jams. Since the town boasts a year-round population of just 1,300, almost every Blowing Rocker is somehow involved with the town's proud tradition as a jewel of the tourism industry. The lodgings, restaurants, shops, and other attractions are owned and staffed by local professionals dedicated to enhancing your enjoyment.

Complementing the human element, the majestic mountain splendor of Blowing Rock is guaranteed to make your stay here memorable. Situated on the Eastern Continental Divide at an altitude of 4,000 feet, the area offers countless dazzling displays of the surrounding mountains' year-round beauty.

History

The town of Blowing Rock has been a mountain refuge since the mid-1800s. During the Civil War, refugees from the Confederacy fled to the relative safety available in North Carolina's High Country. Word spread of the many charms of

the region, and, following the Civil War, vacationers began to visit. They found it a delightful place to escape the oppressive heat of the flatlands, view the spectacular scenery of the mountains, enjoy the rich and varied plant and animal life, and—perhaps most important—get away from a certain lowland insect. As an 1897 advertisement proclaimed, "Happiness for All! Mountain Retreats in Western North Carolina, Where Torrid Heat is Subdued by Cooling Breezes, and the Mosquito Pest is Unknown."

Blowing Rock's founders were ever mindful of promoting tourism. The city charter, passed in 1889, includes an exhaustive array of ordinances imposing various fines for cluttering up the streets with garbage—or hogs, sheep, chickens, or geese.

Most of the postwar tourists who came to Blowing Rock stayed in boarding houses operated out of family homes, but by 1892, Blowing Rock boasted three large and luxurious hotels, including the venerable Green Park Inn. Still in operation today, the hotel preserves its century-old elegance in its spacious lobby and nostalgic atmosphere.

The early 1900s continued to boom for Blowing Rock, augmented by an increasing number of wealthy families known as "cottagers"—summertime residents who built mansions in town and in the surrounding hills. The elegant Inn at Ragged Gardens, with a dozen bedrooms, is one such cozy "cottage" you can stay in today.

Tourism continued to grow through the 1920s, but the Great Depression brought a quick halt to those halcyon days. However, Blowing Rock was not hit as hard as many surrounding communities—the cottagers were sufficiently wealthy to escape the brunt of the impact. Local officials—in particular Grover Robbins, the town mayor—also showed great foresight in their leadership. Thanks in great measure to Robbins' relentless lobbying

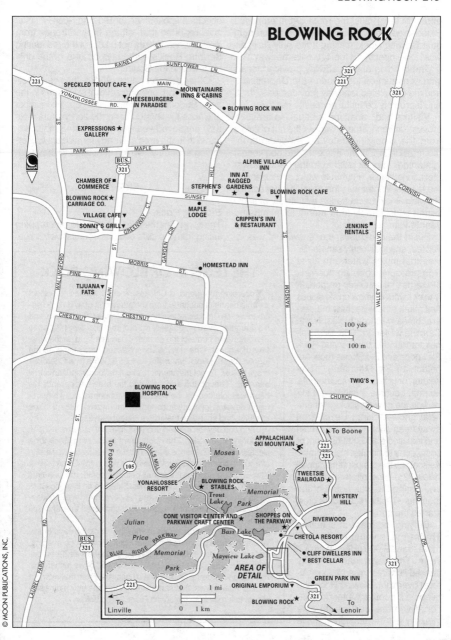

BLOWING ROCK

SPECKLED TROUT CAFE ▼

CHEESEBURGERS ● IN PARADISE

MOUNTAINAIRE ● INNS & CABINS

● BLOWING ROCK INN

EXPRESSIONS ★ GALLERY

CHAMBER OF COMMERCE ■

BLOWING ROCK ★ CARRIAGE CO.

VILLAGE CAFE ▼

SONNY'S GRILL ▼

STEPHEN'S ▼

INN AT RAGGED GARDENS ★

ALPINE VILLAGE INN ●

BLOWING ROCK CAFE ●

MAPLE LODGE ●

CRIPPEN'S INN ● & RESTAURANT

JENKINS ■ RENTALS

HOMESTEAD INN ●

TIJUANA ▼ FATS

BLOWING ROCK HOSPITAL ■

0   100 yds
0   100 m

TWIG'S ▼

AREA OF DETAIL

To Boone →

APPALACHIAN SKI MOUNTAIN ⚡

Moses Cone

YONAHLOSSEE RESORT

BLOWING ROCK ★ STABLES

Trout Lake

Memorial Park

TWEETSIE RAILROAD ★

★ MYSTERY HILL

CONE VISITOR CENTER AND PARKWAY CRAFT CENTER

SHOPPES ON ● THE PARKWAY ▼

RIVERWOOD

Julian Price Memorial Park

Bass Lake

CHETOLA RESORT ●

Mayview Lake

● CLIFF DWELLERS INN ▼ BEST CELLAR

ORIGINAL EMPORIUM ▼

GREEN PARK INN ●

0   1 mi
0   1 km

← To Linville

BLOWING ROCK ★

To Lenoir →

© MOON PUBLICATIONS, INC.

efforts in the 1930s, the route of the proposed Blue Ridge Parkway was adjusted to run right past Blowing Rock, making it the only "full-service" town directly on the 470-mile roadway.

The building of the parkway provided locals with construction jobs during the Depression, and the completed roadway provided easy, fast, and incredibly beautiful access to the town.

Visitors and vacationers began to arrive in droves—in springtime to witness the riot of colors from the blooming catawba rhododendron, mountain laurel, flame azaleas, and dogwoods; in summer to seek relief from the heat at lower elevations; and in autumn to watch the turning of the leaves. Winter was the only slow season for Blowing Rock, because the availability of snow varied considerably from month to month and year to year.

But in the mid-1950s, the "snow gun" was invented, an ingeniously simple device that mixes water and air at high pressures, blasting out miniblizzards that can keep perpetually thick layers of snow on ski slopes that might otherwise thaw out several times during a typical North Carolina winter. In 1962, Bill Thalheimer founded the Blowing Rock Ski Lodge and Ski Slopes (now Appalachian Ski Mountain). Thalheimer, originally from southern Alabama, became a self-taught expert on the new technology of artificial snow-making. He cleared away trees on a nearby mountain and installed a $50,000 network of snow guns to blanket his ski trails. As soon as the temperature dipped below 32°—most often late at night and during the wee hours of the morning—Thalheimer and his crew started the guns.

Defying the mass of skeptics, Thalheimer's venture attracted more than 15,000 skiers in its first year. The town had officially ceased its winter hibernations. Almost overnight, Blowing Rock had become a popular winter destination. Even the local health care industry felt the economic ripple

effects. A spokesman for Blowing Rock Hospital later reported that "all the broken bones from inexperienced skiers got us out of the red" during Blowing Rock's early days as one of the only ski towns in the South.

Other entrepreneurs quickly followed Thalheimer's lead, opening several ski resorts in the area. Suddenly, the year-round population, most of whose livelihoods depended on visitors, was now employed year-round, inspiring major expansion in the area's already formidable tourist-driven economy—which continues to thrive.

SIGHTS

Blowing Rock

The town's namesake is a granite outcropping jutting from the cliffs over the Johns River Gorge.

THE LEGEND OF BLOWING ROCK

According to legend, a Chickasaw chief wanted to protect his beautiful daughter from the attentions of white men encroaching on Chickasaw territory in the Midwest. So the chief and his daughter, Wauhonhassee, moved from the Great Plains to Blowing Rock, home of the eastern Cherokee (and, at the time, free of whites). One day, Wauhonhassee was sitting on the jagged Blowing Rock when she noticed a handsome Cherokee brave below. To get his attention, she flirtatiously shot an arrow near him. Though the arrow missed the brave, apparently his heart was pierced by the beautiful Wauhonhassee. They became devoted lovers, wandering the mountains, fishing in the streams, and spending their days in happy idyll.

Then one day the maiden and the brave noticed a mysterious reddening in the sky. They both went to Blowing Rock for a clearer view of this strange event. The brave realized it was a sign of trouble, commanding him to join in a war in the Great Plains. Knowing she might not see her beloved again, the beautiful maiden begged him not to leave her. Standing on Blowing Rock as he struggled between duty and his devotion to Wauhonhassee, the brave opted for a surprise third choice: he threw himself off the edge of the cliff.

Wauhonhassee remained at Blowing Rock for days in fervent and tearful prayer to the Great Spirit. Finally, one evening, her prayers were answered—the sky reddened as it had before, and a great gust of wind blew her beloved brave, unharmed, back up onto Blowing Rock and into her arms. From that moment on, the legend says, that same strong wind has blown perpetually on this rock from the Johns River Gorge below.

Standing near Blowing Rock offers a breathtaking view of the gorge, which plummets 3,000 feet down to the Johns River below. Facing you is a panorama of some of the tallest mountains east of the Rockies, including Grandfather Mountain, which really does look like a napping, paunchy old man from this vantage point.

But the great view isn't what made this rock one of North Carolina's first tourist attractions. It's the "blowing" part that draws the visitors. The steep walls of the Johns River Gorge form a powerful updraft, causing an almost constant wind to swoop up Blowing Rock's face—an updraft stiff enough to make it "snow up" or return your hat and mittens to you if you toss them over the edge.

Although Blowing Rock offers the allure of history, romance, myth, and natural beauty, be warned that the modest square footage of the gift shop and snack bar just about equals that of the foot trails and overlook platform. For the 15 minutes you'll spend here, you may well find yourself questioning whether the four dollar admission charge isn't a little steep ($1 for kids 6-11). The **Original Emporium** restaurant, just down the road, offers a similarly spectacular view of the Johns River Gorge and much better food than The Rock's snack bar.

The Tweetsie Railroad

If you need to spend several hours entertaining a child under 12, or if you want to bring out your own inner child, then by all means take a ride on The Tweetsie Railroad, tel. (828) 264-9062 or (800) 526-5740. The Tweetsie is more than a railroad—it's a sizeable amusement park. But when we say that, we don't mean to conjure up glitzy images of Disney World. Constructed more of plywood than plastic, the Tweetsie is a 1950s-style Wild West theme park, where attractions tend towards low-tech amusements like panning for gold, riding a chairlift, feeding goats and deer in the petting zoo, and watching live performances like cloggers, bluegrass bands, or saloon-style high-steppers.

Of course the headline attraction is the three-mile, 25-minute train ride on the Tweetsie Railroad. If you're lucky, your train might be one that's carrying the Fort Boone payroll, in which case you're in for a wild ride, complete with train robbers and Native Americans on the warpath.

the Tweetsie engine in special Halloween regalia

(Okay, so all the trains carry the payroll—by the way, for the best views of the unfolding drama, sit on the right side of the train, facing the engine.)

If you're with young kids, you can easily spend a long and delightful afternoon here. The $15 per adult admission ($13 for kids 4-12) covers all rides and attractions but does not include the purchase of the six-shooter cap guns perpetually being fired by the gangs of kindergarten gunslingers who prowl the grounds. The Tweetsie Railroad is located on Highway 321, a five-minute drive from downtown Blowing Rock.

Mystery Hill

It's raining out, and your kids are about to drive you crazy cooped up in your hotel room, so where do you take them? Mystery Hill! Mystery Hill, tel. (828) 264-2792, may seem a little hokey and down-at-the-heels, but little kids will love it. You will see how the "normal laws of gravity are suspended" in the Mystery House, which features water that appears to flow uphill and a ball that seems to roll up instead of down. Other

SAVING THE TWEETSIE

The Tweetsie is a genuine narrow-gauge train which has been in operation since 1881. Originally owned by the Eastern Tennessee and Western North Carolina Railroad, the Tweetsie Railroad carried passengers, farm produce, furniture, lumber, textiles, and other freight through this rugged, road-resistant region for over half a century. Eventually, though, roads, cars, and trucks rendered the Tweetsie obsolete; August 13, 1940, marked the final run on the Tweetsie line (the end was hastened by a flood that wiped out a critical section of track between the towns of Boone and Cranberry).

By 1950, the noble iron pony that had whistled along the Tweetsie line appeared destined for the scrap heap. Then Hollywood stepped in, in the form of Gene Autry, the movies' original singing cowboy, who bought an option on the train, intending to take the Tweetsie to California and make her a star in Hollywood westerns.

But at that point, Grover Robbins, Jr., son of Blowing Rock's mayor, entered the picture and applied some of the same persuasive tenacity that his father had exercised 20 years earlier, when he succeeded in having the Blue Ridge Parkway re-routed to run by Blowing Rock. By 1956, Autry relented and sold back his option on the line. By the next year, an exact replica of Tweetsie's main depot had been constructed, and new track was laid. The first run on the new line took place on June 30, 1957. Over the next three days, more than 2,000 passengers took the 18-minute ride, and today's Tweetsie Railroad Wild West theme park was born.

"mysterious phenomenon" include water flowing from a spigot with no pipe attached, and the Shadow Wall, where your shadow gets lost on a phosphorous wall. The self-guided tour, which can last from half an hour to an hour or more, ends in a room devoted to making gigantic soap bubbles. Admission is $5 for adults and $3.50 for ages 5-12. Mystery Hill is a few hundred yards south of the Tweetsie Railroad, on Highway 321.

OUTDOOR RECREATION

Hiking and Fishing

Beginning in downtown Blowing Rock, the **Glen Burney Trail** follows New Year's Creek into the spectacular Johns River Gorge south of town. The trail descends for 1.6 miles, past breathtaking views of the gorge and two dramatic waterfalls, the 45-foot Glen Burney Falls and 55-foot

Glen Mary Falls. The trail is steep and slippery in parts, so wear footgear with good traction. The entrance to the Glen Burney Trail begins at Annie Cannon Gardens, behind the town park on Main Street. For a trail map, stop by the Chamber of Commerce on Main Street, next to the park.

Two woodsy parks, operated by the National Park Service, lie on the outskirts of Blowing Rock, along the Blue Ridge Parkway between mileposts 293 to 300. **Moses H. Cone Memorial Park** and **Julian Price Memorial Park** cover 7,860 acres and contain more than 35 miles of hiking and bridle trails. Two lakes in these parks are also popular fishing spots, the 22-acre Bass Lake and 16-acre Trout Lake. For more information on the parks, stop by the visitors center at Moses Cone Park, in the 20-room Flat Top Manor, built at the turn of the century by the former owner of most of the park's land, Moses "The Denim King "Cone, who became wealthy making blue jeans in the late 19th and early 20th centuries.

Skiing

With a maximum vertical drop of only 365 feet, the trails down **Appalachian Ski Mountain,** tel. (800) 322-2373, are the tamest of the four major ski resorts in the area. Skiing here feels like a family affair, with lots of little kids flopping around on the snow and running around the lodge. Of the four resorts, Appalachian is the calmest and least crowded, making it the ideal choice for families with young children. This is also the best choice if you're looking to introduce yourself or others to the joys of downhill skiing, for two reasons. First, its slopes provide the least terrifying, least crowded runs, and second, because Appalachian is home to the first-rate French-Swiss Ski College, one of the finer ski schools in the country. Appalachian Ski Mountain features two beginner, four intermediate and three advanced slopes, in addition to an ice-skating rink

($10 includes skate rental), a large video game room, and a day care nursery. Lift tickets are $20 on weekdays and $30 on weekends ($13 and $16 for night skiing, 6-10 p.m.). A full range of lessons are available.

Caving, Rock Climbing, and Whitewater Rafting

At the intersection of Main Street and US 221 in Blowing Rock, you'll find **High Mountain Expeditions,** tel. (800) 262-9036. This experienced outfit offers a panoply of guided outdoor expeditions to choose from, including rock climbing, spelunking, and a half dozen different whitewater rafting trips. They even offer a two-day whitewater adventure for those who really want to "experience the river."

Horseback Riding

Blowing Rock Stables, tel. (828) 295-7847, is located a mile outside downtown Blowing Rock, just off US 221 North, in Moses H. Cone Memorial Park (watch for the sign on 221). This is an ideal place to discover the unique pleasures of horseback riding. The trails through the park are lush, and the horses know what they're doing, even if the riders may not. The guided trail rides are $20 per hour.

If you're a more experienced equestrian, the **Yonahlossee Resort's Saddle Club,** tel. (828) 963-6400 or (800) 962-1986, caters to the more serious rider. Lessons for folks staying at the resort run $25 per hour, but again, this is for riders who aspire to gallop along the resort's cross-country courses or try out the jump course. Many guests bring their own horses. Yonahlossee's lies about five miles northeast of Blowing Rock and six miles from Boone, at the intersection of Shulls Mill Road and Poplar Grove Road.

ACCOMMODATIONS

Bed and Breakfasts

Downtown Blowing Rock contains three elegant bed and breakfasts, all within a few steps of each other on Sunset Drive. The **Inn at Ragged Gardens,** 203 Sunset Dr., tel. (828) 295-9703, was built as a seasonal summer "cottage" back at the turn of the century, when a mountain cottage could be an elegant mansion with stone columns and floors, a dozen bedrooms, and spacious living, dining, and sitting areas. In 1996, Lee and Jama Hyett bought the inn, closed it for three months of renovations, and succeeded in creating an atmosphere of rare elegance. They preserved marvelous original touches like the fine woodwork, old fixtures, chandeliers, and the "ragged" 70-year-old American Chestnut bark shingles that cover the outside. And the Hyetts added equally splendid new touches, including fine antiques, skylights, and jacuzzis. Among their many grand creations and restorations is the Rock Garden Garret. Tucked under the attic eaves, this two-room suite features a king-size bed, English pine antiques, and extras like two skylights, window seat, jacuzzi, and unique indoor rock garden and fountain. Weather permitting, you may enjoy a sumptuous breakfast on the outdoor patio, beside the lovely gardens. This elegance doesn't come cheap, however, with seven of the eight bedrooms and suites going for $135-150 a night. Expensive-Luxury.

A few steps up and across the street, **Maple Lodge** at 152 Sunset Dr., tel. (828) 295-333, offers 11 impeccably decorated rooms, and a two-bedroom, two-bath cottage out back. The rooms begin at $80 a night; the cottage costs up to $150 a night. The rather bland, colonial-style exterior of the lodge, built in 1946, masks the comfortable, country atmosphere inside, including the immaculate rooms and the effortless hospitality of innkeepers Marilyn and David Bateman. Moderate.

Across the street, at 239 Sunset Dr., **Crippen's Country Inn,** tel. (828) 295-0388, is another recently renovated, old kid on the block. Jimmy and Carolyn Crippen and chef extraordinaire James Welch bought the place in 1994, and Crippen's has since become a celebrated "full-service" country inn, complete with a world-class restaurant and elegantly appointed rooms. Although Crippen's doesn't provide the quiet intimacy offered by neighboring bed and breakfasts, the activity of the restaurant and the small bar/lounge on the ground floor affords a comforting yet cosmopolitan atmosphere and fabulous food, ideally suited for couples who struggle between staying at a Hilton or a homey bed and breakfast. Rooms range $80-110 a night, depending upon the season. A private two-room cottage out back is available for $140 a night. Moderate-Expensive.

Inns

Established in 1882, the **Green Park Inn,** tel. (800) 852-2462, located about two miles southeast of downtown Blowing Rock on US 321, still retains its venerable roots as one of the premier mountain meccas of the past century.

When the inn first opened, the town of Blowing Rock didn't exist, and the inn was so isolated that it was, of necessity, a self-sufficient community. It had its own post office, resident physician, farm, dairy, and, although gambling was illegal, a discreet casino and barroom in separate buildings. Listen closely, as you sway back and forth on one of the inn's plentiful wicker rockers, and you might hear the echoes of former guests like Eleanor Roosevelt or J.D. Rockefeller. The 85-room inn includes several roomy suites and extras like a comfy library and lobby, as well as a top-flight continental restaurant and friendly English pub. Although most of the rooms may appear somewhat ordinary by today's standards, the Green Park's rates make this an affordable trip to the splendor of yesteryear. Single rooms start at $69 Dec.-April, and $99 May through November. The variety of suites range $99-165. Moderate-Expensive.

Resorts

Tennis buffs, horseback riders, and their horses board at **Yonahlossee Resort and Club,** located off Shulls Mill Road, off NC 105, tel. (828) 963-6400 or (800) 962-1986. Yonahlossee is geared toward serving visitors who are looking for active relaxation. The resort includes six outdoor tennis courts and three indoor courts for the racket set, cross-country and jumping courses for the equestrian-oriented, and an indoor pool and fitness center. Rooms at the inn begin at $99 a night in season, and cottages start at $149 per night. Private homes and condos are also available for rent, at Luxury prices. Expensive.

Chetola Lodge and Conference Center, tel. (828) 295-5500 or (800) 243-8652, Blowing Rock's heavily marketed major resort, has hospitality roots that extend back to the 1850s, when an inn on this spot served as a way station for folks traveling by horse-drawn coaches. In the early 1900s, lumber baron W.W. Stringfellow bought the property and built the gracious manor house, which is home today to the elegant and expensive Hearthside Restaurant. The rest of the resort, however, has the antiseptic atmosphere common to conference centers. To give Chetola its due, we should mention that it does offer first-class amenities, including an indoor pool, fitness center, sauna, whirlpool, racquetball and tennis courts, and boating on the seven-acre Chetola Lake. Constructed in 1988, the lodge has 42 clean and pleasantly decorated guest rooms and suites that feel more appropriate to corporate retreats than personal vacations. In addition to the lodge's guest rooms, you can rent one of the 51 condos at the resort. Room and condo prices range from $109-350 a night. Premium-Luxury.

Motor Inns

The town of Blowing Rock features several motels where you can rest your car and exercise your legs while exploring the dozens of nearby shops and restaurants. You'll notice a wide range of prices for these accommodations. That's partly because these are not "cookie cutter" lodgings. Most are family-owned, and rooms often differ in size and the number of extras offered, from fireplaces, porches, and balconies to jacuzzis. Certain times of year also have an effect on the price of accommodations, when rooms in Blowing Rock become a much sought-after commodity, particularly during the dog days of summer, when flatlanders long for the feel of a cool mountain breeze, and in mid to late October, when the dazzling leaf-changing season fires up the hillsides with blazing colors.

The **Meadowbrook Inn** on N. Main Street, tel. (828) 295-4300 or (800) 456-5456, offers 46 comfortable rooms (two with fireplaces) and extras like an indoor pool, exercise room, and the on-site Garden Restaurant and lounge. Rates range $79-159. Moderate-Luxury.

The **Blowing Rock Inn** on N. Main Street, tel. (828) 295-7921, also has a pool, though this one is outdoors. Open April-Nov., the inn offers 24 pleasantly decorated rooms ranging in price from $43 in April to $70 during the summer and autumn. You can also try one of the inn's four villas, which each include a kitchen and fireplace. The villas range $59-125. Inexpensive-Premium.

Also on N. Main Street, the **Mountainaire Inn and Log Cabins,** tel. (828) 295-7991, offer a variety of accommodations, in addition to a swimming pool and exercise room. Take your pick between single rooms with one or two beds, two-bedroom suites, and log cabins with or without a loft. The prices vary considerably, from Inexpensive ($45) to Luxury ($170).

If a swimming pool isn't a top priority for you, bustling downtown Blowing Rock contains several motels that offer pleasant, well-maintained rooms. The most inexpensive of these, ranging $35-65, are the **Alpine Village Inn** at 297 Sunset Dr., tel. (828) 295-7206, and the quieter **Homestead Inn,** 153 Morris St., tel. (828) 295-9559.

If you don't mind staying on the outskirts of town, you won't be disappointed by the **Cliff Dwellers Inn** on the US 321 Bypass, just south of the junction with US 221, tel. (800) 322-7380. Although the entrance is located near this rather busy intersection, the lodgings are set up on a steep hillside. For $90-105, you'll receive a spacious room with a balcony looking out over Lake Chetola and the surrounding mountains. A few efficiencies and one- and two-bedroom suites are also available at higher prices. Expensive.

Rentals

Half a dozen real estate companies offer a wide variety of cottages, cabins, condos, and homes in the area. If you're staying a week or more, vacationing with a large family, or sharing a vacation with several others, you should investigate this option. You can often rent a spacious house for less than many of the motels and resorts cost. For the biggest selection of rentals, call **Jenkins Rentals** at (800) 438-7803, which, at last count offered 27 cottages, 10 cabins, 25 condos, and 58 homes. **Blowing Rock Properties,** tel. (828) 295-7921, also offers a full selection of rentals.

FOOD AND DRINK

Blowing Rock is blessed with a bountiful collection of restaurants, appealing to a wide range of palates and wallets.

Fine Dining

Among Blowing Rock's top-notch eateries, **Crippen's,** 239 Sunset Dr., tel. (828) 295-3487, is in a class by itself. Since chef James Welch and partners Jimmy and Carolyn Crippen opened Crippen's Country Inn and Restaurant in January 1995, the good news has traveled fast and far. In addition to recently earning rave reviews from *Country Inns* and *Southern Living* magazines, chef Welch was also recently invited for a command performance to prepare his "New World" cuisine at the prestigious culinary James Beard House in Manhattan.

Though the menu changes daily, you'll have a chance to savor such astonishing appetizers as the fabulous potato fritters with Beluga caviar, chive butter, and sour cream ($13), or the celebrated pan-seared Maine sea scallops "sandwich," served between two crunchy lattices of fried potato, with arugula and tomato in a brown butter vinaigrette ($12). The continental entrees with a Southern flair usually run about $20 and might include the barbecue-rubbed rare grilled yellowfin tuna with vegetable slaw, ham-scallion sauce, and corn-fried oysters ($21). The dining room seats 70 comfortably, with plenty of space between the tables.

Just a few steps away, **Stephen's,** 155 Sunset Dr., tel. (828) 295-4344, serves up slightly more straightforward fare, including a variety of beef, veal, duck, chicken, fish, and seafood entrees in the $10-15 range. Stephen's has a few seating options, from the more reserved dining room on the first floor to the casual seating on the second floor, which includes a lively bar with music on the weekends. Weather permitting, you can sit at one of the handful of tables on the second floor balcony overlooking Sunset Drive and sip one of Stephen's popular coffee drinks, or the even more popular ice cream drinks, made with a variety of liquors and locally famous, delectable Kilwin's ice cream.

Three other fine restaurants are located on the outskirts of downtown Blowing Rock on US 321. **Twig's,** tel. (828) 295-5050, offers entrees that will appeal to a wide array of palates, from the New Zealand rack of lamb ($18) and Texas-style T-bone steak ($20) to more exotic items like linguine tossed with smoked trout, cilantro, tomatoes, and baby corn in a light cream sauce, or the fabulous low-country shrimp and andouille sausage served over cheese grits, topped with a lobster cream sauce (both $17). The portions are hefty, so if your appetite starts to wane, get the remainder of your entree wrapped to go so you can exult in the luscious creations forged daily by pastry chef Mario Pedrino, whose cappuccino mousse cake will make your head spin in caffeinated, gustatory delight. The dining atmosphere is enhanced by many thoughtful touches, including fine antiques, fresh flowers on white tablecloths, and colorful paintings on the walls. You can also dine outside, weather permitting. Twig's also has a lively, friendly bar, which features live acoustic blues and rock on Friday and Saturday evenings.

The Riverwood, on a hillside of US 321 just south of the Blue Ridge Parkway entrance, tel. (828) 295-4162, also offers gourmet fare, with entrees in the $15-20 range. The atmosphere is elegant, with about a half dozen intimate dining rooms, many with a lovely hillside view. Fish, seafood, and fowl are the specialties, along with the notorious "Chef's Five Alarm Dangerously Hot Specialty," with chicken ($15) or shrimp ($19).

The Best Cellar, just south of the Riverwood on the US 321 Bypass, tel. (828) 295-3446, offers similarly fancy fare, with continental entrees featuring seafood, beef, veal, and fowl, for about $15. In addition, the Best Cellar also includes a popular Oyster Bar, where you can sample enticing New England clam chowder, Cajun shrimp cocktail, and of course, oysters on the halfshell ($7.50 a dozen).

Economical Eats

Downtown Blowing Rock offers a variety of moderate and inexpensive eateries to rest your weary wallet while enjoying a good meal.

For an elegant breakfast, lunch, or brunch, the **Village Cafe,** set back about 20 yards behind Main Street, between Sunset Drive and Morris Street, tel. (828) 295-3769, provides a relaxed atmosphere in a "civilized rustic" setting. The downstairs has the feel of a log cabin, complete with a large stone fireplace. Upstairs, gabled ceilings help create the illusion of space in the rather small, intimate rooms. Outside, tables adorn a pleasant, shaded patio, an ideal spot to ease into the day with a Bloody Mary and a plate of eggs Benedict. Entrees range $5-10.

The **Speckled Trout Cafe and Oyster Bar** at US 221 and Main Street, tel. (828) 295-9474, offers a casual, friendly atmosphere and three square meals a day. With omelettes, smoked trout, or bagels and cream cheese in the morning; burgers or fish sandwiches at lunch; and fish, fowl, or beef at dinner, you'll get a solid meal for $5-12. The she-crab soup, usually offered on the dinner menu, is thrilling.

Next door, on US 221, a pebble's throw from Main Street, **Cheeseburgers In Paradise,** tel. (828) 295-1858, serves up some of the tastiest burgers in North Carolina, which is cursed with a state law that forbids serving hamburger that hasn't been "cooked through." If you temporarily tire of Blowing Rock's refined, gustatory splendors and suddenly get hit with an overwhelming urge to devour a good burger, don't miss this ground beef oasis.

The **Blowing Rock Cafe** on Sunset Drive, tel. (828) 295-9683, is a favorite local diner. For $3-10 you'll get heaping helpings of sturdy country food for any meal of the day.

For a change of pace, **Tijuana Fats** on Main Street, tel. (828) 295-9683, offers a relaxed atmosphere and a wide selection of Mexican eats for $5-8, as well as a friendly bar serving the stiffest margaritas in town.

SHOPPING

Downtown Blowing Rock contains enough gift stores, clothing boutiques, specialty shops, galleries, and antique dealers to keep even the speediest window shopper busy for a day or more. This is not like the shopping districts of so many resort towns, where the seemingly cloned storefronts are plastered with identical arrangements of souvenir T-shirts and sweatshirts. From toys to books, Christmas decorations to dulcimers, the wares of dozens of specialty shops in downtown Blowing Rock provide inviting diversions to a lazy walk through the cozy streets of the town.

Although it's unfair to single out any particular shopping destination here, one deserves a special mention. **Expressions Crafts Guild and Gallery** on Main Street, tel. (828) 295-4248, is a cooperative gallery, owned and operated by dozens of local craftspeople who work in jewelry, fiber, photography, glass, wood, pottery, leather, and more. Here you'll find an creative mix of traditional and contemporary arts and crafts.

Blowing Rock also provides the region's only comfort for shoppers who can't resist factory outlets. The **Shoppes On the Parkway,** located on US 321, tel. (828) 295-4248, house 35 name-brand outlets, from Anne Klein and Ralph Lauren to Seiko and Corning Revere.

INFORMATION

For more information, contact the **Blowing Rock Chamber of Commerce,** P.O. Box 406, Blowing Rock, NC 28605, tel. (828) 295-7851 or (800) 295-7851. Or stop in at their office on Main Street, next to the town park.

BANNER ELK AND VICINITY

With three popular ski resorts within a 10-minute drive of the center of town, Banner Elk is the skiing hub of the High Country. During the high season here—mid-November through mid-March—legions of skiers descend upon the area. After the successful opening of Appalachian Ski Mountain in Blowing Rock, a few slopes were carved out in the Banner Elk area, and snow guns pressed into service. Ironically, the goal behind building the first slopes was to provide a small extra perk to attract more home buyers to the area. But it wasn't long before real estate investors realized that the allure of skiing here could fuel a thriving tourist economy as well as a lucrative real estate market. By the mid-1960s, the High Country ski industry was in full bloom.

As you drive along the roads that wind through the towns of Banner Elk, Sugar Mountain, Beech Mountain, and Seven Devils, you'll see the results of the last three decades' building boom. Clean-cut modern chalets abound, and the restaurants, lodgings, and shops exude the same aura of new construction.

It's pretty hard to get lost in the Banner Elk area, once you know where Highway 184 runs. With the exceptions of the Ski Hawksnest resort and the Inn at Elk River, most sites mentioned in this section lie right alongside Highway 184 between Beech Mountain and the junction of Hwy. 184 and NC 105.

SKI RESORTS

Each of the four major ski resorts in the area has its own distinctive flavor. For information on the tamest, most family-friendly resort, see **Appalachian Ski Mountain** under "Skiing" in the Blowing Rock section. All four resorts feature night skiing and private and group lessons for all ages and levels of expertise. Equipment rentals range $9-15 dollars a day, depending upon the resort and the day of the week.

Ski Beech
At a lofty peak elevation of 5,505 feet above sea level, Ski Beech, on Beech Mountain, tel. (800) 438-2093, boasts the highest skiing east of the Rockies. Ski Beech also provides the most elaborate amenities. While the other resorts feature one main lodge building that forms the center of activity off the slopes, Ski Beech comes complete with its own little pre-fab Alpine village, including a 7,800-square-foot ice skating rink. For eats, you can grab a snack at the Pizza Corner or the cavernous View Haus cafeteria, or settle in next to a fireplace at the Beech Tree Restaurant. For quick energy, there's also a bakery and coffee shop. The Ski Beech Sports Shop offers a full selection of ski fashions and accessories, and the Demo Center and Repair Shop handles used equipment and any tune-ups or repairs your equipment might need.

Ski Beech also offers a tube run, a ride providing downhill thrills you can enjoy sitting down. For $15, you can rent an inner tube for a four-hour session, ride up the tubers-only lift, and then plop your behind in your tube and hang on as you sail down the 475-foot-long course in one of three 12-foot-wide flumes.

Ski Beech's 14 ski slopes are divided into three beginner, seven intermediate, and four expert runs. The vertical drop is the region's second deepest, at 830 feet. In addition, there's a half-pipe for snowboarders. Lift tickets are $27 Mon.-Fri., $41 weekends and holidays (eight dollars cheaper for children 12 and under, or folks 65 and over). For the snow report, call (828) 387-2011.

THE WOOLLY WORM FESTIVAL

On a weekend in mid-October, Banner Elk hosts the annual Woolly Worm Festival. This event, now in its 20th year, owes its roots to Pennsylvania's ritual Groundhog Day observation of Punxatawney Phil to determine how much longer winter will last. Banner Elk's festival establishes a forecast for the winter and celebrates the meteorological prowess of the area's dense population of woolly worms—plump caterpillars with alternating black and reddish-brown stripes of varying widths. The black stripes presage harsh storms, snow, and ice; the reddish-brown stripes portend milder weather. Every woolly worm has its own distinctive pattern of stripes, and the purpose of the Woolly Worm Festival is to determine *which* woolly worm has the most accurate stripes.

On a Saturday in mid-October, about 800 human contestants, cradling fat, fuzzy worms, congregate in downtown Banner Elk and coach their worms up vertical strings in dramatic races for a $500 first prize for the fastest caterpillar. The winner is ceremoniously analyzed by the mayor, who promptly decodes its stripes to foretell the severity of the coming winter.

In addition to the races, the festival features local crafts, food, and live entertainment, including a woolly worm dance on Saturday night at the Holiday Inn. For more information, call (828) 898-5605. Admission to the festival is $3 for adults, $1 for children.

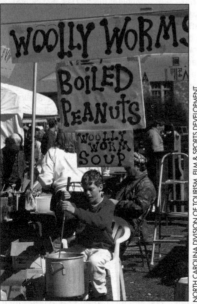

NORTH CAROLINA DIVISION OF TOURISM, FILM & SPORTS DEVELOPMENT

Sugar Mountain

Sugar Ski, tel. (800) SUGAR-MT, prides itself on being number one in North Carolina for the deepest vertical drop (1,200 feet), the longest run (1.5 miles), the largest lift capacity (8,800 people per hour), and the most slopes (19), including seven novice, nine intermediate, and two expert trails, in addition to a snowboard park. Sugar has a peak elevation of 5,300 feet, just 200 feet shorter than Ski Beech. The massive lodge houses two cafeterias, a lounge, restaurant, sports shop, repair shop, and locker room.

Of the four resorts in this area, Sugar Mountain revs at the highest idle, particularly on weekends. If you enjoy the energy and population density of popular dance clubs, you'll love the bustling atmosphere here. While Sugar may be the area's most popular ski resort for folks in their late teens and early 20s, skiers from five to 75 won't feel out of place, as the resort attracts large numbers of families (there's also a nursery for the pre-ski set). Call (828) 898-5256 for the snow report.

Ski Hawksnest

This resort, in Seven Devils, is the favorite of the locals, and it's easy to see why. Ski Hawksnest, tel. (800) 822-HAWK, combines a calmer, less crowded, family-friendly atmosphere with trails at least as challenging as anything Beech and Sugar Ski have to offer. Of the 12 slopes and trails, only two are rated beginner, while five are rated intermediate and five expert, with a maximum vertical drop of 669 feet. What Hawknest's trails lack in length and drop, they make

NORTH CAROLINA DIVISION OF TOURISM, FILM & SPORTS DEVELOPMENT

up for in steepness. The biggest challenge here is the celebrated Top Gun trail, which opened in the 1994-95 ski season. This chilling monster rips along 2,200 feet at an *average* grade of 38 percent.

Ski Hawksnest also offers the most flexible hours of the area's resorts, staying open until 2 a.m. on Friday and Saturday nights, when you can also take in some live music at the lodge's Nest Bar and Grill. If you have a serious desire to ski for an entire day, or if you're a late riser, you can take advantage of Nighthawk, the South's longest continuous ski session (no breaks at all), which begins on Friday at 9 a.m. and concludes 17 hours later at 2 a.m. Saturday.

Lift tickets are $12 Mon.-Fri. (including the marathon Nighthawk session), and $14 on weekends ($2 cheaper for folks younger than 13 and older than 64). For the current snow report, call (828)963-6563.

ACCOMMODATIONS

True to its modern origins as a real estate venture, this area's lodgings are dominated by dozens of real estate companies that manage thousands of condos, cottages, and chalets, while a small number of inns and motels provide just a few hundred rooms. As a consequence, you should seriously consider investigating the rental market, particularly if you're staying a few days or traveling with more than two people. The high season for accommodations is mid Nov.-mid March, when the ski resorts are open. During other times of the year, you can get a great bargain on renting a magnificent home.

Bed and Breakfasts
Hovering near 5,000 feet above sea level, the **Archers Mountain Inn** on Highway 184, tel. (828) 898-9004, rests on a steep hillside near the summit of Beech Mountain. The inn includes 15 elegant rooms, all with their own fireplaces, most with kitchenettes, many with poster beds and chestnut beamed ceilings, a couple with jacuzzis, and 13 with awe-inspiring views of Grandfather and the surrounding mountains. The rooms-with-a-view begin at $80 for a weekday night and $100 on a weekend during the high ski and leaf seasons, and gradually make their way up to $200 for a weekend night in the grand Presidential Suite. Archers also provides ideal accommodations for sprained and sore-muscled skiers, who only have to navigate a few feet from their rooms to the inn's marvelous Jackalope's View restaurant, where guests get a complimentary full breakfast. For a romantic weekend in this area, you can't beat the intimate and spectacular mountain splendor of Archers. Moderate-Luxury.

Country Inns
On the opposite slope of Beech Mountain, still on Highway 184, two Swiss-style inns operated by the same management are located within a few hundred yards of each other. At the **Beech Alpen Inn** and the **Top of the Beech Inn,** tel. (828) 387-2252 for both, you can choose between a variety of lovely rooms, most with exposed beam ceilings and magnificent distant mountain vistas. Even during the high season, these inns provide a great bargain. Stay for two nights Sun.-Thurs., and you can get a room for $45 a night. On weekends, rooms are still just $69. Extra amenities like a fireplace or private

balcony can bring the cost to $59-135 a night. Inexpensive-Premium.

The **Inn at Elk River,** tel. (828) 898-9669, has a few unique attributes. For one, it's located a couple miles east of Banner Elk on Highway 194—not on the main drag of Highway 184, which contains most of the area's commercial lodgings. For another, the Inn at Elk River is the only lodging in the region that bills itself as a "Williamsburg style colonial inn," a change of pace from the typical faux-Swiss-ski-resort-style architecture so prevalent in this area. Amenities include the antique furniture and cozy wood fireplaces in most rooms. A full breakfast is included at the inn's restaurant, which also serves elegant dinners, open to the public. The "lodging tariffs" range $95-145. Expensive-Premium.

Hotel/Motels

The only lodging resembling a conventional, chain-like hotel/motel in the area is the 101-room **Holiday Inn Express,** on Highway 184, a mile north of Sugar Mountain, tel. (828) 898-4571 or (800) HOLIDAY. All rooms have free HBO, and you can have breakfast, lunch, or dinner on the premises at the Elk Cafe. During the warmer seasons, you can enjoy the outdoor pool. Inexpensive-Expensive, depending upon the season and day of the week.

Rental Agencies

The following list is not comprehensive and mentions only some of the many real estate agencies in the Banner Elk area that offer packages of daily, weekend, weekly, and monthly rentals. Rates range Moderate-Luxury.

Accommodations Center of Beech Mountain, 500 Beech Mountain Parkway, Beech Mountain, NC 28604, tel. (828) 387-4246 or (800) 258-6198. 40 cottages, 25 condos.

Bears Real Estate & Rentals, 2904 Tynecastle Hwy., Unit 2, Banner Elk, NC 28604, tel. (828) 898-4546 or (800)543-7551. 12 cottages, 125 condos, 1 cabin.

Beech Mountain Chalet Rentals, 405 Beech Mountain Parkway, Beech Mountain, NC 28604, tel. (828) 387-4231 or (800) 368-7404. 80 cottages, 20 condos.

Beech Mountain Realty and Rentals, 401 Beech Mountain Parkway, Beech Mountain, NC 28604, tel. (828) 387-4291 or (800) 845-6164. 50

cottages, 10 efficiencies, 15 condos, 1 cabin.

Dereka's Sugar Mountain Accommodations Center & Realty, Inc., 106 Sugar Mountain Dr., Banner Elk, NC 28604, tel. (828) 898-9475 or (800) 545-9475. 17 cottages, 6 efficiencies, 130 condos, 1 cabin.

Paramount Realty Co., P.O. Box 1616, Banner Elk, NC 28604, tel. (828) 898-6006. 5 houses, 12 condos, 4 cabins.

Pinnacle Inn Resort, 301 Pinnacle Inn Dr., Beech Mountain, NC 28604, tel. (828) 387-4276 or (800) 438-2097. 180 condos.

FOOD AND DRINK

For food and drink in the Banner Elk vicinity, you never have to stray off the stretch of Highway 184 between Banner Elk and Beech Mountain.

Without question, the premier eatery in the area is the **Louisiana Purchase,** on Highway 184 about 100 yards south of its intersection with Highway 194 in Banner Elk, tel. (828) 898-5656, an elegant restaurant where you can feast on Cajun, Creole, and French delicacies that will transport you to Bourbon Street. From the classy decor and professional wait staff to the luscious food and comprehensive wine list, this place is first-class. For appetizers you'll be tempted with rich crawfish-corn chowder ($3.75) or the fabulous Muscovy Duck, a hickory-smoked Muscovy duck breast on portabella and sundried tomato salad, fresh mozzarella, and roasted garlic herb vinaigrette ($10). Most entrees are under $20, including the jambalaya and Cajun seafood etouffee (both $16), and the blackened fish Bourbon Street, topped with sautéed crawfish tail meat, shallots, and green onions in an etouffee sauce, finished with bernaise ($18). Live jazz is performed on weekend evenings. Open for dinner only; reservations are recommended.

Just across the street, but far across the restaurant spectrum, the humblest joint in the area serves $3 breakfasts, lunches that peak at $5, and dinner entrees that max out under $7. Open 7 a.m.-10 p.m., the **Banner Elk Cafe,** tel. (828) 898-4040, may not have much atmosphere, but their Formica tables fill up quickly around mealtimes. If you have to wait for a table during ski season, you might find it to be a slightly chaotic affair, based upon a "survival of the boldest and rudest" theory. But once you're seated, the food comes fast and tastes fine. Takeout is also available.

A few dozen yards away, at the intersection of Highways 184 and 194, the **Corner Palette,** tel. (828) 898-8668, also provides three square meals a day, as well as slightly fancier fare. A favorite of the locals, the wood-paneled rooms and the bright, cozy porch provide a pleasant, relaxing atmosphere. Full breakfasts generally cost $3-5, with a delightful eggs Benedict for $6.25. For lunch, you can choose between burgers, pasta, and chicken or fish sandwiches, which average $6. You can have the same sandwiches for dinner (at the same prices), or opt for steaks, pastas, poultry, or fish for about $12 per entree.

On the hillside of Beech Mountain, between Banner Elk and the town of Beech Mountain on Highway 184, **Jackalope's View** at Archers Inn, tel. (828) 898-9004, serves good food, but what makes this a great place to eat are its magnificent views of Grandfather and Sugar Mountains and the valley stretching out before you for miles. Dinner offerings include seafood, steaks, poultry, and pasta ($11-20). You can also get full breakfasts; eggs, pancakes, French toast, omelettes, (and often, quiches or crepes) run about $6.

Between "downtown" Beech Mountain and the Ski Beech resort, the **Alpen Inn Restaurant** at the Beech Alpen Inn on Highway 184, tel. (828) 387-2252, offers similar fare at similar prices, and, depending upon your table, a similarly magnificent view from the opposite side of Beech Mountain. Dinner entrees, including the highly recommended crab cakes, hover in the $14-20 range. The relaxed, Swiss mountain lodge atmosphere helps to make this a pleasant spot to dine.

For an inexpensive snack ($2-4), the **Backside Deli,** tel. (828) 387-4838, at Fred's General Mercantile Company in the town of Beech Mountain, serves soups, sandwiches and desserts you can enjoy on a bright, enclosed patio. Fred's can also pack a picnic basket for you.

SHOPPING

Fred's General Mercantile Company, tel. (828) 387-4838, in the town of Beech Mountain, presents a nouveau version of the venerable Mast General Store in nearby Valle Crucis. Fred's bold motto reads "If we don't have it, you don't need it," and the vast variety of stuff available here backs up Fred's claim. In addition to the above-mentioned deli, Fred's provides groceries, clothing, hardware, crafts, gifts, mountain gear, candy, and a full array of skiing equipment, plus a separate section called the Wildbird Supply Company (open April-Nov.), a mecca for birders. In a separate building right beside Fred's is the affiliated **Wizards Toy Shop.** It may be small, but it's packed from floor to ceiling with thousands of engaging toys and games.

INFORMATION

For visitor information about this area, contact the **Banner Elk Chamber of Commerce,** P.O. Box 335, Banner Elk, NC 28604, tel. (828) 898-5605 or (800) 972-2183.

VALLE CRUCIS

In the tiny town of Valle Crucis stands the venerable **Mast General Store,** tel. (828) 963-6511, built in 1883 and little changed over the years. Reach into the old-fashioned freezer and grab a Coke, then sit a spell beside the old potbellied woodstove inside, or head out to the swings on the back porch. Or better yet, wander up and down the aisles, enjoy the creaky, century-old floorboards, and gaze at the wondrously diverse merchandise stuffed into every available space. The store is not quaint for quaint's sake—it's an actual working store, transporting you back to a time long before malls, when you could get almost anything at the local general store.

Accommodations

Since 1987, the talented husband-and-wife team of Roland and Chip Schwab have run **The Inn At Taylor House,** on N.C. 194 in Valle Crucis, tel. (828) 963-5581. Roland, whose family owned a small hotel in Switzerland, is a fifth-generation innkeeper who graduated from the prestigious École Hôtelière de Lausanne, and Chip formerly operated the noted Truffles Cooking School in Atlanta. Together, they have created an inn whose ambience pays high tribute to the

High Country's turn-of-the-century moniker of "America's Switzerland." Built in 1911, this two-story farmhouse with a wraparound porch, is decorated with an eclectic mix of European and American country antiques, along with fine Oriental rugs. The six guest rooms include a suite with a sitting room and fireplace. The $110-145 rates include Chip's gourmet breakfasts. Open April-December. Premium.

The **Mast Farm Inn,** on route 1112 a couple miles east of the Mast General Store, tel. (828) 963-5857 or (888) 963-5857, provides both immaculate lodgings and the best cooking (open to the public) in town. Built in the 1880s, the Inn's charming, country decor rooms range Moderate-Luxury, depending upon whether you'd prefer one of two smaller dormer rooms for $75 a night, the more spacious guest rooms in the farmhouse that range $100-125 a night, or the luxury cottages, which are also restored structures from the 19th century, including the Loom House, the Blacksmith and Woodworker's Shops, and the top-of-the-line Granary, which includes two bedrooms, two baths, a whirlpool tub and kitchen for $185 a night. The two-story cottages and Granary, with meticulously restored woodwork, provide particularly romantic, memorable lodgings.

If you're staying at the Mast Farm Inn, a full country breakfast is included (guests only for breakfast). If you're not staying there, you might want to try the inn Thurs.-Sat. for dinner, or Sunday for brunch at 12:30 and 2 p.m. The dining area consists of two cozy, wood-paneled rooms, where, for a fixed price of about $15, you'll be treated to a hearty family-style meal, including an appetizer, entree, dessert, and non-alcoholic beverage. A typical night's menu might be sautéed mountain trout, followed by Beef Burgundy, vegetable strudel, garden vegetables, coleslaw, corn bread, and your choice of pie or cake. You're welcome to bring your own wine ($1.25 corkage fee). Call (828) 963-5857 for a reservation.

FOSCOE AND SEVEN DEVILS

About six miles south of Boone, just off NC 105 in Foscoe, the **Hound Ears Club,** tel. (828) 963-4321, offers rooms, suites, chalets, and extras that make this resort an ideal destination for the athletically oriented traveler. In addition to the tennis courts and heated pool, the Hound Ears has two small ski slopes (one beginner, one intermediate), a magnificent golf course, and a first-class restaurant. Although the rates are Premium April-Nov., they include both breakfast and a gourmet dinner. The same accommodations, without meals, come at Moderate prices from early November through the first week in April.

Riches await you at the **Greater Foscoe Mining Company,** 7.5 miles from Boone, tel. (828) 963-5928. Here, you buy a bucket of dirt and dip a screen into a water flume to sift for jewels. The buckets of dirt are "enriched" gem ore (i.e., gems are added), so you're almost guaranteed to find some pretty stones in every bucket. This is a fabulous hit with young kids, whose rapt attention at the flumes approaches video-game levels. Buckets come in a wide range of sizes, costing $5-100. Gems can be polished, cut, and set on the premises.

About 12 miles south of Boone along NC 105, about a mile north of the turnoff for Ski Hawknest resort, **Smoketree Lodge,** tel. (828) 963-6505, gives you a lot of bang for your buck, including large rooms and a sizeable indoor pool with adjacent whirlpool and weight room. A creek with a small waterfall curls around the lodge, set on a hillside. Smoketree is a great bargain, offering studios, one- and two-bedroom suites, all with kitchenettes, from $55-90 a night, $300-475 a week. Inexpensive-Expensive.

Along NC 105 between Boone and Route 184, you'll know you're near Foscoe and Seven Devils when you start seeing lots of antique stores along the side of the road. Near the end of this antique row, a few yards from the turn-off to Ski Hawksnest Resort, at the junction of NC 105 and Skyland Drive, you can pull off the road and walk to four antique shops, all in a row. **Gilded Age Antiques** features fine English, French, and French Country pieces, the **Mulberry Cat** displays garden furniture, accessories, and other antiques, while **Marjori's Antiques** and **Stoney Creek Antiques** cater more to the "trash and treasure" crowd, hunting for old bottles, weather vanes, and other fun furniture and accessories.

ROAN MOUNTAIN AND THE APPALACHIAN TRAIL

The peerless Appalachian Trail winds for about 15 miles through this region, beside the Tennessee-North Carolina border. Beginning at US 19 E. at Elk Park, NC in the north, the A.T. traverses five summits over 5,400 feet above sea level, reaching an apex at breathtaking Roan Mountain (altitude 6,285 feet) at the southern end of this stretch. The summits here are grassy, treeless meadows, which provide such spectacularly panoramic views that you wouldn't be surprised to find Julie Andrews spinning around next to you, belting out "The Hills Are Alive. . . ."

The last couple of weeks in June, Roan Mountain's 600 acres of wild gardens explode with catawba rhododendron blooms, inspiring the 50-year-old **North Carolina Rhododendron Festival,** featuring crafts, food, and entertainment, in nearby Bakersville, NC. For more information on the festival, usually held the third weekend in June, call (800) 227-3912. You can drive to the celebrated Cloudland rhododendron gardens on Roan Mountain. The easiest way to get there from the Banner Elk area is to take Highway 194 east to Elk Park, NC, then proceed north on US 19E into Tennessee to the town of Roan Mountain, where you'll then take Route 143 south to Roan's summit. If you're coming from Asheville, make your way to Highway 261 and proceed north from Bakersville.

GRANDFATHER MOUNTAIN

Rising to 5,964 feet, Grandfather Mountain represents the high point of the Blue Ridge Mountains in more ways than just elevation. Due to its vast biodiversity, this extraordinary mountain has been designated by the United Nations as one of 324 International Biosphere Reserves in the world.

Grandfather Mountain is unique even among those biospheres—it's the only one that's privately owned, by a fellow named Hugh Morton, who is largely responsible for preserving this treasure and who in recent years has donated most of his mountain to the Nature Conservancy. This guy knows how to run a mountain. More than 30 miles of spectacular trails wind around the mountain, home to countless exotic species of plants, as well as 42 rare and endangered animal species.

But you don't need to strap on a backpack and hiking boots to enjoy spending hours with Grandfather (who, appropriately, is great with the kids). In several natural habitat enclosures, you'll get to view and interact with black bears, deer, otters, bald eagles, and cougars, as well as wild chipmunks and groundhogs who make walk-on appearances trying to steal the show and procure some of the peanuts and dried fruit that visitors buy to feed the more celebrated animals.

Grandfather's Nature Museum displays several Smithsonian-level exhibits on topics like the rare flora, fauna, and minerals found here, as well as fun tidbits like a writing sample reputedly carved on a Grandfather tree by a legendary mountain man, which reads "D. BOON KILLD A BAR O THIS TRE 1775." The museum also includes a cozy movie theater showing a variety of documentary films about Grandfather every hour. The museum also houses a cafeteria, restrooms, and a gift shop well stocked with fun and informative materials.

From the habitat enclosures and museum, you can drive up the mountain to the parking lot, where a short flight of steps will lead you to the celebrated Mile-High Swinging Bridge, strung over a chasm that plunges a few hundred feet below. Although engineers maintain that the steel-cabled bridge could support hundreds of visitors, the imposed limit is 40 folks at a time. Even that seems a bit high—*five* people on the bridge at one time, with or without a gusting wind, is enough to inspire visions of cables unraveling and bodies plummeting into the chasm. (Not surprisingly, a recent study found that 16.5% of the folks who come to the bridge refuse to cross it.) Whether or not you choose to cross the bridge, your breath will be taken away by the grand vistas of the southern Appalachians.

Across the parking lot from the swinging bridge begins Grandfather Trail, the park's most popular trail. The first major summit on the trail is Macrae Peak (elevation 5,939 feet), the tallest summit visible from the parking lot. Although this trail is only nine-tenths of a mile to Macrae, it's a *long* nine-tenths. It includes ladder climbs and is often quite slippery and muddy (you should wear shoes with good traction—hiking boots are best). Believe the warnings at the trailhead cautioning you that this is a difficult trail, but don't be intimidated by them (or by our caveats); it's not a *dangerous* trail, and if you're up to it, you'll find that the extra effort will reward you with unforgettable views and an appreciation for the rugged nature of this mountain. The trailhead sign doesn't mention that you should tote some water and snacks, but you'll be glad if you do (incidentally, pack those refreshments, rather than carrying them—you'll need both hands to negotiate several spots).

Grandfather got its name because its ridgeline looks remarkably like the profile of your average grandfather, stretched out on his back, snoring away on the sofa. Similarly, although he can be cantankerous at times, you'll find Grandfather Mountain's treats well worth the visit. Admission is $9 for adults and $5 for kids ages 5 through 12). The museum, animal habitats, and some picnic areas are accessible to visitors with disabilities. The entrance to the mountain is two miles east of Linville on US 221. For more information, call (800) 468-7325.

Grandfather Mountain Highland Games

During the second full weekend in July, the slopes of Grandfather erupt with the blare of bagpipes and bold plaids, as more than 100 Scottish clans and societies gather on Macrae Meadows on US 221 to hold the annual Grandfather Mountain Highland Games. In addition to traditional Scottish contests, such as the tossing of cabers and track and field events, there's pageantry aplenty, beginning with the torchlight ceremony that inaugurates the games on Thursday night. Traditional food, highland dancing, and lots of inspired piping and drumming add a unique flavor to this energetic festival.

Eseeola Lodge

For grand lodging, dining, and golf in the shadow of Grandfather Mountain, **Eseeola Lodge** in Linville, tel. (828) 733-4311 or (800) 742-6717, provides all three, par excellence. Open mid-May through late October, Eseeola has been one of the premier mountain resorts in North Carolina since its creation at the turn of the century. Rebuilt after a fire destroyed most of the original lodge in 1936, the lodge exudes an elegant country decor, from the masterful stonemasonry and woodwork to the fine furniture and manicured grounds.

Eseeola is home to the famed **Linville Country Club golf course,** one of legendary designer Donald Ross's proudest jewels. Built in the 1920s, this course recently won *Golf Digest's* highest distinction as a "Super Value," one of only 25 courses in the nation earning that designation. Greens fees for guests of the lodge run about $55.

Whether you spend your day on Grandfather Mountain, in the lodge's heated pool, or on the clay tennis courts or golf course, return to Esseola for a magnificent continental dinner. Dining is a formal affair, so gents must wear a jacket and tie. The lodge's Luxury rates include both breakfast and the fabulous gourmet dinner. (Nonguests must make a reservation for the prix fixe dinners, about $30 per person.)

ASHEVILLE AND VICINITY

As you glide through the glorious Blue Ridge Mountains and enter Asheville, you can see why, in the late 1700s, the first settlers of this city called it "Eden Land." It nestles in a wide, gently sloping valley, with the dramatic skyline of the Blue Ridge Mountains rising in the distance and presenting an ever-changing panorama. Downtown, the man-made skyline blends examples of at least four architectural styles with effortless grace. The 62,000 citizens of Asheville affect a similarly eclectic but harmonious mix, as the Armani-suited, polyester-clad, and tie-dyed mingle at the friendly cafes and coffeehouses. The climate is mild (though winter can bring some snow), the cultural scene vibrant and thriving, the restaurants diverse, the nightlife hopping, and the recreational opportunities endless. From a descriptive standpoint, Asheville is a city of superlatives, whose boundless charms make it an enchanting base for exploring the mountains of North Carolina.

History

In 1784, William Davidson took his wife and children up into the mountains seeking a solitary life. They became the first European settlers to make a home in this valley, but they weren't alone for long. By the following year, a handful of other homesteaders arrived, and a permanent settlement was established. A few more pioneer families arrived each successive year, and within only seven years there was enough of a municipal presence for Davidson and his friend Colonel David Vance to succeed in officially establishing Buncombe County on December 5, 1791.

The next year, a politically savvy fellow named John Burton finagled a land grant from the state government for 21 acres in the county (this includes today's downtown). He called his purchase Morristown, in honor of Robert Morris, who played a major part in financing the American Revolution, and who owned land in the region.

Though politically adept, Burton was not the shrewdest of real estate developers. He divided his land into 42 half-acre parcels and sold those for $2.50 apiece. Burton's hundred-buck bonanza brought enough people to the area that by 1797 Burton incorporated the town and renamed it in honor of another powerful figure who controlled a lot of land, Samuel Ashe, the governor of North Carolina from 1795 to 1798.

But try as they might, Burton and other chamber-of-commerce types could not attract enough settlers to create the glistening mountain metropolis of their dreams. By 1840, Asheville's population had grown to only 500 citizens. In 1824, city fathers took action to have the Buncombe Turnpike routed near Asheville. When

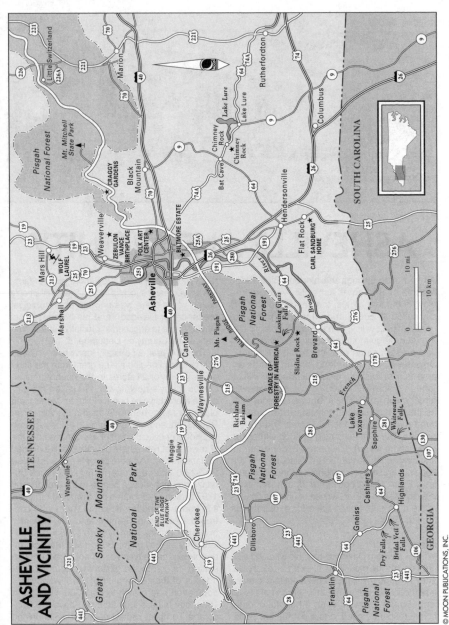

ASHEVILLE AND VICINITY

© MOON PUBLICATIONS, INC.

ASHEVILLE'S MILD MOUNTAIN CLIMATE

At an altitude of 2,500 feet above sea level, Asheville has long attracted visitors for its temperate summer weather. But its southern location also tempers the winter here. The following are average highs and lows throughout the year. Asheville is an ideal spot to dress in layers.

MONTH	HIGH	LOW
Jan.	42° F	23° F
Feb.	52° F	29° F
March	60° F	35° F
April	72° F	45° F
May	73° F	48° F
June	83° F	62° F
July	80° F	63° F
Aug.	82° F	65° F
Sept.	75° F	54° F
Oct.	66° F	45° F
Nov.	63° F	37° F
Dec.	53° F	35° F

completed, in 1828, the Buncombe united "the two Greenvilles"—in South Carolina and Tennessee. This road wasn't anywhere close to what we think of as a turnpike today; it wasn't much more than a narrow clearing cut through the forest, and its uneven surface was dominated not by carriage-riding travelers from the East but rather by drovers herding livestock to market from Tennessee and Kentucky. As a result, Asheville's main streets frequently reeked of cow, sheep, and hog manure. However, in spite of its small population and pungent streets, word began to spread about the region and the city.

In 1851, the Asheville and Greenville Plank Road was completed, and the first wealthy tourists began visiting, arriving in four- and six-horse stagecoaches. The inns that had opened to accommodate cattle and sheep herders slowly multiplied. During the Civil War, Asheville became a transportation hub for Confederate supplies, exposing thousands of Dixie's loyal troops to the town's appeal. When federal troops occupied the city during the final months of the war, they burned only the armory before returning home, where they, too, spread glowing reviews of Asheville.

The fledgling hospitality industry continued to expand. In 1880, the railroad came to town, and with it modern industry. Lumber and textile mills sprang up alongside tobacco warehouses and markets.

Of all the things the railroad brought to Asheville, perhaps the most lasting legacy came in the form of a young bachelor from New York City. In 1888, at the age of 26, George Vanderbilt, one of the heirs to America's premier railroad empire, was traveling with his mother when he stopped in Asheville. Although he had toured much of the globe, Vanderbilt christened the area "the most beautiful place in the world" and decided to live there. He soon bought 125,000 acres of land, beginning at the southern outskirts of Asheville and spreading south (including much of what is today Pisgah National Forest). Vanderbilt engaged the nation's top architects and designers to fashion him a French Renaissance-style chateau and working estate. From 1890 to 1895, employing hundreds of America's and Europe's best artisans and construction workers, they built the incomparable Biltmore Estate. With 255 rooms in the main house, Vanderbilt's chateau accommodated lots of highbrow visitors, who infused the conversation of high society circles from New York to Paris with tales of the astonishing beauty of "George's place."

Luxury inns and hotels began to sprout up to accommodate the wealthy folks who couldn't wrangle an invitation to Biltmore but still wanted to experience the neighborhood's majesty. The most celebrated and enduring of these lodgings, still thriving today, is the Grove Park Inn, built in 1913 on Sunset Mountain, overlooking the city. The inn drew widespread praise from notables including Thomas Edison, F. Scott Fitzgerald, Henry Ford, Will Rogers, and Calvin Coolidge. By the mid-1920s, Asheville had become a major mountain mecca for the rich and famous.

For decades, the city had sought and received huge loans from local banks to erect grand buildings, from City Hall to schools and everything in between. As a result, when the stock market crashed in 1929, Asheville won the dubious honor of possessing the highest per-capita civic debt of any city in America. Unlike many cities, Asheville's city government steadfastly refused

THE EVOLUTION OF "BUNKUM"

Asheville's home county, Buncombe, was established in 1792 and named for Edward Buncombe, a hero in the Revolutionary War. In the 1820s, though, his name would acquire a much greater (and profoundly unheroic) currency. In a controversial debate during North Carolina's Sixteenth Congress, Buncombe County's congressman, Felix Walker, rose on the floor of the House and delivered a passionate oration expressing the merits of both sides of the issue at hand (carefully omitting his actual opinion).

Justifiably confused, a colleague rose and asked for which side Walker was speaking. Walker rose briefly and replied, "I was just talking for Buncombe."

Walker served only one term—1819-1821—but his talent for lofty but empty equivocation inspired use of the word "buncombe" to mean, in the words of one dictionary, "empty speech-making for political effect or to please constituents." The spelling eventually evolved into "bunkum," and the word (and its diminutive, "bunk," and antonymous verb, "debunk") is still with us.

to default on a single bond. In fact, the city didn't pay off all of its Depression-era debts until 1977. For architecture lovers, this pay-what-you-owe policy reaped tangible benefits. During the 1950s, '60s, and '70s, while other cash-cow cities elected to invest in razing their old neighborhoods in favor of vast assemblages of steel and glass "business districts," Asheville chose the cheaper path of touching up the graceful stone, brick, and tile of its existing downtown buildings. This gives Asheville today an invitingly walkable downtown, generously peppered with cafes, bistros, fine restaurants, shops, and office and apartment buildings—all preserving the richly eclectic architectural history of this lovely city.

SIGHTS

Asheville and the surrounding area teem with diversions. Parks, gardens, museums, and historical sites abound.

The Museums at Pack Place

At the center of town (easternmost end of Patton Ave.), the **Pack Place Education, Arts & Science Center,** on Pack Square, tel. (828) 257-4500, includes four museums.

At **Health Adventure,** a hit with kids, a five-foot brain details the workings our little gray cells. The Bodyworks Gallery takes you on a quick 60,000-mile-tour of the human body's circulatory system and invites you to test your leaping abilities on the jumping wall or see how many pounds you can levitate at the safe lifting station. The NutriSpace Gallery includes a grocery counter enumerating the fat, sugar, salt, and fiber content of various foods and lets you walk on a giant set of dentures. At the Miracle of Life Gallery, a glass-skinned model leads you through a tour of human reproduction. The Creative Playspace encourages kids under eight to dress up in various garbs from cowboys to pirates, slide down a giant tongue, skipper a boat, and engage in other imaginative role-playing. Lots of other hands-on exhibits will delight kids and adults' "inner children."

The **Colburn Gem and Mineral Museum** features a dazzling display of more than 1,500 minerals and gems from North Carolina and around the world. This is a great place to learn about the rock-hounding history of North Carolina and see diamonds, rubies, emeralds, and sapphires, along with extraordinary examples of the variety of stones you might pick up in one of the area's prolific roadside gem mines—like a 229-carat blue topaz and a 376-pound aquamarine crystal.

The collection at the **Asheville Art Museum** emphasizes 20th-century works in various media, from paintings and textiles to lithographs and bronze. The museum focuses on the thriving contemporary arts and crafts of the region, through both permanent and changing exhibits.

The **YMI Cultural Center** is housed in an elegant Tudor building, around the corner from Pack Square, at the corner of S. Market and Eagle Streets. Built in 1892 by George Vanderbilt as a community center for the "colored" craftsmen working at Biltmore Estate, the craftsmen bought the Young Men's Institute in 1905. Today, the center, long a hub of African-American arts and culture, continually features a broad array of traveling exhibits, in addition to an impressive permanent collection of African and African-American artworks.

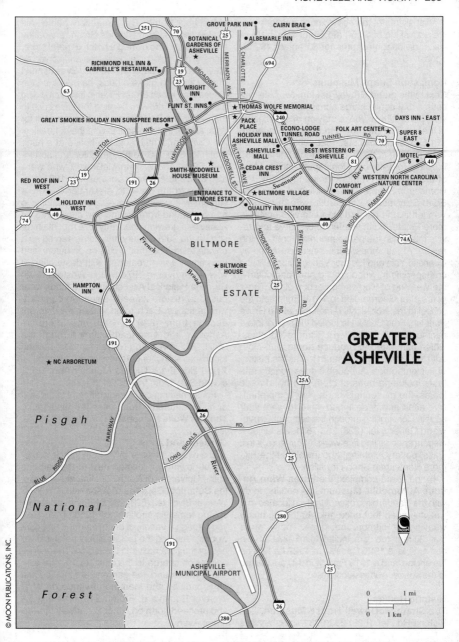

GREATER ASHEVILLE

Visit all four of the above museums for a single admission of $6.50 ($4.50 for kids 4-15) or visit individual museums for $3 apiece ($2 for ages 4-15).

Homespun Shops Museums

Next to the grand Grove Park Inn, two little museums that don't charge admission are worth a visit, particularly if you're staying or sightseeing at the inn. The **Biltmore Homespun Museum,** 111 Grovewood Rd., tel. (828) 253-7651, is an English-style cottage, one of the original shop buildings of Biltmore Homespun Shops. More of a school than a manufacturing facility, the Homespun Shops were established in 1901 by Edith Stuyvesant Vanderbilt, wife of George Vanderbilt, the railroad magnate who built Biltmore Estate. Edith wanted to preserve and revive interest in the native mountain crafts of the region. At the shops, expert instructors, led by Charlotte Yale and Eleanor Vance, tutored young craftspeople in woodcarving and, particularly, the weaving of woolen homespun cloth. Three years after George died in 1914, Edith sold the school to the architect and manager of the Grove Park Inn, Fred Seely. He turned the school into a mini-textile mill and called it Biltmore Industries, which continued to produce homespun cloth until the 1980s. The museum traces the history of this enterprise. Although it does contain artifacts including bolts of cloth and handmade looms, the museum is not a very comprehensive affair and is designed more to whet your appetite for strolling through the adjacent **Grovewood Gallery,** tel. (828) 253-7651, a spacious, elegant shop selling fine works of furniture, rugs, glass, pottery, clothing, and jewelry in the Biltmore Homespun Shops tradition.

In the same complex, the **Estes-Winn Antique Automobile Museum** has nothing to do with the Vanderbilts, except that it's located in a weaving shed that once held 40 looms, busily weaving for Biltmore Industries. Today, more than 20 restored cars, including a 1927 La Salle convertible, a 1926 Cadillac, a 1922 La France fire engine, and a 1913 Ford Model T, are parked in the space. Admission is free.

Historic Homes

The **Smith-McDowell House Museum,** 283 Victoria Rd., tel. (828) 253-9231, is Asheville's oldest brick home. The three-story home was built in the 1840s by James Smith, a wealthy entrepreneur who owned a hotel, general store, tannery, and gold mine in the area and served as Mayor of Asheville in the 1840s. Ever mindful of new ways to make a buck, he built a bridge across the French Broad River in town, providing a short-cut for drovers herding their livestock to markets in the Southeast and charging a toll for each animal that crossed. Before the outbreak of the Civil War, Smith sold the house at a huge profit, for $10,000, to his daughter and son-in-law, Sarah and William McDowell, who were also active in Asheville business. In 1881, McDowell sold the home to Alexander Garrett, a supremely successful real estate speculator who had emigrated from Ireland and capitalized on Asheville's growing popularity as a mountain resort. In the 20th century, the home served as a private residence, then a college dormitory, and then finally was threatened with destruction. It was taken over in 1974 by the Western North Carolina Historical Association, and funds were raised to restore its early splendor, complete with antiques. Each room features a different decade from 1840 to 1900 and interprets Asheville and American history through the Smith, McDowell, and Garrett families, making for an interesting tour. Admission is $3 for adults, $1.50 kids 6-12. Closed Monday April-Dec., closed Sat.- Mon. the rest of the year.

For something completely different in the way of historic homes, don't miss the fascinating **Thomas Wolfe Memorial** in downtown Asheville.

Gardens and Zoos

Just a couple minutes' drive from the skyscrapers of downtown, located next to the campus of the University of North Carolina at Asheville, the **Botanical Gardens of Asheville,** 151 W.T. Weaver Blvd., tel. (828) 252 5190, have been inspiring romantic strolls since 1960. Trails lead you through a variety of bright gardens and dark woods, featuring the extraordinary botanical variety of the flora native to the region. There is no admission charge to the intimate 10-acre site. Open year-round, the gardens are located just off Broadway and Merrimon Avenue on W.T. Weaver Boulevard. From I-240, take exit 5A and proceed north on either Broadway or Merrimon Avenue.

BUT DO YOU *WANT* TO GO HOME AGAIN?

The **Thomas Wolfe Memorial,** 48 Spruce St., tel. (704) 253-8304, in downtown Asheville, is a worthwhile stop even if you've never heard of Thomas Wolfe and don't plan to read any of his work (including the classics *Of Time and the River, The Web and the Rock,* and *You Can't Go Home Again*). In 1929, Wolfe published his autobiographical coming-of-age masterwork, *Look Homeward, Angel,* based on his unusual upbringing in Asheville. The book immediately established Wolfe as one of America's great novelists, a designation that has fallen into dispute over the ensuing decades.

Visiting the Wolfe Memorial, including the boarding house in which he grew up, will give you an intriguingly concrete yet ghostly insight into the writer's unique roots—evidence that truth really is stranger than fiction.

First, a bit of background: Thomas Clayton Wolfe was born in 1900, the last of eight children, the son of William Wolfe, a successful carver of tombstones and homemaker wife, Julia, a former schoolteacher. When Tom was six, Julia decided that she wanted to buy the 18-room Old Kentucky Home boarding house just a few yards up the block. Her husband said he didn't want any part of it—Julia could buy it, but he'd never stay there. She did buy it, and her husband did refuse to spend a night there (until he became ill with cancer and stayed there nonstop from 1921 to 1922).

In 1906, Julia moved up the street and took over the boarding house. She brought only Tom—her youngest—to live with her, separating him from his father and siblings. At first, Tom stayed in a front bedroom with his mother. But after a year or two, Julia decided to rent that room out. She moved to a tiny room off the kitchen. The room was too small to share with Tom, who was getting too old to share a room with her anyway. But giving Tom a room of his own would deprive her of that much rent. So Julia

decided that Tom—from age seven until he left to attend Harvard, a decade later—never had a room he could call his own. He moved around from room to room, often sharing quarters with one or more of the boarders. (Although *Look Homeward, Angel* was largely simple autobiography, his strange, almost Dickensian upbringing led critics to herald it as the work of a powerful imagination.)

Thomas Wolfe died in 1938. When his mother died, in 1945, nothing in the boarding house was removed, so everything you see there today is pretty much the way it looked when she lived and died here. Her big shoes lie next to her bed in the cubicle she occupied next to the kitchen/laundry room. The original furnishings remain. The lighting is the same as it was when Julia expanded the house in 1916 to 29 rooms and added electricity—a lone electric bulb hangs by a cord from the ceiling in the center of each room. A few mementos of Tom's have been incorporated—his typewriter, briefcase, overcoat, *his* size-13 shoes (Wolfe was six and a half feet tall—truly a literary giant).

Although by today's standards, this would be a comfortable bed and breakfast inn, Wolfe referred to it as "having all of the charm and conveniences of a modern jail." His ghost, and that of his mother, haunt a terrific half-hour tour through the house.

Just as this book was going to press, the Wolfe boarding house was fire-bombed by an arsonist, causing extensive damage. The house will be authentically restored, but an estimate of the completion of the restoration was unavailable at press time. The visitors center, however, remains open, showing films and audio-visual presentations about Wolfe's life. Visitors center hours are Mon.-Sat. 9 a.m.-5 p.m. and Sunday 1-5 p.m. April-Oct., Tues.-Sat. 10 a.m.-4 p.m. and Sunday 1-4 p.m. the rest of the year. Admission is $1 for adults, 50 cents for students.

A little farther from downtown, in the southwest outskirts of Asheville near the crossroads of the Blue Ridge Parkway and I-26, the **North Carolina Arboretum,** tel. (828) 665-2492, is a young, ambitious work-in-progress. The gates formally opened on this 424-acre site in the summer of 1996. Although major improvements and additions will continue over the next several years, the arboretum today includes a visitor education center, a greenhouse complex, and a loop trail that leads through showcase gardens featuring native plants. Located on the edge of Pisgah National Forest, this arboretum promises to become one of the most popular attractions in Asheville, particularly when a spur road is connected to the Blue Ridge Parkway. To get there, choose exit 2 on I-26 or the Blue Ridge Parkway at the I-26/US 191 exit. Take US 191 south, turn right onto Bent Creek Branch Road, and right onto Wesley Branch Road. Thanks to its affiliation with the University of North Carolina system, admission to the arboretum is free.

If you want some native fauna to go with your flora, the **Western North Carolina Nature Center,** tel. (828) 298-5600, offers plenty of both, although the emphasis is clearly on the animals. Kids will enjoy this educational center. Your visit begins indoors, where informative, though stat-

ic, archeological displays alternate with vibrant, living exhibits like the working beehive, the reptile and amphibian sections complete with slithering snakes, or the darkened room where you can watch bats, owls, and other nocturnal critters. There's also an aviary. Outside, native animals run a wide gamut, from cougars, wolves, bears, and foxes to deer, turtles, raccoons, sheep, goats, and chickens, some of which you can meet up-close-and-personal in the petting zoo. The engaging nature trails include a boardwalk through treetops. Open daily 10 a.m.-5.p.m. The center is located on route 81, just off I-240, a mile north of the I-240/I-40 junction. Plenty of signs make getting there easy.

BILTMORE ESTATE

"The driveway is measured in miles. The floor plan is measured in acres," proclaim the brochures on Biltmore Estate. What the brochures can't tell you is how utterly captivated you will be by the extraordinary house, gardens, restaurants, shops, and winery that make up Biltmore Estate. Plan to spend at least one full day here. The gates open at 9 a.m., and you won't regret arriving close to that time, so you can leisurely take in

The Biltmore House was under construction from 1889 through 1895.

THE BILTMORE COMPANY, ASHEVILLE, NC

the splendors of this glorious, living monument to the grandeur of the Gilded Age.

Located in south Asheville, nestled in the heart of the Blue Ridge Mountains overlooking Pisgah National Forest, the 250-room mansion, completed in 1895, was conceived by one of the wealthiest industrialists of his time, railroad baron George Vanderbilt, and designed by the foremost architect of the Gilded Age, Richard Morris Hunt. The 75 acres of gardens, park, and grounds surrounding the house were designed by America's premier landscape architect of the 19th and 20th centuries, Frederick Law Olmstead, the designer of New York City's Central Park.

The mansion may seem familiar to you, due to its use as the setting for movies like *Being There* and *Richie Rich,* and for its frequent appearance in print and television ads, when Madison Avenue wants to evoke an image of unparalleled luxury.

Vanderbilt fell in love with this particular spot in North Carolina's Blue Ridge Mountains in the late 1880s. He purchased land, ultimately amassing 125,000 acres, and began planning his dream home. After six years of toil by more than a thousand workers, including hundreds of stonecutters and artisans, Vanderbilt officially opened his house on Christmas Eve 1895. Even today, it is America's largest private residence, with 34 bedrooms, 43 bathrooms, 65 fireplaces, three kitchens, a bowling alley, exercise room, indoor swimming pool, and public rooms of extraordinary beauty.

From I-40, the estate is located just north of exit 50 or 50B on Highway 25. From the Blue Ridge Parkway, the estate is about four miles from the Highway 25 North exit. Phone number is (828) 274-6333 or (800) 543-2961. Open every day except Christmas and Thanksgiving days, Biltmore Estate admission is $30 adults, $23 ages 10-15, free for ages under 10. Make sure to bring extra cash along to take advantage of the restaurants and shops.

The House

Start your visit by taking the self-guided tour of the Vanderbilts' home. The tour will take an hour or two, depending on how much you want to linger, so you might want to visit the restrooms to the right of the main entrance before you enter the residence (an option you won't have inside the house). The addition of the audio tour ($4 per headset) is highly recommended. A brochure, included with the basic admission price, gives thumbnail sketches of most of the rooms on the house tour, but the audio tape allows you the freedom to drink in the extraordinary visual detail of the rooms. The tape is gracefully conceived and executed, and the narrator transports you back a century, helping you imagine that you're one of George and Edith Vanderbilt's guests being given a personalized tour of their singular home at the turn of the century.

In 1895, this house was a model of modern invention, fitted with almost unheard-of amenities, including hot and cold running water, bathrooms off most of the guest rooms, electricity, central heat, mechanical refrigeration, telephones, and even an elevator. Some of Thomas Edison's original light bulbs were placed in the house when it was first built. The showers with hot and cold running water were such a novel invention that permanent instructions were etched onto the faucets.

For more insights into the workings of the house, and for an extra fee, you can take the "Behind-the-Scenes" tour, where you can see the mechanics behind the actual running of the house, including several unrestored rooms (only about 90 of the 250 original rooms have been restored and are open to the public). Don't bother with this particular tour if this is your first visit to Biltmore—there's too much else to experience.

The house contains a vast collection of artworks by masters like Pierre Auguste Renoir, John Singer Sargent, Albrecht Dürer, and Karl Bitter, as well as a rare and stunning ceiling canvass by 18th-century Italian muralist Giovanni Antonio Pellegrini adorning the library ceiling. Ten thousand volumes of the Vanderbilts' massive book collection still remain, while magnificent paintings and prints, sculpture, carvings, tapestries, decorative objects, fabrics, and wall coverings give ubiquitous testimony to the Vanderbilts' love of beauty.

The house, while obviously formal and suited to a more formal age and grand lifestyle, nonetheless exudes an atmosphere of relaxed elegance and comfort. The home's museum-full of rare art treasures are incorporated into the design of each room in a remarkably understated manner, lending the place a uniquely homey feel without the antiseptic ostentation of many palaces of the rich and famous.

For example, in one corner of the airy salon, two comfortable, velvet-cushioned Louis XV-style chairs sit on either side of a small, thin-legged, square walnut table, just a bit wider than the inlaid chess board on the top surface. Small red and white ivory chess pieces, ornately carved in the various human shapes of pawns, knights, bishops and royalty, stand in two lines on opposing sides of the board, ready to do battle. What sets this particular chess set apart from others is that the Vanderbilts' guests knew that when they played with these pieces, they were commanding the same ivory armies on the same walnut battlefield that Napoleon engaged daily during his exile on St. Helena 1815-1821.

A few feet away from Napoleon's chess table, several French doors lead out to the first floor veranda, where guests could take in the grand vistas of the Vanderbilts' backyard, extending to the boundary marker at misty Mount Pisgah, 19 miles away.

When you get through with your tour of the house, head over a few dozen yards to your left, to what used to be the stables. Instead of horses, today you can find mementos to take home from your visit, including toys, books, candy, Christmas ornaments, and other Victorian goodies. You might want to make this first visit a window-shopping one, however, since your next Biltmore Estate excursion should be to explore the gardens surrounding the house.

The Gardens

As you first enter the estate's gates, cruising along the three-mile entrance drive, you'll think you're driving through pleasant, varied, pristine forest. On closer inspection, you'll realize that this is a meticulously planned landscape. The grounds surrounding the Vanderbilt mansion, including thousands of acres extending to the winery and beyond, are an equally magnificent rendering of nature-inspired splendor. The trail-blazing landscape architect who invented this subtle form, Frederick Law Olmstead, planned this "natural-looking" flora almost from scratch. Early photos show a rather barren patch of land denuded by loggers.

Olmstead's beautifully subtle landscaping seems to spring naturally from the earth of the estate as it winds freely across several acres, inviting strolls that can last for hours along the esplanade, terraces, Italian garden, pergola and surrounding bower, shrub garden, walled garden, rose garden, spring garden, azalea garden, conservatory, deer park, bass pond, lagoon, and forest areas. Considering the tireless work required to maintain this intricate botanical network, it's easy to see why the young horticulturist Chauncey Beadle, hired temporarily in 1890 to oversee Olmstead's plan for the grounds, came for a month and stayed a lifetime, until his death in 1950.

Something is always blooming here—in the gardens from early April to November, and in the huge conservatory all year. These garden areas provide striking and subtle contrasts of formal gardens and "natural landscapes." Step out on the Library Terrace next to the house in the early spring and drink in the heavy fragrance of century-old wisteria vines, and then stroll along the adjacent Italian gardens, based on a 16th-century design that includes three lovely pools. The shrub garden, similar to Olmstead's beloved "ramble" in Manhattan's Central Park, offers comfortable walking over steep terrain (it's particularly pleasant in spring, when azaleas and dogwoods bloom). The walled garden next to the conservatory is modeled after an Old English "pleasure garden" and dazzles the eye and nose.

The spacious conservatory provides the stunning flowers and plants that you see walking through Biltmore House. Take a 20-minute walk through this maze of exotic flora and marvel at all the wondrous varieties you could grow for *your* house—if only your backyard had a greenhouse complex half the size of a football field. At The Gardener's Place shop, in the conservatory, you can purchase the beginnings of your own Biltmore gardens.

If you're looking to get away from the crowds for a couple of hours, take the trail to Bass Pond, next to the conservatory. This wonderful stroll leads through the 20-acre azalea garden, a marvel in the spring. On the way back from the pond, take a different route through the azalea garden and veer off to the spring garden, through groves of white pine and hemlock and a cool green meadow, returning you to Biltmore House, where you can take a shuttle bus back to your car.

Once back in your own driver's seat, you can choose to enjoy a meal at the Stable Cafe next to the house, drive to the Deerpark Restaurant for an elegant lunch, or proceed to the winery.

The Winery

Biltmore Estate was conceived as a self-sufficient working estate, patterned after the great noblemen's estates in France and England. In fact, Biltmore House is based on three 16th-century chateaux in the Loire Valley in France. Still self-sufficient today, Biltmore Estate is privately owned and operated and does not receive government subsidies or private grants. The estate is supported by a variety of ventures, including guest admissions, restaurants, a winery, selective logging, and the sale of souvenirs and reproduction furnishings. Employing 650 people, the estate is one of the region's largest employers.

The most recent addition to the estate, the winery is housed in what was once the Vanderbilts' calving barn. The winery opened its production facility in 1984 and has since won over 100 awards for its distinctive wines and earned the title of "the most visited winery in America."

The Biltmore winery is a terrific way to end your trip to Biltmore Estate. The five-mile drive from the parking lots leads you along the winding Swananoa River, past rolling hills populated by grazing cattle, meadows chock full of crops, and Olmstead's subtly enhanced, natural landscapes. If you've ever visited the Provence region of France, this drive will bring back memories.

All Biltmore wines are made solely from grapes picked from the estate's vineyards. The self-guiding tour through the winery can last 10 minutes to half an hour, depending on whether you view the 10-minute introductory film or wait for your kids to do "the grape stomp" in a bucket of grapes (the kids get to keep their grape-juiced footprints on a sheet of paper). At the end, you arrive at the tasting room. In this bright and cheery space, you'll be offered free tastings of one premium and three not-premium-yet-surprisingly-tasty Biltmore vintages. At the adjoining wine shop, for a small charge, you can imbibe more generously poured samples of other varieties of Biltmore's stunning premium wines, including champagnes. For $5, two people can get a few generous sips of three premium wines.

Restaurants

As you might have guessed, all this activity can work up an appetite. Three restaurants plus an ice cream parlor offer plenty of variety. Adjacent to Biltmore House, the **Stable Cafe** originally housed George Vanderbilt's riding and driving horses. Now renovated into a charming restaurant with seating in former stalls and a hay loft, the cafe serves hamburgers, steaks, rotisserie chicken, and salads for $5-10, open 11 a.m.-5 p.m. Next door, the ice cream parlor serves a continental breakfast in the morning and other tasty treats, including fabulous ice cream, 9 a.m.-5 p.m.

Located on the way to the winery, the **Deerpark Restaurant** offers a huge and varied luncheon buffet 11 a.m.-3 p.m. The Deerpark has an airy garden atmosphere with a tree- and plant-filled open courtyard, surrounded by two rows of enclosed tables behind folding glass doors that are opened, weather permitting. The $13 buffet, which changes seasonally, offers several types of salads, and entrees that might include Biltmore trout, hand-carved pork loin, or London broil. Desserts, like chocolate cheesecake with coulis of estate-grown raspberries, cost an extra $3-4. Beer and wine are also extra.

At the winery, the **Bistro** has an outdoor terrace and elevated views of surrounding fields that create the atmosphere of a Provence-style bistro. Lunch and dinner menu items include salads, sandwiches ($5-10), and wood-fired pizzas ($10), as well as fancier fare, including homemade pastas, beef bourguignon with garlic mashed potatoes ($14), or herb- and gorgonzola-roasted leg of lamb *au jus* ($17). A $22 prix fixe dinner includes a limited but delectable choice of appetizers, entrees, and desserts.

Festivals and Events

Biltmore Estate hosts many special events throughout the year. At the end of March, the annual **Easter Egg Hunt** delights kids and adults alike. Early April to early May, during the **Festival of Flowers,** the estate's grounds burst with blossoms, and live music wafts through the gardens, including musical vignettes performed on the Italian Garden stage. Evenings during the Festival of Flowers feature "Amusements of the Gilded Age," including performances inside the house and in surrounding courtyards, with characters created by Shakespeare and Strauss, mountain dancers, and mystics. Dinner is served by candlelight. Reservations are required for these separate-admission evenings ($35, not including dinner).

Christmas at Biltmore is a special time. From mid-November to the end of December, holiday music is performed daily, the halls are decked with holly, wreaths, poinsettias, and 35 decorated Christmas trees, including a magnificent 40-foot Fraser fir in the cavernous banquet hall. In the evenings, the inside of the house is illuminated by candles and fireplaces, and choirs, wind trios, and brass quintets perform holiday compositions. These "candlelight Christmas evenings" require reservations and a separate admission fee ($35 Sun.-Thurs., $37 Friday and Saturday).

RECREATION

Unless you count the exotic hiking trails suffusing Biltmore Estate, the biggest recreational attraction actually in town is **golfing** at the Grove Park Inn, tel. (828) 252-2711 or (800) 438-5800. The course first opened in 1899 and was subsequently redesigned by legendary golf course architect Donald Ross in 1924. Located in a gently sloping valley beneath the Grove Park Inn, the 6,500-yard, par 71 course is not particularly dramatic, but it is utterly immaculate. The thrill of playing here is further enhanced by the knowledge that legends like Bobby Jones, Ben Hogan, Arnold Palmer, and Jack Nicklaus have preceded you along the manicured fairways, greens, and sand traps.

Skiing brings lots of folks to town in the winter, although the closest slopes lie in Mars Hill, about a 45-minute drive north of Asheville on US 23. The newest of Western North Carolina's ski areas, the family-friendly **Wolf Laurel** ski resort, tel. (828) 689-4111or (800) 817-4111, boasts 16 slopes, including a half-pipe for snowboarders and a tubing run. With a peak elevation of 4,600 feet and a vertical drop of 700 feet, Wolf Laurel includes 54 acres of skiable terrain and a double and a quad chairlift. Lift tickets are $20 on weekdays, $30 on weekends. Night skiing is also available 6-10 p.m. Call for more information about the resort and ski packages available at nearby lodgings.

The French Broad River rolls gently through Asheville, but half an hour's drive north of town

rapids roar, particularly in the spring, when the water is highest. Several outfitters offer thrilling **whitewater rafting** adventures on the French Broad. The renowned **Nantahala Outdoor Center,** based in Bryson City, tel. (800) 232-7238, offers three different options at its satellite operation on US 25/70, five miles west of Marshall, NC, a 30-minute drive from Asheville. All of the rafting excursions lead through lush Pisgah National Forest. The half-day trip takes two and a half to three hours and costs $36 ($40 on Saturday). Another half-day trip, covering the same terrain, tacks on another hour and offers a more relaxed pace and time out for a deli lunch ($44-48). Three miles longer than the half-day trips, a full-day excursion including lunch runs four to six hours, depending on the speed of the river ($52-56).

SHOPPING

In 1972, with the opening of the Asheville Mall on Tunnel Road, a slow exodus of the downtown department stores began. But, as the big department stores left, they were eventually replaced by smaller shops and restaurants. Consequently, downtown Asheville streets are lined with loads of antique stores, boutiques, bookstores, galleries, specialty shops, and dozens of spots to stop and enjoy a snack, meal, or libation in between. At **Malaprop's Bookstore and Cafe,** 61 Haywood St., tel. (828) 254-6734, you can wander along creaky floorboards through towering stacks of books, and then get some refreshment in the basement cafe, a favorite local hangout for Asheville's literary set. Even if you're not interested in Malaprop's wares, its location at the corner of Haywood and Walnut Streets is in the heart of one of the most varied and interesting shopping districts in town, making it a good place to start your shopping expedition.

At the entrance to Biltmore Estate, south of downtown, the tree-lined streets of **Biltmore Village** are invitingly walkable, peppered with upscale shops, galleries, and eateries. North of downtown, next to the Grove Park Inn, the **Grovewood Gallery,** tel. (828) 253-7651, features top-of-the-line contemporary and tradiional arts and crafts.

ACCOMMODATIONS

Asheville has two accommodations referral agencies, which do a top-notch job at finding lodgings appropriate to your desires and budget. Both services are free and handle inns, B&Bs, resorts, lodges, cabins, hotels, and motels in Asheville and much of the western North Carolina region. Call **Four Star Accommodations of Asheville** at (828) 232-0001 or (800) 816-8449, or **Asheville Accommodations** at (828) 299-9882 or (800) 770-9055.

Bed and Breakfasts

Asheville is blessed with literally dozens of marvelous bed-and-breakfast inns, ranging from historic Victorian mansions to more modern mountain chalets. The following are just representative

of the excellence that pervades Asheville's inns. If they're booked, or you're looking for something different, you should consider contacting one of the accommodations referral agencies listed above.

Situated on a promontory overlooking the French Broad River, just a five-minute drive from downtown, the **Richmond Hill Inn,** 87 Richmond Hill Dr., tel. (828) 252-8726 or (800) 545-9238, combines new and old with gracious ease. The focal point of the inn is the glorious Queen Anne-style mansion, built in 1889. A century later, the present owners plowed $3 million into restoring the residence to its glory days of the 1890s, outfitting every room with fine antiques and fixtures. Every penny appears to have been efficiently spent, from the extraordinary oak woodwork and Georgian paneling to the claw-footed bathtubs. In addition to the 12 guest rooms in the mansion,

---

ASHEVILLE CHAIN ACCOMMODATIONS

If you're searching for the reliability of chain lodgings, Asheville has plenty to choose from. Unless specified otherwise, all places listed below have the usual amenities of a swimming pool, in-room telephones, and cable TV. In Asheville, peak season generally lasts from the beginning of June until the end of October (during the rest of the year, most rates dip near or below $50 per night).

Best Western Asheville-Central Hotel, 22 Woodfin St., at exit 5A on I-240, tel. (704) 253-1851 or (800) 528-1234. Within walking distance of downtown. Moderate-Expensive.

Best Western of Asheville, 501 Tunnel Rd. (US 70), half mile from exit 7 on I-240, tel. (704) 298-5562 or (800) 528-1234. Moderate.

Comfort Inn, 800 Fairview Rd., at exit 8 on I-240, tel. (704) 298-9141 or (800) 836-6732. Whirlpool and basketball court. Expensive-Luxury.

Days Inn-East, 1500 Tunnel Rd. (US 70), off exit 55 on I-40, tel. (704) 298-5140 or (800) DAYS-INN. Moderate.

Econo Lodge Tunnel Road, 190 Tunnel Rd. (US 70), off exit 7 on I-240, tel. (704) 254-9521 or (800) 553-2666. No pool. Small pets okay. Moderate.

Great Smokies Holiday Inn SunSpree Golf and Tennis Resort, 1 Holiday Inn Drive, off exit 3 on

I-240, tel. (704) 254-3211 or (800) HOLIDAY. Indoor and outdoor tennis courts, 18-hole golf course, two pools, basketball court, and exercise room. Expensive-Premium.

Hampton Inn, 1 Rocky Ridge Rd., at exit 2 on I-26, tel. (704) 667-2022 or (800) HAMPTON. Indoor pool, sauna, whirlpool, and exercise room. Moderate-Expensive.

Holiday Inn Asheville Mall, 201 Tunnel Rd. (US 70), off exit 7 on I-240, tel. (704) 252-4000 or (800) HOLIDAY. Small pets okay. Moderate-Expensive.

Best Western Biltmore West, 275 Smoky Park Highway, off exit 44 on I-40, tel. (704) 667-4501 or (800) 528-1234. Indoor pool, sauna, whirlpool, and exercise room.

Motel 6, 1415 Tunnel Rd. (US 70), off exit 55 on I-40, tel. (704) 299-3040. Inexpensive.

Quality Inn Biltmore, 115 Hendersonville Rd. (US 25), off exit 50 on I-40, tel. (704) 274-1800 or (800) 221-2222. Expensive-Premium.

Red Roof Inn-West, 16 Crowell Rd., off exit 44 on I-40, tel. (704) 667-9803 or (800) THE-ROOF. Pets okay. No pool. Moderate.

Super 8 East, 1329 Tunnel Rd. (US 70), off exit 55 on I-40, tel. (704) 298-7952. Inexpensive.

the inn has two new sets of lodgings, built in the early 1990s. The 15 rooms in the Garden Pavilion overlook a gorgeous parterre garden, complete with waterfall. Nine rooms are located in the Croquet Cottages, situated around a neatly manicured croquet lawn. Though obviously more modern than the century-old mansion, the interiors of the pavilion and cottage rooms emulate the opulence of the main residence. Two superb restaurants are located on-site, including the regal Gabrielle's (see "Food and Drink"), where guests are served a sumptuous breakfast. Luxury rates begin at $150 and climb into the $300 range.

Even older, the **Cedar Crest Inn,** 674 Biltmore Ave., tel. (828) 252-1389 or (800) 252-0310, built in 1891, is another Queen Anne-style beauty, situated on a four-acre estate with Victorian gardens, located just three blocks from the entrance to Biltmore Estate. Some of the artisans who worked on Vanderbilt's Biltmore chateau created the marvelous oak interiors of Cedar Crest. The rooms are charmingly appointed with lovely 19th-century collectibles and antiques like canopied beds, encouraging the "passage to 1890" that the owners seek to provide (though the passage is accompanied by modern amenities like air-conditioning, telephones, and gas fireplaces). Rates range from $120 for regular rooms, $185 for a jacuzzi suite and $210 for the two-bedroom guest cottage, built in 1915, adjoining the house. Premium-Luxury.

The **Wright Inn & Carriage House,** 235 Pearson Dr., tel. (828) 251-0789, is yet another of Asheville's celebrated Queen Anne Victorians. Built in 1899, the eight guest rooms and one suite are all impeccably decorated with an-

THE GROVE PARK INN

Since its opening in 1913, this grand hotel has been hosting a relentless cavalcade of America's rich and famous. As you drive up to the inn, you know you're in for something special. Your first impression is of the red clay roof, which from a distance looks as if it's been melted over the stone frame of the building, á la Salvador Dali, drooping over windows and ledges, bereft of any sharp corners. As you get closer, the stone walls gain more dimension. On close inspection, the exterior walls look like a completely unstable agglomeration, as if someone attempted to cover the structure using only bubble gum and stones, trying to stick the rocks in place so that you can't see the gum. The walls have a wildly uneven, sharp surface. Split-open geodes are stuck willy-nilly next to granite shards and boulders, the placement of every rock seeming to maximize its sharpest edge, pointing out.

As you enter the cavernous lobby, notice the gigantic stone fireplaces to your right and left, hearths that can handle twelve-foot logs. In front of you, grand picture windows look out over the valley of Asheville and to the mountains miles away. For a quick trip back in time, walk over to the massive fireplace on your left. A few feet from the hearth, you'll see an indentation in the rock. That's the elevator, which rides up the stone chimney. This small elevator accommodates only five people comfortably, including the elevator-operator, who will ask you what floor you want. Tell him three. When you get off, you'll find a spacious sitting room with a five-floor atrium soaring overhead, complete with skylight. This is the heart of the original inn.

The 142 guest rooms and common areas in this section have recently undergone a meticulous restoration to return the elegant simplicity of the pure Mission style that originally graced the rooms of the inn. Interior-design magazines, including *Architectural Digest,* have praised this thoughtful multimillion-dollar restoration. If you can get a reservation in the original part of the inn, it affords a clear sense of the look and feel of the inn in its heyday.

The dramatic architecture was the result of an unusual alliance. In the early 1900s, Edwin Wiley Grove made millions by inventing and marketing Grove's Tasteless Chill Tonic and Grove's Bromo-Quinine—concoctions claiming health benefits considered dubious today. Grove visited a rustic mountain lodge in Yellowstone Park and wanted to build a replica in Asheville. Stubbornly, he rejected all the fancy architects' renderings. Seeing an opportunity, his son-in-law, Fred Seely, a reporter for an Atlanta newspaper with no architectural experience, drew up some sketches. Fred embellished his sketches with descriptive details, like walls honed from granite boulders on nearby Sunset Mountain and a roof made of red clay tiles from Tennessee.

Grove liked his son-in-law's drawings, and construction began in 1912. The 150-room inn was

tiques and heirlooms from the early 1900s, as is the carriage house, which includes three bedrooms, living and dining rooms, kitchen, and two baths. Prices range $90-130, and $200 for the carriage house. Breakfast is included for folks staying at the inn, but not for those staying in the carriage house. Expensive-Premium.

A five-minute walk from downtown, the **Flint Street Inns,** 100-116 Flint St., tel. (828) 253-6723, are two adjacent homes. All eight guest rooms and the common rooms are filled with antiques and collectibles emphasizing the turn-of-the-century construction of the homes. Three rooms have fireplaces, and all have private baths. Rates begin at $95 and include a full Southern-style breakfast. Expensive.

The **Albemarle Inn,** 86 Edgemont Rd., tel. (828) 255-0027 or (800) 621-7435, a couple of miles from downtown, offers 11 spacious, tastefully decorated rooms, including one suite, in a 1909 Greek Revival mansion. The Albemarle offers the unusual extra of an outdoor pool. The rates, which include breakfast and evening beverages, begin at $90 and rise to $150 for the suite. Expensive.

Though only about three miles from downtown, **Cairn Brae,** 217 Patton Mountain Rd., tel. (828) 252-9219, is far removed from the bustle of city living. Situated on a rocky hillside (the Scottish definition of "Cairn Brae"), this modern mountain chalet lies along an unpaved road leading up Patton Mountain. The mountain view of Asheville spreads out through the large picture windows of the three guest rooms and one two-bedroom suite. Breakfast is served in the "treehouse" dining room, which, like the

---

completed in less than a year, with the help of a small army of stonemasons. Seely became the manager of the hotel, which soon earned a reputation as one of the finest resort hotels in the nation, attracting wealthy visitors in droves, including celebrities and dignitaries like Thomas Edison, Woodrow Wilson, and Will Rogers.

With the death of Edwin Grove in 1927, a new era began. Seely was fired as manager, and the inn was sold to a group of bankers in Baltimore. When the Great Depression hit, the bankers, and consequently the inn, fell on hard times, although it still attracted guests including Franklin and Eleanor Roosevelt and F. Scott Fitzgerald (who lived in room 441 during much of 1935-1936, while his wife, Zelda, was confined to an Asheville mental hospital).

The Grove Park Inn played a highly unusual role during World War II. The U.S. government took command of the inn, temporarily transforming it into a confinement center for Axis diplomats. As the war progressed, authorities decided that the inn could be put to better use than as a jail and designated it a rest-and-recreation center for American naval officers and wounded sailors. At the end of the war, the inn resumed normal operations, but by that time, the original furnishings, rugs, linens, drapes and plumbing had deteriorated.

A new era began in 1955, when Charles Sammons purchased the inn. Over the next 33 years, until his death, Sammons financed an enormous restoration and expansion program. Under Sammons' ownership, the biggest changes occurred in 1984 and 1988, when two huge wings were added to either side of the original inn. The wings more than tripled the number of guest rooms, transforming the regal 150-room hotel into a vast, 510-room complex complete with indoor and outdoor pools, tennis courts, four restaurants; and a fitness center.

As a result of this major expansion, the Grove Park Inn today is a slightly confusing place, combining the dual roles of the richly historic and grand Arts and Crafts-style mountain retreat of 1920 and the state-of-the-art convention facility of the 1990s. Most of the original inn, in the center of the structure, remains intact.

Staying Here Today

For visitors, staying in this amazing old hotel is a special experience. For maximum atmosphere, you'll want to stay in the original inn section of the hotel. The modern rooms in other sections are comfortable and more spacious than most of those in the original section, but they're not as stylish or evocative. All rooms that look out over the valley offer marvelous views—it's worth specifying such a room when you reserve.

Rates vary according to the season and the type of room desired. For a small "value" room (no valley view) in the original inn, prices start at $79 January 1-April 3 and rise to $109 the rest of the year ($10 more on weekends). Bigger rooms with views in the old section range $150-200, as do the rooms in the modern wings. Suites range $350-500. The inn is located at 209 Macon Avenue, a 10-minute drive from downtown. Call (704) 252-2711 or (800) 438-5800 for information and reservations.

rooms, features an inspiring view. Walking trails wind through the wooded acreage surrounding this elegant retreat. Rates range from $90 up to $140 for the suite. To get there, get off I-240 at the Charlotte Street exit, proceed south about 50 yards to College Street, and turn left. Make another left shortly on Town Mountain Road, and proceed for one mile until you reach Patton Mountain Road. Cairn Brae lies another mile along this gravel road.

Downtown

Two fine downtown hotels put you right in the thick of Asheville city life. **The Haywood Park Hotel,** One Battery Park Ave., tel. (828) 252-2522 or (800) 228-2522, just a decade ago was a cavernous, empty retail space, abandoned by Ivey's Department Store. Thanks to some ingenious architects, this former department store has been magically transformed into a luxurious hotel consisting of 33 spacious and elegant suites, a superb restaurant and cafe, and a 24-hour fitness center. Extras in every suite include wet bars, Spanish marble and ceramic baths, and a continental breakfast delivered to your room. It's located at the corner of Haywood Street and Battery Park Avenue, surrounded by some of downtown's finest shopping and dining. The rates range $150-300. Luxury.

The 12-story **Radisson Hotel Asheville,** One Thomas Wolfe Memorial Plaza, tel. (828) 252-8211 or (800) 333-3333, provides dazzling views of downtown Asheville and the surrounding landscape. Towering over the humble boarding house next door, where novelist Thomas Wolfe grew up, the Radisson offers a fitness room, outdoor pool, coffee shop, and a full-service rooftop restaurant. Prices for the 281 rooms are $90 from Nov. 16-March 31, and rise to $110 the rest of the year. Suites are also available. Expensive.

FOOD AND DRINK

Special Spots

Although Asheville boasts a large and varied selection of great eateries, a few spots deserve special mention for guaranteeing a particularly memorable repast.

You'll never forget any meal you have at the **Sunset Terrace,** on the veranda of the Grove Park Inn, tel. (828) 252-2711. Cradled in stone, with an open-air view of a gorgeous valley and mountain range in the distance, this dining spot provides a supremely romantic setting for any meal. As the name suggests, the time around sunset tints the scenery in particularly enchanting hues. The $12 breakfast buffet provides a full array of breakfast foods, from eggs Benedict to cereal and fruit. Lunch includes offerings like burgers ($8) and a grilled portabella mushroom sandwich ($9), as well as more exotic fare like the sautéed Black Tiger shrimp with basil couscous, served with Sauce Neapolitan ($13). Dinner features a variety of meat, fish, and poultry, in addition to at least one vegetarian entree. Prix fixe dinners include an appetizer, soup or salad, and dessert. Depending on your choice of entree, the price varies from $26 for the vegetarian option to $42 for the steak and shrimp combo. For a culinary delight, try the North Carolina mountain trout served with crawfish, morel mushroom ragout, and basil couscous ($34). Though the food is excellent, it's really the open-air atmosphere and grand view that make the terrace such a magical dining spot. The terrace is only open when the weather is warm enough. (The veranda does have a roof, so rain is not a problem). On the weekends, singer Maddy Winer and her band play standards to accompany dinner, a tradition dating back to 1979. Reservations are a must for dinner and highly recommended for lunch. When the terrace is closed, the same menu is available at the **Carolina Cafe,** indoors next to the terrace. Though it has the same view, it's just not as good through picture windows.

The Grove Park Inn's spot for fine dining is the posh **Horizons,** tel. (828) 252-2711. Gents wear jackets and ties, and a pianist provides classy background music. Upholstered booths provide luxurious comfort, and most tables have a lovely view of the valley and mountains. Horizons prides itself on both its innovative and classic cuisine. You'll be tempted by appetizer selections like the timbale of cold water lobster paired with rosettes of applewood-smoked salmon and salmon caviar, complemented with lemon curd créme fraiche ($11). Classic entrees include grilled tuna ($24) and mesquite-smoked Angus beef ($34). More innovative entree options include sliced roast ostrich ($30) or the truly novel mixed grill, a trio of grilled boar, antelope, and Australian lamb chops garnished with an assortment of forest mushrooms and roasted shallot marmalade finished with a natural glaze ($36). Reservations are a must.

At the Richmond Hill Inn, 87 Richmond Hill Dr., **Gabrielle's**, tel. (828) 252-7313, provides the ultimate in elegance. You can savor Gabrielle's utterly superb continental cuisine with a Southern flavor in one of two dining rooms. The 1899 mansion's formal dining room, with its rich cherry paneling and three-tier chandelier, exudes the stately ambience of the 1890s. The glass-enclosed sun porch with charming wicker furniture, ceiling fans, and majestic views of the mountains also offers a superb dining experience. The food presentation and quality and the service are all outstanding, ensuring you'll enjoy a memorable meal. The menu changes to take advantage of the freshest ingredients available, but you can usually depend on a few revered house standards like Gabrielle's signature mountain apple and Vidalia onion soup gratinée with aged Gruyére, or the roasted rack of New Zealand lamb with Dijon mustard brûlée and three-mushroom pilaf served with mint-apple butter. Plan to spend at least $35 per person for a full dinner, more if you take advantage of the marvelous wine list. Semi-formal attire is requested, and be sure to make a reservation.

Downtown

At the Haywood Park Hotel, at the corner of Haywood Street and Battery Park Avenue, **23 Page,** tel. (828) 252-3685, serves fabulous American cuisine with an international flair. The menu changes to accommodate the freshest ingredients, but you might start your meal with the summery "Ain't that a Peach" salad—fresh spinach and peaches served with a peach vinaigrette, topped with fried oysters—or the foie gras sautéed with port wine and grapes garnished with a brioche. One of the house's signature dishes is the shrimp Michelle le Borgne, which is fresh shrimp (flown in from New Orleans twice weekly), green apples, and aromatic vegetables braised in organic carrot juice with far East spices and angel hair pasta ($23). Entrees range $16-27. Casual but proper attire is requested (no shorts or T-shirts). Reservations are recommended. Only dinner is served. Downstairs, the affiliated **New**

French Bar serves a selection of wines, coffees, baguettes, and pastries, making it an ideal spot for an afternoon or evening rendezvous.

The **Flying Frog Cafe,** 76 Haywood St., tel. (828) 254-9411, has something for almost everyone. If you're going out to eat with folks who want "ethnic" food, but you just can't decide which kind, the Flying Frog is the perfect choice. The eclectic menu features French, Cajun, Indian, Caribbean, and Italian specialties. You can start with something like escargots, crawfish, or dahl, then move on to linguine al pesto, crab cakes, bouillabaisse, roast duck, jerk chicken, frog legs, coq au vin, Creole crawfish broil, or tandoori chicken tikka, to name just a few of the myriad options. There's lots of space between the tables at this romantic bistro, whose atmosphere is enhanced by a varied collection of large paintings by local artists. Dinner entrees range $13-19. Lunch is also available at reduced prices. There's live piano music on Friday and Saturday evenings.

Vincenzo's, 10 North Market St., tel. (828) 254-4698, features a full menu of Northern Italian delights. From the calamari and antipasto appetizers, through a dozen pastas, to creamy chicken, veal, and vegetarian entrees, this popular trattoria offers some of the best Italian fare available in the entire North Carolina mountain region. Most of the pastas are available as side dishes, as well as entrees, like the risotto with sautéed calamari, red peppers, onions, tomatoes, garlic, and parmesan cheese ($5.50 as side dish, $10.50 as entree). Some house favorites include sautéed veal medallions topped with a blend of wild mushrooms, capers, and artichoke hearts ($15.50), and the marvelous zuppa de pesce, with whitefish, scallops, mussels, shrimp, and tomatoes in a white wine pesto sauce ($17.50). The restaurant also features a piano bar. Vincenzo's is also open for lunch with a more limited menu, when the salads, sandwiches, pastas, and specials average about $6. The downstairs bistro features live jazz, blues, and standards nightly.

If you're looking for a breathtaking view to go along with your food, the **Top of the Plaza** on the 12th floor of the downtown Radisson Hotel, tel. (828) 252-8211, won't disappoint you. This penthouse eatery features panoramic views of downtown and the surrounding mountains. In addition to the scenery, it offers tasty treats like the flounder Theresa, stuffed with crab meat and served with a veil of caper butter. Top of the Plaza serves breakfast and dinner; the first meal of the day will run about $5, and the dinner entrees range $15-22. Be sure to reserve a window table.

At the corner of Market and Walnut Streets, **Magnolia's Raw Bar & Grille,** tel. (828) 251-5211, specializes in fresh seafood and steaks. The restaurant offers three different rooms, including the casual raw bar; a year-round, covered outdoor patio; and the elegant Magnolia room. The house favorite is the steam pot, with lobster, snow crab legs, oysters, clams, and mussels, along with a couple vegetables like corn on the cob or potatoes ($33 for two). Magnolia's also serves lunch, with meals running $3-7, including a daily Blue Plate special for $4.25, which might consist of meatloaf or roasted chicken with mashed potatoes and bread. On Thursday, Friday and Saturday nights, starting around 10 p.m., live music is performed, ranging from rock to blues to oldies.

For vegetarians looking to hang out with their own kind, the **Laughing Seed Cafe,** 40 Wall St., tel. (828) 252-3445, serves exclusively vegetarian fare, like the popular Harmony Bowl, a marvelous meal all in one bowl, with layers of brown rice, beans, steamed veggies, grilled tofu, and sesame ginger sauce ($6). Specials include a sea vegetable and smoothie of the day. Lunch and dinner are served seven days a week, with entrees costing about $5-7. Downstairs, the affiliated **Jack of the Wood** brewery and bakery features great desserts, breads, coffees, and house-brewed, preservative- and additive-free beers.

Everyone is welcome at the **Bean Street Cafe,** Broad and College Streets, tel. (828) 255-8180, the favorite hangout for caffeine aficionados with a bohemian bent. This haunt of the hip, young and old, offers a full range of gourmet coffees, in addition to food like waffles, bagels, sandwiches, soups, and desserts, all under $3. Once you collect your order at the counter, proceed into the two spacious sitting rooms, filled with furniture collected over many a yard sale, from card tables to old sofas of fine, aged Naugahyde. The lighthearted decor includes kitschy local art adorning the brick walls, a couple of mannequins' arms poking through the dropped ceiling, chess tables, and bookshelves stocked with eclectic volumes.

Pack Square

On Biltmore Avenue, next to Pack Square, several eateries have blossomed, including several cafes with outdoor seating, further contributing to Asheville's burgeoning reputation as "the Paris of the South." The **Cafe on the Square,** tel. (828) 251-5565, with a chic, black-and-white Art Deco interior, as well as sidewalk seating, offers tasty delights like a butternut squash and brie soup crowned with puff pastry, and entrees like angel hair pasta with sun-dried tomato pesto, artichoke hearts, and capers, or the sensational chipotle-rubbed pork tenderloin seasoned with smoked jalapeño, finished with a Southwestern apple chutney. Entrees range $10-15.

Next door, the **Bistro 1896,** tel. (828) 251-1300, which also combines indoor and outdoor seating, serves appetizers like fried calamari ($4.50) and oysters on half shell ($7), more filling options like apricot-mustard-glazed spare ribs ($6), and entrees that average about $10.

Still looking out to Pack Square, next door on Biltmore Avenue, **La Catarina Trattoria,** tel. (828) 254-1148, also providing both indoor and outdoor seating, serves splendid southern Italian fare. In addition to making its own blends of succulent sausages, Catarina's makes mouth-watering mozzarella cheese each day, which, during tomato season, forms a fabulous mozzarella-tomato-basil appetizer. Their homemade bresaola is another great choice for an appetizer—wine-cured, air-dried beef served on greens with a horseradish vinaigrette. Also made on the premises, the ravioli are pillows from heaven, as opposed the belly bombs you can get at other Italian eateries. Other entrees include southern Italian pasta dishes, like the nido di Columba, an angel hair nest with poached egg and shaved prosciutto in a light cream sauce, or meatier options like osso bucco or lamb tenderloin. The entrees range $9-17, the appetizers $5-7. Open for lunch, dinner, and brunch.

Just a few yards south of Pack Square, still along Biltmore Avenue, a few pubs have sprouted up, including the celebrated **Barley's Taproom,** tel. (828) 255-0504. Locals voting in the weekly newspaper christened it Asheville's best place to drink beer, best place to eat pizza, and best place to be seen. This bustling pub offers 24 beers on tap and a full menu (including great pizza). Barley's hops at night to live rock, jazz, and blues, with no cover charge. If Barley's is too packed, try next door at the **Blue Rooster Brewhouse,** tel. (828) 281-4500, a similar combination pub, restaurant, and microbrewery.

ENTERTAINMENT

Downtown Nightlife
In addition to the live music at restaurants and pubs mentioned above, Asheville offers several hopping nightclubs. The premier venue for national acts, **Gatsby's,** 13 Walnut St., tel. (828) 254-4248, has wood floors and booths that have been graced by artists from alternative rock to sultry blues. Covers vary according to the performers. **45 Cherry,** 45 Cherry St., tel. (828) 254-9173, located in a downtown warehouse, features R&B, reggae, funk, and grunge. The cover charge varies. If you've been dining at the Grove Park Inn and are looking to top off your elegant meal with some strobe lights, the three-tier **Elaine's,** tel. (828) 252-2711, delivers energetic live rock and country.

For a genuine taste of traditional Asheville nightlife, complete with bluegrass and country beats you can stomp your boots to, the celebrated **Mountain Smokehouse,** 20 South Spruce St., tel. (828) 253-4871, is guaranteed to provide you with a rip-roaring good time. Cover charges vary and can include country-style dinners.

Festivals and Events
Asheville and the surrounding area feature dozens of different intimate and crowded festivals and events. For a complete listing, call the Asheville Convention and Visitors Bureau, tel. (800) 257-1300. Two related festivals, however, stand out from all the others. Every Saturday, from the first weekend in July through Labor Day, Asheville's **Shindig-on-the-Green,** on the city/county plaza just east of Pack Square, erupts with traditional mountain music, complete with banjo pickers, fiddlers, guitar players, and country crooners, inspiring the crowds to get up and dance. If you're in town on any summer Saturday, don't miss this free, enthusiastic get-together. The only weekend the Shindig doesn't happen, the last weekend in July, it's replaced by the even more festive, full-blown **Bele Chere** festival, which runs Saturday morning to Sunday evening, featuring a variety of country music dancers and musicians, as well as a cornucopia of traditional mountain foods and crafts.

INFORMATION

If you call the **Asheville Convention and Visitors Bureau,** tel. (800) 257-1300, they'll mail you a brochure listing Asheville accommodations and attractions, maps, and an updated brochure listing the dozens of festivals and events that occur in and around Asheville every year. It's well worth the toll-free call. The **Asheville Chamber of Commerce,** 151 Haywood St., just off exit 4C of I-240, tel. (828) 258-6109, provides an exhaustive array of brochures and detailed maps, as well as friendly advisors who will help you match Asheville's bounteous diversions and attractions with your desires.

AROUND ASHEVILLE

THE LOWER BLUE RIDGE PARKWAY

In the northern High Country, the Blue Ridge Parkway is the major roadway, the quickest way to get around in the region. Not so in North Carolina's central mountains, where highways like I-40 make for much speedier transit. Consequently, this southern stretch of the parkway, from Little Switzerland to Cherokee, is traveled less by impatient locals and more by Sunday-driver types, who often slow down and pull off the road to absorb the rippling vistas of the tallest mountains east of the Rockies.

Parkway Highlights
At milepost 331, the **Museum of North Carolina Minerals,** tel. (828) 765-9483, provides a sparkling introduction to the rich gem-mining history of North Carolina's Southern Mountains. From rough rocks to cut, polished sapphires and emeralds, and loads of geodes and jewels in

between, the exhibits cover the culture and techniques of past and present rock-hounders, who have been unearthing treasures in these hills for centuries. Admission is free.

Located directly on the Parkway, at milepost 334, the **Switzerland Inn & Chalet Restaurant,** tel. (828) 765-2153 or (800) 654-4026, sits regally near a summit in the Black Mountains, offering a dazzling, panoramic view. Styled like a Swiss alpine chalet, the inn includes 55 guest rooms, most with balconies, and five two-bedroom cottages, open May-October. Rates range Moderate-Premium. Rooms without the staggering mountain view start at $75; rooms with the view start at $90. The cottages run $130. A full breakfast is included. The Chalet Restaurant serves three meals a day and is open to the public. Breakfast and lunch average $4-6, including the popular, broiled Chalet hot sandwich consisting of ham, turkey, and Swiss cheese on toast with blue cheese dressing. At dinner, fresh fish and seafood reigns, including the local favorite, rainbow trout sautéed in lemon butter, with sautéed grapes and walnuts ($14). The chicken pot pie is another staple, $8 for lunch or dinner. Call ahead to reserve a window table in the Mountain View dining room.

Crabtree Meadows, at milepost 339.5, tel. (828) 675-5444, provides picnic areas, restrooms, 70 tent campsites, and 20 trailer campsites (no hookups). But the big attraction here is the moderately steep, 2.5-mile loop trail leading to the postcard-perfect, 70-foot cascade of Crabtree Falls. Next to the trailhead, you can enjoy a snack at the **Crabtree Meadows Coffee Shop,** tel. (828) 765-2153, open May-October.

At milepost 355.4, NC 128 leads you immediately into popular, 1,677-acre **Mt. Mitchell State Park,** tel. (828) 675-4611, home of Mt. Mitchell, the highest peak east of the Mississippi. Towering 6,684 feet above sea level, the summit of this majestic mountain is very popular with visitors, in part, because you can drive there. From the Parkway, NC 128 winds along for five miles, concluding at Mt. Mitchell's summit parking lot and observation tower. You'll notice lots of dead trees at this high altitude. The culprit is the balsam woolly adelgid, a tiny but destructive European insect that has devastated the wild Fraser firs in North Carolina. On clearer days, the views of the surrounding peaks

are staggering, sometimes enhanced by fog moving through the valleys below the summit. Don't be surprised, however, if the summit is shrouded in clouds. The weather at the summit is notoriously fickle, averaging 100 inches of snow a year, closing the road to the summit in the winter. In fact, you might want to call the park about weather conditions if you're making a special trip to visit the summit. You can depend on one thing: it will be windy and chilly atop Mt. Mitchell, even on a sunny summer day. In addition to several hiking trails, the park includes a small natural history museum and tent camping area. About two-thirds of the way up the mountain along NC 128, a restaurant serves three standard American meals a day, open April-October.

The **Craggy Gardens Visitors Center** at milepost 364.4, tel. (828) 298-0495, provides a full selection of books and brochures about the Parkway, in addition to nature exhibits, picnic tables, and restrooms. Two splendid trails lead from different parking lots. The **Craggy Pinnacle Trail,** north of the visitors center (near the tunnel), rises at a moderate grade through woods and rhododendron thickets for seven-tenths of a mile, leading to the breathtaking 360-degree view from the summit of Craggy Dome. The **Craggy Gardens Trail** begins south of the visitors center. The same length as the pinnacle trail, but a little steeper, this self-guiding nature trail winds through lush woods and emerges onto magnificent meadows bursting with wildflowers.

Between mileposts 375 and 376, you'll see signs to turn off for the **Zebulon B. Vance Birthplace,** tel. (828) 645-6706, which lies about five miles away from the Parkway exit. This historic site commemorates the life of one of North Carolina's most influential public servants, Zebulon B. Vance, born in 1830. At the age of 24, Vance was first elected to public office, serving in the North Carolina House of Commons. It was the first of many elections he would win, including three terms as governor of North Carolina and four terms as U.S. Senator from North Carolina, an office he held from 1879 until his death in 1894. Best known for his gubernatorial leadership during and after the Civil War, Vance's career is detailed at the visitors center. A guided tour takes you through seven reconstructed 18th and 19th century buildings, including the two-story main house, smoke-house, spring house, corn crib, loom house, tool house, and slave house. Antique furnishings, including some original pieces owned by Vance, contribute to the authentic feel of this homestead. Hours are Mon.-Sat. 9 a.m.-5 p.m. and Sunday 1-5 p.m. April-Oct., Tues.-Sat. 10 a.m.-4 p.m. and Sunday 1-4 p.m. the rest of the year. Free admission.

For an exquisite history of the artistic traditions of this region, stop by the **Folk Art Center** just east of Asheville at milepost 382, tel. (828) 298-7928. This attractive, modern, alpine-style building serves as headquarters for the 700-member Southern Highland Craft Guild and displays changing exhibits featuring past and current works from the guild's permanent collection. In addition, the **Allanstand Craft Shop** at the center sells a vast variety of pieces made by guild members. Truly fine work composed by master craftspeople, the dazzling handmade pieces cover a variety of media, including pottery, wood, jewelry, baskets, glass, furniture, ceramics, and quilts. If you're looking to bring a crafts souvenir back home, this is the place to come. It won't take more than half an hour to tour the center, but it may take you at least that long to decide which piece of artwork to purchase.

South of Asheville, the **Pisgah Inn** at milepost 408.6, tel. (828) 235-8228, provides 50 comfortable rooms, all with private balconies, situated 5,000 feet above sea level on a slope of Mt. Pisgah. Every room at the inn commands an eye-popping view of the undulating mountains and valleys below. Remarkably, this mountain splendor comes relatively inexpensively, with rooms ranging $65-75, and a two-bedroom suite costing $110. Make sure to call well ahead of time (months ahead for the fall leaf season) to reserve one of these popular rooms; the inn and restaurant are open early April to mid-November. Moderate.

Even if you're not staying at the inn, you can enjoy this mountain retreat by eating at the inn's restaurant, which serves three meals a day, open 7:30 a.m.-10:30 p.m. The spacious dining room, paneled with knotty pine, has three walls of adjoining picture windows, offering the same stupendous mountain views as the guest rooms. Breakfasts run about $4 for eggs with bacon or sausage, $7 for the hearty country ham. Lunch

and dinner include sandwiches, salads, and steaks for $5-9. The specialty of the house is the fresh mountain trout, baked in lemon butter or char-grilled. At $9.75, the trout is the most expensive item on the menu, but it's also probably the best value. Plus you get the fun show of watching your waitperson perform delicate tableside surgery, cleanly filleting and removing the trout skeleton. If you're not up for a whole trout, sample the smoked mountain trout appetizer with chopped Bermuda onion, capers, lemon, and a tangy mustard-dill sauce. Beer and wine are available.

Half a dozen trails converge at the Pisgah Inn and surrounding parking lots, including the moderately strenuous, 1.5-mile **Mt. Pisgah Trail** leading to the summit of the 5,721-foot peak.

At milepost 412, the Parkway crosses US 276. Take this route south for four miles to reach the **Cradle of Forestry in America,** tel. (828) 877-3130, the nation's first forestry school. It was founded in 1898 by railroad magnate George Vanderbilt and Carl Schenck, the brilliant Prussian forester Vanderbilt hired to maintain the forests of his 125,000-acre holdings. Together, Vanderbilt, Schenck, and other scientists inaugurated new logging and replanting techniques that no longer devastated vast tracts of forests for generations, as most American logging before the turn of the century did. In addition to an 18-minute film about the history of the school, the Cradle offers many exhibits about forestry science. Live demonstrations include craftspeople that show you how to weave a basket from a tree. Guided tours lead through forests and along streams, with exploratory stops like an old saw mill and logging train. Admission is $4 adults, $2 kids 6-17.

After your trip to the Cradle, take US 276 another mile south, until you come to **Looking Glass Falls,** a stunning 30-foot-wide by 60-foot-high cascade alongside the road. A short flight of steps leads from the road down to the base of these popular falls, a perfect spot for shutterbugs in search of a picturesque waterfall shot. Two miles farther south, 7.4 miles from the Blue Ridge Parkway on US 276, you'll see signs and a spacious parking lot for the celebrated **Sliding Rock,** located a few yards off the road. Known locally as "bust-yer-butt falls," this slippery rockface provides a thrilling, 60-foot long, natural waterslide plunging into a seven-foot-deep pool. Kids can, and often do, take this free ride repeatedly for hours. Beware: this popular and addictive spot is not the place to test out your fancy new swimsuit; old denim is the fabric of choice, for good reason. Lifeguards are on duty Memorial Day to Labor Day.

Back on the Parkway, the 55-mile stretch between its junction with US 276 and its southern terminus at Great Smoky Mountains National Park, leads through the highest elevations along the 469-mile route. The zenith of the Parkway, 6,053 feet in elevation, lies alongside Richland Balsam Mountain at the **Haywood-Jackson Overlook** at milepost 431. The soaring views of the Great Balsam Range are terrific, but to get a fuller feel for this heavenly high elevation, take the **Richland Balsam Trail,** a moderately strenuous, 1.5-mile looping trail leading to the mountain's 6,540-foot summit. On the way, you'll pass through an eerie Fraser fir forest, which, like Mount Mitchell's summit, has been ravaged by a destructive European aphid that has killed most of the trees.

From Richland Balsam Mountain, the Parkway continues its glorious path through the clouds, past misty coves and dramatic peaks. The end of the Parkway, at milepost 469, forms the gateway to another adventure, joining up with US 441 at the entrance to the magical Great Smoky Mountains National Park.

SOUTH TO THE LAND OF WATERFALLS AND GEMS

South of Asheville, the crowds thin out, and so do the roads. But the mountains remain majestic, and several small towns hidden in these hills have developed deserved reputations as inviting "mountain getaways." Just driving to these places is an adventure unto itself. US Route 64 links the most popular half-dozen of these little resort towns, beginning with Chimney Rock in the east, stretching to Franklin in the west. As you negotiate this route's relentless hairpin turns, curling steeply up towering mountains and swerving down into deep valleys, marvel at the gorgeous scenery and gain a renewed appreciation for the tireless reliability of your vehicle's transmission and brakes.

CHIMNEY ROCK AND LAKE LURE

About half an hour's drive southeast from Asheville will take you to Chimney Rock Village, located on US 64/74A. The town itself is about a half-mile long by 50 yards wide, situated in a deep gorge and lined with souvenir shops, craft galleries, ice cream parlors, inns, restaurants, and other businesses catering to tourists. If you've been keeping your eyes on the road, you may wonder why this particular spot features one of the biggest concentrations of commercial enterprises in North Carolina's southern backcountry region. To answer this question, you need only look up. In the distance, you'll see the sparkling sprays of 404-foot Hickory Nut Falls, next to some rocky cliff faces, the attractions that draw all the visitors. In the center of town, you'll see the stone walls of the entrance to the park that puts you on top of these scenic wonders.

Chimney Rock Park

Enter through the gates on US 64/74A, crossing the wooden plank bridge over the Rocky Broad River, and drive about a mile along a rising road to the ticket plaza. Although this privately owned and operated park encompasses more than 1,000 acres, visitors only get to traverse a few dozen of them. In fact, the park's network of hiking trails total only about 2.5 miles. But what trails they are!

Prepare to be elevated.

After driving about two miles along a steeply rising, serpentine road, you'll eventually reach the football-field-size parking area at the base of Chimney Rock. Vertical cliffs rise straight up from the parking lot like stone skyscrapers. You can take an elevator from the basement parking lot to the 26th floor, up a vertical shaft blasted through the insides of the solid granite cliff in 1949. The elevator lets you off at the Sky Lounge snack bar and gift shop onto a level, wheelchair-accessible promenade. As you look out from this sidewalk, you'll gasp and feel a wobble in your knees. On a clear day, the view of Hickory Nut Gorge and Lake Lure extends out over the foothills of the North Carolina Piedmont as far as Kings Mountain, 75 miles away, just over the South Carolina border. To intensify the wobbly-knee effect, climb the 20-yard staircase extending from the promenade over a plunging chasm, leading to the free-standing Chimney Rock.

You don't have to take the elevator to Chimney Rock. If you're looking for a quick, challenging workout to start your visit, or if you've brought along a four-legged member of the family (leashed pets are welcome in the park but can't use the elevator), you can take staircases up through the rocky cliffs. The difference is that the elevator takes you up 258 feet in about 40 seconds, whereas the network of staircases requires at least 10-20 minutes. One advantage of these staircases is that they provide a few stopping off points, where you can take in awe-inspiring views while you catch your breath.

Once you get to the Chimney Rock, take the Skyline Trail, which leads you higher along the mountain, through thickets of Carolina rhododendron, past dozens of different varieties of wildflowers, plants and trees. Make sure to tote some water with you. For the first 20 or 30 minutes of this roughly two-hour hike, you'll be climbing steeply uphill on a well-trod dirt path and several staircases, until you reach Exclamation Point, the highest point in the park accessible to visitors, at 2,480 feet. From there, it's all downhill, but the views continue their relentless, panoramic beauty. Among the many highlights, you'll get to stand atop **Hickory Nut Falls,** which plunges straight down in a 404-foot free fall. When you get to the waterfall, you can take your shoes off and wade in pools in the stream, or you can cool off by walking underneath "nature's shower bath," a 15-foot waterfall just before the deep plunge of Hickory Nut Falls. From the falls, take the heady Cliff Trail, which descends along the rocky cliff faces of the park back to the parking lot.

For a different view of the park, take the Forest Stroll, a less strenuous 1.4-mile roundtrip trek following the base of the massive cliffs on the north side of Chimney Rock Mountain. Rising about 200 feet, this self-guiding nature trail winds through dense hardwood forests of oak, hickory, maple, and basswood, past dozens of species of exotic flora, like broad-leaved tickseed and little sweet Betsy, marked by signs that coordinate with a pamphlet that fills you in on the botanical details. The trail's thrilling terminus places you at the bottom of Hickory Nut Falls, perhaps the most dramatic view of these memorable falls.

The park provides several picnic and grilling areas. But whether or not you bring your own food and beverages, there's one set of supplies you'll definitely want to bring: a camera and plenty of film (you can buy more film at the Sky Lounge when you run out).

The park is open daily. Admission is $9.50 adults and $5 kids 6-15 (under 6 admitted free). From mid-November to mid-April, when the trails to the waterfall are closed, rates drop to $6 for adults, $3 for children.

Accommodations and Food

Chimney Rock Village's bustling, half-mile-long commercial strip on US 64/74 contains a few small lodgings. The best choice is **The Dogwood Inn,** tel. (828) 625-4403 or (800) 922-5557. Originally a stagecoach stop between Asheville and Charlotte, this beautifully preserved and comfortably appointed 1890s bed and breakfast offers four relaxing porches and six rooms with private baths, two with jacuzzis, as well as four rooms with shared baths. Rates range $75-135 and include a full breakfast. Moderate-Premium.

A five-minute drive south along US 64/74 will land you at the sandy public beach in the tiny downtown of Lake Lure, an inviting spot to take a dip after challenging the heights of Chimney Rock Park. Across from the beach, you'll find the **Lake Lure Inn,** tel. (828) 625-2525 or (800) 277-5873, an elegant mountain hotel that's been hosting luminaries since 1927, from FDR and F. Scott Fitzgerald to Patrick Swayze (he filmed *Dirty Dancing* in this area). The comfortable rooms in the Georgian/colonial-style inn have ceiling fans and air conditioning, and the black-and-white checkered tile floors of the bathrooms evoke the inn's long history. The spacious lobby includes a quaint little bar with a huge moose head looming over the sole table. Rates begin at $110 during the peak summer season. Premium.

The Lake Lure Inn also has a lovely restaurant with two serving rooms, including a veranda and a more formal dining room. Seven pairs of French doors in the dining room enhance the airy feel. Dinner fare includes appetizers like escargots or oysters in angel nest (both $6). For an entree, choose between steaks, crispy roasted duck, rainbow trout, or the delectable scampi fettuccine ($13.50). The restaurant is open for lunch Mon.-Sat., dinner Tues.-Sat., and Sunday brunch, and guests are served a continental breakfast daily.

If you want to enjoy a meal directly on the waters of Lake Lure, you have only one choice, **Jimmy's Original Seafood and Steak,** three miles east of town along US 64/74, tel. (828) 625-4075. The lunch menu is mostly sandwiches ($4-5). The dinner entrees are more varied but feature steaks and—the most popular choice— native trout sautéed in lemon butter with a pecan crust (both $15). The food is fine, but it's the location, directly on the water, that makes Jimmy's so popular. With three docks, Jimmy's is even accessible by boat. Both the upstairs dining room and the downstairs tavern serve lunch and dinner.

A couple minutes' drive farther south will take you to the Lake Lure municipal golf course. Across from the golf course, turn onto Charlotte Drive., next to the Fire Department, to reach Lake Lure's only lodging directly on the water, the celebrated **Lodge on Lake Lure,** tel. (828) 625-2789 or (800) 733-2785. This inviting bed and breakfast is situated at the end of a wooded drive on a sloping hillside, high enough to afford a sweeping view of the lake, including the stony cliffs of Rumbling Bald Mountain across the water. You enter via the greatroom, a warmly furnished space with vaulted ceilings made of hand-hewn beams, walls of wormy chestnut, and a 20-foot-tall stone fireplace. Common areas include the greatroom, living room, sun porch, and a reading room stocked with hundreds of magazines and books. Downstairs, the lakeside veranda is lined with rocking chairs. From here, a terraced walkway meanders down the hillside to the boathouse and deck, outfitted with paddle boats and canoes.

The inn's atmosphere is an interesting combination, part elegant country inn, part casual bed and breakfast, typified by the complimentary beverage time in the afternoon, when guests gather to savor jug wine in fine crystal glasses.

Carl Sandburg Home

The 12 spacious guest rooms exude a comfortable mountain charm, with fine antiques side by side with family photos and collectibles gathered by the entertaining and outgoing innkeepers, Robin and Jack Stanier. Open year-round; rates are $96-135. Expensive-Premium.

Carl Sandburg Home

About 15 miles southwest of Chimney Rock, along US 64, take a three-mile detour south from Hendersonville on US 25 to visit **Connemara,** in Flat Rock, tel. (828) 693-4178, the estate where writer Carl Sandburg spent the last 22 years of his life. Although access to the grounds is free, we recommend starting your visit by taking the 25-minute guided tour of the main house ($2) to get a feel for this inspiring property. Though Sandburg died in 1969, it feels almost as if he just stepped out for a moment. Books and magazines are stacked and scattered everywhere, evidence of Sandburg's voracious reading and pack rat proclivities. Carl's wife, Paula, spent her time breeding prized goats at the estate. A brief stroll through the woods will bring you to the goat barn, where you can pet the descendants of Paula's stock. Plan to spend at least a couple of hours watching the introductory film at the visitors center and exploring the house, barn, other farm buildings, and hiking trails.

West on US 64 to Highlands

Twenty miles west of Hendersonville along US 64, three miles before Brevard, you'll pass junction US 276. Take 276 north for about eight miles to reach the trio of attractions discussed above: Sliding Rock (a natural waterslide), Looking Glass Falls, and the Cradle of Forestry in America museum. Or continue west on US 64, where the twisting and turning, rising and descending roadway curls past the little mountain towns of Brevard, Rosman, Lake Toxaway, Sapphire, and Cashiers, where you'll be able to take a break (and rest your brakes) and enjoy a meal and a stroll through these quaint communities.

At the junction of US 64 and Route 28 near the Georgia border, you'll come to a favorite haunt of Atlanta's well-to-do. The mountain retreat of **Highlands,** the highest incorporated town east of the Mississippi, is situated on a plateau at a heady elevation of 4,120 feet. Though only a couple blocks long, the tiny downtown area is crammed with dozens of upscale shops, inns, and restaurants.

Highlands wears its wealth with a casual, inviting ease. You don't necessarily have to drain your bank account to shop, stay, or eat here, and there's no dress code for the restaurants. Two inns, located across Main Street from each other in downtown, offer meticulously preserved and restored lodgings that have been serving travelers for more than a century. The 1878 **Highlands Inn,** tel. (828) 526-9380 or (800) 964-6955, offers 31 comfortable rooms furnished in the style of the late 1800s. Rates are $90-125 year-round and include a continental breakfast. Expensive-Premium. The inn, open April-Nov., is also home to the **Kelsey Place** restaurant, serving dinner only. The constantly changing menus of pasta, beef, poultry, and seafood entrees fall in the $15-20 range.

The 1876 **Old Edwards Inn,** tel. (828) 526-9319 or (888) 526-9319, provides 19 rooms furnished in 1800s style, complete with lots of antiques. Open year-round; rates range $95 for single rooms to $115 for two-room suites. Expensive. The **Central House Restaurant,** on the premises, is open for lunch and dinner. This dining room evokes its century-old history, from the wood floors and thick posts to the ponderous wrought iron chandelier. The lunch menu includes lots of sandwich options in the $5 range and tops out with the Cajun shrimp for $10. Dinner entrees include chicken with a light cream sauce($14), lamb curry ($19), and the deservedly celebrated chateaubriand ($37 for two).

If you prefer lodgings constructed in the 20th century, the modern **Highlands Suite Hotel,** 205 Main St., tel. (828) 526-4502 or (800) 221-5078, offers 28 spacious two-room suites ranging $160-180 during the peak summer season. Luxury.

Northwest to Franklin

From Highlands to Franklin, a distance of about 20 miles, US 64 snakes through spectacular Cullasaja River Gorge, where the sun makes limited appearances during the day. The cliff-lined scenery through this deep canyon is stunningly dramatic, but if you're the driver of your vehicle, you should miss most of it. From Highlands for another 10 or so miles, this narrow, steeply descending stretch of roadway defines the phrase "serpentine curves." If a traveling companion says "Wow! Look at that!" don't glance away from the road for more than a split second. US 64 offers plenty of overlooks to stop and take in the canyon views.

Dozens of alluring waterfalls plunge over the canyon's cliffs, but most are inaccessible by foot, unless you're extremely adventurous. A few, however, fall right by the roadside. At the head of the gorge, about 2.5 miles northwest of Highlands, the road brushes by **Bridal Veil Falls,** named for the lace-like delicacy of the 120-foot cascade's water patterns. You'll see where US 64 used to run underneath the falls—you can still take this side road today to feel the falls' spray. Another mile northwest along US 64, you'll see the pull-off for **Dry Falls.** From the parking area, where you can't see the falls but can hear their thundering bass, you'll imagine there's nothing dry about them. But after strolling the brief descent to the base of this dramatic 75-foot cascade, you'll see the appropriateness of the name after you take the dry path passing underneath these falls.

Franklin

US 64 levels out a bit as you approach the town of Franklin. A relatively sleepy little town, Franklin is not a destination unto itself, but a convenient way station at the crossroads of US 64, US 441/23 and Highway 28, the latter two routes leading north to Great Smoky Mountains National Park. Though it's nicknamed "the jewel of the Southeast," that moniker would be more accurately worded as "the town with North Carolina's densest concentration of commercial gem mine operations."

Around the turn of the century, this area yielded a few big rubies and sapphires, spurring a 20-year era of ubiquitous gem-mining in the area. As these mining operations failed to break even, the local mining industry waned until a few decades later, when the concept of commercial gem mines was born. These roadside

SIFTING FOR SAPPHIRES

While the southern mountain region of North Carolina provides some of the most dramatic and panoramic scenery east of the Rockies, a more microscopic glance at the ground beneath your feet may inspire a similar, albeit more mercenary, reverence. Why? There are big jewels hidden in this dirt.

In 1540, driven by a lust for gold, Spanish explorer Hernando De Soto was the first white man to barge aggressively into this Cherokee territory. Finding no gold, he left without discovering the treasure trove of sapphires and rubies he and his men had trod upon. Four and a half centuries later—after more than 100 years of aggressive mining—these hills are still yielding multimillion-dollar treasures, such as the 10.5-pound, 9,700-carat star sapphire unearthed in these hills in 1989.

For a little guaranteed excitement, stop at any of the dozens of gem mines peppering this region. At these mines, you can purchase buckets or bags of "gem ore"—hunks of dirt containing tiny sprinklings of pretty stones. At most mines, the ore is "enriched" (i.e., it's been salted with at least a few little gems) and usually costs around $5 for a 10-pound bag.

Once you have your bucket in hand, you head over to one of the flumes (troughs full of flowing water). You dip a handful of ore into the flume and let the water rinse away the dirt, perhaps revealing a nice little garnet or two—or, if you're extremely lucky, a little ruby, sapphire, or emerald.

Of course, the chances are extremely remote that you'll unearth a jewel worth thousands of dollars—however, it *has* been known to happen at these tourist mines. And it's that unlikely but not unreal possibility that gives rise to the thrill of rinsing your way through a bag of dirt. Also, unlike buying a handful of lottery tickets, you'll almost always come away with *something*—a pretty little souvenir that most mines will mount for you for a small fee while you wait, if you like.

gem mines, which surround Franklin, may appear crassly commercial and a bit run-down. But don't underestimate their allure. Far from the antiseptic, automatic motions of gambling machines in Cherokee, the gritty, tactile thrills of sifting through buckets of gem ore yield much more dependable thrills (see special topic "Sifting for Sapphires").

If Franklin is a convenient spot to spend the night, try the Inexpensive but clean and comfortable **Franklin Motel,** 17 W. Palmer St., at the motel-rich junction of US 23, 64, 441 and highway 28, tel. (828) 524-4431 or (800) 433-5507. Or, for equally pleasant motel rooms in town, along the US 441 business route (Main Street), try the **Country Inn,** 277 E. Main St., tel. (828) 524-4451 or (800) 233-7555, or **Days Inn,** 525 E. Main St., tel. (828) 524-6491 or (800) DAYS-INN. Both are Inexpensive.

Within walking distance of these lodgings, you'll find spots serving burgers, pizza, fried chicken, meatloaf, and other similar fare. The most enjoyable of these eateries is the **Hickory Ranch Restaurant,** 126 Palmer St. (Bus. 441N), tel. (828) 369-9909, serving lunch and dinner, where you can chow down on ribs, chicken, and steaks for under $10, or visit the Hickory Ranch's ice cream parlor or wine bar.

GREAT SMOKY MOUNTAINS NATIONAL PARK AND VICINITY

From your first views of the of the Great Smoky Mountains, you'll appreciate the appropriateness of the name. Grand mountains rise dramatically from valleys shrouded in a smoky mist, inspiring memories of childhood tales about enchanted forests prowled by fairies and goblins. At lower elevations, massive trees form a canopy above foliage so dense you could imagine you're in a tropical rainforest. The weather often contributes to that image—the park averages more than 55 inches of precipitation each year. As lovely, dark, and deep as the valleys are, however, it's the soaring mountains that make this park so special. The Great Smoky Mountains exhibit a dizzying diversity—some are rounded, others jagged, some mossy and wooded, others boulder-strewn and bald on top. All of them are enticing.

The combination of the mountains' moist climate and pervasive winds have produced one of the most botanically diverse environments in the world, earning Great Smoky Mountains National Park a designation as one of the 300-plus "international biospheres" protected by the United Nations. With more than 1,200 species of flowering plants, 2,000 species of mosses, lichen and fungi, and 125 species of trees, we could spend endless pages describing the flora alone. Suffice it to say that in the spring, particularly during May and June, your eyes will be utterly dazzled by the lush profusion of blossoms of every color, and your nose will experience exotic scents never inhaled before. In the fall, especially October, the dense forests coating the valleys and mountainsides are transformed into exquisitely colorful carpets woven with plush threads of red, orange, yellow, green, and brown, which fade into misty indigo and violet in the distance.

The most popular national park in the U.S.— attracting more than nine million visitors a year— Great Smoky Mountains National Park covers 520,000 acres of unspoiled and surprisingly uncrowded atmosphere. The uncrowded adjective, however, doesn't apply to the roads. During peak periods—summer and the autumn leaf-changing season—don't be surprised to encounter traffic like you'd find in a Manhattan or

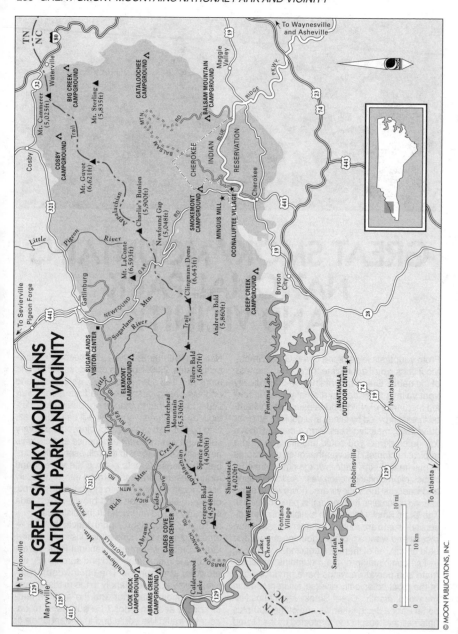

GREAT SMOKY MOUNTAINS
NATIONAL PARK AND VICINITY

© MOON PUBLICATIONS, INC.

Los Angeles rush hour. The reason the roads get so crowded is that there are so few of them.

In order to truly experience the mysterious splendor of the place, you have to park the car and hike off into the mist (this alone will separate you from more than 90% of the park's visitors, who never stray much beyond a hundred yards from the road).

About 900 million years ago, these mountains slowly eroded into the sea, where, for about 500 million years, they collected a layer of limestone and inorganic sediment pressurized into metamorphic rock. Then North America and Africa collided, and the resultant buckling and folding formed the Appalachians, including the Great Smoky Mountains.

Safety in the Park

As winds sweep eastward across the plains of the Midwestern United States, they rise over the Great Smokies. There, they cool off, often dropping rain or snow. During the winter, some areas average more than six feet of snow per year, and the temperature can dip as low as -20°. Other times of year, you may start out on a hike under a cloudless blue sky and soon find yourself drenched by a sudden downpour and buffeted by cool, blustery winds. You won't regret having invested in a rain poncho when you hike these mountains.

If you hear a rustling in the bushes, don't panic. The park's critters won't attack you if you leave them alone. Do *not* traipse into the woods to investigate the rustling. Chances are, what you're hearing is a woodchuck, white-tailed deer, or similarly harmless creature of the forest, but it could also be a black bear or a European wild hog. (About 500 members of both species live in the park.) If you're lucky enough to catch a glimpse of the cute and cuddly-looking bears, ignore the temptation to try to engage in a friendly interaction with them. If you happen to run across one, rangers advise you to calmly turn around and keep walking until you get back to where you started or until the bear scurries off into the underbrush. Above all, *do not feed the bears.* Offering a bear a handful of food could cost you not only your hand, but also the criminal penalties of a $5,000 fine and six months in jail.

The park's not-so-cuddly wild hogs, descendants of wild boars who escaped from a game preserve at the turn of the century, can weigh more than 200 pounds, have sharp tusks, and are mainly nocturnal foragers, rarely encountered by visitors. Their diet consists mainly of acorns and berries, but don't let their vegetarian bent lull you into complacency. If you happen to encounter one, *immediately* back off. These wild boars are fierce if they're cornered and have been known to eviscerate dogs that pursued them.

The most vicious critter in the park is harmless to humans, but murder to evergreens. At the highest elevations in the park, you'll see tracts of red spruce and Fraser fir forest that have been ravaged by the balsam woolly adelgid, a tiny European insect that made its way to these mountains in 1963. The little bugger feeds on the bark of the Fraser fir, secreting a toxin which prevents the fir from producing cones and eventually kills the tree. So far, the adelgid has claimed about 95% of the park's mature Fraser firs.

New revelations of nature's relentless diversity greet you around every bend in the trail here. If you camp overnight in the park, you may hear the plaintive howls of the park's two dozen or so red wolves, an endangered species reintroduced into the park in 1991 (these little wolves don't hunt in packs and never bother humans). As you're hiking along a stream, you may glimpse one of the 150-plus river otters who live in the park. And turning a corner on a trail, you may hear a sudden commotion in the woods and witness a wild turkey burst into flight.

History

Inhabited by the Cherokee for millennia, then joined by a few hundred European mountain settlers in the late 19th century, the lands constituting today's park remained pristine until lumber-hungry loggers arrived in the early 1900s. By 1925, almost every accessible big tree in the park had been chopped down. Among the 6,000 folks living there in 1925, the vast majority depended on the logging enterprises of cutting, hauling, and processing trees, and building roads to haul the trees out of the mountains. The timber industry was king, and the citizens were, for the most part, pawns.

In the 1920s, one of those pawns would begin an ultimately successful rebellion. Horace Kephart was a librarian from St. Louis. In 1904, Kephart traveled to these mountains to reinvigorate his health. The mountain cure worked, and he stayed, though he was sickened by the devastation wrought by the lumber industry.

In 1916, the National Park Service was established but did not select the Great Smoky Mountains as a national park. Kephart immediately began a grassroots campaign to right that wrong. Unfortunately, soon after the creation of the National Park Service, the federal government stopped allocating funds to buy land. The librarian from St. Louis didn't give up. Uniting every citizen group he could find in Tennessee, North Carolina, and throughout the country, Kephart's coalition solicited millions of donations, from pennies collected at Sunday schools to a $5 million grant from John D. Rockefeller, Jr. The North Carolina and Tennessee legislatures, recognizing the growing popularity of the concept, eventually joined the movement. Lumber barons and most other landowners were bought off (some settled for lifelong occupancy rights), and, in 1934, Great Smoky Mountains National Park was established.

SIGHTS AND RECREATION

Auto-Touring

Although the park boasts 238 miles of paved roadway, you'll have plenty of company almost everywhere you drive (unless you're grinding along the unpaved routes). This particularly applies to the two-lane, 32-mile long **Newfound Gap Road (US 441),** which cuts across the center of the park, uniting Cherokee, NC, and Gatlinburg, TN, the two most popular places for park visitors to sleep overnight. That said, we still recommend that you first enter the park via this popular route, for a few reasons. First, you should visit one of the two main visitors centers along this road, at the Tennessee and North Carolina entrances, to gather basic information and timely tips about special events from guided nature tours to music festivals. In addition, the road also provides easy access to many interesting trails and dozens of spots to pull off the road and gape at the wondrous scenery. Although commercial vehicles are prohibited on Newfound Gap Road, RVs and trailers aren't. But even if you get stuck behind one of these lumbering homes on wheels, you'll still find this

route enchanting as it weaves through valleys and up and down mountainsides, perpetually revealing dazzling views.

As you enter the park from the south, along US 441/Newfound Gap Road, stop at the **Oconaluftee visitor center,** the only visitor center in the North Carolina portion of the park. After you pick up a healthy collection of brochures, guidebooks, and maps, stroll next door to the stone cabin whose displays will give you a feel for what life was like for the settlers who moved here in the 19th century. As you proceed half a mile north, pull into the parking area marked **Mingus Mill.** A short stroll through yellow poplar forest leads to a gristmill built in 1876. From April through November, the mill is open 9 a.m.-5 p.m., although its cast iron turbine is not always in operation.

You'll have plenty of opportunities to pull off US 441 and drink in grand scenes of rivers, waterfalls, mountains, and valleys. In the center of the park, Newfound Gap Road crosses the Appalachian Trail (A.T.) at **Newfound Gap,** where the highest peaks in the Great Smokies form some of the park's most dynamic skylines. The large parking lot at Newfound Gap is a favorite jumping-off spot for day-hikers.

Just before you reach the A.T. and the Tennessee border, the spur of **Clingman's Dome Road** beckons off to your left, climbing six miles south from US 441 to Clingman's Dome, the highest summit in the park at 6,642 feet. This suspenseful drive, closed in winter, cuts through deep, often foggy woods and veers along sharp cliffs toward "the dome," as it's called. The road doesn't extend all the way to the summit. To reach the top of the dome, you still have a stiff half-mile hike ahead of you. From the parking lot, a steep, though wheelchair-accessible, asphalt path winds up the mountain and eventually rolls out onto an observation platform, where the panoramic views of the rippling ridgelines and thickly carpeted, misty valleys are unsurpassed. Even if it's rainy and foggy, this trip is worthwhile; you'll enjoy the ghostly aura of the red spruce and Fraser fir forests you'll pass through, where the dead firs loom like skeletons in the mist.

Newfound Gap Road proceeds north into Tennessee. At the park's northern entrance, the **Sugarland Visitors Center** offers the same wealth of materials as its North Carolinian counterpart across the park, as well as an interesting little natural history museum that includes entertaining and informative short films and lots of dramatic dioramas, complete with stuffed bears, early settlers, and other creatures of the forest.

Along US 441, a few minutes after you leave the park, but before you reach downtown Gatlinburg, you'll see signs for **Roaring Fork Motor Nature Trail.** This paved, one-way, 5.5-mile loop leads you through a variety of woods. At several spots, signposts invite you to pull over and explore the forest on foot.

Cades Cove, one of the park's most popular attractions, lies about 23 miles west of the Sugarland visitor center, along Little River Road. In 1821, a few hardy pioneers established a little village in this picturesque valley. During its prime, in 1850, the Cove boasted a population of 650. Soon after, most residents moved on; when the park was created in the '30s, virtually everyone moved away. But many of the buildings were preserved. The 11-mile **Cades Cove Loop** features 19 stops, all wheelchair accessible, where you can hop out of the car and explore restored, historic structures like farmhouses, barns, churches, and a working gristmill. For 50 cents, you can pick up an auto-tour booklet at one of the visitor centers, including the **Cades Cove visitors center,** located about halfway through the loop. From spring through September, the loop is closed to auto traffic on Saturday until 10 a.m., when bicyclists temporarily rule the road. Be forewarned that during the summer and the fall foliage season, traffic along the narrow, one-way loop is often bumper-to-bumper. Nonetheless, the comprehensive and informative restorations of this mountain village of the past make Cades Cove a worthwhile tour and an ideal diversion during days when weather conditions aren't right for a hike, or if you're sore from yesterday's climbs.

In the opposite, southeastern corner of the park, in North Carolina, the secluded hamlet of **Cataloochee Valley** also retains several historic buildings. Not as interesting as Cades Cove, Cataloochee Valley attracts comparatively few visitors, in part because getting there requires driving about 10 miles on Cove Creek Road, a twisting and turning, mostly gravel and mud route beginning at US 276 just before its terminus at I-40. Cataloochee Valley does, however, offer a campground that will appeal to folks who want to get off the beaten paths around the park

Hiking

For hiking variety, you can't beat the 800 miles of well-maintained trails that wind through this park. During a single day hike, you can experience a microcosm of the entire Appalachian Trail, which extends from Georgia to Maine. You'll start out in a valley with lush and dense woods; as you ascend one of the towering peaks, the landscape becomes more rugged, until you near the 6,000-foot ridgelines, where the red spruces and Fraser firs look more like flags than trees, fighting the wind, hanging on for dear life to the rocky turf.

The park's most celebrated trails lead to one or more of the 16 peaks topping 6,000 feet in elevation. These are generally strenuous hikes, but you aren't out of luck if you prefer gentler strolls: the park has plenty of leisurely alternatives, with almost 200 trails to choose from. Free trail maps are available at the visitors centers, although you should consider buying one of the more comprehensive guidebooks at the centers if you're going to do any "serious" hiking.

From late October through early April, expect wintry temperatures, which can quickly dip below freezing at the highest elevations. Any time of year, you're well advised to bring an extra layer of clothing for any hikes that take you above 5,000 feet. And, as mentioned earlier, always pack a rain poncho. The park averages 40 inches of rainfall a year, and storms form quickly and unexpectedly. Even more important than rain gear, always make sure to tote water with you. As attractive and pristine as the glistening mountain streams may appear, their water may contain microscopic critters whose vengeful wrath eclipses Montezuma's.

The Appalachian Trail

Beginning at Fontana Dam in the south, the Appalachian Trail winds 71 miles northeast, through the middle of the park, dancing along the North Carolina and Tennessee border. Following the main ridge of the Great Smokies, the trail leads through old-growth forests and across spectacular summits. The A.T. also traverses several **balds,** grassy meadows appearing unexpectedly at elevations over 5,000 feet. The lack of trees affords these balds grand, panoramic views of the surrounding peaks and valleys, making them ideal spots to stop and enjoy a picnic. How these balds were created remains a mystery. Probably, they first emerged through fires caused by lightning or set by the Cherokee. Once established, animals like deer, bison, elk, and eventually cattle, grazed in these meadows, maintaining them as pastures. Most of these balds slowly are being reclaimed by forest, although two, Gregory and Andrews Balds, are defended by the Park Service, which removes encroaching trees from these spectacular meadows.

The Appalachian Trail is the park's most popular trail, and the most popular stretch of the A.T. within the park is the portion that crosses Newfound Gap Road. (US 441). From the Newfound Gap parking lot, both directions of the trail lead uphill. Heading south, the trail rises 1,600 feet in elevation by the time you reach **Clingman's Dome,** the highest peak in the park, about 7.5 miles from the parking lot. This is a dramatic, high-elevation hike, offering marvelously distant views, but it's strenuous. If you have two cars, you can park near the summit of Clingman's Dome, and hike one-way in either direction between the dome and the Newfound Gap parking lot.

Heading north from the Newfound Gap parking lot, a very popular stretch rises a little more moderately, leading along ridges offering breathtaking vistas. The trail culminates four miles away, where you can stand atop dramatic **Charlie's Bunion,** a sheer 1,000-foot cliff. The vast majority of A.T. hikers don't stray much beyond the stretch between Clingman's Dome and Charlie's Bunion. If you prefer less crowded hiking, the Appalachian Trail offers about 50 miles of more solitary, spine-tingling trekking within the park.

If you plan to stay overnight on the A.T., you have to stay in one of the three open-air shelters along the trail, consisting of three walls at right angles covered by a roof—cozy, but big enough to allow 20 folks in sleeping bags to spend the night together without being slugged by the errant arm of a fellow camper having a nightmare. One

aspect makes these shelters different from most others on the A.T. These have a partial "fourth wall" to close the rectangle—a wire fence to keep out the bears. If you plan to stay at one these A.T. shelters in the park, you must register in advance. Call the **Backcountry Reservation Office,** tel. (423) 436-9564, at least a month beforehand.

Other Trails

Plunk down a quarter at one of the visitors centers to purchase the **Walks and Hikes** brochure and fold-out map, which catalogues 62 well-maintained trails in the park, including 11 self-guided nature trails. Or pick up the superb guidebook *Hiking Trails of the Smokies* ($17), which exhaustively covers 149 trails in the park.

In selecting certain trails to recommend exploring in this mountain paradise, we feel like parents trying to choose which children we love most. We recommend them all. Each one has distinctive flavors and rhythms, and we briefly mention the following hikes as typical examples of the glorious diversity of these trails.

The **Forney Ridge Trail** begins at the Clingman's Dome parking area, stretching four miles to the grassy summit of Andrews Bald. This thrilling hike is among the highest in the park, and, except for the brief but steep initial descent over rocky terrain, one of the most moderate of the high-elevation hikes, which tend to be quite strenuous.

At the Deep Creek campground and picnic area near Bryson City, you can choose between three trails leading to three picturesque waterfalls. The easy trail to **Toms Branch Falls** stretches just half a mile, while the equally easy, but longer **Indian Creek Falls Trail** meanders for two miles. The slightly more difficult **Juneywhank Falls Trail** climbs for 1.5 miles.

The 11 self-guided nature trails are all easy hikes, taking you through fascinating foliage. The exception to this leisurely inclined rule, *if* you hike the entire 5.5-mile route, is the popular **Alum Cave Bluff Self-Guiding Nature Trail,** beginning at Signpost 8 on Newfound Gap Road. in Tennessee. The first mile and a half winds merrily along Alum Creek through thick hemlock and birch forest, tempting you to lock elbows, start skipping, and burst into a chorus of "We're off to see the wizard." At Arch Rock, a natural tunnel, the trail starts climbing steeply, until you reach dramatic open heath balds another mile and a half up the trail. From these bluffs, it's another strenuous 2.5 miles to the top of Mt. LeConte. This trail, by the way, is the shortest route to the celebrated, super-rustic LeConte Lodge.

The **Noah "Bud" Ogle Self-Guiding Nature Trail,** off Cherokee Orchard Road near Gatlinburg, roams for three-fourths of a mile around the Ogle farm, past the long-abandoned homestead, barn, fields, orchards, and the stone foundation of "the weaner cabin," where Bud's sons and daughters-in-law spent their first year of marriage.

Along the roads, you'll see spots with signs saying, "Quiet Walkways," where two or three cars can pull off the road. These are brief strolls of a half mile or shorter, leading to streams, waterfalls, colorful thickets, and other woodsy delights. Because not many vehicles can park at the entrances to these walkways, they're never crowded.

Other Recreation

More than 700 miles of rivers, creeks and streams flow through the park, making **fishing** a popular pastime. Rainbow and brown trout predominate. The year-round trout season lures anglers far, wide, and frequently. Three restrictions apply: First, you need either a North Carolina or Tennessee fishing license, which you must purchase outside the park. Either license allows fishing anywhere in the park. Two, you need artificial lures. Organic bait is prohibited. Three, if you happen to hook the endangered brook trout, you must toss your catch back into the water.

Several stables in the park rent horses for guided **horseback rides.** In North Carolina, call **Smokemont Riding Stables** at (828) 497-2373. In Tennessee, try **Cades Cove Riding Stables,** tel. (423) 448-6286. If you bring your own horse, call the park headquarters at (423) 436-1200 for guidelines.

Because of the heavy traffic and ubiquitous blind curves, **bicycling** on the park's paved roads can be a combative, harrowing experience. On Saturday mornings, however, the Cades Cove Loop is closed to automotive traffic until 10 a.m., providing a temporary haven for bicyclists. Various back roads provide inviting biking, but the uneven road surfaces demand that you pay a lot of attention to the rocks and pits in your path, at the cost of absorbing the ethereal surroundings.

ACCOMMODATIONS AND FOOD

If you're fond of modern frills (like electricity), you'll have to find lodgings outside the park. However, the park can claim one celebrated hostelry. **LeConte Lodge** is one of the most sought-after, unique lodgings in the nation. With its lack of luxuries including phones, central heating, showers, baths, and electricity, the lodge is a testament to the first three laws of real estate—location, location, location. Built in the 1920s, this ageless lodge is situated miles from the closest road, high atop towering 6,593-foot Mt. LeConte, the second-tallest peak in the park. The shortest route to the lodge is via the strenuous 5.5-mile Alum Caves Bluff Trail, but four other (longer) trails also climb up to the lodge. With a capacity of 50 guests per night, the Lodge provides beds in both shared sleeping lodges and small, private cabins. The $75/night tariff includes breakfast and dinner served family-style, made from provisions toted up the mountain by llamas three times a week. Extras include kerosene lanterns and heaters, bed linens and wool blankets, bunk beds, and the big luxury—flush toilets!

Despite, or more accurately, because of its unique "rusticity," the lodge draws loads of repeat visitors who manage to reserve space by calling months ahead. Closed late November to mid-March, the lodge starts taking reservations for the following year on the first business day in October. Call (423) 429-5704 to see if they can squeeze you in (no credit cards accepted).

Campgrounds

The campgrounds in the park have a similar rustic feel. No showers here, and no flush toilets (except a few that are engaged at the bigger campgrounds when the crowds descend during peak seasons). Although the campgrounds can accommodate most RVs, there are no electrical or plumbing hook-ups. During the summer and fall, stays are limited to seven days, and during the rest of the year, two weeks. Pets are permitted but must be restrained. You can reserve sites at the Cades Cove, Smokemont, and Elkmont campgrounds up to two months in advance (these are also the only sites that can accommodate RVs over 26 feet long) by calling (800) 365-2267. The rest are first-come, first-served. Overall, the park offers 1,008 campsites, spread unevenly between ten campgrounds. Here's a quick summary, from smallest to largest:

Big Creek, nine sites, near the northeastern corner of the park in North Carolina, open May 1-Nov. 2.

Abrams Creek, 16 sites, near the northwestern corner of the park in Tennessee, open April 2-Nov. 2.

Cataloochee, 27 sites, near the eastern edge of the park in North Carolina, open spring through October.

Balsam Mountain, 46 sites, at the southeastern corner of the park in North Carolina, open May 20-Oct. 18.

Look Rock, 92 sites, at the western edge of the park in Tennessee, open mid-April to October.

Deep Creek, 108 sites, near Bryson City, NC, at the southern edge of the park, open May-November.

Smokemont, 140 sites, directly north of Cherokee, NC, just off US 441, open year-round.

Cades Cove, 161 sites, in Tennessee, open year-round, the only campground with a store.

Cosby, 175 sites, directly south of Cosby, TN, open spring through October.

Elkmont, 220 sites, closest campground to Gatlinburg, TN, open year-round.

Backcountry Camping
The park provides almost 100 sites where backpackers can pitch a tent in the wilderness. These spots can accommodate eight to 20 campers each. Though backcountry camping is free, permits are required, and you can't stay more than three days at any one site. Call (423) 436-9564, stop by one of the visitors centers, or write to Backcountry Permits, Great Smoky Mountains National Park, Gatlinburg, TN 37738.

Food and Drink
Bring your own. There are no restaurants in the park. Especially, be sure to carry water with you on hikes.

INFORMATION

For more information, contact Great Smoky Mountains National Park, 107 Park Headquarters Road, Gatlinburg, TN 37738, tel. (423) 436-1200. Set aside a few minutes when you call this main number, which leads you through a dizzying array of touch-tone menus. If you want to speak to a live human, it's best to pretend that you have a rotary phone. Allow at least two weeks to receive any information you request by mail. Despite the minor hassle and delay involved, you won't regret gathering some informational material before you visit.

THE CHEROKEE INDIAN RESERVATION

HISTORY

Founding Culture

For thousands of years, the southern Appalachian Mountains, extending from southern West Virginia to northern Georgia, belonged to the Cherokee Nation, or "Ani'-Yun'wiya" ("principal people").

The principal people's main responsibility was to keep the world in harmony and balance. When a Cherokee hunter killed a deer, tradition demanded that the hunter pray over the body of the deer, begging forgiveness from the deer's spirit for having taken its life, explaining that hungry Cherokee families needed the deer for food and clothing. This emphasis on balance also applied to human lives. The loss of any Cherokee in combat required taking an equal number of lives from the tribe responsible for the Cherokee deaths. Similarly, if one Cherokee killed another, the murderer's life, or that of a member of his family, was forfeited to keep the balance.

The primary duties of men in Cherokee society were to hunt, patrol the hunting grounds, and dance. Women bore the brunt of the work, including farming, gathering food, cooking, rearing children, and making clothes, baskets, and cookware.

But true to the ideal of balance, because women worked harder, they held more power in Cherokee society. When a woman decided who she wanted to marry, the intended either had to build a new house or come to live in the wife's home. In either case, the home was the woman's property, as were any children from the marriage. In addition, it was the sole prerogative of the mother to kill any unwanted and/or deformed newborns; if the father killed an infant, he was guilty of murder and subject to execution.

Women also had the right to divorce their mates. To get a divorce, the wife simply stuffed her husband's clothes in a sack and set it outside the door. Divorce and remarriage were not uncommon.

In late autumn, winter, and early spring, groups of 20 to 40 male warriors would patrol their territories, hunting deer and attacking any trespassers. True to the matriarchal orientation of Cherokee society, any trespassers captured in these attacks were taken back to the Cherokee village, where the women of the village were put in charge of determining the fate of the captives. Captured women and children were often adopted into Cherokee families, while adult males, more often than not, were tied to a stake, beaten, or otherwise tortured to death.

Conquistadors Come and Go

The first contact between the Cherokees and Europeans took place in 1540, when Spanish conquistador Hernando De Soto launched his first expedition into what is today the southeastern United States. De Soto and his heavily armed entourage were convinced that the Indians were hiding gold, which had been discovered in great quantities by other Spanish explorers in Mexico and Peru.

De Soto's routine, upon encountering Native Americans, was to torture a few of them to death in the noblest Spanish-Inquisition fashion, in hopes of getting them to reveal their hidden gold mines. This tactic always failed, because tribes like the Cherokee didn't value, and therefore didn't mine, gold. Captives who weren't tortured were enlisted as bearers, guides, and translators, then taken back to Spain to be sold as slaves.

Even though De Soto and his band of merry Spaniards were traipsing over significant stores of gold, sapphires, rubies, and emeralds, these riches went undiscovered. Subsequent expeditions by conquistador Juan Pardo in the 1560s also failed to unearth any significant wealth. Consequently, the Cherokee lands in the rugged southern Appalachians were left relatively undisturbed by Europeans for another two centuries.

Trading Hub

This changed in the early 1700s when British and French traders set up shop in the mountains, bartering for deer skins, a valuable commodity in the colonies and Europe at the time.

The traders had a significant impact on Cherokee traditions and values. No longer did deer

SEQUOYAH'S ALPHABET

Beginning in the late 18th century, many Cherokees encouraged their children to attend missionary schools. The intention was for the children to learn the intricacies of the European-dominated American culture and become better able to succeed in the new America. Many of these schools were boarding schools, designed to wean young Cherokee children away from the ways of their parents and ancestors, who were derided as savage and illiterate.

One child, born in 1771, whose white father named him George Gist but whose Cherokee mother called him Sequoyah, would go on to bridge the literacy gap between the Cherokee and English languages. Sequoyah Gist never attended school, but, as a gifted artisan, he made a decent living as a silversmith—enough to support his wife and daughter. To keep his business books, the "illiterate" Sequoyah devised an unusual ledger system, whereby various customers' accounts were identified not by name, but by the portraits Sequoyah drew of them.

Sequoyah

Various stories exist to explain how Sequoyah, at the age of 50, became the first and only single human being ever known to devise a successful alphabet of his own. Some say he got the idea when he became jealous of a relative who stayed with his family and who, a graduate of the missionary system, wrote letters to friends during his stay. Others maintain that Sequoyah—a notorious drunkard—created his syllabary in response to a challenge at a local bar, when Sequoyah said something like "reading, writing, there's no secret to it—it's just marks on paper or stone that stand for sounds."

The truth of how Sequoyah devised the Cherokee alphabet is, of course, not that simple. He saw that the Cherokee oral tradition was being lost, squeezed out by written English. Creating a written Cherokee language, he knew, could help preserve and maintain their heritage. For years, he labored obsessively to become literate in English and Greek, at the same time creating and refining his own private syllabary specially geared to render into writing the sounds of the Cherokee language (which didn't include English letter sounds such as B, Ch, J, P, R, or Z). Borrowing characters from the McGuffey Reader, the Bible, and various Greek texts, Sequoyah finally settled on a set of 86 characters to represent the Cherokee language.

Initially, his creation, far from earning him great renown, had the opposite effect. A respected friend pleaded with him to give up his embarrassing al-

play quite so sacred a role in keeping nature's balance. Whereas deer previously were hunted for both hide and meat, now the value of the deer's skin took precedence, and the carcasses could be left in the woods. Prayers to the spirit of the slain deer were now revised to give thanks for the nifty metal knives, hoes, guns, and ammunition that the deer's hide could procure for the family.

Skills such as carving stone into knives and arrowheads, and hunting with blowguns and bows and arrows, evaporated in favor of European technology. The change came swiftly. In 1708, the Cherokees sold about 50,000 deerskins to traders. By 1735, sales topped a million.

Other Cherokee traditions quickly evolved, geared toward gaining more European goods. Cherokee hunting patrols actively sought to round up as many captives of other tribes as possible and sell off the prisoners to slave-traders. This became an extremely lucrative enterprise for almost all native American tribes, greatly increasing the aggressions between them. Rather than making war to avenge past

D R T ♂ O i
a   e   i   o   u   v

ga ka ge yi yo ju gv

ha he hi ho hu hv

la le li lo lu lv

ma me mi mo mu

na hna gna ne ni no nu nv

gwa gwe gwi gwo gwu gwv

∧ as in FATHER
E as A in HATE OR SHORT as in PIT
I as I in PIQUE OR SHORT as in PIT
O as in LOW SHORT as in NOT
U as OO in FOOT SHORT as in PULL
V SHORT U NAZALIZED

sa s se si so su sv

da ta de te di ti do du dv

dla tla tlo tli tlo tlu tlv

tsa tse tsi tso tsu tsv

wa we wi wo wu wv

ya ye yi yo-yu yv

THERE WAS NO SOUND OF P, B, J, R, CH or Z

The entire language could be spoken without closing the lips except for the sound of 'M'

Cherokee alphabet

phabetical obsession. Sequoyah replied, "What I have done I have done from myself. If our people think I am making a fool of myself, you may tell our people that what I am doing will not make fools of them. They did not cause me to begin and they shall not cause me to give up. If I am no longer respected, what I am doing will not make our people the less respected, either by themselves or others; and so I shall go on and so you may tell our people."

Soon after, Sequoyah's wife and children moved out of his house to a place a few miles away. Sequoyah responded by building a house near them, so he could remain in close contact with his family. He taught his six-year-old daughter, Atoyah, his syllabary. A clever girl, Atoyah caught on quickly. Sequoyah and Atoyah soon astonished their neighbors and Sequoyah's drinking buddies. You could whisper in Sequoyah's ear that his daughter should pick up a certain glass or repeat a certain phrase,

Sequoyah would write down on a piece of paper whatever had been whispered, and Atoyah would repeat it or perform the requested task perfectly.

The brother of Chief John Watts became enamored of Sequoyah's alphabet and convinced his brother to allow Sequoyah and Atoyah to demonstrate their "written language" before the Cherokee Tribal Council. The politicians loved it. Suddenly, there was a way to immortalize in print their speeches and decisions—verbatim and *in the Cherokee language.*

By 1828, a year after their unified declaration of independence, the Cherokee Nation established a national bilingual newspaper, half English and half Cherokee, using Sequoyah's alphabet. In the twilight of his life, Sequoyah became one of the most venerated figures in Cherokee and American history. He died in 1843 at the age of 72, during a diplomatic mission to New Mexico.

killings or to protect their hunting grounds, the primary motivation of inter-tribal aggression was now mercenary. The balanced equation of "avenge one killing by taking one life" was supplanted by "take as many prisoners alive as possible, and sell them for the best price."

The heightened value of deerskins and Indian prisoners had an immediate impact on the gender roles in Cherokee life. Suddenly, the warriors became the main providers. Selling deerskins and hostages to traders could buy everything that Cherokee women had previously pro-

duced, from clothing and kettles to cornmeal and cutlery. The matriarchal foundation of Cherokee society gave way to the dominance of the male warrior-providers, whose wealth soon dominated tribal councils.

War, European-Style

Through the 1700s, the Cherokees fought as allies with both the British and the French, as those two colonial powers sought to divide up the Cherokee territory. The more the Cherokee fought alongside European allies, the more territory they lost. During the French and Indian War, between 1756 and 1763, most Cherokees started out as allies of the British, but then switched allegiance to the French—who, of course, lost the war.

Although the Cherokees were forced to give up huge chunks of their hunting grounds after their defeat, the British "compromised" by barring English settlement west of the foothills of the Appalachian mountains. For that reason, most Cherokees supported the British during the American Revolution. In the summer of 1776, at Britain's request, the Cherokees raided settlements in the Carolinas, Georgia, and Virginia. In response, General Griffith Rutherford, commander of the North Carolina colonial troops, led a brutal retaliation, wiping out more than 50 Cherokee towns, scalping all the adults, and selling all the children into slavery.

With the defeat of the British, the Cherokees were forced to cede more land to the new American government. The young Americans were apparently as eager as the Cherokees to avoid a continuance of warfare, and the two cultures embarked upon a period of cooperation marked by the establishment of schools and churches run by missionaries and government agents.

The "Europeanization" of the Cherokees progressed swiftly. The role of Cherokee women continued to diminish. Hunting was severely restricted, and men were now expected to do all the farming and decision-making, while the women were largely relegated to cooking, cleaning, and child-rearing.

Government, American-Style

Prior to the 19th century, the Cherokees' political structure was fragmented, a combination of hundreds of relatively autonomous town councils who met occasionally and informally at central gatherings. In 1817, the Cherokees created a unified republic, divided into eight distinct electoral districts which sent representatives to an official national council. The Cherokees established a unified Supreme Court in 1822 and adopted a formal constitution in 1827. The constitution established two legislative bodies, tailored along the lines of the U.S. House and Senate, with representatives democratically elected.

This creation of a unified Cherokee Republic precipitated an immediate response from the Georgia legislature, which accused the Cherokee of violating state sovereignty. Georgia passed a series of bills outlawing the Cherokee judicial and political systems, barring court testimony by Cherokees against whites, forbidding the Cherokees to mine gold, and—most punitive of all—creating the Georgia Guard, a brutal police force whose key responsibility was to beat, rob, imprison, and generally harass the Cherokees until they left Georgia.

By this time, however, the Cherokees' willingness to explore the white man's educational institutions had produced a brave new brand of Cherokee warriors—effective lawyers. Through a series of legal battles, the Cherokees ultimately prevailed in 1832, in *Worcester v. Georgia,* in which the U.S. Supreme Court ruled that the Cherokee Nation was not subject to Georgia state law.

Unfortunately, this legal victory proved hollow, since the federal government failed to enforce the ruling. In fact, two years earlier, in 1830, the U.S. Congress passed the Indian Removal Act, which authorized President Andrew Jackson to "negotiate" the relocation of all Indians to reservations west of the Mississippi. By the time the Supreme Court ruled for the Cherokees, the federal government was already busily pushing Indians throughout the East to move to reservations out West.

The Cherokees refused to budge. By 1835, Jackson's "negotiations" with them were deemed a complete failure, and the U.S. government resorted to force. By a margin of one vote, the U.S. Senate ratified a bogus treaty signed by 20 Cherokees. The ridiculous treaty called for the exchange of all Cherokee territory in the southeastern United States for $5.6 million and a tract of land in northeast Oklahoma, to take effect within two years.

After the two years had passed, the Cherokees refused to budge. More than 15,000 Cherokees—about 90% of the adult population—signed a petition repudiating the treaty. In response, in the summer of 1838, President Martin Van Buren dispatched General Winfield Scott and thousands of soldiers to relocate the Cherokees. The soldiers captured 16,000 people and imprisoned them in hastily built concentration camps. That fall and winter, the captive Cherokees were marched to various reservations in the Midwest. During this death march, called The Trail of Tears, between 10% and 25% of the Cherokee population perished.

About 1,000 Cherokees evaded capture in the 1838 roundup. Known as the Oconaluftee band, they pled their case the following year before the North Carolina legislature, were tacitly recognized as North Carolina citizens, and were allowed to buy property. By 1870, the federal government officially recognized the 56,000 acres of today's Qualla Boundary as a semi-autonomous Cherokee reservation—now home to about 8,000 Cherokees.

THE TOWN OF CHEROKEE

Regardless of which route you take to enter the town of Cherokee, you'll be hard pressed not to feel a tingle of anticipation upon entering an unspoiled paradise, protected by grand peaks. Then, as you descend for miles from the towering mountains along hairpin turns, you'll start to pass ever-increasing numbers of gift shops with handwritten signs, until you eventually reach the valley housing the town of Cherokee.

At first, driving along the streets of Cherokee, you might deduce that Cherokee culture revolves around silk-screened T-shirts and beaded moccasins. Souvenir shops abound, like the Honest Injun Trading Post or the Hiawatha Moccasin Shop (she wasn't even a Cherokee), packed with goods as kitschy as their names. Other commercial ventures like the Tee Pee Village Casino (the Cherokees didn't even build tepees), or the Cherokee Cyclorama Wax Museum, tend to color the town of Cherokee with the ambience of a tourist boardwalk without the ocean. Some visitors are repelled by the pervasive commercial atmosphere, but a few attractions provide insightful and entertaining glimpses into Cherokee culture and history. And if you think of the rest of it as an entertaining cornucopia of kitsch, you'll find plenty of amusing diversions to choose from, particularly if you're traveling with young children. Kids will long remember getting their picture taken with a "real" Indian, and parents will have a tough time peeling those new moccasins off their children's feet.

The four major attractions that impart an authentic understanding of Cherokee heritage all lie within walking distance of each other, at or near the intersection of US 441 and Drama Road.

Oconaluftee Village

First, visit the Oconaluftee Village, tel. (828) 497-2111, to experience a typical Cherokee village circa 1750. Kids especially will enjoy this guided one-hour tour. Friendly and knowledgeable re-enactors demonstrate activities like preparing food, weaving clothing and baskets, carving arrows and blowguns, and burning out canoes. Feel free to linger and ask questions—you can always join the next tour, which will be along in a few minutes. After your tour, stroll around the surrounding gardens. Located on Drama Road, the village lies about a half mile from its intersection with US 441. Admission is $9 for adults, $5 for kids 6-13. Open daily May 15-Oct.25. Tours begin every ten minutes.

Museum of the Cherokee Indian

Next, proceed to the Museum of the Cherokee Indian, at the intersection of US 441 and Drama Road, tel. (828) 497-3481. In addition to hundreds of artifacts, some dating back 10,000 years, the museum houses six mini-theaters that show brief videos about Cherokee history and culture, from prehistory to the present. Though it's packed with enough information to satisfy a hungry history Ph.D., the museum remains very kid-friendly, loaded with interactive exhibits like strapping on a headset and listening to how familiar English texts sound, spoken in Cherokee. Open daily, except major holidays; admission is $4 for adults, $2 for kids 6-12.

Qualla Arts and Crafts Mutual, Inc.

Admission to the art gallery and gift shop at the Museum of the Cherokee Indian is free, but before you purchase items there, stroll a few yards across Drama Road to check out Qualla Arts and Crafts Mutual, Inc., tel. (828) 497-3103, an artist cooperative featuring the work of more than 300 Cherokee craftspeople. This is *the* spot to purchase authentic Cherokee art and crafts. The stunning collections of beautiful and intricate masks, weaving, pottery, woodcarving, dolls, and jewelry have deservedly made this venture the most successful Indian-owned and - operated arts and crafts cooperative in the nation. Open daily; admission is free.

Outdoor Drama

For an effortless and entertaining history of the Cherokee, you can't beat the outdoor drama *Unto These Hills,* performed nightly except Sunday, from mid-June through late August at the 2,800-seat Mountainside Theatre on Drama Road, just off US 441, tel. (828) 497-2111. This elaborately staged play, energetically performed by more than 100 actors, recounts the history of the Cherokees from the time of Hernando De Soto's visit here in 1540 through the tragic Trail of Tears. The most popular of North Carolina's nine outdoor dramas, Kermit Hunter's moving tale has been packing in audiences since 1950.

Kids, especially, will be mesmerized by the flashy performance, complete with blazing torch dances and a vibrant musical score. Although the nearby Museum of the Cherokee Indian presents a much more comprehensive history of the Cherokee, the performance of *Unto These Hills* provides audiences with a memorable introduction to Cherokee history.

In June and July, performances start at 8:10 p.m., and in August at 7:50 p.m. The show includes half an hour of pre-drama musical entertainment. Reserved seats are $11 for all ages. General admission is $9 for adults and $5 for kids 12 and younger. Tickets are available 9 a.m.-6:30 p.m. at the box office at the intersection of US 441 and Drama Road. After 6:30, go directly to the Mountainside Theatre, about 200 yards up Drama Road.

Cherokee "Commercial Museums"

A number of stores bill themselves as museums. Some are as transparently named as the American Indian Museum and Chairlift, at Tomahawk Mall (and in fact, the chairlift *is* more fun than some museum tours), or the Cherokee Heritage Museum and Art Gallery, one of the few shops in Cherokee that sells fine Cherokee arts and crafts.

Santa's Land Fun Park & Zoo

Visit this combination amusement park/zoo/living history museum *only if you've got small children* (if they're older than eight, skip it). The "hot" rides include a one-mile train trip, an acrophobic-friendly Ferris wheel, and the exceedingly tame "Rudi Coaster," whose first car sports the bust of the most famous reindeer of all. Live entertainment includes the juggling and magic show at The Jingle Bell Theater.

The hottest attraction at Santa's Land is the zoo, where kids can feed and pet kids (goats, that is), deer, and other domesticated animals, as well as observe bears, monkeys, and other more exotic species. Other stops include various "heritage exhibits," where children can see grain ground into flour, or watch brooms be assembled. Santa and his elves, Frosty the Snowman, and other engaging, perpetually jovial, costumed characters stroll around the grounds. Santa's Land, located on NC 19 (Soco Road) in downtown Cherokee, tel. (828) 497-9191, is open daily May-October. Admission is $12, with kids under two admitted free.

Mineral Gambling

In the final analysis, the **Smoky Mountain Gem Mine,** tel. (828) 497-6574, is still Cherokee's

CHEROKEE GAMBLING

In North Carolina, where the state legislature promptly kills any attempts to legalize gambling, including perennial campaigns to establish a state lottery, Cherokee has the only games in the state.

For years, gambling in Cherokee was a rather dismal affair, characterized by dingy halls. But that changed in late 1997, with the grand opening of **Harrah's Cherokee Casino,** 7777 Casino Dr., tel (828) 497-7777. Located just off US 19, about a mile from downtown, the sprawling 175,000-square-foot Harrah's operation features 60,000 square feet of cavernous gaming space in the main hall. For veterans of Las Vegas and Atlantic City, however, don't get your hopes up—the only gaming consists of 2,300 video gambling machines. Also, as throughout the Cherokee reservation, no alcohol is available. But Harrah's does boast some big-name entertainment acts, who perform in the 1,500-seat pavilion (tickets start at $20). The casino is open 24 hours a day every day.

About a mile from Harrah's (two miles from downtown), also on US 19, **Tribal Bingo,** tel. (828) 497-4320 or (800) 410-1254, provides games nightly. Doors open at 4 p.m. daily and jackpots often reach $1,500 and higher.

best gambling venue. You can take your choice between fluming for gold ($4.50 a bag) or rubies and sapphires ($3.25 a bag). At least you'll get an aquamarine, amethyst, garnet, or other pretty pebble for your money. The mine is located on US 441, a few hundred yards north of the intersection with Drama Road.

OUTDOOR RECREATION

As you drive along the Oconaluftee River, you'll notice that **fishing** is extremely popular. It's also usually productive, thanks to the Cherokee Fish and Game Management, tel. (828) 497-5201, who twice a week stocks 30 miles of streams and three ponds with thousands of rainbow and brown trout. Although you don't need a state license, anglers must get a Tribal Fishing Permit ($5 per day), available at dozens of Cherokee shops. The daily creel limit is 10 per permit holder. Fishing is allowed year-round, except during most of March (the season closes March 1 and reopens the last Saturday in March).

Cherokee River Trips, located on US 19, two miles south of the Holiday Inn, tel. (828) 497-2821, offers relatively tame, two-hour **rafting** excursions down four miles of the Oconaluftee River. Guided trips are $15 per person ($12.50 unguided).

Glorious **hiking** opportunities lie just minutes away in Great Smoky Mountains National Park. If you'd like some thorough guidance before you head into the hills, or if you need any hiking or camping equipment, from maps and water bottles to backpacks and stoves, stop by **Queen's Trading Post & Outfitters,** a mile south of the Great Smoky Mountains National Park entrance on US 441, tel. (828) 497-HIKE. The staff there are veteran hikers who know these hills well.

ACCOMMODATIONS

Elegant lodgings like historic hotels or bed and breakfasts simply don't exist in Cherokee. However, there are lots of other options. Cherokee is riddled with dozens of Inexpensive independent lodgings, like the Papoose Motel, Wigwam Motel, the Redskin Motel, and lots of cabin rentals. Un-

characteristically, we recommend sticking to the chains in Cherokee, with the following exceptions, all Inexpensive: the best-buy **Pioneer Motel and Cabins** on US 19, a mile south of the junction with US 441, tel. (828) 497-2435, $28-64; the plain-as-its-name, but very clean and comfortable **Craig's Motel** on US 19 (Soco Road), a mile north of the junction with US 441, tel. (828) 497-3821, $42-63; and the pleasant **Pageant Hills Motel,** on US 441, a mile north of the junction with US 19, tel. (828) 497-5371, $30-48.

The chain lodgings in central Cherokee are pretty interchangeable. Here's a quick, alphabetical summary of the options available within a couple miles of Cherokee's focal intersection of US 19 and US 441. During non-summer months, the rates of most of these chains are reduced by a third or half, dipping close to or below the $50 per night level. Rates described below are for two persons during the peak season, June-August. Even during this peak season, rates sometimes vary depending on the day.

Best Western Great Smokies Inn, Acquoni Rd., just off US 441N, tel. (828) 497-2020 or (800) 528-1234. Moderate-Expensive.

Budgetel Inn, Acquoni Rd., just off US 441N, tel. (828) 497-2101 or (800) 4-BUDGET. Moderate-Expensive.

Comfort Inn, US 19, just west of junction of US 19 and 441, tel. (828) 497-2411 or (800) 228-5150. Moderate.

Days Inn, tel. (828) 497-9171 or (800) DAYS-INN. Moderate-Expensive.

Econo Lodge, Acquoni Rd., just off US 441N, tel. (828) 497-2226 or (800) 55-ECONO. Moderate.

The Hampton Inn, at junction of US 19S and 441S, tel. (828) 497-3115 or (800) HAMPTON. Moderate.

Holiday Inn, on US 19S, about a mile from junction of US 19 and 441, tel. (828) 497-9181 or (800) HOLIDAY. Moderate-Expensive.

Quality Inn, on US 441 Bypass, about a mile from junction of US 19 and 441, tel. (828) 497-4702 or (800)-228-5151. Moderate-Expensive.

Campgrounds

No fewer than 26 campgrounds, providing more than 2,000 campsites, are located within a five-minute drive of downtown Cherokee. The 35-acre **Cherokee KOA** on Big Cove Road a couple miles north of the Blue Ridge Parkway, tel. (828) 497-9711 or (800) 825-8352, includes 420 campsites, from primitive tent sites to paved sites with full hook-ups. Sites average about $20. KOA also offers 100 inexpensive one- and two-bedroom log cabins, many alongside the Oconaluftee River. The campground includes extras like a swimming pool, tennis courts, a big jacuzzi, game rooms, and movies. Call for a free brochure.

Another whopper of a campground is the 100-acre, 210-site (50 riverfront) **Yogi in the Smokies,** about five miles north of the Blue Ridge Parkway on Big Cove Road, tel. (828) 497-9151. If you want to camp in town, try the 60-site **Cherokee Campground** located at the junction of US 19 and US 441 Business, tel. (828) 497-9838.

Pick up a listing of the area campgrounds at the Cherokee Visitor Center, at the junction of US 19 (Soco Road) and Business US 441 (Acquoni Road), tel. (828) 497-9195 or (800) 438-1601.

FOOD AND DRINK

With one exception, the closest you'll come to haute cuisine in Cherokee is Ponderosa Steak House. The exception is the **Tee Pee Restaurant** on US 441, next to the *Unto These Hills* ticket office at US 441 and Drama Road, tel. (828) 497-5141. With a lovely view overlooking the Oconaluftee River, the Tee Pee is considered by the locals to be not only one of the best places to eat out in Cherokee, but the *only* spot in town to enjoy a really good meal. Specializing in rainbow trout and country ham, both $9, the Tee Pee is open daily 6:30 a.m.-9 p.m. On the first and third Thursdays of every month, the Tee Pee cooks "Traditional Indian Food Dinners" ($5 for lunch, $9 for dinner),when you can try some hearty bean bread and fatback and other traditional dishes. The Tee Pee closes from Thanksgiving through January.

If you'd like glass of wine with your meal, you'll have to leave town. No alcohol is sold on the reservation.

INFORMATION

The **Cherokee Visitors Center** is located at the junction of US 19 (Soco Road) and Business US 441 (Acquoni Road). Call (828) 497-9195 or (800) 438-1601 for a free 20-page brochure. The mailing address is Cherokee Tribal Travel and Promotion, P.O. Box 460, Cherokee, NC 28719.

BEYOND CHEROKEE

Several other, smaller towns near Great Smoky Mountains National Park offer hospitable lodgings, hearty country cooking, and entertaining diversions from skiing to kayaking, rail excursions to roller coasters.

MAGGIE VALLEY

You won't get lost here—Maggie Valley consists mostly of one road, US Route 19, running through a deep valley between two towering walls of the Balsam Mountains. This main drag is lined with chain motels and restaurants, as well as dozens of gift shops. In addition to its proximity to Great Smoky Mountains National Park, about 15 miles west of the park entrance just north of Cherokee, Maggie Valley offers some popular attractions of its own.

During the winter, legions of skiers descend on the valley to schuss down the mile-high slopes of **Cataloochee Ski Area,** located on Fie Top Road, four miles off US Route 19 (Soco Road), tel. (828) 926-0285 or (800) 768-0285. Nine slopes, serviced by two chairlifts, zig and zag down 5,400-foot Moody Top Mountain, with a maximum vertical drop of 740 feet. The Omigosh run starts at the mountain summit, zipping steeply down for 2,200 feet, then joins with the Lower Omigosh slope, which descends for another 1,800 feet to the lodge. Lift tickets for adults are $20 on weekdays and $33 Saturday and Sunday. Night skiing, 6-10 p.m. is available Tuesday through Saturday, with lift tickets costing

$14 Tues.-Thurs. and $16 Friday and Saturday. Thanks to its mile-high location and lots of snow-making machines, skiing continues into March. Equipment rentals and lessons are available for skiers of all sizes and levels of expertise.

On Route 19 in downtown Maggie Valley, you'll see a narrow clearing, where a steep chairlift and incline railway lead straight up to the mile-high, Wild West theme park, **Ghost Town In the Sky,** tel. (828) 926-1140 or (800) 446-7886. Although you can take a shuttle bus, choose the chairlift or incline—they are two of the most exciting rides at this park. Make no mistake about it, this is a kids-only attraction—and fairly young kids at that. Most of the rides are pretty tame, like the spinning, tilting roulette wheel. For courageous kids, the Red Devil roller coaster is the big fear-monger of the park, featuring a loop-the-loop. Inside the red velvet walls of the Silver Dollar Saloon, live bands play country music, and the honky-tonk piano blasts out the can-can, complete with high-stepping showgirls flipping and twirling their colorful petticoats. At Fort Cherokee, kids can watch live performance of authentic Cherokee dances. In all, the park has about 30 rides and shows to keep the kids entertained, along with several spots to eat. If you hang out on Main Street awhile, you'll also be sure to encounter a jail break or bank robbery. Don't worry though, the ghost town's busy marshall is used to several gunfights a day and is sure to gun down or round up the bad guys before they get away. Tickets are $17 for adults, $12 for kids 3-9, and include admission to all rides and shows.

Golfers won't want to miss the **Maggie Valley Resort & Country Club,** 340 Country Club Rd., off Route 19, tel. (828) 926-1616 or (800) 438-3861. Famed for its scenic split-personality, the front nine of the championship course winds through rolling valley terrain, and the back nine snakes through the mountains. Greens fees for golfers not staying at the resort are $29 Mon.-Thurs. and $34 Fri.-Sunday. Carts cost $14.50/per person and are mandatory until 2:30 p.m. If you stay at the resort, greens fees are reduced by $10. Two-day, three-night golf packages start at $175 per person and include two breakfasts, two dinners, and three rounds of golf.

Accommodations and Food

You don't have to play golf to stay at the Maggie Valley Resort, which also offers two tennis courts and a large, heated outdoor swimming pool. From March to November, standard rooms with two double beds start at $100. During the ski season, rates drop to about $75. Spacious one- and two-bedroom villas are also available. All 64 rooms have balconies, most with a view of the golf course. Moderate-Expensive. The Valley Room at the resort serves full country breakfasts for $5-8, and steaks, fish, and poultry for dinner ($15-25).

Cataloochee Ranch lies three miles up Fie Top Road, off US 19, tel. (828) 926-1401 or (800) 868-1401. And we mean up. At an elevation of 5,000 feet, this 1,000-acre resort offers a heady lodging experience. As the name implies, this is a working ranch, and horses make up some of the livestock. Guided horseback rides will take you through high-elevation forests and across peaks with vistas of distant ranges. Horseback and hiking trails lead from the ranch into adjacent Great Smoky Mountains National Park. Just a mile down Fie Top Road from Cataloochee ski area, the ranch provides the closest lodgings for Maggie Valley skiers. In addition to 15 regular guest rooms and two two-bedroom suites, the ranch also has 11 cabins that can sleep two to eight people. Summer rates range $140-220 and include family-style breakfasts and dinners. Meals aren't included in the winter, when the rates are reduced by about half. Premium-Luxury.

Maggie Valley is home to dozens of relatively interchangeable chain and chain-like motels, all along US 19 (Soco Road). The **Best Western Mountainbrook Inn,** 1021 Soco Rd., tel. (828) 926-3962 or (800) 528-1234, includes a heated outdoor pool and indoor hot tub. Moderate. The **Jonathan Creek Inn,** 1314 Soco Rd., tel. (828) 926-1232 or (800) 577-7812, includes a small, heated indoor pool and some hot tub suites. Rates vary depending on the season and type of room you want. Inexpensive-Expensive. The **Laurel Park Inn,** 109 Soco Rd., tel. (828) 926-1700 or (800) 451-4424 offers a small, heated pool, and Inexpensive rates Sun.-Thurs. even during peak season. On Friday and Saturday, rates rise to Moderate. The **Comfort Inn,** 848

Soco Rd., tel. (828) 926-9106 or (800) 221-2222, includes an outdoor pool and whirlpools in some suites. Moderate-Expensive.

Eating in Maggie Valley is a family affair, with lots of places to get burgers and other sand-wiches for lunch and dinner. A pleasant excep-tion, **J. Arthur's Steakhouse,** 801 Soco Rd. (US Route 19), tel. (828) 926-1817, specializes in steak and seafood. Specialties of the house in-clude a creamy gorgonzola cheese salad and fresh mountain trout. The two-story, pine-paneled dining room includes fireplaces to warm snow-weary bones. A popular cocktail lounge sup-plies beverages to warm you up from the inside. Dinner entrees range $10-22. Closed Sunday and Monday during the winter, J. Arthur's is open daily for dinner the rest of the year.

Nightlife

From May through October, the **Stompin' Ground** on US 19, tel. (828) 926-1288, hosts country clogging per-formances nightly. You can join in on Friday and Saturday. For the most popular dancing spot in town, try the **Maggie Valley Opry House** on US 19, tel. (828) 926-9336, hopping nightly May-Oct. with blue-grass and country music.

WAYNESVILLE

Whereas Maggie Valley consists largely of one long, modern commer-cial strip appealing to tourists, Waynesville re-tains the atmosphere of a small, mountain town with a long history. Much quieter than Maggie Valley, Waynesville is located on US 23/74, four miles from the Blue Ridge Parkway and about 25 miles from both the Great Smoky Mountains National Park and Asheville, making it an attrac-tive base for folks wanting to explore the big city and big mountains of this region. There's not a whole lot to do in Waynesville's two-block down-town, except taking a very leisurely afternoon stroll through the dozen or so antique and gift shops, craft studios, and galleries. For a tasty sandwich or calorie-concentrated treat during your downtown wanderings, stop by **Whitman's**

Bakery, 113 N. Main St., tel. (828) 4456-8271.

Hard-core handicraft buffs won't want to miss the **Museum of North Carolina Handicrafts** on the corner of US 276 South and Shelton Street, two blocks off Main Street, tel. (828) 452-1551. The gorgeously preserved two-story Shelton House, a Charleston-style farm home built be-tween 1875-80, now houses an elaborate selection of traditional handicrafts created by some of North Carolina's most renowned artisans. Wares in-clude Ed Presnell's ornate mountain dulcimers, Bill Crowe's tiny carved Cherokee boots, Sea-grove pottery, and dozens of quilts and coverlets.

In all, the museum collection numbers more than 2,000 pieces of pottery, bas-kets, woodcarvings, textiles, jewelry, and other hand-made crafts. Admis-sion is $4 for adults, $1 for kids under 12. Open Tues.-Fri. May-October.

Golf reigns at the **Waynesville Country Club Inn,** 1 Country Club Dr., tel. (828) 456-3551 or (800) 627-6250, where 27 pic-turesque holes wind through mountain streams and ponds, with soaring peaks rising in the distance. Tennis courts, a swim-ming pool, two restaurants, and a lounge serving beer and wine provide entertaining diver-sions from your golf game. Less than a five-minute drive from downtown, the modern resort includes 94 spacious guest rooms and eight one-bedroom cot-tages. Luxury rates include gourmet breakfasts and dinners, and of course, golf. During the winter season, rates go down to $100 or less.

For $65, two can stay in one of the four guest rooms at the **Belle Meade Inn,** 804 Balsam Rd., tel. (828) 456-3234. The restored 1908 crafts-man-style house, complete with chestnut wood-work and a large fieldstone fireplace, elegantly blends antique and traditional furnishings. Rates in-clude a full country breakfast and afternoon tea or sherry. Moderate.

For lunch, dinner, or drinks downtown, try **Bo-gart's,** 222 South Main St., tel. (828) 452 1313. The menu varies considerably at this popular tavern and restaurant, from burgers to steaks to rainbow trout. The stained-glass windows accentuate the tavern atmosphere, making this Waynesville's most popular night spot. Prices range $5-15 for lunch and dinner.

BRYSON CITY AREA

If you've never been **whitewater rafting** but always wanted to try it, then look no further than the **Nantahala Outdoor Center,** 13 miles southwest of Bryson City along US 19, tel. (800) 232-7238. Here, you'll share a raft with three or five others for a three-and-a-half-hour ride on the clear, cool water of the Nantahala River, through deep, lush Nantahala Gorge, accompanied by a guide in every two or three rafts.

At first, you'll be enchanted by secluded valley scenery and the relatively languid pace, as you float by the forested riverbanks. Then, you'll start to hear the whisper of rushing water around the bend. The whisper swells into a roar, your pulse quickens with anticipation mixed with a little fear, and then, you're sucked into a narrow, swirling current, defying gravity, swishing up, down, around boulders, your raftmates are yelling and paddling like mad, and, after a frenetic minute or two, you're back to more tranquil waters. By the way, don't worry about falling out in a rapid. As the guides will teach you, if you just thrust your feet out in front of you, the current will steer you clear of the rocks, and the life jackets will keep your head above water, except for some momentary dunkings.

This section of the river is dam-controlled, so the water level remains constant all year. The rafting season begins in March and ends in mid-November. Guided trips cost $25-31, the most expensive time being Saturdays July 4-August 15. If you're an experienced rafter and don't need a guide, you can rent equipment, either rafts or inflatable one- or two-person kayaks, at lower prices.

Shuttle buses take you to the appropriate "put-in" point, and your river excursion concludes at the center. Guaranteed, you'll have built up a considerable appetite from all that paddling. **Relia's Garden** restaurant, at the center, tel. (828) 488-2175, provides burgers (both beef and grain varieties), chicken and hummus sandwiches ($5-6), rainbow trout ($11-13), various linguine dishes($8-14), and during lunch, the hearty Carolina jambalaya—smoked sausage and shrimp in a mildly spicy tomato sauce served over rice ($8). Dinner options include all the foregoing plus steaks ($14). Relia's also serves full country breakfasts ($3-5).

Incidentally, for hard-core rafters' looking for class IV rapids, the center also sponsors trips in Tennessee and South Carolina, as well as trips around the globe, to wild rivers in Costa Rica, Nepal, Turkey, and other exotic destinations.

Running rapids isn't the only adventure available at the center. For $75 you can also take one-day mini-courses on **mountain biking, rock climbing,** and **kayak touring.** For a free brochure about all of the center's programs, including in-depth clinics, call (888) 662-1662.

The center has very limited accommodations, mostly bunk-house-style, and most are reserved for students studying at the center's various clinics, including the world-renowned kayaking school. The center will send you a listing of recommended lodgings in the Bryson City area. The closest is also among the best, **Nantahala Village,** about three miles north of the center and 10 miles from Bryson City along US 19, tel. (828) 488-2826 or, outside NC, (800) 438-1507. Here, you can stay in one of 41 pleasant cabins or 12 privately owned homes. All have kitchens. Most of the cabins have two bedrooms, but one-, three-, and four-bedroom cabins are available. Some of the private homes have hot tubs. From May to October, the cabins and homes range $85-245, with a two-night minimum. You can also stay in guest rooms at the main lodge, which was mostly gutted by a fire in late 1996 and undergoing a major renovation as this edition went to press, but which should now be open, with a restaurant. The village is closed Nov. 30-March 20.

The Great Smoky Mountain Railway

With depots in Dillsboro, Bryson City and Andrews, this first-class operation has been chugging through the Great Smoky Mountains for a decade, utilizing rail lines dating back to the 1840s. The railway, tel. (800) 872-4681, operates four diesel-electric locomotives and one steam locomotive, No. 1702, which served the Army during World War II. Passengers ride in reconditioned coaches, open cars, or the fancier club cars ($7 extra). Excursions powered by No. 1702 cost an extra $5. Depending on your destination, roundtrips cost $18-24, $9 for kids under 12. The excursions last three and a half to four and a half hours, including a one-hour layover for a meal or brief sightseeing. All of the trips provide dazzling scenery and the nostalgic charm of experiencing the mountainous terrain via train.

To experience the ultimate romance of these rails, make a reservation for the **twilight dinner train,** departing from Dillsboro. During this two-and-a-half-hour, adults-only trip, you'll be served a gourmet dinner featuring entrees like chateaubriand, roasted rosemary hen, or beef tenderloin, as you watch the sun play hide and seek with the mountain skylines. Tickets are $50. Another regularly running favorite is the seven-hour **raft 'n' rail,** combining a train trip and a rafting adventure guided by the Nantahala Outdoor Center. Departing from Bryson City,

this two-in-one excursion costs $52-57 for adults and $42 for kids.

Railroad buffs will enjoy touring the 5,000-square-foot **Historic Train Museum** next to the Dillsboro depot. Crammed with more than 3,000 articles of railroading history, the museum has operating model trains and shows informative videos, including "Riding on Steam Engine #1702," "History of the Railroad," and "The Railway and the Community"—an ideal introduction for kids about to ride the rails. Admission is $3 for adults, $2 for kids under 12.

The railway also offers a number of special trips, like the **murder mystery excursions** staged monthly May-Oct. with help from members of the Asheville Community Theatre. Trains don't run in January or February and have limited schedules in March, November, and December. For reservations and information about the railway's many options, call (800) 872-4681.

BOOKLIST

DESCRIPTION AND TRAVEL

Alexander, John, and James Lazell. *Ribbon of Sand—the Amazing Convergence of the Ocean and the Outer Banks.* Chapel Hill: Algonquin Books, 1992, 240 pp. The distinguished authors of this unusual book have rendered the physical and sociological history of the Outer Banks in a superbly readable, informative, and entertaining style.

Bailey, Anthony. *The Outer Banks—Exploring An Enticing & Endangered Stretch of the Carolina Coastline.* New York: Farrar, Straus Giroux, 1989. This marvelous personal travelogue, portions of which first appeared in *The New Yorker,* is a terrific read, giving readers an intimate feel for what exploring the Outer Banks felt like a decade ago. Bailey is a consummate stylist who gives his adventurous trip along the Outer Banks a dramatic immediacy.

Barefoot, Daniel W. *Touring the Backroads of North Carolina's Lower Coast.* Winston-Salem: John F. Blair, 1995. One of three wonderfully detailed guides (see other Daniel W. Barefoot and Carolyn Sakowski entries) delivering comprehensive historic details about places in the coastal and mountain areas of North Carolina.

Barefoot, Daniel W. *Touring the Backroads of North Carolina's Upper Coast.* Winston-Salem: John F. Blair, 1995. (See previous entry.)

Biggs, Walter C., and James F. Parnell. *State Parks of North Carolina.* Winston-Salem: John F. Blair, 1995, 342 pp. A fact-packed guide to North Carolina's state parks and state recreation areas, this guide is marvelously comprehensive, listing the various activities, hiking trails, flora and fauna, and camping facilities.

Handmade in America, Inc. *The Craft Heritage Trails of Western North Carolina.* Asheville, NC: Handmade in America, Inc., 145 pp. (copies are available by calling 828-252-0121 or stopping at any of hundreds of arts-and-crafts galleries and stores throughout North Carolina's western mountain region). The ultimate bible for anyone seeking to explore the richesse of traditional Appalachian arts and crafts practiced throughout the state's western mountain region. This guidebook provides not only a series of efficiently plotted routes to hundreds of great galleries and stores, but also provides authoritative background on the area's renowned artistic traditions, as well as providing helpful hints for hospitable lodging and convenient spots to eat during your craft search.

Lord, William G. *Blue Ridge Parkway Guide.* Birmingham, NC: Menasha Ridge Press, 1992. This terrific two-volume guide, originally published in 1981, details all 469 miles of the Blue Ridge Parkway. Written by a naturalist who started working as a ranger on the Parkway in 1948. As it describes virtually every feature and overlook you'll encounter as you glide along this magnificent road, the guide seamlessly weaves together nature, history, and folklore.

Roe, Charles E. *North Carolina Wildlife Viewing Guide.* Helena, MT: Falcon Press, 1992. If you're looking for just one illustrated nature guide to the state, this is your best bet. Clean, lively prose.

Sakowski, Carolyn. *Touring the Western North Carolina Backroads.* Winston-Salem: John F. Blair, 1995. Like the other two books in this series (see entries under Daniel W. Barefoot, above), this guide is written with the energetic voice of a scholarly researcher who can bring history to life and help you see a single sight through many different periods.

CULTURE AND HISTORY

Barrett, John G. *The Civil War In North Carolina.* Chapel Hill and London: University of North Carolina Press, 1987, 486 pp. This scholarly tome thoroughly covers the history of the Civil War years in the state, including details of the 11 battles and 73 skirmishes fought here.

Claiborne, Jack, and William Price, editors. *Discovering North Carolina.* Chapel Hill and London: University of North Carolina Press, 1991, 380 pp. An absolutely mesmerizing, highly entertaining anthology of histories, biographies, diaries, short stories, and novel excerpts, and newspaper and magazine pieces chronicling 400 years of North Carolina history. North Carolina-born, -bred, and -educated Charles Kuralt described the book as "a lively, rich compendium, funny and poignant and inspiring, like North Carolina. And full of surprises," and called it "the most interesting book about North Carolina I've ever read—and one of the most interesting books about *anything.*"

Coombs, Harry B. *Kill Devil Hill—Discovering the Secret of the Wright Brothers.* Boston: Houghton Mifflin Co., 1979, 386 pp. This intriguing history, written by a veteran pilot who first soloed in a biplane in WW I and later rose to become president of Lear Jets, artfully combines science and history to reveal how the two bicycle mechanics from Ohio achieved in four years what many of the world's greatest scientific minds had failed to accomplish in all of history.

Kuralt, Charles, and Loonis McGlohon. *North Carolina Is My Home.* Charlotte: East Woods Press, Fast & McMillan, Publishers, 1986, 105 pp. An endearing homage to Kuralt's home state, this book is an outgrowth of Kuralt's grand effort to write the book (i.e., the lyrics) for McGlohon's musical about North Carolina. Every page is packed with wonderful photos. The book exudes the characteristic sense of discovery and appreciation with which Kuralt suffused his *On The Road* series and pieces and also offers a unique glimpse into Kuralt's natural feel for verse.

Luebke, Paul. *Tarheel Politics—Myths and Realities.* Chapel Hill and London: The University of North Carolina Press, 1990. In just 200 pages, Luebke (Professor of Sociology at the University of North Carolina at Greensboro and a state representative) delivers a scholarly, comprehensive history of North Carolina politics. Among many other political and sociological mysteries, Luebke helps to explain why in the 1990s North Carolina—a traditionally liberal Democratic state—was simultaneously represented in the U.S. Senate by one of that body's most liberal and educated members (Terry Sanford) and one of its most conservative, anti-intellectual ones (Jesse Helms).

North Carolina: the WPA Guide To The Old North State. Columbia, SC: The University of South Carolina Press, 1989 (orig. published by The University of North Carolina Press in Chapel Hill in 1939). Virtually unchanged from the 1939 edition, except for a 10-page introduction, this rich guide provides a comprehensive snapshot of the state, as viewed by a team of professional writers and historians. Though obviously dated, the book is full of elegantly presented information still frequently used by writers, historians, and travelers today.

Powell, William. *North Carolina—Through Four Centuries.* Chapel Hill and London: The University of North Carolina Press, 1989. William Powell is known as the premier textbook writer about North Carolina history. This 650-page volume is scholarly yet readable.

Rogers, Dennis. *Crossroads.* Raleigh: Raleigh News & Observer Publishing Company, 1984. For more than two decades, native Tarheel Rogers has been a columnist for the daily *Raleigh News & Observer* newspaper, capturing just about every facet of the experience of North Carolina. The paper's publishing company has released four collections of Rogers' finest columns, all highly recommended.

Rogers, Dennis. *Home Grown.* Raleigh: Raleigh News & Observer Publishing Company, 1979.

Rogers, Dennis. *It's Bad News When The Bartender Cries.* Raleigh: Raleigh News & Observer Publishing Company, 1988.

Rogers, Dennis. *Second Harvest.* Raleigh: Raleigh News & Observer Publishing Company, 1981.

Wolfe, Thomas. *Look Homeward Angel.* Available in virtually any library or bookstore, this magnificently personal work, first published in the 1920s, tells the tale behind Wolfe's bizarre youth in Asheville. Although Wolfe defied the literary convention of his time—preferring long, complicated sentences to short, clear ones—this masterpiece remains justly revered today and constitutes a wonderfully readable, dramatic history.

RECREATION

De Hart, Allen. *North Carolina Hiking Trails.* Boston: Appalachian Mountain Club, 1998 (3rd ed.). Incomparable comprehensive guide to hiking in the state.

Young, Claiborne. *Cruising Guide to Coastal North Carolina.* Winston-Salem: John F. Blair, Publisher, 1997 (4th ed.). With more than 3,000 miles of shoreline, North Carolina presents a panoply of opportunities for boaters. Young, a gifted writer, navigator, and boater, has been compiling detailed guides for boaters for several years. In addition to details on virtually every marina, cove, and cape on the North Carolina coast, he also provides a wealth of history and current local color in this marvelous guide.

CONTEMPORARY FICTION

North Carolina is the birthplace and home of an extraordinary number of renowned writers of fiction. This selective list (which includes only one of each author's many wonderful titles) is geared toward generally lighthearted reading (Charles Frazier's celebrated novel is the one exception), appropriate for vacationing, that also gives you a feel for rich, authentic North Carolina voices.

Chappel, Fred. *I Am One of You Forever.* Louisiana State University Press, 1985, 184 pp. As this travel guide went to press, Mr. Chappel was serving as the state's Poet Laureate. A wonderfully gifted poet, fiction writer, and literary critic, Chappel first won our hearts with the funny and elegant coming-of-age tales in this short story collection.

Edgerton, Clyde. *Raney.* New York: Ballantine Books, 1997 (orig. published 1985). Edgerton delights readers with colorfully bizarre yet believable characters whose interaction and dialogue propel you effortlessly through his works.

Frazier, Charles. *Cold Mountain.* New York: Atlantic Monthly Press, New York, 1997, 356 pp. This much-celebrated first novel, set during the last months of the Civil War, won the 1997 National Book Award for fiction. The novel details the ordeal of a wounded Civil War soldier making his way home across North Carolina after his final battle. (This is anything but light reading.)

Gibbons, Kaye. *Ellen Foster.* New York: Vintage Press, 1990, 128 pp. (orig. published 1987). A brilliant young Tarheel voice, Gibbons burst upon the national literary scene with this, her first novel, as she was graduating college. The heroine of this enthralling, hilarious contemporary novel has frequently been referred to in reviews as "a Southern, female Holden Caulfield." This was one of the first selections of Oprah Winfrey's book club.

McCorkle, Jill. *Carolina Moon.* Chapel Hill: Algonquin Books, 1996. This novel, revolving around Quee Purdy, a sixty-something entrepreneur from the wrong side of small-town tracks, is characteristic of McCorkle's expertly crafted, ingeniously plotted novels featuring a vast range of surreal yet reality-based characters.

Smith, Lee. *Black Mountain Breakdown.* New York: Ballantine Books, 1980. Smith is the author of several utterly beautiful novels and short story collections that deftly tread the line separating fact from fiction.

ACCOMMODATIONS INDEX

RESTAURANT INDEX

INDEX

FISHING

ABOUT THE AUTHORS

Rob Hirtz is a freelance writer, born and raised in Pittsburgh, Pennsylvania. While attending the University of Pennsylvania, he was editor-in-chief of Penn's literary magazine before graduating in 1980 with degrees in English and psychology. After a decade of work as a political consultant, Rob returned to a writing career. He chronicled the big and little issues (and juicy gossip) of Pennsylvania politics as a columnist for Philadelphia City Paper and as a weekly commentator on WHYY, Philadelphia's National Public Radio station. After moving to North Carolina in the early 1990s, Rob fell in love with his adopted home state and started writing about it. In 1996, he co-authored, with his brother, Bill, *Tales of Orp,* a music instruction book for second-year piano students.

Jenny Daughtry Hirtz is a Southerner by birth, rearing, and heritage. After earning a bachelor's degree in political science, she spent 11 years in Washington, D.C. and Philadelphia, working as national field director and state executive director for political lobbying groups and as a consultant to several political campaigns and nonprofit organizations. Jenny traveled frequently to North Carolina for vacations as a child and for both work and pleasure as an adult, and longed to make the state her home. In 1994 she got her wish. She currently works as a writer and a sales representative who regularly travels throughout the state.

Rob and Jenny live in Durham with their beautiful, adored mutt-from-the-animal-shelter, Sparky, a veteran travel researcher who specializes in reviews of pet-friendly accommodations and restaurants that provide doggy bags.

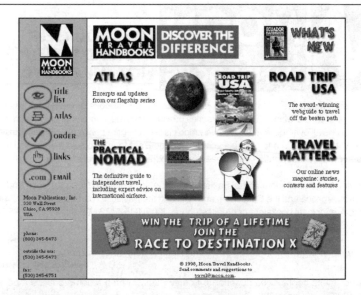

www.moon.com

Enjoy our travel information center on the World Wide Web (WWW), loaded with interactive exhibits designed especially for the Internet.

ATTRACTIONS ON MOON'S WEB SITE INCLUDE:

ATLAS
Our award-winning, comprehensive travel guides cover destinations throughout North America and Hawaii, Latin America and the Caribbean, and Asia and the Pacific.

PRACTICAL NOMAD
Extensive excerpts, a unique set of travel links coordinated with the book, and a regular Q & A column by author and Internet travel consultant Edward Hasbrouck.

TRAVEL MATTERS
Our on-line travel zine, featuring articles; author correspondence; a travel library including health information, reading lists, and cultural cues; and our new contest, **Destination X,** offering a chance to win a trip to the mystery destination of your choice.

ROAD TRIP USA
Our best-selling book, ever; don't miss this award-winning Web guide to off-the-interstate itineraries.

Come visit us at: **www.moon.com**

LOSE YOURSELF IN THE EXPERIENCE, NOT THE CROWD

For 25 years, Moon Travel Handbooks have been the guidebooks of choice for adventurous travelers. Our award-winning Handbook series provides focused, comprehensive coverage of distinct destinations all over the world. Each Handbook is like an entire bookcase of cultural insight and introductory information in one portable volume. Our goal at Moon is to give travelers all the background and practical information they'll need for an extraordinary travel experience.

The following pages include a complete list of Handbooks, covering North America and Hawaii, Mexico, Latin America and the Caribbean, and Asia and the Pacific. To purchase Moon Travel Handbooks, check your local bookstore or order by phone: (800) 345-5473 M-F 8 am.-5 p.m. PST or outside the U.S. phone: (530) 345-5473.

> "An in-depth dunk into the land, the people and their history, arts, and politics."
> —*Student Travels*

> "I consider these books to be superior to Lonely Planet. When Moon produces a book it is more humorous, incisive, and off-beat."
> —*Toronto Sun*

> "Outdoor enthusiasts gravitate to the well-written Moon Travel Handbooks. In addition to politically correct historic and cultural features, the series focuses on flora, fauna and outdoor recreation. Maps and meticulous directions also are a trademark of Moon guides."
> —*Houston Chronicle*

> "Moon [Travel Handbooks] . . . bring a healthy respect to the places they investigate. Best of all, they provide a host of odd nuggets that give a place texture and prod the wary traveler from the beaten path. The finest are written with such care and insight they deserve listing as literature."
> —*American Geographical Society*

> "Moon Travel Handbooks offer in-depth historical essays and useful maps, enhanced by a sense of humor and a neat, compact format."
> —*Swing*

> "Perfect for the more adventurous, these are long on history, sightseeing and nitty-gritty information and very price-specific."
> —*Columbus Dispatch*

> "Moon guides manage to be comprehensive and countercultural at the same time . . . Handbooks are packed with maps, photographs, drawings, and sidebars that constitute a college-level introduction to each country's history, culture, people, and crafts."
> —*National Geographic Traveler*

> "Few travel guides do a better job helping travelers create their own itineraries than the Moon Travel Handbook series. The authors have a knack for homing in on the essentials."
> —**Colorado Springs** *Gazette Telegraph*

MEXICO

"These books will delight the armchair traveler, aid the un-decided person in selecting a destination, and guide the seasoned road warrior looking for lesser-known hideaways."

—*Mexican Meanderings* Newsletter

"From tourist traps to off-the-beaten track hideaways, these guides offer consistent, accurate details without pretension."

—*Foreign Service Journal*

Archaeological Mexico	**$19.95**
Andrew Coe	420 pages, 27 maps
Baja Handbook	**$16.95**
Joe Cummings	540 pages, 46 maps
Cabo Handbook	**$14.95**
Joe Cummings	270 pages, 17 maps
Cancún Handbook	**$14.95**
Chicki Mallan	240 pages, 25 maps
Colonial Mexico	**$18.95**
Chicki Mallan	400 pages, 38 maps
Mexico Handbook	**$21.95**
Joe Cummings and Chicki Mallan	1,200 pages, 201 maps
Northern Mexico Handbook	**$17.95**
Joe Cummings	610 pages, 69 maps
Pacific Mexico Handbook	**$17.95**
Bruce Whipperman	580 pages, 68 maps
Puerto Vallarta Handbook	**$14.95**
Bruce Whipperman	330 pages, 36 maps
Yucatán Handbook	**$16.95**
Chicki Mallan	400 pages, 52 maps

LATIN AMERICA AND THE CARIBBEAN

"Solidly packed with practical information and full of significant cultural asides that will enlighten you on the whys and wherefores of things you might easily see but not easily grasp."

—Boston Globe

Belize Handbook	**$15.95**
Chicki Mallan and Patti Lange	390 pages, 45 maps
Caribbean Vacations	**$18.95**
Karl Luntta	910 pages, 64 maps
Costa Rica Handbook	**$19.95**
Christopher P. Baker	780 pages, 73 maps
Cuba Handbook	**$19.95**
Christopher P. Baker	740 pages, 70 maps
Dominican Republic Handbook	**$15.95**
Gaylord Dold	420 pages, 24 maps
Ecuador Handbook	**$16.95**
Julian Smith	450 pages, 43 maps
Honduras Handbook	**$15.95**
Chris Humphrey	330 pages, 40 maps
Jamaica Handbook	**$15.95**
Karl Luntta	330 pages, 17 maps
Virgin Islands Handbook	**$13.95**
Karl Luntta	220 pages, 19 maps

NORTH AMERICA AND HAWAII

"These domestic guides convey the same sense of exoticism that their foreign counterparts do, making home-country travel seem like far-flung adventure."

—Sierra Magazine

Alaska-Yukon Handbook	**$17.95**
Deke Castleman and Don Pitcher	530 pages, 92 maps
Alberta and the Northwest Territories Handbook	**$17.95**
Andrew Hempstead and Nadina Purdon	530 pages, 72 maps,
Arizona Traveler's Handbook	**$17.95**
Bill Weir and Robert Blake	512 pages, 54 maps
Atlantic Canada Handbook	**$17.95**
Nan Drosdick and Mark Morris	460 pages, 61 maps
Big Island of Hawaii Handbook	**$15.95**
J.D. Bisignani	390 pages, 23 maps

Boston Handbook		**$13.95**
Jeff Perk		200 pages, 20 maps
British Columbia Handbook		**$16.95**
Jane King and Andrew Hempstead		430 pages, 69 maps
Colorado Handbook		**$18.95**
Stephen Metzger		480 pages, 59 maps
Georgia Handbook		**$17.95**
Kap Stann		370 pages, 50 maps
Hawaii Handbook		**$19.95**
J.D. Bisignani		1,030 pages, 90 maps
Honolulu-Waikiki Handbook		**$14.95**
J.D. Bisignani		400 pages, 20 maps
Idaho Handbook		**$18.95**
Don Root		610 pages, 42 maps
Kauai Handbook		**$15.95**
J.D. Bisignani		320 pages, 23 maps
Maine Handbook		**$18.95**
Kathleen M. Brandes		660 pages, 27 maps
Massachusetts Handbook		**$18.95**
Jeff Perk		600 pages, 23 maps
Maui Handbook		**$15.95**
J.D. Bisignani		420 pages, 35 maps
Michigan Handbook		**$15.95**
Tina Lassen		300 pages, 30 maps
Montana Handbook		**$17.95**
Judy Jewell and W.C. McRae		480 pages, 52 maps
Nevada Handbook		**$18.95**
Deke Castleman		530 pages, 40 maps
New Hampshire Handbook		**$18.95**
Steve Lantos		500 pages, 18 maps
New Mexico Handbook		**$15.95**
Stephen Metzger		360 pages, 47 maps
New York Handbook		**$19.95**
Christiane Bird		780 pages, 95 maps
New York City Handbook		**$13.95**
Christiane Bird		300 pages, 20 maps
North Carolina Handbook		**$14.95**
Rob Hirtz and Jenny Daughtry Hirtz		275 pages, 25 maps
Northern California Handbook		**$19.95**
Kim Weir		800 pages, 50 maps
Oregon Handbook		**$17.95**
Stuart Warren and Ted Long Ishikawa		588 pages, 34 maps
Pennsylvania Handbook		**$18.95**
Joanne Miller		448 pages, 40 maps

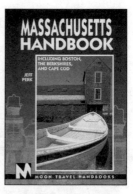

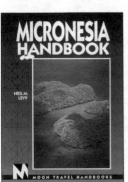

Road Trip USA	**$22.50**
Jamie Jensen	800 pages, 165 maps
Santa Fe-Taos Handbook	**$13.95**
Stephen Metzger	160 pages, 13 maps
Southern California Handbook	**$19.95**
Kim Weir	720 pages, 26 maps
Tennessee Handbook	**$17.95**
· Jeff Bradley	530 pages, 44 maps
Texas Handbook	**$18.95**
Joe Cummings	690 pages, 70 maps
Utah Handbook	**$17.95**
Bill Weir and W.C. McRae	490 pages, 40 maps
Virginia Handbook	**$15.95**
Julian Smith	340 pages, 30 maps
Washington Handbook	**$19.95**
Don Pitcher	870 pages, 113 maps
Wisconsin Handbook	**$18.95**
Thomas Huhti	590 pages, 69 maps
Wyoming Handbook	**$17.95**
Don Pitcher	610 pages, 80 maps

ASIA AND THE PACIFIC

"Scores of maps, detailed practical info down to business hours of small-town libraries. You can't beat the Asian titles for sheer heft. (The) series is sort of an American Lonely Planet, with better writing but fewer titles. (The) individual voice of researchers comes through."

—Travel & Leisure

Australia Handbook	**$21.95**
Marael Johnson, Andrew Hempstead, and Nadina Purdon	940 pages, 141 maps
Bali Handbook	**$19.95**
Bill Dalton	750 pages, 54 maps
Bangkok Handbook	**$13.95**
Michael Buckley	244 pages, 30 maps
Fiji Islands Handbook	**$14.95**
David Stanley	300 pages, 38 maps
Hong Kong Handbook	**$16.95**
Kerry Moran	378 pages, 49 maps
Indonesia Handbook	**$25.00**
Bill Dalton	1,380 pages, 249 maps

Micronesia Handbook	$14.95
Neil M. Levy	340 pages, 70 maps
Nepal Handbook	**$18.95**
Kerry Moran	490 pages, 51 maps
New Zealand Handbook	**$19.95**
Jane King	620 pages, 81 maps
Outback Australia Handbook	**$18.95**
Marael Johnson	450 pages, 57 maps
Philippines Handbook	**$17.95**
Peter Harper and Laurie Fullerton	670 pages, 116 maps
Singapore Handbook	**$15.95**
Carl Parkes	350 pages, 29 maps
South Korea Handbook	**$19.95**
Robert Nilsen	820 pages, 141 maps
South Pacific Handbook	**$22.95**
David Stanley	920 pages, 147 maps
Southeast Asia Handbook	**$21.95**
Carl Parkes	1,080 pages, 204 maps
Tahiti-Polynesia Handbook	**$15.95**
David Stanley	380 pages, 35 maps
Thailand Handbook	**$19.95**
Carl Parkes	860 pages, 142 maps
Vietnam, Cambodia & Laos Handbook	**$18.95**
Michael Buckley	760 pages, 116 maps

OTHER GREAT TITLES FROM MOON

"For hardy wanderers, few guides come more highly recommended than the Handbooks. They include good maps, steer clear of fluff and flackery, and offer plenty of money-saving tips. They also give you the kind of information that visitors to strange lands—on any budget—need to survive."

—*US News & World Report*

Moon Handbook	**$10.00**
Carl Koppeschaar	141 pages, 8 maps
The Practical Nomad: How to Travel Around the World	**$17.95**
Edward Hasbrouck	575 pages
Staying Healthy in Asia, Africa, and Latin America	**$11.95**
Dirk Schroeder	230 pages, 4 maps

MOONBELTS

Looking for comfort and a way to keep your most important articles safe while traveling? These were our own concerns and that is why we created the Moonbelt. Made of heavy-duty Cordura nylon, the Moonbelt offers maximum protection for your money and important papers. Designed for all-weather comfort, this pouch slips under your shirt or waistband, rendering it virtually undetectable and inaccessible to pickpockets. It features a one-inch high-test quick-release buckle so there's no fumbling for the strap nor repeated adjustments. This handy buckle opens and closes with a touch, but won't come undone until you want it to. Moonbelts accommodate traveler's checks, passport, cash, photos, etc. Measures 5 x 9 inches and fits waists up to 48".

Available in black only. **US$8.95**
Sales tax (7.25%) for California residents
$1.50 for 1st Class shipping & handling.

To order, call (800) 345-5473
outside the US (530) 345-5473 or fax (530) 345-6751

Make checks or money orders payable to:
MOON TRAVEL HANDBOOKS
PO Box 3040, Chico, CA 95927-3040 U.S.A.
We accept Visa, MasterCard, or Discover.

MOON TRAVEL HANDBOOKS

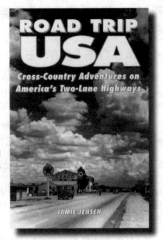

THE PRACTICAL NOMAD

✈ TAKE THE PLUNGE

"The greatest barriers to long-term travel by Americans are the disempowered feelings that leave them afraid to ask for the time off. Just do it."

✈ TAKE NOTHING FOR GRANTED

"Even 'What time is it?' is a highly politicized question in some areas, and the answer may depend on your informant's ethnicity and political allegiance as well as the proximity of the secret police."

✈ TAKE THIS BOOK

"Full of hard-won road wisdom."
—*San Francisco Examiner*

$17.95   576 pages

With experience helping thousands of his globetrotting clients plan their trips around the world, travel industry insider Edward Hasbrouck provides the secrets that can save readers money and valuable travel time.
An indispensable complement to destination-specific travel guides, *The Practical Nomad* includes:

> **airfare strategies**
>
> **ticket discounts**
>
> **long-term travel considerations**
>
> **travel documents**
>
> **border crossings**
>
> **entry requirements**
>
> **government offices**
>
> **travel publications**
>
> **Internet information resources**

WHERE TO BUY MOON TRAVEL HANDBOOKS

BOOKSTORES AND LIBRARIES: Moon Travel Handbooks are distributed worldwide. Please contact our sales manager for a list of wholesalers and distributors in your area.

TRAVELERS: We would like to have Moon Travel Handbooks available throughout the world. Please ask your bookstore to write or call us for ordering information. If your bookstore will not order our guides for you, please contact us for a free catalog.

> **Moon Travel Handbooks**
> **P.O. Box 3040**
> **Chico, CA 95927-3040 U.S.A.**
> **tel.: (800) 345-5473, outside the U.S. (530) 345-5473**
> **fax: (530) 345-6751**
> **e-mail: travel@moon.com**

IMPORTANT ORDERING INFORMATION

PRICES: All prices are subject to change. We always ship the most current edition. We will let you know if there is a price increase on the book you order.

SHIPPING AND HANDLING OPTIONS: Domestic UPS or USPS first class (allow 10 working days for delivery): $4.50 for the first item, $1.00 for each additional item.

Moonbelt shipping is $1.50 for one, 50 cents for each additional belt.

UPS 2nd Day Air or Printed Airmail requires a special quote.

International Surface Bookrate 8-12 weeks delivery: $4.00 for the first item, $1.00 for each additional item. Note: We cannot guarantee international surface bookrate shipping. We recommend sending international orders via air mail, which requires a special quote.

FOREIGN ORDERS: Orders that originate outside the U.S.A. must be paid for with an international money order, a check in U.S. currency drawn on a major U.S. bank based in the U.S.A., or Visa, MasterCard, or Discover.

TELEPHONE ORDERS: We accept Visa, MasterCard, or Discover payments. Call in your order: (800) 345-5473, 8 a.m.-5 p.m. Pacific standard time. Outside the U.S. the number is (530) 345-5473.

INTERNET ORDERS: Visit our site at: www.moon.com

ORDER FORM

Prices are subject to change without notice. Be sure to call (800) 345-5473,
or (530) 345-5473 from outside the U.S. 8 a.m.–5 p.m. PST for current prices and editions.
(See important ordering information on preceding page.)

Name: _____ Date: _____

Street: _____

City: _____ Daytime Phone: _____

State or Country: _____ Zip Code: _____

QUANTITY	TITLE	PRICE

Taxable Total_____
Sales Tax (7.25%) for California Residents_____
Shipping & Handling_____
TOTAL_____

Ship: ☐ UPS (no P.O. Boxes) ☐ 1st class ☐ International surface mail

Ship to: ☐ address above ☐ other _____

_____

_____

Make checks payable to: **MOON TRAVEL HANDBOOKS**, P.O. Box 3040, Chico, CA 95927-3040
U.S.A. We accept Visa, MasterCard, or Discover. **To Order**: Call in your Visa, MasterCard, or Discover number,
or send a written order with your Visa, MasterCard, or Discover number and expiration date clearly written.

Card Number: ☐ **Visa** ☐ **MasterCard** ☐ **Discover**

☐ ☐ ☐ ☐ ☐ ☐ ☐ ☐ ☐ ☐ ☐ ☐ ☐ ☐ ☐ ☐

Exact Name on Card: _____

Expiration date:_____

Signature: _____